THE MAKING OF THE WEST

PEOPLES AND CULTURES

A CONCISE HISTORY

Volume I: To 1740

LYNN HUNT
University of California at Los Angeles

THOMAS R. MARTIN
College of the Holy Cross

BARBARA H. ROSENWEIN
Loyola University Chicago

R. PO-CHIA HSIA
Pennsylvania State University

BONNIE G. SMITH
Rutgers University

BEDFORD/ST. MARTIN'S   Boston   ◆   New York

FOR BEDFORD/ST. MARTIN'S

Publisher for History: Mary Dougherty
Executive Editor for History: Katherine Meisenheimer
Director of Development for History: Jane Knetzger
Developmental Editor: Sara Wise
Production Editor: Deborah Baker
Senior Production Supervisor: Dennis Conroy
Executive Marketing Manager: Jenna Bookin Barry
Editorial Assistant: Kate Macmillan
Copyeditor: Susan Free
Proofreaders: Lisa Wehrle, Jan Cocker
Text Design: Wanda Kossak, Joan O'Connor
Indexer: EdIndex
Cover Design: Donna Lee Dennison
Composition: Techbooks
Cartography: Mapping Specialists Limited
Printing and Binding: R.R. Donnelley & Sons Company

President: Joan E. Feinberg
Editorial Director: Denise B. Wydra
Director of Marketing: Karen Melton Soeltz
Director of Editing, Design, and Production: Marcia Cohen
Managing Editor: Elizabeth M. Schaaf

Library of Congress Control Number: 2005938009

For information, contact: Bedford/St. Martin's, 75 Arlington Street, Boston, MA 02116 (617-399-4000)
bedfordstmartins.com

ISBN-10: 0–312–43937–7 (paperback complete edition)   ISBN-13: 978–0–312–43937–8
0–312–43945–8 (paperback Volume I)   978–0–312–43945–3
0–312–43946–6 (paperback Volume II)   978–0–312–43946–0

Cover and Title Page Art: Workshop of Filippino Lippi. *The Worship of the Egyptian Bull God, Apis,* ca. 1500. Oil and egg (identified) on wood. National Gallery, London.

Preface

THE IDEA OF "THE WEST" is now urgently under discussion. The end of the cold war after 1989 presented new challenges for historical interpretation, but these had hardly been digested when the shock of September 11, 2001, reverberated throughout the world. Conflict now takes place on a global stage, and globalization of the economy and culture has become a subject of passionate debate. These momentous issues and events present extraordinary challenges for authors of Western civilization textbooks. We welcome the challenges, for they have deepened our commitment to our project's basic goal and approach. From the very beginning, we have insisted on an expanded vision of the West that includes the United States, fully incorporates eastern Europe, and emphasizes Europe's relationship with the rest of the world, whether through trade, colonization, migration, cultural exchange, or religious and ethnic conflict.

Every generation of students needs new textbooks that synthesize recent findings. Textbooks conceived during the era of the cold war are, of course, oriented toward explaining the clash between a West unquestionably identified as western Europe and the United States and its eastern-bloc opponents, eastern Europe and the Soviet Union. Since much of eastern Europe has now joined the European Union, the notion of Europe—and the West—has to change. New histories must reflect these dramatic changes. We feel confident that ours meets the challenge. Our post–cold war conception applies not only to our coverage of recent events, but informs our entire treatment of Western Civilization—from antiquity to the present. By adopting a wider view of the West from the start, our book offers a more coherent and convincing view of the important issues in the making of the West to help students understand the world in which they live.

Central Themes and Approach

Our title—*The Making of the West: Peoples and Cultures, A Concise History*—makes three enduring points about our themes and approach: (1) that the history of the West is the story of a process that is still ongoing, not a finished result with only one fixed meaning; (2) that "the West" includes many different peoples and cultures; that is, that there is no one Western people or culture that has existed from the beginning until now. To understand the historical development of the West and its position in the world today, it is essential to place the West's emergence in a larger, global context that reveals the cross-cultural interactions fundamental to the shaping of the Western identity. Finally, (3), that a "concise" approach is ideally suited to meet the needs of instructors who wish to assign additional supplementary readings, who need to cover the entire introduction to Western civilization in a single semester, or who find a comprehensive textbook too detailed and daunting for their students. By reworking, condensing, and combining thematically related sections throughout the text ourselves, we've created a brief edition that preserves the narrative flow, balance, and power of our full-length work.

Our task as authors, moreover, is to integrate the best of social and cultural history with the enduring developments of political, military, and diplomatic history, offering a clear, compelling narrative that sets all the key events and stages of the West's evolution in a broad, meaningful context.

We know from our own teaching that introductory students need a solid chronological framework, one with enough familiar benchmarks to make the material readily digestible, but also one with enough flexibility to incorporate the new varieties of historical research. That is one reason we present our account in a straightforward, chronological manner. Each chapter treats all the main events, people, and themes of a period together; thus students are not required to learn about political events in one chapter, and then backtrack to concurrent social and cultural developments in the next. The chronological organization also accords with our belief that it is important, above all else, for students to see the interconnections among varieties of historical experience— between politics and cultures, between public events and private experiences, between wars and diplomacy and everyday life. Our chronological synthesis allows students to appreciate these relationships while it, we hope, captures the spirit of each age and sparks students' historical imaginations. For teachers, our chronological approach ensures a balanced account, allows the flexibility to stress themes of one's own choosing, and perhaps best of all, provides a text that reveals history not as a settled matter but as a process that is constantly alive, subject to pressures, and able to surprise us.

In writing *The Making of the West: Peoples and Cultures, A Concise History*, it has been our aim to communicate the vitality and excitement as well as the fundamental importance of history. If we have succeeded in conveying some of the vibrancy of the past and the thrill of historical investigation, we will be encouraged to start rethinking and revising—as historians always must—once again.

Textual Changes

Unlike most scholarly books, a textbook offers historians the rare chance to revise the original work, to keep it fresh, and to make it better. It has been a privilege to bring our own scholarship and teaching to bear on this rewriting. In this second edition, we have kept our emphasis on a strong central story line that incorporates the best of new research, but we have worked to make the narrative even more focused and accessible by reviewing every line of text and recrafting the headings to provide better signposts for readers.

To illustrate our conception of the history of the West as an ongoing process, the first chapter opens with a new discussion of the origins and contested meaning of "Western civilization." In this conversation, we emphasize our theme of cultural borrowing between the peoples of Europe and their neighbors that has characterized Western civilization from the beginning. We continue to incorporate the experiences of borderland regions and the importance of global interactions into the historical narrative and in many of our new art selections.

Of course, the recent past is the most pressing arena in which to examine the West as an evolving construct. The impact of recent events is reflected most dramatically in the last two chapters, which have been completely rewritten and now divide at 1989, the year that marks the beginning of a new era after the cold war.

Throughout each chapter, we've added new material and drawn on new scholarship on topics such as Zoroastrianism and the influence of Persian religion on later faiths (Chapter 1); criticisms of radical democracy (Chapter 2); the origins of Islam (Chapter 7); Byzantine court culture (Chapter 8); the prominence of the flagellant movement (Chapter 11); sugar grinding in the colonies (Chapter 14); the role of peasants in the French Revolution (Chapter 16); nineteenth-century French efforts to transform Saigon (Chapter 18); Japan's imperialist activity in the 1920s (Chapter 20); discontent in the colonies during the depression (Chapter 21); postwar recovery in Scandinavia and the contributions of immigrants to postwar European economies (Chapter 22); the rise in the study of social sciences (Chapter 23); and the impact of global outsourcing (Chapter 24).

Pedagogy and Features

More and more is required of students these days, and not just in Western Civilization courses. We know from our own teaching that students need all the help they can get in assimilating information, acquiring skills, and learning about historical debate. With these goals in mind, we retained the class-tested learning and teaching aids that contributed to the first edition, but we have also added more such features.

Each chapter begins with a ***vivid anecdote*** that draws readers into the atmosphere and issues of the period and raises the chapter's main themes, supplemented by a full-page illustration that echoes the anecdote and similarly reveals the temper of the times. To help students check their comprehension of main ideas, we have added new *review questions* strategically placed at the end of each major section. Bolded *key terms* in the text are defined in a new *Glossary of Key Terms* at the end of the book. Each chapter closes with a list of *important dates* and a strong *chapter conclusion* that reviews main topics and ties together the chapter's thematic strands. Two new *Making Connections questions* at the end of each chapter encourage students to analyze chapter material or make comparisons within or beyond the chapter.

To reflect the richness of the themes in the text and to enliven the past with many more original sources, in the second edition we have greatly expanded the companion sourcebook that accompanies this textbook, *Sources of THE MAKING OF THE WEST: A CONCISE HISTORY*. There are now five documents per chapter, which vary in length to offer instructors the flexibility to use them in the classroom or for outside assignments. Nothing can give a more direct experience of the past than original voices, and we have endeavored to let those voices speak in the sourcebook, whether it is Seneca describing everyday life in the Roman Empire (Chapter 3), student impressions of university life in the twelfth and early thirteenth centuries (Chapter 9), or a child's view of war-torn Sarajevo in the early 1990s (Chapter 24). *Sources of THE MAKING OF THE WEST* is available free when packaged with *A Concise History*, or at a nominal charge if purchased separately.

The map program of the first edition was widely praised as the most comprehensive in any brief survey text. In each chapter we offer a set of three types of maps, each with a distinct role in conveying information to students. On average, three to four *full-size maps* show major developments, one to three *"spot" maps*—small maps that emphasize a detailed area from the discussion—aid students' understanding of specific but crucial issues, and *Mapping the West* summary maps at the end of each chapter provide a snapshot of the West at the close of a transformative period and help students visualize the West's changing contours over time. For this edition, we have carefully considered each map, improved the colors for better contrast, and clarified and updated borders and labels where needed. In addition to the *more than 160 maps,* numerous charts and graphs visually support the narrative, including innovative *Taking Measure* features, which highlight a chart, table, graph, or map of historical statistics that illuminates an important political, social, or cultural development.

It has been our intention to integrate art as fully as possible into the narrative and to show its value for teaching and learning. *Over 260 illustrations,* carefully chosen to reflect this edition's broad topical coverage and geographic inclusion, reinforce the text and show the varieties of visual sources from which historians build their narratives and interpretations. All artifacts, illustrations, paintings, and photographs are contemporaneous with the chapter; there are no anachronistic illustrations—no fifteenth-century peasants tilling fields in a chapter on the tenth century! We know that today's students are very attuned to visual sources of information, yet they do not always receive systematic instruction in how to "read" or think critically about such visual sources. Our substantive captions for the maps and art help them learn how to make the most of these informative materials, and new to the second edition, we have frequently included specific questions or suggestions for comparisons that might be developed. Specially designed visual exercises in the Online Study Guide supplement this approach.

Supplements

Because textbook supplements take on special importance in classrooms in which a brief survey text is assigned, we have taken care in revising and augmenting the comprehensive and well-integrated set of print and electronic resources for students and instructors that support the second edition of *The Making of the West: A Concise History.*

For Students

Sources of THE MAKING OF THE WEST: A CONCISE HISTORY, Second Edition— Volumes I (to 1740) and II (since 1340)—by Katharine J. Lualdi, University of Southern Maine. For each chapter in *The Making of the West,* this companion sourcebook now features five important political, social, and cultural documents that reinforce or extend discussions in the textbook, encouraging students to make connections between narrative history and primary sources. The second edition provides instructors with even more flexibility with 35 percent more documents and the addition of visual sources. This edition also pays more attention to geographic areas beyond Europe and includes an improved balance between traditional documents and selections that provide a fresh perspective. Short chapter summaries and document headnotes contextualize the wide array of sources and perspectives represented, while discussion and new comparative questions guide students' reading and promote historical thinking skills. *Available free when packaged with the text.*

Online Study Guide at bedfordstmartins.com/huntconcise.   The popular Online Study Guide for *The Making of the West: A Concise History* is a free and uniquely personalized learning tool to help students master themes and information in the textbook and improve their historical skills. Assessment quizzes let students evaluate their comprehension and provide them with customized plans for further study through a variety of activities. Instructors can monitor students' progress through the online Quiz Gradebook or receive e-mail updates.

NEW The Bedford Glossary for European History.   This handy supplement for the European history survey course provides students with clear, concise definitions of the political, economic, social, and cultural terms used by historians and contemporary media alike. All terms are placed within their historical context to aid comprehension. *Available free when packaged with the text.*

The Bedford Series in History and Culture—Advisory Editors Lynn Hunt, University of California, Los Angeles; David W. Blight, Yale University; Bonnie G. Smith, Rutgers University; Natalie Zemon Davis, Princeton University; and Ernest R. May, Harvard University. European titles in this highly praised series combine first-rate scholarship, historical narrative, and important primary documents for undergraduate courses. Each book is brief, inexpensive, and focused on a specific topic or period. To see a complete list of titles in this series, please go to bedfordstmartins.com/wwbshc. *Package discounts are available.*

NEW Trade Books.   Titles published by our sister companies Farrar, Straus and Giroux; Henry Holt and Company; Hill and Wang; Picador; and St. Martin's Press are available at a discount when packaged with the text. For a list of titles, please see bedfordstmartins.com/tradeup.

A Student's Online Guide to History Reference Sources at bedfordstmartins.com/benjamin.   This Web site provides links to history-related databases, indexes, and journals, plus contact information for state, provincial, local, and professional history organizations.

Research and Documentation Online at bedfordstmartins.com/resdoc.   This Web site provides clear advice on how to integrate primary and secondary sources into research papers, how to cite sources correctly, and how to format in MLA, APA, *Chicago,* or CBE style.

The St. Martin's Tutorial on Avoiding Plagiarism at bedfordstmartins.com/plagiarismtutorial.   This online tutorial reviews the consequences of plagiarism and explains what sources to acknowledge, how to keep good notes, how to organize research, and how to integrate sources appropriately. The tutorial includes exercises to help students practice integrating sources and recognize acceptable summaries.

Bedford Research Room at bedfordstmartins.com/researchroom.   The Research Room, drawn from Mike Palmquist's *The Bedford Researcher,* offers a wealth of resources—including interactive tutorials, research activities, student writing samples, and links to hundreds of other places online—to support students in courses across the disciplines. The site also offers instructors a library of helpful instructional tools.

For Instructors

Instructor's Resource Manual to Accompany THE MAKING OF THE WEST, A CONCISE HISTORY, ***Second Edition,*** by Dakota Hamilton, Humboldt State University. This helpful manual offers both first-time and experienced teachers a wealth of tools for structuring and customizing Western Civilization history courses of different sizes. For each chapter in the textbook, the *Instructor's Resource Manual* includes an outline of chapter themes; a chapter summary; lecture and discussion topics; film and literature suggestions; writing and class-presentation assignments; research topic suggestions; and in-class exercises for working with maps, illustrations, and sources. The new edition includes a chapter-by-chapter guide to all of the supplements available with *The Making of the West: A Concise History,* answers to the new in-text Review questions and Making Connections questions, and a brief guide for using the book companion site.

Transparencies.   A set of over 200 full-color acetate transparencies of maps and images in the parent text broaden the art program in *A Concise History* to help instructors present images and teach students important map-reading skills. A correlation guide that shows how the transparencies align with the brief text appears in the *Instructor's Resource Manual* and on the book companion Web site.

Book Companion Web site at **bedfordstmartins.com/huntconcise.**   The companion Web site for *The Making of the West: A Concise History* gathers all the electronic resources for the text—including the Online Study Guide and related Quiz Gradebook—at a single Web address, providing convenient links, and lecture, assignment, and research materials such as PowerPoint chapter outlines and the digital libraries at Make History.

Computerized Test Bank by Joseph Coohill, Pennsylvania State University at New Kensington, and Frances Mitilineos, Loyola University Chicago. This fully updated test bank offers over 80 exercises per chapter, including multiple-choice, identification, timelines, map labeling and analysis, and full-length essay questions. Instructors can customize quizzes and add or edit both questions and answers, as well as export questions and answers to a variety of formats, including WebCT and Blackboard. The disc includes answer keys and essay outlines.

Instructor's Resource CD-ROM.   This disc provides instructors with ready-made and easily customized PowerPoint multimedia presentations built around chapter outlines, maps, figures, and selected images from the textbook. The disc also includes selected images from the textbook in JPEG format, an electronic version of the *Instructor's Resource Manual,* outline maps in PDF format for quizzing or handouts, and a quick-start guide to the Online Study Guide.

NEW *Make History* at bedfordstmartins.com/makehistory. Comprising the content of our acclaimed online libraries—Map Central, DocLinks, and HistoryLinks—Make History provides one-stop access to relevant digital content including maps, documents, and Web links. Students and instructors can search this free, easy-to-use database by keyword, topic, date, or specific chapter of *The Making of the West: A Concise History* and can download any content they find. Instructors using *The Making of the West: A Concise History* can also create entire collections of content and store them online for later use or post their collections to the Web to share with students.

Using the Bedford Series in History and Culture with THE MAKING OF THE WEST: A CONCISE HISTORY, Second Edition at bedfordstmartins.com/usingseries. This online guide helps instructors integrate volumes from the highly regarded Bedford Series in History and Culture into their Western Civilization survey course. The guide correlates themes from each series book with relevant chapters in *A Concise History.*

Course Management Content. E-content is available for this book in Blackboard, WebCT, Angel, and Desire2Learn. This e-content includes nearly all of the offerings in the book's Online Study Guide, as well as the book's test bank.

Videos and Multimedia. A wide assortment of videos and multimedia CD-ROMs on various topics in European history is available to qualified adopters. Contact your Bedford/St. Martin's sales representative for more information.

Acknowledgments

In the vital process of revision, the authors have benefited from repeated critical readings by many talented scholars and teachers. Our sincere thanks go to the following instructors, as well as three anonymous reviewers, whose comments often challenged us to rethink or justify our interpretations and who always provided a check on accuracy down to the smallest detail: Michael Anderson, George Mason University; Marjorie Berman, Red Rocks Community College; Stephen Bourque, California State University, Northridge; Scott Bruce, University of Colorado at

Boulder; Elspeth Carruthers, University of Illinois at Chicago; Elizabeth Dennison, University of Alaska Anchorage; Constantina Scourtis Gaddis, Onondaga Community College; Richard Golden, University of North Texas; Richard Jobs, Pacific University; Bill Kamil, Sinclair Community College; Joseph Lepore, University of South Alabama; Steven Marks, Clemson University; John Moser, Ashland University; Larry Ping, Southern Utah University; Jana Pisani, Ferris State University; Jennifer Popiel, St. Louis University; Mark Potter, University of Wyoming; Thomas Saylor, Concordia University, St. Paul; Barbara Shepard, Longwood University; Heath Spencer, Seattle University; Daniel Thiery, Iona College; and William Virden, University of Northern Colorado.

Many colleagues, friends, and family members have helped us develop this work as well. They know how grateful we are. We also wish to acknowledge and thank the publishing team at Bedford/St. Martin's who did so much to bring this revised edition to completion: Joan Feinberg, Denise Wydra, Elizabeth Welch, Mary Dougherty, Jane Knetzger, Sara Wise, Deborah Baker, Jenna Bookin Barry, Katherine Meisenheimer, Kate Macmillan, Danielle Slevens, and Gillian Speeth. Our students' questions and concerns have shaped much of this work, and we welcome all our readers' suggestions, queries, and criticisms. Please contact us at our respective institutions or via history@bedfordstmartins.com.

L. H.   T. R. M.   B. H. R.   R. P. H.   B. G. S.

Brief Contents

1   Foundations of Western Civilization, to 500 B.C.E.   *3*

2   The Greek Golden Age, c. 500–400 B.C.E.   *51*

3   From the Classical to the Hellenistic World, c. 400–30 B.C.E.   *91*

4   The Rise of Rome, c. 753–44 B.C.E.   *129*

5   The Roman Empire, c. 44 B.C.E.–284 C.E.   *171*

6   The Transformation of the Roman Empire, c. 284–c. 600 C.E.   *213*

7   The Heirs of the Roman Empire, 600–750   *259*

8   Unity and Diversity in Three Societies, 750–1050   *295*

9   Renewal and Reform, 1050–1200   *339*

10   An Age of Confidence, 1200–1340   *385*

11   Crisis and Renaissance, 1340–1500   *425*

12   Struggles over Beliefs, 1500–1648   *473*

13   State Building and the Search for Order, 1648–1690   *523*

14   The Atlantic System and Its Consequences, 1690–1740   *567*

Contents

Preface   *v*

Brief Contents   *xiv*

Maps and Figures   *xxx*

Authors' Note: The B.C.E/C.E. Dating System   *xxxiv*

About the Authors   *xxxvii*

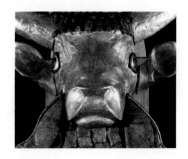

Foundations of Western Civilization, to 500 B.C.E. 3

Making Civilization, to 1000 B.C.E.   *5*

Paleolithic and Neolithic Life, c. 400,000–4000 B.C.E.   *5*   ◆   The Birth of Cities and Empire in Mesopotamia, c. 4000–1000 B.C.E.   *8*   ◆   Mesopotamian Legacies: Commerce, Law, and Learning, c. 2200–1000 B.C.E.   *13*

Early Civilizations in Egypt, the Levant, and Anatolia, c. 3100–1000 B.C.E.   *15*

Religion and Rule in Egypt, c. 3100–2190 B.C.E.   *16*   ◆   Life in the Egyptian and Hittite Kingdoms, 2190–1000 B.C.E.   *21*

Shifting Empires in the Ancient Near East, to 500 B.C.E.   *25*

From Neo-Assyrian to Babylonian to Persian Empire, c. 900–500 B.C.E.   *26*   ◆   Creating Hebrew Monotheism, c. 1000–539 B.C.E.   *30*

Greek Civilization, to 750 B.C.E.   *33*

Minoan and Mycenaean Civilization, c. 2200–1000 B.C.E.   *33*   ◆   The Greek Dark Age, c. 1000–750 B.C.E.   *36*

Remaking Greek Civilization, c. 750–500 B.C.E.   *38*

Citizenship and Freedom in the City-State   *39*   ◆   New Ways of Thought and Expression   *45*

Conclusion   *48*

The Greek Golden Age, c. 500–400 B.C.E. 51

The Persian Wars, 499–479 B.C.E. *52*

The Ionian Revolt and the Battle of Marathon, 499–490 B.C.E. *52*
◆ Xerxes' Invasion of 480–479 B.C.E. *54*

Athenian Confidence in the Golden Age, 479–431 B.C.E. *56*

The Establishment of the Athenian Empire, 479–c. 460 B.C.E. *56*
◆ Radical Democracy and Pericles' Leadership, 461–445 B.C.E. *59*
◆ The Urban Landscape of Golden Age Athens *61*

Tradition and Innovation in Athens's Golden Age *65*

Religious Tradition in a Period of Change *66* ◆ Women, Slaves, and
Metics in Traditional Society *68* ◆ Education and Intellectual Innovation
73 ◆ The Development of Tragedy and Comedy *79*

The End of the Golden Age, 431–403 B.C.E *83*

The Peloponnesian War, 431–403 B.C.E. *84* ◆ The Rule of the Thirty
Tyrants, 404–403 B.C.E. *86*

Conclusion *88*

From the Classical to the Hellenistic World, c. 400–30 B.C.E.

From the Classical to the Hellenistic World, c. 400–30 B.C.E.   91

Disunity in Classical Greece, c. 400–350 B.C.E.   *93*

The Aftermath of War and the Trial of Socrates   *93*   ◆   The Philosophy of Plato and Aristotle   *95*   ◆   The Fracturing of Greece   *98*

The Rise of Macedonia, 359–323 B.C.E.   *99*

Philip II and the Background of Macedonian Power   *99*   ◆   Exploits of Alexander the Great, 336–323 B.C.E.   *102*

The Hellenistic Kingdoms, 323–30 B.C.E.   *106*

The Structure of Hellenistic Kingdoms   *106*   ◆   Hierarchy in Hellenistic Society   *110*

Hellenistic Culture   *112*

The Arts under Royal Support   *112*   ◆   Philosophy for a New Age   *115*   ◆   Innovation in the Sciences   *118*   ◆   A New East-West Culture   *120*

Conclusion   *125*

The Rise of Rome, c. 753–44 B.C.E.   129

Social and Religious Traditions   *131*

Roman Values *131* ◆ The Patron-Client System *132* ◆ The Roman Family *134* ◆ Education for Public Life *136* ◆ Religion for Public and Private Interests *137*

From Monarchy to Republic, c. 753–287 B.C.E.   *139*

Rule by Kings, c. 753–509 B.C.E. *140* ◆ The Early Roman Republic, 509–287 B.C.E. *142*

Consequences of Roman Imperialism, Fifth to Second Centuries B.C.E.   *146*

Roman Expansion in Italy *147* ◆ Wars with Carthage *148* ◆ Greece's Influence on Rome's Literature, Philosophy, and Art *152* ◆ Imperialism's Effects on Republican Society *156*

The Destruction of the Republic, c. 133–44 B.C.E.   *158*

The Gracchus Brothers and Political Rupture *159* ◆ Gaius Marius and the First Client Armies *160* ◆ Sulla and Civil War *161* ◆ Pompey, Caesar, and the End of the Republic *163*

Conclusion   *168*

The Roman Empire, c. 44 B.C.E.–284 C.E. 171

Creating "Roman Peace"   *173*

From Republic to Principate, 44–27 B.C.E.   *173*   ◆   Augustus's "Restoration,"
27 B.C.E.–14 C.E.   *174*   ◆   Life in Augustan Rome   *177*   ◆   Art and
Literature to Please the Emperor   *182*

Maintaining "Roman Peace"   *184*

Making Monarchy Permanent, 14–180 C.E.   *185*   ◆   Life under the Five
Good Emperors, 96–180 C.E.   *189*

The Emergence of Christianity   *195*

The Teachings of Jesus   *196*   ◆   Growth of a New Religion   *199*
◆   Competing Beliefs   *202*

The Crisis of the Third Century   *205*

Defending the Frontiers   *205*   ◆   The Severan Emperors and
Catastrophe   *206*

Conclusion   *210*

The Transformation of the Roman Empire, c. 284–c. 600 C.E. 213

Reorganizing the Empire 214

Imperial Reform and Fragmentation *215* ◆ Financial Reform and Social Consequences *219* ◆ Religious Reform: From Persecution to Conversion *220*

Christianizing the Empire 222

The Spread of Christianity *222* ◆ Competing Visions of Religious Truth *227* ◆ The Beginning of Christian Monasticism *232*

Non-Roman Kingdoms in the West 235

Migrations into the Empire *235* ◆ Mixing Traditions *243*

The Byzantine Empire in the East 245

Byzantine Society *245* ◆ The Reign of Justinian, 527–565 *249* ◆ Preserving Classical Literature *252*

Conclusion 255

CHAPTER 7

The Heirs of the Roman Empire, 600–750 259

Byzantium: A Christian Empire under Siege *260*

Wars on the Frontiers, c. 570–750 *261* ◆ From an Urban to a Rural Way of Life *263* ◆ Religion, Politics, and Iconoclasm *266*

Islam: A New Religion and a New Empire *268*

The Rise and Development of Islam, c. 610–632 *268* ◆ Muhammad's Successors, 632–750 *273* ◆ Peace and Prosperity in Islamic Lands *274*

The Western Kingdoms *275*

Frankish Kingdoms with Roman Roots *276* ◆ Economic Activity in a Peasant Society *280* ◆ The Powerful in Merovingian Society *282* ◆ Christianity and Classical Culture in the British Isles *286* ◆ Unity in Spain, Division in Italy *288*

Conclusion *292*

Unity and Diversity in Three Societies, 750–1050   295

Byzantium: Renewed Strength and Influence   *296*

Imperial Might *297* ◆ The Macedonian Renaissance, c. 870–c. 1025 *299* ◆ New States under the Influence of Byzantium *301*

From Unity to Fragmentation in the Islamic World   *303*

The Abbasid Caliphate, 750–c. 950 *304* ◆ Regional Diversity *305* ◆ The Islamic Renaissance, c. 790–c. 1050 *307*

The Creation and Division of a New Western Empire   *309*

The Rise of the Carolingians *310* ◆ Charlemagne and His Kingdom, 768–814 *311* ◆ The Carolingian Renaissance *314* ◆ Charlemagne's Successors, 814–911 *315* ◆ Land and Power *317* ◆ Vikings, Muslims, and Magyars Invade *318*

The Emergence of Local Rule in the Post-Carolingian Age   *323*

Public Power and Private Relationships *323* ◆ War and Peace *327* ◆ Political Communities in Italy, England, and France *329* ◆ Emperors and Kings in Central and Eastern Europe *332*

Conclusion   *336*

Renewal and Reform, 1050–1200   339

The Commercial Revolution   *340*

Centers of Commerce and Commercial Life   *340*   ◆   Business Arrangements   *343*   ◆   Self-Government for the Towns   *345*

Church Reform and Its Aftermath   *346*

Beginnings of the Reform Movement   *346*   ◆   Gregorian Reform and the Investiture Conflict, 1073–1085   *349*   ◆   The Sweep of Reform   *351* ◆   Early Crusades and Crusader States   *352*   ◆   The Jews as Strangers   *356*

The Revival of Monarchies   *358*

Byzantium in Its Prime   *359*   ◆   Norman and Angevin England   *360* ◆   Praising the King of France   *365*   ◆   Remaking the Empire   *366* ◆   The Courtly Culture of Europe   *367*

New Forms of Scholarship and Religious Experience   *369*

Schools, Scholars, and the New Learning   *370*   ◆   Benedictine Monks and Artistic Splendor   *373*   ◆   New Monastic Orders of Poverty   *375* ◆   Religious Fervor and Dissent   *377*

Conclusion   *382*

An Age of Confidence, 1200–1340 385

War, Conquest, and Settlement   *386*

The Northern Crusades *386* ◆ The Capture of Constantinople *387* ◆ The Spanish Reconquista Advances *390* ◆ Putting Down the Heretics in Their Midst *391* ◆ The Mongol Takeover *396*

Politics of Control   *398*

France: From Acorn to Oak *398* ◆ England: Crisis and Consolidation *401* ◆ Papal Monarchy *402* ◆ Power Shifts in the Italian Communes *406* ◆ New-Style Associations amid the Monarchies *406* ◆ The Birth of Representative Institutions *407*

Religious and Cultural Life in an Age of Expansion   *409*

Lay Religious Fervor *409* ◆ Scholastics and Scholasticism *411* ◆ New Syntheses in Writing and Music *413* ◆ The Order of High Gothic *415*

Conclusion   *422*

Crisis and Renaissance, 1340–1500   425

A Multitude of Crises   *426*

Economic Contraction and the Black Death   *426*   ◆   The Hundred
Years' War, 1337–1453   *430*   ◆   Ottoman Conquest and New Political
Configurations in Eastern Europe   *436*   ◆   Hard Times   *439*   ◆   The
Crisis of the Papacy   *440*   ◆   Stamping Out Dissenters, Heretics, Jews, and
Muslims   *444*   ◆   End of the Reconquista and Expulsion of the Jews from
Spain, 1492   *447*

New Forms of Thought and Expression: The Renaissance   *448*

Renaissance Humanism   *448*   ◆   New Perspectives in Art and Music   *452*
  ◆   Republics and Principalities in Italy   *457*   ◆   The Intersection of Private
and Public Lives   *459*

On the Threshold of World History   *463*

The Divided Mediterranean   *463*   ◆   Portuguese Confrontations   *465*
  ◆   The Voyages of Columbus   *466*   ◆   A New Era in Slavery   *467*
  ◆   Europeans in a New World   *468*

Conclusion   *471*

Struggles over Beliefs, 1500–1648   473

The Protestant Reformation   *474*

Popular Piety and Christian Humanism   *474*   ◆   Martin Luther and the German Nation   *476*   ◆   Huldrych Zwingli and John Calvin   *479*   ◆   Reshaping Society through Religion   *481*   ◆   Catholic Renewal and Missionary Zeal   *484*

State Power and Religious Conflict, 1500–1618   *486*

Wars among Habsburgs, Valois, and Ottomans   *487*   ◆   French Wars of Religion   *489*   ◆   Challenges to Habsburg Power and the Rise of the Dutch Republic   *491*   ◆   England Goes Protestant   *494*

The Thirty Years' War and the Balance of Power, 1618–1648   *498*

Origins and Course of the War   *498*   ◆   The Effects of Constant Fighting   *500*   ◆   The Peace of Westphalia, 1648   *501*   ◆   Growth of State Authority   *503*

From Growth to Recession   *504*

Causes and Consequences of Economic Crisis   *505*   ◆   The Economic Balance of Power   *507*

A Clash of Worldviews   *509*

The Arts in an Age of Religious Conflict   *509*   ◆   The Natural Laws of Politics   *512*   ◆   Origins of the Scientific Revolution   *514*   ◆   Magic and Witchcraft   *517*

Conclusion   *520*

CHAPTER 13

State Building and the Search for Order, 1648–1690   523

Louis XIV: Model of Absolutism   *524*

The Fronde, 1648–1653 *525* ◆ Court Culture as an Element of Absolutism *526* ◆ Enforcing Religious Orthodoxy *528* ◆ Extending State Authority at Home and Abroad *529*

Absolutism in Central and Eastern Europe   *532*

Brandenburg-Prussia and Sweden: Militaristic Absolutism *533* ◆ An Uneasy Balance: Austrian Habsburgs and Ottoman Turks *535* ◆ Russia: Foundations of Bureaucratic Absolutism *537* ◆ Poland-Lithuania Overwhelmed *539*

Constitutionalism in England   *540*

England Turned Upside Down, 1642–1660 *541* ◆ The "Glorious Revolution" of 1688 *545*

Other Outposts of Constitutionalism   *548*

The Dutch Republic *548* ◆ Freedom and Slavery in the New World *551*

The Search for Order in Elite and Popular Culture   *552*

Social Contract Theory: Hobbes and Locke *553* ◆ Newton and the Consolidation of the Scientific Revolution *554* ◆ Freedom and Order in the Arts *556* ◆ Women and Manners *559* ◆ Reforming Popular Culture *561*

Conclusion   *565*

The Atlantic System and Its Consequences, 1690–1740   567

The Atlantic System and the World Economy   *569*

Slavery and the Atlantic System   *569*   ◆   World Trade and Settlement   *574*   ◆   The Birth of Consumer Society   *577*

New Social and Cultural Patterns   *578*

Agricultural Revolution   *578*   ◆   Social Life in the Cities   *581*   ◆   The Growing Public for Culture   *582*   ◆   Religious Revivals   *586*

Consolidation of the European State System   *586*

The Limits of French Absolutism   *587*   ◆   British Rise and Dutch Decline   *589*   ◆   Russia's Emergence as a European Power   *592*   ◆   The Balance of Power in the East   *594*   ◆   The Power of Diplomacy and the Importance of Numbers   *597*   ◆   Public Hygiene and Health Care   *598*

The Birth of the Enlightenment   *600*

Popularization of Science and Challenges to Religion   *600*   ◆   Travel Literature and the Challenge to Custom and Tradition   *602*   ◆   Raising the Woman Question   *604*

Conclusion   *606*

Suggested References   *SR-1*

Glossary of Key Terms   *G-1*

Index   *I-1*

Maps and Figures

MAPS

Chapter 1

The Ancient Near East   7

SPOT MAP   The Ancient Levant   16

Ancient Egypt   17

Expansion of the Neo-Assyrian
    Empire, c. 900–650 B.C.E.   26

Expansion of the Persian Empire,
    c. 550–490 B.C.E.   29

Greece and the Aegean Sea,
    c. 1500 B.C.E.   33

Archaic Greece, c. 750–500 B.C.E.   39

SPOT MAP   Sparta and the Peloponnese,
    c. 750–500 B.C.E.   43

SPOT MAP   Ionia and the Aegean,
    c. 750–500 B.C.E.   46

MAPPING THE WEST   Mediterranean
    Civilizations, c. 500 B.C.E.   47

Chapter 2

The Persian Wars, 499–479 B.C.E.   53

SPOT MAP   The Delian and
    Peloponnesian Leagues   57

Fifth-Century B.C.E. Athens   62

The Peloponnesian War,
    431–404 B.C.E.   86

MAPPING THE WEST   Greece, Europe,
    and the Mediterranean,
    c. 400 B.C.E.   88

Chapter 3

SPOT MAP   Expansion of Macedonia
    under Philip II, r. 359–336 B.C.E.
    101

Conquests of Alexander the Great,
    336–323 B.C.E.   103

Hellenistic Kingdoms, c. 240 B.C.E.
    107

MAPPING THE WEST   The Fall of the
    Hellenistic Kingdoms, to 30 B.C.E.
    124

Chapter 4

Ancient Italy, c. 500 B.C.E.   141

SPOT MAP   Rome and Central Italy,
    Fifth Century B.C.E.   147

SPOT MAP   Roman Roads, c. 110 B.C.E.
    148

Roman Expansion, c. 500–44 B.C.E.
    153

MAPPING THE WEST   The Roman World
    at the End of the Republic,
    c. 44 B.C.E.   168

Chapter 5

The Expansion of the Roman Empire, 30 B.C.E.–117 C.E. *188*

Natural Features and Languages of the Roman World *191*

SPOT MAP Palestine in the Time of Jesus, 30 C.E. *197*

Christian Populations in the Late Third Century C.E. *201*

MAPPING THE WEST The Roman Empire in Crisis, c. 284 C.E. *209*

Chapter 6

Diocletian's Reorganization of 293 *217*

SPOT MAP The Division of the Empire, c. 395 *218*

The Spread of Christianity, 300–600 *226*

Migrations and Invasions of the Fourth and Fifth Centuries *236*

Peoples and Kingdoms of the Roman World, c. 526 *243*

MAPPING THE WEST The Byzantine Empire and Western Europe, c. 600 *254*

Chapter 7

Byzantine and Sassanid Empires, c. 600 *261*

SPOT MAP The Byzantine Empire, c. 700 *263*

SPOT MAP Arabia in Muhammad's Lifetime *269*

Expansion of Islam to 730 *272*

The Merovingian Kingdoms in the Seventh Century *276*

SPOT MAP The British Isles *286*

SPOT MAP Lombard Italy, Early Eighth Century *289*

MAPPING THE WEST Europe and the Mediterranean, c. 750 *291*

Chapter 8

The Expansion of Byzantium, 860–1025 *298*

SPOT MAP The Balkans, c. 850–950 *302*

Islamic States, c. 1000 *306*

Expansion of the Carolingian Empire under Charlemagne *312*

Viking, Muslim, and Magyar Invasions of the Ninth and Tenth Centuries *319*

SPOT MAP The Fragmentation of France, c. 1000 *326*

SPOT MAP England in the Age of King Alfred, r. 871–899 *330*

SPOT MAP The Ottonian Empire, 936–1002 *332*

MAPPING THE WEST Europe and the Mediterranean, c. 1050 *335*

Chapter 9

Medieval Trade Routes in the Eleventh and Twelfth Centuries *341*

SPOT MAP The World of the Investiture Conflict, c. 1070–1122 *349*

The First Crusade, 1096–1098 *353*

SPOT MAP The Crusader States in 1109 *355*

SPOT MAP Norman Conquest of England, 1066 *360*

Europe in the Age of Frederick Barbarossa and Henry II, 1150–1190 *363*

MAPPING THE WEST Major Religions in the West, c. 1200 *380*

Chapter 10

Crusades and Anti-Heretic Campaigns, 1150–1204   *388*

The Reconquista Triumphs, 1212–1275   *391*

Europe in the Time of Frederick II, r. 1212–1250   *394*

SPOT MAP   Italy at the End of the Thirteenth Century   *395*

The Mongol Invasions to 1259   *397*

SPOT MAP   The Consolidation of France under Philip Augustus, r. 1180–1223   *398*

France under Louis IX, r. 1226–1270   *400*

SPOT MAP   Growth of the Swiss Confederation to 1353   *407*

MAPPING THE WEST   Europe, c. 1340   *420*

Chapter 11

Advance of the Plague   *427*

The Hundred Years' War, 1337–1453   *432*

Ottoman Expansion in the Fourteenth and Fifteenth Centuries   *436*

Eastern Europe in the Fifteenth Century   *438*

The Great Schism, 1378–1417   *442*

SPOT MAP   Unification of Spain, Late Fifteenth Century   *447*

Exploitation and Exploration in the Sixteenth Century   *464*

MAPPING THE WEST   Renaissance Europe, c. 1500   *469*

Chapter 12

SPOT MAP   The Peasants' War of 1525   *478*

Spread of Protestantism in the Sixteenth Century   *482*

Habsburg-Valois-Ottoman Wars, 1494–1559   *487*

SPOT MAP   Protestant Churches in France, 1562   *490*

The Empire of Philip II, r. 1556–1598   *493*

SPOT MAP   The Netherlands during the Revolt, c. 1580   *494*

The Thirty Years' War and the Peace of Westphalia, 1648   *502*

MAPPING THE WEST   The Religious Divisions of Europe, c. 1648   *519*

Chapter 13

SPOT MAP   The Fronde, 1648–1653   *525*

Louis XIV's Acquisitions, 1668–1697   *531*

State Building in Central and Eastern Europe, 1648–1699   *535*

SPOT MAP   England during the Civil War   *542*

Dutch Commerce in the Seventeenth Century   *549*

MAPPING THE WEST   Europe at the End of the Seventeenth Century   *564*

Chapter 14

European Trade Patterns, c. 1740   *570*

Europe, c. 1715   *588*

Russia and Sweden after the Great Northern War, 1721   *595*

SPOT MAP   Austrian Conquest of Hungary, 1657–1730   *596*

MAPPING THE WEST   Europe in 1740   *605*

FIGURES

Cuneiform Writing   *13*

Egyptian Hieroglyphs   *18*

Triremes, the Foremost Classical Greek Warships   *58*

Styles of Greek Capitals   *64*

TAKING MEASURE   Military Forces of Athens and Sparta at the Beginning of the Peloponnesian War   *84*

TAKING MEASURE   Census Records of Adult Male Roman Citizens during the First and Second Punic Wars   *151*

Cutaway Reconstruction of the Forum of Augustus   *176*

TAKING MEASURE   The Falling Value of Roman Imperial Coinage, 27 B.C.E.–300 C.E.   *207*

TAKING MEASURE   Viking Coin Hoards, c. 865–895   *321*

Floor Plan of a Romanesque Church *375*

Floor Plan of a Cistercian Monastery *376*

TAKING MEASURE   Sentences Imposed by an Inquisitor, 1308–1323   *393*

Elements of a Gothic Cathedral *417*

TAKING MEASURE   Population Losses and the Plague, 1340–1450   *429*

TAKING MEASURE   The Rise and Fall of Silver Imports to Spain, 1550–1660 *504*

TAKING MEASURE   The Seventeenth-Century Army   *534*

African Slaves Imported into American Territories, 1701–1810   *571*

TAKING MEASURE   Relationship of Crop Harvested to Seed Used, 1400–1800 *579*

AUTHORS' NOTE
The B.C.E./C.E. Dating System

"WHEN WERE YOU BORN?" "What year is it?" We customarily answer questions like these with a number, such as "1987" or "2006." Our replies are usually automatic, taking for granted the numerous assumptions Westerners make about how dates indicate chronology. But to what do numbers such as 1987 and 2006 actually refer? In this book the numbers used to specify dates follow a recent revision of the system most common in the Western secular world. This system reckons the dates of solar years by counting backward and forward from the traditional date of the birth of Jesus Christ, over two thousand years ago. Using this method, numbers followed by the abbreviation B.C.E., standing for "before the common era" (or, as some would say, "before the Christian era"), indicate the number of years counting backward from the assumed date of the birth of Jesus Christ. B.C.E. therefore indicates the same chronology marked by the traditional abbreviation B.C. ("before Christ"). The larger the number following B.C.E. (or B.C.), the earlier in history is the year to which it refers. The date 431 B.C.E., for example, refers to a year 431 years before the birth of Jesus and therefore comes earlier in time than the dates 430 B.C.E., 429 B.C.E., and so on. The same calculation applies to numbering other time intervals calculated on the decimal system: those of ten years (a decade), of one hundred years (a century), and of one thousand years (a millennium). For example, the decade of the 440s B.C.E. (449 B.C.E. to 440 B.C.E.) is earlier than the decade of the 430s B.C.E. (439 B.C.E. to 430 B.C.E.). "Fifth century B.C.E." refers to the fifth period of 100 years reckoning backward from the birth of Jesus and covers the years 500 B.C.E. to 401 B.C.E. It is earlier in history than the fourth century B.C.E. (400 B.C.E. to 301 B.C.E.), which followed the fifth century B.C.E. Because this system has no year "zero," the first century B.C.E. covers the years 100 B.C.E. to 1 B.C.E. Dating millennia works similarly: the second millennium B.C.E. refers to the years 2000 B.C.E. to 1001 B.C.E., the third millennium to the years 3000 B.C.E. to 2001 B.C.E., and so on. To indicate years counted forward from the traditional date of Jesus' birth, numbers are followed by the abbreviation C.E., standing for "of the common era" (or "of the Christian era"). C.E. therefore indicates the same chronology marked by the traditional abbreviation A.D., which stands for the Latin phrase *anno Domini* ("in the year of the Lord"). A.D. properly comes before the date being marked. The date A.D. 1492, for example, translates as "in the year of the Lord 1492," meaning 1,492 years after the birth of Jesus. Under the B.C.E./C.E. system, this date would be written as 1492 C.E. For dating centuries, the term "first century C.E." refers to the period from 1 C.E. to 100 C.E. (which is the same period as A.D. 1 to A.D. 100). For dates C.E., the smaller the number, the earlier the date in history. The fourth century C.E. (301 C.E. to 400 C.E.) comes before the fifth century C.E. (401 C.E. to 500 C.E.). The year 312 C.E. is a date in the early fourth century C.E., while 395 C.E. is a date late in the same century. When numbers are given without either B.C.E. or C.E., they are presumed to be dates C.E. For example, the term *eighteenth century* with no abbreviation accompanying it refers to the years 1701 C.E. to 1800 C.E. No standard system of numbering years, such as B.C.E./C.E., existed in antiquity. Different people in different places identified years with varying names and numbers. Consequently, it was difficult to match up the years in any particular local system with those in a different system. Each city of ancient Greece, for example, had its own method for keeping track of the years. The ancient Greek historian Thucydides, therefore, faced a problem in presenting a chronology for the famous Peloponnesian War between Athens and Sparta, which began (by our reckoning) in 431 B.C.E. To try to explain to as many of his readers as possible the date the war had begun, he described its first year by three different local systems: "the year when Chrysis was in the forty-eighth year of her priesthood at Argos, and Aenesias was overseer at Sparta, and Pythodorus was magistrate at Athens." A Catholic monk named Dionysius, who lived in Rome in the sixth century C.E., invented the system of reckoning dates forward from the birth of Jesus. Calling himself *Exiguus* (Latin for "the little" or "the small") as a mark of humility, he placed Jesus' birth 754 years after the foundation of ancient Rome. Others then and now believe his date for Jesus' birth was in fact several years too late. Many scholars today calculate that Jesus was born in what would be 4 B.C.E. according to Dionysius's system, although a date a year or so earlier also seems possible. Counting backward from the supposed date of Jesus' birth to indicate dates earlier than that event represented a natural complement to reckoning forward for dates after it. The English historian and theologian Bede in the early eighth century was the first to use both forward and backward reckoning from the birth of Jesus in a historical work, and this system gradually gained wider acceptance because it provided a basis for standardizing the many local calendars used in the Western Christian world. Nevertheless, B.C. and A.D. were not used regularly until the end of the eighteenth century. B.C.E. and C.E. became common in the late twentieth century. The system of numbering years from the birth of Jesus is far from the only one in use today. The Jewish calendar of years, for example, counts forward from the date given to the creation of the world, which would be calculated as 3761 B.C.E. under the B.C.E./C.E. system. Under this system, years are designated A.M., an abbreviation of the Latin *anno mundi*, "in the year of the world." The Islamic calendar counts forward from the date of the prophet Muhammad's flight from Mecca, called the *Hijra*, in what is the year 622 C.E. The abbreviation A.H. (standing for the Latin phrase *anno Hegirae*, "in the year of the Hijra") indicates dates calculated by this system. Anthropology commonly reckons distant dates as "before the present" (abbreviated B.P.). History is often defined as the study of change over time; hence the importance of dates for the historian. But just as historians argue over which dates are most significant, they disagree over which dating system to follow. Their debate reveals perhaps the most enduring fact about history—its vitality.

About the Authors

LYNN HUNT, Eugen Weber Professor of Modern European History at the University of California, Los Angeles, received her B.A. from Carleton College and her M.A. and Ph.D. from Stanford University. She is the author of *Revolution and Urban Politics in Provincial France* (1978); *Politics, Culture, and Class in the French Revolution* (1984); and *The Family Romance of the French Revolution* (1992). She is also the coauthor of *Telling the Truth about History* (1994); coauthor of *Liberty, Equality, Fraternity: Exploring the French Revolution* (2001, with CD-ROM); editor of *The New Cultural History* (1989); editor and translator of *The French Revolution and Human Rights* (1996); and coeditor of *Histories: French Constructions of the Past* (1995), *Beyond the Cultural Turn* (1999), and *Human Rights and Revolutions* (2000). She has been awarded fellowships by the Guggenheim Foundation and the National Endowment for the Humanities and is a fellow of the American Academy of Arts and Sciences. She served as president of the American Historical Association in 2002.

THOMAS R. MARTIN, Jeremiah O'Connor Professor in Classics at the College of the Holy Cross, earned his B.A. at Princeton University and his M.A. and Ph.D. at Harvard University. He is the author of *Sovereignty and Coinage in Classical Greece* (1985) and *Ancient Greece* (1996, 2000) and one of the originators of *Perseus 1.0: Interactive Sources and Studies on Ancient Greece* (1992, 1996, and www.perseus.tufts.edu), which, among other awards, was named the EDUCOM Best Software in Social Sciences (History) in 1992. He also wrote the lead article on ancient Greece for the revised edition of the *Encarta* electronic encyclopedia. He serves on the editorial board of STOA (www.stoa.org) and as codirector of its DEMOS project (online resources on ancient Athenian democracy). A recipient of fellowships from the National Endowment for the Humanities and the American Council of Learned Societies, he is currently conducting research on the comparative historiography of ancient Greece and ancient China.

BARBARA H. ROSENWEIN, professor of history at Loyola University Chicago, earned her B.A., M.A., and Ph.D. at the University of Chicago. She is the author of *Rhinoceros Bound: Cluny in the Tenth Century* (1982); *To Be the Neighbor of Saint Peter: The Social Meaning of Cluny's Property, 909–1049* (1989); *Negotiating Space: Power, Restraint, and Privileges of Immunity in Early Medieval Europe* (1999); and *A Short History of the Middle Ages* (2001). She is the editor of *Anger's Past: The Social Uses of an Emotion in the Middle Ages* (1998) and coeditor of *Debating the Middle Ages: Issues and Readings* (1998) and *Monks and Nuns, Saints and Outcasts: Religion in Medieval Society* (2000). A recipient of Guggenheim and National Endowment for the Humanities fellowships, she is currently working on a history of emotions in the early Middle Ages.

R. PO-CHIA HSIA, Edwin Erle Sparks Professor of History at Pennsylvania State University, received his B.A. from Swarthmore College and his M.A. and Ph.D. from Yale University. He is the author of *Society and Religion in Münster, 1535–1618* (1984); *The Myth of Ritual Murder: Jews and Magic in Reformation Germany* (1988); *Social Discipline in the Reformation: Central Europe 1550–1750* (1989); *Trent 1475: Stories of a Ritual Murder Trial* (1992); and *The World of the Catholic Renewal* (1997). He has edited *The German People and the Reformation* (1988); *In and Out of the Ghetto: Jewish-Gentile Relations in Late Medieval and Early Modern Germany* (1995); *Calvinism and Religious Toleration in the Dutch Golden Age* (2002); and *A Companion to the Reformation World* (Blackwell Companion Series, 2004). An academician at the Academia Sinica, Taiwan, he has also been awarded fellowships by the Woodrow Wilson International Society of Scholars, the National Endowment for the Humanities, the Guggenheim Foundation, the Davis Center of Princeton University, the Mellon Foundation, the American Council of Learned Societies, and the American Academy in Berlin. Currently he is working on the cultural contacts between Europe and Asia between the sixteenth and eighteenth centuries.

BONNIE G. SMITH, Board of Governors Professor of History at Rutgers University, earned her B.A. at Smith College and her Ph.D. at the University of Rochester. She is the author of *Ladies of the Leisure Class* (1981); *Confessions of a Concierge: Madame Lucie's History of Twentieth-Century France* (1985); *Changing Lives: Women in European History Since 1700* (1989); *The Gender of History: Men, Women and Historical Practice* (1998); and *Imperialism* (2000). She is also the coauthor and translator of *What Is Property?* (1994); editor of *Global Feminisms Since 1945* (2000) and *Women's History in Global Perspective* (3 vols. 2004–2005); coeditor of *History and the Texture of Modern Life: Selected Writings of Lucy Maynard Salmon* (2001), *Gendering Disability* (2004), and *Sources of the Medieval and Early Modern World* (2005); and general editor of the forthcoming *Oxford Encyclopedia of Women in World History*. She has received fellowships from the Guggenheim Foundation, the National Endowment for the Humanities, the National Humanities Center, the Davis Center of Princeton University, and the American Council of Learned Societies. Currently she is studying the globalization of European culture since the seventeenth century.

SECOND EDITION

THE MAKING OF THE WEST

PEOPLES AND CULTURES

A CONCISE HISTORY

Volume I: To 1740

Foundations of Western Civilization

To 500 B.C.E.

ACCORDING TO THE MESOPOTAMIAN *EPIC OF CREATION*, the gods created the universe in a violent struggle. The goddess Tiamat, furious over her husband's murder, threatened to destroy the other gods. In response, they pledged to make the male god Marduk their king if he protected them. The fierce Marduk—"four were his eyes, four were his ears; when his lips moved, fire blazed forth"—crushed Tiamat and her army of snaky monsters in a gory battle. He then created human beings from the blood of her fiercest monster to be the gods' servants.

This myth showed how important it was for people to please the gods, who could crush them if humans made them angry. The precariousness of life implied by this story was real. Before civilization, in the Stone Age, tens and tens of thousands of years ago, people hunted and gathered food in the wild, using tools that they made from stone, bone, and wood. They roamed constantly to find enough food for their families and still have some left over for offerings to the gods that they believed controlled nature. Around ten or twelve thousand years ago, this way of life slowly began to change when people living in southwestern Asia began to cultivate wild plants and domesticate wild animals to become farmers and herders. The

■ **Gold Bull's Head Decoration for a Musical Instrument from Ancient Iraq**
This bull's head, made of gold leaf and lapis lazuli (a semiprecious stone prized for its vivid blue color), decorated a lyre—a stringed instrument similar to a harp. It was found in a tomb in the royal cemetery at Ur in what is today Iraq and was probably made in the period 2650–2550 B.C.E. The scenes below the beard, carved from mother of pearl, show animals walking upright like human beings and a mythological figure who appears to be a combination of a man and perhaps a scorpion. The donkey shown just above him is playing a lyre like this one. The meaning of the bull's head and the scenes remains a mystery. (© University of Pennsylvania Museum [neg. S4=142913].)

invention of agriculture and the domestication of animals made life in permanent settlements possible and produced surpluses of grain, fruit, vegetables, and meat that allowed people to do jobs besides farming. Some settlements gradually grew larger, until by 4000–3000 B.C.E., the first cities developed in Mesopotamia, the region between the Euphrates and Tigris Rivers (today southern Iraq). This was the start of civilization: life based in cities operating as political states, each having its own territory, ruler, taxes, and sense of local identity. Religion was the center of Mesopotamian civilization. Remembering the Marduk myth, rulers believed that the gods held them responsible for maintaining order on earth and for making sure that people honored the gods. The Egyptians, whose civilization emerged about 3100–3000 B.C.E., also held strong religious beliefs. Religion, combined with extraordinary architectural skills, inspired them to build fabulous temples and the pyramids.

Civilizations arose at different times in different places. Starting about 2500 B.C.E., they emerged in India, China, and the Americas. By 2000 B.C.E., civilizations had appeared in Anatolia (today Turkey), on islands in the eastern Mediterranean Sea, and in Greece. The early civilizations of Mesopotamia, Egypt, the eastern Mediterranean, and Greece began the history of Western civilization by interacting with each other. Building on concepts they took from their Near Eastern neighbors, the Greeks passed on to us today the idea of the West as a region with its own type of civilization. They identified Europe as the West (where the sun sets) and different from the East (where the sun rises).

The Greeks also inherited from their Near Eastern neighbors the idea that regional differences meant that one people's way of life was better than another's. This ancient dispute continues today in ongoing arguments about whether Western, Eastern, or some other civilization is best. One point is clear: the story of Western civilization is the story of cultural borrowings between the peoples of Europe and their neighbors near and far. That borrowing involved ideas, technologies, and goods. In short, the story of Western civilization concerns cultural, political, and economic interchange both among the West's diverse peoples and between them and other peoples around the globe. The West is a constantly evolving concept, not a fixed region with unchanging borders or members. It is wrong to take the word *Western* in Western civilization to mean "fenced off in the West from the rest of the world."

Early Western civilization developed when trade and war brought peoples in the Near East and Europe into contact. This cultural interaction provided opportunities for different people to learn from one another and to adapt for their own use the traditions, beliefs, and technology of others. These exchanges generated intended and unintended consequences. Metallurgical technology, for example, created ever better tools and weapons but also increased social differences among people. Just as the gods insisted on their superiority to human beings, people also developed **hierarchy**, or status differences, among themselves.

Making Civilization, to 1000 B.C.E.

The background of the story of civilization reaches far back into time. About four hundred thousand years ago, people whose brains and bodies resembled ours appeared first in Africa. These people, called *Homo sapiens*, or "wise human beings" by scientists, were the immediate ancestors of modern human beings. They spread out from there and gradually populated the rest of the earth. Anthropologists call this time the "Stone Age" because people made tools and weapons from stone; these early humans did not yet know how to work metals. The Stone Age is divided into two parts to mark an enormous transformation in the way people lived: the earlier part is the Paleolithic ("Old Stone") period, and the later part is the Neolithic ("New Stone"), which began about ten to twelve thousand years ago (c. 10,000–8000 B.C.E.). At this time, many human populations gradually transformed their ways of acquiring food by learning to farm—with enormous consequences for later history. This change was so radical that historians call it the "Neolithic Revolution."

Eventually, the Neolithic Revolution led to what historians traditionally identify as the features of **civilization**: cities with large buildings for community purposes (especially religion); political systems; production of textiles, pottery, and other crafts for local use and trade; and writing. In Mesopotamia, where the first cities arose about 4000 to 3000 B.C.E., the invention of bronze, an alloy of copper and tin used to make tools, weapons, and jewelry, led archaeologists to call the period from approximately 4000 to 1000 B.C.E. the "Bronze Age." The rulers of Bronze Age cities battled one another for glory, territory, and, especially, access to copper and tin. The drive to acquire metal ores pushed the Akkadians (named after Akkad, their capital city on the Tigris River) to create the first **empire**, a political unit controlling formerly independent territories subjected to a single ruler.

Paleolithic and Neolithic Life, c. 400,000–4000 B.C.E.

Paleolithic peoples lived as hunter-gatherers, meaning they roamed around looking for food; they did not know how to farm and did not live in settled communities. They probably banded together in groups of twenty to fifty, frequently changing their location to hunt animals and gather plants, fruits, and nuts. Finding food was the responsibility of both men and women. Women of childbearing age had to nurse their young, so they usually stayed close to camp; the food they gathered provided the group's most reliable supply of nourishment. Women beyond childbearing age, unburdened by infants, performed many different tasks for the group. Men probably did most of the hunting of dangerous wild animals far from camp, although recent archaeological evidence shows that women also participated, especially in hunting with nets.

Hunter-gatherer societies perhaps started out as egalitarian (meaning all adults enjoyed a rough equality in making decisions for the group), but hierarchy eventually developed. Men could acquire prestige from hunting large beasts and bringing back meat. Older women and men earned respect because of their wisdom from long experience and because their age set them apart at a time when illness and accidents killed most people before age thirty. Some Paleolithic graves contain weapons, tools, animal figurines, seashells, ivory beads, and bracelets. These individuals probably were especially prestigious members of their group. The care with which the dead were buried, decorated with red paint, flowers, and seashells, indicates concern with the mystery of death and perhaps some belief in an afterlife. Paleolithic artists also sculpted statuettes of human figures, probably for religious purposes.

Items found in burials indicate that hunter-gatherer bands traded energetically with one another. Trade spread knowledge—especially technological advances, such as ways to start fires or make tools, and artistic techniques for creating beauty and expressing beliefs—that changed lives. The use of fire for cooking was a far-reaching technological innovation because cooking made it possible for people to eat plants, such as wild grain, that they could not digest raw.

The Neolithic Revolution took place when people learned to farm and to domesticate animals about ten to twelve thousand years ago. The first farms emerged in the foothills of the Near East's Fertile Crescent, an arc of territory that curved up from what is today the

■ **Prehistoric Venus Figurine**
Archaeologists have discovered small female figures, like this one from Romania, at many late Paleolithic and Neolithic sites in Europe. They predate writing, so we cannot be sure of their significance, but many scholars assume that their hefty proportions are meant to signal a special concern for fertility. These female figures may represent pre-historic people's vision of rare good fortune: having enough food to become fat and produce healthy children. The statuettes are called Venus figurines after the Roman goddess of love.
(Erich Lessing/Art Resource, NY.)

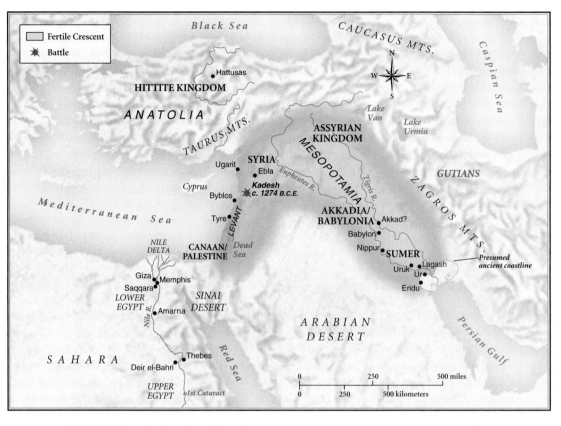

■ MAP 1.1 The Ancient Near East

The large region we call the ancient Near East included a variety of landscapes, climates, peoples, and languages; monarchy was the usual form of government. Trade by land and sea for natural resources, especially metals, kept the peoples of the region in constant contact with one another, as did the wars of conquest that the region's kings regularly launched.

Jordan Valley in Israel, through eastern Turkey, and down into the foothills and plains of Iraq and Iran (Map 1.1).* The revolution started when a climate change brought more rainfall and increased the amount of wild grains to gather. This larger food supply meant people could support more children, but, the more hungry mouths were born, the greater became people's need for food. After thousands of years of trial and error, people in the Fertile Crescent invented agriculture by sowing seeds from one crop to produce another. Since women had more experience foraging for plants, they probably played the major role in developing farming, while men continued to hunt.

---

*The meanings of the terms *Near East* and *Middle East* have changed over time. Both originally reflected a European geographic point of view. During the nineteenth century, *Middle East* usually meant the area from Iran to Burma, especially the Indian subcontinent (then part of the British Empire); *Near East* meant the Balkan peninsula (today the countries of Croatia, Slovenia, Bosnia-Herzegovina, Macedonia,

During this same period, people learned to domesticate animals for meat, starting with sheep about 8500 B.C.E. By about 7000 B.C.E., keeping herds for food had become common in the Near East, which was home to various kinds of wild animals such as goats, pigs, and cattle, that turned out to be suitable for domestication.

Some bands moved around to find grazing land for their animals, living as pastoralists, but farmers had to reside in a permanent location to raise crops year after year. Settling down marked a turning point in the relation between human beings and the natural environment. Farmers cut down trees and diverted streams for irrigation. By 4000 B.C.E., people migrating from the Fertile Crescent had spread knowledge of agriculture to the European shores of the Atlantic Ocean. Eventually, farmers were able to produce more food than they needed to feed themselves and their families. The creation of agricultural surpluses allowed some people to specialize in architecture, art, crafts, metalwork, textile production, and trade. This change opened the way for cities to develop.

The Neolithic Revolution created greater social hierarchy because new levels of management were needed to supervise irrigation. Greater economic activity also created a new division of labor by gender. Men began to dominate agriculture when heavy wooden plows pulled by oxen were invented, sometime after 4000 B.C.E. Not having to bear and nurse babies, men also took over long-distance trade. Women and older children took on new domestic labor as they turned milk into cheese and yogurt and made their families' clothing. This gendered division of labor arose as an efficient response to the conditions and technologies of the time, but it also increased men's status.

The Birth of Cities and Empire in Mesopotamia, c. 4000–1000 B.C.E.

The first cities emerged in Mesopotamia by about 4000 B.C.E. in the plains between and around the Tigris and Euphrates Rivers (Map 1.1). Agriculture had begun in the Fertile Crescent's well-watered hills, but there was not enough good farmland to support large settlements. The flatland bordering the rivers was huge but hard to farm: temperatures soared to 120 degrees Fahrenheit and little rain fell, yet the rivers flooded unpredictably. Mesopotamians transformed this harsh environment into lush farmland by irrigating the plains with water channeled from the rivers. A vast

---

Yugoslavia, Albania, Greece, Bulgaria, Romania, and the European portion of Turkey) and the eastern Mediterranean. The term *Far East* referred to the Asian lands that border the Pacific Ocean. Today, *Middle East* usually refers to the area encompassing the Arabic-speaking countries of the eastern Mediterranean region, Israel, Iran, Turkey, Cyprus, and much of North Africa. Ancient historians, by contrast, commonly use the term *ancient Near East* to designate Anatolia (often called Asia Minor, today occupied by the Asian portion of Turkey), Cyprus, the lands around the eastern end of the Mediterranean, the Arabian peninsula, Mesopotamia (the lands north of the Persian Gulf, today Iraq and Iran), and Egypt. Some historians exclude Egypt from this group on strict geographic grounds because it is in Africa (the rest of the region lies in Asia). In this book, we observe the common usage of the term *Near East* to mean the lands of southwestern Asia and Egypt.

system of canals allowed farmers to turn the desert green with crops and controlled flooding. The increase in food production created surpluses, which allowed the population to swell and nonagricultural occupations to flourish. Thus city life began.

The need to construct and maintain irrigation canals promoted centralization in Mesopotamian cities, which controlled the farmland lying outside their fortified walls. This arrangement—an urban center exercising political and economic control over the nearby countryside—is called a **city-state**. Mesopotamian city-states were independent communities competing with each other for land and resources. Travelers from one to another would first come to irrigated fields on a city's outskirts, then villages housing agricultural workers, and finally the city's walls. Ships transporting grain and goods would be docked nearby on the river-bank. Inside the walls were private houses and apartments, the huge royal palace, and immense temples.

The people of Sumer, the name for southern Mesopotamia, built the earliest cities. Unlike other Mesopotamians, the Sumerians did not speak a Semitic language (the group of languages from which Hebrew and Arabic came); the origins of their language remain a mystery. By 3000 B.C.E., the Sumerians had created twelve independent city-states, such as Uruk, Eridu, and Ur, which repeatedly fought each other over territory. By 2500 B.C.E., these cities had each expanded to twenty thousand residents or more. The rooms in Sumerians' mud-brick houses surrounded open courts. Large homes had a dozen rooms or more. Everyone was in danger from contaminated water because no sewerage system existed. Pigs and dogs scavenged in the garbage dumped in the streets.

Agriculture and trade made these cities prosperous. Sumerians bartered grain, vegetable oil, woolens, and leather with one another, and they acquired metals, timber, and precious stones from foreign trade. Traders traveled as far as India, where the cities of Indus civilization emerged about 2500 B.C.E. Technological innovation also strengthened the Mesopotamian economy, especially around 3000 B.C.E., when Sumerians invented a wheel for use on wagons. Temples and the rulers' families dominated the Sumerian economy because they both controlled large farms and gangs of laborers, but some private households also amassed wealth.

Hierarchy, which had initially emerged from the organization of irrigation during the Neolithic Revolution, dominated Sumerian society. Slaves, owned by temples and by individuals, had the lowest status. People became slaves by being captured in war, by being born to slaves, by voluntarily selling themselves or their children (usually to escape starvation), or by being sold by their creditors when they could not repay loans (known as "debt slavery"). Children whose parents dedicated them as slaves to the gods could rise to prominent positions in the temple administrations. In general, however, slaves existed in near-total dependency on other people and were excluded from normal social relations. They usually worked without pay and lacked almost all legal rights. They could be bought, sold, beaten, or even killed by their masters because they were considered property.

Slaves worked in domestic service, craft production, and farming, but scholars dispute whether they or free laborers were more important to the economy. Free persons performed most government labor, paying their taxes with work rather than with money, which was measured in amounts of food or precious metal (coins were not invented until about 700 B.C.E., in Anatolia). Most slaves had little chance of gaining freedom. Masters' wills could liberate them, or they could purchase their freedom from earnings that some owners would let them keep.

Hierarchy became so strong in Mesopotamian society that its most powerful man became a king—a sole ruler whose son inherited his father's position. To display their exalted status, royal families lived in elaborate palaces that served as administrative centers and treasure-houses. Archaeologists excavating royal graves in Ur have revealed the rulers' dazzling riches—spectacular possessions crafted in gold, silver, and precious stones. These burials also yielded grisly evidence of the top-ranking status of the king and queen: servants sacrificed to look after their royal masters after death.

Patriarchy—domination by men in political, social, and economic life— already existed in Mesopotamian city-states. A Sumerian queen was respected because she was the king's wife and the mother of the royal children, but her husband held supreme power. The king formed a council of older men as his advisers, but he publicly acknowledged the gods as his rulers; this concept made the state a theocracy (government by gods) and gave priests and priestesses public influence. The king's greatest responsibility was to keep the gods happy and to defeat attacks from rival cities. The king demanded taxes from the working population to support his family, court, palace, army, and officials. The kings, along with the priests of the large temples, regulated most of the economy in their kingdoms by controlling the exchange of food and goods between farmers and crafts producers in a system known as a **redistributive economy**.

Mesopotamians practiced **polytheism**: they worshipped many gods whom they believed controlled different aspects of life, such as the weather, fertility, and war. They believed that their safety depended on the goodwill of the gods, and each city-state honored one deity as its special protector. To please their gods, city dwellers offered sacrifices and built ziggurats (temple towers) soaring as high as ten stories. Mesopotamians believed that if human beings angered the gods, divinities such as the sky-god Enlil and Inanna (also called Ishtar), goddess of love and war, would punish them by sending disease, floods, famine, and defeats in war.

Mythical stories such as the *Epic of Creation* and the *Epic of Gilgamesh* described the unbridgeable gap between gods and human beings. Gilgamesh was a legendary king of Uruk, who lusted to cheat death. He forced the young men of Uruk to toil like slaves and the young women to sleep with him. When his mistreated subjects begged Aruru, mother of the gods, to grant them a protector, she created a man of nature, Enkidu, "hairy all over . . . dressed as cattle are."

A week of sex with a prostitute tamed this brute, preparing him for civilization: "Enkidu was weaker; he ran slower than before. But he had gained judgment, was wiser." After wrestling Gilgamesh to a draw, he and the king became friends and conquered Humbaba (or Huwawa), the ugly giant of the Pine Forest, and the Bull of Heaven. The gods doomed Enkidu to die soon after these triumphs. Depressed about the human condition, Gilgamesh sought the secret of immortality, but a thieving snake ruined his quest. He decided that the road to immortality for mortals was to win fame for deeds. Only memory and gods could live forever.

A late version of the Gilgamesh story recounted how the gods sent a huge flood over the earth. They warned one man, Utnapishtim, telling him to build a boat. He loaded his vessel with his relatives, workers, possessions, domesticated and wild animals, and "everything there was." After a week of torrential rains, they left the boat to repopulate the earth. This story recalled the devastating floods of Mesopotamia and looked ahead to the later biblical account of the flood and Noah's ark. Mesopotamian myths, living on in poetry, song, and art, greatly influenced Greek mythology.

The invention of writing helped these stories live on. Sumerians originally invented this new technology to do accounting. Before writing, people drew small pictures on clay tablets to keep count of objects or animals. Writing started when people created symbols instead of pictures to represent the sounds of speech. Sumerian writing did not use an alphabet (a system in which each symbol represents the sound of a letter), but rather a system of wedge-shaped marks pressed into clay tablets to represent the sounds of syllables and entire words (see Figure 1.1, page 13). Other Mesopotamians adopted this form of writing, which is today called **cuneiform** (from *cuneus*, Latin for "wedge"). For a long time, writing was a professional skill for accounting mastered by only a few men and women, known as scribes.

■ The Ziggurat of Ur in Sumer

King Ur-Nammu and his son Shulgi built this huge temple to honor the gods in their city of Ur (in what is today southern Iraq) in the early twenty-first century B.C.E. It had three massive terraces, one above another, connected by stairways. The mud-brick core of the structure was covered with baked bricks held in place with tar. The walls were more than seven feet thick to support the enormous weight of the terraces. The total height is uncertain, but the first terrace alone soared some forty-five feet above ground level.

(Hirmer Fotoarchiv,
Munich, Germany.)

■ A Cuneiform Letter in Its Envelope

Written about 1900 B.C.E., this cuneiform text records a merchant's complaint that a shipment of copper contained less metal than he had expected. His letter, written on a clay tablet several inches long, was enclosed in an outer clay shell marked with the sender's private seal. This envelope protected the inner text from tampering or breakage. (© Copyright The Trustees of The British Museum.)

Eventually, scribes began to record nature lore, mathematics, foreign languages, and literature. Written poems and stories then provided a powerful new way to pass on traditions. The world's oldest written poetry by a known author was composed in the twenty-third century B.C.E. by Enheduanna, the daughter of King Sargon of the city of Akkad. Written in Sumerian, her poetry praised the life-giving goddess of love, Inanna: "the great gods scattered from you like fluttering bats, unable to face your intimidating gaze . . . knowing and wise queen of all the lands, who makes all creatures and people multiply." Later princesses who wrote love songs, lullabies, dirges, and prayers continued the Mesopotamian tradition of royal women becoming authors.

Metallurgy was another influential technology that developed in this period; its invention indirectly helped produce the world's first empire, in Akkadia (see Map 1.1). After figuring out how to smelt ore and forge metal alloys, Bronze Age smiths could make new luxury goods, such as jewelry, as well as better tools and weapons. Bronze, a copper-tin alloy hard enough to hold a razor edge, produced durable swords and spearheads. Rich men found a new way to display their status by paying artisans to decorate their weapons with ornate engravings and inlays, as on costly guns today. Metal weapons also emphasized the differences between men's and women's roles in society because they marked the masculine roles of hunter and warrior that had emerged long ago in the division of labor among hunter-gatherers. The development of metallurgy helped lead to the first empires because Mesopotamian kings craved a reliable supply of metals to support their royal status: those who had no ore in their territory had to get it by trade or by conquest.

The first empire arose about 2350 B.C.E., when Sargon, king of the city of Akkad, launched invasions north and south of his homeland in mid-Mesopotamia seeking metals and glory. His violent campaigns conquered lands from Sumer all the way to the Mediterranean Sea. Sargon's grandson Naram-Sin continued this foreign conquest. By 2250 B.C.E., he had attacked Ebla, a large city whose site was recently discovered in modern Syria. Archaeologists at Ebla have unearthed many cuneiform tablets, some in multiple languages, suggesting Ebla thrived as a center for learning.

The conquests that created empire also spread Mesopotamian literature and art throughout the Near East. Although the Akkadians spoke a Semitic language, not Sumerian, after conquering Sumer they adopted much of the defeated land's

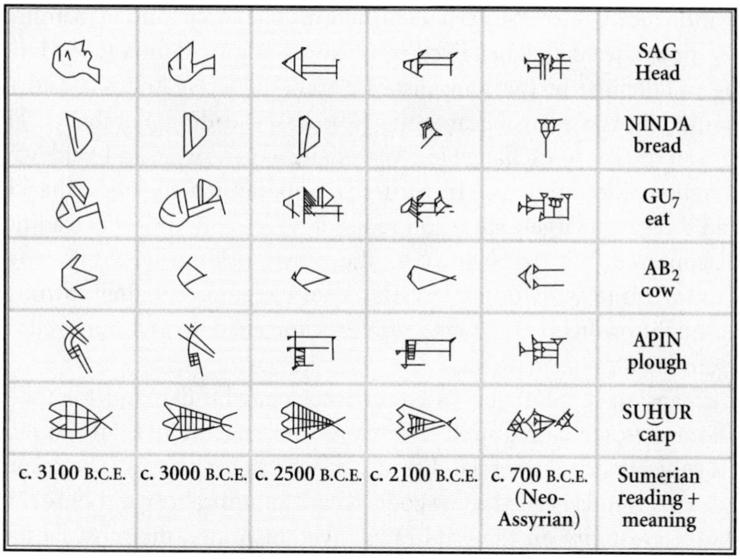

					SAG Head
					NINDA bread
					GU$_7$ eat
					AB$_2$ cow
					APIN plough
					SUHUR carp
c. 3100 B.C.E.	c. 3000 B.C.E.	c. 2500 B.C.E.	c. 2100 B.C.E.	c. 700 B.C.E. (Neo- Assyrian)	Sumerian reading + meaning

■ **FIGURE 1.1 Cuneiform Writing**

*The earliest known form of writing developed in different locations in Mesopotamia in the late
3000s B.C.E., when meaning and sound were associated with signs such as these. The scribes who
mastered the system used sticks or reeds to press dense rows of small wedge-shaped marks into damp
clay tablets or chisels to engrave them on stone. Cuneiform was used for at least fifteen Near Eastern
languages and continued to be written for three thousand years.*

religion, literature, and culture. Other peoples later conquered by the Akkadians
were thus exposed to Sumerian beliefs and traditions, which they in turn adapted to
their own purposes. In this way, war indirectly promoted cultural interaction
between peoples.

Neighboring hill peoples, the Gutians, defeated the Akkadian empire around
2200 B.C.E. A Mesopotamian poet gave a religious explanation for this catastrophe:
King Naram-Sin, enraged at the god Enlil when his capital's prosperity waned,
reduced Enlil's temple to "dust like a mountain mined for silver." Enlil then punished the Akkadians by sending the Gutians swooping down from their "land that
rejects outside control, with the intelligence of human beings but with the form and
stumbling words of a dog." This account reflected the Mesopotamians' deep-seated
belief that the gods held ultimate power over human destiny.

Mesopotamian Legacies: Commerce, Law, and Learning, c. 2200–1000 B.C.E.

Two kingdoms, Assyria and Babylonia, emerged in the second millennium B.C.E. to
replace the Akkadian Empire. Their innovations in private commerce, law, and

learning influenced later Western civilization. The Assyrians, a Semitic people descended from the Akkadians, lived in northern Mesopotamia (see Map 1.1). By becoming middlemen in the long-distance trade between Anatolia and southern Mesopotamia, the Assyrians became the Near East's leading merchants. They produced woolen textiles to exchange for Anatolian copper, silver, and gold, which they sold throughout Mesopotamia. In earlier Mesopotamian societies, the kings and priests had directed a largely state-run redistributive economy. This tradition never totally disappeared, but by 1900 B.C.E., the Assyrian kings were allowing private individuals to trade with other city-states and regions on their own. Assyrian investors sought profits by financing donkey caravans to travel hundreds of rocky and dangerous miles to Anatolia.

The expansion of profit-based commerce created a demand for the enforcement of contracts, which required law. It was the king's sacred duty to render justice to his subjects in commercial disputes as well as for crimes. The record of the king's decisions is today called a law code. King Hammurabi (r. c. 1792–1750 B.C.E.) of Babylon, a great city on the Euphrates River, instituted the most famous set of early laws. Hammurabi proclaimed he was showing Shamash, the Babylonian sun-god and god of justice, that he was fulfilling a king's responsibility imposed on him by the gods—to ensure justice and the moral and material welfare of his people: "So that the powerful may not oppress the powerless, to provide justice for the orphan and the widow . . . let the victim of injustice see the law which applies to him, let his heart be put at ease."

Hammurabi's code divided society into three categories: free persons, commoners, and slaves. We do not know what made the first two categories different, but free persons outranked commoners in the hierarchy of Babylonian society. An attacker who caused a pregnant woman of the free class to miscarry, for example, paid twice the fine levied for the same offense against a woman of the commoner class. A member of the free class who killed a commoner was fined instead of executed. For social equals, the code specified "an eye for an eye."

The people themselves assembled in courts to determine most cases. The laws primarily concerned the king's interests as a property owner who leased innumerable tracts of land to tenants in return for rent or services. For offenses against property, the laws imposed severe penalties, including mutilation or a gruesome death for crimes as varied as theft, wrongful sales, and careless construction. In this patriarchal society, women had limited legal rights, but they could make business contracts and appear in court. A wife could divorce her husband for cruelty; a husband could divorce his wife for any reason. Since, however, divorced wives were entitled to recover the property they had brought to the marriage, husbands had to think twice before ending their marriages.

Hammurabi's laws reveal much about urban life in Bronze Age Mesopotamia. Burglary and assault apparently plagued city dwellers. Marriages were arranged by the groom and the bride's father, who sealed the agreement with a legal contract.

Laws about surgery inform us about the work of doctors. Because people believed that angry divinities caused many diseases, Mesopotamian medicine included magic as well as potions and specific diets. Magicians treated illness by interpreting signs, such as the patient's dreams or hallucinations, and casting spells.

Archaeological excavations and cuneiform records reveal that Mesopotamian cities had numerous wine shops, often run by women proprietors, offering drinks and a place to relax. Residents also found relief from the odors and crowding in the streets in open spaces set aside as parks. The world's oldest known map, an inscribed clay tablet showing the outlines of the Babylonian city of Nippur about 1500 B.C.E., indicates that a sizeable section of the city was parkland.

Mapmaking required sophisticated calculations and spatial knowledge, which point to Mesopotamia's most influential achievements: knowledge in mathematics and astronomy. Mathematicians used algebra to solve complex problems and knew how to derive the roots of numbers. They invented place-value notation and a system of reckoning based on sixty, still used in our division of a circle into hours, minutes, and degrees. Mesopotamians' skill in describing the paths of the stars and planets probably arose from a desire to make predictions about the future, based on the astrological belief that the movements of celestial objects affect human life. The charts and tables compiled by Mesopotamian stargazers laid the foundation for later advances in astronomical knowledge.

■ **REVIEW:** *How did life change for people in Mesopotamia when they began to live in cities?*

Early Civilizations in Egypt, the Levant, and Anatolia, c. 3100–1000 B.C.E.

Africa was home to the second great civilization to shape the West: Egypt. It lay close enough to Mesopotamia to learn from that culture but was geographically set apart enough to develop its own distinct culture. Egyptians created a wealthy, deeply religious, and strongly traditional civilization ruled by kings. Unlike Mesopotamia, Egypt was politically united under a strong central authority. The Egyptian kings' desire for immortality in the afterlife led them to build some of the largest tombs in history, the pyramids. Egyptian architecture and art inspired later Mediterranean peoples, especially the Greeks.

The height of Egyptian power came under the New Kingdom (c. 1569–1081 B.C.E.*); the Hittite kingdom in Anatolia was then Egypt's most aggressive rival

---

*Every date in Egyptian history is approximate and controversial, and different scholars use different dates because the evidence is often contradictory. Those used here are taken from the articles and "Egyptian King List" in *The Oxford Encyclopedia of Ancient Egypt*, edited by Donald B. Redford (2001).

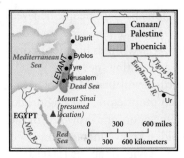

The Ancient Levant

(see Map 1.1). The Hittites had become a powerful people by about 1750 B.C.E. They flourished because they inhabited a fertile, upland region and controlled trade there and southward into the Levant[*] (modern Jordan, Syria, Lebanon, and Israel), the commercial crossroads of the eastern Mediterranean and the persistent site of conflict among Near Eastern powers.

Religion and Rule in Egypt, c. 3100–2190 B.C.E.

The first large-scale Egyptian state emerged about 3100–3000 B.C.E., when King Menes united Upper (southern) Egypt and Lower (northern) Egypt. (*Upper* and *Lower* refer to the direction in which the Nile River flows—from south of Egypt northward to the Mediterranean Sea.) By around 2687 B.C.E., the kings following Menes had forged a centralized state, today known as the Old Kingdom, which lasted until around 2190 B.C.E. (Map 1.2). Egypt's people lived mainly in farming villages in a narrow band of land along the Nile. Their irrigated farms extended several miles away from the river's banks on both sides. The Nile overflowed its banks once every year for several weeks, when melting snow from the mountains of central Africa gradually swelled its flow. This predictable and gentle flood enriched the soil near the river with nutrients from silt and diluted harmful deposits of mineral salts. Unlike the random deluges in Mesopotamia, the Nile's flood recurred at the same season every year and benefited the land. Trouble came only if dry weather in the mountains kept the river from overflowing.

Deserts east and west of the Nile protected Egypt from invasion, except through the Nile delta in the north and on the southern frontier with Nubia. Deposits of metal ores, trade by sea, and lush agriculture made Egypt prosperous, but it had fewer and smaller cities than in Mesopotamia. From their ample supplies of grain, the Egyptians made bread and beer, the most common beverage. Egypt's population included a diversity of people, whose skin color ranged from light to very dark. Many ancient Egyptians would be regarded as black by modern racial classification (unknown to ancient peoples). The modern controversy over whether Egyptians were people of color is anachronistic; ancient Egyptians presumably identified themselves by geography, language, religion, and social traditions. Later peoples, especially the Greeks, admired Egyptian civilization for its great antiquity and religious devotion. Some nineteenth-century historians minimized the Egyptian contribution to Western civilization, but ancient peoples did not.

---

[*]The name *Levant*, French for "rising (sun)"—that is, the East—reflects the European perspective on the area's location.

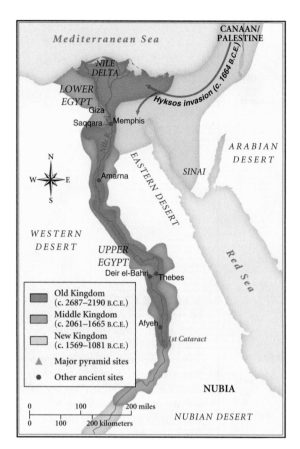

■ **MAP 1.2 Ancient Egypt**
The Nile River, closely embraced by arid deserts, provided Egyptians with water to irrigate their fields and a highway for traveling north to the Mediterranean Sea and south to Nubia. The only easy land route into and out of Egypt lay through the Nile delta region into the northern Sinai peninsula and on into the coastal area of the Levant; Egyptian kings therefore always fought to control these areas to secure the safety of their land.

Like everyone else in history, Egyptians learned from other peoples. For example, they probably learned the technology of writing from the Sumerians, but they developed their own scripts rather than adopting cuneiform. To write formal and official texts, they used an ornate, picture-based script known as hieroglyphs (see Figure 1.2 on page 18). Looking southward, Egyptians saw that the Nubians had already built extensive settlements and produced complex art by Menes' time. At places such as Afyeh near the Nile's First Cataract, a Nubian social elite lived in dwellings much grander than the small huts housing most of the population. Egyptians constantly interacted with Nubians while trading for raw materials such as gold, ivory, and animal skins, and Nubia's hierarchical organization perhaps influenced the development of centralized authority in Egypt's Old Kingdom. Eventually, however, Egypt's power overshadowed that of its southern neighbor.

The strength or weakness of the central authority determined Egyptian political history. When the kings were strong, as during the Old Kingdom, the country was stable, and trade flourished with the Levant and other Mediterranean areas.

Hieroglyph	Meaning	Sound value
	vulture	glottal stop
	flowering reed	consonantal I
	forearm and hand	ayin
	quail chick	W
	foot	B
	stool	P
	horned viper	F
	owl	M
	water	N
	mouth	R
	reed shelter	H
	twisted flax	slightly guttural
	placenta (?)	H as in "loch"
	animal's belly	slightly softer than h
	door bolt	S
	folded cloth	S
	pool	SH
	hill	Q
	basket with handle	K
	jar stand	G
	loaf	T

■ **FIGURE 1.2 Egyptian Hieroglyphs**

Ancient Egyptians developed their own system of writing about 3100 B.C.E., using pictures such as these. Because this formal script was used mainly for religious inscriptions on buildings and sacred objects, Greeks referred to it as ta hieroglyphica *("the sacred carved letters"), from which comes the modern term* hieroglyphs. *Egyptian hieroglyphs employ around seven hundred pictures in three categories: ideograms (signs indicating things or ideas), phonograms (signs indicating sounds), and determinatives (signs clarifying the meaning of the other signs). Eventually (the chronology is unsure), Egyptians also developed the handwritten cursive script called* demotic *(Greek for "of the people"), a much simpler and quicker form of writing.*

However, when regional governors or prominent priests, whose status was second only to that of the royal family, refused to support the king, political instability resulted.

The king's success depended on his properly fulfilling his religious duties. Egyptians worshiped many gods, often depicted as creatures with both human and animal features such as the head of a jackal or a bird atop a human body. They did not worship animals; rather, they believed that each god had a particular animal to serve as the bearer of the god's divine soul. A picture or statue of a divinity had to include the animal so the image would include the soul. Egyptian religion told lively stories about the passion-filled lives of the gods to explain their powers. Deities were associated with powerful natural objects, emotions, qualities, and technologies, such as the sun-god Re; Isis, goddess of love and fertility; and Thoth, god of wisdom and the inventor of writing.

Egyptians regarded their king as a god in human form, but they recognized that the man on the throne was mortal. That is, they saw a difference between the individual king's human existence and the divine origin of his rule. The monarchy as a system was divine because it represented on earth the supernatural, eternal force that created harmony and stability in the universe. This force was called Maat, often translated as "truth" or "justice" or "correct balance." The king had to rule according to Maat by keeping the forces of nature in balance for the benefit of his people. The Egyptian kings' religious identity made them different from Sumerian kings, who ruled only as men, though their kingdoms were devoted to the gods.

An Egyptian king ensured his people's safety and prosperity by strictly observing ritual. For example, he had to keep to a specific time for taking a bath, going for a walk, or having sex with his wife. Above all, the king was responsible for summoning the divine power that made the Nile overflow. If he failed to make the flood occur, he gravely weakened his authority. If he could not produce annual floods and keep the people well fed, then he had lost his Maat—and might lose his kingdom.

Old Kingdom rulers used expensive building programs to demonstrate their devotion to the gods and proclaim their status atop the social hierarchy. Their great buildings were mainly the temples or tombs that were constructed outside their cities. In the suburbs of Memphis, the first capital (south of modern Cairo), these kings erected the most stunning proofs of their piety and status—huge tombs in the form of pyramids. These monuments formed the centerpieces of groups of buildings for royal funerals and religious ceremonies. Although the pyramids were not the first monuments built from enormous, worked stones (that title goes to temples on the Mediterranean island of Malta), they rank as the grandest.

The Old Kingdom rulers spent vast sums of money on these huge complexes because they cared so much about protecting their mummified bodies for the afterlife. In the twenty-sixth century B.C.E., King Cheops commissioned the biggest of them all—the so-called Great Pyramid at Giza. At about 480 feet high, it stands taller than a forty-story skyscraper. Covering over thirteen acres and extending 760 feet on each side, it required more than two million blocks of limestone, some of which weighed fifteen tons apiece. Quarried in the desert, the stone was floated to the site on river barges and dragged on rollers and sleds up earthen ramps into position.

The kings' lavish preparations for death reflect the strong Egyptian belief in life after death. A prayer from about 2300 B.C.E. expresses that idea: "O divine Atum, put your arms around King Neferkare Pepy II, around this construction work, around this pyramid. . . . May you guard lest anything evil happen to him throughout the course of eternity." So they would be comfortable in their new existence, the royal family packed their tombs with gilded furniture, sparkling jewelry, and luxury goods of all kinds. Archaeologists have uncovered two full-size cedar ships buried next to the Great Pyramid, meant to carry King Cheops on his voyage into eternity.

Their need to direct the labor and expenses for their mammoth projects led Old Kingdom rulers to centralize their administration and strengthen the social hierarchy. The king and queen topped the social order. Brothers and sisters in the royal family could marry each other, perhaps because such matches were believed necessary to preserve the purity of the royal line or to imitate the marriages of the gods. The priests, royal administrators, regional governors, and commanders of the army ranked next in the hierarchy. The common people, who did all the manual labor, made up the great majority of free people in Egypt. (Slaves became more common after the Old Kingdom.) Free workers had heavy obligations to the state. For example, although they were not slaves, they were required to work on the pyramids. On occasion they received wages, but mostly their labor was a

■ **The Pyramids at Giza in Egypt**
The kings of Old Kingdom Egypt constructed enormous stone pyramids for their tombs. Pyramids were the centerpieces of large complexes of temples and courtyards stretching to the banks of the Nile or along a canal leading to the river. The burial chambers lay at the end of long, narrow tunnels snaking through the pyramids' interiors. The largest pyramid shown here is the nearly five-hundred-foot high Great Pyramid of King Cheops, erected in the twenty-sixth century B.C.E. (© John Lawrence/SuperStock.)

way of paying taxes. Rates of taxation reached 20 percent on the produce of free farmers.

Women generally had the same legal rights as men. They could own land and slaves, inherit property, pursue lawsuits, transact business, and initiate divorces. Old Kingdom portrait statues display the equal status of wife and husband: each figure is the same size and sits on the same kind of chair. Men dominated public life, while women devoted themselves mainly to private life, managing their households and property. When their husbands went to war, however, women often took on men's work. As a result, some women held government posts, served as priestesses, managed farms, and practiced medicine.

The formal, even rigid appearance of Egypt's art illustrates how much its people valued religion, order, and predictability. Almost all sculptures and paintings belonged to tombs or temples, testimony to the desire to please the gods. Old Kingdom artists excelled in stonework, from carved ornamental jars to massive portrait statues of kings and queens. These statues represent the person either standing stiffly with the left leg advanced or sitting on a chair or throne, stable and poised. Concern for appropriate behavior also appears in the Old Kingdom literature the Egyptians called instructions, known today as wisdom literature. These texts instructed high officials how to act. In the *Instruction of Ptahhotep*, for example, the king advises his minister Ptahhotep to tell his son, who will follow him in office, not to be arrogant or overconfident just because he is well educated and to seek advice from ignorant people as well as from the wise.

Life in the Egyptian and Hittite Kingdoms, 2190–1000 B.C.E.

The Old Kingdom's stability disintegrated when climate change shrank the annual Nile flood. This disaster caused starvation, which caused civil unrest, which discredited the kings. By 2190 B.C.E., regional governors seized and held onto power until King Mentuhotep II finally restored central authority, initiating what historians call the Middle Kingdom (c. 2061–1665 B.C.E.). This restoration of the monarchy gave Egyptians pride in their homeland, to judge from the period's vigorous literature. The Egyptian narrator of *The Story of Sinuhe*, for example, reports that he lived luxuriously during a forced stay in Syria but still pined to return: "Whichever deity you are who ordered my exile, have mercy and bring me home! Please allow me to see the land where my heart dwells! Nothing is more important than that my body be buried in the country where I was born!" The Middle Kingdom fell apart, however, around 1665 B.C.E., when irregular Nile floods again undermined royal power.

A foreign invasion worsened the situation when a Semitic people from the Syria-Palestine region, whom the Egyptians called the Hyksos, took over Lower Egypt around 1664 B.C.E. (see Map 1.2). Recent archaeological discoveries have revealed the Hyksos transplanted elements of foreign culture to Egypt. The invaders brought bronze-making technology, horses and war chariots, more powerful bows, new musical instruments, hump-backed cattle, and olive trees, and they promoted contact with other Near Eastern states. As with the foreign wars of the Akkadians, so, too, the Hyksos invasion generated cultural interchange.

The leaders of Thebes in southern Egypt eventually reunited Egypt by defeating the Hyksos around 1569 B.C.E. and starting the New Kingdom (c. 1569–1081 B.C.E.). Its kings, known as pharaohs (meaning "the Great House," that is, the royal palace and estate), rebuilt central authority by restricting the power of regional governors. Recognizing that knowledge about the world was important for safety, they established diplomatic contacts with foreign states, such as the Hittite kingdom in Anatolia.

The New Kingdom pharaohs also used war to promote Egypt's interests. They earned the title "warrior pharaohs" by invading Nubia and the Sudan to the south, seeking gold and other precious materials, and by fighting in Palestine and Syria to control trade routes. As in the earlier kingdoms, religion remained the kings' most important activity. The principal festivals of the gods, for example, involved lavish public celebrations. A calendar based on the moon governed the dates of religious ceremonies. (The Egyptians also developed a calendar for administrative and fiscal purposes that had 365 days divided into twelve months of thirty days each, with the extra five days added before the start of the next year. Our modern calendar comes from it.) The royal family in the New Kingdom also built most of Egypt's magnificent temples, whose sculpted columns set a precedent for later Greek architecture. Queen Hatshepsut in the fifteenth century B.C.E., for example, erected a massive sanctuary at Deir el Bahri near Thebes. After her husband (who was also her half-brother) died, Hatshepsut proclaimed herself "female king" as co-ruler with her young stepson. To observe Egyptian political traditions, which did not include a queen ruling on her own, she had official artists portray her as a man, sporting a king's beard and male clothing.

So intense were Egyptians' religious feelings that they threatened the stability of the New Kingdom in the fourteenth century B.C.E., when the pharaoh Akhenaten reformed official religion. He made the cult of Aten, the shining disk of the sun, the centerpiece of royal worship and excluded other deities and their supporters. Akhenaten's reforms did not aim at pure **monotheism** (belief in the existence of only one god, as in Judaism, Christianity, and Islam) because they did not change the divine status of the king. His wife, Queen Nefertiti, tried to restrain him when she realized the hostility that his changes were generating in the priesthood and the general population, but he kept on, even neglecting the defense of Egypt to devote himself to religion. His religious reform died with him; during the reign of his successor Tutankhamun (r. 1355–1346 B.C.E.), famous today through the discovery in 1922 of his unlooted tomb, the traditional solar cult of Amun-Re reclaimed its leading role.

Whether Egypt was at peace or in turmoil, Egyptians' daily lives focused on work (mainly farming and craft production) and religion. Ordinary people devoted much attention to deities outside the royal cults, especially to gods they believed protected them. They venerated Bes, for instance, a dwarf with the features of a lion, as a protector of the household. They carved his image on amulets, beds, headrests, and the handles of mirrors. Magic also played a large role in people's lives. They used spells and charms to ward off demons, smooth the course of love, take revenge on enemies, and find relief from disease and injury. Egyptian doctors made medicinal use of herbs, knowledge that was passed on to later civilizations, and they could perform surgeries, including opening the skull.

Like royalty, ordinary people prepared for the afterlife. Those who could afford it arranged to have their bodies mummified and their tombs outfitted with all the goods needed for the journey to their new existence. A mummy's essential equipment included a copy of the *Book of the Dead*—a collection of magic spells to ward off danger and gain a successful verdict from the divine jury that put every

■ **The "Opening of the Mouth" Ceremony in an Egyptian Funeral**
This picture from a papyrus scroll containing the Egyptian Book of the Dead, *instructions for the afterlife, shows priests, mourners, and the god Anubis performing the Opening of the Mouth funeral ceremony. In this ritual, the deceased's mummy was touched on the mouth by sacred instruments that released the person's individual personality (ba) to join the rest of his or her spirit for a happy new existence in the afterlife.* (© Copyright The Trustees of The British Museum.)

soul on trial. To avoid experiencing death a second time, the *Book* instructed, dead people had to convince the jury of gods by sworn statements such as "I have not committed crimes against people; I have not mistreated cattle; I have not robbed the poor; I have not caused pain; I have not caused tears." Souls who received positive judgments experienced a mystical union with the god Osiris, the head judge of the dead.

The greatest external threat to the safety of New Kingdom Egyptians came from the aggressive wars of the Hittite kingdom in Anatolia (see Map 1.1). Unrelated to the Egyptians, the Hittites spoke an Indo-European language from the family of languages that eventually spread over most of Europe. The original Indo-European speakers had migrated as separate groups into Anatolia and Europe from somewhere in western Asia. Recent archaeological discoveries there of graves of women buried with weapons suggest that Indo-European women originally occupied positions of leadership alongside men; the prominence of Hittite queens in official documents perhaps sprang from that tradition.

Hittite kingship was based on religion—the worship of Indo-European gods and local Anatolian deities. The king served as high priest of the storm-god and had to maintain strict purity. His drinking water, for example, was always strained, and his water carrier was executed if so much as a hair was found in a drink. Like Egyptian kings, Hittite rulers felt responsible for maintaining divine goodwill toward their subjects. One of them, King Mursili II (r. 1321–1295 B.C.E.), issued a set of prayers begging the gods to end a plague: "What is this, o gods, that you have done? Our land is dying. . . . We have lost our wits, and we can do nothing right. O gods, whatever sin you behold, either let a prophet come forth to identify it . . . or let us see it in a dream!"

The Hittite rulers launched long-range military campaigns to acquire metals and control trade routes. The Hittites did not owe their success in war to a special knowledge of making weapons from iron, as once thought, because iron weapons did not become common until well after 1200 B.C.E. They did excel in the use of war chariots, however. Hittite kings particularly wanted to dominate the lucrative trade from Mesopotamia and Egypt. In 1595 B.C.E., therefore, their army raided as far as Babylon, overthrowing that kingdom.

They also invaded the Levant, the principal trade highway to Egypt. Previously, independent Canaanite city-states, such as the bustling ports of Ugarit, Byblos, and Tyre, had dominated the Levant. There, the interaction of traders and travelers from different cultures created about 1600 B.C.E. a supremely important innovation in writing technology: the alphabet. In this new system, a simplified picture—that is, a letter—stood for only one sound in the language. This offered a dramatic improvement in ease of writing over cuneiform and hieroglyphic scripts. The Canaanite alphabet later became the basis for the Greek and Roman alphabets, from which came modern Western alphabets.

The New Kingdom pharaohs fiercely resisted Hittite expansion in the Levant, but they could not defeat the Hittites at the climactic battle of Kadesh in Syria about 1274 B.C.E. Diplomacy finally created a balance of power between the kingdoms when, around 1259 B.C.E., the Hittite king Hattusili III signed a treaty with the Egyptian king Ramesses II and gave Ramesses his daughter in marriage to seal the agreement. Remarkably, both Egyptian and Hittite copies of this landmark in diplomatic history survive. In it the two monarchs pledged to be "at peace and brothers forever."

■ **REVIEW:** *How did religion guide the lives of people in the early civilizations of Egypt, the Levant, and Anatolia?*

Shifting Empires in the Ancient Near East, to 500 B.C.E.

A widespread spasm of attacks, apparently generated by invasions of separate bands of shipborne raiders known to us as the "Sea Peoples" (their history remains mysterious), afflicted the eastern Mediterranean region from about 1200 to 1000 B.C.E. The turmoil wiped out many communities, producing what scholars call a "Dark Age" because economic conditions became gloomy for many people, and because our view of what happened is so dim. In the Near East, recent archaeological excavation suggests that this Dark Age lasted about a century. Egypt lost its international power forever during this troubled period when the New Kingdom fell apart about 1081 B.C.E.

By 900 B.C.E., a powerful Assyrian kingdom had reemerged from the Near East's Dark Age. From their Mesopotamian homeland, these Assyrians ruthlessly carved out a centralized empire even larger than the one their ancestors had created. The riches and power of this Neo-Assyrian ("New Assyrian") Empire later inspired the Babylonians and then the Persians to create their own empires when the Assyrians lost their power. This constant striving for imperial wealth and territory kept the Near East on the same violent political and military path—monarchy and empire—that the region had followed in the past.

Hebrew (or Israelite) civilization, centered in the southern Levant, lost its independence to these Near Eastern empires, but its religion—Judaism—became influential in Western civilization. The Hebrews' religion, originally reflecting influences from their polytheistic Canaanite neighbors, took a long time to develop into monotheism. Eventually, however, the Hebrew ideas of belief in one god and basing a religion on scripture became essential concepts for major religions that deeply influenced Western civilization.

From Neo-Assyrian to Babylonian to Persian Empire, c. 900–500 B.C.E.

The collapse of the Egyptian and Hittite kingdoms by around 1000 B.C.E. allowed the aggressive warriors of Assyria to seize supplies of metal and control land and sea trade routes. By about 900 B.C.E., the armies of the Neo-Assyrian kingdom were relentlessly driving westward against the Aramaean states in Syria until they punched through to the Mediterranean coast (Map 1.3). Neo-Assyrian monarchs constantly pursued foreign expansion, and for the first time, their armies made foot soldiers the principal striking force instead of cavalry. Trained infantrymen excelled in the use of military technology such as siege towers and battering rams; archers rode in chariots. Campaigns against foreign lands brought back plunder to supplement the kingdom's agriculture and long-distance trade. Conquered peoples had to pay annual tribute to the Assyrians, supplying raw materials and luxury goods such as incense, wine, dyed linens, glass, and ivory.

Neo-Assyrian kings treated conquered peoples brutally to keep order. They herded large numbers of people from their homelands to Assyria, forcing them to build temples and palaces. One unexpected consequence of this merciless policy was that the kings undermined their native language: so many Aramaeans were deported from Canaan to Assyria that Aramaic largely replaced Assyrian as Assyria's everyday language by the eighth century B.C.E.

When not waging war, Neo-Assyrian men loved to hunt—the more dangerous the animal, the better. The king hunted lions as proof of his vigor and power. Royal lion hunts provided a favorite subject for sculptors, who carved long relief sculptures

■ **MAP 1.3 Expansion of the Neo-Assyrian Empire, c. 900–650 B.C.E.**
Like their Akkadian, Assyrian, and Babylonian predecessors, the Neo-Assyrian kings dominated a vast region of the Near East to secure a supply of metals, access to trade routes on land and sea, and imperial glory. They built the largest empire the world had yet seen. Also like their predecessors, they treated disobedient subjects harshly and intolerantly to try to prevent their diverse territories from rebelling.

telling a connected story. Although the Neo-Assyrian imperial administration preserved countless documents in its archives, literacy apparently mattered less to the
kingdom's males than war, hunting, and practical technology. King Sennacherib
(r. 704–681 B.C.E.), for example, boasted that he invented new irrigation equipment
and a novel method of metal casting. Ashurbanipal (r. 680–626 B.C.E.) is the only
king to proclaim his scholarly accomplishments: "I have read complicated texts,
whose versions in Sumerian are obscure and in Akkadian hard to understand. I do
research on the cuneiform texts on stone from before the Flood." Women of the
social elite probably learned to read, but they were excluded from the male dominions of hunting and war. Public religion, which included deities adopted from
Babylonia, also reflected the prominence of war in Assyrian culture: even the
Assyrian cult of Ishtar (the Babylonian name for Inanna), the goddess of love and
fertility, glorified warfare.

The Neo-Assyrian kings' harshness made their own people dislike their rule,
especially the social elite. Rebellions were common, and in the seventh century
B.C.E., they crippled the kingdom. The Medes, an Iranian people, and the Chaldeans,
a Semitic people who had driven the Assyrians from Babylonia, combined forces to
invade. They destroyed the Neo-Assyrian capital at Nineveh in 612 B.C.E. and ended
its kings' imperial power.

Sprung from seminomadic herders along the Persian Gulf, the Chaldeans established the Neo-Babylonian Empire, which became the most powerful empire in
Babylonian history. King Nebuchadnezzar II (r. 605–562 B.C.E.) drove the Egyptian
army from Syria at the battle of Carchemish in 605 B.C.E. Nebuchadnezzar spent lavishly to turn Babylon into an architectural showplace, rebuilding the great temple
of its chief god, Marduk; creating the famous Hanging Gardens (so named because
lush plants drooped over its terraced sides); and constructing a dazzling city gate
dedicated to the goddess Ishtar. Blue-glazed bricks and lions molded in yellow, red,
and white decorated the gate's walls, which soared thirty-six feet high.

The Chaldeans adopted traditional Babylonian culture and preserved much
ancient Mesopotamian literature, such as the *Epic of Gilgamesh*. They also created
many new works of prose and poetry, which the few educated people often read
aloud publicly for the enjoyment of the many illiterate members of the population.
Particularly popular were fables, proverbs, essays, and prophecies that taught morality and proper behavior. This so-called wisdom literature, a Near Eastern tradition
going back at least to the Egyptian Old Kingdom, greatly influenced the later religious writings of the Hebrews.

The Chaldeans' advances in astronomy became so influential in the ancient
Mediterranean world that the word *Chaldean* became the Greeks' word for
"astronomer." People's main reason for observing the stars was the belief that the
gods communicated their will to humans through events in nature, such as eclipses
and the movements of the stars and planets, abnormal births, smoke curling upward
from a fire, and the trails of ants. The interpretation of these events as messages

from the gods was characteristic of the mixture of science and religion in ancient Near Eastern thought, which so deeply influenced the Greeks.

The Persian kingdom, the Near East's last and greatest empire, began when Cyrus (r. 559–530 B.C.E.) overthrew Median rule in Persia (today Iran). Relying on his skills as a general and a diplomat who respected others' religious beliefs, he conquered Babylon in 539 B.C.E. A rebellion there had weakened the Chaldean dynasty when King Nabonidus (r. c. 555–539 B.C.E.) provoked a revolt among Marduk's priests by promoting a different deity. Cyrus profited from this religious crisis by promising to restore traditional Babylonian religion, thereby winning local support. According to an ancient inscription, he proclaimed: "Marduk, the great lord, caused Babylon's generous residents to adore me."

Later Persian kings expanded their rule by following Cyrus's principles of military strength and cultural tolerance. Darius I (r. 522–486 B.C.E.) vastly extended Cyrus's conquests by pushing Persian power eastward to the Indus Valley and westward to Thrace (Map 1.4). Organizing this vast territory into provinces, he assigned each region taxes payable in the form best suited to its local economy—precious metals, grain, horses, or slaves. He required each region to send soldiers to staff the royal army. A network of roads and a courier system for royal mail aided contact among the far-flung provincial centers. The Greek historian Herodotus reported that neither snow, rain, heat, nor darkness slowed the couriers from completing their routes as swiftly as possible (an achievement later transformed into the U.S. Postal Service motto). The kings' belief in their divine right to rule everyone, everywhere would provoke great conflicts—above all, the war between Persians and Greeks that would break out around 500 B.C.E.

The revenues flowing into the imperial treasury made the Persian king wealthy beyond imagination and supported his exalted status. So special was the monarch that servants held their hands before their mouths in his presence so that he would not have to breathe the same air as they. In sculpture adorning the immense palace at Persepolis, artists carved royal figures larger than other people. The king's purple robes were more splendid than anyone else's, and no other person could walk on the red carpets spread before him. To show that he used his gargantuan resources to help his loyal subjects, the king often provided meals for fifteen thousand nobles, courtiers, and other followers at one sitting—although he himself ate hidden from the view of his guests. Lawbreakers or rebels the king punished harshly, mutilating their bodies and executing their families. Greeks, in awe of the Persian monarch's power and luxury, referred to him as "The Great King."

So long as his subjects—numbering in the millions and of many different ethnicities—remained peaceful, the king left them alone to live and worship as they pleased. The empire's smoothly functioning administrative structure sprang from Assyrian precedents: provincial governors (satraps) ruled enormous territories with little interference from the king. In this decentralized system, the governors' duties included keeping order, enrolling troops, and sending revenues to the royal treasury.

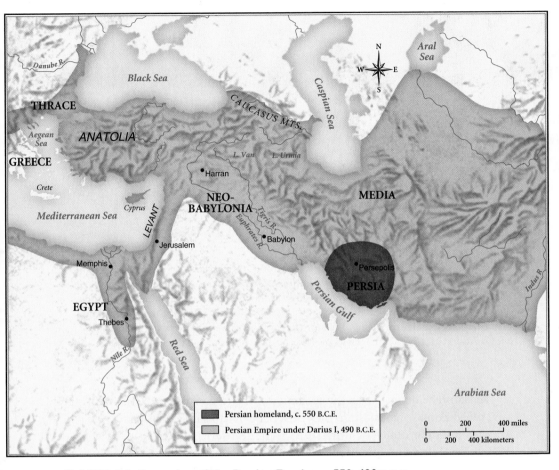

■ **MAP 1.4 Expansion of the Persian Empire, c. 550–490 B.C.E.**
*Cyrus (r. 559–530 B.C.E.) founded the Persian Empire, which his successors expanded to be even
larger than the Neo-Assyrian Empire, which it replaced. By the later years of Darius's reign
(r. 522–486 B.C.E.), the Persian Empire had expanded east as far as the western edge of India; to the
west, it reached Thrace, the eastern edge of Europe. Persian kings, unlike their imperial predecessors,
won their subjects' loyalty with tolerance and religious freedom, although they treated rebels
harshly.* **For more help analyzing this map,** *see the map activity for this chapter in the* ONLINE
STUDY GUIDE *at* bedfordstmartins.com/huntconcise.

Ruling as absolute autocrats and therefore possessing the power to make the
rules for everyone else, the Persian kings believed they were superior to all humans.
They regarded themselves not as gods but as the agents of Ahura Mazda, the
supreme god of Persia. As Darius said in his autobiography that was carved into a
mountainside in three languages, "Ahura Mazda gave me kingship . . . by the will of
Ahura Mazda the provinces respected my laws."

■ **The Great King of Persia**
Like their Assyrian predecessors, the Persian kings decorated their palaces with large relief sculptures emphasizing royal dignity and success. This one from Persepolis shows officials and petitioners giving the king proper respect when entering his presence. To symbolize their elevated status, the king and his son, who stands behind the throne, are depicted as larger than everyone else. **For more help analyzing this image,** see the visual activity for this chapter in the ONLINE STUDY GUIDE at bedfordstmartins.com/huntconcise. (Courtesy of the Oriental Institute of the University of Chicago.)

Persian religion, based on the teachings of the legendary prophet Zarathustra (and called Zoroastrianism from the Greek name for this holy man), made the god Ahura Mazda the center of worship. It seems, however, not to have been pure monotheism. Its most important doctrine was a moral dualism: perceiving the world as the arena for an ongoing battle between the opposing forces of good and evil. Ahura Mazda's two children, according to Persian belief, made different moral choices: one chose the way of the truth, but the other chose the way of the lie. Humans, too, could freely decide between purity and impurity, and their judgment had consequences: Zoroastrianism promised that salvation awaited those following the way of the truth, while damnation would strike those electing the way of the lie. The Persian religious emphasis on ethical behavior had a lasting influence on others, especially the Hebrews.

Creating Hebrew Monotheism, c. 1000–539 B.C.E.

The Hebrews' enduring impact on Western civilization comes from the book that became their sacred scripture, the Hebrew Bible (known to Christians as the Old Testament). It deeply affected the formation of not only Judaism but also Christianity and, later, Islam. Unfortunately, no source provides clear information on the origins of the Hebrews or their religion. The Bible tells stories to explain

God's moral plan for the universe, not the full history of the Hebrews, and archaeology has not yielded a clear picture.

The Hebrew Bible reports that the patriarch Abraham led his followers from the Mesopotamian city of Ur to ancient Palestine, at the southeast corner of the Mediterranean Sea where the Canaanites ruled (see Map 1.1). Traditionally said to have been divided into twelve tribes, the Hebrews never formed a political state in this period, about 1900 B.C.E. The biblical story of Joseph bringing Hebrews to Egypt may belong between 1600 and 1400 B.C.E., during the time of Hyksos rule. By the thirteenth century B.C.E., the pharaohs had conscripted the male Hebrews into labor gangs for farming and construction work.

According to the book of Exodus, around 1250 B.C.E. the Hebrew deity Yahweh instructed Moses to lead the Hebrews out of bondage in Egypt against the will of the king. The biblical narrative then relates the central event in Hebrew history: the sealing of a covenant between the Hebrews and Yahweh at Mount Sinai. This agreement declared that, if the Hebrews promised to worship Yahweh as their only God and to live by his laws, Yahweh would make them his chosen people and lead them into a promised land of safety and prosperity. This binding arrangement demanded human obedience to divine law and promised punishment for unrighteousness. As God described himself, he was "compassionate and gracious, patient, ever constant and true . . . forgiving wickedness, rebellion, and sin, and not sweeping the guilty clean away; but one who punishes sons and grandsons to the third and fourth generation for their fathers' iniquity" (Exodus 34:6–7). The religious and moral code that bound the Hebrews was written down in the Ten Commandments and the Pentateuch (the first five books of the Hebrew Bible), or Torah.

Many of the laws in the Pentateuch recalled earlier Mesopotamian rules, such as those of Hammurabi, but Hebrew law differed because it applied the same rules and punishments to everyone, regardless of their social position. Hebrew law also ruled out vicarious punishment—a Mesopotamian tradition ordering, for example, that a rapist's wife be raped. Hebrew women had less extensive legal rights than men, such as in seeking a divorce. Crimes against property never carried the death penalty, as they frequently did in other Near Eastern societies, and Hebrew laws protected slaves against glaring mistreatment.

The earliest parts of the Hebrew Bible were probably composed about 950 B.C.E., some three centuries after the exodus from Egypt. Many uncertainties cloud our understanding of how the Hebrews acquired their monotheism. It seems that it took much longer to evolve than the biblical account suggests. In the time of Moses, Yahweh-religion was not yet monotheistic because it did not deny the existence of other gods, such as Baal of Canaan. Fully developed Hebrew monotheism did not emerge until well after 1000 B.C.E., by which time the first Hebrew kingdom had formed. Solomon (r. c. 961–922 B.C.E.) brought the united nation to the height of its prosperity, largely from trade. He displayed his wealth by building in Jerusalem a temple to Yahweh richly decorated with gold leaf; it became the center of Hebrew religion.

After Solomon, the monarchy split into two kingdoms: Israel in the north and Judah in the south. The Assyrian king Tiglath-pileser III conquered Israel in 722 B.C.E. and deported its population to Assyria. In 597 B.C.E., the Neo-Babylonian king Nebuchadnezzar II conquered Judah; ten years later he destroyed Solomon's temple and sent most of the Hebrews into exile in Babylon. When the Persian king Cyrus overthrew the Babylonians in 539 B.C.E., he permitted the Hebrews to return to Palestine, which was called *Yehud* from the name of the southern Hebrew kingdom, Judah. From this geographical term came the name *Jews,* a designation for the Hebrews after their Babylonian exile. Cyrus allowed them to rebuild their Jerusalem temple and practice their religion. After returning from exile, the Jews in the ancient world remained a people subject to the political domination of various Near Eastern powers, except for a period of independence during the second and first centuries B.C.E.

Jewish prophets, both men and women, preached that the Hebrews' defeats were divine punishment for neglecting the Sinai covenant and mistreating the poor. Some prophets also predicted the coming end of the present world following a great crisis, a judgment by Yahweh, and salvation leading to a new and better world. Yahweh would save the Hebrew nation, the prophets thundered, only if Jews learned to observe divine law strictly. This **apocalypticism** ("uncovering" of the future), which recalled Babylonian prophetic wisdom literature, would later influence Christianity.

Jewish religious leaders developed strict regulations requiring people to maintain ritual and ethical purity in all aspects of life. Ethics applied not only to obvious crimes but also to financial dealings. Jews had to pay taxes and offerings to support Yahweh's temple, and they had to forgive debts every seventh year. Jews therefore created laws based on ethics as the focus of the world's first complete monotheism. They retained their cultural identity by following their religious laws, regardless of where they lived. In this way, Jews who did not return to their homeland could maintain their identity while living among foreigners. Over time, the Diaspora ("dispersion of population") came to characterize the history of the Jewish people.

Hebrew monotheism made the preservation and understanding of a sacred text, the Hebrew Bible, the key to a religious life. Making scripture important to religion became a crucial development for the history not only of Judaism but also of Christianity and Islam because these later religions placed their own sacred texts, the Christian Bible and the Qur'an, respectively, at the centers of their belief and practice. The Hebrews thus passed on ideas that have endured to this day, such as the belief in monotheism, the importance of scripture in religion, and a commitment to a covenant between God and a people who are promised salvation if they obey divine will.

■ **REVIEW:** *How did religion affect the history of the Near East from c. 1000 B.C.E. to c. 500 B.C.E.?*

Greek Civilization, to 750 B.C.E.

Neolithic settlements of Indo-European speakers dotted the mountainous Greek mainland and the islands of the Aegean Sea by 8000 B.C.E. By 6000 B.C.E., Anatolian peoples had migrated to the large island of Crete, southeast of the Greek mainland. The type of language spoken by these early Cretans, called *Minoans,* remains uncertain, but they created the first civilization in this part of the world in the late third millennium B.C.E. Eventually, they lost their preeminence and power to their warlike northern neighbors, the Mycenaean Greeks.

When Mycenaean civilization was destroyed during the tumult that affected the entire eastern Mediterranean from about 1200 to 1000 B.C.E., the aftermath— a prolonged Dark Age of depopulation and poverty—threatened doom for Greek civilization.

Minoan and Mycenaean Civilization, c. 2200–1000 B.C.E.

With its fertile plains, adequate rainfall, and sheltered ports for fishing and seaborne trade, Crete offered a fine home for settlers (Map 1.5). By 2200 B.C.E., the inhabitants

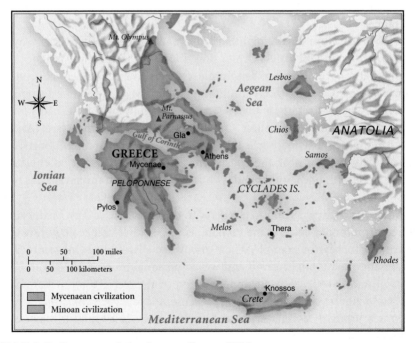

■ **MAP 1.5 Greece and the Aegean Sea, c. 1500 B.C.E.**
Mountains, islands, and sea defined the geography of Greece. The rough terrain and seasonally stormy sailing made travel a chore. The distance from the mainland to the largest island in this region, Crete, where Minoan civilization arose, was sufficiently long to keep Cretans isolated from the turmoil of most of later Greek history.

of Crete created what scholars have named a palace society, referring to the sprawling, many-chambered buildings that seem to have been both the residences of the rulers and centers of political, economic, and religious administration. The palaces seem to have been independent; no one ruler controlled Crete. We call this civilization Minoan because a famous archaeologist, Arthur Evans (1851–1941), believed that one of its rulers was King Minos, renowned in Greek myth because his wife gave birth to the half-man, half-bull Minotaur ("Minos's bull").

Minoan farmers developed Mediterranean polyculture—growing olives, grapes, and grain all on the same farm. This innovation made the best use of agricultural labor because these crops' different growing cycles allowed the same laborers to take care of them all. Farmers could thus produce valuable and versatile products such as olive oil and wine. This combination of crops provided a healthy diet that stimulated population growth.

The storage areas in the Cretan palaces, such as the vast one at Knossos, suggest that Minoan rulers enforced a redistributive economic system. The Knossos palace, for example, held hundreds of gigantic jars holding 240,000 gallons of olive oil and wine. The rulers evidently decided how much each farmer or crafts producer had to contribute to the palace storehouse and how much of those contributions would then be redistributed to each person in the community for basic subsistence or as an extra reward.

Greek civilization on the mainland also had a redistributive economy controlled by independent rulers. Emerging about the same time as the Hittite kingdom, in the early second millennium B.C.E., this civilization derives its modern designation—Mycenaean—from the hilltop site of Mycenae in the Peloponnese (the large peninsula forming southern Greece), which by 1400 B.C.E. had a fortified settlement dominated by a palace and dotted with rich tombs (see Map 1.5). Because mountainous Greece had little fertile land but many useful ports, settlements tended to arise near the coast. Greeks always depended on the sea: for food, for trade with one another and with foreign lands, and for naval raids on rich targets.

Seaborne commerce involved Greeks with the rest of the eastern Mediterranean region and promoted cultural interaction, as underwater archaeology reveals. Off Uluburun in Turkey, for example, divers discovered a late-fourteenth-century B.C.E. ship carrying such a mixed cargo and varied personal possessions—from Greece, Egypt, Canaan, Cyprus, Babylon, and elsewhere in the Near East—that attaching a single "nationality" to this vessel makes no sense.

The sea brought Mycenaeans and Minoans into close contact. Many objects found on the mainland display designs clearly inspired by Cretan traditions. At the same time, the two civilizations remained different in important ways. The Mycenaeans burned offerings to the gods; the Minoans did not. The Minoans scattered sanctuaries across the landscape in caves, on mountaintops, and in country villas; the Mycenaeans kept their sanctuaries inside their palaces. When the Mycenaeans

■ Minoan Wall Painting from the Island of Thera

Minoan artists painted with vivid colors on plaster to enliven the walls of buildings. They depicted a wide variety of subjects, from lively animals and flowering plants to young boxers and women of the court in splendid dress. Unfortunately, time and earthquakes have severely damaged most Minoan wall paintings, and the versions we see today are largely reconstructions, painted around surviving fragments of the originals. This wall painting was found on the island of Thera (or Santorini), whose volcano exploded in the seventeenth century B.C.E., blowing out the entire center of the island and burying its Minoan settlements. Some scholars think the explosion of Santorini was the inspiration for the story of the lost land of Atlantis. (Julia M. Fair.)

started building palaces in the fourteenth century B.C.E., unlike the Minoans, they designed them around megarons—rooms with prominent ceremonial hearths and thrones for the rulers. Some Mycenaean palaces had more than one megaron, which could tower two stories high with columns to support a roof above the second-floor balconies.

A cache of clay tablets discovered in the Knossos palace shows that Mycenaeans achieved dominance over Crete, possibly in a war over international trade. These documents were written in a script that archaeologists call Linear B, a picture-based script that evolved from an earlier script called Linear A. Linear B, we now know, was used to write the Mycenaeans's language: Greek. Because the Linear B tablets date from before the final destruction of Knossos in about 1370 B.C.E., they reveal that the palace administration had been keeping its records in this non-Minoan language for some time and therefore that Mycenaeans controlled Crete well before the end of Minoan civilization.

Later Greeks recalled this conquest of Crete with the myth describing how Theseus of Athens defeated the Minotaur monster: when Minos forced the Athenians to send youths for the creature to devour in his labyrinth, Theseus slew the brute and found his way out of the maze by backtracking along the thread that the king's daughter Ariadne, who had fallen in love with the handsome hero, told him to leave to mark his path.

By the time Mycenaeans ruled Crete, war at home and abroad was the principal concern of well-off Mycenaean men. Contents of Bronze Age tombs in Greece reveal that no wealthy man went to his grave without his war equipment. The expense of these grave goods shows that armor and weapons were so central to a Mycenaean male's identity that he could not leave them behind even in death.

Their warlike spirit, however, probably ruined the Mycenaeans during the Sea Peoples period (c. 1200–1000 B.C.E.). At this time, the palace settlements of eastern Greece constructed such massive defensive walls that later Greeks believed giants had built them. These fortifications would have protected coastal palaces against invading Sea Peoples, so these marauders most likely did not destroy Mycenaean civilization. The great wall around the palace at Gla, far inland where foreign sea raiders could not easily reach, suggests instead a land-based threat; that is, the Mycenaeans at Gla and elsewhere were defending themselves against other Mycenaeans. Archaeologists therefore speculate that internal turmoil, made worse by earthquakes, destroyed the order and prosperity of Mycenaean civilization by about 1000 B.C.E.

The loss of their redistributive economies devastated most Mycenaeans, who depended on their rulers' system for their subsistence. The catastrophic fall of Mycenaean civilization led to the Greek Dark Age.

The Greek Dark Age, c. 1000–750 B.C.E.

Greek culture came close to vanishing in the Dark Age (c. 1000–750 B.C.E.). Political organization faded, the economy collapsed, and the population dwindled. Conditions were so depressed that Greeks even lost the technologies of writing and of illustrating people and animals in art.

When the powerful rulers of Mycenaean Greece disappeared, competition for leadership in Dark Age society was wide open. The men and women who proved themselves excellent in action, words, and religious knowledge became the new social elite. Excellence—*aretê* in Greek—became a competitive value: men and women earned high social status by outdoing others. Men displayed aretê through prowess in war and persuasiveness in speech; women, through savvy management of a bustling household of children, slaves, and the family's storerooms. Members of the elite accumulated wealth by controlling agricultural land, which people of lower status worked for them as tenants or slaves.

The rebuilding of Greek social and political life after the Dark Age required the reestablishment of values. The poetry of Homer and Hesiod provided the elite with its ideals. Greeks believed that Homer was a blind poet from Ionia (today Turkey's western coast) who composed the epics the *Iliad* and the *Odyssey*, whose stories explore the consequences of making excellence the principal social value. Homer probably lived in the eighth century B.C.E. and belonged to a long line of poets who, influenced by Near Eastern mythology, had been singing these stories for centuries. The *Iliad* tells the story of the Greek army in the Trojan War (one of the many wars of the Sea Peoples period). The manliest Greek hero is Achilles, who displays his surpassing excellence by choosing to die gloriously in battle rather than return home safely but without glory. The *Odyssey* describes the hero Odysseus's ten-year adventure finding his way home to his family after the fall of Troy, and the struggle of his wife, Penelope, to protect their household from schemes and threats while her husband is missing. Penelope proves herself the best of women, showing her aretê by outwitting treacherous neighbors and thereby preserving her family's prosperity.

The *Iliad* and *Odyssey* reveal how the quest for excellence could produce both wondrous deeds and brutal inhumanity. As Achilles prepares to duel with Hector, the prince of Troy, he coldly rejects the Trojan's proposal for the winner to return the loser's corpse to his family and friends: "Do wolves and lambs agree to cooperate? No, they hate each other to the roots of their being." After Achilles kills Hector, he mutilates his body. When Hecuba, the queen of Troy and Hector's mother, sees this outrage, she bitterly shouts, "I wish I could sink my teeth into his liver in his guts to eat it raw." Homer's poems suggest that the gods could promote reconciliation, but they also reveal that the level of suffering in the human condition means excellence comes at a supremely high price.

Hesiod's poetry stressed the human need for justice. Like Homer a poet of the eighth century B.C.E., Hesiod told stories influenced by Near Eastern myths, such as the Mesopotamian *Epic of Creation*. His poems explain that existence, even for deities, entails sorrow and violence. They also show that justice is part of the divine order of the universe. In *Works and Days*, Hesiod identifies Zeus, king of the gods, as the source of justice: "Zeus ordained that fishes and wild beasts and birds should eat each other, for they have no justice; but to human beings he has given justice, which is far the best." Hesiod emphasizes that men from the social elite should demonstrate excellence by promoting justice through persuasion instead of force: "When his people in their assembly get on the wrong track, [a good leader] gently sets matters right, persuading them with soft words." Hesiod proclaims that the divine origin of justice should be a warning to "bribe-devouring chiefs" who impose "crooked judgments." By the end of the Dark Age, the outrage that ordinary people felt at not receiving just treatment was producing pressure for a new form of social and political organization in Greece.

During the Dark Age, the Greeks remained in contact with the Near East, and about 800 B.C.E., they learned to write again in a new way when Phoenician traders from Canaan taught them their alphabet. Eastern art inspired Greeks once more to include lively figures in their paintings. Most important, trade brought to Greece the new technology of iron metallurgy. Because iron ore was available in Greece, iron was cheaper than bronze. The relatively low cost of iron tools helped revive farming, which in turn rebuilt the population. By the eighth century B.C.E., Greece was emerging from its Dark Age.

■ **REVIEW:** *What factors contributed to the onset of the Greek Dark Age?*

Remaking Greek Civilization, c. 750–500 B.C.E.

The Greeks' ties with Egypt and the Near East had kept them going economically and culturally during their Dark Age; beginning in the eighth century B.C.E., they gradually remade their civilization on new social and political principles, inventing citizenship based on freedom and sharing power in government. In doing so, they created their version of the city-state complete with new directions in politics, art, literature, philosophy, and science.

The best evidence of Greece's revival is the founding of the Olympic Games, traditionally dated to 776 B.C.E. Every four years, the games took place during a religious festival at Olympia, in the northwest Peloponnese, in a huge sanctuary dedicated to Zeus. There, male athletes from elite families competed in sports based on activities needed for war: running, wrestling, jumping, and throwing. Horse and chariot racing were added to the program later, but the main event remained a two-hundred-yard sprint, the *stadion.* Women were barred on pain of death, but they had their own separate Olympic festival on a different date in honor of Hera, queen of the gods; only unmarried women could compete.

Athletes competed as individuals, not on national teams as in the modern Olympic Games. Only first prizes were awarded; winners received no financial rewards, only a garland made from wild olive leaves that signified the prestige of victory. Later, full-time athletes dominated the Olympics, earning their living from appearance fees and prizes at games held throughout the Greek world. The most famous winner was Milo, from Croton in Italy. Six-time Olympic wrestling champion, he stunned audiences with demonstrations of strength such as holding his breath until his veins expanded so much that they snapped a cord tied around his head.

Historians date the end of the Dark Age and the beginning of the Archaic Age (c. 750–500 B.C.E.) near the time when the Olympics began. The Archaic Age gave birth to the Greek **polis** as an independent community of citizens inhabiting a city and the countryside around it. Greece's geography, dominated by mountains and islands, promoted the creation of city-states that remained fiercely independent communities (Map 1.6). The ancient Greeks never constituted a united nation.

During the Archaic Age, Greeks established settlements around the Mediterranean in a process traditionally called Greek colonization. This modern

■ MAP 1.6 Archaic Greece, c. 750–500 B.C.E.

The Greek heartland lay in and around the Aegean Sea, in what is today the nation of Greece and the western edge of the nation of Turkey (ancient Anatolia). The "mainland," where Athens, Corinth, and Sparta are located, is the southernmost tip of the mountainous Balkan peninsula. The many islands of the Aegean area were home mainly to small city-states, with the exception of the large islands just off the western Anatolian coast, which were home to populous ones.

term, however, is misleading because it implies that governments originated and administered foreign colonies. In truth, individuals' desire for profit from trade, especially in raw materials such as metals, and from acquiring farmland on foreign shores drove the founding of most new settlements. By about 580 B.C.E., Greeks had settled in Spain, present-day southern France, southern Italy and Sicily, North Africa, and along the Black Sea coast. Greek settlements in the east were fewer, perhaps because the monarchies there restricted foreign immigration.

Citizenship and Freedom in the City-State

Greeks lived in more than a thousand separate city-states, most no larger than several hundred to a thousand or so in population. The Greek city-state was a new form of political organization because all free inhabitants were considered citizens and, usually, all free men could participate in governance. Some historians argue that the Greeks modeled their city-states on the older city-states on the island of Cyprus and in Phoenicia in the Levant, but this conclusion seems flawed because those city-states were ruled by kings and were not based on the concept of free citizens sharing power in governing, which was a defining characteristic of most Greek city-states. The most famous ancient analyst of Greek politics and society, the philosopher Aristotle (384–322 B.C.E.), insisted that the city-state was natural: "Humans are beings who by nature live in a city-state." Anyone who existed outside such a community, Aristotle concluded, must be either a simple fool or superhuman.

Citizenship was a new concept because it assumed a basic level of political and legal equality—above all, the expectation of equal treatment under the law for citizens regardless of their social status or wealth. Women had the protection of the law, but they were barred from participation in politics on the assumption that female judgment was inferior to male. The most dramatic indication of political equality in a Greek city-state was the right of all free, adult male citizens to vote on laws and policies in a political assembly. Not all city-states reached this level of power sharing and participation, however. In some, the social elite kept a stranglehold on politics, with a small group or, more rarely, a single person or family dominating. Rule by a small elite group is called oligarchy. Rule by one person is called tyranny.

Even if the Greeks' implementation of citizenship and equality before the law remained imperfect, the fact that they developed these concepts at all is remarkable because legal inequality between rich and poor in the free population was the rule in the ancient Near East and in Greece itself before the polis came into existence. Given the lack of precedent, how and why the poor in Greece gained citizenship and equality before the law remains a mystery. The greatest population increase in the late Dark Age and in the Archaic Age occurred in the ranks of the poor. These families raised more children to help farm more land, which otherwise would have lain idle because of the depopulation brought on by the worst of the Dark Age. There was no precedent for extending even limited political and legal power to this growing segment of the population, but most Greek city-states did so.

For a long time, historians attributed the general widening of political and legal rights to a so-called hoplite revolution, but recent research undermines this theory. Hoplites were infantrymen who wore metal body armor, carried a large shield in one hand, and wielded a spear with the other. They constituted the main strike force of the volunteer militia that defended each city-state. In the eighth century B.C.E., a growing number of men could afford to buy hoplite equipment (the use of iron had cut its cost). It seems likely that the new hoplites believed they were entitled to a say in politics because they bought their own equipment and voluntarily trained hard to defend their community. According to the hoplite revolution theory, the new hoplites forced the social elite to share political power by threatening to refuse to serve in the militia. The problem with that theory is that hoplites were not poor. How, then, did poor men, too, win political rights, especially the vote in the

■ **A Hoplite's Breastplate**

This bronze armor protected the chest of a sixth-century B.C.E. hoplite. It had to be fitted to his individual body; the design is meant to match the musculature of his chest and symbolize his manliness. The Greek soldier would have worn a cloth or leather shirt underneath to prevent the worst chafing, but such a heavy and hot device could never be comfortable, and soldiers often removed them despite the danger. A slave would have carried the soldier's armor for him until the moment of battle, when he would have donned his protective gear just before facing the enemy. (Olympia Museum © Archaeological Receipts Fund.)

assembly? The answer is unknown. Perhaps poor men earned respect and political rights by fighting as lightly armed fighters, disrupting the enemy's infantry by hurling barrages of rocks. Whatever the reason for the designation of poor men as citizens with roughly the same rights as the rich, this unprecedented decision constituted the most innovative feature of the transformation of Greek society in the Archaic Age.

The inclusiveness of the Greek city-state did not extend to slaves. As the notion of freedom became stronger, the practice of slavery—the opposite of freedom—became ever more widespread in Archaic Age Greece. Individual Greeks and the city-states themselves owned slaves. Public slaves sometimes lived on their own, performing specialized tasks such as detecting counterfeit coins. Temple slaves "belonged" to the deity of the temple, for whom they worked as servants. Private slaves totaled perhaps a third of the population by the fifth century B.C.E. They did all sorts of jobs, from household chores to crafts production to farm labor. Their masters controlled their lives and could punish them or demand sexual favors at will. Most owners did not brutalize their slaves because that damaged their human property. Lacking any right to family life and having no property or legal rights, slaves were completely alienated from polis society. As Aristotle put it, slaves were "living tools." Sometimes owners let slaves earn money to purchase their freedom, or promised freedom at a future date to encourage hard work. Slaves who gained their freedom did not become citizens but instead joined the population of noncitizens

■ **A Greek Woman at an Altar**

This vase painting from the center of a large drinking cup shows a woman in rich clothing pouring a libation to the gods onto a flaming altar. In her other arm, she carries some sort of religious object. This scene illustrates the most important and frequent role of women in Greek public life: participating in religious ceremonies, both at home and in community festivals. This painting style is called red figure because the picture's details are painted over the reddish color of the baked clay, which shows through to depict the surfaces of the figures, such as skin or clothing.

(The Toledo Museum of Art, Toledo, Ohio. Purchased with funds from the Libbey Endowment, Gift of Edward Drummond Libbey [1972.55].)

(metics) officially allowed to live in the city-state. Despite the bitter nature of their existence, Greek slaves rarely revolted on a large scale except in Sparta, perhaps because elsewhere they were of too many different origins and nationalities to organize. No Greek is known to have called for the abolition of slavery.

Women, like slaves, lacked the right of political participation in the city-state. Freeborn women, however, did count as citizens, enjoyed the protection of the laws, and—in a crucial role respected by everyone—performed numerous religious functions. Citizen women had recourse to the courts in disputes over property, although they usually had to have a man speak for them. Before marriage, a woman's father served as her legal guardian; after marriage, her husband did. The paternalism of Greek society—men acting as "fathers" to regulate the lives of women and safeguard their interests as men defined them—demanded that all women have male guardians to protect them physically and legally.

The expansion of slavery in the Archaic Age increased the size of households and added new responsibilities for women. While their husbands farmed, participated in politics, and met with their male friends, wives managed the household: raising children, supervising the cooking, keeping the family's financial accounts, making clothing, directing the slaves, and tending them and other family members when they were ill. Poor women worked outside the home, tilling gardens and selling produce and small goods such as ribbons and trinkets in the market found at the center of every settlement. Women rich and poor attended funerals, state festivals, and public rituals, and they controlled cults reserved exclusively for female worshippers. Their religious functions gave them freedom of movement and prestige. At Athens, for example, by the fifth century B.C.E. they officiated as priest-esses for more than forty different deities and enjoyed benefits such as salaries paid by the state.

Greek paternalism allowed men to control human reproduction and therefore the inheritance of property. Families arranged marriages, and everyone was expected to marry and produce children. The bride brought to the marriage a dowry of property (land yielding an income, if she was wealthy) that her children would inherit. Her husband was legally obligated to preserve this dowry and to return it to his wife if they divorced. A husband could divorce his wife at will. Legally, a wife could leave her husband on her own initiative to return to the guardianship of her male relatives, but her husband could force her to stay if her family refused to help her. Except in certain cases in Sparta, monogamous marriage was the rule in Greece, as was a nuclear family (that is, husband, wife, and children living together without other relatives in the same house). Citizen men could have sexual relations without penalty with slaves, foreign concubines, female prostitutes, or willing pre-adult citizen males. Citizen women, single or married, had no such freedom. Sex between a married woman and anyone other than her husband car-ried harsh penalties for both parties.

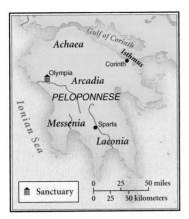

Sparta and the Peloponnese, c. 750–500 B.C.E.

Sparta differed from other city-states because it ranked regimentation and obedience as the highest social values. Spartans placed military readiness above personal concerns because Sparta's survival was threatened by its economic foundation: the great mass of slaves called helots, who were owned by the community and did almost all the work. Helots were Greeks from neighboring towns and regions that the Spartans had conquered, especially Messenia, a fertile region to the west that Sparta captured by about 700 B.C.E. The helots greatly outnumbered Sparta's citizens. They toiled as farmers and servants so that Spartans would not have to stoop to ordinary tasks. Spartan men wore their hair very long to show that they were "gentlemen," not laborers.

The helots faced constant humiliation and violence. Every year Spartan officials formally declared war on them so that a citizen could kill without penalty any helot thought to be disobedient or dangerous. To control the helots and intimidate other city-states, Spartans devoted their lives to constant preparation for war. Boys left home at age seven to live in barracks, drilling and eating together to learn discipline. Any youth unable to complete the harsh training fell into disgrace and lost citizen rights.

Adolescent boys in Sparta often were involved in homosexual relationships with older men. A boy would be chosen as a special favorite by the man to promote love for a fellow soldier at whose side he would one day march into battle; their relationship could include sex. The elder partner was supposed to help educate the young man in politics and community values and not just exploit him for physical pleasure. Both were expected to marry. Homoerotic sex between adult males was considered disgraceful, as it was between women of all ages (at least according to the reports of men).

Spartan women were known throughout the Greek world for the freedom of their lives, especially being able to exercise in public in short outfits. (Greek women elsewhere lacked exercise facilities and had to keep their bodies modestly covered.) Citizen women were expected to use their liberty from labor, which helots provided, to stay fit so they could bear healthy children to sustain the Spartan population. They could own property, including land. Women also were expected to teach their children Spartan values. One mother became legendary for handing her son his shield on the eve of battle and sternly telling him, "Come back with it—or on it!"

Athens differed from Sparta politically, socially, and economically. During the Archaic Age, it took the first steps toward democracy, a new system of government that gave equal political and legal rights to all male citizens, and toward an economy based on international trade by sea. In 594 B.C.E., an economic crisis that pitted rich against poor unexpectedly promoted change when Solon, appointed as a mediator, outlawed debt slavery and created a council to guide the legislative work of the assembly. The council's members were chosen by lottery and could serve only two annual terms (not in succession), ensuring wide participation. Equally important was Solon's decision to empower any citizen to bring charges in court on behalf of any victim and to appeal any magistrate's judgments to the assembly. These reforms gave ordinary citizens a real share in the administration of justice. Finally, Solon convinced the Athenians to improve the economy by exporting olive oil.

Some elite Athenians vehemently opposed Solon's political reforms because they wanted oligarchy. The unrest they caused opened the door temporarily to tyranny at Athens, and the family of Peisistratus held power from 546 to 510 B.C.E. by championing the interests of the poor. A rival elite family finally got the tyranny overthrown by denouncing it as unjust and inducing the Spartans, the self-proclaimed defenders of Greek freedom, to "liberate" Athens. Cleisthenes, an ambitious politician, found that he could win prominence only by promising greater democracy to the masses. Beginning in 508 B.C.E., he delivered on his promises and came to be remembered as the "father of Athenian democracy" for his reforms. His complex political reorganization achieved its goal of promoting participation in governance by as many male citizens as possible. It would take another fifty years of controversy before Athens's democracy reached its fullest form, but Cleisthenes' changes opened the way to an unprecedented way of life based on people persuading, not compelling, each other to achieve common goals. Athenian citizens believed in the rule of law, but they chose personal freedom and responsibility for themselves (though not for their slaves) over forced social regimentation like that at Sparta.

New Ways of Thought and Expression

The political idea that people should make decisions based on persuasion, rather than force or social status, matched the spirit of intellectual change rippling through Greece in the late Archaic Age. In city-states all over the Greek world, new ways of thought were inspiring artists, poets, and philosophers. Ongoing contacts with the Near East exposed the Greeks to traditions from which to learn and create something new. Artists became expert at rendering fully three-dimensional figures—whether goddesses, warriors, or monsters from myth—in an increasingly realistic style. Sculptors made their statues less stiff and more varied, from gracefully clothed young women to muscular male nudes, and made them come alive with gleaming paint.

Poets expanded the Near Eastern tradition of expressing personal emotions in poetry by developing lyric, a new type of verse similar to popular songs. Composed in diverse rhythms and performed to the music of a lyre (a kind of harp that gives

■ Archaic Age Sculpture of a Dead Athenian Warrior
This Athenian marble statue dating from about 530–520 B.C.E. shows the stiff posture and smiling expression that Archaic Age Greek sculptors used for "heroic nudes" depicting dead young men. These kouros ("young male") statues had a striding stance recalling the style of Egyptian art and were painted in bright colors; this one retains traces of red paint. A base probably belonging to this six-feet four-inch tall statue bore an inscription addressed to people passing by: "Stand and mourn at this monument of Croesus, now dead; raging Ares [the Greek war god] destroyed him as he battled in the front ranks."
(The Art Archive/National Archeological Museum Athens/Dagli Orti.)

its name to the poetry), Greek lyric poems could be short and for one singer or long and for a chorus. Archilochus of Paros, who lived in the early 600s B.C.E., became infamous for his unheroic lines about throwing down his shield in battle so he could run away to save his life: "Oh, the hell with it; I can get another one just as good." Sappho, a lyric poet from Lesbos born about 630 B.C.E., became famous for her love poems, writing, "Some would say the most beautiful thing on our dark earth is an army of cavalry, others of infantry, others of ships, but I say it's whatever a person loves." In this poem Sappho was expressing her longing for a woman she loved, who was far away.

**Ionia and the Aegean,
c. 750–500 B.C.E.**

Greek philosophers in the Archaic Age developed radically new explanations of the nature of the universe and its relation to the gods. Most of these thinkers came from Ionia. This location placed them in close contact with Near Eastern knowledge, especially astronomy, mathematics, and myth. Because there were no formal schools, pupils who studied privately with these philosophers helped spread the new ideas. Inspired by Babylonian astronomy, Ionian Greek philosophers such as Thales (c. 625–545 B.C.E.) and Anaximander (c. 610–540 B.C.E.) of Miletus expressed the bold idea that laws of nature, not the whims of gods, governed the universe. Pythagoras, who emigrated from the island of Samos to the Greek city-state Croton in southern Italy about 530 B.C.E., taught that patterns and relationships of numbers explained the entire world and promoted the systematic study of mathematics and its relation to music.

Ionian philosophers insisted that they could discover the workings of the universe because nature was not random but rather determined by what we today call the laws of physics. They named the universe *cosmos,* meaning an orderly arrangement that is beautiful. The order of the cosmos encompassed not only the motions of stars and planets but also the weather, the growth of plants and animals, human health, and so on. Because the universe was ordered, it could be understood; because it could be understood, its events could be explained by thought and research. Early Greek philosophers therefore looked for the first or universal cause of things, a problem that scientists still pursue. The philosophers who taught these ideas about the cosmos believed they needed to give reasons for their conclusions and to persuade others by arguments based on evidence. That is, they used logic. This mode of thought, called **rationalism**, was a crucial first step toward science and philosophy as these disciplines endure today. This rule-based explanation of the causes of things developed by these philosophers contrasted sharply with the traditional mythological explanation that the gods controlled the universe. Naturally, many people had difficulty accepting such a

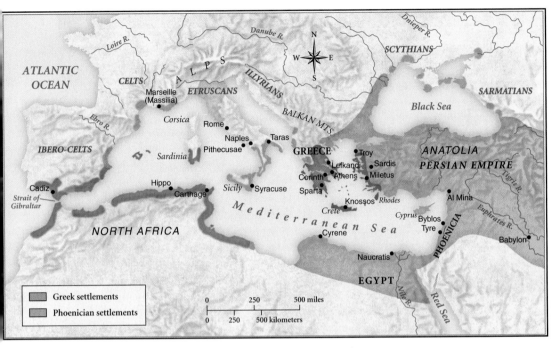

■ **MAPPING THE WEST** Mediterranean Civilizations, c. 500 B.C.E.

At the end of the sixth century B.C.E., the Persian Empire was far and away the most powerful civilization touching the Mediterranean. Its vast territory and riches gave it resources that no Phoenician or Greek city could match. The Phoenicians dominated economically in the western Mediterranean, while the Greek city-states in Sicily and southern Italy rivaled the power of those in the heartland. In Italy, the Etruscans were the most powerful civilization; the Romans were still a small community struggling to replace monarchy with a republic.

startling change in their understanding of the world, and the older tradition explaining events as the work of gods lived on alongside the new idea.

The idea that people must give reasons to explain their beliefs, rather than just make assertions that others must believe without evidence, was the Ionian philosophers' most important achievement. This insistence on logic, coupled with the belief that the world could be understood through logic, gave people hope that they could improve their lives through their own efforts. As Xenophanes from Colophon (c. 580–480 B.C.E.) put it, "The gods have not revealed all things from the beginning to mortals, but, by seeking, human beings find out, in time, what is better." This saying well expressed the value Archaic Age Greek philosophers attached to intellectual freedom, a new idea corresponding to the value given to the new idea of a citizen's freedom and legal equality in the city-state, however imperfect it may have been in reality.

■ **REVIEW:** *How did the Greeks recover from their Dark Age?*

IMPORTANT DATES			
c. 10,000–8000 B.C.E.	The "Neolithic Revolution" (the development of agriculture and domestication of animals)	c. 1400 B.C.E.	Mycenaeans take over Minoan Crete
c. 4000–1000 B.C.E.	Bronze Age in southwestern Asia, Egypt, and Europe	c. 1200–1000 B.C.E.	The Sea Peoples period
		c. 1000–750 B.C.E.	Greece's Dark Age
c. 4000–3000 B.C.E.	First cities established and writing developed in Mesopotamia	c. 950 B.C.E.	Earliest Hebrew scripture composed
2500s B.C.E.	The Great Pyramid is built in Egypt	c. 900 B.C.E.	Neo-Assyrians create an empire
		776 B.C.E.	Traditional date of first Olympic Games in Greece
c. 2350 B.C.E.	Sargon establishes the first empire in Akkadia in Mesopotamia	775–500 B.C.E	Greeks establish many new settlements around the Mediterranean
c. 2200 B.C.E.	Earliest Minoan palaces on Crete	c. 750 B.C.E.	Greeks begin to create city-states
c. 1792–1750 B.C.E.	Reign of Hammurabi, king of Babylon, in Mesopotamia	559 B.C.E.	Cyrus founds the Persian Empire
c. 1750 B.C.E.	Beginning of Hittite kingdom in Anatolia	508 B.C.E.	Cleisthenes strengthens Athenian democracy

Conclusion

Fundamental characteristics of Western civilization slowly emerged as human life changed in the lengthy period from the Stone Age to 1000 B.C.E. The Neolithic Revolution turned many people into farmers living in settled communities; from these, the first cities arose in Mesopotamia by 4000 to 3000 B.C.E. International trade and wars of conquest generated cultural interaction. The development of metallurgy, large-scale architecture, mathematics, and the alphabet in the eastern Mediterranean region during the Bronze Age deeply influenced later ages.

After the devastation wrought by the Sea Peoples (1200–1000 B.C.E.), the traditional political pattern of empire under a strong central authority revived in the Near East. The Neo-Assyrians, then the Neo-Babylonians, and then the Persians succeeded one another as rulers of enormous empires. The moral dualism of Persian Zoroastrianism influenced later religions, most importantly Hebrew monotheism, whose expression in the Torah created the first religion based on scripture.

The destruction of the Mycenaean palaces about 1000 B.C.E. opened the way to remaking Greek civilization after the Dark Age. Recovering from economic and population decline, Greeks in the Archaic Age invented the polis (city-state) as a new form of social and political organization based on the notions of citizenship and equal protection of the laws as essential components of justice. The Greek city-state treasured the notion of personal freedom for men, but only in limited ways for women and not at all for slaves. Equally revolutionary were new ways of thought. By arguing that the universe was based on laws of nature that humans could discover through reason and research, Greek philosophers established rationalism as the basis for science and philosophy.

In this way, ideals with a lasting significance for Western civilization began to emerge in Greece. But the Greek world and its new values would soon face a grave threat from the awesome empire of Persia.

■ MAKING CONNECTIONS

1. *How did the Greek city-state differ from the political and social organizations of earlier civilizations?*

2. *How were the ideas of Ionian philosophers different from mythic traditions?*

■ FOR FURTHER EXPLORATION

For further reading and online research ideas, see the Suggested References on page SR-1 at the back of the book.

For practice quizzes, a customized study plan, and other study tools, see the ONLINE STUDY GUIDE at **bedfordstmartins.com/huntconcise**.

For primary-source material from this period, see Chapter 1 in *Sources of THE MAKING OF THE WEST: A CONCISE HISTORY*, Second Edition.

The Greek Golden Age

c. 500–400 B.C.E.

FAILED DIPLOMACY IGNITED THE GREATEST DANGER ever to threaten ancient Greece. In 507 B.C.E., the Athenians, fearing a Spartan invasion, sent ambassadors to the Persian king, Darius I (r. 522–486 B.C.E.), to request a protective alliance. The Persian Empire was then the greatest power in the ancient world. The diplomats met with one of the king's governors at Sardis, the Persian regional headquarters in western Anatolia (modern Turkey). After the royal administrator heard their plea, he reportedly replied, "But who in the world are you and where do you live?"

This incident reveals the background to the wars that would dominate the military and political history of mainland Greece during the fifth century B.C.E. First, the two major powers of mainland Greece—Athens and Sparta—distrusted each other. Second, the Persian kingdom had taken over Ionia (today western Turkey), including the Greek city-states there. Yet neither the Persians nor the mainland Greeks knew much about each other. Their mutual ignorance sparked a bloody conflict.

Although the fifth century B.C.E. saw almost continuous warfare, first between Greeks and Persians and then between Greek city-states themselves, it was also the period of Greece's most enduring cultural and artistic achievements. Athenian accomplishments in the fifth century B.C.E. had such a lasting impact that historians call this period a Golden Age. This Golden Age opens the Classical Age of Greek

■ **A Greek Warrior Leaves Home for Battle**
This vase, made about 450 B.C.E. to hold wine, shows a well-armed Greek infantryman (hoplite) leaving for battle. The vase painter portrayed the warrior in full armor to make the scene more dramatic; in real life, a slave would have carried the nearly seventy pounds of metal armor to the battlefield, where the soldier would put it on at the last minute. The warrior holds a thrusting spear, his main battle weapon, but also wears a sword for close-in fighting. The man on the left is probably the warrior's father, his age indicated by his cane. The woman is probably his wife, who is ready both to pour a libation to the gods for her husband's safety and give him a last drink before he leaves home on his dangerous mission. (© Copyright The Trustees of The British Museum.)

history, a modern title that covers the period from about 500 B.C.E. to the death of Alexander the Great in 323 B.C.E.

Despite the pressures of war, Athenians in the Golden Age created Greece's leading state, developing a "radical" democracy at home while establishing an empire abroad. They generated enormous prosperity and artistic and cultural accomplishments that dazzled the Greek world. More than any other city-state, Golden Age Athens was home to innovations in drama, art, architecture, and thought that have deeply influenced Western civilization. Some of these changes angered Greeks at the time, however, because they conflicted with ancient traditions, especially people's religious fear that abandoning their ancestors' beliefs and practices would offend the gods and bring disaster.

The Peloponnesian War, a bitter struggle between Athens and Sparta that dragged on from 431 to 404 B.C.E., ended the Golden Age in the closing decades of the fifth century B.C.E. This period of cultural blossoming therefore both began and finished with destructive wars, with Greeks standing together in the first one and tearing each other apart in the concluding one.

The Persian Wars, 499–479 B.C.E.

The most famous series of wars in ancient Greek history had its roots in the Athenian-Persian meeting at Sardis in 507 B.C.E. There the Athenian ambassadors accepted the customary Persian terms for an alliance: admitting Persian superiority by presenting symbolic tokens of earth and water to the king's representative. Although the Athenian assembly expressed outrage when they learned that their diplomats had submitted to a foreign power, they never informed King Darius that they were rejecting the alliance. He therefore continued to believe that Athens remained an obedient ally. This misunderstanding started a chain of events that led to two Persian invasions of Greece, the so-called Persian Wars.

The Persian kingdom surpassed Greece in every category of material resources, from precious metals to soldiers. The clash between Persia and Greece pitted the equivalent of an elephant against a pack of undersized dogs. Greek victory in such a mismatch seemed unthinkable. Making the situation gloomier was the habit of the Greek city-states of quarreling with one another. Their usual lack of unity made it seem unlikely that they could work together to fight the Persians.

The Ionian Revolt and the Battle of Marathon, 499–490 B.C.E.

War broke out in 499 B.C.E., when the Ionian Greek city-states rebelled against their Persian-installed tyrants. Athenian troops sent to aid the rebels burned Sardis, but a Persian counterattack sent them fleeing and crushed the revolt by 494 B.C.E. (Map 2.1).

■ **MAP 2.1 The Persian Wars, 499–479 B.C.E.**

The Persian Wars originated in the failed revolt (499–494 B.C.E.) of the Greek city-states in Ionia against Persian control. To punish the Greeks, the Persian king Darius (r. 522–486 B.C.E.) first sent an expedition by sea whose infantry the Athenians defeated on the Marathon plain in 490 B.C.E. Darius's son Xerxes (r. 486–465 B.C.E.) then led a mammoth invasion of Greece, starting from Sardis in Ionia. The Persians' unexpected defeats at sea at Salamis (480 B.C.E.) and on land at Plataea and Mycale (479 B.C.E.) ended the Persians' attempt to extend their empire into Europe. Compare the relative sizes of Greece and the Persian Empire to get an idea of how bold an idea it was for Greeks to attack Persians in Asia.

King Darius erupted when he learned that the Athenians had aided the Ionian revolt: not only had they dared attack his kingdom, but they had done it after, as far as he knew, pledging loyalty to him. To remind himself to punish this betrayal, Darius ordered a slave to say to him three times at every meal, "Sire, remember the Athenians." In 490 B.C.E., he launched a fleet with orders to punish them by installing their exiled tyrant, Hippias, as his puppet ruler, who would force the Athenians to pay heavy taxes and obey the king's orders.

The Persians expected Athens to surrender without a fight. The Athenians, however, met the fearsome invaders at Marathon, on the northeastern coast of Athenian territory. The Athenian soldiers, who had never before seen Persians, grew nervous just seeing their strange (to Greek eyes) outfits—pants instead of the short tunics and bare legs that Greeks regarded as manly dress. The Athenian generals never let their men lose heart. Planning their tactics to shorten the time their men would be exposed to Persian arrows, the commanders sent their hoplites against the enemy at a dead run. The Greeks dashed across the Marathon plain in their clanking metal armor (seventy pounds per man) under a hail of missiles to engage the Persians in hand-to-hand combat. The hoplites' heavier weapons gave them the edge. After a furious struggle, they drove their opponents backward into a swamp; the Persians who failed to splash their way to their ships were slaughtered.

The Athenian army then hurried the twenty-six miles from Marathon to Athens to guard the city against a Persian naval attack. (Today's marathons recall the legendary run of a messenger who raced ahead to announce the victory, after which he dropped dead from the exertion.) The Persians then sailed home, leaving the Athenians to rejoice in disbelief at their victory. For decades thereafter, the greatest honor a family could claim was that one of its men had once been a "Marathon fighter."

The symbolic importance of the battle of Marathon far outweighed its military significance. His expedition's defeat enraged Darius because it injured his prestige, not because it threatened his kingdom's security. The Athenians' success demonstrated the depth of their commitment to preserve their freedom. The unexpected victory at Marathon boosted Athenian self-confidence, and the city-state's citizens ever after boasted that they had withstood the feared Persians on their own, without Sparta's help.

Xerxes' Invasion of 480–479 B.C.E.

The Marathon victory encouraged Greeks to resist the gigantic Persian invasion of Greece that Darius's son and successor, Xerxes (r. 486–465 B.C.E.) led in 480 B.C.E. So immense was Xerxes' army, the Greeks claimed, that it took seven days and seven nights of continuous marching to cross a pontoon bridge over the Hellespont strait, the narrow passage of sea between Anatolia and mainland Greece. Xerxes expected the Greek city-states to surrender immediately once they learned the size of his forces.

Some did, but thirty-one city-states united to fight the Persians. This alliance, known as the Hellenic League, accomplished the incredible: protecting their

■ **Greek against Persian in Hand-to-Hand Combat (detail)**
This red-figure painting appears on the inside a Greek wine cup. Painted during the Persian Wars (about 480 B.C.E.), it shows a hoplite about to kill a Persian warrior at the ultimate moment in battle— hand-to-hand combat with swords. The Greek has lost his principal weapon, a spear, and the Persian can no longer shoot his weapon, the bow and arrow. The scene expresses multiple messages: the realistic rendering of the Persian's colorful outfit with sleeves and pants stresses the "otherness" of the enemy in Greek eyes; representing the fighters with bare feet is an artistic convention to make the scene more heroic; and their serene expressions at a moment of extreme stress dignify the horror of killing in war. (© The Trustees of the National Museums of Scotland.)

independence from the world's strongest power. They succeeded without the aid of the city-states in Italy and Sicily, such as Syracuse, the powerful ruler of a regional empire. Those western Greeks refused to join the league because they were occupied fighting Carthage, a Phoenician settlement in North Africa that was aggressively trying to monopolize commerce in the west.

The united Greeks chose Sparta as their leader because of its famous hoplite army. The Spartans demonstrated their courage when three hundred of their men held off Xerxes' huge army for several days at the narrow pass called Thermopylae ("warm gates") in central Greece. A hoplite summed up the Spartans' bravery with his response to a remark that the Persian archers were so numerous that their arrows darkened the sky in battle. "That's good news," said the Spartan warrior. "We'll fight in the shade." They all died fighting.

When the Persians marched south, the Athenians evacuated their city instead of surrendering. They believed their city-state and its freedom would survive so long as its people survived, regardless of what happened to their property. The Persians promptly burned the empty city. In the summer of 480 B.C.E., Themistocles of Athens tricked the other, less aggressive Greek leaders into facing the larger Persian navy in a sea battle in the narrow channel between the island of Salamis and the west coast of Athenian territory. The narrowness of the channel prevented the Persians from using all their ships at once and let the heavier Greek ships win victory by ramming the flimsier Persian vessels. When Xerxes observed that his most aggressive naval commander appeared to be the one woman among his admirals, Artemisia, ruler of

Caria (the southwest corner of Anatolia), he shouted, "My men have become women, and my women, men." In 479 B.C.E., the Greek infantry headed by the Spartans defeated the remaining Persian land forces at Plataea (see Map 2.1).

The Greeks' superior weapons and clever use of Greece's geography to overcome the Persians' greater numbers help explain their military victories. But most remarkable is the decision of the thirty-one Greek city-states to unite in a coalition. They could easily have agreed to become Persian subjects to save themselves; for most of them, Persian rule would have imposed little interference in their internal affairs. Instead, they chose to fight for absolute independence against seemingly overwhelming odds. Because the Greek forces included not only the social elite and hoplites but also thousands of poorer men who rowed the warships, the effort against the Persians cut across social and economic divisions. The Hellenic League's decision to fight the Persian Wars demonstrated both courage and a commitment to the ideal of political freedom that had emerged in the Archaic Age.

> ■ **REVIEW:** *How did differences in Persian and Greek political and military organization determine the course of the Persian Wars?*

Athenian Confidence in the Golden Age, 479–431 B.C.E.

Victory ruptured the alliance that the Persian threat had forged between Sparta and Athens. Out of this fractured partnership arose the so-called Athenian Empire, a modern label to describe the Athenians' new vision of grander international power that emerged following the Persian Wars. The growth of Athens's power internationally went hand in hand with more democracy and vast spending on public buildings, art, and festivals.

The Establishment of the Athenian Empire, 479–c. 460 B.C.E.

After the Persian Wars, Sparta and Athens both built up their own alliances to strengthen their positions against each other. Relying on long-standing treaties with city-states located mainly in the Peloponnese, Sparta headed forces stronger in infantry than in warships, with the notable exception of Corinth, a naval power. The Spartan allies, called the Peloponnesian League, met in a representative assembly, but no action could be taken unless the Spartan leaders approved.

By 477 B.C.E., under the leadership of the Athenian upper-class leader Aristides (c. 525–465 B.C.E.), Athens allied with city-states exposed to possible Persian retaliation—in northern Greece, on the islands of the Aegean Sea, and along the western coast of Anatolia. Most Athenian allies had strong navies, and all solemnly swore never to desert the coalition. This alliance, called the **Delian League** because its treasury was originally located on the island of Delos, also had an assembly. Supposedly, every ally had an equal say in making decisions, but in practice Athens was in charge.

The special arrangements for financing the alliance's naval operations allowed the Athenians to dominate. Each ally paid annual "dues" based on its size and prosperity. Because they were required, these dues were actually "tribute." Larger member states supplied entire triremes (warships) complete with crews and their pay (Figure 2.1); smaller states could share the cost of a ship and crew or contribute cash instead.

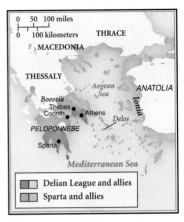

The Delian and Peloponnesian Leagues

Over time, more and more members paid cash. It proved beyond their capacities to build warships and to train crews (170 rowers each); the recent reconstruction of a full-size trireme has shown how difficult it was to build one and train an effective crew. Athens, far larger than most league members, possessed the necessary shipyards as well as many men eager to earn pay as rowers. Many oarsmen came from Athens's poor, and they earned not only money but also political influence in Athenian democracy, as naval strength became the city-state's principal source of military power. Without them, Athens had no navy.

The decision of many Delian League allies to let Athens supply warships eventually left them without any navies of their own. Therefore, they had no power if they disagreed with Athens's policy. The Athenian assembly could simply order its fleet to compel discontented allies to comply and continue paying their tribute. As the Athenian historian Thucydides observed, rebellious allies "lost their independence," and the Athenians became "no longer as popular as they used to be." This unpopularity was the price Athenians paid for making themselves the leading naval power in the eastern Mediterranean. They insisted that their dominance of the Delian League was justified because it kept the alliance strong enough to protect Greece from the Persians.

By about 460 B.C.E., their fleet had expelled almost all the Persian garrisons that had held out along the northeastern Aegean coast. The alliance drove the enemy fleet from the Aegean Sea, quashing any Persian threat to Greece for the next fifty years. Athens meanwhile grew rich off spoils captured from Persian outposts and the league's tribute.

The Athenian assembly decided how to spend this revenue. Rich and poor alike had a stake in keeping the fleet active and the league members paying for it. The poor men who rowed the ships came to depend on the pay they earned on league expeditions. Members of the social elite enhanced their social status by commanding campaigns and spending their portion of the plunder on public festivals and buildings.

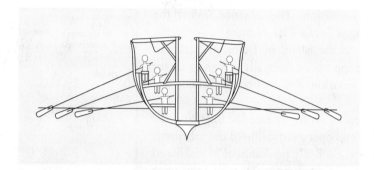

■ **FIGURE 2.1 Triremes, the Foremost Classical Greek Warships**

Innovations in military technology and training fueled a naval arms race in the fifth century B.C.E.,
when Greek shipbuilders devised larger and faster ramming ships called triremes. The boats were
powered by 170 rowers seated in three rows, one above each other as shown in the illustration of the
rowers from behind (top). These ships' radical new design with triple banks of oars made them
expensive to build and required extensive crew training. Only wealthy and populous city-states such
as Athens could afford to maintain large fleets of triremes. No ancient trireme survives to show
exactly how such a warship was built, but this relief sculpture (bottom) found on the Athenian
acropolis and dating from about 400 B.C.E. gives a glimpse of what a trireme looked like from the
side when being rowed into battle. Sails were used to power the ship only when not in combat.
(The Art Archive/Acropolis Museum Athens/Dagli Orti.)

Wealthy Athenians were expected to make financial contributions for public
works and festivals to win popular support. They did not form political parties but
gathered informal circles of friends and followers to support their agendas.
Arguments about policy tended to revolve around how Athens should exercise its
growing power internationally, not whether it was right to treat allies as subjects.

Radical Democracy and Pericles' Leadership, 461–445 B.C.E.

As the Delian League grew, the poorer men who powered the Athenian fleet came to recognize that they provided a cornerstone of Athenian security and prosperity. They felt the time had come to increase their political power by making the judicial system of Athens just as democratic as the process of passing laws in the assembly, which was open to all male citizens over eighteen years of age. The leaders of this initiative were members of the elite, who competed for popular support to win elective office. One of Athens's most socially prominent citizens, Pericles (c. 495–429 B.C.E.), became the leading Golden Age politician by supporting the masses' desire for greater democracy.

Golden Age Athenian democracy gradually became so sweeping, compared with most ancient governments, that today it is called **radical democracy**. Its principles were clear: direct and widespread participation by male citizens in the assembly to make laws and policy by majority rule; random selection and rotation for members of the Council of 500 (which prepared the agenda for the assembly), most magistrates, and jurors; elaborate precautions to prevent corruption; and equal protection under the law for citizens regardless of wealth. At the same time, excellence was recognized by making the top public offices—the board of ten "generals," who managed the city-state's military and financial affairs—elective annually and without limits on how many terms a man could serve.

Reforming the judicial system was essential to radical democracy. Ever since Cleisthenes' reforms at the end of the sixth century B.C.E, most judicial verdicts had been rendered by archons (magistrates) and the Areopagus Council of exarchons (separate from the Council of 500). Although archons were now chosen annually by lottery to make their selection democratic, they and the Areopagus members were still susceptible to bribery and pressure from the social elite. Since even democratically enacted laws meant little if applied unfairly, the masses demanded reforms to halt corruption in trials.

The opportunity for change arose in 461 B.C.E., when a prominent member of the elite, Ephialtes, sought the people's political support by sponsoring a reformed court system. Ephialtes' reforms made it nearly impossible to bribe or pressure jurors. They were selected by lottery from male citizens over thirty years old, the selection was made only on the day of the trial, all trials were concluded in one day, and juries were large (from several hundred to several thousand). No judges presided; only one official was present—to stop fistfights. Jurors voted after hearing speeches from the accuser and the accused, who had to speak for themselves although they might pay someone else to compose their speeches and ask others to speak in support. A majority vote of the jurors ruled, and no appeals were allowed.

Majority rule was the operative principle for enforcing accountability in Athenian radical democracy. Any citizen could call for a trial to judge an official's conduct in office, but the most striking example of this principle was the procedure called **ostracism** (from *ostracon*, meaning a "piece of broken pottery," the material used for casting ballots). Once a year, all male citizens could scratch on a ballot the name of one man they thought should be ostracized (exiled for ten years). If at least six thousand ballots were cast, the man who received the most "votes" was expelled from Athenian territory. He suffered no other penalty, and his family and property remained behind undisturbed. Ostracism was not a criminal penalty, and ostracized men recovered their citizen rights after their exile.

This process was meant to protect radical democracy; a man therefore could be ostracized if the majority perceived his prominence as a threat to their interests. An anecdote about the politician Aristides illustrates this possibility. He was nicknamed "the Just" because he had proved himself so fair-minded in setting the dues for Delian League members. On the day of the balloting, an illiterate farmer handed Aristides a pottery fragment and asked him to scratch the name of the man's choice for ostracism on it.

> *"Certainly," said Aristides. "Which name shall I write?"*
> *"Aristides," replied the countryman.*
> *"Very well," remarked Aristides as he proceeded to inscribe his own name.*
> *"But tell me, why do you want to ostracize Aristides? What has he done to you?"*
> *"Oh, nothing. I don't even know him," sputtered the man. "I just can't stand hearing everybody refer to him as 'the Just.'"*

True or not, this tale demonstrates that Athenians assumed that the right way to protect democracy was always to trust the majority vote of freeborn, adult male citizens, without any restrictions on a man's ability to decide what he thought was best for democracy. It also shows that men seeking political success in Athenian democracy had to be ready to pay the price that jealousy or spite could exact.

Like his distant relative Cleisthenes before him, Pericles became the most influential Athenian politician of his era by devising innovations to strengthen the egalitarian tendencies of Athenian democracy. The Golden Age's most spellbinding public speaker, Pericles repeatedly persuaded the assembly to pass laws increasing its political power. In return, he gained such popularity that he was regularly elected as a general.

Pericles' most important democratic innovation was pay for service in public jobs filled by lottery. This allowed poorer men to leave their regular work to serve in government. Early in the 450s B.C.E., he convinced the assembly to use state revenues to pay a daily stipend to men who served in the Council of 500, on juries, and in numerous other posts. The amount was approximately what an unskilled worker could earn in a day. The generals received no pay because the prestige of their position was considered its own reward.

In 451 B.C.E., Pericles strengthened citizen identity, which even the poor possessed under democracy, by sponsoring a law making citizenship more exclusive and enhancing the status of Athenian mothers. This law mandated that citizenship would be given only to children whose mother and father were both Athenian by birth. Thereafter, men avoided seeking wives outside the citizen body.

Finally, Pericles supported the interests of poorer men by recommending frequent naval campaigns against Spartan and Corinthian interests in Greece and against Persian control of Cyprus, Egypt, and the eastern Mediterranean. The assembly's confidence reached such a fever pitch that they voted to carry on as many as three different major expeditions simultaneously. The Athenians' ambitions at last exceeded their resources, however, and by 450 B.C.E., they had to pull back from the eastern Mediterranean and stop fighting against the Peloponnesian League. In the winter of 446–445 B.C.E., Pericles engineered a peace treaty with Sparta designed to freeze the balance of power in Greece for thirty years and thus preserve Athenian control of the Delian League. Pericles dropped his aggressive foreign policy because he realized that preserving radical democracy at home depended on Athens not losing its power over its allies.

The Urban Landscape of Golden Age Athens

The Delian League's fleet protected seaborne trade, and Athens became a flourishing commercial center for traders, merchants, and crafts producers from around the Mediterranean world. The city's new riches flowed mainly into public building projects, art, and festivals rather than private luxury. People's homes in the city and the countryside remained modest. Farmhouses usually clustered in villages, while homes in the city wedged tightly against one another along narrow, winding streets. Houses grouped bedrooms, storerooms, and dining rooms around small, open-air courtyards. People only rarely decorated their rooms with paintings or art, and their furniture was kept to a minimum. Toilets usually consisted of a pit dug outside the front door, which was emptied by collectors paid to dump the excrement outside the city at a distance set by law. Poorer people rented small apartments.

Generals who became rich plundering Persian outposts in the eastern Mediterranean used this wealth to beautify the city, not to build themselves mansions. They paid for public landscaping that included shade trees, running tracks for exercise, and gathering places such as the colorful Painted Stoa. A stoa was a narrow building open along one side whose purpose was to provide shelter from sun or rain. One successful general's family built the Painted Stoa in the heart of the city, on the edge of the central market square, the **agora**. The crowds who came to the agora daily to shop and chat about politics would cluster inside this shelter. There they could gaze at its bright paintings, which depicted the glorious exploits of the general's family and thus publicized its dedication to the city-state. Wealthy citizens also paid for other major public expenses, such as equipment for warships and entertainment at city festivals. This custom was essential because Athens, like most Greek city-states, had no regular direct taxes on income or property.

Huge buildings paid for by public funds were the most prominent new architecture in Golden Age Athens. In 447 B.C.E., Pericles persuaded the assembly to fund

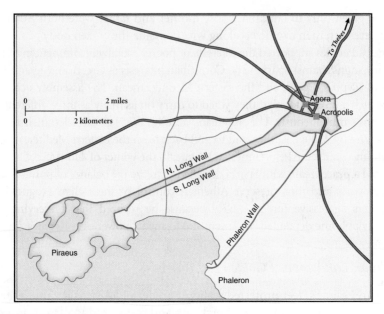

■ MAP 2.2 Fifth-Century B.C.E. Athens

The urban center of Athens with the agora and acropolis at its heart measured about one square mile, surrounded by a stone wall with a perimeter of some four miles. Fifteen large gates flanked by towers and various smaller doors allowed traffic in and out of the city; much of the Athenian population lived in the many villages (demes) of the surrounding countryside. Most of the city's water supply came from wells and springs inside the walls, but, unusually for a Greek city, Athens also had water piped in from outside. The Long Walls provided a protected corridor connecting the city to its harbor at Piraeus, where the Athenian navy was anchored and grain was imported to feed the people.

the city's greatest building project ever, on the rocky hill at the center of the city called the *acropolis* (Map 2.2). The project's centerpieces were a mammoth gate building with columns straddling the western entrance of the acropolis and a new temple of Athena housing a huge statue of the goddess. Comparing the value of a day's wage then and now, we can calculate that these buildings easily cost more than the modern equivalent of a billion dollars, a phenomenal sum for a Greek city-state. Pericles' political rivals denounced him for squandering public funds. Scholars disagree about whether the assembly spent Delian League dues to help finance the program; it is certain that substantial funds were taken from sales taxes, harbor taxes, and the financial reserves of the sanctuaries of the goddess Athena, which derived from private donations and public support.

The vast new temple built for Athena—the Parthenon ("the house of the virgin goddess")—became Greece's most famous building. As the patron goddess of Athens, Athena had long had another sanctuary on the acropolis. Its focus was an olive tree regarded as the goddess's sacred symbol as protector of the city-state's economic health. The Parthenon honored her in a different capacity: as the divine

■ **The Acropolis of Athens**

Like most Greek city-states, Athens grew up around a prominent hill (acropolis) whose summit served as a special sanctuary for the gods and as a fortress to which the population could retreat when an enemy attacked. The invading Persians burned the buildings on the Athenian acropolis in 480 B.C.E. The Athenians left the charred remains in place for thirty years to remind themselves of the sacrifice they had made for their freedom. In the 440s B.C.E., they began erecting the magnificent temples and other public buildings that have made the city famous for its monumental marble architecture. (© AKG-Images, London/John Hios.)

champion of Athenian military power. Inside the temple stood a gold and ivory statue nearly forty feet high depicting the goddess in battle armor, holding in her outstretched hand a six-foot statue of Victory (*Nike* in Greek).

Like all Greek temples, the Parthenon was built to be a house for its divinity, not as a gathering place for worshipers. Its design followed standard temple architecture: a rectangular box on a raised platform, a plan the Greeks probably derived from Egyptian temples. Columns on a raised porch surrounded the box on all sides. The Parthenon's columns were carved in the simple style called Doric, in contrast to the more elaborate Ionic and Corinthian styles, often imitated in modern buildings (see Figure 2.2 on page 64). Only priests and priestesses could enter the temple usually; public religious ceremonies took place out front.

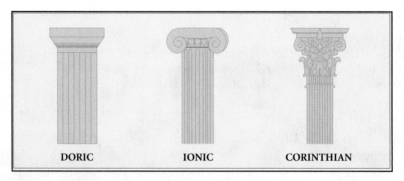

■ FIGURE 2.2 Styles of Greek Capitals

The Greeks decorated the capitals, or tops, of columns in these three styles to fit the different architectural "canons" (their word for precise mathematical systems of proportions) that they devised for designing buildings. The "pillow" atop Doric columns evolved into the Ionic style sporting "ears" (volutes). Corinthian capitals with their elaborately carved leaves were a later outgrowth of Ionic. These styles were widely imitated in later times, as on many U.S. state capitols and the U.S. Supreme Court Building in Washington, D.C.

The Parthenon proclaimed the self-confidence of Golden Age Athens. Constructed from twenty thousand tons of Attic marble, it stretched nearly 230 feet in length and 100 feet wide, with eight columns across the ends instead of the six normally found in Doric style and seventeen instead of thirteen along the sides. Its massive size conveyed an impression of power. The temple's sophisticated architecture demonstrated Athenian ability to construct order that was both apparent and real: because perfectly rectangular shapes in large-scale architecture appear curved to the human eye, subtle curves and inclines were built into the Parthenon to produce an illusion of completely straight lines and emphasize its massiveness.

The elaborate sculptural frieze of the Parthenon announced the temple's most innovative and confident message: Athens's citizens possessed the special goodwill of the gods. The frieze, a continuous band of figures, was carved in relief around the top of the walls inside the porch that ran along all four sides of the building. This sort of decoration usually appeared only on Ionic-style buildings. Adding it to a Doric-style temple was a striking departure meant to attract attention. The Parthenon's frieze portrayed Athenian men, women, and children in a parade in the presence of the gods. Depicting the procession in motion, like a filmstrip in stone, the frieze included youths riding spirited horses and women carrying sacred implements. As usual on Greek temples, brightly colored paint and shiny metal attachments enlivened the figures of people and animals.

No other city-state had ever gone beyond the traditional function of temples—glorifying and honoring the community's protector gods—by adorning a temple with representations of its citizens. The Parthenon frieze made a unique statement about how Athenians perceived their relationship to the gods. A temple adorned with pictures of citizens being viewed by the gods amounted to a claim of special closeness between the city-state and the gods. This assertion reflected the Athenians' interpretation of their success in helping turn back the Persians, in achieving leadership of a powerful naval alliance, and in amassing wealth that made Athens richer than all its neighbors in mainland Greece. Their success, the Athenians believed, proved that the gods were on their side.

Like the Parthenon frieze, the changes that Golden Age artists made in free-standing sculpture broke with tradition. Archaic male statues had only one pose: arms pressed to their sides and left leg striding forward, imitating the unchanging posture of Egyptian statuary. This style gave them an appearance of stability; even a hard shove seemed unlikely to budge them. By the time of the Persian Wars, Greek sculptors began to express motion in their art. Male statues could have bent arms and the body's weight on either leg. Female statues, too, had more relaxed poses and clothing that hung in a way that hinted at the shape of the curves underneath. The faces of Golden Age sculptures were self-confidently calm rather than smiling like Archaic Age figures. This spirited new style suggested the confident energy of the times but also hinted at the possibility of instability: Golden Age sculptors took more chances with the balance of their statues.

Statues were meant to be displayed in public to broadcast a message, regardless of whether private individuals or the city-state paid for them. Art was not yet used to decorate homes. Instead, wealthy families would pay for statues of gods to be housed in a sanctuary as symbols of devotion. They also placed statues of their deceased members above their graves as memorials of their virtue, especially if they had died young in war or in childbirth.

REVIEW: *What factors prompted political change in fifth-century B.C.E. Athens?*

Tradition and Innovation in Athens's Golden Age

Fifth-century B.C.E. Athens generated unprecedented accomplishments in architecture, art, drama, and ways of thought, but many central aspects of its social and religious life remained unchanged. Conflicts between innovation and tradition created social tensions, especially concerning religion. Women's roles in public life did not change, and they continued to make essential contributions by managing the household, participating in religious ceremonies, and, if they were poor, working in commerce and agriculture to help support their families. The greatest tension arose from the startling ideas of teachers called **sophists** and the ethical views of the philosopher Socrates. The most visible reflection of the tension was the growing popularity of state-funded theater: plays—both tragedies and comedies—whose plots explored problems in city-state life.

Religious Tradition in a Period of Change

Greeks maintained their polytheistic religious traditions with sacrifices and public festivals and by seeking a personal relationship with the gods in the rituals of hero cults and **mystery cults**. City-states were officially religious communities: each honored a particular god or goddess, such as Athena at Athens, as its protector and patron, while also worshiping many other deities. The twelve most important gods were envisioned assembling for banquets atop Mount Olympus, the highest peak in mainland Greece. Zeus headed this immortal pantheon; joining him were Hera, his wife; Aphrodite, goddess of love; Apollo, sun god; Ares, war god; Artemis, moon goddess; Athena, goddess of wisdom and war; Demeter, goddess of agriculture and fertility; Dionysus, god of pleasure, wine, and disorder; Hephaestus, god of fire and technology; Hermes, messenger god; and Poseidon, sea god.

Like the peoples of the ancient Near East, the Greeks believed that humans, as individuals and as communities, must honor the gods to thank them for blessings received and to receive blessings in return. This idea of reciprocity between gods and humans underlay the Greeks' understanding of the nature of the gods. Deities did not love humans, though in some mythological stories they took earthly lovers and produced half-divine children. Rather, they supported humans who paid them honor and did not anger them. Gods offended by humans could punish them by sending calamities such as famine, earthquake, epidemic disease, or defeat in war. The Greeks did not expect to achieve paradise on earth at some future time when evil forces would finally be vanquished forever.

Each god's cult—the set of prayers and rituals for worshiping a particular divinity—had its own practices, but sacrifice provided the focus. Sacrifices ranged from bloodless offerings—fruits, vegetables, and small cakes—to large animals roasted for eating. The speechwriter Lysias (c. 445–380 B.C.E.), a Syracusan who lived in Athens, explained the importance of state-sponsored sacrifices in a speech composed for an Athenian official: "Our ancestors handed down to us the most powerful and prosperous community in Greece by performing the prescribed sacrifices. It is therefore fitting for us to offer the same sacrifices they did, for the sake of the success that those rites have brought us." Sacrificing large animals, such as cattle and sheep, provided occasions for the community to assemble and reaffirm its ties to the divine world and for the worshippers, by sharing the roasted meat from the sacrifice, to benefit personally from their relationship with the gods. People who were not rich—the great majority of the population—particularly loved the feasting that followed a large-animal sacrifice because meat was too costly for them to buy regularly.

The bloody killing of the animal followed strict rules to prevent ritual contamination. The victim had to be an unblemished domestic animal, specially decorated with garlands and made to approach the altar as if willing to be sacrificed. The assembled crowd maintained strict silence to avoid possibly impure remarks. The official in charge of the sacrifice sprinkled water on the animal's head so it would shake its head and appear to consent to die. After washing his hands, the official scattered barley grains on the altar fire and on the animal's head and then cut a lock of the animal's hair and threw it on the fire. Following a prayer, he swiftly cut the animal's throat while musicians played flutelike pipes and female worshipers screamed, presumably to express the group's ritual sorrow at the victim's death. The carcass was then butchered, and some portions of it were thrown on the altar fire so that the aromatic smoke could waft its way upward to the cult's god. The rest of the meat was cooked for the worshipers to eat.

Public festivals featured not just sacrifices but also elaborate ceremonies, such as parades and musical performances. Athens boasted of having the most festivals, with nearly half the days of the year featuring one. Its biggest festival, the Panathenaia, honored Athena with sacrifices, parades, and contests with valuable prizes for music, dancing, poetry, and athletics. Some occasions were for women only, such as the three-day festival for married women in honor of Demeter.

Greek religion included many activities besides the civic cults of the twelve Olympian gods. People took a keen interest in religious actions meant to improve their personal relations with the divine. Families marked significant moments such as birth, marriage, and death with prayers, rituals, and sacrifices. They honored their ancestors with offerings made at their tombs, consulted seers about the meanings of dreams and omens, and sought out magicians for spells to improve their love lives or curses to harm their enemies.

Hero cults and mystery cults had special appeals. The former were rituals performed at the tomb of an extraordinarily famous man or woman. Local heroes' remains were thought to retain special power to reveal the future through oracles, to heal illnesses and injuries, and to provide protection in battle. The only hero to whom cults were established all over

■ **Cup with Symbols to Avert Evil**
Ancient Greeks had a healthy respect for the ability of nature and their fellow human beings to do them harm. Like prayer, magical symbols were thought to have power to ward off bad luck and other evils. Sometimes items from everyday life, such as this cup, were decorated with these symbols as a way of providing the object's owner with some hope of averting evil fortune both large and small. Here the god Dionysus is seated between two large eyes as sources of magical power. What objects do people use for similar purposes today?
(Kanellopoulos Museum © Archaeological Receipts Fund.)

the Greek world was the strongman Heracles (or Hercules, as his name was later spelled by the Romans). His superhuman feats gave him an appeal as a protector in many city-states.

The Athenian mystery cult of Demeter and her daughter Kore (also called Persephone), headquartered in the village of Eleusis, attracted men and women from all over the Mediterranean world because it offered the hope of protection in this life and the afterlife. The central rite of this cult was the Mysteries: a series of initiation ceremonies into the secret knowledge of the cult. The main initiation occurred during an annual festival lasting nearly two weeks, which built up to the revelation of Demeter's central secret, after a day of fasting. The most eloquent proof of how seriously people took these Mysteries is that no one ever revealed the secret throughout the thousand years during which the rites were celebrated; some hints reveal that it promised initiates a better life on earth and a happier fate in the afterlife.

Other mystery cults also emphasized protection for initiates in their current lives, whether against ghosts, illness, poverty, shipwrecks, or the countless other dangers of life. People received divine protection as a reward for appropriate worship, not for abstract faith. The ancient Greeks believed that the gods expected visible honors and rites, and their religion required action from worshipers. Greeks had to pray and sing hymns praising the gods, perform sacrifices, and undergo ritual purification. Preserving religious tradition mattered deeply to most people because it offered a safeguard against the precarious conditions of human life in a world in which early death from disease, accident, or war was commonplace.

Women, Slaves, and Metics in Traditional Society

The power and status of Athenian women came from their roles in the family and in religion. Upper-class women devoted their lives to running their households, meeting female friends, and participating in the city-state's religious cults. Poorer women helped support themselves and their families, often as small-scale merchants and crafts producers.

Women's exclusion from politics meant that men might overlook women's contributions to the city-state. In his play *Medea* of 431 B.C.E., the Athenian dramatist Euripides had his heroine insist that women who bear children are owed at least as much respect as are hoplites, a plausible claim given the high risks of childbirth under the medical conditions of antiquity:

> *People say that we women lead a safe life at home, while men have to go to war. What fools they are! I would much rather fight in the army three times than give birth to a child even once.*

Women, like men, could own property, including land (the most valued possession in Greek society), and they were supposed to preserve it to hand down to their

■ Vase Painting of a Woman Buying Shoes

Greek vases were frequently decorated with scenes from daily life instead of mythological stories. Here, a woman is being fitted for a pair of custom-made shoes by a craftsman and his apprentice. Her husband has accompanied her on the expedition and, to judge from his gesture, is participating in the discussion of the purchase. This vase was painted in so-called black-figure technique, in which the figures are rendered as black outlines, with their details incised into a background of red clay. Painters later reversed this technique on red-figure vases so that they could draw pictures with greater precision and elegance of line. **For more help analyzing this image,** see the visual activity for this chapter in the ONLINE STUDY GUIDE at bedfordstmartins.com/huntconcise.

(Museum of Fine Arts, Boston. Henry Lillie Pierce Fund. Photograph © 2007 Museum of Fine Arts, Boston [01.8035].)

children. A daughter's share in her father's estate usually came to her as her dowry (the money and property a woman brought to her marriage). Husband and wife co-owned the household's common property. The husband was legally responsible for preserving the dowry and using it for the support and comfort of his wife and any children she bore. Upon her death, her children inherited the dowry. In a divorce, the wife got her property back.

Athenian laws concerning heiresses reveal the society's goal of enabling males to establish and maintain households. If a father died leaving only a daughter, his property went to her, but she could not dispose of it as she pleased. Instead, the law required her father's closest male relative—her official guardian after her father's death—to marry her, with the aim of producing a son. This child inherited the property when he reached adulthood. This law applied regardless of whether the heiress was already married (without any sons) or whether the male relative already had a wife. The heiress and the male relative were both supposed to divorce their present spouses and marry each other (although in practice the rule could be circumvented by legal subterfuge) to preserve the father's line and keep the property in his family.

Athenian women from the urban propertied class were expected to avoid close contact with men who were not family members or good friends. They were supposed to spend much of their time in their own homes or the homes of women friends. Women dressed and slept in rooms set aside for them, which opened onto a walled courtyard where they could walk in the open air, talk, supervise the family's slaves, and interact with other members of the household and visitors, male and female. Here in her "territory" a woman would spin wool for clothing, converse with friends, play with her children, and give her opinions on various matters to the men of the house as they came and went. Poor women had little time for such activities because they, like their husbands, sons, and brothers, had to leave their homes, usually crowded rental apartments, to work. They often set up small stalls to sell bread, vegetables, simple clothing, or trinkets.

A woman with servants who answered the door herself would be reproached as careless of her reputation. A proper woman left her home only for an appropriate reason, but Athenian life offered many occasions for women to get out: religious festivals, funerals, childbirths at the houses of relatives and friends, and trips to workshops to buy shoes or other domestic articles. Sometimes her husband escorted her, but more often a woman was accompanied only by a servant and could act independently. Social tradition required men not to speak the names of respectable women in public conversations or in court speeches unless absolutely necessary.

Rich women maintained pale complexions because they stayed out of the sun. This paleness was much admired as a sign of an enviable life of leisure and wealth. Women regularly used powdered white lead to give themselves a suitably pallid look. Many upper-class women most likely viewed their limited contact with men outside the household as a badge of superior social status. In a gender-segregated society such as that of upper-class Athens, a woman's primary personal relationships were probably with her children and other women.

Men restricted women's freedom of movement partly to reduce uncertainty about the paternity of their children and to protect their daughters' virginity from seducers and rapists. Since citizenship guaranteed the city-state's political structure and a man's personal freedom, Greeks felt it crucial to ensure that a boy truly was his father's son and not the child of a foreigner or a slave. Women who bore legitimate children earned higher status and greater freedom in the family, as an Athenian man explained in this excerpt from a court case:

> When I decided to marry and had brought a wife home, at first my attitude towards her was this: I did not wish to annoy her, but neither was she to have too much of her own way. . . . I kept an eye on her as was proper. But later, after my child had been born, I came to trust her, and I handed all my possessions over to her, believing that this was the greatest possible proof of affection.

Bearing male children brought special honor to a woman because sons meant security for parents. Sons could appear in court in support of their parents in lawsuits and protect them in the streets of Athens, which for most of its history had no police force. By law, sons were required to support elderly parents. So intense was the pressure to produce sons that stories were common of women who smuggled in male babies born to slaves and passed them off as their own. Such tales, whose truth is hard to gauge, were credible because husbands customarily stayed away at childbirth.

A small number of Athenian women were able to ignore traditional restrictions because they gave up the usual expectations of marrying or were too rich to care what others thought. The most talked-about of the former group were called companions. Often foreigners, they were physically attractive, witty in conversation, and able to sing and play musical instruments. They often entertained at a **symposium** (a male dinner party without wives), and sometimes they sold sexual favors for a high price. Their independent lives set companions apart from citizen women, as did the freedom to control their own sexuality. Equally distinctive was their skill in conversing with men in public. Companions charmed men with their witty, joking conversation. Their characteristic skill at clever remarks and verbal jabs allowed companions a freedom of speech denied to "proper" women.

■ Vase Painting of a Symposium

Upper-class Greek men often spent their evenings at a symposium, a drinking party that always included much conversation and usually featured music and entertainers; wives were not included. The discussions could range widely, from literature to politics to philosophy. Here, a female musician, whose nudity shows she is a hired prostitute, entertains the guests, who recline on couches, as was customary. The man on the right is about to fling the dregs of his wine, playing a messy game called kottabos.

(Reproduction by permission of the Syndics of the Fitzwilliam Museum, Cambridge. Master and Fellows of Corpus Christi College, Cambridge, The Parker Library.)

Some companions lived precarious lives subject to exploitation and even violence at the hands of their male customers, but the most skillful could attract lovers from the highest levels of society and live in luxury on their own. The most famous companion was Aspasia from Miletus, who became Pericles' lover and bore him a son. She dazzled Athens's upper-class males with her brilliant conversation and confidence. Ironically, Pericles' own law of 451 B.C.E. restricting citizenship to children of two Athenian parents meant that their child was not a citizen.

Only the wealthiest citizen women could speak to men openly with the frankness of companions. One such was Elpinike, a member of a super-rich Athenian family of great military distinction. She once publicly criticized Pericles for having boasted about the Athenian conquest of a rebellious ally. When some other Athenian women praised Pericles for his success, Elpinike sarcastically remarked, "This really is wonderful, Pericles, . . . that you have caused the loss of many good citizens, not in battle against Phoenicians or Persians, like my brother Cimon, but in suppressing an allied city of fellow Greeks." Ancient sources confirm that ordinary women, too, remained engaged and interested in issues affecting the city-state as a whole. They often had strong opinions on politics and public policy, but they had to express their views privately to their husbands, children, and relatives.

In contrast to citizen women, slaves and **metics** (immigrants who were granted permanent residency in Athens in exchange for paying taxes and serving in the military) had no political influence because they were "outsiders" living inside Greek society. Individuals and the city-state alike owned slaves, who could be purchased from traders or bred in the household. Unwanted newborns abandoned by their parents (a practice called infant exposure) were often picked up by others and raised as slaves. Athens's commercial growth in this period increased the demand for slaves to provide manual labor. Although no reliable statistics survive, slaves probably made up 100,000 or more of the city-state's estimated 250,000 residents in Pericles' time. (This population made Athens an extraordinarily large city-state.) Slaves worked in homes, on farms, in crafts shops, and, if they were truly unfortunate, in the cramped and dangerous silver mines whose riches boosted Athens's prosperity. Unlike Sparta's helots, Athens's slaves never rebelled, probably because they originated from too many different places to be able to unite.

Golden Age Athens's wealth and cultural vitality attracted numerous metics who worked in Athens as traders, crafts producers, entertainers, and laborers. By the start of the Peloponnesian War in 431 B.C.E., these immigrants made up perhaps half the free population. Metics had to pay for the privilege of working in Athens through a special foreigners' tax and military service. Citizens valued metics' contributions to the city's prosperity but only rarely offered them citizenship.

Metics sometimes found themselves forced into making a living outside the mainstream, especially as prostitutes. Men, unlike women, were not penalized for sexual activity outside marriage. "Certainly you don't think men beget children out of sexual desire?" wrote the upper-class author Xenophon. "The streets and the brothels are swarming with ways to take care of that." Men could have sex with female or male slaves, who could not refuse their masters, or they could have sex with various classes of prostitutes, depending on how much money they wanted to spend.

Education and Intellectual Innovation

Education was privately funded in Golden Age Athens; public schools did not yet exist. Well-to-do families paid private tutors to teach their sons to read, write, and perhaps sing or play a musical instrument, and trainers to instruct them in athletics. Physical fitness was considered vital for men because it was thought to be disgraceful not to be in shape and because all male citizens and metics could be called up for military service from ages eighteen to sixty. Therefore, men exercised daily in public, open-air facilities paid for by wealthy families. Men frequently discussed politics and exchanged news at these gymnasia. The daughters of wealthy families usually learned to read, write, and do arithmetic; a woman with these skills would be better prepared to manage a household and help her future husband run their estate.

Poorer girls and boys learned a trade and perhaps a bit of reading and arithmetic by assisting their parents in their daily work; if they were fortunate, they would become apprentices learning from skilled crafts producers. Scholars disagree about how many people could read and write, but most likely they were a small minority. The predominance of oral rather than written communication meant that people usually absorbed information by ear: songs, speeches, narrated stories, and lively conversation were central to Greek life.

Young men from prosperous families traditionally acquired the skills to participate successfully in the public life of Athenian democracy by observing their fathers, uncles, and other older men as they debated in the Council of 500 and the assembly, served as public officials, and made speeches in court. In many cases, an older man would choose an adolescent male as his special favorite to educate. The younger man would learn about public life by spending his time in the company of the older man and his adult friends. During the day, the youth would observe his mentor talking politics in the agora, help him perform his duties in public office, and work out with him in a gymnasium. Their evenings would be spent at a symposium, where the entertainment ranged from serious political and philosophical discussion to riotous partying fueled by endless cups of wine.

This type of relationship could lead to sexual relations between the youth and the older male, who would normally be married. Although both male homosexuality between adults and female homosexuality in general were regarded as wrong throughout the Greek world, sexual relations between older mentors and younger favorites were considered acceptable in many, though not all, city-states. These differing attitudes about homosexual behavior reflected the complexity of Greek ideas of masculinity, about what made a man a man and what unmade him. In any case, a mentor was never supposed to exploit his younger partner physically or neglect his political education. If this ideal was observed, Athenian society accepted the relationship as part of a complicated range of bonds among males, from political and military activity to training of mind and body to sexual relations.

By the time democracy at Athens had become "radical," young men eager to become skilled political speechmakers could study with a new kind of expert. These teachers of public speaking and clever arguments were called *sophists* ("wise men"), a label that later became an insult (preserved in the English word *sophistry*) because ordinary people thought sophists were dangerously persuasive in making misleading arguments. Sophists created bitter controversy because they taught unprecedented skills in public speaking, but also because they expressed ideas about the nature of human existence and religion that challenged traditional beliefs. The earliest sophists were foreigners who began moving to Athens about 450 B.C.E., at the height of the city-state's prosperity, to attract pupils who could pay the high tuition that sophists charged.

Sophists primarily taught what every ambitious young man needed to learn to gain power in Athens's radical democracy: techniques for persuasive public speaking for the political debates in the assembly and the councils or lawsuits in court. Wealthy men therefore flocked to the dazzling demonstrations these foreign teachers put on to showcase their new methods of persuasion. In some cases, the sophists charged stiff fees to write speeches that customers could deliver as their own compositions.

The sophists alarmed traditionalists, who feared this new and seductive eloquence would undermine communal social and political traditions in favor of individual interests. In ancient Greek culture, where codes of proper behavior, moral standards, and religious ideals were handed down in speech from generation to generation, a persuasive and charismatic speaker could potentially wield as much power as an army of warriors. Sophists made people anxious because political leaders, such as Pericles, flocked to hear them. Many citizens feared that selfish politicians would use the silver-tongued style of the sophists to mislead the assembly and the councils.

The sophists' innovative ideas about human existence and religion deeply upset many people. One especially controversial sophist was Protagoras, a contemporary of Pericles from Abdera in northern Greece. He immigrated to Athens around 450 B.C.E., when he was about forty, and spent most of his career there. His views proved extremely controversial, especially his agnosticism (the belief that human beings cannot know anything about the supernatural): "Whether the gods exist I cannot discover, nor what their form is like, for there are many barriers to knowledge, [such as] the difficulty of the subject and the short span of human life." Ideas like this implied that traditional religion had no meaning, and people worried that they might provoke divine anger.

Equally controversial was Protagoras's denial of any absolute standard of truth: he asserted that every issue had two, irreconcilable sides. For example, he argued, if one person feeling a breeze thinks it warm, whereas another person thinks it cool, neither judgment can be absolutely correct because the wind simply is warm to one and cool to the other. Protagoras summed up his **subjectivism**—the belief that there is no absolute reality behind and independent of appearances—in the much-quoted opening of his work *Truth*: "Man is the measure of all things, of the things that are that they are, and of the things that are not that they are not." *Man* (*anthropos* in Greek, hence our word *anthropology*) in this passage refers to the individual human, male or female, whom Protagoras makes the sole judge of his or her own impressions.

These ideas and other similarly unsettling ones taught by sophists deeply worried many people. They feared that sophists would convince others that human institutions and values were only matters of convention, custom, or law (*nomos*) and not products of nature (*physis*), and that because truth was subjective, speakers should be able to argue either side of a question with equal persuasiveness. The first view implied that traditional human institutions were arbitrary rather than grounded in nature, and the second made morality irrelevant to politics. The combination of the two ideas amounted to moral relativism, the idea that there were no absolute moral values, which threatened the shared public values of the democratic city-state.

Protagoras tried to meet such objections by insisting that his doctrines were not hostile to democracy, arguing that every person had an innate capability for "excellence" and that human survival depended on the rule of law based on a sense of justice. Members of the community, he explained, must be persuaded to obey the laws not because they are based on absolute truth, which does not exist, but because it was advantageous for people to live by them. A thief, for example, would have to be persuaded that the law forbidding theft was to his advantage because it protected his own property and the city-state in which he, like others, had to live in order to survive.

Other sophists taught other disturbing ideas. Anaxagoras of Clazomenae, for example, offended believers in traditional religion by arguing that the sun was nothing more than a lump of flaming rock, not a deity. Leucippus of Miletus, whose doctrines were made famous by his pupil Democritus of Abdera, invented an atomic theory of matter to explain how change was constant. Everything, he argued, consisted of tiny, invisible particles in eternal motion. Their random collisions caused them to combine and recombine in an infinite variety of forms. This physical explanation of the source of change, like Anaxagoras's theory about the sun, implied that traditional religion, which explained events as the outcome of divine forces, was invalid.

Because only wealthy men could afford instruction from sophists, this new education worked against the egalitarian principles of Athenian democracy by giving an advantage to the rich. In addition, moral relativism and the physical explanation of the universe struck many Athenians as dangerous: they feared that the teachings of the sophists could bring divine punishment on the whole community.

The ideas of Socrates of Athens (469–399 B.C.E.), the most famous philosopher of the Golden Age, added to the tension that the sophists provoked. He was not a sophist and offered no courses, but his views became well known because his lifestyle was so distinctive. Socrates devoted his life to conversation combating the notion that justice should be equated with the power to impose one's will on others. His passionate concern to discover valid guidelines for leading a just life and to prove that justice is better than injustice under all circumstances gave a new direction to Greek philosophy: an emphasis on individual ethics. Although other thinkers before him

■ Statuette of the Philosopher Socrates

The controversial Socrates, the most famous philosopher of Athens in the fifth century B.C.E., joked that he had a homely face and a bulging stomach. This small statue is an artist's impression of what Socrates looked like; we cannot be sure of the truth. Socrates was famous for his irony, and he may have purposely exaggerated his physical unattractiveness to show his disdain for ordinary standards of beauty, which valued a fit body, and his own emphasis on the quality of one's soul as the true measure of a person's worth.

had dealt with moral issues, especially poets and dramatists, Socrates was the first to make the ethics and morality of the individual a central concern for philosophy.

Socrates lived a life that attracted attention. He paid so little notice to his physical appearance and clothes that he seemed eccentric. Sporting a stomach, in his words, "somewhat too large to be convenient," he wore the same cheap cloak summer and winter and went barefoot in all weather. His tirelessness as a hoplite and his ability to outdrink anyone at a symposium amazed his companions. Unlike the sophists, he lived in poverty and disdained material possessions, somehow managing to support a wife and several children. He may have inherited some money, but he certainly received gifts from wealthy admirers.

Socrates spent his time in conversations: participating in a symposium, strolling in the agora, or watching young men exercise in a gymnasium. He wrote nothing; our knowledge of his ideas comes from others' writings, especially those of his pupil Plato (c. 428–348 B.C.E.). Plato portrays Socrates as a relentless questioner of his fellow citizens, foreign friends, and leading sophists. Socrates' questions aimed at making his conversational partners examine the basic assumptions of their way of life. Giving few answers, Socrates never directly instructed anyone; instead, he led them to draw conclusions in response to his asking probing questions that picked apart their unexamined assumptions. Teaching this way is today called the **Socratic method**.

This indirect method of searching for the truth often left people uncomfortably baffled because they were forced to conclude that they were ignorant of what they had assumed they knew very well. Socrates' questions showed that normal careers—pursuing success in politics or business or art—were excuses for avoiding genuine virtue. Socrates insisted that he was ignorant of the best definition of virtue but that his wisdom consisted of knowing that he did not know. He vowed that he was trying to improve, not undermine, people's beliefs in morality, even though, as a friend put it, a conversation with Socrates made a man feel numb—just as if he had been stung by a stingray. Socrates especially wanted to use reasoning to discover universal standards justifying individual morality. He fiercely attacked the sophists, who dismissed traditional morality as "chains that bind nature." This idea, he protested, equated human happiness with power and "getting more."

Socrates passionately believed that just behavior was better for people than injustice and that morality was priceless because it guaranteed happiness. Essentially, he argued that just behavior, or virtue, was identical to knowledge and that true knowledge of justice would inevitably lead people to choose good over evil. They would therefore live truly happy lives, regardless of how rich or poor they were. Since Socrates believed that moral knowledge was all a person needed for the good life, he argued that no one knowingly behaved unjustly and that behaving justly was always in the individual's interest. It was simply ignorant to believe that the best life was the life of unlimited power to pursue whatever one desired. The most desirable human life was focused on virtue and guided by reason, not by dreams of personal gain.

Socrates' effect on many people was as disturbing as the sophists' doctrines that questioned traditional morality. Socrates' attacks on his fellow citizens' ideas about the importance of wealth and public success made some men extremely upset because his ideas seemed to mean that people should not bother thinking about the community, only about their individual virtue. Unhappiest of all were the fathers whose sons, after listening to Socrates reduce someone to utter bewilderment, came home to try the same technique on their parents by arguing that the public accomplishments their family held dear were old-fashioned, even worthless. Men who experienced this reversal of the traditional educational hierarchy—fathers were supposed to educate sons—felt that Socrates was undermining the stability of society by making young men question Athenian traditions. The ancient sources fail to reveal what Athenian women thought of Socrates, or he of them. His thoughts about human capabilities and behavior could be applied to women as well as to men, and he probably believed that women and men both had the same basic capacity for justice.

People's worry that Socrates presented a danger to traditional society inspired playwright Aristophanes to write his comedy *Clouds* (423 B.C.E.). He portrayed Socrates as a cynical sophist operating a Thinking Shop who, for a fee, offered instruction in Protagoras-like techniques of making the weaker argument the stronger.

When Socrates' curriculum transforms a youth into a public speaker arguing that a son has the right to beat his parents, his father burns down Socrates' school. None of these plot details was real; what was genuine was the fear that Socrates' uncompromising views on individual morality endangered the traditional practices of the community at a time when new ways of thought were angering many Athenians.

One especially significant intellectual innovation that emerged in the Golden Age was historical writing as a critical vision of the past. Herodotus of Halicarnassus (c. 485–425 B.C.E.) and Thucydides of Athens (c. 455–399 B.C.E.) became Greece's most famous historians and established Western civilization's tradition of history writing. By 428–425 B.C.E., Herodotus had finished his groundbreaking work called *Histories* (meaning "inquiry" in Greek) to explain the Persian Wars as a clash between East and West; by Roman times he had been christened "Father of History." Herodotus achieved an unprecedented depth for his book by giving it a wide geographical scope, an investigative approach to evidence, and a lively story. Herodotus searched for the origins of the Persian-Greek conflict both by delving deep into the past and by examining the cultural traditions of all the peoples involved. He recognized the relevance and the delight of studying other cultures as a component of historical investigation.

Thucydides took another giant step in this process by writing contemporary history influenced by what today is called political science. His *History of the Peloponnesian War* made power politics, not divine intervention, the primary force in history. Deeply affected by the war's brutality, he used his personal experiences as a politician and military commander to make his history vivid and frank in describing human moral failings. His insistence that historians should spare no effort in seeking out the most reliable sources and evaluating their testimony with objectivity set a high standard for later writers.

Equally innovative were the medical doctrines of Hippocrates of Cos, a fifth-century B.C.E. contemporary of Thucydides, who became Greece's most famous physician. He is remembered today in the oath bearing his name that doctors swear at the beginning of their professional careers. Hippocrates made great strides in putting medical diagnosis and treatment on a scientific basis. Earlier medicine had depended on magic and ritual. Hippocrates viewed the human body as an organism whose parts must be understood in relation to the whole. Some attributed to him the view, profoundly influential in later times, that four humors (fluids) made up the human body: blood, phlegm, black bile, and yellow bile. Health depended on keeping the proper balance among them; being healthy was to be in "good humor." This intellectual system corresponded to philosophers' division of the physical world into four parts: the elements earth, air, fire, and water. Hippocrates taught that the physician's most important duty was to base his knowledge on careful observation of patients and their response to remedies. Clinical experience, not theory, he insisted, was the best guide to effective treatments. Although various cults in Greek religion offered healing to worshippers, Hippocratic medical doctrine apparently made little or no mention of any role for the gods in illnesses and their treatments.

The Development of Tragedy and Comedy

The complex relationship between gods and humans formed the basis of Golden Age Athens's most influential cultural innovation: tragic drama. Greek plays, still read and produced onstage today, were presented over three days at the major annual festival of the god Dionysus, which was held in the spring. They were staged in a drama contest with prizes for the best plays, in keeping with the competitive spirit characteristic of many events honoring the gods. By presenting shocking stories exploring tensions in the city-state, tragedy inspired its large audiences to ponder the danger that ignorance, arrogance, and violence presented to Athens's democratic society. Following the tradition of Homer and Hesiod, Golden Age playwrights treated themes ranging from individual freedom and responsibility in the polis, to the underlying nature of good and evil.

Every year, Athens's government held a competition to choose three authors to present four plays each: three tragedies in a row (a trilogy), followed by a semicomic play featuring satyrs (mythical half-man, half-animal beings) to end the day on a lighter note. The term *tragedy*—derived for reasons now lost from the Greek words for "goat" and "song"—referred to plays with plots that presented fierce conflicts among characters representing powerful forces. Tragedies were written in verse and used solemn language; they were often based on stories about the violent consequences of interaction between gods and humans told in myth. The plots often ended with a resolution to the trouble—but only after great suffering.

The performance of Athenian tragedies took place during the daytime in an outdoor theater sacred to Dionysus, built into the southern slope of Athens's acropolis. This theater held about fifteen thousand spectators overlooking an open, circular area in front of a slightly raised stage. Every tragedy had to have eighteen cast members, all of whom were men: three actors to play the speaking roles (both male and female characters) and fifteen chorus members. Although the chorus leader sometimes engaged in dialogue with the actors, the chorus primarily performed songs and dances in the circular area in front of the stage, called the *orchestra*.

A successful tragedy presented a vivid spectacle. The chorus wore decorative costumes and performed intricate dance routines. The actors wore masks and used broad gestures and booming voices to reach the upper tier of seats. A powerful voice was crucial to a tragic actor because words represented the heart of a tragedy, in which dialogue and long speeches were far more common than physical action. Special effects, however, were part of the spectacle. For example, a crane allowed actors playing the roles of gods to fly suddenly onto the stage. The actors playing lead roles, called the *protagonists* ("first competitors"), competed against one another to win an award for best actor. So important was a first-rate protagonist to a successful tragedy that actors were assigned by lottery to the playwrights to give all three an equal chance to have the finest cast. Great protagonists became international celebrities.

■ **Theater of Dionysus at Athens**

Tragedies, satyr plays, and comedies produced at this theater in daytime festivals riveted the attention of the city. The theater held about fifteen thousand spectators. In the Classical period, the seating, the stage, and scenery were not yet permanent installations. The seating and stone stage building foundations are remnants of much later changes. What qualities in an actor do you think would be most important under these conditions? (John Elk III/Bruce Coleman, Inc.)

Most playwrights came from the social elite because only men of property could afford the amount of time and learning their work demanded; they served as author, director, producer, musical composer, choreographer, and sometimes even actor. The prizes awarded in the tragedy competition were modest, but the fame was enormous. As citizens, playwrights also fulfilled the normal military and political obligations of Athenian men. The best-known Athenian tragedians—Aeschylus (525–456 B.C.E.), Sophocles (c. 496–406 B.C.E.), and Euripides (c. 485–406 B.C.E.)— all served in the army, held public office at some point in their careers, or did both.

Athenian tragedy was a public art form. Its performances were subsidized with public funds, and its plots explored the ethical problems of humans in conflict with the gods and with one another in a city-state. Even though most tragedies were based on stories that referred to a legendary time before city-states existed, such as tales of the Trojan War, the moral issues the plays explored always concerned the society and obligations of citizens in a city-state. To take only a few examples: in his trilogy *Oresteia* (458 B.C.E.), Aeschylus explains the importance of democratic

Athens's court system by reworking the story of how the gods stopped the murderous violence in the family of Orestes, son of the Greek leader against Troy. The plays suggest that human beings have to learn by suffering but that the gods will provide justice in the long run. Sophocles' *Antigone* (441 B.C.E.) presents the sad story of the family of Oedipus of Thebes as a drama of harsh conflict between a courageous woman, Antigone, who insists on her family's moral obligation to bury its dead in obedience to divine command, and her uncle Creon, the city-state's stern male leader, who defends the need to preserve order and protect community values by prohibiting the burial of traitors. In a horrifying story of anger and suicide centered on one of the most famous heroines of Western literature, Sophocles deliberately exposes the right and wrong on each side of the conflict. His play offers no easy resolution to the possible conflict between divine and human laws. Euripides' *Medea* (431 B.C.E.) implies that the political order of a city-state depends on men treating their wives and families with honor and trust: when Medea's husband betrays her for a younger woman, she takes revenge by destroying their children and the community's political leadership with her magical power.

We cannot reconstruct precisely how the audiences of the drama competition of the Dionysian festival understood the messages of tragedies. At the very least, however, they must have been aware that the central characters of the plays were figures who fell into disaster from positions of power and prestige. The characters' reversals of fortune came about not because they were absolute villains but because, as humans, they could fail through a lethal combination of error, ignorance, and **hubris** (violent arrogance). The Athenian Empire was at its height when audiences at Athens attended the tragedies of these three great playwrights. Thoughtful spectators may have reflected on the possibility that Athens's current power and prestige, managed as they were by humans, remained hostage to the same forces that controlled the fates of the heroes and heroines of tragedy. Tragedies certainly appealed to audiences because they were entertainment, but they also had an educational function: to remind male citizens, who made policy for the city-state, that success created complex moral problems that could not be solved casually or arrogantly.

Athens also developed theatrical comedy as another innovative form of public art. Like tragedies, comedies were written in verse, were performed in a competition in the city's large outdoor theater during festivals honoring the god Dionysus, and were subsidized with public funds. Unlike tragedies, comedies made direct comments about public policy, criticized current politicians and intellectuals by name, and devised plots of outrageous fantasy to make their points. Comic choruses of twenty-four actors, for example, could feature characters colorfully dressed as talking birds or dancing clouds.

The immediate goal of a comic playwright was to win the award for the festival's best comedy by creating beautiful poetry, raising laughs with constant jokes and puns, and mocking prominent men. Much of the humor concerned sex and bodily functions, delivered in a stream of imaginative profanity. Well-known male citizens were targeted for insults as cowardly or sexually effeminate. Women characters who were made fun of, however, seem to have been fictional.

Comedy's remarkable freedom of speech promoted frank, even brutal, commentary on current issues and personalities. Even during the Peloponnesian War, comic playwrights presented plays that criticized the city-state's policy, for example by recommending an immediate peace settlement. It was no accident that this energetic, critical drama emerged in Athens at the same time as radical democracy, in the mid-fifth century B.C.E. The principle that all voters should have a stake in determining government policies evidently fueled a passion for using biting humor to keep the community's leaders from becoming arrogant and aloof.

Athenian comedies often blamed particular political leaders for government policies that had been approved by the assembly, similar to the way ostracism singled out individuals for punishment. As the leading politician of radical democracy, Pericles came in for fierce criticism in comedy. Comic playwrights mocked his policies, his love life, and his looks ("Old Turnip Head" was a favorite insult). Cleon, the most prominent politician after Pericles, was so outraged by the way that he was parodied on stage by Aristophanes (c. 455–385 B.C.E.), Athens's most famous comic playwright, that he sued him. When Cleon lost the case, Aristophanes responded by pitilessly mocking him as a slavish foreign slob in *The Knights* (424 B.C.E.).

The most remarkable of Aristophanes' comedies are those in which the main characters are powerful women who force the men of Athens to change their policy to preserve family life and the city-state. Most famous is *Lysistrata* (411 B.C.E.), named after the female lead character of the play. In it, the women of Athens and Sparta unite to force their husbands to end the Peloponnesian War. To make the men agree to a peace treaty, they first seize the acropolis, where Athens's financial reserves are kept, to prevent the men from spending them on the war. They then beat back an attack on their position by the old men who have remained in Athens while the younger men are out on campaign. When their husbands return from battle, the women refuse to have sex with them. This strike, which is portrayed in a series of risqué episodes, finally coerces the men of Athens and Sparta to agree to a treaty.

Lysistrata presents women acting bravely and aggressively against men who seem bent on destroying their traditional family life—they are staying away from home for long stretches while on military campaigns and are ruining the city-state by prolonging a pointless war. Lysistrata insists that women have the intelligence and judgment to make political decisions: "I am a woman, and, yes, I have brains. And I'm not badly off for judgment. Nor has my education been bad, coming as it has from my listening often to the conversations of my father and the elders among the men." Her old-fashioned training and good sense allow her to see what needs to be done to protect the community. Like the heroines of tragedy, Lysistrata is a reactionary; she wants to put things back the way they were. To do that, however, she has to act like an impatient revolutionary. That irony well sums up the challenge that

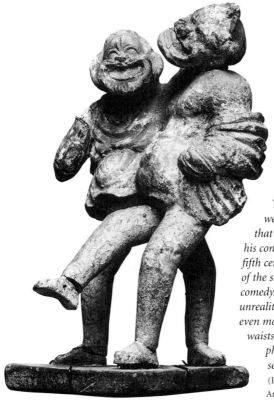

■ **Statuettes of Comic Actors**
These little statues portray comic actors wearing the kinds of masks and costumes that became popular after Aristophanes and his contemporaries wrote their comedies in the fifth century B.C.E., and they give a vivid sense of the slapstick acting that characterized Greek comedy. In Aristophanes' day, the grotesque unreality of comic costumes would have been even more striking because attached below the waists of the male actors were large leather phalluses that were props for all sorts of sex-related jokes.
(Bildarchiv Preussischer Kulturbesitz/ Art Resource, NY.)

Golden Age Athens faced in trying to balance its reliance on tradition with the energy of the period's innovation in so many fields.

■ **REVIEW:** *How did new ways of thinking in the Golden Age threaten cherished traditions?*

The End of the Golden Age, 431–403 B.C.E.

A war between Athens and Sparta that lasted a generation (431–404 B.C.E.) ended the Athenian Golden Age. Called Peloponnesian today because it pitted Sparta's Peloponnese-based alliance against Athens's alliance, the war arose at least in part as a result of Pericles' policies. The most powerful politician in Athens—he won election as a general for fifteen years in a row beginning in 443 B.C.E.—Pericles nevertheless had to withstand severe criticism of the huge public spending on his building program and harsh measures against Delian League allies; his rivals said these policies soiled Athens's reputation. He faced his greatest challenge, however, when relations with Sparta worsened in the mid-430s B.C.E. over Athenian actions against Corinth and Megara, crucial Spartan allies. Finally, Corinth told Sparta to attack Athens, or Corinth would change sides to the Athenian alliance. Sparta's leaders therefore gave Athens an ultimatum—stop mistreating our allies—which Pericles convinced the Athenian assembly to reject as unfair because Sparta was refusing arbitration of the disputes. In this way, the relations of Athens and Sparta with lesser city-states propelled the two powers over the brink into war. Pericles' critics claimed he was insisting on war against Sparta to revive his popularity. By 431 B.C.E., the thirty-year peace made in 446–445 B.C.E. had been shattered beyond repair.

The Peloponnesian War, 431–403 B.C.E.

Dragging on longer than any previous war in Greek history, the Peloponnesian War took place above all because Spartan leaders feared that the Athenians would use their superior long-distance offensive weaponry—the naval forces of the Delian League—to destroy Spartan control over the Peloponnesian League. (See "Taking Measure," below.) The duration of the struggle reflects the unpredictability of war

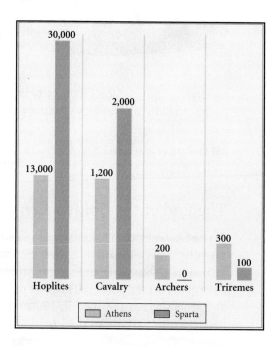

■ **TAKING MEASURE Military Forces of Athens and Sparta at the Beginning of the Peloponnesian War**
These figures give estimates of the comparative strengths of the military forces of the Athenian side and the Spartan side when the Peloponnesian War broke out in 431 B.C.E. The numbers come from ancient historical sources— above all, the Athenian general and historian Thucydides, who fought in the war. The bar graphs reveal the different characteristics of the competing forces: Athens relied on its navy of triremes and its archers (the fifth-century B.C.E. equivalent of artillery and snipers). Sparta was preeminent in the forces needed for land battles—hoplites (heavily armed infantry) and cavalry (shock troops used to disrupt opposing infantry). These differences dictated the strategies and tactics of each side. Athens tried to launch surprise raids from the sea, and Sparta tried to force decisive confrontations on the battlefield.

and the consequences of the repeated refusal of the Athenian assembly to negotiate lasting peace terms.

Thucydides dramatically revealed the absolute refusal of the Athenians to find a compromise solution with these words of Pericles to the assembly:

> *If we do go to war, harbor no thought that you went to war over a trivial affair. For you this trifling matter is the assurance and the proof of your determination. If you yield to their demands, they will immediately confront you with some larger demand, since they will think that you only gave way on the first point out of fear. But if you stand firm, you will show them that they have to deal with you as equals. . . . When our equals, without agreeing to arbitration of the matter under dispute, make claims on us as neighbors and state those claims as commands, it would be no better than slavery to give in to them, no matter how large or how small the claim may be.*

Pericles advised Athens to use its superior navy to raid enemy lands while avoiding battles with the Spartan infantry, even when they invaded the Athenian countryside and destroyed citizens' property there. In the end, he predicted, the superior resources of Athens would enable it to win a war of attrition. With his unyielding leadership, this strategy might have prevailed, but unexpected trouble struck. From 430 to 426 B.C.E., an epidemic disease ravaged Athens's population, killing thousands—including Pericles in 429 B.C.E. The Athenians fought on, but they lost the clear direction that Pericles' costly strategy had required. The generals after him followed increasingly risky plans, culminating in an overambitious campaign against Sparta's allies in Sicily, far to the west. Dazzling the assembly in 415 B.C.E. with the dream of conquering that rich island, Alcibiades, the most innovative and brashest commander of the war, persuaded the Athenians to launch their largest naval expedition ever. His political rivals got him recalled from his command, however, and the invasion force suffered a catastrophic defeat in 413 B.C.E. (see Map 2.3 on page 86).

The Spartans then launched the final phase of the war by establishing a permanent base of operations in the Athenian countryside for year-round raids. The agricultural economy was devastated, and revenues fell drastically when twenty thousand slave workers crippled production in Athens's publicly owned silver mines by deserting to the enemy. Distress over the war's losses led to a group of antidemocratic citizens briefly overturning the democracy in 411 B.C.E., but other citizens soon restored democratic government. Athens fought on. The end came when Persia sent money to help the Spartans finally build a strong navy.

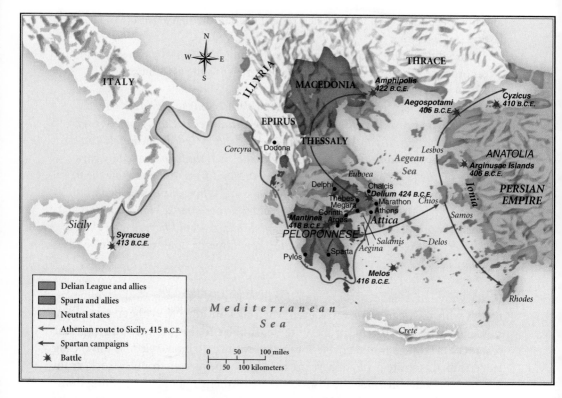

■ MAP 2.3 The Peloponnesian War, 431–404 B.C.E.
During the first ten years of the war, most of the battles took place in mainland Greece. Sparta, whose armies usually avoided long-distance campaigns, shocked Athens when its general Brasidas led successful attacks against Athenian forces in northeast Greece. In the war's next phase, Athens stunned the Greek world by launching a naval expedition against Spartan allies in Sicily. In the last ten years of the war, the action moved to the east, on and along the western coast of Anatolia and its islands; this was the western boundary of the Persian Empire, which helped the Spartans build a navy to defeat the Athenian fleet and win the war. **For more help analyzing this map,** see the map activity for this chapter in the ONLINE STUDY GUIDE at bedfordstmartins.com/huntconcise.

Aggressive Spartan action at sea forced Athens to surrender in 404 B.C.E. After twenty-seven years of near-continuous war, the Athenians were at the mercy of their enemies.

The Rule of the Thirty Tyrants, 404–403 B.C.E.

The victorious Spartans installed a regime of antidemocratic Athenians, members of the social elite who became known as the Thirty Tyrants. Brutally suppressing democratic opposition, these rulers embarked on an eight-month period of terror in 404–403 B.C.E. The speechwriter Lysias, for example, reported that

IMPORTANT DATES			
c. 499–494 B.C.E.	Ionian revolt against Persian control	446–445 B.C.E.	Athens and Sparta sign a peace treaty meant to last thirty years
490 B.C.E.	Battle of Marathon		
480 B.C.E.	Battles of Thermopylae and Salamis	431 B.C.E.	Peloponnesian War between Athens and Sparta begins
477 B.C.E.	Athens forms the Delian League	c. 428–425 B.C.E.	Herodotus finishes the *Histories*
469–399 B.C.E.	Life of Socrates	411 B.C.E.	Aristophanes presents the comedy *Lysistrata*
461 B.C.E.	Ephialtes' political and judicial reforms strengthen Athenian democracy	404 B.C.E.	Athens surrenders to Sparta, ending the Peloponnesian War
458 B.C.E.	Aeschylus presents the trilogy *Oresteia*	404–403 B.C.E.	Thirty Tyrants suspend democracy at Athens but are soon overthrown; Athenian democracy is restored but weakened economically
450 B.C.E.	The sophist Protagoras comes to Athens		
447 B.C.E.	Construction begins on the Parthenon in Athens		

the tyrants' thugs seized his brother for execution as a way of stealing the family's valuables, down to the gold earrings ripped from the ears of his brother's wife. An Athenian democratic resistance movement soon arose and expelled the Thirty Tyrants in 403 B.C.E. with a series of bloody street battles. Fortunately for the democrats, a split in the Spartan leadership, propelled by the competing ambitions of its two most prominent men, prevented Spartan military support for the tyrants.

This civil war made Athenians so angry at each other that internal strife threatened to tear the community apart even after democracy was restored. The assembly therefore proclaimed the first known amnesty in Western history, a truce forbidding any official charges or revenge for crimes committed during the rule of the Thirty Tyrants. Athens's government was once again a functioning democracy, but its financial and military strength was shattered. Worse, its society harbored bitterness that no amnesty could fully dissolve. The end of the Golden Age left Athenians worriedly wondering how to remake their lives and restore the luster that their city-state's innovative accomplishments had produced in that wondrous period.

■ **REVIEW:** *How did unexpected events contribute to the outcome of the Peloponnesian War?*

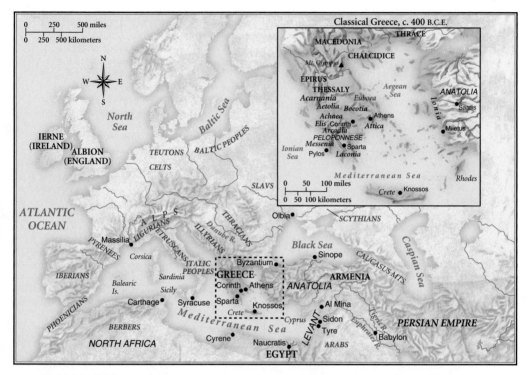

■ **MAPPING THE WEST** Greece, Europe, and the Mediterranean, c. 400 B.C.E.
No single power controlled the Mediterranean region at the end of the fifth century B.C.E. In the west, the Phoenician city of Carthage and the Greek cities of Sicily and southern Italy were rivals for the riches to be won by trade. In the east, the Spartans, made ambitious by their victory over Athens in the Peloponnesian War, tried to become an international power outside the mainland for the first time in their history by sending campaigns into Anatolia and, they hoped, further east still. This aggressive action aroused stiff opposition from the Persians because it was a threat to their western-most imperial provinces.

Conclusion

Athens's Golden Age in the fifth century B.C.E. was a time of prosperity, political stability, international power, and artistic and cultural accomplishment. Its citizens had won great glory in the unexpected victory of the Greek alliance against the Persians at the beginning of the century. This stunning triumph occurred, the Athenians believed, because the gods smiled upon them with special favor and because they displayed superior courage, intelligence, and virtue.

Athens soon rivaled Sparta for the leadership of the Greek world, and by the mid-fifth century B.C.E. it was enjoying unprecedented confidence and prosperity. As the money poured in, the city-state built glorious temples, instituted pay for service in many government offices, and assembled the Mediterranean's most powerful navy. The poorer men who rowed the ships demanded greater democracy, leading to a judicial system guaranteeing fair treatment for all. Pericles became the most famous politician of the Golden Age by leading the drive for radical democracy.

Traditional boundaries remained in place for women and for religious worship, but the scale of intellectual change was as dramatic as that in politics. Art and architecture broke out of old forms, promoting an impression of precarious motion rather than stability. Tragedy and comedy developed at Athens as public art forms commenting on contemporary social and political issues. Sophists' new ideas about the nature of the universe and morality disturbed traditionally minded people, as did Socrates' strict ethics denying the value of the ordinary pursuit of wealth and success.

Wars framed the Golden Age. The Persian Wars sent the Athenians soaring to imperial power and prosperity, but their high-handed treatment of allies and enemies helped bring on the disastrous Peloponnesian War. Nearly three decades of battle brought the stars of the Greek Golden Age thudding back to earth: the Athenians by 400 B.C.E. found themselves in the same situation as in 500 B.C.E., fearful of Spartan power and worried whether the world's first democracy could survive. As it turned out, the next great threat to Greek stability and independence would once again come from outside, not from the east this time but from the north.

■ **MAKING CONNECTIONS**

1. *What were the most significant differences between Greece in the Archaic Age and in the Golden Age?*

2. *What did Greeks in the Golden Age believe it was worth spending public funds to pay for and why?*

■ **FOR FURTHER EXPLORATION**

For further reading and online research ideas, see the Suggested References on page SR-1 at the back of the book.

For practice quizzes, a customized study plan, and other study tools, see the ONLINE STUDY GUIDE at bedfordstmartins.com/huntconcise.

For primary-source material from this period, see Chapter 2 in *Sources of THE MAKING OF THE WEST: A CONCISE HISTORY*, Second Edition.

3

From the Classical to the Hellenistic World

c. 400–30 B.C.E.

A BOUT 255 B.C.E., AN EGYPTIAN CAMEL TRADER in Syria paid a bilingual scribe to write a letter to his Greek employer, Zeno, back in Egypt, to complain about his treatment by Zeno's Greek assistant, Krotos: "You know that when you left me in Syria with Krotos I followed all your instructions concerning the camels and behaved blamelessly towards you. But Krotos has ignored your orders to pay me my salary; I've received nothing despite asking him for my money over and over. He just tells me to go away. I waited a long time for you to come, but when I no longer had enough to live on and couldn't get help anywhere, I had to run away to keep from starving to death. . . . I am desperate summer and winter. . . . They have treated me with contempt because I am not a Greek. I therefore beg you, please, command them to pay me my salary so that I won't go hungry just because I don't know how to speak Greek."

The camel trader's name has been lost, but his desperate plea reveals that not being Greek contributed to his mistreatment. His difficult situation—having to

■ **Solving the Mystery of Egyptian Writing**
The three kinds of writing on this stone found by Napoleon's army in 1799 C.E. near Rosetta in Egypt's Nile River delta unlocked the thousand-year mystery of how to read ancient Egyptian hieroglyphs. The three bands of text repeat the same message (praise for King Ptolemy V of Egypt decreed by priests in 196 B.C.E.) in three different scripts: at the top, hieroglyphs (Egypt's oldest writing system, c. 3100–3000 B.C.E.), then demotic (a cursive form of Egyptian invented around 600 B.C.E.), and finally a translation in Greek. Scholars in the nineteenth century C.E. deciphered the hieroglyphs by comparing them to the Greek version, which they could read. Most Egyptians, like the mistreated camel trader stranded in Syria, could not read Greek, and most Greeks living in Egypt under the rule of the Ptolemaic kings could not read Egyptian, so bilingual texts such as the Rosetta Stone were necessary to reach the widest possible audience in Hellenistic Egypt. (Art Resource, NY.)

communicate persuasively with a foreigner holding power in his homeland—reveals the challenges facing the eastern Mediterranean world as it moved from the Classical period (500–323 B.C.E.) to the Hellenistic period (323–30 B.C.E.). These challenges were created by the large-scale movement of Greeks into the Near East and the resulting interaction between the local cultures and the culture of the newcomers. War brought these changes. The Peloponnesian War (431–404 B.C.E.) had accustomed many Greeks to making a living as soldiers, and after the war thousands of them became mercenaries serving Near Eastern rulers. The migration of Greeks to the Near East accelerated when the Macedonian king Alexander the Great (356–323 B.C.E.) conquered the Persian Empire and left behind colonies of Greeks from Egypt and the Near East to present-day Afghanistan.

Nineteenth-century scholars coined the term **Hellenistic** to designate the period of Greek and Near Eastern history from Alexander's death in 323 B.C.E. to the death of Cleopatra VII, the last Macedonian queen of Egypt, in 30 B.C.E. The term expresses the idea that a mixed, more international form of social and cultural life, combining Hellenic (that is, Greek) and local, Near Eastern traditions, emerged in the aftermath of Alexander's conquest of the Persian Empire.

The kings who followed Alexander revived monarchy in the Greek world by carving Macedonian and Near Eastern territory into kingdoms whose wealth made them dominant and reduced Greece's city-states to second-rate powers. The city-states retained their local political and social institutions but lost their independence in foreign policy: Hellenistic kings decided international politics. The kings hired Greeks to fill royal offices, man their armies, and run businesses throughout their Near Eastern territories; this policy created tension with their non-Greek subjects. Immigrant Greeks, such as Zeno in Egypt, formed a social and political elite dominating the kingdoms' local populations. Egyptians, Syrians, or Mesopotamians who wanted to rise in society had to win the support of these Greeks and learn their language. Otherwise, they might find themselves as powerless as the hungry camel trader.

Over time, however, the local cultures in the Near East interacted with the culture of the Greek overlords. The result was a new, multicultural mixture. Locals married Greeks, shared their religious traditions with the newcomers, taught them their agricultural and scientific knowledge, and sometimes learned Greek to win administrative jobs. The social tension between Greeks and non-Greeks never disappeared in the Hellenistic kingdoms, but their blending of Greek and Near Eastern traditions nevertheless promoted innovations in art, science, philosophy, and religion.

The Hellenistic kingdoms ended during the second and first centuries B.C.E., when the Romans overpowered all of them. The complex mixing of peoples and ideas that occurred in the Hellenistic period greatly influenced Roman civilization and thus later Western civilization. Hellenistic religious developments, for example, provided the background for Christianity. The period's cultural achievements remained influential long after the glories of Greece's Golden Age had faded away.

Disunity in Classical Greece, c. 400–350 B.C.E.

Sparta's victory over Athens in the Peloponnesian War brought a violent end to the Golden Age of Greece in the fifth century B.C.E. Once the Athenians had restored their democracy following the fall of the Thirty Tyrants, their city-state's economy gradually recovered, but the stability of daily life did not remove the hatred that democratic Athenians felt toward their fellow citizens whom they blamed for the Tyrants' violent rule. This bitterness led to the execution of Socrates in 399 B.C.E. Outraged at Socrates' fate, Plato and Aristotle created Greece's most famous philosophies about right and wrong and how human beings should live.

The Spartans tried to use their victory to turn their city-state into an international power, but their harsh leadership and collaboration with the Persian king stirred up fierce resistance from Greek city-states, especially Thebes and Athens. By the 350s B.C.E., the Greeks had become so disunited by their bloody battles with one another that they were too weak to prevent the expansion of their ambitious northern neighbors, the Macedonians.

The Aftermath of War and the Trial of Socrates

Spartan invaders during the Peloponnesian War had wrecked the homes of many Athenians living in the countryside and devastated Athens's agriculture and trade. Especially hard hit were moderately well-off women whose husbands and brothers died in the war. These women traditionally did weaving at home and supervised household slaves while the men earned the family's income by farming or commerce. Without male providers, many war widows had to find work outside the home. The jobs open to them were low-paying occupations, some traditional for women, such as wet nurses or weavers, or some for which there were not enough men, such as vineyard laborers.

Some Athenian families found ways to profit from women's skills. Socrates' friend Aristarchus, for example, became poverty-stricken supporting several widowed sisters, nieces, and female cousins. Socrates reminded his friend that his relatives knew how to make cloaks, shirts, capes, and smocks, "the work considered the best and most fitting for women." The women had been making clothing only for family members. Socrates suggested that they sell it for profit. The plan succeeded financially, but the women complained that Aristarchus was the only member of the household who ate without working. Socrates advised his friend to reply that the women should think of him as sheep viewed a guard dog—earning his food by keeping the wolves away.

■ **Vase Painting of Women Fetching Water**
This painting shows a scene from everyday life in a Greek city-state: women filling water jugs at a covered public fountain to take back to their homes. Few Greek homes had running water, so it was the duty of freeborn and slave women in a household to gather water for drinking, cooking, wash-ing, and cleaning. Prosperous cities built attractively decorated fountain houses, such as the one shown here, where a regular supply of fresh water was available from springs or was piped in through aqueducts. These fountains were popular spots for women's conversations outside the house. The women in this scene wear the long robes and hair coverings characteristic of the time.
(Museum of Fine Arts, Boston. William Francis Warden Fund. Photograph © 2004 Museum of Fine Arts, Boston [61.195].)

Economic recovery stumbled when revenue fell in Athens's biggest enterprise—the state-owned silver mines, which were leased to private citizens who owned crews of slave miners. Economic conditions gradually improved as households and business owners revived trade and the production of goods in their homes and in small shops, such as metal foundries and pottery workshops. Businesses, usually family run, were small; the largest known was a shield-making company owning 120 slaves. The return of prosperity, coupled with the more flexible work roles that war had created, apparently led to changes in gender-defined occupations. The earliest evidence for men working alongside women in cloth production occurs in this postwar period, when commercial weaving shops sprang up for the first time. Previously, only women made cloth and did so at home. Later in the fourth century B.C.E., there is also evidence that women made careers in the arts, especially painting and music, which men traditionally dominated.

Even in the improved postwar economy, most workers earned just enough to feed and clothe their families. They customarily ate two meals a day, a light lunch in midmorning and a heavier evening meal. Bread baked from barley provided the main part of their diet; only rich people could afford wheat bread. A family bought its bread from small bakery stands, often run by women, or made it at home. Most people ate greens, beans, onions, garlic, olives, fruit, and cheese with their bread;

they had meat only at animal sacrifices paid for by the state. Everyone drank wine, diluted with water. Water was fetched from public fountains in jugs by women or slaves. All but the poorest families owned at least one or two slaves to do household chores and to look after the children.

The restored stability in the everyday lives of Athenians did not erase their memories of the murderous rule of the Thirty Tyrants and the civil war of 404–403 B.C.E. Socrates became the best-known victim of this lingering bitterness dividing Athenians when he was blamed for the violent crimes of his follower Critias, one of the Thirty. In fact, Socrates had put himself at risk by refusing to cooperate with the tyrants, but some prominent Athenians believed his philosophy had turned Critias into a traitor. Since the amnesty blocked prosecution for offenses during the civil war, Socrates' opponents indicted him on a charge of impiety in 399 B.C.E. At his trial they accused him of not believing in the city-state's gods and of introducing new divinities, and also of turning young men away from Athenian moral traditions. When Socrates spoke in his own defense, he repeated his unyielding dedication to goading his fellow citizens into examining their unexamined assumptions about individual virtue. He vowed to remain their stinging gadfly.

After the jury narrowly voted to convict, the prosecutors proposed death. In such a case, the defendant was then expected to propose exile as an alternative, which the jury usually accepted. Socrates, however, said that he deserved a reward rather than a punishment, until his friends at the trial made him propose a fine as his penalty. The jury, however, chose death. Socrates accepted his sentence calmly because, as he put it, "nothing evil can happen to a good man, either in life or in death." He was executed in the customary way, with a poisonous drink concocted from powdered hemlock. Later sources report that many Athenians soon came to regret the execution of Socrates as a tragic mistake and a severe blow to their reputation.

The Philosophy of Plato and Aristotle

Socrates' trial and execution turned the world upside down for his most famous follower, Plato (c. 429–348 B.C.E.). Tormented by anger and grief, Plato turned his back on marriage and a public career and devoted himself to thinking about the nature of a world in which an evil fate could befall such a good man as Socrates. He established a philosophical "school," the Academy, in Athens around 386 B.C.E. The Academy was an informal association of educated people—mostly men but also some women—who studied philosophy, mathematics, and theoretical astronomy; it attracted intellectuals to Athens for the next nine hundred years.

Plato's ideas on ethics and politics have remained central to philosophy and political science since his day. He presented his ideas in written dialogues that read like plays instead of philosophy textbooks; he wanted them to make readers reflect thoughtfully on difficult philosophical questions. His views apparently changed

■ Mosaic of Plato's Academy
This mosaic from the Roman period portrays philosophers—identified by their beards—at Plato's school in Athens, called the Academy, holding discussions among themselves. Founded around 386 B.C.E., the Academy became one of Greece's most famous and long-lasting organizations, attracting scholars and students until it closed around 530 C.E. The columns and tree express the Academy's harmonious blend of the natural and built environments, a setting meant to promote pleasant and productive discussions. (Erich Lessing/Art Resource, NY.)

over time—nowhere did he present a fully worked out list of doctrines. Nevertheless, he always maintained one essential idea: moral qualities in their ultimate reality are universal and absolute, not relative.

To support this idea, Plato argued that absolute virtues, such as Goodness, Justice, Beauty, and Equality, existed as metaphysical realities he called Forms (or Ideas). He explained that the Forms are invisible, invariable, and eternal entities located in a higher realm beyond the daily world. According to Plato, the Forms are the only true reality; what we experience through our senses in everyday life are only dim and imperfect representations of these flawless realities, as if, he said, we were watching their shadows cast on the wall of a cave. His theory of Forms made **metaphysics**—the consideration of the ultimate nature of reality beyond the reach of the human senses—into a central issue for philosophers.

Plato's idea that humans possess immortal souls distinct from their bodies established the concept of **dualism**, a separation between spiritual and physical being. This notion influenced much of later philosophical and religious thought. Plato believed the proper goal for humans is to seek order and purity in their own souls by using reason to control their irrational desires, which are harmful. The desire to drink wine to excess, for example, is irrational because the drinker fails to consider the hangover to come the next day. Finally, because the soul is immortal and the body is not, our present, impure existence is only one part of our true existence.

Plato presented the most famous version of his utopian political ideas in his dialogue *The Republic.* This work, whose Greek title means "system of government," primarily concerns the nature of justice and the reasons people should be just. According to Plato, justice is impossible in a democracy and requires hierarchy. The trial of Socrates convinced him that most citizens were incapable of rising above self-interest. He therefore ranked people in his ideal society by their ability to grasp the truth of the Forms.

Women could rank as high as men because they possess the same virtues. To minimize distraction, the highest-ranking members of Plato's utopia are to have neither private property nor individual families. These men and women are to live together in barracks, eat in mess halls, and exercise in the same gymnasiums. They are to have sexual relations with various partners so that the best women can mate with the best men to produce the best children, who will be raised in a common environment by special caretakers. Those who achieve the highest level of knowledge in Plato's ideal society qualify to rule over it as philosopher-kings. Plato did not think such a society was truly possible, but he did believe that imagining it was important in teaching people to live justly. For this reason above all, he passionately believed the study of philosophy mattered to human life.

Plato was also influential because he trained an extremely famous pupil, Aristotle (384–322 B.C.E.). From 342 to 335 B.C.E., Aristotle tutored the young Alexander the Great in Macedonia. He then created his own practical philosophy for living a happy life and founded his own "school" in Athens, the Lyceum, in 335 B.C.E. Later called the Peripatetic School after the covered walkway (*peripatos*) where students conversed protected from the sun, Aristotle's Lyceum became world famous. He lectured with dazzling intelligence on nearly every branch of learning: biology, medicine, anatomy, psychology, meteorology, physics, chemistry, mathematics, music, metaphysics, rhetoric, political science, ethics, and literary criticism.

Aristotle's vast writings made him one of the most influential scientists and philosophers in Western history. His great reputation rests on his development of rigorous systems of logical argument and his scientific investigation of the natural world. Creating a sophisticated system of logic to identify the forms of valid arguments, Aristotle established rules to tell the difference between a logically proven case and a merely persuasive one. Furthermore, Aristotle insisted on explanations based on common sense rather than metaphysics. He denied the validity of Plato's theory of Forms, for example, on the grounds that the separate, unverifiable existence Plato asserted for them did not make sense. As for scientific investigation, Aristotle believed that the best way to understand objects and beings was to observe them in their natural settings. The first scientist to try to collect all available information on animals, Aristotle recorded facts about more than five hundred different species, including insects. His recognition that whales and dolphins are mammals, which later writers on animals overlooked, was not rediscovered for another two thousand years.

Like Plato, Aristotle criticized democracy because it allowed uneducated instead of "better" people to control politics. Some of Aristotle's views justified inequalities characteristic of his time. He regarded slavery as natural, arguing that some people were by nature meant to be slaves because their souls lacked the rational part that should rule in a human. He also concluded, based on faulty notions of biology, that women were by nature inferior to men, a conclusion with disastrous influence on later thought.

In ethics, Aristotle emphasized the need to develop habits of just behavior and not just good intentions. People should achieve self-control by training their minds to win out over instincts and passions. Self-control did not mean denying human desires and appetites; rather, it meant striking a balance between suppressing and heedlessly indulging physical yearnings, of finding "the mean." Aristotle claimed that the mind should rule in finding this balance because the intellect is the finest human quality and the mind is the true self—indeed, the godlike part of a person.

The Fracturing of Greece

During the fifty years following the Peloponnesian War, Sparta, Thebes, and Athens each in turn tried to dominate Greece. None succeeded. Their struggles with one another left Greece too weak to prevent outside interference and undermined the political independence of the Classical city-states. In the 390s to 370s B.C.E., the Spartans did the most to provoke this fatal disunity by trying to conquer other city-states. Thebes, Athens, Corinth, and Argos responded by forming an anti-Spartan coalition because Spartan aggression threatened their interests at home and abroad. The Spartans counterbalanced the alliance by making a treaty with the Persian king. Blatantly renouncing their commitment to defend Greek freedom, the Spartans acknowledged the Persian ruler's right to control the Greek city-states of Anatolia— in return for permission to pursue their own interests in Greece without Persian interference. This treaty of 386 B.C.E., called the *King's Peace*, deprived the Anatolian Greeks of the freedom won in the Persian Wars. The Athenians rebuilt their military strength to combat Sparta. By 377 B.C.E., Athens had again become the leader of a naval alliance. This time, league members insisted that their rights be specified in writing to prevent any imperialistic Athenian behavior.

The Thebans became Greece's main land power in the 370s B.C.E. Attacking the Spartan homeland, they destroyed Sparta's power forever by freeing many helots.

This Theban success so frightened the Athenians, whose city lay only forty miles from Thebes, that they made a temporary alliance with the Spartans. Their combined armies confronted the Thebans in the battle of Mantinea in the Peloponnese in 362 B.C.E. Thebes won the battle but lost the war when its best general was killed and no capable replacement could be found.

The battle of Mantinea left the Greek city-states in impotent disunity. As the contemporary historian Xenophon said: "Everyone had supposed that the winners of this battle would be Greece's rulers and its losers their subjects; but there was only more confusion and disturbance in Greece after it than before." By the 350s B.C.E., then, the Greek city-states' struggle for supremacy over one another had left them in a stalemate of exhaustion. Failing to cooperate, they opened the way for the rise of a new power—the kingdom of Macedonia, which would threaten their cherished independence.

■ **REVIEW:** *What were the major philosophical ideas of Plato and Aristotle?*

The Rise of Macedonia, 359–323 B.C.E.

The rulers of Macedonia took advantage of the Greek city-states' disunity to make their kingdom an international superpower. That this previously weak kingdom would seize the leadership of Greece and conquer the Persian Empire ranks as one of the greatest surprises in ancient political and military history. Two aggressive and charismatic kings produced this amazing transformation: Philip II (r. 359–336 B.C.E.) and his son Alexander the Great (r. 336–323 B.C.E.). Their conquests marked the end of the Classical period and set in motion the cultural interactions of the Hellenistic age.

Philip II and the Background of Macedonian Power

The Macedonians' power sprang from the characteristics of their society and their ethnic pride. The Macedonian people demanded the freedom to tell their monarchs what needed to be improved, and a king could govern effectively only as long as he maintained the support of the other Macedonian men heading powerful families, who were the king's social equals and controlled large bands of followers. Fighting, hunting, and heavy drinking were these men's favorite pastimes. The king was expected to excel in these activities to prove he was capable of ruling. Queens and royal mothers received respect in this male-dominated society because they came from powerful Macedonian families or the ruling houses of lands bordering Macedonia.

■ **Dancing Figures on a Gilded Bowl from Macedonia**
Archaeologists discovered this large metal wine bowl, made of bronze plated with gold, at Derveni in Macedonia. Its artistic style dates it to the 330s B.C.E. Wealthy Macedonian men at a Greek-style drinking party (symposium) used these expensive bowls to dilute wine so they could drink large amounts of it. The excited conditions of the two figures—a satyr and a female worshipper of Dionysus, the god of wine and pleasure—expressed the ecstasy that the partygoers hoped to achieve. Since erect penises were shown frequently in Greek and Macedonian art associated with Dionysus, representing hopes for fertility and sexual pleasure, pictures like this were not regarded as obscene.
(Thessalonike, Archaeological Museum, © Archaeological Receipts Fund.)

Macedonians thought of themselves as Greek by blood and took pride in their identity. They had their own language, but wealthy Macedonians routinely learned to speak Greek. Macedonians looked down on their southern relatives as being too soft for the adversities of northern life. The Greeks returned this scorn. The famed Athenian orator Demosthenes (384–322 B.C.E.) lambasted Philip II as "not only not a Greek nor related to the Greeks, but not even a barbarian from a land worth mentioning; no, he's a plague from Macedonia, a region where you can't even buy a slave worth his salt."

Until Philip II's reign, rivalry between the king and the other leading families kept Macedonia from mobilizing its full military strength. Indeed, kings so feared violence from their own countrymen that they stationed bodyguards outside the royal bedroom. A military disaster brought Philip to the throne at a desperate moment. The Illyrians, hostile neighbors to the north, had slaughtered the previous Macedonian king and four thousand troops. Philip restored the army's confidence by teaching the infantry an unstoppable new tactic. Arming his infantry with long thrusting spears that extended fourteen to sixteen feet and took two hands to wield, and arranging these troops in a phalanx formation, he created deep blocks of soldiers bristling with outstretched spears like a lethal porcupine. Using cavalry to disrupt the enemy's battle line and protect his own infantry's flanks, Philip smashed the Illyrians with his revived army.

Philip soon embarked on a whirlwind of diplomacy, bribery, and military action that turned Macedonia into an international power. A Greek contemporary, the historian Theopompus of Chios, labeled Philip "never satisfied, extravagant—he did everything in a hurry . . . he never spared the time to reckon up his income and expenses." By the late 340s B.C.E., Philip had persuaded or forced most of northern Greece to follow his lead in foreign policy. Seeking the glory of avenging Greece and fearing the potentially destabilizing effect his victorious army would have on his kingdom if the soldiers had nothing to do, Philip planned to lead a united Macedonian and Greek army against the Persian Empire. To launch this grandiose invasion, he needed to control the forces of southern Greece.

Expansion of Macedonia under Philip II, r. 359–336 B.C.E.

Philip found in Greek history the justification for attacking Persia: revenge for the Persian Wars. But some Greeks remained unconvinced. Demosthenes used stirring rhetoric to criticize Greeks for their failure to resist Philip. They stood by, he thundered, "as if Philip were a hailstorm, praying that he would not come their way, but not trying to do anything to head him off." Finally, Athens and Thebes headed an alliance of southern Greek city-states to try to block Philip, but in 338 B.C.E. the king and his Greek allies trounced the coalition's forces at the battle of Chaeronea in Boeotia. The defeated city-states retained their internal freedom, but Philip forced them to form a league under his leadership. The course of later history showed the battle of Chaeronea to be a turning point in Greek history: although Philip promised the league city-states freedom from interference in their internal affairs, they had to yield to him their power to decide foreign policy. As it turned out, the Greeks would never again regain the freedom to make such decisions on their own without some outside ruler looking over their shoulder.

Exploits of Alexander the Great, 336–323 B.C.E.

Alexander III stepped onto center stage in 336 B.C.E., when a Macedonian assassinated his father. Unconfirmed rumors speculated that Alexander's mother, Olympias, had arranged the murder to seize the throne for her twenty-year-old son. Alexander soon murdered potential rivals for the crown and, in several lightning-fast wars, subdued Macedonia's enemies on the west and north. Then Alexander compelled the southern Greeks, who had defected from the Macedonian-led league after Philip's death, to rejoin. To demonstrate the price of disloyalty, in 335 B.C.E. he destroyed Thebes for rebelling.

The following year Alexander embarked on the most astonishing military campaign in ancient history by leading a Macedonian and Greek army against the Persian Empire to fulfill his father's dream of avenging Greece. Alexander's astounding success in conquering everything from Turkey to Egypt to Uzbekistan while still in his twenties earned him the title "the Great" in later ages and inspired countless legends. His greatness came from his ability to inspire his men to follow him into unknown lands and to lead daring cavalry charges to disrupt the enemy's infantry. Alexander regularly rode his warhorse Bucephalus ("Oxhead") into the heart of the enemy's front line, sharing the danger of the common soldier. No one could miss him in his plumed helmet, vividly colored cloak, and armor polished to reflect the sun. He alarmed his principal adviser by giving away nearly all his property to create new landowners who would furnish troops. "What," the adviser asked, "do you have left for yourself?" "My hopes," Alexander replied. Those hopes centered on being a warrior as splendid as the matchless Achilles of Homer's *Iliad*; he always slept with a copy of the *Iliad* and a dagger under his pillow.

Alexander displayed his heroic ambitions as his army advanced relentlessly eastward through Persian territory (Map 3.1). In Anatolia, he visited Gordion, where an oracle had promised the lordship of Asia to whoever could loosen a seemingly impenetrable knot of rope tying the yoke of an ancient chariot preserved in the city. The young king, so the story goes, cut the knot with his sword. When his army later forced the Persian king, Darius III, to abandon his wives and daughters, Alexander treated the captured women with honor. His polite behavior toward the royal women won him respect from the peoples of the Persian Empire.

Alexander complemented his bravery and courtesy toward women with a keen eye for innovative military technology. When Tyre, a fortified city on an island off the coast of the Levant, refused to surrender in 332 B.C.E., he built a massive stone pier as a platform for armored battering rams and catapults flinging boulders to breach the walls of the city. The capture of Tyre demonstrated to walled city-states that they could no longer expect to hold out indefinitely in a siege; this awareness that a well-equipped army could penetrate fortification walls made it difficult for cities to remain united in the face of attacks and easier for Alexander to convince them to surrender.

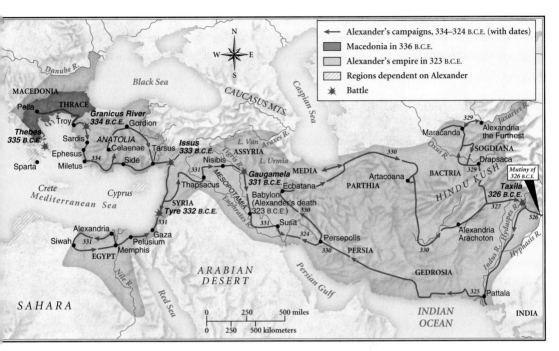

■ MAP 3.1 Conquests of Alexander the Great, 336–323 B.C.E.

The huge extent of Alexander's military campaigns in Asia made him a legend. From the time he led his army out of Macedonia and Greece in 334 B.C.E. until his death in Babylon in 323 B.C.E., he never stopped fighting. His careful intelligence gathering combined with his charismatic and brilliant generalship produced an unbroken string of victories. His skillful choice of regional administrators, founding of garrison cities and colonies, and preservation of local governing structures kept his conquests stable after he moved on. **For more help analyzing this map**, see the map activity for this chapter in the ONLINE STUDY GUIDE at bedfordstmartins.com/huntconcise.

After conquering Egypt and the Persian heartland, Alexander revealed his strategy for ruling a vast empire: establish colonies of Greeks and Macedonians in conquered territory but keep the area's traditional administrative system. The first new colony he established, in 331 B.C.E., was a city in Egypt on the Mediterranean coast to the west of the Nile River. He named it Alexandria, after himself. In Persia, he proclaimed himself king of Asia but left the existing Persian administrative system in place, even retaining some high-ranking Persian officials. That a Macedonian became Persian king hardly changed the lives of the local populations of the Persian Empire. They continued to send the same taxes to a still remote master, whom they rarely if ever saw.

Alexander's goal seems to have been to outdo even the heroes of legend by marching to the end of the world. Reducing his army to lessen the need for supplies, he led his forces northeast into lands previously unknown to Greeks, Bactria and

Sogdiana (modern Afghanistan and Uzbekistan). On the Jaxartes River (Syr Darya), he founded a city called Alexandria the Furthest to show that he had penetrated deeper into this region than even Cyrus, founder of the Persian Empire. When it proved impossible to pin down the fast-moving locals, however, Alexander settled for an alliance sealed by his marriage to the Bactrian princess Roxane. He then headed east into India. Seventy days of marching through monsoon rains extinguished his soldiers' fire for conquest. In the spring of 326 B.C.E., they mutinied on the banks of the Hyphasis River in western India and forced Alexander to turn back. A difficult march brought him back to Persia by 324 B.C.E.; he immediately began planning an invasion of the Arabian peninsula and, after that, North Africa.

His conquests changed Alexander. He was no longer keeping the promise to the league city-states to respect their internal freedom. He ordered them to restore citizenship to the many war-created exiles whose status as wandering, stateless

■ **Mosaic of Alexander the Great at the Battle of Issus**
This large mosaic, which served as a floor in an upscale Roman house, was a copy of a famous earlier painting of the battle of Issus of 333 B.C.E. It shows Alexander the Great on his warhorse Bucephalus (at left) confronting the Persian king Darius in his chariot. Darius reaches out in compassion for his warriors, who are sacrificing themselves to protect him. The original artist was an extremely skilled painter. Notice the dramatic foreshortening of the horse directly in front of Darius and the startling effect of the face of the dying warrior reflected in the polished shield just to the right of the horse. Alexander usually wore a helmet; why do you think the artist portrayed him bareheaded? (Erich Lessing/Art Resource, NY.)

persons was creating unrest. Even more startling was his announcement that he wished to receive the honors due a god. At first bewildered by these instructions, most Greek city-states soon complied by sending honorary religious delegations to him. The Spartan Damis expressed the only prudent position on Alexander's deification: "If Alexander wishes to be a god, then we'll agree that he be called a god." Personal rather than political motives best explain Alexander's wish. He almost certainly had come to believe he was actually the son of Zeus; after all, Greek mythology contained many stories of Zeus mating with a human female and producing children. Alexander's feats exceeded the bounds of human possibility, demonstrating that he had achieved godlike power and therefore must be a god himself.

Alexander's plans for more conquest ended when he unexpectedly died of an illness, made worse by heavy drinking, in Babylon in 323 B.C.E. Roxane gave birth to a child a few months after Alexander's death, but, like Pericles, Alexander had made no plans about who should rule in his place if he suddenly disappeared. The story goes that when his commanders asked him on his deathbed to whom he bequeathed his kingdom, he replied, "To the most powerful."

Modern scholars disagree on almost everything about Alexander. They offer varying judgments on his character, ranging from bloodthirsty monster interested only in endless conquest to romantic dreamer aiming to create a multiethnic world open to all cultures. The ancient sources suggest that Alexander had interlinked goals: the conquest and rule of the known world and the exploration and possible colonization of new territory beyond. Conquest through military action was a time-honored pursuit for Macedonian leaders like Alexander and suited his restless, ruthless, and incredibly energetic nature. He included non-Macedonians in his administration and army because he needed their skills. Alexander's explorations benefited numerous scientific fields, from geography to botany, because he took along scientifically minded writers to collect and catalog the new knowledge they acquired; he regularly sent reams of new scientific information to his old tutor Aristotle. The far-flung cities that Alexander founded served as outposts to warn headquarters about local uprisings. They also created new opportunities for trade in valuable goods such as spices that were not produced in the Mediterranean region.

The Athenian orator Aeschines (c. 397–322 B.C.E.) summed up the stunned reaction of many people to Alexander's deeds: "What strange and unexpected event has not occurred in our time? The life we have lived is no ordinary human one, but we were born to be an object of wonder to later ages." Aeschines predicted correctly. Stories of fabulous deeds attributed to Alexander became popular folktales throughout the world, reaching even distant regions where Alexander had never set foot, such as southern Africa. The popularity of his legend as a warrior-hero lasted into later ages because his achievements seemed incredible. That the worlds of Greece and the Near East had been brought into closer contact than ever before represented another long-lasting effect of his astonishing career, which drew the curtain on the Classical period and opened the next act in the drama of Western history, the Hellenistic period.

■ **REVIEW:** *How were Philip II and his son Alexander able to establish such a powerful empire?*

The Hellenistic Kingdoms, 323–30 B.C.E.

The innovative political, cultural, and economic developments of the Hellenistic period arose from the interaction of Greek and Near Eastern civilizations. War set this process in motion, and its changes created tension between conquerors and subjects and produced uneven results. Greek ideas and practices had their greatest impact on the urban populations of Egypt and southwestern Asia. The many people who farmed in the countryside had much less contact with Greek ways of life. Later on, the Hellenistic world's cultural achievements greatly influenced the Romans.

The dominant Hellenistic political structures were new kingdoms, which reintroduced monarchy into Greek history; kings had been rare in Greece since the fall of Mycenaean civilization nearly a thousand years earlier. Commanders from Alexander's army created the new kingdoms by seizing portions of his empire for themselves after his death and declaring themselves kings. Between 306 and 304 B.C.E., after more than twenty years of struggle, their families established themselves as dynasties ruling Hellenistic kingdoms.

The Structure of Hellenistic Kingdoms

Alexander's commanders divided his conquests into three major parts (Map 3.2): Antigonus (c. 382–301 B.C.E.) took over in Anatolia, the Near East, Macedonia, and Greece; Seleucus (c. 358–281 B.C.E.), in Babylonia and the East as far as India; and Ptolemy (c. 367–282 B.C.E.), in Egypt. These new rulers—historians call them **successor kings** because they succeeded Alexander—had to create their own form of kingship because they did not inherit their positions legitimately: they were self-declared monarchs with neither blood ties to any traditional royal family line nor any personal relationship to a particular territory. For this reason, historians often characterize their type of rule as "personal monarchy."

By the middle of the third century B.C.E., the three major Hellenistic kingdoms had reached a balance of power that prevented them from expanding much beyond their core territories. The Antigonids had been reduced to a kingdom in Macedonia, but they also controlled mainland Greece, whose city-states had to follow royal foreign policy even though they retained much internal freedom. The Seleucids ruled in Syria and Mesopotamia, but they had been forced to yield their easternmost

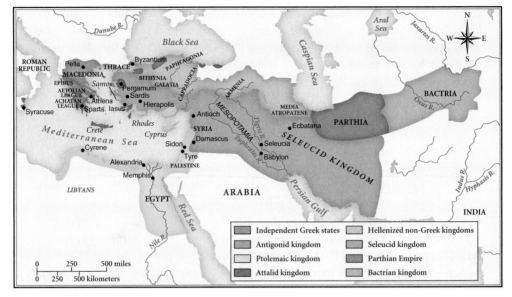

■ MAP 3.2 Hellenistic Kingdoms, c. 240 B.C.E.

Although the traditional Greek city-states kept their internal independence in the Hellenistic period, monarchy became the dominant political system in the areas of Alexander's former conquests. By about eighty years after his death in 323 B.C.E., the most striking changes to the three major kingdoms originally established by his successors were that the Seleucids had given up their easternmost territories and the Attalid kingdom had carved out an independent local reign in western Anatolia.

territory to the Indian king Chandragupta (r. 323–299 B.C.E.), founder of the Mauryan dynasty. They also lost most of Persia to the Parthians, a northern Iranian people. The Ptolemies retained control of the rich land of Egypt.

Conflicts frequently arose over contested border areas. The armies of the Ptolemaic and Seleucid kingdoms, for example, periodically battled over the lands of the Levant, just as the Egyptians and Hittites had done a thousand years earlier. Sometimes the struggles between the major kingdoms left openings for smaller, regional kingdoms to establish themselves. The most famous of these was the kingdom of the Attalids in western Anatolia, with the wealthy city of Pergamum as its capital. In Central Asia (in modern Afghanistan), Greek colonists settled by Alexander broke off from the Seleucid kingdom in the mid–third century B.C.E. to found their own regional kingdom in Bactria. Between 239 and 130 B.C.E., it flourished from the trade in luxury goods between India and China and the Mediterranean world.

The Hellenistic kings realized that establishing the legitimacy of their rule was essential if their royal lines were to endure. To gain it, they tried to incorporate local traditions into their rule. For the Seleucids, this meant combining Macedonian with Near Eastern royal customs; for the Ptolemies, Macedonian with Egyptian. The strength of successor kings ultimately rested on their personal ability and power. A letter from the city of Ilion (on the site of ancient Troy) summed up the situation in its praise of the Seleucid king Antiochus I (c. 324–261 B.C.E.): "His rule depends mostly on his own excellence [*aretê*], and on the goodwill of his friends and on his forces." In the end, then, Hellenistic monarchy amounted to foreign rule over original local populations by kings and queens of Macedonian descent. Seleucus, for one, claimed this right as a universal truth: "It is not the customs of the Persians and other people that I impose upon you, but the law which is common to everyone, that what is decreed by the king is always just."

The survival of Hellenistic dynasties depended on their ability to create strong armies, effective administrations, and cooperative urban elites. Hellenistic militaries provided security against internal unrest as well as external enemies. To develop their forces, the Seleucid and Ptolemaic kings vigorously promoted immigration by Greeks and Macedonians, who received land grants in return for service as professional soldiers. When this source of manpower gave out, the kings had to employ more local men as troops. Military expenses eventually became a problem because the kings faced continual pressure to pay large numbers of mercenaries and because military technology had become so expensive. To compete effectively, a Hellenistic king had to provide giant artillery, such as catapults capable of flinging a projectile weighing 170 pounds a distance of nearly two hundred yards.

Hellenistic kings had to create large administrations to collect the revenues they needed. They recruited immigrant Greeks and Macedonians to be their top officials. Local men who wanted a job as a lower official bettered their chances if they learned to read and write Greek in addition to their native language. This bilingualism qualified them to communicate official orders, especially tax laws, to farmers and crafts producers. Greeks and Macedonians generally saw themselves as too superior to mix with the locals, so Greeks and non-Greeks tended to live in separate communities.

Agriculture and trade generated the wealth of the kingdoms, and cities old and new were their economic and social hubs. Many Greeks and Macedonians lived in new cities founded by Alexander and his successors in Egypt and the Near East, and they also moved to old cities. Hellenistic kings promoted this urban emigration to build communities supportive of their rule. These rulers adorned their new cities with the traditional features of classical Greek city-states, such as gymnasiums and theaters. Although these cities often had the political institutions of the polis, such as councils and assemblies for citizen men, the requirement to follow royal policy limited their freedom. The kings treated the cities considerately because they needed the Greek and Macedonian urban elites to keep order and ensure a steady flow of tax revenues. Wealthy people had the crucial responsibility of collecting taxes from the surrounding countryside, as well as from their city, and sending the money

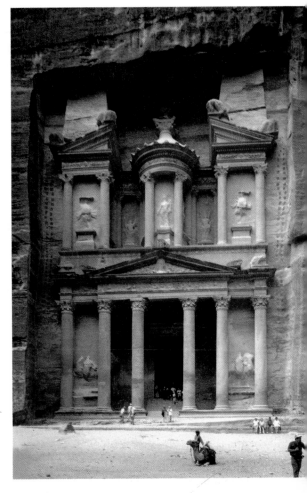

■ **Hellenistic Architecture in the Jordanian Desert**

This decorative front for a structure carved into a sheer rock cliff in probably the first century B.C.E. stands at the entrance to the ancient settlement of Petra, the capital of the Nabatean Arabs (in what is today Jordan). This desert people grew rich by controlling caravan trade from Asia across the deserts to the Mediterranean coast. In true Hellenistic spirit, they took Greek architectural models and adapted them to express their own style. For example, this carved front has Greek triangular pediments but also makes a break in the upper pediment to include a round gazebo. What do you think the visual effect of this innovation would be as the sunlight moves during the day?
(Z. Radovan, www.BibleLandPictures.com.)

on to the royal treasury. In turn, the kings honored and flattered members of the cities' social elites.

The kings' reliance on local elites led them to establish close relationships with well-to-do non-Greeks living in the old cities of Anatolia and the Near East, such as Sardis, Tyre, and Babylon. In addition, non-Greeks and non-Macedonians from eastern regions began moving westward to the new Hellenistic Greek cities in increasing numbers. Jews in particular moved from Palestine to Anatolia, Greece, and Egypt. The Jewish community eventually became an influential minority in Egyptian Alexandria, the most important Hellenistic city.

All the Hellenistic kingdoms eventually fell to the Romans. The Ptolemaic kingdom survived the longest. The end came when Queen Cleopatra VII, a descendant of Ptolemy and the last Macedonian to rule Egypt, chose the losing side in the Roman civil war between Mark Antony, her lover at that time, and the future emperor Augustus in the late first century B.C.E. In 30 B.C.E., an invading Roman army ended her reign and three centuries of Hellenistic monarchy.

Hierarchy in Hellenistic Society

People in the eastern Mediterranean Hellenistic world lived in a social hierarchy with the royal family and the king's friends ranking highest. The Greek and Macedonian elites of the major cities ranked next. Just under them came the non-Greek wealthy elites of the cities, the leaders of large minority urban populations, and the traditional lords and princes of local groups who maintained their ancestral domains in rural regions. Lowest of the free population were the masses of small merchants, artisans, and laborers. Slaves had no social standing.

The growth of the kingdoms apparently increased the demand for slave labor throughout the eastern Mediterranean. The centrally located island of Delos established a market where up to ten thousand slaves were bought and sold daily. The fortunate ones would become servants at court and live physically comfortable lives; the luckless ones would toil, and soon die, in the mines. Enslaved children often were taken far from home and put to work. A sales contract from 259 B.C.E. shows that Zeno, to whom the camel trader wrote, bought a girl about seven years old named Sphragis ("Gemstone") to work in an Egyptian textile factory. This was not her first job. Originally from Sidon in the Levant, she had previously been the slave of a Greek mercenary soldier employed by Toubias, a Jewish cavalry commander in the Transjordan region.

Even with power based in the cities, most of the population continued to live in small villages. Most farmers were forced tenants on royal land who were not allowed to move away or stop working. Free peasants still worked their own small plots as well as the farms of wealthy landowners. Perhaps 80 percent of all adult men and women had to work the land to produce enough food to sustain the population. In the cities, the poor worked as small merchants, peddlers, and artisans. Men could sign on as deckhands on the merchant ships that sailed the Mediterranean Sea and Indian Ocean.

Women's status in the Hellenistic world depended on the social layer to which they belonged. Like their Macedonian predecessors, Hellenistic queens enjoyed enormous riches and high honor. Because the Ptolemaic royal family observed the Egyptian royal tradition of brother-sister marriage, daughters could rule alongside sons. For example, Arsinoe II (c. 316–270 B.C.E.), the daughter of Ptolemy I, first married the Macedonian successor king Lysimachus, who gave her four towns as her personal domain. After Lysimachus's death she married her brother Ptolemy II and exerted at least as much influence on Egyptian policy as he did. The virtues publicly praised in a queen reflected traditional Greek values for women. When the city of Hierapolis around 165 B.C.E. passed a decree honoring Queen Apollonis of Pergamum, for example, it praised her piety toward the gods, her reverence toward her parents, her distinguished conduct toward her husband, and her harmonious relations with her "beautiful children born in wedlock."

Elite women continued to live separated from nonfamily males; poor women still worked in public. Greeks continued to abandon infants they could not or would not raise—girls more often than boys. Other populations, such as the Egyptians and the Jews, did not practice abandonment, or exposure, as it is called. Exposure differed from infanticide because the parents expected someone else to find the child and raise it, albeit usually as a slave.

In some limited ways, women achieved greater control over their own lives in the Hellenistic period. A woman of exceptional wealth could enter public life by making donations or loans to her city and being rewarded with an official post in local government. Such positions were less prestigious than in the days of the independent city-states because the king and his top administrators now controlled the real power. In Egypt, women acquired greater say in the family because marriage contracts, the standard procedure, gradually evolved from an agreement between the groom and the bride's parents to one in which the bride made her own arrangements with the groom.

■ **Egyptian-Style Statue of Queen Arsinoe II**
Arsinoe II (c. 316–270 B.C.E.), daughter of Ptolemy I and widow of the Macedonian "successor" king Lysimachus, married her brother Ptolemy II to unify the monarchy. Hailed as Philadelphoi *("Brother-Loving"), the couple set a precedent for brother-sister marriages in the Ptolemaic dynasty. One of the most remarkable women of the Hellenistic period, Arsinoe was the first Ptolemaic ruler whose image was placed in Egyptian temples as a "temple-sharing goddess." This eight-foot-tall, red granite statue portrays her in the traditional sculptural style of the pharaohs.* (Vatican Museums.)

During this period, it became more common for the wealthy to follow the example of royalty and show concern for the poor. On the island of Samos, for example, prosperous citizens funded a foundation to distribute free grain. Donor-sponsored schools sprang up in various cities, and sometimes girls as well as boys could attend. Many cities also began sponsoring doctors. Donors were repaid by the respect and honor they earned from their fellow citizens. In this system, the welfare of the masses depended on the generosity of the rich; without democracy, the poor had no political power to demand reforms. This strongly hierarchical arrangement reflected the top-down structure of Hellenistic society.

■ **REVIEW:** *What were the biggest challenges faced by the Hellenistic kings?*

Hellenistic Culture

Hellenistic culture reflected three principal characteristics of the age: the effects of royal wealth, ordinary people concentrating on private matters more than public life, and the increased interaction of diverse peoples. In keeping with the era's hierarchical trends, the kings almost single-handedly determined developments in literature, art, science, and philosophy by deciding which fields and which scholars and artists to support financially. The kings' status as sole rulers and the source of law meant that authors and artists did not have freedom to criticize public policy and thus concentrated on individual emotions and aspects of private life. Nevertheless, royal support did produce an expansion and diversification of knowledge. Cultural interaction between Greek and Near Eastern traditions happened most prominently in language and religion. These developments eventually became extremely influential in Roman culture; in this way, "captive Greece captured its fierce victor," as the Roman poet Horace (65–8 B.C.E.) expressed the effect of Hellenistic culture on his own.

The Arts under Royal Support

The Hellenistic kings supported scholarship and the arts on a vast scale, competing with one another to lure the best scholars and artists to their capitals with magnificent salaries and benefits. They paid for many intellectual innovations but for little applied technology except for military use. The Ptolemies assembled the Hellenistic world's most intellectually distinguished court by turning Alexandria into the Mediterranean's leading center of the arts. There they established the first scholarly research institute. Its massive library had the ambitious goal of trying to collect all the books (that is, manuscripts) in the world; it grew to hold a half-million scrolls, an enormous number for the time. Linked to it was a building in which the hired scholars dined together and produced encyclopedias of knowledge such as

The Wonders of the World and *On the Rivers of Europe* by Callimachus, a learned prose writer as well as a poet. The name of this building, the Museum (meaning "place of the Muses," the Greek goddesses of learning and the arts), is still used to designate institutions that preserve and promote knowledge. The output of the Alexandrian scholars was huge. Their champion was Didymus (c. 80–10 B.C.E.), nicknamed "Brass Guts" for his tireless writing of nearly four thousand books of research; it is a sad commentary on the preservation of ancient sources that not a single one has survived.

The writers and artists whom Hellenistic kings paid had to please their employers with their works. The poet Theocritus (c. 300–260 B.C.E.), for example, relocated from his home in Syracuse to the Ptolemaic court. In a poem expressly praising his employer, Ptolemy II, he spelled out their professional relationship: "The spokesmen of the Muses [that is, poets] celebrate Ptolemy in return for his benefactions." Theocritus and other poets succeeded by avoiding political subjects and stressing the division in society between the intellectual elite—to which the kings belonged—and the uneducated masses. Their poetry centered on individual emotions and broke new ground in demanding great intellectual effort as well as emotional engagement from the audience. Only people with a deep literary education could appreciate the allusions and complex references to mythology that these poets employed in their elegant poems.

Theocritus was the first Greek poet to express the divide between town and countryside that was becoming a Hellenistic reality. The *Idylls*, his pastoral poems, emphasized the discontinuity between the elegant environment of the city and the simple life in the country, reflecting the fundamental social division of the Ptolemaic kingdom between the food consumers of the town and the food producers of the countryside. He presented a city dweller's idealized dream that country life must be peaceful and stress free; this fiction deeply influenced later literature.

Women poets made important contributions to literature in the Hellenistic period, apparently without any royal support. They excelled in writing **epigrams**, a style of short poem originally meant for tombstones. Elegantly worded poems written by women from diverse regions of the Hellenistic world—Anyte of Tegea in the Peloponnese, Nossis of Locri in southern Italy, Moero of Byzantium—still survive. Women, from "companions" to respectable matrons, figured as frequent subjects in their work and expressed a wide variety of personal feelings, love above all. Nossis's poem on the power of Eros (Greek for "Love"), for example, proclaimed, "Nothing is sweeter than Eros. All other delights are second to it—from my mouth I spit out even honey. And this Nossis says: whoever Aphrodite has not kissed knows not what sort of flowers are her roses." No Hellenistic literature better conveys the depth of human emotion than the epigrams of women poets.

The Hellenistic theater also presented stories of individual emotion; no longer did dramatists offer open criticism of politics or contemporary leaders as they had in Golden Age comedy. Comic playwrights such as Menander (c. 342–289 B.C.E.)

composed plays with timeless plots concerning the trials and tribulations of fictional lovers. These comedies of manners, as they are called, proved enormously popular because, like modern situation comedies, they offered a humorous view of situations and feelings that occur in daily life and cleverly made fun of social conditions. Recent papyrus finds have allowed us to recover almost complete plays of Menander, the most famous Hellenistic playwright, and to appreciate his subtle skill in depicting personality. He presented his first comedy at Athens in 324 or 323 B.C.E. No tragedies written in this period have survived intact, but we know that they could involve the interaction among peoples and cultures at this time. Ezechiel, for example, a Jew living in Alexandria, wrote *Exodus*, a tragedy in Greek about Moses leading the Hebrews out of captivity in Egypt.

Like poet and dramatists, Hellenistic sculptors and painters featured human emotions prominently in their works. Classical-era artists had given their subjects' faces a serenity that represented an ideal rather than reality. Numerous examples, usually surviving only in later copies, show that Hellenistic artists portrayed individual emotions more naturally in a variety of types. In portrait sculpture, Lysippus's widely copied bust of Alexander the Great captured the young commander's passionate dreaminess. A sculpture from Pergamum by an unknown artist commemorated the third-century B.C.E. Attalid victory over the plundering Gauls (one of the Celtic peoples, called *Galatians*) by showing a defeated Gallic warrior stabbing himself after killing his wife to prevent her enslavement by the victors. A large-scale painting of Alexander battling the Persian king Darius (see page 104) portrayed Alexander's intense concentration and Darius's horrified expression. The artist, probably either Philoxenus of Eretria or a Greek woman from Egypt named Helena (one of the first female artists known), used foreshortening and strong contrasts between shadows and highlights to increase the picture's emotional impact.

To appreciate fully the appeal of Hellenistic sculpture, we must remember that, like earlier Greek sculpture, it was painted in bright colors. But Hellenistic art differed from classical art in its social context. Works of classical art had been paid for by the city-states for public display or by wealthy individuals to donate to their city-state as a work of public art. Now sculptors and painters created their works primarily for royalty and the urban elites who wanted to show they had artistic taste like the royal family. The increasing diversity of subjects that emerged in Hellenistic art presumably represented a trend approved by kings, queens, and the elites. Sculpture best reveals this new preference for showing humans in a wide variety of poses, mostly from private life (in contrast with classical art). Hellenistic sculptors portrayed subjects never before shown: foreigners, drunkards, battered athletes, wrinkled old people. The female nude became a particular favorite. A statue of Aphrodite, which Praxiteles sculpted completely nude as an innovation in portraying this goddess, became so famous as a religious object and tourist attraction in the city of Cnidos that the king of Bithynia later offered to pay off the citizens' entire public debt if they would give him this work of art. They refused.

■ **Dying Celts**
*Hellenistic artists excelled in portraying
deeply emotional scenes such as this scene
of a Celtic warrior, who is committing
suicide after killing his wife to prevent
their capture by the enemy after defeat in
battle. Celtic women followed their men
to the battlefield and willingly exposed
themselves to the same dangers. The original statues (these are Roman imita-
tions) were in bronze, forming part of a
large sculptural group that Attalus I,
king of Pergamum from 241 to 197
B.C.E., set up on his acropolis to commemorate his defeat around 230 B.C.E. of
the Celts, called Galatians, who had
moved into Anatolia in the 270s B.C.E. in
order to conduct raids throughout the area.
Why do you think that Attalus celebrated his
victory by erecting a monument that portrayed
the defeated enemy as brave and noble?* **For
more help analyzing this image,** see the
visual activity for this chapter
in the ONLINE STUDY GUIDE at
bedfordstmartins. com/
huntconcise.
(Erich Lessing/Art Resource, NY.)

Philosophy for a New Age

New philosophies arose in the Hellenistic period, all asking the same question: what
is the best way for humans to live? They recommended different paths to the same
answer: individual humans must find personal serenity, to achieve freedom from
the turbulence of outside forces, especially chance. For Greeks in particular, the
changes in political and social life accompanying the rise to dominance of the
Macedonian and, later, the Hellenistic kings made this focus necessary. Outside
forces—aggressive kings—had robbed the city-states of their freedom of action
internationally, and the fates of entire communities as well as individuals rested in
the hands of distant, unpredictable monarchs. More than ever before, human life

and opportunities for free choice seemed out of individuals' control. It therefore made sense, at least for those wealthy enough to spend time philosophizing, to look for personal, private solutions to the unsettling new conditions of life in the Hellenistic Age. More women than ever before joined in this quest.

Few Hellenistic thinkers concentrated on metaphysics. Instead they focused on philosophical **materialism,** a doctrine asserting that only things made up of matter truly exist. It denied the concept of soul that Plato described and ignored any suggestion that nonmaterial phenomena could exist. Hellenistic philosophy was regularly divided into three related areas: *logic,* the process for discovering truth; *physics,* the fundamental truth about the nature of existence; and *ethics,* the way humans should achieve happiness and well-being as a consequence of logic and physics. The era's philosophical thought greatly influenced Roman thinkers and many important Western philosophers who followed them.

One of the two most significant new philosophical schools of thought was **Epicureanism.** It took its name from its founder, Epicurus (341–271 B.C.E.), who settled his followers in Athens in a house about 307 B.C.E. amid a shady park (hence "The Garden" as his school's name). Under Epicurus the study of philosophy broke with tradition because he admitted not only women but also slaves as regular members of his group. His lover, the "companion" Leontion, became well known for her treatise criticizing the views of Theophrastus (c. 370–285 B.C.E.), Aristotle's most famous pupil.

People should above all be free of worry about death, Epicurus taught, because all matter consists of microscopic atoms in random movement and death is nothing more than the painless separating of the body's atoms. Moreover, all human knowledge must be empirical—that is, derived from experience and perception. Despite the common belief, the gods do not cause thunder, drought, and other natural events. The gods live far away in perfect peacefulness, paying no attention to human affairs. People therefore have nothing to fear from the gods, in life or in death.

Epicurus believed people should pursue pleasure, but his notion of true pleasure had a special definition: he insisted that it consists of the "absence of disturbance" from pain and everyday troubles, passions, and desires. A sober life spent with friends apart from the cares of the world could best provide this essential peace of mind. His teaching represented a serious challenge to the traditional ideal of Greek citizenship, which required men of means to participate in local politics and citizen women to engage in public religious cults.

The other important new Hellenistic philosophy, Stoicism, did not call for people to retire from public life. Its name derived from the Painted Stoa in Athens, where Stoic philosophers discussed their doctrines. Zeno (c. 333–262 B.C.E.) from Citium on Cyprus founded **Stoicism,** but Chrysippus (c. 280–206 B.C.E.) from Cilicia in Anatolia did the most to make it a complete guide to life. Stoics believed that life is fated but that people should still pursue virtue as their goal. Virtue, they said, consists of putting oneself in harmony with the divine, rational force of universal Nature by developing the virtues of good sense, justice, courage, and moderation. These doctrines applied to women as well as men. In fact, the Stoics advocated equal citizenship for women and doing away with marriage and families as the Greeks knew them. Zeno even proposed unisex clothing as a way to obliterate unnecessary distinctions between women and men.

The belief that fate determines everything created the question of whether humans truly have free will. Employing some of the subtlest reasoning ever applied to this fundamental issue, Stoic philosophers concluded that purposeful human actions do have significance. Nature, itself good, does not prevent evil from occurring because virtue would otherwise have no meaning. What matters in life is the striving for good, not the result. A person should therefore take action against evil by, for example, participating in politics. To be a Stoic also meant to shun desire and anger while enduring pain and sorrow calmly, an attitude that yields the modern meaning of the word *stoic*. Through endurance and self-control, followers of Stoic philosophy attained personal serenity. They did not fear death because they believed that people live over and over again infinitely in identical fashion to their present lives.

Numerous other philosophies emerged in the Hellenistic period to compete with Epicureanism and Stoicism. Some of them carried on the work of famous earlier thinkers such as Plato and Pythagoras. Still others struck out in new directions. Skeptics, for example, aimed at the same state of personal serenity as did Epicureans and Stoics, but from a completely different assumption about reality. Pyrrho (c. 360–270 B.C.E.) of Elis in the Peloponnese established the principles of Skepticism; his ideas were influenced by the Indian ascetic wise men (the magi) he met while a member of Alexander the Great's expedition. Skeptics believed that secure knowledge about anything is impossible because the human senses yield contradictory information about the world. All that people can do, they insisted, is depend on appearances while withholding judgment about their reality.

The philosophers called *Cynics* boastfully rejected every convention of ordinary life, especially wealth and material comfort. They believed that humans should aim for complete self-sufficiency. Whatever is natural is good, they said, and can be done without shame before anyone. According to this idea, public defecation and fornication were acceptable, and women and men alike were free to have sex however and whenever they pleased. Above all, Cynics rejected traditional human behavior as ridiculous. The most famous early Cynic, Diogenes (d. 323 B.C.E.) from Sinope on the Black Sea, had a reputation for wearing borrowed clothes and sleeping in a giant storage jar. Almost as notorious was Hipparchia, a Cynic of the late fourth century B.C.E. She once bested an obnoxious philosophical opponent named Theodorus the Atheist with the following argument: "That which would not be considered wrong if done by Theodorus would also not be considered wrong if done by Hipparchia.

Now if Theodorus strikes himself, he does no wrong. Therefore, if Hipparchia strikes Theodorus, she does no wrong." The name *Cynic,* which meant "like a dog," reflected the ancient evaluation of this unconventional way of life; our word *cynical* recalls the Cynics' biting criticism of what others regarded as normal.

In the Hellenistic period, Greek philosophy reached a wider audience than ever before. Although the working poor had neither the leisure nor the money to attend philosophers' lectures, affluent members of society studied philosophy in growing numbers. Theophrastus lectured to crowds of up to two thousand in Athens. Most philosophy students continued to be men, but women could join the groups attached to certain philosophers. Kings competed to attract famous thinkers to their courts, and Greek settlers took their interest in philosophy with them, even to the most remote Hellenistic cities. Archaeologists excavating a Hellenistic city located thousands of miles from Greece on the Oxus River in Afghanistan, for example, turned up a Greek philosophical text as well as inscriptions of moral advice imputed to Apollo's oracle at Delphi.

Innovation in the Sciences

Science first became an activity separated from philosophy during the Hellenistic period. Scientific investigation of the physical world so benefited from this divorce that historians have dubbed this era the Golden Age of ancient science. Various factors contributed to this flourishing of thought and discovery: the expeditions of Alexander had encouraged curiosity and increased knowledge about the extent and differing features of the world, royal wealth supported scientists financially, and the concentration of scientists in Alexandria promoted an exchange of ideas that could not have taken place otherwise.

The greatest advances came in geometry and mathematics. Euclid, who taught at Alexandria around 300 B.C.E., made revolutionary progress in the analysis of two- and three-dimensional space. The usefulness of Euclidean geometry continues today. Archimedes of Syracuse (287–212 B.C.E.) was a mathematical genius who calculated the approximate value of *pi* and devised a way to manipulate very large numbers. He also invented hydrostatics (the science of the equilibrium of a fluid system) and mechanical devices such as a screw for lifting water to a higher elevation. Archimedes' shout of delight "I have found it" (*heureka* in Greek) when he solved a problem while soaking in his bathtub lives on in the modern expression "Eureka!"

The sophistication of Hellenistic mathematics affected other fields that also required complex computation. Aristarchus of Samos early in the third century B.C.E. became the first to propose the correct model of the solar system: the earth revolves around the sun, which is far larger and far more distant than it appears. Later astronomers rejected Aristarchus's heliocentric model in favor of the traditional geocentric one (with the earth at the center) because calculations based on

■ **Bronze Astronomical Calculator**
Underwater archaeologists found these fragments in an ancient shipwreck off Anticythera, south of the Peloponnese. This bronze object, which its discoverers at first could not identify, was being transported to Italy in the early first century B.C.E. *as part of a shipment of metalwork and other valuable objects. Historians of science have figured out that it was a calculator to determine the position of stars and planets. Its intermeshed gears controlled rotating dials. The sophisticated applied engineering and astronomical knowledge necessary to design and build this machine reveal the high level of achievement of Hellenistic science.* (National Archaeological Museum, Athens. Archaeological Receipts Fund.)

the orbit he calculated for the earth failed to correspond to the observed positions of the planets. Aristarchus had made an unfortunate mistake: assuming a circular orbit instead of an elliptical one. Eratosthenes of Cyrene (c. 275–194 B.C.E.) pioneered mathematical geography. He calculated the circumference of the earth with astonishing accuracy by simultaneously measuring the length of the shadows of widely separated but identically tall structures. The ideas and procedures of these Hellenistic researchers gave Western scientific thought an important start toward the principle scientists now take for granted: the need to verify theory through observation and measurement in experiments.

Hellenistic science maintained a spirit of discovery despite the enormous difficulties imposed by technical limitations. Many experiments were not possible because no technology existed for the precise measurement of very short intervals of time. Measuring tiny quantities of matter was also next to impossible. The science of the age was as quantitative as it could be given these limitations. Ctesibius of Alexandria (b. c. 310 B.C.E.), a contemporary of Aristarchus, invented the scientific field of pneumatics by creating machines operated by air pressure. He also built a working water pump, an organ powered by water, and the first accurate water clock. A later Alexandrian, Hero, continued the Hellenistic tradition of mechanical ingenuity by building a rotating sphere powered by steam. As in most of Hellenistic science, these inventions did not lead to uses in daily life. The scientists and their royal supporters were more interested in new theoretical discoveries than in practical results, and the metallurgical technology to produce the pipes, fittings, and screws needed to build powerful machines did not yet exist.

Military technology was the one area in which Hellenistic science produced practical inventions. The kings hired engineers to design powerful catapults and wheeled siege towers many stories high to batter down the defenses of walled cities. The most famous large-scale application of technology for nonmilitary purposes was the construction of a lighthouse three hundred feet tall (the Pharos) for the harbor at Alexandria. Using polished metal mirrors to reflect the light from a large bonfire, it shone many miles out over the sea. Grateful sailors regarded it as one of the wonders of the world.

Medicine also benefited from the thirst for new knowledge characteristic of Hellenistic science. The increased contact between Greeks and people of the Near East in this period made the medical knowledge of the ancient civilizations of Mesopotamia and Egypt better known in the West and promoted study of human health and illness. Around 325 B.C.E., Praxagoras of Cos discovered the value of measuring the pulse in diagnosing illness. A bit later, Herophilus of Chalcedon (b. c. 300 B.C.E.), working in Alexandria, became the first scientist in the West to study anatomy by dissecting human cadavers and, it was rumored, the bodies of condemned criminals while they were still alive; he had this gruesome opportunity because the king authorized his research. Some of the anatomical terms Herophilus invented are still used. Other Hellenistic advances in understanding anatomy included the discovery of the nerves and nervous system.

As in science, however, Hellenistic medicine was limited by its inability to measure and observe things not visible to the naked eye. Unable to see what really occurred under the skin in living patients, for example, doctors thought many illnesses in women were caused by displacements of the womb, which they wrongly believed could move around in the body. These mistaken ideas could not be corrected because the technology to evaluate them did not yet exist.

A New East-West Culture

Wealthy non-Greeks increasingly adopted Greek ways as they adapted to the new social hierarchy of the Hellenistic world. To give only one example: Diotimus of Sidon in the Levant adopted a Greek name and pursued the premier Greek sport, chariot racing. He traveled to Nemea in the Peloponnese to enter his chariot in the race at the prestigious festival of Zeus. He announced his victory in an inscription written in Greek, which had become the language of international commerce and culture in the Hellenistic world. The explosion in the use of a simplified version of Greek called **Koine** ("shared" or "common") reflected the emergence of an international culture based on Greek models; this was why the Egyptian camel trader stranded in Syria had to communicate in Greek with a high-level official such as Zeno.

The most striking evidence of this cultural development comes from Afghanistan. There, King Ashoka (r. c. 268–232 B.C.E.), who ruled most of the Indian subcontinent, used Greek as one of the languages in his public inscriptions to announce his efforts to introduce his subjects to Buddhist traditions of self-control, such as not eating meat. Local languages did not disappear in the Hellenistic kingdoms, however. In one region of Anatolia, people spoke twenty-two different languages.

The diversity of Hellenistic religion matched the variety of many other areas of life in this period of cultural interaction. The traditional cults of Greek religion remained very popular, but new cults, such as those that made gods of ruling kings, responded to changing political and social conditions. Preexisting cults that previously had only local significance, such as that of the Greek healing god Asclepius or the mystery cult of the Egyptian goddess Isis, grew prominent all over the Hellenistic world. In many cases, Greek cults and local cults from the eastern Mediterranean influenced each other. Their beliefs meshed well because these cults shared many assumptions about how to remedy the troubles of human life. In other instances, local cults and Greek cults existed side by side, with some overlap. The inhabitants of villages in the Fayum district of Egypt, for example, continued worshiping their traditional crocodile god and mummifying their dead according to the old ways but also worshiped Greek deities. In the tradition of polytheistic religion, people could worship in both old and new cults.

New cults picked up a prominent theme of Hellenistic thought: anxiety about the relationship between individuals and the unpredictable power of the divinities Luck and Chance. Although Greek religion had always been concerned with the unpredictability of life, the chaotic course of Greek history since the Peloponnesian War had made human existence seem more uncertain than ever. Since advances in astronomy revealed the mathematical precision of the heavens, religion now had to address the seeming disconnect between that celestial uniformity and the shapeless chaos of life on earth. One increasingly popular approach to bridging that gap was to rely on astrology for guidance derived from the movement of the stars and planets, thought of as divinities. Another very common choice was to worship Tyche (Chance) as a god in the hope of securing good luck in life.

The most revolutionary approach in seeking protection from the unpredictable tricks of Chance or Luck was to pray for salvation from a king regarded as a god, worshiped in what are known as **ruler cults**. Various populations established these cults to honor royal benefactors. The Athenians, for example, deified the Macedonians Antigonus and his son Demetrius as savior gods in 307 B.C.E., when these commanders liberated the city and bestowed magnificent gifts on it. Like most ruler cults, this one expressed both spontaneous gratitude and a desire to flatter the rulers in the hope of obtaining additional favors. Many cities in the Ptolemaic and Seleucid kingdoms created ruler cults for their kings and queens. An inscription put up by Egyptian priests in 238 B.C.E. described the qualities appropriate to a divine king and queen:

> *King Ptolemy III and Queen Berenice, his sister and wife, the Benefactor Gods, . . . have provided good government . . . and [after a drought] sacrificed a large amount of their revenues for the salvation of the population, and by importing grain . . . they saved the inhabitants of Egypt.*

As these words make clear, the Hellenistic rulers' tremendous power and wealth gave them the status of gods to the ordinary people who depended on their generosity and protection in times of danger. The idea that a human being could be a god, present on earth to be a "savior" delivering people from evils, was firmly established and would prove influential later in Roman imperial religion and Christianity.

Healing divinities offered another form of protection to anxious individuals. Scientific Greek medicine had rejected the notion of supernatural causes and cures for disease ever since Hippocrates had established his medical school on the Aegean island of Cos in the late fifth century B.C.E. Nevertheless, the cult of the god Asclepius, who offered cures for illness and injury at his many shrines, grew popular during the Hellenistic period. Suppliants seeking Asclepius's help would sleep in special dormitories at his shrines to await dreams in which he prescribed healing treatments. These prescriptions emphasized diet and exercise, but numerous inscriptions set up by grateful patients also testified to miraculous cures and surgery performed while the sufferer slept. The following example is typical:

> *Ambrosia of Athens was blind in one eye. . . . She . . . ridiculed some of the cures [described in inscriptions in the sanctuary] as being incredible and impossible. . . . But when she went to sleep, she saw a vision; she thought the god was standing next to her. . . . He split open the diseased eye and poured in a medicine. When day came she left cured.*

People's faith in divine healing gave them hope that they could overcome the constant, unpredictable danger of illness.

Mystery cults promised secret knowledge as a key to salvation during life and after death. The cults of the Greek god Dionysus and, in particular, the Egyptian goddess Isis gained many followers in this period. The popularity of Isis, whose powers extended over every area of human life, received a boost from King Ptolemy I, who established a headquarters for her cult in Alexandria. He also promoted the cult of the Egyptian deity Sarapis, Isis's consort, as his dynasty's protector; Sarapis reportedly performed miracles of rescue from shipwreck and illness. The cult of Isis, who became the most popular female divinity in the Mediterranean, involved

■ **Marble Head of the Greco-Egyptian God Sarapis**
Sarapis was originally an Egyptian god incorporating aspects of Osiris, the consort of Isis, and the sacred Apis bull. In the early Hellenistic period, the Ptolemaic royal family adopted Sarapis as its divine protector. Eventually, worshippers spread the cult of Sarapis around the Hellenistic world. They identified Sarapis as a transcendent god combining the powers of Zeus with those of other divinities, and they looked to him for miracles. He was commonly portrayed with a food container or measure on his head, as here, to signify his concern for human prosperity in this world and in the afterlife. That this head was found in a Roman-era temple in Britain indicates the long-lasting and widespread appeal of this deity.
(Museum of London Photographic Library.)

extensive rituals and festivals mixing features of Egyptian and Greek religion. Followers of Isis hoped, in return for a virtuous life, to gain the goddess's help against the demonic influence of Chance; they also expected she would reward them with a happier fate after death. That an Egyptian deity like Isis could achieve enormous popularity among Greeks (and Romans in later times) alongside the traditional gods of Greek religion is the best evidence of the cultural cross-fertilization of the Hellenistic world.

The history of Judaism in the Hellenistic period shows especially strong evidence of cultural interaction. King Ptolemy II had the Hebrew Bible translated into Greek (the Septuagint) in Alexandria in the early third century B.C.E. Many Jews, especially those living in the large Jewish communities that had grown up in Hellenistic cities outside Palestine, adopted the Greek language and many aspects of Greek culture. Nevertheless, these Hellenized Jews largely retained the ritual practices and habits of life that defined traditional Judaism, and they did not worship Greek gods. Hellenistic politics also affected the Jewish community in Palestine, which was controlled militarily and politically first by the Ptolemies and then by the Seleucids. Both allowed the Jews to live according to their ancestral tradition under the political leadership of a high priest in Jerusalem.

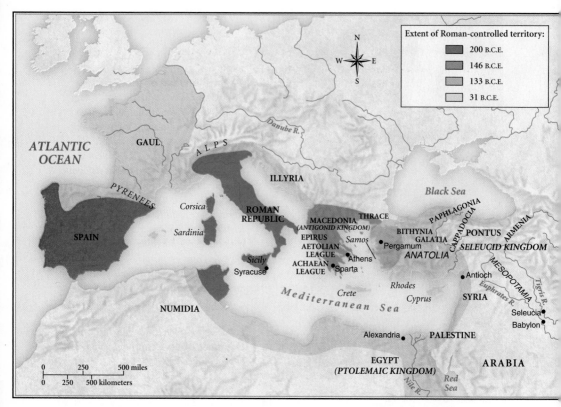

■ MAPPING THE WEST The Fall of the Hellenistic Kingdoms, to 30 B.C.E.

By 30 B.C.E. (the death of Cleopatra VII, the last Ptolemaic monarch of Egypt), the Roman republic had conquered or absorbed the Hellenistic kingdoms of the eastern Mediterranean. Competition for the tremendous wealth that Romans captured in this expansion helped fuel bitter and divisive feuds between Rome's most ambitious generals and political leaders. The territories of the former Hellenistic kingdoms became the main part of the eastern half of the Roman Empire.

Internal conflicts among Jews erupted in second-century B.C.E. Palestine over the amount of Greek influence that traditional Judaism could accept. The Seleucid king Antiochus IV (r. 175–163 B.C.E.) intervened in the conflict in support of the Jerusalem Jews who were most Greek-like in their ways. In 167 B.C.E., Antiochus converted the main Jewish temple there into a Greek temple and outlawed the practice of Jewish religious customs, such as observing the Sabbath and circumcision. A revolt led by Judah the Maccabee eventually won Jewish independence from the Seleucids after twenty-five years of war. The most famous episode of this revolt was the retaking of the Jerusalem temple and its rededication to the worship of the Jewish god Yahweh—a triumphant moment celebrated by Jews ever since on the holiday of Hanukkah. That Greek culture attracted some Jews in the first place, however, provides a striking example of the transformations that affected many—though far from all—people of the Hellenistic world. By the time of the Roman Empire, one of those transformations would be Christianity, whose beliefs had roots in the cultural interaction of Hellenistic Jews and Greeks and their ideas on religion.

■ **REVIEW:** *How did political changes in the Hellenistic period affect art and science?*

IMPORTANT DATES			
399 B.C.E.	Trial and execution of Socrates at Athens	**331 B.C.E.**	Alexander founds Alexandria in Egypt
386 B.C.E.	Sparta makes a peace with Persia ceding control over the Anatolian Greek city-states; Plato founds the Academy in Athens	**324 or 323 B.C.E.**	Menander presents his first comedy at Athens
		323 B.C.E.	Alexander dies in Babylon
362 B.C.E.	Greek city-states weakened by fighting one another at battle of Mantinea	**c. 307 B.C.E.**	Epicurus founds "The Garden" in Athens
		306–304 B.C.E.	Alexander's successors declare themselves kings
338 B.C.E.	Philip II, Macedonian king, defeats Greek alliance at Chaeronea to become the leading power in Greece	**239–130 B.C.E.**	Independent Greek kingdom in Bactria (Afghanistan)
		167 B.C.E.	Jewish revolt in Jerusalem
336 B.C.E.	Philip II is murdered; Alexander becomes king	**30 B.C.E.**	Death of Cleopatra VII and takeover of the Ptolemaic kingdom by Rome
335 B.C.E.	Aristotle founds the Lyceum in Athens		
334 B.C.E.	Alexander leads an army of Greeks and Macedonians against the Persian Empire		

Conclusion

Greece's Classical period came to an end in the fourth century B.C.E. The violence and bitterness of the Peloponnesian War and its aftermath led ordinary people as well as philosophers to question the basis of morality. The characteristic disunity of Greek international politics proved disastrous because the

Macedonian kingdom developed aggressive leaders, Philip II and Alexander the Great, who made themselves masters of the quarreling city-states to their south. Inspired by Greek heroic ideas, Alexander conquered the entire Persian Empire and set in motion the great political, social, and cultural changes of the Hellenistic period.

When Alexander's generals transformed themselves into Hellenistic kings, they made use of the governmental structures they found already established in the lands they conquered, but they also added an administrative staff of Greeks and Macedonians. Local elites as well as Greeks and Macedonians cooperated with the Hellenistic monarchs in governing and financing their society, which was divided into a hierarchy along ethnic lines. To enhance their image of magnificence, the kings and queens of the Hellenistic world supported writers, artists, scholars, philosophers, and scientists, thereby encouraging Hellenistic intellectual innovation. The traditional city-states continued to exist in Hellenistic Greece, but their freedom extended only to local affairs; they lost their independence in foreign policy to the period's powerful kings.

The diversity of the Hellenistic world included much that was new, especially because cultural interaction between different peoples became more common than ever before. An outgrowth of the greater opportunities created by this interaction and change was anxiety about the role of chance in life. In response, people looked to new religious experiences to satisfy their yearning for protection from dangers. In the midst of so much novelty, however, the most fundamental elements of the ancient world remained unchanged—the labor, the poverty, and the limited opportunities for the mass of ordinary people working in fields, vineyards, and pastures.

In the end, the longest lasting effect of the Hellenistic period came in the changes it brought to Roman society and culture; Romans had increasingly close contact with the multicultural traditions of the Hellenistic kingdoms as they gradually rose to become the Mediterranean's dominant political state. That rise to power, however, took centuries because Rome originated as a tiny, insignificant place that no one except Romans ever expected to amount to anything on the world stage.

■ **MAKING CONNECTIONS**

1. *What were the central political, economic, and social developments of the Hellenistic world?*

2. *Compare life for people of all social classes in the Hellenistic kingdoms with that of people living in the Classical Greek city-state.*

■ **FOR FURTHER EXPLORATION**

For further reading and online research ideas, see the Suggested References on page SR-2 at the back of the book.

For practice quizzes, a customized study plan, and other study tools, see the ONLINE STUDY GUIDE at bedfordstmartins.com/huntconcise.

For primary-source material from this period, see Chapter 3 in *Sources of THE MAKING OF THE WEST: A CONCISE HISTORY*, Second Edition.

The Rise of Rome

c. 753–44 B.C.E.

ROMANS TREASURED THE LEGENDS describing their state's slow, violence-plagued transformation from a tiny village to a world power. They especially loved stories about their legendary first king, Romulus, because they remembered him as a passionate leader. According to the legend later known as the "Rape of the Sabine Women," Romulus's Rome was a small settlement without enough women to bear children to increase the population and defend the community in war. The king therefore begged the nearby peoples of central Italy to allow Romans to intermarry with them. Everyone turned him down, out of contempt for Rome's poverty and weakness. Enraged, Romulus hatched a plan: he invited the neighboring Sabines to a festival honoring the gods and had his Roman men kidnap the unmarried Sabine women and fight off their relatives' frantic attempts to rescue them. The kidnappers immediately married the women, persuading them of their good intentions by promising to cherish them as beloved wives and new citizens. When the Sabine men returned to attack Rome, the newly married women rushed into the bloody battle, yelling at their brothers, fathers, and new husbands to stop the slaughter either by laying down their weapons or killing all the women. The men immediately made peace and agreed to unite their populations under Roman rule.

■ **Temple of Castor and Pollux in the Roman Forum**
From the time of Romulus, Rome's first king, Romans believed that the gods supported their city and that citizens needed to show their gratitude in visible ways. These columns belonged to one of Rome's most prominent temples, originally constructed at the heart of the city in the forum in the fifth century B.C.E. to honor the divine twins Castor and Pollux for their help in battle. It was rebuilt several times; the remains seen today date to the time of Augustus (c. 27 B.C.E.–14 C.E.). The temple served important state functions: the Senate often met inside, and it held the official standards for weights and measures as well as treasuries for the emperors and wealthy individuals. Its architectural detail is famous for its elegance. Notice the sculpted capitals atop the forty-foot-high columns.
(Sonia Halliday Photographs.)

This legend emphasizes that Rome, unlike the city-states of Greece, expanded by absorbing outsiders into its citizen body, sometimes violently, sometimes peacefully. Rome's growth became the ancient world's largest expansion of population and territory, as a people originally housed in a few huts slowly created a state that, after centuries of war, came to control most of Europe, North Africa, Egypt, and the eastern Mediterranean. The social, cultural, political, legal, and economic traditions that the Romans developed in ruling this vast area created closer connections among its diverse peoples than ever before or since. Unlike the Greeks and Macedonians, the Romans maintained the unity of their state for centuries. Alexander the Great's conquests won him everlasting fame as the ancient world's most fearless hero, but not even he equaled the Romans in affecting the course of Western civilization: the history of Europe and its colonies, including the United States, has deep roots in Rome.

Roman culture sprang from the traditions of ancient Italy's many peoples, but Greek literature, art, and thought deeply influenced Romans as they gained international power. Of course, they did not just passively absorb other civilizations' traditions or change them only in superficial ways, such as giving Latin names to Greek gods. Whatever Romans took over from others they adapted to their own purposes in complex ways. The cross-cultural contact that so greatly influenced Rome was a kind of competition in innovation rather than an "advanced" Greek culture improving a "primitive" Roman culture.

The kidnapping legend belongs to the earliest period of Rome, when kings ruled (c. 753–509 B.C.E.), but the majority of Roman history comes in two later periods of about five hundred years each—the republic and the empire. These terms refer to the system of government in each period: under the republic (founded 509 B.C.E.), an oligarchy (the social elite) governed; under the empire (founded at the end of the first century B.C.E.), monarchs (the Roman emperors) once again ruled.

Rome's greatest expansion came during the republic. The confidence that fueled this amazing growth sprang from Romans' faith that the gods wanted them to rule the world by military might and law and improve it through social and moral values. The foundation legend illustrates Romans' faith in their divine destiny: Romulus employs a religious festival as a cover for kidnapping. Romans' firm belief that values should drive politics showed in their using persuasion to convince the captive women that loyalty and love would wipe out the crime that had forcibly turned them into wives and Romans.

In addition to the devotion to family that the legend implied, Roman values under the republic emphasized selfless service to the community, individual honor and public status, the importance of laws, and shared decision making. By the first century B.C.E., however, tension between these values had erupted into open conflict because powerful individuals were placing their personal and family interests ahead of the common good. Blinded by ambition, Rome's politician-generals began a civil war that destroyed the republic.

Social and Religious Traditions

Romans regulated their lives by traditional values stressing personal connections, education for public service, religious duties, and hierarchy. Just as Greeks had emphasized excellence as a social value, Romans believed that men and women should show courage in all aspects of life. In public life, Roman men connected with one another as patron or client, each with obligations to the other. In private life, men as the heads of households held power over their children and slaves, but most wives lived independent of their husband's control. In religion, the gods' power over human life meant that everyone had to pray for divine favor to protect the family and the community.

Roman Values

Romans believed that their ancestors had handed down their values from ancient times. They therefore referred to their values as **mos maiorum**, "the way of the ancestors." The Romans treasured their ancient values because, for them, "old-fashioned" meant "good because tested by long experience," while "new" suggested "dangerous because not tested by any experience." Roman morality made honor the reward for right conduct, which required uprightness, faithfulness, and respect for others. Uprightness defined how a person related to others. In the second century B.C.E., the poet Lucilius defined it as virtue:

> Virtue is to know the human relevance of each thing,
> To know what is humanly right and useful and honorable,
> And what things are good and what are bad, useless, shameful,
>   and dishonorable. . . .
> Virtue is to pay what in reality is owed to honorable status,
> To be an enemy and a foe to bad people and bad values
> But a defender of good people and good values. . . .
> And, in addition, virtue is putting the country's interests first,
> Then our parents' interests, with our own third and last.

Faithfulness (*fides*, from which the English word *fidelity* derives) had many forms, for women as well as for men. Basically, it meant to keep one's obligations, no matter the cost. Failing to meet an obligation offended the community and the gods. Faithful women remained virgins before marriage and avoided adultery afterward. Faithful men kept their word, paid their debts, never had sex with another man's wife, and treated everyone justly—which did not mean treating everyone the same, but rather treating people appropriately according to whether they were equals, superiors, or inferiors.

Faithfulness was one aspect of respect, a very complex value. Respect's supreme form was devotion to the gods, to one's own dignity, and to one's family, especially elders. Honoring the gods required carefully planned worship, prayers, and sacrifices performed in a state of strict purity. Respect for one's self meant maintaining self-control and displaying only limited emotion. So strict was this expectation that not even wives and husbands could kiss in public without seeming emotionally out of control. Respect also required never giving up, regardless of difficulties. Standing firm and overcoming all obstacles to do one's duty were thus fundamental Roman values.

Honor was the Romans' reward for living by these values. Women earned honor—a good reputation—especially by bearing legitimate children and educating them morally. Honor for upper-class men brought concrete rewards: election to government office and public recognition of their military bravery and other contributions to the common good. A man who had gained the status bestowed by honor commanded so much respect that others would obey him regardless of whether he exercised formal power over them. A man earning this much prestige was said to possess "authority."

Finally, Romans believed that family background influenced a person's values. Being born in an elite family was therefore a two-edged sword. It automatically carried greater status, but at the same time it imposed a stricter demand to behave morally. Originally, wealth had nothing to do with Roman moral virtue. Over time, however, it became overwhelmingly important to the elite to spend money in displays of conspicuous consumption, social entertainments, and gifts to the community. By the later centuries of the Roman republic, ambitious men required vast fortunes to buy honor, and they became willing to abandon other values to acquire riches.

The Patron-Client System

The hierarchy of Roman society was rooted in the **patron-client system**, an interlocking network of personal relationships linking Romans to one another morally and legally. A patron was a man of superior status who was obliged to provide benefits to certain men of lower status, who paid special attention to him. These were his clients, who in return owed him duties. Both sets of obligations centered on financial and political help. The system had multiple levels: a patron of others was often himself the client of a more distinguished man. The Romans called this hierarchy "friendship"—with clearly defined roles for each party. A sensitive patron would greet a social inferior as "my friend," not as "my client." A client, however, showed respect by addressing his superior as "my patron."

■ Sculpted Tomb of a Family of Ex-Slaves

The husband and wife depicted on this tomb, which perhaps dates to the first century B.C.E., *started life as slaves but gained their freedom and thus became Roman citizens. Their son, in the background holding a pet pigeon, was a free person. One of the remarkable features of Roman civilization, and a source of its demographic strength, was that it granted citizenship to ex-slaves. This family had done well enough financially to afford a sculpted tomb. The tablets the man is holding and the carefully groomed hairstyle of the woman are meant to show that their family was educated and stylish. What do you think it means that the couple are shown holding hands?*

(German Archeological Institute/Madeline Grimoldi.)

Benefits and duties took various forms. A patron benefited his clients by providing gifts or loans in hard times, supporting them when they started political careers, and speaking for them in lawsuits. Clients' duties included lending money when patrons needed it to pay for public works or their daughters' expensive dowries, or aiding their campaigns for public office by soliciting votes. Furthermore, because it was a mark of great status for a man to have numerous clients thronging around like a swarm of bees, a patron expected them to gather at his house early in the morning and accompany him to the forum, the city's public center. A Roman leader needed a large, fine house to accommodate this throng and to entertain his social equals; a crowded house signified social success.

These mutual obligations endured over generations. Ex-slaves, for example, who automatically became the clients of the masters who freed them, passed on this relationship to their children. Wealthy Romans could acquire clients among foreigners, sometimes even entire communities. With its emphasis on duty and permanence, the system epitomized the Roman view that social stability and well-being were achieved by faithfully maintaining people's obligations to one another.

The Roman Family

The family was the bedrock institution of Roman society because it taught values and determined the ownership of property. Men and women shared the duty of teaching values to their children, though by law the father possessed the *patria potestas* ("power of a father") over his children of any age and over his slaves. This power gave him legal ownership of all the property acquired by his dependents. As long as he was alive, no son or daughter could own anything, accumulate money, or possess any independent legal standing—in theory at least. In practice, adult children controlled personal property and money, and favored slaves might accumulate savings. Fathers also held legal power of life and death over these members of their households, but they rarely exercised it on anyone except unwanted or deformed newborns. Abandoning babies so that they would die, be adopted, or be raised as slaves by strangers was an accepted practice to control the size of families and dispose of physically imperfect infants. Baby girls probably suffered this fate more often than boys—a family enhanced its power by investing its resources in its sons.

As the emphasis in Roman values on shared decision making required, fathers regularly conferred with others on important family issues. Each Roman man identified a circle of friends and relatives, his "council," whom he always consulted before making important decisions. A man brooding over the drastic decision to execute an adult member of his household, for example, would never have made the decision on his own. His council would recommend this violent exercise of a father's power only in the most extreme circumstances, as in 63 B.C.E. when a father had his son executed because the youth had committed treason by joining a conspiracy to overthrow the government.

Patria potestas did not allow a husband to control his wife because "free" marriages—in which the wife formally remained under her father's power for as long as he lived—eventually became common. Many Roman wives were relatively independent because their fathers were dead, and their husbands did not legally control their lives (four out of five parents died before their children reached thirty). Legally, a woman needed a male guardian to conduct business for her, but guardianship became an empty formality by the first century B.C.E. As one legal expert said about Roman women's freedom of action: "The common belief, that because of their instability of judgment women are often deceived and that it is only fair to have them controlled by the authority of guardians, seems more specious than true. For women of full age manage their affairs themselves." Upper-class women could express their opinions publicly. In 195 B.C.E., for example, they blocked Rome's streets for days until the men ended a wartime law meant to reduce tensions between rich and poor by limiting the amount of gold jewelry and fine clothing women could wear and where they could ride in carriages.

Roman women had to grow up fast to assume their duties as teachers of values to children and managers of their household's resources. Tullia (c. 79–45 B.C.E.), daughter of the renowned politician and orator Marcus Tullius Cicero (106–43 B.C.E.), was engaged at twelve, married at sixteen, and widowed by twenty-two. As a married Roman woman of wealth, she oversaw the household slaves, including wet nurses for infants, kept account books for the property she personally owned, and accompanied her husband to dinner parties—something Greek wives never did.

Roman mothers won public honor for managing their households well and shaping their children's moral outlook. Cornelia, an aristocrat of the second century B.C.E., won extraordinary fame after her husband died by refusing an offer of marriage from the Ptolemaic king of Egypt so she could instead oversee the family estate and educate her surviving daughter and two sons. (Her other nine children had died.) The boys, Tiberius and Gaius Gracchus, grew up to be among the most influential and controversial officials of the late republic. Wealthy women such as Cornelia wielded political influence, if only indirectly, by expressing their opinions to the male members of their families. Marcus Porcius Cato (234–149 B.C.E.), a famous politician and author, hinted at the behind-the-scenes reality of women's

■ Sculpture of a Woman Running a Store

This relief sculpture shows a woman selling food from behind the counter of a small shop, while customers make purchases or converse with each other. Roman women could own property, so the woman may be the store owner. The man immediately to her right behind the counter could be her husband or a servant. Market areas in Roman towns were packed with small family-run stores like this that sold everything imaginable, much like the malls of today. (Art Resource, NY.)

power with a biting comment directed at his fellow leaders: "All mankind rule their wives, we rule all mankind, and our wives rule us."

Women accumulated property in many ways, from inheritance to entrepreneurship. Recent archaeological discoveries suggest that by the late republic some women owned large businesses. Poor women, like poor men, toiled to help support their families by selling vegetables or charms or colorful ribbons from stands. Slightly more prosperous families crafted furniture or clothing at home, the location of most Roman production, with the men cutting, fitting, and polishing the wood, leather, and metal. The poorest women could earn money only as prostitutes, which was legal but considered disgraceful. Prenuptial agreements to outline the rights of both partners in marriage were common, and divorce was a simple matter, with fathers usually keeping the children.

Education for Public Life

Education for both women and men aimed to make them supporters of traditional values and, for different purposes, effective speakers. As in Greece, most children received their education in the family; only the rich could afford to pay teachers. Wealthy parents bought literate slaves to tend and teach their children. By the late republic, they often chose Greek slaves so their children could be taught to speak Greek and read Greek literary classics, which most Romans regarded as the world's best. Parents might also send their children, from about seven years old, to classes offered by independent schoolmasters in their lodgings. Repetition was the usual teaching technique. Teachers slapped and hit students to keep them attentive.

In upper-class families, both daughters and sons learned to read. The girls were also taught literature, perhaps some music, and, especially, how to make educated conversation at dinner parties. Another principal aim of women's education was to prepare them for the important role of teaching their children traditional social and moral values.

Fathers taught their sons a man's life, especially physical training, fighting with weapons, and courage, but the crown of an upper-class boy's education was rhetoric—skill in persuasive public speaking. Rhetorical training was crucial to a successful public career. A boy would accompany his father to public meetings and court sessions. By listening to speeches, he would learn to imitate winning techniques. Cicero, Rome's most famous orator, agreed with his brother's advice that a young man must learn "to become an excellent public speaker. This is the way to control men at Rome, winning them over to your side and keeping them from harming you. You really have power when you are a man who can cause your rivals the greatest fears of meeting you [as a speaker] in a trial." Roman rhetoric owed much to Greek techniques. This was only one of the crucial ways in which Greek culture influenced Rome.

Kreshnik - Mirahit27@Hotmail. Com.

Religion for Public and Private Interests

Romans followed Greek models in religion, too, worshiping many divinities that corresponded directly with Greek gods. Romans viewed their chief god, Jupiter, who corresponded to the Greek god Zeus, as a powerful, stern father. Juno (Greek Hera), queen of the gods, and Minerva (Greek Athena), goddess of wisdom, joined Jupiter as the three central gods of the state cults. This divine triad shared Rome's most revered temple on its acropolis, the Capitoline hill.

The goal of Roman religion was to preserve Rome's safety and prosperity; above all, people prayed to the gods for victory in war and fertility in agriculture. Many official prayers implored divine aid for growing crops, preventing disease, and spurring healthy reproduction for animals and people. In times of crisis, Romans sought foreign gods to protect them, such as when the government brought the cult of the healing god Asclepius from Greece in 293 B.C.E. to fight a plague. In 204 B.C.E., officials imported the pointed black stone representing Cybele ("the Great Mother"), whose chief sanctuary was in Phrygia in Asia Minor (the Roman term for Anatolia), to promote fertility.

Romans supported many other cults with special guardian responsibilities. The shrine of Vesta, goddess of the hearth and a protector of the family, housed the official eternal flame of Rome, which guaranteed the state's permanent existence. Vestal Virgins, six unmarried women who were sworn to chastity at age six to ten for terms of thirty years, tended Vesta's shrine. Their chastity symbolized Roman family values and thus the preservation of the republic itself. As Rome's only female priesthood, the Vestals earned high status and freedom from their fathers' control by performing their most important duty: keeping the flame from going out. As the Greek historian Dionysius of Halicarnassus reported in the first century B.C.E., "The Romans dread the extinction of the fire above all misfortunes, looking upon it as an omen which means the destruction of the city." Should the flame go out, the Romans assumed that one of the women had broken her vow of chastity and that this Vestal had to be buried alive as punishment.

At home, families maintained a sacred space for small shrines housing statuettes of their Penates (spirits of the household) and Lares (spirits of the ancestors), protectors of their well-being and moral traditions. Upper-class families hung death masks of famous ancestors in the main room in their homes and wore them at funerals to express the current generation's responsibility to live up to the family's virtuous past. In sum, tradition represented the main source of Roman morality. The shame of losing status by tarnishing one's reputation, not the fear of divine punishment, was the strongest deterrent to immoral behavior.

Romans performed many rituals to combat life's uncertainty, in activities as diverse and commonplace as breast-feeding babies and fertilizing crops. Many public religious gatherings promoted the community's health and stability. For example, during the February 15 Lupercalia festival (whose name recalled the wolf, *luper*

■ **Household Religious Shrine from Pompeii**

This colorfully painted shrine stood inside the entrance to a house at Pompeii known as the House of the Vettii, from the name of its owners. Successful businessmen, they spared no expense in decorating their home: with 188 frescoes (paintings done by applying pigments to damp plaster) adorning its walls, the interior blazed in a riot of color. This type of shrine for family religion, found in every Roman home, is called a lararium because it housed the Lares (spirits of the ancestors), who are shown here flanking a central figure, who represents the spirit (genius) of the father of the family. The snake, poised to drink from a bowl probably holding milk set out for it, also symbolizes a protective force, as it did for Greeks as well. The scene sums up the role Romans expected their gods to play: staving off harm and bad luck. Why do you think these ancient peoples regarded snakes as symbols of divine protection? (Scala/Art Resource, NY.)

in Latin, which legend said had reared Romulus), naked young men streaked around the Palatine hill, lashing any woman they met with strips of goat skin. Women who had not yet borne children would run out to be struck, believing this would make them fertile. The December 17 Saturnalia festival, honoring the Italian god of liberation, Saturnus, temporarily turned the social order upside down to release tensions caused by the inequalities between masters and slaves. As the playwright and scholar Accius (c. 170–80 B.C.E.) described the occasion, "People joyfully hold feasts all through the country and the towns, each owner acting as a waiter to his slaves." This reversal of roles reinforced slaves' ties to their owners by symbolizing patrons' benefits, which slaves were expected to repay with faithful service.

Roman tradition did not regard the gods as the guarantors of the Romans' moral code. Like the Greek gods, Roman gods were more connected to national security and prosperity than to human morality, as Cicero explains: "We call Jupiter the Best (*Optimus*) and Greatest (*Maximus*) not because he makes us just or sober or wise but, rather, healthy, unharmed, rich, and prosperous." Therefore, every official action was preceded by "taking the auspices"—seeking Jupiter's approval by observing natural "signs" such as the direction of the flights of birds, their eating habits, or the presence of thunder and lightning. Romans gave human moral actions a religious dimension by hailing their values, such as faithfulness, as divine forces. Also regarded as divine was piety (*pietas*), the sense of devotion and duty to family, friends, and the republic. Rome's temple to pietas housed a statue personifying it as a female divinity. The religious importance attached to the cults of moral qualities emphasized that they were supreme human values that all Romans should practice.

Roman government and public religion had a common goal: to preserve the community. Priests were supposed to ensure the gods' goodwill toward the state, a crucial relationship the Romans called the *pax deorum* ("peace of/with the gods"). Men from the top of the social hierarchy served as priests by conducting sacrifices, and presiding at festivals and other rituals conforming strictly to ancestral tradition. They were not professionals devoting their lives solely to religious activity but, rather, citizens performing public service. The most important official, the *pontifex maximus* ("highest priest"), served as the head of state religion and the ultimate authority on religious matters affecting government; Rome's most prominent men sought this priesthood for its political influence.

Disrespect for religious tradition brought punishment. Naval commanders, for example, took the auspices by feeding sacred chickens on their ships: if the birds ate energetically before a battle, Jupiter favored the Romans and an attack could begin. In 249 B.C.E., the commander Publius Claudius Pulcher grew frustrated when his chickens, probably seasick, refused to eat. Determined to attack, he finally hurled them overboard in a rage, sputtering, "Well then, let them drink!" When he suffered a huge defeat, he was fined very heavily.

■ **REVIEW:** *What role did family and values play in Roman society?*

From Monarchy to Republic, c. 753–287 B.C.E.

Rome's community-focused values provided the unity necessary for its astounding growth from a tiny settlement into the Mediterranean's greatest power. This process took centuries, while the Romans reinvented their government and expanded their territory and population. Rome's first government was a monarchy, the most common type of government in the ancient world. This rule by kings lasted from 753 to

509 B.C.E, when members of the social elite overthrew it in anger at the royal family's violent behavior. The elite then created a new political system—the republic—that lasted until almost the end of the first century B.C.E. The **Roman republic**, from the Latin *res publica* ("the people's matter" or "the public business"), was based on shared political decision making and the election of officials in assemblies of male citizens organized by social hierarchy. Rome acquired land and population by winning aggressive wars and by absorbing other peoples. Its economic and cultural growth depended on contact with peoples around the Mediterranean.

Rule by Kings, c. 753–509 B.C.E.

Legend taught that Rome's original government had seven kings in succession from 753 (the most commonly given date for the city's founding) to 509 B.C.E.; in truth, little reliable evidence exists for this period. The kings probably created the Senate, a body of advisers chosen from the city's leading men to serve as the ruler's council, in keeping with the Roman principle that decisions should be made by consensus. This institution advised government leaders for two thousand years, as Rome changed from a monarchy to the republic and back to a monarchy under the empire.

Rome's policy of making conquered outsiders into citizens or allies produced tremendous expansion, promoted ethnic diversity, and contrasted sharply with the exclusionary citizenship policies of Greek city-states. Another important Roman policy—also different from Greek tradition—was to grant citizenship to freed slaves. These freedmen and freedwomen, as ex-slaves were called, became clients of their former owners. They were barred from elective offices or military service but in all other ways possessed full civil rights, such as legal marriage. Their children enjoyed citizenship without any limitations. By the late republic, many Roman citizens were descendants of freed slaves.

By around 550 B.C.E., the Romans controlled three hundred square miles of the area around Rome, called Latium—enough agricultural land to support a population of thirty thousand to forty thousand people. Geography and contact with other cultures, especially Greek, drove Rome's growth. The city lay at the natural center of both Italy and the Mediterranean world. As the historian Livy (59 B.C.E.–17 C.E.), our source for the heroic legends of early Rome, expressed it, "Gods and men chose this site for good reasons: all its advantages make it the best place in the world for a city destined to grow great." Those advantages were fertile farmland, control of a river crossing on the major north-south route in the peninsula, a nearby harbor on the Mediterranean Sea, and easy access to the surrounding areas in Italy. Most important, Rome was ideally situated for contact with the outside world. The Italian peninsula stuck out so far into the Mediterranean that east-west ship traffic naturally stopped in its ports (Map 4.1).

Ancient Italy was home to a diverse population, and contact with their neighbors profoundly influenced the Romans' cultural development. The people of

■ **MAP 4.1 Ancient Italy, c. 500 B.C.E.**

When the Romans ousted the monarchy to found a republic in 509 B.C.E., they inhabited a relatively small territory in central Italy between the western coast and the mountain range that runs down the peninsula from north to south. Numerous different peoples lived in Italy at this time. The most prosperous occupied fertile agricultural land and sheltered harbors on the peninsula's west side. The early republic's most urbanized neighbors were the Etruscans to the north and the Greek city-states to the south and on the island of Sicily.

Latium were poor villagers like the Romans and spoke the same Indo-European language, an early form of Latin. Flourishing Greek city-states dotted Italy to the south, however, and contact with them had the greatest effect on Rome. Greeks had established colonies in the Campanian plain, such as Naples, from the 700s B.C.E. These settlements grew rich thanks to their ideal location for participating in international trade. Romans developed a love-hate relationship with Greeks, admiring their literature and art but despising their lack of military unity. They adopted many elements from Greek culture—from ethical values to gods, from the model for their poetry and prose to architectural design and style.

The Etruscans, a people north of the Tiber River, also influenced the Romans. They lived in prosperous, independent towns nestled on central Italian hilltops. Vividly colored wall paintings, which survive in some tombs, portray funeral banquets and games testifying to their society's splendor. Etruscans crafted fine artwork, jewelry, and sculpture, but they also loved importing luxury objects from Greece and other

Mediterranean lands. Most of the intact Greek vases known today, for example, were found in Etruscan tombs. The Etruscans' international contacts encouraged cultural interaction: gold tablets inscribed in Etruscan and Phoenician and discovered in 1964 at the port of Pyrgi (thirty miles northwest of Rome) reveal that at about 500 B.C.E., the Etruscans dedicated a temple to the Phoenician goddess Astarte, whom they had learned about by trading with Carthage. That rich city, founded in western North Africa (modern Tunisia) by Phoenicians around 800 B.C.E., dominated seaborne commerce in the western Mediterranean and would later become the Romans' most feared rival.

The extent of Etruscan influence on Rome remains controversial. Until recently, scholars speculated that the Etruscans conquered Rome and dominated it politically in the sixth century B.C.E. The Etruscans were also seen as more culturally refined, mainly because so much Greek art has been found at Etruscan sites; they were therefore assumed to have reshaped Roman culture during this period of supposed domination. New scholarship, however, stresses the independence of Romans in developing their own cultural traditions: they borrowed from Etruscans, as from Greeks, whatever appealed to them and adapted it to fit their local circumstances. Romans took over the Etruscans' procedures for religious rituals, and adopted their magistrates' elaborate garments and musical instruments. They also learned Etruscan divination techniques for discovering the gods' will by identifying clues in the shapes of the internal organs of slaughtered animals. Romans may also have adopted from Etruscan society the tradition of wives joining husbands at dinner parties.

Many features of Roman culture formerly seen as examples of Etruscan influence were probably part of the ancient Mediterranean's shared cultural environment. The organization of the Roman army, a citizen militia of heavily armed infantry troops fighting in formation, reflected not just Etruscan precedent but that of other peoples. The Romans' alphabet, which they first learned from the Etruscans, was Greek; the Greeks had acquired it through their contact with the Levant. The engineering necessary to urbanize Rome has been said to have been done by the Etruscans, but it is too simplistic to assume that cultural developments of this size resulted from one superior culture "instructing" another, less-developed one. Rather, at this time in Mediterranean history, similar cultural developments were under way in many places. The Romans, like so many others, found their own way in navigating through this common cultural sea.

The Early Roman Republic, 509–287 B.C.E.

The social elite's hatred of kings created the Roman republic. Their belief that monarchy always turned into tyranny was expressed in Livy's story of the rape of Lucretia, the most famous legend about the creation of the republic. Like most of Livy's stories, it stressed the role of moral virtue in Roman history. The assault on

■ Banquet Scene Painted in an Etruscan Tomb

Painted about 480–470 B.C.E., this brightly colored fresco at Tarquinia decorated a wall in an Etruscan tomb (known today as the "Tomb of the Leopards," from the animals painted just above this scene). Wealthy Etruscan men and women filled their tombs with pictures such as these, which simultaneously represented the funeral feasts held to celebrate the life of the dead person and the social pleasures experienced in this life and expected in the next. The banqueters recline on their elbows in Greek style. (Scala/Art Resource, NY.)

Lucretia, a chaste wife in the social elite, took place when the swaggering son of King Tarquin the Proud violently raped her to demonstrate his superior power. Despite pleas from her husband and father not to blame herself, she committed suicide after identifying her attacker.

Declaring themselves Rome's liberators from tyranny, her relatives and friends, led by Lucius Junius Brutus, expelled Tarquin in 509 B.C.E. They then created a new political system—the republic—to ensure the sharing of power by the elite and to block rule by one man or family. Thereafter, the Romans prided themselves on living under a freer political system than that of their neighbors. The legend of the warrior Horatius at the bridge, for example, advertised the republic's dedication to national freedom. As Livy told the story, Horatius single-handedly blocked the Etruscan army's march on Rome when they wanted to put a king back in charge of the city. While hacking at his opponents, Horatius cursed them as slaves who had lost their freedom because they were ruled by arrogant kings. Horatius's legend made clear that Romans created the republic to prevent a leader from abusing power by ruling alone.

Conflict over how to achieve this goal persisted for over two hundred years after 509 B.C.E., a period called the **struggle of the orders**. Bitter turmoil between a closed circle of elite families (called the patricians) and the rest of Rome's citizen population (the plebeians), the two "orders" of the republic's social hierarchy, centered on social and economic issues. The patricians inherited their status by being born into one of the about 130 wealthy families controlling important religious activities. Some plebeians, however, were also rich, and they resented the patricians' arrogance in monopolizing political elections, banning intermarriage with plebeians, and advertising their social superiority by wearing special red shoes (later they changed to black footwear adorned with a shiny metal crescent).

Poor plebeians demanded relief from crushing debts and a fairer distribution of farmland. To pressure the patricians, plebeians periodically took the extreme step of leaving the city (secession) for a temporary settlement and refusing to serve in the army. This tactic worked because they made up the majority of Rome's military. A secession provoked by a patrician's violence against a plebeian woman led to the earliest Roman laws, called the Twelve Tables from the bronze tablets on which they were engraved for display between 451 and 449 B.C.E. In Livy's words, these laws prevented the patrician government officials who judged most legal cases from "arbitrarily giving the force of law to their own preferences." So important did the Twelve Tables become as a symbol of the Roman commitment to justice for all citizens that for the next four hundred years children were required to memorize them.

These laws were, however, only a first step toward greater sharing of political power; that process occurred mainly through hammering out the different and sometimes overlapping responsibilities of Rome's assemblies. At these outdoor meetings, adult male citizens elected officials, passed laws, decided government policies, and held some trials. Assemblies were only for voting, not discussion, but every session was preceded by a public gathering to hear speeches. Everyone, including women and noncitizens, could listen to these addresses. The crowd loudly expressed its agreement or disagreement by applauding or hissing. Speakers therefore had to pay close attention to public opinion in forming the proposals that they put before the male citizens who then voted them up or down in the assemblies.

A significant restriction on the democratic aspect of assemblies was that each one was divided into groups according to the social hierarchy determined by status and wealth. Voting took place by groups. Each group, not each individual, had a vote, and a small group had the same vote as a large group. The hierarchy of the voting groups in the Centuriate Assembly, which elected the major officials (consuls and praetors), reflected the organization of the army: it confined the huge population of men too poor to afford military weapons, the **proletarians**, to one group that cast only one out of the total of 193 votes. The Plebeian Assembly excluded patricians and grouped itself into thirty-five tribes based on where voters lived; it elected special officials (tribunes) responsible for protecting plebeians, and it passed resolutions called **plebiscites**, which were originally not recognized as law by patricians. The conflict of the orders finally ended in 287 B.C.E., when patricians conceded that plebiscites had the status of laws. In a third grouping, the Tribal Assembly, patricians joined plebeians as voters grouped by residence. This assembly, in which plebeians greatly outnumbered patricians, eventually became the republic's most important institution for making policy, passing laws, and, until separate courts were created in the second century B.C.E., conducting judicial trials.

Annually elected officials ran the republic's government; they served in groups, numbering from two to more than a dozen, to ensure shared rule. The highest officials were consuls; two were elected each year, and their most important duty was commanding Rome's army legions. Winning a consulship was the greatest political honor a Roman man could achieve, and it bestowed high status on his descendants forever, entitling them to be called nobles. To be elected consul, a man traditionally had to work his way up a **ladder of offices**. After ten years of military service beginning about age twenty, he would seek election as a quaestor, a financial administrator. Continuing to climb the ladder, he would next be elected to the board of aediles, officials overseeing the city's streets, sewers, aqueducts, temples, and markets. Each rung up the ladder was more competitive, and few men reached the next office, that of praetor, which performed judicial and military command duties. The most successful praetors then reached for the gold ring of Roman public office, the consulship.

Ex-consuls could also compete to become one of the censors, prestigious senior officials elected every five years to conduct censuses of the citizen body and select new members of the three-hundred-man Senate, which advised the consuls (as it had the kings). The special role of the Senate in the republic's government made clear the Roman principle of making decisions by consensus. The Senate had no authority to pass laws; it could only give advice. But its prestige was so enormous that no high official or assembly would disregard the senators' advice, unless they wished to start a political crisis. Following the Roman tradition that status should be visible, the senators wore special black high-top shoes and robes embroidered with a broad purple stripe.

The struggle of the orders extended to control of the elective offices. The patricians tried to monopolize the highest ones, but the plebeians resisted fiercely. Through violent struggle from about 500 to 450 B.C.E., the plebeians forced the patricians to yield another important concession besides the Twelve Tables: the creation of a special panel of ten annually elected officials, called tribunes. Their responsibility was to stop actions that would harm the plebeians and their property. The tribunate's purpose made it stand apart from regular ladder offices. Tribunes, who had to be plebeians, based their power on the sworn oath of the other plebeians to protect them against all attacks; this protected status, called sacrosanctity, allowed tribunes the right to use a veto (Latin, meaning "I forbid") to block the actions of officials, suspend elections, and even counter the advice of the Senate. The tribunes' extraordinary power to halt government action sometimes made them the sources of bitter political disputes.

Roman values motivated men to compete for honor, not money, in pursuing a public career. By 367 B.C.E., the plebeians had pushed their way fully into this competition by requiring that at least one consul every year must be a plebeian. Only welloff men could run for election because officials earned no salaries. On the contrary, they were expected to spend large sums to win popular support by entertaining the electorate with, for example, spectacles featuring gladiators (trained fighters) and wild beasts, such as lions imported from Africa. Once elected, a magistrate had to benefit the people by paying for public works, such as roads, aqueducts, and temples.

When Rome later won control of more and more overseas territory through warfare, the desire for the status that money could buy in financing successful election campaigns overcame the values of faithfulness and honesty. By the second century B.C.E., military officers could enrich themselves by seizing booty from enemies in successful foreign wars and by extorting bribes from the local people while administering conquered territory. They could then use these profits of war to finance their political careers at home. In this way, acquiring money became more important in the late republic than winning honor through honest public service.

Outrage over corrupt officials dismissing complaints about each other's conduct led to the creation of a court system with jury trials in the second century B.C.E. Since most officials were also senators, the Senate self-interestedly tried to have these juries be manned only by its members, while nonsenators agitated to be included. Both accusers and accused had to speak for themselves in court or have friends speak for them. Prominent men, usually senators with legal knowledge, played a central role as advisers in the Roman judicial system. These jurists, as they were called (from the Latin *jus, juris*, "law"), operated as private citizens, not official judges, in providing legal advice. This reliance on jurists reflected the Roman tradition of consulting councils of advisers to reach decisions. Roman law developed over centuries, sometimes adapting laws from other peoples, and became the basis for many later European legal codes still in use today.

These centuries of conflict over how to organize the republic did not produce coordinated political and judicial systems. Republican Rome had a jumbled network of overlapping institutions. Several different assemblies voted on laws or, in the Senate's case, opinions that guided lawmaking. Legal cases could be decided by magistrates, assemblies, or juries. Rome had no highest judicial authority, such as the U.S. Supreme Court, to resolve disputes about conflicting laws or verdicts. The republic's stability therefore depended on observing tradition, the mos maiorum. This reliance on tradition ensured that the most socially prominent and the richest Romans dominated government and society—because they defined the "way of the ancestors."

■ **REVIEW:** *What issues fueled the struggle of the orders?*

Consequences of Roman Imperialism, Fifth to Second Centuries B.C.E.

Expansion through war made military service and conquest central to the lives of Romans under the republic. During the fifth, fourth, and third centuries B.C.E., they fought war after war in Italy until they became the most powerful state on the peninsula. In the third and second centuries B.C.E., they began warring far from home in the west, the north, and the east, but above all they battled Carthage to the south. Their success in these campaigns made Rome the premier power in the Mediterranean.

Fear and ambition motivated this imperialism. Worries about national security made the senators recommend preemptive attacks against others perceived as enemies of Rome, and everyone longed to capture wealth on foreign military campaigns. Poorer soldiers hoped their gains would pull their families out of poverty. The elite longed to increase their riches and acquire glory as commanders, to promote their public careers.

The consequences of repeated wars in Italy and abroad transformed Romans culturally and socially. Astonishingly, they had no literature before about 240 B.C.E. Cultural interaction with others during overseas expansion stimulated Romans to write their first history and poetry and deeply influenced their art, especially portraits. Endless military campaigns far from home created stresses on family life and small farmers in the army, while the novel demands of ruling conquered territory undermined the government's stability. The importation of huge numbers of war captives to work as slaves on the estates of the rich put free laborers out of work. The conquests and spoils of war from Rome's great victories in the third and second centuries B.C.E. thus turned out to be a two-edged sword: they brought expansion and wealth, but their unexpected social and political consequences disrupted traditional values and the community's stability.

Roman Expansion in Italy

The Romans believed they were successful militarily because they respected the will of the gods. Cicero claimed, "We have defeated all the nations of the world, because we have realized that the world is directed and governed by the gods." Believing that the gods supported defensive wars as just, the Romans always insisted they fought only in self-defense, even when they attacked first. After a victory over their Latin neighbors in the 490s B.C.E., the Romans spent the next hundred years warring with the Etruscan town of Veii, a few miles north of the Tiber River. Their 396 B.C.E. victory doubled Roman territory. A devastating sack of Rome in 387 B.C.E. by Gauls (a Celtic group) from beyond the Alps proved only a temporary military setback, but it made Romans forever fearful of foreign invasion. By around 220 B.C.E., Rome controlled all of the peninsula south of the Po River.

Rome and Central Italy, Fifth Century B.C.E.

The Romans sometimes forced defeated opponents to give up large amounts of land or even enslaved them, yet they also often struck generous peace terms with former enemies. Some defeated Italians immediately became Roman citizens; others gained limited citizenship without the right to vote; still other communities received treaties of alliance. No conquered Italian peoples had to pay taxes to Rome. All, however, had to send soldiers for future wars. These new allies then received a share of the booty, chiefly slaves and land, from victorious campaigns against a new crop of enemies. In this way, the Romans used the sharing of the profits of conquest to turn former opponents into partners, an arrangement that only made Rome more powerful.

Roman Roads, c. 110 b.c.e.

To strengthen Italy's security, the Romans planted colonies of citizens and constructed roads up and down the peninsula to allow troops to march faster. These roads also connected the diverse peoples of Italy, speeding the creation of a more unified culture dominated by Rome. Latin, for example, came to be the common language, although local tongues lived on, especially Greek in the south. The wealth flowing from Rome's first two centuries of expansion in Italy attracted hordes of people to the city because these riches financed new aqueducts to provide fresh, running water—a rarity in the ancient world—and a massive building program employing poor laborers. By around 300 b.c.e., perhaps 150,000 people lived within Rome's walls. Outside the city, about 750,000 free Roman citizens inhabited various parts of Italy on land taken from local peoples. Much conquered territory was declared public land, open to any Roman to use for grazing herds of cattle.

Rich patricians and rich plebeians cooperated to exploit the expanding Roman territories; the old hierarchy separating the orders had become a technicality for the wealthy. This merged elite derived its wealth mainly from agricultural land and plunder acquired during military service. Since Rome levied no regular income or inheritance taxes, families could pass down their assets from generation to generation.

Wars with Carthage

Rome fought three wars against the powerful and wealthy North African city of Carthage. Also governed as a republic, Carthage by the third century b.c.e. controlled an empire stretching across the northwest African coast, part of Libya, Sardinia, Corsica, Malta, and the southern portion of Spain. Geography therefore ensured that an expanding Rome would sooner or later bump up against Carthage's

■ **Aqueduct at Nîmes in France**
Like the Greeks, the Romans supplied fountains and public baths in their towns with water by constructing aqueducts. They excelled at building complex systems of tunnels, channels, and bridges to move water over great distances. One of the best-preserved sections of a major aqueduct is the so-called Pont-du-Gard near present-day Nîmes in France, erected in the late first century B.C.E. to serve the flourishing town of Nemausus. Built of stones fitted together without clamps or mortar, the span soars 160 feet high and is 875 feet long, carrying water from 35 miles away in a channel constructed to fall only 1 foot in height for every 3,000 feet in length, so that the flow would remain steady but gentle. What sort of social and political organization would be necessary to construct such a system? **For more help analyzing this image,** see the visual activity for this chapter in the ONLINE STUDY GUIDE at bedfordstmartins.com/huntconcise. (© Hubertus Kanus/Photo Researchers, Inc.)

interests, which depended on the sea; the Carthaginians fielded a strong fleet but had to hire mercenaries to field a sizable infantry. To Romans, remembering the invasion by the Gauls, Carthage seemed a dangerous rival, as well as a fine prize because of its riches. Roman hostility was also fueled by horror at the Carthaginian tradition of sacrificing infants in times of trouble in the belief that this would placate their gods.

A coincidence ignited open conflict with Carthage, taking Roman troops outside Italy and across the sea for the first time; the three wars that followed are called the Punic Wars, from the Roman term *Punici,* meaning "Phoenicians" (the ancestors of the Carthaginians). The First Punic War (264–241 B.C.E.) began when a band of mercenaries stranded in a local war at Messana, on Sicily's northeastern tip, appealed for help to Rome and Carthage simultaneously. Both states sent troops. The Carthaginians wanted to protect the profits they earned from Sicilian trade; the Romans wanted to keep Carthaginian troops from moving close to their territory and to win plunder. The clash between their forces exploded into a war that lasted a generation. Its bloody battles revealed why the Romans so consistently conquered their rivals. In addition to being able to draw on the Italian population for reserves of manpower, they were prepared to lose as many troops, vote as much money, and fight as long as necessary to win. Previously unskilled at naval warfare, they spent vast sums to build warships to combat Carthage's experienced navy; they lost more than five hundred ships and 250,000 men while learning how to win at sea. (See "Taking Measure," page 151.)

Victory in the First Punic War made the Romans masters of Sicily, where they set up their first province (a foreign territory ruled and taxed by Roman officials). This innovation proved so profitable that they created another province by seizing the islands of Sardinia and Corsica from Carthage's control. Acquiring these foreign territories whetted the Romans' appetite for more, and they also feared a renewal of Carthage's power (Map 4.2). Pressing their advantage, they next made alliances with local peoples in Spain, where the Carthaginians were expanding from their original trading posts in the south.

The Senate's harsh warning to Carthage not to expand any further convinced the Carthaginians that another war was inevitable, so they decided to strike back. In the Second Punic War (218–201 B.C.E.), the daring Carthaginian general Hannibal (247–182 B.C.E.) shocked the Romans by marching troops and war elephants over the snowy Alps into Italy. After slaughtering a Roman army at the battle of Cannae in 216 B.C.E.—thirty thousand men died in the bloodiest defeat in Roman history—Hannibal tried to convince Rome's Italian allies to come over to his side. Disastrously for him, most Italians remained loyal to Rome. Hannibal's alliance in 215 B.C.E. with King Philip V of Macedonia (238–179 B.C.E.) forced the Romans to fight on a second front in Greece (their first presence in that region), but they refused to crack despite Hannibal's ravaging Italy for fifteen years before retreating to Africa in 203 B.C.E. The Romans finally won by turning the tables and invading the Carthaginians' homeland. Their general Scipio trained his soldiers to keep formation and then swivel out of the way of Hannibal's war elephants, even when facing dozens of the beasts charging so hard they shook the earth. At the decisive battle of Zama in 202 B.C.E., Scipio crushed Carthage's forces. The Senate imposed a punishing settlement on the Carthaginians in 201 B.C.E., forcing them to eliminate their navy, pay huge fines for fifty years, and hand over their rich territory in Spain, which Rome made into provinces famous for their mines.

The Third Punic War (149–146 B.C.E.) broke out when the Carthaginians, who had revived financially, struck back against an aggressive African neighbor and Roman ally. After defeating Carthage for a third time, the Romans followed the advice of the tough-minded senator Cato: "We must destroy Carthage." They destroyed the city and converted its territory into a province. This disaster did not obliterate Carthaginian language and culture, however, and under the Roman

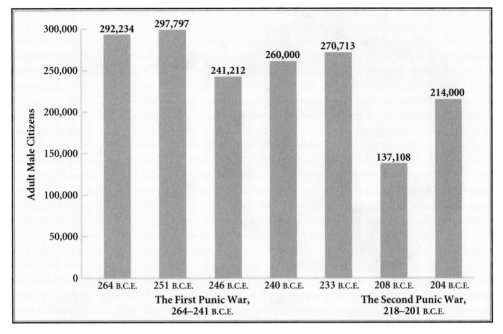

■ TAKING MEASURE Census Records of Adult Male Roman Citizens during the First and Second Punic Wars

Livy (59 B.C.E.–17 C.E.) and Jerome (c. 347–420 C.E.) provide these numbers from Roman censuses conducted during and between the first two wars against Carthage. Only adult male citizens (the men eligible for Rome's regular army) were counted. The drop in the total for 246 B.C.E., compared with the total for 264 B.C.E., reflects losses in the First Punic War. The low total for 208 B.C.E. reflects losses in battle and defections by communities such as Capua in 216 B.C.E. Because the censuses did not include the Italian allies fighting on Rome's side, the numbers understate the wars' total casualties. Scholars estimate that the first two Punic Wars took the lives of nearly a third of Italy's adult male population—perhaps a quarter of a million soldiers killed.

Empire this part of North Africa became renowned for its economic and intellectual vitality, which emerged from a combination of Roman and Punic traditions.

Rome's conquests in the Punic Wars led to the extension of Roman power to Macedonia, Greece, and part of Asia Minor. After defeating Philip in Macedonia for revenge and to prevent any threat of his invading Italy, the Roman commander Flamininus proclaimed the "freedom of the Greeks" in 196 B.C.E. to show respect for Greece's tradition of fighting for independence. The Greek cities and federal leagues naturally interpreted the proclamation to mean they could behave as they liked. They misunderstood. The Romans meant them to behave as clients and follow their new patrons' advice; the Greeks thought, as "friends" of Rome, that they were truly independent. Trouble then developed because the two sides failed

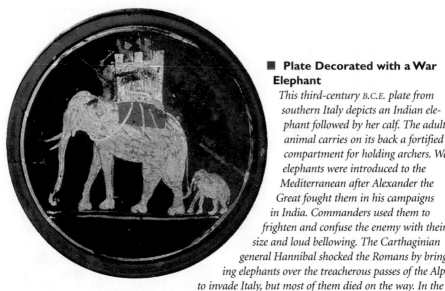

■ **Plate Decorated with a War Elephant**

This third-century B.C.E. plate from southern Italy depicts an Indian elephant followed by her calf. The adult animal carries on its back a fortified compartment for holding archers. War elephants were introduced to the Mediterranean after Alexander the Great fought them in his campaigns in India. Commanders used them to frighten and confuse the enemy with their size and loud bellowing. The Carthaginian general Hannibal shocked the Romans by bringing elephants over the treacherous passes of the Alps to invade Italy, but most of them died on the way. In the long run, however, armies gave up on elephants because they were too expensive to feed and too difficult to control when panicked or wounded in battle. (Scala/Art Resource, NY.)

to realize that common and familiar words such as *freedom* and *friendship* could carry very different meanings in different societies. To make the kingdom of Macedonia and the Greeks observe their obligations as clients, the Romans repeatedly sent armies. Frustrated by continuing Greek resistance, the Senate in 146 B.C.E. ordered the destruction of Corinth for asserting its independence and converted Macedonia and Greece into a province. In 133 B.C.E., the Attalid king of Pergamum boosted Roman power with an astonishing gift: he left his rich Asia Minor kingdom to Rome in his will. In 121 B.C.E., when the Greek city of Massilia on the southern coast of Gaul asked for protection against local tribes, the Romans made the lower part of Gaul across the Alps (modern France) into a province. By this date, then, Rome governed and profited from two-thirds of the Mediterranean region; only the easternmost Mediterranean lay outside its control (see Map 4.2).

Greece's Influence on Rome's Literature, Philosophy, and Art

Although Romans looked down on Greeks for their military weakness, they admired their literature, philosophy, and art. The wars that brought Roman armies to Greece also brought increased Greek cultural influence on Romans. In about 200 B.C.E., the first Roman historian, Fabius Pictor, wrote in Greek to compose his account of Rome's foundation and the Punic War. Greece also directly inspired the earliest literature in Latin: an adaptation of Homer's

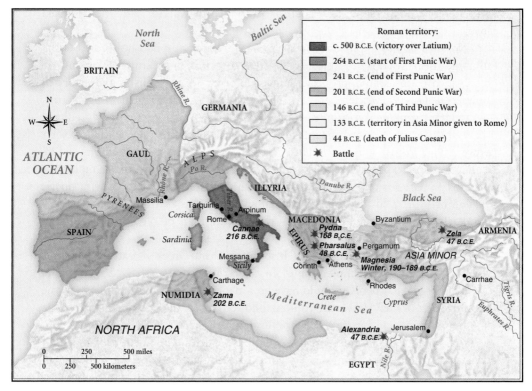

■ MAP 4.2 Roman Expansion, c. 500–44 B.C.E.

During the first two centuries of its existence, the Roman republic used war and diplomacy to extend its power north and south on the Italian peninsula. In the third and second centuries B.C.E., conflict with Carthage to the south and west and with the Hellenistic kingdoms to the east extended Roman power far outside Italy and led to the creation of provinces from Spain to Greece. The first century B.C.E. saw the conquest of the Levant by Pompey and of Gaul by Julius Caesar. **For more help analyzing this map,** see the map activity for this chapter in the ONLINE STUDY GUIDE at bedfordstmartins.com/huntconcise.

Odyssey by a Greek ex-slave, Livius Andronicus, written sometime after the First Punic War.

Like Livius, many of the most famous early Latin authors were not native Romans. Their widespread origins reveal the mixing of cultures under the republic. The poet Naevius (d. 201 B.C.E.) came from Campania in southern Italy; the poet Ennius (d. 169 B.C.E.) from even farther south, in Calabria; the comic playwright Plautus (d. 184 B.C.E.) from north of Rome, in Umbria; his fellow comedy writer Terence (c. 190–159 B.C.E.) from North Africa. They all found inspiration in Greek literature. Roman comedies, for example, took their plots and standard characters from Hellenistic Greek comedy, which raised laughs from family life and stereotyped personalities, such as the boastful warrior and the obsessed lover.

Not all Romans applauded Greek influence. Cato, although he studied Greek himself, insisted that the "feeble" Greeks were corrupting the "sturdy" Romans. He established Latin as an appropriate language for prose by publishing a history of Rome, *The Origins* (written between 168 and 149 B.C.E.), and instructions for running a large farm, *On Agriculture* (published about 160 B.C.E.). He glumly predicted that if the Romans ever became infected with Greek literature, they would lose their power. In fact, as usual in cultural interactions, early Roman authors employed foreign models to express their own values in new ways. Ennius, for example, was inspired by Greek epic poetry to compose his own Latin epic *Annals,* a poetic version of Roman history, but he praised ancestral Roman tradition, as a much-quoted line demonstrated: "On the ways and the men of old rests the Roman commonwealth."

Later Roman writers also took inspiration from Greek literature. Lucretius (c. 94–55 B.C.E.), for example, published a long poem entitled *On the Nature of Things* to argue that people should have no fear of death, which only inflamed "the running sores of life." His work's content followed closely the "atomic theory" of the nature of existence of the Greek philosopher Epicurus (341–270 B.C.E.) and described matter as composed of tiny, invisible particles. The poem explained that death meant only that the atoms temporarily forming a person's body once again separated, without pain or suffering. There could be no eternal punishment—or reward—after death, indeed no afterlife at all, because a person's soul, itself made up of atoms, dissolved along with the body.

Hellenistic Greek authors inspired Catullus (c. 84–54 B.C.E.), whose witty poems satirized prominent politicians for their sexual behavior and revealed his own disastrous love life. His most notorious erotic poems detailed his passion for a married woman named Lesbia, whom he begged to think only of immediate pleasures: "Let us live, my Lesbia, and love; the gossip of stern old men is not worth a cent. Suns can set and rise again; we, when once our brief light has set, must sleep one never-ending night. Give me a thousand kisses, then a hundred, then a thousand more."

The orator Cicero wrote not only speeches and letters but also many essays on philosophy, ethics, theology, and political science that built on the work of Greek philosophers. He adapted Greek ideas to Roman life—above all expressing the value of appreciating the uniqueness of each human personality. He wrote his most influential philosophical works in one period of furious activity while in political exile in 45 and 44 B.C.E. His doctrine of **humanitas** ("humanness, the quality of humanity") combined various ideas from Greek philosophy, especially Stoicism, to express an ideal for human life based on generous and honest treatment of others and an abiding commitment to morality derived from natural law

■ **Actors in a Comedy**

This relief sculpture dating to the first century B.C.E. shows actors portraying characters in one of the various kinds of comedy popular during the Roman republic. In this variety, which derived from Greek New Comedy of the Hellenistic period, the actors wore exaggerated masks designating stock personality types and strove for broad, slapstick comedy. The plots ranged from burlesques of famous mythological stories to stereotypes of common family problems. Here, on the right, an irresponsible son returns home after a night of drinking, supported by his slave and preceded by a hired female musician. On the left, his enraged father is restrained by a friend from beating the prodigal son with his cane. (Scala/Art Resource, NY.)

(the right that exists for all people by nature, independent of the differing laws and customs of different societies). The spirit of humanitas that Cicero passed on to later ages was perhaps the most attractive ideal to emerge from republican Rome.

Greece influenced Rome not only in literature but also in art and architecture, from the style of sculpture and painting to the design of public buildings. As usual, Romans adapted Greek models to their own purposes, most strikingly in portrait sculpture. Hellenistic artists had pioneered the sculpting of realistic statues that showed the damage old age and stress did to the human body. These Greek statues, however, portrayed human stereotypes (the "old man," the "drunken woman"), not specific people; Greek portrait sculpture, by contrast, presented real individuals in the best possible light, much like a retouched photograph today.

Roman artists in the later republic transferred the Greek tradition of realistic sculpture to portrait statues. Roman sculptures of specific men did not conceal unflattering features: protruding noses, receding chins, deep wrinkles, bald heads, careworn eyes. Portraits of women, however, were more idealized, perhaps to represent the traditional vision of a happy marriage. Portraits of children were not popular during the republic, perhaps because offspring were not seen as contributing to public life until they were grown. Because either the men shown in the portraits or their families paid for their statues, they must have wanted the faces sculpted realistically—showing the toll of age and effort—to emphasize how hard the men had worked to serve "the people's matter" that was the republic.

Imperialism's Effects on Republican Society

Before the long campaigns required to defeat Carthage, Macedonia, and Greece in the third and second centuries B.C.E., Roman warfare, like Greek, had followed a pattern of short campaigns timed not to interfere with the labor needs of farming. Rome's long wars abroad had the unintended consequence of disrupting the traditional rhythm of Roman agricultural life and forcing many poor people to move to the capital. Furthermore, the years of conquest led to hard times for the poorer families in Italy, who constituted the principal source of soldiers. A farmer absent on prolonged military expeditions had two choices: relying on a hired hand or slave to manage his crops and animals or having his wife take on what was traditionally man's work in the fields in addition to her usual domestic tasks. The story of the consul Regulus, who led a Roman army to victory in Africa in 256 B.C.E., revealed the severe problems a man's absence could cause. When the man who managed his $4\frac{1}{3}$-acre farm died while the consul was away fighting Carthage, a hired hand ran off with all the farm's tools and livestock. Regulus begged the Senate to send a general to replace him so he could return home to save his wife and children from starving. The senators saved Regulus's family and property from ruin because they wanted to retain him as a commander in the field.

Ordinary soldiers could expect no such special aid, and these troubles hit poorer families particularly hard when in the second century B.C.E., for reasons that remain unclear, there was not enough farmland to support their children from generation to generation. Scholars have usually concluded that the rich had deprived the poor of land, but recent research suggests that the problem stemmed from an astonishing growth in the number of young people in the population. Not all regions of Italy suffered as severely as others, and some impoverished farmers and their families managed to remain in the countryside by working as day laborers for others. In any case, the number of poor people without a way to make a living had created a social crisis by the late second century B.C.E. Many homeless people migrated to Rome, where the men looked for work as menial laborers and women sought piecework making cloth but often were forced into prostitution.

This influx of desperate, landless people swelled the poverty-level urban population. The difficulty they experienced just surviving made them an important factor in Roman politics, as ambitious politicians competed for their support by promising welfare benefits. The state had to feed them to avert riots, and by the late second century B.C.E., Rome was importing food to support this swollen population of urban poor. Their demand for rations of low-priced (and eventually free) grain distributed at the state's expense became one of the most explosive issues in late republican politics.

At the other end of the social hierarchy, Rome's elite reaped abundant rewards from imperialism. The increased need for commanders to lead military campaigns

■ **Wall Painting of a Woman Playing a Lyre**

This painting done in about 40–30 B.C.E. covered part of a wall in a rich family's house at Boscoreale, near Pompeii in southern Italy. Wealthy Romans loved brightly colored rooms elaborately decorated on every wall. This painting shows an unnamed woman playing a kind of concert lyre or harp known as a kithara. The gilding on her instrument and her gold jewelry identify her as a wealthy person. She and the young girl stare out into the room in a style popular at the time. What effect do you think this pose was meant to have on spectators?

(The Metropolitan Museum of Art, Rogers Fund, 1903 [03.14.5]. Photograph © 1986 The Metropolitan Museum of Art.)

overseas created opportunities for successful generals to enrich themselves and their families. By using their gains to finance public buildings, the elite built up their reputations while benefiting the general population. Building new temples, for example, was thought to increase everyone's security by pleasing the gods. In 146 B.C.E., a victorious general paid for Rome's first temple built of marble, finally bringing this Greek style to the capital city.

The financial troubles of small farmers suited rich landowners because they could buy bankrupt plots to create large estates. They further increased their holdings by illegally occupying public land carved out of the territory of defeated peoples. The rich worked their large estates, called latifundia, with slaves as well as free laborers. Many free but poor Romans now found it hard to get work as laborers because the rich had bought workers from the many slaves taken captive during the foreign wars. The growing size of the slave crews working on latifundia was a mixed blessing for their wealthy owners because the presence of so many slave workers in one place led to periodic revolts that required the army to suppress.

The elite also profited from Rome's expansion by filling government offices in the new provinces; they could enrich themselves if they ignored the traditional value of uprightness. Since Roman provincial officials ruled by martial law, no one in the provinces could curb a greedy governor's appetite for graft, extortion, and plunder. Not all governors were corrupt, but some did use their unsupervised power to extort everything they could from the provincials. Until jury trials were created, such offenders faced little or no punishment because in the Senate they and their colleagues would routinely excuse one another's crimes.

The new desire for luxury, financed by the fruits of expansion abroad, fractured the traditional values of moderation and frugality. Before, a general like Manius Curius (d. 270 B.C.E.) represented the ideal: despite his glorious military victories, he was said to have boiled turnips for his meals in a humble hut. Now, the elite acquired showy luxuries, such as large country villas for entertaining friends and clients, to proclaim their social superiority. Money had become more valuable to them than the good of "the people's matter."

■ **REVIEW:** *What were some of the unintended consequences of Rome's victories over foreign peoples?*

The Destruction of the Republic,
c. 133–44 B.C.E.

Placing their own interests ahead of the traditional values of community service, ambitious leaders from the Roman elite destroyed the republic in civil war. When the tribunes Tiberius and Gaius Gracchus agitated for reforms to help poor

Romans, their opponents in the Senate resorted to murder to curb them. When a would-be member of the elite, Gaius Marius, opened army service to the poor to boost his personal status, his creation of "client armies" undermined faithfulness to the republic. When the people's unwillingness to share citizenship with Italian allies sparked a war in Italy and the clashing ambitions of the "great men" Sulla, Pompey, and Julius Caesar burst into civil war, the republic shattered beyond repair.

The Gracchus Brothers and Political Rupture

The aristocratic brothers Tiberius and Gaius Sempronius Gracchus won election as tribunes by advocating a much higher level of financial help for poor citizens. This policy set them at odds with many of the elite, into whose order they had been born: their grandfather Scipio had defeated Hannibal, and their mother was the Cornelia whom the king of Egypt had courted after their father died. Tiberius, the elder brother, spoke bluntly about the horrible lives of the landless poor, according to the biographer Plutarch (c. 50–120 C.E.):

> The wild beasts that roam over Italy have their dens. . . . But the men who fight and die for Italy enjoy nothing but the air and light; without house or home they wander about with their wives and children. . . . They fight and die to protect the wealth and luxury of others; they are styled masters of the world, and have not a clod of earth they call their own.

In 133 B.C.E., when the Senate blocked Tiberius's proposed reforms, he outflanked his opponents by having the Plebeian Assembly pass laws redistributing public land to landless Romans. He further shattered tradition by defying the Senate in financing his land reform: before the Senate could decide whether to accept the gift of the Attalid kingdom from the ruler of Pergamum, Tiberius had the plebeians pass another law specifying that the kingdom's riches be distributed to the poor so they could buy equipment and livestock to start a farm.

Tiberius then announced his intention to run for reelection as tribune, violating the tradition against consecutive terms. His senatorial enemies boiled over: Tiberius's own cousin led a band of senators and their clients in an ambush against him to, as they shouted, "save the republic." Pulling their togas up over their left arms so they would not trip in the attack, they clubbed to death the tribune and many of his followers. Their assault marked a turning point in the republic's history: murder now became a political tool.

Gaius, elected tribune for 123 B.C.E. and, contrary to tradition, elected again the next year, followed his brother's lead by pushing measures that outraged the elite: more land reform, greatly subsidized prices for grain, public works projects throughout Italy to provide employment for the poor, and colonies abroad with farms for the landless. His most revolutionary proposals were to grant Roman citizenship to many Italians and to establish new courts that would try senators accused of corruption as provincial governors. The new juries would be manned not by senators but by *equites* ("equestrians" or "knights"). These were landowners from outside the city, wealthy businessmen whose choice of commerce over a public career set them apart from senators. Because they did not serve in the Senate, equestrians could convict corrupt senators without fear of peer pressure. Gaius's proposal marked the emergence of the equestrians as a political force in Roman politics and angered the Senate. When the senators blocked his plans, Gaius in 121 B.C.E. assembled an armed group to threaten them. They responded by instructing the consuls "to take all measures necessary to defend the republic," meaning the use of force. To escape arrest and certain execution, Gaius had one of his slaves cut his throat; hundreds of his supporters were then murdered by the senators and their supporters.

The violent deaths of the Gracchus brothers and so many of their followers introduced a deep rupture in Roman elite politics. From now on, members of the elite divided themselves either as "supporters of the common people" (*populares*), or "supporters of the best people" (*optimates*). Some identified with one side or the other from genuine allegiance to its policies; others based their choice on self-interest, supporting whichever side better promoted their own political advancement. This split in the elite made political cooperation in service of the republic a lost cause.

Gaius Marius and the First Client Armies

The rupture in the elite broke the nobles' stranglehold on political power, allowing a new kind of leader to arise: men from the elite but with no consul among their ancestors. These men relied on sheer ability to force their way to fame, fortune, influence, and—their ultimate goal—election as consul. The most controversial of them was Gaius Marius (c. 157–86 B.C.E.), an equestrian from Arpinum in central Italy. Ordinarily, a man from this background had no chance of cracking the nobles' hold on the consulships. When Marius succeeded as a general against a rebel in Africa where nobles had failed, however, the people's enthusiasm powered him to election as consul for 107 B.C.E. In Roman terms, this election made him a "new man"—that is, the first man in the history of his family to become consul. Marius's further successes in great crises, especially against German tribes who attacked southern France and then Italy, led the people to elect him consul for six terms, including consecutive service, by 100 B.C.E. This overturned Roman political tradition.

Marius became so famous that the Senate voted him a triumph, Rome's highest—and rarest—military honor. On the day of the ceremony, the general paraded through Rome in a chariot. His face was painted red for reasons Romans no longer remembered. Huge crowds cheered him, while his army teased him with off-color jokes to avert the evil eye at this moment of supreme glory. For a similar reason, a slave rode with him to keep whispering in his ear, "Look behind you, and remember that you are a mortal."

The optimates never accepted Marius, despising him as a dangerous upstart. His support came mainly from the common people, who loved him for his reform of military service. Previously, only men with property could enroll as soldiers. Marius opened enlistment to proletarians, men who owned almost nothing. For them, serving in the army meant an opportunity to better their lot by acquiring plunder and a grant of land to retire on.

This change had a consequence fatal to the republic: creating armies more loyal to their commander than to the community. Proletarian troops felt tremendous goodwill toward a commander who led them to victory and then divided the loot with them generously. Poor soldiers thus began to behave like an army of clients following their general as their patron. They naturally supported his personal ambitions. Marius was the first to promote his own career in this way, but he lost his political importance after 100 B.C.E. because he stopped commanding armies and tried to gain acceptance from the optimates. When later generals used client armies to advance their political careers more violently than Marius ever had, the republic's doom was sealed.

Sulla and Civil War

Taking Marius's lesson to heart, a noble named Lucius Cornelius Sulla (c. 138–78 B.C.E.) exploited the dirty secret of politics in the late republic: traditional values no longer restrained commanders who prized their own advancement and the enrichment of their troops above peace and the good of the community. Sulla wielded his client army as a weapon to extort the consulship and dominate the Senate, perverting the Roman notion of honor. His opportunity came when Rome's Italian allies rebelled in frustration at their being denied citizenship. The Italians' discontent finally erupted in 91–87 B.C.E. in the Social War (so named because the Latin word for "ally" is *socius*). The allies lost the war and 300,000 men, but they won the political battle: Romans granted citizenship to all freeborn peoples of Italy south of the Po River. Most important, their men were now entitled to vote in Rome's assemblies.

Sulla's successful command in the Social War won him election as consul for 88 B.C.E. His luck continued when, in that same year, the king of Pontus on the southern coast of the Black Sea, Mithridates VI (120–63 B.C.E.), organized a murderous rebellion against Rome's control of Asia Minor, especially its greedy tax collectors, who squeezed provincials to pay much more than they owed. Denouncing Romans as "the common enemies of all mankind," Mithridates persuaded the locals to slaughter all the Italians they could locate—tens of thousands of them—in a single day. As retaliation for this treachery, the Senate advised a military expedition;

victory would mean unimaginable plunder because Asia Minor held many wealthy cities.

Born to a patrician family that had lost most of its status and all of its money, Sulla craved the command against Mithridates. When the Senate advised giving Sulla the appointment, his jealous rival Marius, now an old man, immediately plotted to have it transferred to himself by plebiscite. Outraged, Sulla marched his client army against Rome itself. All his officers except one deserted him in horror at this unthinkable outrage. But common soldiers united behind him; neither they nor their commander shrank from civil war. Capturing Rome, Sulla murdered or exiled his opponents and let his men rampage through the city. He then led them off to fight Mithridates, ignoring a summons to stand trial and sacking Athens on the way to Asia Minor.

Sulla's violence generated more violence from his rivals. In Sulla's absence, Marius and his friends embarked on their own reign of terror in Rome. In 83 B.C.E., Sulla returned after defeating Mithridates and allowing his soldiers to plunder Asia Minor. Civil war began again for two years until Sulla crushed his enemies and their Italian allies. The climactic battle took place in 82 B.C.E. before the gates of Rome. An Italian general whipped his troops into a frenzy by shouting, "The last day is at hand for the Romans! These wolves that have made such ravages upon our liberty will never vanish until we have cut down the forest that harbors them."

This passionate cry for freedom failed. Sulla won and destroyed everyone who had opposed him. To speed the extermination, he devised a merciless procedure called proscription—posting a list of those supposedly guilty of treasonable crimes so that anyone could kill them without a trial. Because the property of those proscribed was confiscated, the victors listed the name of anyone whose wealth they desired. The Senate in terror appointed Sulla dictator—an emergency office supposed to be held only temporarily—without any limitation of term. He reorganized the government in the interest of "the best people"—his social class—by making senators the only ones allowed to judge cases against their colleagues and forbidding tribunes to offer legislation on their own or hold any other office after their term.

Convinced by an old prophecy that he had only a short time to live, Sulla surprised everyone by retiring to private life in 79 B.C.E. and indeed dying the next year. His bloody career revealed the sad fate of the traditional values of the republic. First, success in war had long ago changed its meaning from defense of the community to acquiring profits for commanders and common soldiers alike. Second, the patron-client system had mutated to make poor soldiers feel stronger ties of obligation to their generals than to the republic; Sulla's men obeyed his order to attack Rome because they owed obedience to him as their patron and could expect benefits from him in return. He fulfilled his obligations to them by permitting the plundering of Roman and foreign opponents alike.

Finally, the traditional desire to win honor now worked both for and against political stability. So long as that value motivated men from leading families to seek office to promote the welfare of the population as well as the status of their families—the traditional ideal of a public career—it exerted a powerful force for social peace and general prosperity. But pushed to its extreme, the concern for prestige and wealth could overshadow all considerations of public service, even to the point of unleashing civil war. The republic was doomed once its leaders and followers abandoned the "way of the ancestors" that valued respect for the peace, prosperity, and traditions of the republic above personal gain.

Pompey, Caesar, and the End of the Republic

The generals whose names dominate the history of the republic after Sulla all took him as their model: while claiming to be serving the community, in truth they cared most about their own careers. Their motivation—the belief that a Roman noble could never have too much glory or too much wealth—was a corruption of the republic's finest ideals of public service. Two Roman nobles, Pompey and Julius Caesar, fanned the flames of political conflict more than anyone else. They ended up fighting a civil war that ended the republic: for peace to revive, monarchy had to return to Rome after an absence of nearly five hundred years.

The career of Gnaeus Pompey (106–48 B.C.E.) shows how weak the traditional restraints on an individual's power became after Sulla. At only twenty-three years of age, Pompey gathered a private army from his father's clients to fight for Sulla in 83 B.C.E. So splendid were his victories that his shameless demand for a triumph could not be refused. Awarding the supreme honor to such a young man, who had not held a single public office, shattered tradition, but Pompey's personal power was too great to refuse. As he told Sulla, "People worship the rising, not the setting, sun."

Pompey won victory after victory. In 71 B.C.E., he claimed the credit for stopping a massive slave rebellion led by Spartacus, a fugitive gladiator who had terrorized southern Italy for two years and defeated consuls with his army of 100,000 escaped slaves. Stealing the glory from the real victor, the commander Marcus Licinius Crassus (c. 115–53 B.C.E.), Pompey demanded and won election to the consulship in 70 B.C.E., without climbing the ladder of offices or reaching the legal age of forty-two. Three years later, he received unlimited powers to eradicate the pirates infesting the Mediterranean. He smashed them in a matter of months. This success made him wildly popular with the urban poor, who depended on a steady flow of imported grain; with wealthy shippers, who depended on safe sea lanes; and with coastal communities that had suffered from the pirates' raids. Next he won the first Roman victories in the Levant and made Syria a province in 64 B.C.E., thereby ending the Seleucid kingdom and extending Rome's power to the eastern edge of the Mediterranean. He marched as far south as Jerusalem, capturing it in 63 B.C.E. Jews had lived in Rome since the second century B.C.E., but most Romans knew little about their religion; Pompey inspected the Jerusalem temple to satisfy his curiosity and remove its treasures.

Pompey's victories were so spectacular that people compared him to Alexander the Great and referred to him as *Magnus* ("the Great"). No fan of modesty, he boasted that he had increased Rome's provincial revenues by 70 percent and distributed plunder equal to twelve and a half years' pay to his soldiers. He treated foreign policy as his personal business: in the east he operated on his own and ignored the tradition of commanders consulting the Senate to decide on new political arrangements for conquered territories. For all practical purposes, he behaved abroad more like an independent king than a Roman officer. He explained his attitude when replying to some foreigners after they objected to his actions as unjust: "Stop quoting the laws to us," he told them. "We carry swords."

Fearing his power, Pompey's enemies at Rome tried to strengthen their own positions by proclaiming their concern for the common people. By the 60s B.C.E., Rome's population had soared to over half a million people. Hundreds of thousands of them lived crowded together in shabby, multistory apartment buildings no better than slums and depended on subsidized food. Work was hard to find. Danger haunted the crowded streets because the city had no police force. Even the propertied class was in trouble: Sulla's confiscations had produced a credit crunch by flooding the real estate market with properties for sale and caused land values to crash. Overextended investors were trying to borrow their way back to financial health, with no success.

Pompey's return to Rome in 62 B.C.E. lit the fuse to this political powder keg. The Senate, eager to bring "the Great" down a notch, refused to approve his arrangements in the Levant or his grants of land to his veterans. This setback forced Pompey to negotiate with his fiercest political rivals, Crassus and Julius Caesar (100–44 B.C.E.). In 60 B.C.E., these three joined in an unofficial power-sharing arrangement called the **First Triumvirate** ("coalition of three men"). Their combined power proved unstoppable: Pompey rammed through laws confirming his eastern arrangements and guaranteeing land for his troops, thus affirming his status as a generous patron; Caesar gained the consulship for 59 B.C.E. along with a special command in Gaul, allowing him to build his own client army financed with plunder; and Crassus received financial breaks for the Roman tax collectors in Asia Minor, whose support gave him political clout and in whose business he had invested.

This alliance of former political enemies shared no common philosophy of governing; its only cohesion came from personal connections. To cement his bond with Pompey, Caesar married his daughter, Julia, to Pompey in 59 B.C.E., even though she had been engaged to another man. Pompey soothed Julia's jilted fiancé by having him marry his own daughter, who had been engaged to yet somebody else. Through these marital connections, the two powerful rivals now had a common interest: the well-being of Julia, Caesar's only daughter and Pompey's new wife. (Pompey had earlier divorced his second wife after Caesar allegedly seduced her.) Pompey and Julia apparently fell deeply in love in their arranged marriage. As long as Julia lived, Pompey's affection for her restrained him from an outright break with her father.

■ Coin Portrait of Julius Caesar

Julius Caesar (100–44 B.C.E.) was the first living Roman to have his portrait appear on a Roman coin. Roman republican coinage had annually changing types—the images and words stamped on the front and back of coins—chosen by the officials in charge of minting. Tradition mandated that only persons who had died could be shown (the same rule applies to U.S. currency), but after Caesar won the civil war in 45 B.C.E., he broke that tradition, as he did many others, to show that he was Rome's supreme leader. Here, he wears the laurel wreath of a conquering general. The realistic portrait conforms to late republican style. Caesar's wrinkled neck and careworn expression emphasize the suffering he endured—and imposed on others—to reach the pinnacle of success. Do you think a portrait is more impressive if it shows the person's blemishes or if it is idealized? (Bibliothèque nationale de France.)

Caesar won the loyalty of his client army with years of victories and plunder in central and northern Gaul, which he added to the Roman provinces; he awed his troops with his daring by crossing the channel to campaign in Britain. His political enemies at Rome dreaded him even more as his military successes mounted, and the bond linking him to Pompey vanished in 54 B.C.E. when Julia died in childbirth. With Caesar's followers agitating to win the masses' support for his return to the capital, the two sides' rivalry exploded into violence. By the mid-50s B.C.E., political gangs of young men roamed the alleys of Rome in search of opponents to assault or murder. Street fighting reached such a level of violence in 53 B.C.E. that it prevented elections; no consuls could be chosen until the year was half over. The triumvirate completely dissolved that same year with the death of Crassus in battle against the Parthians at Carrhae in northern Mesopotamia. Feeling inferior to Pompey and Caesar in military glory, Crassus—without the Senate's authorization—had taken a Roman army across the Euphrates River to fight the Parthians, an Iranian people who ruled a vast territory stretching from the Euphrates to the Indus River. A year later, Caesar's enemies took the extraordinary step of having Pompey appointed sole consul. The traditions of republican government had crumbled.

When the Senate ordered Caesar to surrender his command and thus open himself to prosecution by his enemies, he led his army against Rome. As he crossed the Rubicon River, the official northern boundary of Italy, in early 49 B.C.E., he uttered the famous words signaling that he had chosen civil war: "The die is cast." His troops followed him without hesitation, and the people of Italy cheered him on enthusiastically. He had many backers in Rome, too, from the masses who looked forward to his legendary generosity and from poverty-stricken members of the elite hoping to make money through proscriptions.

The enthusiasm for Caesar led Pompey and most senators to flee to Greece to prepare to fight back. Caesar entered Rome peacefully but soon departed to defeat the army his enemies had raised in Spain; he then sailed to Greece in 48 B.C.E. There he nearly lost the war when his supplies ran out, but his soldiers remained loyal even when they were reduced to eating bread made from roots. When Pompey saw what his opponent's troops were willing to live on, he cried, "I am fighting wild beasts." Pompey's weak generalship gave Caesar a decisive victory at the battle of Pharsalus in 48 B.C.E. Pompey fled to Egypt, where the ministers of the boy-king Ptolemy XIII (63–47 B.C.E.) murdered him, mistakenly thinking this would please Caesar.

Caesar then invaded Egypt, winning a difficult campaign that ended when the young pharaoh drowned in the Nile. Caesar restored Cleopatra VII (69–30 B.C.E.) to the Egyptian throne. As intelligent as she was ruthless, Cleopatra charmed the invader into sharing her bed and supporting her rule. This attachment shocked Caesar's friends and enemies alike: they believed Rome should seize power from foreigners, not yield it to them. Still, so effective were Cleopatra's powers of persuasion that Caesar maintained the love affair and guaranteed her rule over a rich land that his army otherwise would have plundered.

By 45 B.C.E., Caesar had won the civil war but faced the problem of how to govern a shattered republic: only a strong, sole ruler seemed capable of ending the cycle of violence, but the oldest tradition of the republic's elite was its hatred of monarchy. The second-century B.C.E. senator Cato, notorious for his advice in favor of destroying Carthage, had best expressed this feeling: "A king," he said, "is an animal that feeds on human flesh." Caesar's solution was to rule as king in everything but name. First, he had himself appointed dictator in 48 B.C.E.; his term in this temporary office was extended to a lifetime tenure around 44 B.C.E. "I am not a king," he insisted, but the distinction was hard to see. As dictator, he controlled the government despite the appearance of normal procedures. Elections for offices continued, for example, but Caesar controlled the results by recommending candidates to the assemblies, which his supporters dominated. Naturally his recommendations were followed.

Caesar introduced changes that he hoped would strengthen Rome: a moderate cancellation of debts; a limitation on the number of people eligible for subsidized grain; a large program of public works, including the construction of public libraries; colonies for his veterans in Italy and abroad; the rebuilding of Corinth and Carthage as commercial centers; and a revival of the ancient policy of giving citizenship to non-Romans, such as the Cisalpine Gauls (those on the Italian side of the Alps). He also admitted non-Italians to the Senate when he expanded its membership from six hundred (the size established by Sulla) to nine hundred.

Unlike Sulla, Caesar did not proscribe his enemies. Instead he prided himself on his clemency, the recipients of which were, by Roman custom, bound to be his grateful clients. In return, he received unprecedented honors, such as a special golden seat in the Senate house and the renaming of the seventh month of the year after him (July). He also regularized the Roman calendar by having each year include 365 days, a calculation based on an ancient Egyptian calendar that formed the basis for our modern one.

His rule pleased most Romans but outraged the optimates. They resented being dominated by one of their own, a "traitor" who had deserted to the people's side. A band of senators formed a conspiracy, led by Caesar's former close friend Marcus Junius Brutus and inspired by the legend about Brutus's ancestor Lucius Junius Brutus having led the violent expulsion of Rome's original monarchy. They cut Caesar to pieces with daggers in the Senate house on March 15 (the Ides of March on the Roman calendar), 44 B.C.E. When his friend Brutus stabbed him, Caesar, according to some ancient reports, gasped his last words—in Greek: "You, too, my son?"

The "liberators," as they called themselves, had no concrete plans for reviving the republic. They apparently believed that it would automatically spring back to life, overlooking the horrible political violence of the previous forty years and the distortion of Roman values that it brought, with ambitious individuals honoring their own interests and those of their clients above those in the community. Panicked by the loss of their patron, the masses rioted at Caesar's funeral to vent their anger against the elite that had robbed them of their benefactor. Failing to form a united front, the elite resumed their feuds with one another over personal political power. By 44 B.C.E., the republic was lost beyond recovery.

■ **REVIEW:** *How did the actions and policies of individual leaders destroy the republic?*

IMPORTANT DATES			
753 B.C.E.	Traditional date of Rome's founding	**133 B.C.E.**	Tiberius Gracchus elected tribune and then assassinated
509 B.C.E.	Roman republic established	**91–87 B.C.E.**	Social War between Rome and its Italian allies
509–287 B.C.E.	Struggle of the orders		
451–449 B.C.E.	Creation of the Twelve Tables, Rome's first written law code	**60 B.C.E.**	First Triumvirate (Caesar, Pompey, and Crassus)
264–241 B.C.E.	First Punic War	**49–45 B.C.E.**	Civil war, with Caesar the victor
218–201 B.C.E.	Second Punic War	**45–44 B.C.E.**	Cicero writes his philosophical works on humanitas
168–149 B.C.E.	Cato writes *The Origins*, the first history of Rome in Latin	**44 B.C.E.**	Caesar appointed dictator for life and then assassinated
149–146 B.C.E.	Third Punic War		
146 B.C.E.	Destruction of Carthage and Corinth		

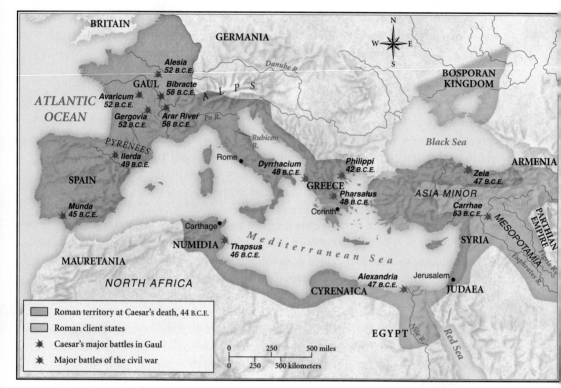

■ **MAPPING THE WEST** The Roman World at the End of the Republic, c. 44 B.C.E.

Upon Julius Caesar's assassination in 44 B.C.E., the territory that Rome would control during the coming centuries was almost complete. Caesar's young relative Octavian (the future Augustus) would conquer and add Egypt in 30 B.C.E. Geography and distance were the primary factors preventing further expansion, which Romans never stopped thinking of as desirable even when practical difficulties made this goal only a dream. The deserts of Africa and the Near East worked against expansion southward or eastward against the powerful peoples located beyond, and trackless forests and fierce resistance from local inhabitants made expansion into central Europe and the British Isles impossible to sustain.

Conclusion

From its beginnings in 509 B.C.E., Rome's republic flourished because its values stressed the common good, it incorporated outsiders, and its small farmers produced agricultural surpluses. These surpluses supported a growing population to supply soldiers for a strong army. Romans' willingness to endure tremendous losses of life and property—the proof that they valued faithfulness—helped make them unbeatable: Rome might lose battles but never wars. Because warfare brought profits, peace seemed a wasted opportunity. Elite commanders craved victories because they brought glory and riches to raise their status in Rome's social hierarchy.

The long wars against Carthage, Macedonia, and Greece, however, had unexpected and harmful consequences. In ways still hard to determine, they created a shortage of farmland for Italy's rural poor. When landless people flocked to Rome, they created an unstable political force: the urban mob demanding subsidized food. Members of the elite upped their competition with each other for the increased career opportunities presented by constant war. These rivalries became unmanageable when successful generals began to extort advantages for themselves by acting as patrons to their client armies of poor troops. In this hypercompetitive environment, force became the preferred means of settling political disputes. But violent actions provoked violent responses; community values were drowned in the blood of civil war. No reasonable Roman could have been optimistic about the chances for an enduring peace in the aftermath of Caesar's assassination in 44 B.C.E. That another "great man" would forge such a peace less than fifteen years later would have seemed an impossible dream.

■ **MAKING CONNECTIONS**

1. Compare the political and social values of the Roman republic with those of the Classical Greek city-state.

2. What were the positive and negative consequences of war for the Roman republic?

■ **FOR FURTHER EXPLORATION**

For further reading and online research ideas, see the Suggested References on page SR-2 at the back of the book.

For practice quizzes, a customized study plan, and other study tools, see the ONLINE STUDY GUIDE at bedfordstmartins.com/huntconcise.

For primary-source material from this period, see Chapter 4 in *Sources of THE MAKING OF THE WEST: A CONCISE HISTORY*, Second Edition.

The Roman Empire

c. 44 B.C.E.–284 C.E.

I N 203 C.E., VIBIA PERPETUA, wealthy and twenty-two years old, nursed her infant in a Carthage jail while awaiting execution. She had received a death sentence for refusing to offer a sacrifice to the gods for the Roman emperor's health and safety. One morning, the jailer dragged her off to the city's main square, where a crowd gathered. Perpetua described in her journal what happened next when the local governor attempted to persuade her to save her life:

> My father came carrying my son, crying "Perform the sacrifice; take pity on your baby!" Then the governor pleaded, "Think of your old father; show pity for your little child! Offer the sacrifice for the health of the emperor's family." "I refuse," I answered. "Are you a Christian?" asked the governor. "Yes." When my father would not stop trying to change my mind, the governor ordered him thrown to the ground and whipped with a rod. I felt sorry for my father; it seemed they were beating me. I pitied his pathetic old age.

Nevertheless, she did not give in. Later, gored by a bull and stabbed by a gladiator, she died still proclaiming her faith.

■ **Executing a Criminal in Public**
This mosaic shows a convicted criminal being killed by a leopard at a public execution. Romans believed that serious criminals deserved disgraceful deaths before crowds of spectators. Martyrs charged with treason, like Perpetua, often were executed by "being condemned to the beasts." Here the prisoner is tied to a stake on a chariot so the handlers can push him into the face of the leopard to provoke an angry leap; wild animals frequently would not attack without such provocation. Dated to about Perpetua's time, c. 200 C.E., the mosaic covered a villa floor in North Africa in what is today Libya. The villa's owner perhaps ordered this subject for his floor to show visitors that he had paid for the expensive spectacle that included this grisly execution. (© Roger Wood/Corbis.)

The clash of traditional Roman values of faithfulness and loyalty doomed Perpetua: she believed that her faith in Christ required her to refuse the state's demand for loyalty to the "way of the elders" in public religion and her father's pleas to preserve her family. Her refusal to observe traditional values in traditional ways echoed the refusal of ambitious Roman commanders in the late republic to value the community's interests over their own private ambitions. The civil wars they fought ended the republic. A bloodbath followed Julius Caesar's assassination in 44 B.C.E.: seventeen more years of Roman fighting Roman. Augustus (63 B.C.E.–14 C.E.) finally restored peace in 27 B.C.E. by inventing a special kind of monarchy—the **principate**—that claimed to restore traditional values. His new political and social system opened the pivotal period in Western civilization known to us as the Roman Empire.

Augustus disguised his government as a restoration of the republic so that he could seem to satisfy the Roman elite's insistence of maintaining the tradition of shared political decision making. He retained old institutions—the Senate, the consuls and other officials, the courts—while reshaping political power by making himself a sole ruler who was not called a king. He masked his monarchy by taking the title "first man" (*princeps*, hence the term *principate* for his new system of government), a traditional honorary title for the leading senator. Princeps was therefore the actual title for the ruler today we call "the Roman emperor" (from Latin *imperator*, "commander").

The principate transformed Rome into a disguised monarchy with a fundamental weakness: since the ruler was officially not a king, he could not automatically pass on his rule to a son as his successor and legitimate ruler. In traditional, acknowledged monarchies, the king's son inherited his father's position and political legitimacy. Augustus had to create a new process to try to ensure a peaceful succession that everyone would regard as legitimate: the princeps would train a successor to be approved by the Senate. If that approved successor just happened to be the princeps's son, so be it. This new system of government brought stability for two hundred years, except during a few brief struggles over who, with the Senate's approval, should become the next princeps. This stability came at a price: since Augustus's successors did not have automatic, inherited legitimacy as rulers, they were always quick to try to suppress any sign of disloyalty or rebellion. Perpetua's refusal to sacrifice, for example, was considered treason and impiety, which was punishable by death because it disrespected the princeps and angered the gods, thereby threatening the safety of the entire community.

Romans welcomed the principate's peacefulness, which historians call the **Pax Romana** ("Roman peace"). In the third century C.E., however, rivalry over the succession reignited civil war, leading to economic crisis. By the 280s, Roman imperial government again desperately needed to transform its political system to restore traditional values of loyalty and public service. Diocletian, a military commander from the provinces, would begin that process by winning rule over the Roman world in 284 C.E.

Creating "Roman Peace"

Inventing tradition takes time. Augustus developed his new political system gradually; as the biographer Suetonius (c. 70–130) expressed it, Augustus "made haste slowly." The principate produced an extended period of peace, although its rulers periodically fought to expand imperial territory, suppress rebellions, and repel invaders. Augustus succeeded in reinventing monarchy as an effective form of Roman government because he won the civil war and, during his long rule, found new ways to inspire loyalty by promoting an image of himself as a dedicated leader.

From Republic to Principate, 44–27 B.C.E.

The principate was born in blood. Julius Caesar's assassination in 44 B.C.E. set off another civil war between generals. The leading opponents were Mark Antony and Octavian (the future Augustus), Caesar's eighteen-year-old grandnephew, who by Caesar's will became his adopted son and heir. Despite his limited military experience, Octavian won the loyalty of Caesar's soldiers by taking his new father's name and promising them rewards from their murdered general's wealth. Marching these veterans to Rome, in 43 B.C.E. the teenager forced his election as consul without, like Pompey before him, ever having been elected to any post on the ladder of offices.

Octavian, Antony, and a general named Lepidus then joined forces to eliminate rivals, especially Caesar's assassins. In late 43 B.C.E., the three formed the so-called Second Triumvirate, which they forced the Senate to recognize as an official emergency panel for "rebuilding the state." With no checks on their power, they began to murder their enemies and confiscate their property. Octavian and Antony soon forced Lepidus into retirement and, too ambitious to cooperate, began civil war with each other.

Antony made the eastern Mediterranean his base, joining forces with Cleopatra VII (69–30 B.C.E.), the Ptolemaic queen of Egypt who had earlier allied with Caesar. Enchanted by Cleopatra's wit and intelligence, Antony became her ally and lover. Skillfully playing on Romans' fear of foreign attack, Octavian rallied support by claiming that Antony planned to make Cleopatra queen of Rome. He persuaded the residents of Italy and the western provinces to swear a personal oath of loyalty to him, making them all his clients. Octavian's victory at the naval battle of Actium in northwest Greece in 31 B.C.E. won the war (see Map 5.1). Cleopatra and Antony fled to Egypt, where they both committed suicide in 30 B.C.E., choosing their own deaths to rob their enemy of celebrity hostages. The general first stabbed himself, bleeding to death in his lover's embrace. The queen then ended her life by letting a poisonous snake, a symbol of Egyptian royal authority, bite her. Octavian's capture of Egypt made him Rome's richest citizen and its unrivaled leader.

Augustus's "Restoration," 27 B.C.E.–14 C.E.

After distributing land to his soldiers and creating colonies in the provinces, Octavian announced in 27 B.C.E. that he had restored the republic. It was now, he proclaimed, the duty of the Senate and the Roman people to preserve it. Awed by Octavian's power, the Senate begged him to do whatever was necessary to safeguard the restored republic, granted him special civil and military powers, and gave him the honorary name **Augustus**, meaning "favored by the gods." Octavian had considered changing his name to Romulus, after Rome's legendary first king, but as the historian Cassius Dio (c. 164–230) later wrote, "When he realized people thought this idea meant he wanted to be their king, he accepted the other title instead, as if he were more than human; for everything that is most treasured and sacred is called *augustus*."

■ Priests on the Altar of Augustan Peace

After four years of construction, Augustus dedicated the Altar of Augustan Peace in northwest Rome on his wife's birthday in 9 B.C.E. The altar stood inside four walls measuring about thirty-four feet long, thirty-eight feet wide, and twenty-three feet high and was open to the sky. Relief sculptures covered the walls. This section shows a religious procession. The figures wearing leather caps with spikes are priests called flamines, who had to wear this headgear whenever they went outside; the man holding a staff is their attendant. The hooded man at the right is probably Marcus Agrippa, Augustus's greatest general. The laurel wreaths worn on bare heads signify both religious devotion and victory; as Augustus commented in his Res Gestae ("Accomplishments") 13, "Peace was achieved through victories." The altar can be seen today in its original form because it was reconstructed by Benito Mussolini, Fascist dictator of Italy from 1926 to 1943, who wanted to associate his regime with Augustus's glory. (Scala/Art Resource, NY.)

In the years following 27 B.C.E., Augustus maintained the appearance of republican government by continuing the annual election of consuls and other officials, the passing of legislation in public assemblies, and respect for the Senate. He served several times as consul, the republic's premier official. To preserve the tradition that no official should hold more than one post at a time, he had the Senate grant him the powers of a tribune without his holding the office. He possessed the authority to act and to compel citizens as if he were a tribune protecting the rights of the people, but he left the posts open for members of the plebeian elite to occupy, as they had done under the republic. Augustus also kept his own appearance "republican" instead of royal: he dressed and acted like a regular citizen, not an aloof king.

Augustus's taking *princeps* as his only title of office was a cleverly calculated move. In the republic, the "first man" had guided Rome because of the respect (***auctoritas***) he had earned; he had no more formal power (*potestas*) than any other leader. By choosing the title *princeps*, Augustus appeared to carry on this valued tradition, but in fact he revised the basic power structure. Previously, no one could have exercised the powers of both consul and tribune simultaneously. The reality of the principate was that it was a monarchy masked as a restored and improved republic, headed by an emperor cloaked as the princeps.

Augustus and his successors exercised supreme power because they controlled the army and the treasury. Augustus made the military the basis for his moral authority as restorer of the republic by turning the republican army—a part-time militia—into a full-time professional force. He completed the transformation of the princeps into the troops' patron by establishing set lengths of service, regular pay, and substantial benefits upon retirement. To cover the added costs, Augustus imposed an inheritance tax on citizens. The rich hated this innovation, but the grateful army obeyed and protected the emperor. Another change Augustus made was to station soldiers—the **praetorian guard**—in Rome itself for the first time. These troops prevented rebellion in the capital and provided an imperial bodyguard, a visible reminder of the emperor's dominance.

To broadcast the political legitimacy he claimed, Augustus communicated his image as protector and patron using objects from coins to buildings. As the only mass-produced source of official messages, coins functioned like modern political advertising. They proclaimed slogans such as "Father of his Country" to remind Romans of their emperor's moral authority over them, or "Roads have been built" to emphasize his personal generosity in paying for highway construction.

To fulfill the tradition that rich politicians and generals should spend money for the public good, Augustus erected huge buildings in Rome paid for by the fortune he had inherited from Caesar and then increased in war. The huge Forum of Augustus best illustrates his skill at communicating through bricks and stone (Figure 5.1). Its plaza centered on a temple to Mars, the Roman god of war. Two-story colonnades stretched out from the temple like wings, sheltering statues of famous Roman heroes as inspirations to future leaders. Augustus's Forum provided gathering space for religious rituals

Temple of Mars Ultor Colonnades (porches)   Statues of
                      lined with columns   Roman heroes

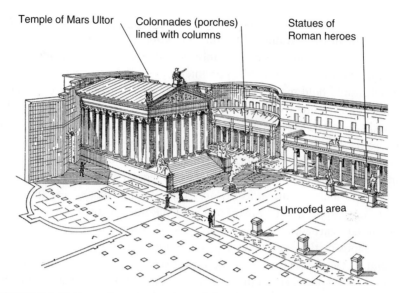

Unroofed area

■ **FIGURE 5.1 Cutaway Reconstruction of the Forum of Augustus**
Augustus built this large forum (120 × 90 yards) to commemorate his victory over the assassins of his adoptive father, Julius Caesar. Dedicated in 2 B.C.E., its centerpiece was a marble temple dedicated to the god Mars Ultor ("The Avenger"). Inside the temple he placed statues of Mars, Venus (the divine ancestor of Julius Caesar), and Julius Caesar (as a god), as well as Caesar's sword and works of art. The two curved spaces flanking the temple featured statues of Aeneas and Romulus, Rome's founders. The porches stretching along the open courtyard housed other statues of Roman heroes. The ceremony marking teenaged boys' passage into adulthood took place here, where they were surrounded by images of the valorous and glorious men whom they were expected to imitate.

and ceremonies marking the passage into adulthood of upper-class boys, but it also stressed the themes Augustus wanted to communicate about his new system: peace restored through victory, the foundation of a new age, devotion to the gods who led Rome to victory, respect for tradition, and unselfishness in spending money for the community. These messages communicated Augustus's justification for his rule.

Augustus never revealed his deepest motives in establishing the principate. Was he a cynical tyrant working to destroy the freedoms of the republic? Did he have no choice but to impose a disguised monarchy to reunite a society ripped apart by civil war? Or did his motives lie somewhere in between? Perhaps it is best to see him as a revolutionary bound by tradition. His problem had been the one always facing Roman politicians—how to balance his own personal ambitions, the need for peace, and Rome's tradition of shared rule. Augustus's goals were stability, order, and legitimacy for his system, not political freedom for citizens; his strategy was to employ traditional values to justify changes, as in his reinventing the meaning of the title "first man." Above all, he extended the patron-client system to politics by making the emperor everyone's most important patron, possessing the moral authority to guide the lives of all. This process reached its peak when the Senate proclaimed him "Father of his Country" in 2 B.C.E. Declaring that this title was the greatest honor Rome could grant, he treasured it because it agreed with his image of himself as princeps: a leader governing Romans like a father, stern but caring, requiring obedience and loyalty from his children but dedicated to taking care of them in return.

Despite frequent illnesses, Augustus ruled until he died at age seventy-five in 14 C.E. The length of his rule—forty-one years—gave his innovations time to become traditions. As the Roman historian Tacitus (c. 56–120) remarked, by the time Augustus died, "almost no one was still alive who had seen the republic." Augustus transformed republican Rome into imperial Rome by his long life, his military and financial innovations, his care for the capital's poor people, and his manipulation of the traditional vocabulary of politics to disguise his power and proclaim his legitimacy.

Life in Augustan Rome

A crucial factor in Augustus's success was trying to better the lives of ordinary people. Their problems were most serious in Rome. Archaeology and literature let us sketch a picture of life in Augustus's Rome. Although some of the sources refer to times after Augustus and to cities other than the capital, they nevertheless help us understand this period; economic and social conditions were essentially the same in all larger cities throughout the early centuries of the empire.

The population of Augustan Rome—probably far over half a million—was vast for the ancient world. Indeed, no European city would have nearly as many people again until London in the 1700s. The streets were packed: "One man jabs me with his elbow, another whacks me with a pole; my legs are smeared with mud, and from all sides big feet step on me" was the poet Juvenal's description of walking in Rome in the early second century C.E. To ease congestion in the narrow streets, wagon traffic was banned in the daytime. This regulation made nights noisy with the creaking of axles and the shouting of drivers caught in traffic jams.

Most urban residents lived in small apartments in multistoried buildings called islands (so named because originally each building had an open strip around it). Outnumbering private houses by more than twenty to one, apartment buildings usually housed shops, bars, and simple restaurants on the first floor. Graffiti—political endorsements, personal insults, advertising, messages of all kinds—covered many outside walls. The higher the floor, the cheaper were the apartments; the poorest people lived on the top floors in single rooms that they rented by the day. Aqueducts delivered fresh water to public fountains, but because apartments had no plumbing, residents had to lug buckets up the stairs. The wealthy few had piped-in water at ground level. Most tenants lacked bathrooms and had to use public latrines or pots for toilets at home. Some buildings had cesspits, or buckets could be carried down to the streets to be emptied by people who made their living collecting excrement. Lazy tenants flung the foul-smelling contents of these containers out the window.

Because the city generated about sixty tons of human waste every day, sanitation presented an ongoing problem that Roman officials constantly worked to overcome. By 33 B.C.E., Augustus's general Marcus Agrippa had improved the city's main sewer, but its untreated contents emptied directly into the Tiber River, which ran through the city. The technology for sanitary disposal of waste simply did not exist. People sometimes left human and animal corpses in the streets, to be gnawed by vultures and dogs until the city's officials had them removed. The poor were not the only people affected by such conditions: a stray mutt once brought a human hand to the table where Vespasian, who would be emperor from 69 to 79, was eating lunch. Flies buzzing everywhere and a lack of mechanical refrigeration contributed to frequent digestive illness: the most popular jewelry of the time was supposed to ward off stomach trouble. Although the wealthy could not eliminate such discomforts, they made their lives more pleasant with luxuries such as snow rushed from the mountains to ice their drinks and slaves to clean their houses, which were built around courtyards and gardens to let in air and sunshine.

Public baths helped residents keep clean. Because admission fees were low, almost everyone could afford to go daily. Many baths dotted the city, serving like modern health clubs as centers for exercising and socializing as well as washing. Bathers progressed through a series of increasingly warm, humid areas until they reached a sauna-like room. They swam naked in their choice of hot or cold pools. Women went to the public baths, but the genders bathed apart, either in separate rooms or at different times of the day. Since bathing was thought to help sick people but doctors did not yet understand the danger of infections, the untreated pools could spread disease.

City residents faced hazards beyond infectious disease. Tenants routinely threw broken dishes and other trash out their apartment windows, to fall like missiles onto the streets below. "If you are walking to a dinner party in Rome," Juvenal warned, "you would be foolish not to make out your will first. For every open window is a source of potential disaster." The apartment buildings could also be dangerous because they sometimes collapsed. Roman engineers, despite their skill in using concrete, brick, and stone as building materials, lacked the technology to calculate precisely how much weight their constructions could stand. Builders trying to cut costs paid little attention to engineering safeguards in any case. Augustus upgraded public safety by imposing a height limit of seventy feet on new apartment buildings. Fire presented the greatest risk; one of Augustus's most important innovations to improve people's lives was to provide Rome with the first public fire department in Western history. He also established the first permanent police force, despite his fondness for stopping to watch the fistfights that often broke out in Rome's crowded streets.

Many city dwellers had too little to eat and few chances for jobs. Augustus aided them by guaranteeing an adequate food supply. This service was his responsibility as Rome's supreme patron, and he freely drew upon his personal fortune to pay for

■ **Downtown Street in Herculaneum**

Like Pompeii, the prosperous town of Herculaneum on the shore of the Bay of Naples was frozen in time by the massive eruption of the neighboring volcano, Mount Vesuvius, in 79 C.E. A flood of mud from the eruption buried the town and preserved its buildings until they were excavated beginning in the eighteenth century. Typical of a Roman town, it had straight roads paved with large, flat stones and flanked by sidewalks. Balconies jutted from the upper stories of houses, offering residents a shady viewing point for the lively traffic in the urban streets. Instead of having yards in front or back, houses often enclosed a garden courtyard that was open to the sky. Why do you think urban homes were arranged in this way? (Scala/Art Resource, NY.)

imported grain. Distributing grain at public expense to the capital's poor citizens had been a tradition for decades, but Augustus's welfare system reached the unprecedented size of 250,000 recipients, plus their families. This statistic suggests that between 600,000 and 700,000 people depended on the government for food to survive. Poor Romans usually boiled this grain to make a sticky soup, which they washed down with cheap wine. If they were lucky, they might have some beans, onions, or cheese on the side. The rich, as we learn from an ancient cookbook, ate costlier foods, such as roast pork or shellfish, served very spicy with pepper, a salty condiment, or sweet-and-sour sauce made from honey and vinegar.

By Augustus's time, many wealthy Romans were spending more money on luxuries and costly political careers than on raising children. Fearing that this decline in the birthrate would destroy the elite on which Rome relied for leadership, Augustus passed laws to strengthen marriage and encourage larger families by granting special legal privileges to the parents of three or more children. He made adultery a crime. So seriously did Augustus back these reforms that he exiled his own daughter—his only child—and a granddaughter for sex scandals. His laws had little effect, however, and the old elite families dwindled over the coming centuries. Recent research suggests that up to three-fourths of senatorial-rank families lost their official status (by losing the wealth required for that designation) or died out every generation. Equestrians and men from the provinces who won the ruler's favor took their places in the social hierarchy and in the Senate.

Slaves occupied the lowest rung in society's hierarchy. Unlike Greece, however, Rome gave citizenship to freed slaves, a policy meaning, over the long term, that many Romans were the descendants of slaves. All slaves could hope to acquire the rights of a free citizen, and their descendants, if they became wealthy, could become members of the social elite. This possibility gave slaves reason to work harder and cooperate with their masters. Conditions of slavery varied widely according to occupation. Slaves in agriculture and manufacturing had harsh lives. Most such workers were men, although women might assist the foremen who managed gangs of rural laborers. The second-century novelist Apuleius wrote this grim description of slaves at work in a flour mill: "Through the holes in their ragged clothes you could see scars from whippings all over their bodies. Some wore only loincloths. Letters had been branded on their foreheads and shackles bound their ankles." Worse than the mills were the mines, where the foremen constantly flogged the miners to keep them digging out metal ores in dangerous conditions.

Household slaves had an easier physical existence. Most Romans owned slaves to work in their homes, from one or two in modestly well-off families to large numbers in rich houses and, above all, the imperial palace. Domestic slaves were often women, working as nurses, maids, kitchen help, and clothes makers. Some male slaves ran businesses for their masters, and, to encourage them to work hard, they were allowed to keep part of the profits to save toward purchasing their freedom someday. Women had less opportunity to earn money. Masters sometimes granted tips for sexual favors, and female prostitutes (many of whom were slaves) could earn money for themselves. Slaves who managed to earn money would sometimes buy slaves themselves, thereby creating their own hierarchy. A male slave might buy a woman for a mate. They could then have an imitation of normal family life, though a legal marriage was impossible because they remained their master's property, as did their children. If truly fortunate, slaves could slowly accumulate enough to buy themselves from their masters or could be freed by their masters' wills. Some inscriptions on tombs testify to masters' affectionate feelings for slaves, but even household servants had to endure violent treatment if their masters were cruel. If they attacked their owners because of brutal treatment, the punishment was death.

While slaves always faced potential violence, actual violence was common in Roman public entertainment. The emperors regularly provided mass spectacles featuring hunters killing fierce beasts, wild African animals such as lions mangling condemned criminals, mock naval battles in flooded arenas, gladiatorial combats, and chariot races. Spectators jammed stadiums for these shows, seated according to their social rank and gender following an Augustan law; the emperor and senators sat close to the action, while women and the poor sat in the upper tiers. These spectacles communicated a political message claiming legitimacy for the new system of government by showing that the emperors were generous in providing expensive entertainment for their subjects, powerful enough to command life-and-death exhibitions, and dedicated to preserving the social hierarchy.

Gladiators were men and, rarely, women, who underwent long and expensive training; war captives, criminals, slaves, and free volunteers performed as gladiators. Gladiatorial combats, which originated under the republic as part of the ceremony at extravagant funerals, became so popular under Augustus that they attracted crowds in the tens of thousands. Gladiatorial fights were bloody but usually fought to the death only for captives and criminals; professional fighters could have extended careers. To make the fights more exciting, gladiators used a variety of weapons. One favorite bout pitted a lightly armored fighter, called a net man because he used a net and a trident, against a more heavily armored fish man, so named from the design of his helmet crest. Betting was a great attraction, and spectators could be rowdy. As the Christian theologian Tertullian (c. 160–240) complained: "Look at the mob coming to the show—already they're out of their minds! Aggressive, mindless, already in an uproar about their bets! They all share the same suspense, the same madness, the same voice."

Champion gladiators won riches and celebrity but not social respectability. Early in the first century C.E., the senators became alarmed at what they regarded as the disgrace caused by members of the upper class fighting as gladiators. They therefore banned the elite and all freeborn women under twenty from appearing in gladiatorial shows. Daughters trained by their gladiator fathers had first competed during the republic, and women continued to compete until the emperor Septimius Severus (r. 193–211) banned them.

Gladiatorial shows, chariot races, and theater productions became an opportunity for ordinary citizens to express their feelings on civic conditions to the emperors, who were expected to attend. On more than one occasion, for example, poorer Romans rioted at shows to protest a shortfall in the free grain supply. In this way, public entertainment served as a two-way form of communication between ruler and ruled.

■ **Gladiators Sculpted on a Tomb**

This relief sculpture, which adorned a tomb near Rome dating to about 30–10 B.C.E., shows gladiators competing in games held to honor the deceased. Gladiatorial combats originated as part of funeral ceremonies because they portrayed with dramatic energy the violent and inevitable struggle to avoid death. Only the very wealthy could afford to have gladiators perform at their funerals or in spectacles meant to win the people's favor. These gladiators represent a traditional form of fighting called provocator ("challenger"). A challenger, who fought gladiators only of the same type, used a short sword, a curved shield, a metal belt cinching up a loincloth, forearm and lower-leg guards, a partial chest protector, and a plumed helmet. These men's muscular bodies show the great strength required to be a successful fighter. (© Alinari/Art Resource, NY.)

Art and Literature to Please the Emperor

Elite culture changed under Augustus to serve the same goal as public entertainment: to express the legitimacy of his transformed system of government. In particular, oratory—the highest attainment of Roman education—lost its bite. Under the republic, rhetorical skill in making stinging speeches to criticize political opponents had been such a powerful weapon that it could catapult a "new man" like Cicero, who lacked social and military distinction, to international fame. Under the principate, the emperor's supremacy ruled out freewheeling debate and open decision making; political criticism was now out of bounds. Speakers now turned their rhetorical skills to praising the emperor at public festivals meant to advance his image as a competent, compassionate, and legitimate ruler.

Education for oratory remained a privilege of wealthy men. Rome had no free public schools, so the poor had to get basic learning from their parents. Most people had time only for training in practical skills. A character in *Satyricon*, a satirical literary work of the first century by Petronius, expressed this hardheaded attitude toward education: "I didn't study geometry and literary criticism and worthless junk like that. I just learned how to read the letters on signs and how to work out percentages, and I learned weights, measures, and the values of the different kinds of coins."

Although Roman tradition called for mothers to teach children right from wrong, servants usually looked after the offspring of rich families. These children attended private elementary schools from age seven to eleven to learn reading, writing, and basic arithmetic. Teachers used rote methods in the classroom and physical punishment for mistakes. Some children went on to the next three years of school, in which they were introduced to literature, history, and grammar. Only a few boys then proceeded to the study of oratory.

Advanced studies for men covered literature, history, ethical philosophy, law, and dialectic (reasoned argument). Mathematics and science were rarely studied as separate subjects, but engineers and architects learned to calculate. Much reading was done aloud. The rich owned educated slaves who would read to them. Books consisted of continuous scrolls made from papyrus or animal skin, not bound pages.

So much new literature emerged at this time that modern scholars call Augustus's reign the Golden Age of Latin literature. The emperor himself composed verse and prose and served as the patron of a circle of writers and artists. His favorites were Horace (65–8 B.C.E.) and Virgil (70–19 B.C.E.). Horace delighted audiences with the rhythms and wit of his short poems on public and private subjects. His poem celebrating Augustus's victory over Antony and Cleopatra at Actium became famous for its opening line, "Now it's time to drink!"

Virgil later became the most popular poet of Augustus's time for his epic poem, the *Aeneid*, in which he mixed praise and subtle criticism of Augustus. Virgil took great pains with his poem, and it remained unfinished at his death. He wanted it burned, but Augustus preserved it. Inspired by Homer's *Iliad* and *Odyssey*, the *Aeneid* told the legend of the Trojan Aeneas, the most distant ancestor of the Romans. Virgil mixed his praise of the principate with recognition of the pain that success required. The *Aeneid* therefore spoke to the complex mix of gain and loss that followed Augustus's transformation of politics and society. Above all, it expressed a moral code for all Romans: no matter how tempting the emotional pull of revenge and pride, be merciful to the conquered but destroy the arrogant.

Authors had to be careful not to anger the ruler. Livy (54 B.C.E.–17 C.E.) composed a lengthy history of Rome in which he recorded the ruthless actions of Augustus and his supporters. The emperor was unhappy, but he did not punish Livy because his history did explain that success and stability depended on traditional values of loyalty and self-sacrifice. Ovid (43 B.C.E.–17 C.E.) was punished. In his poems *Art of Love* and *Love Affairs*, he mocked the emperor's laws on marriage and adultery with tongue-in-cheek tips for conducting secret love affairs and picking up other men's wives at festivals. His *Metamorphoses* ("Transformations") undermined the idea of hierarchy as natural by telling bizarre stories of supernatural shape changes, with people becoming animals and confusion between the human and the divine. In 8 C.E., Augustus exiled Ovid to a bleak town on the Black Sea after the poet became mixed up in a scandal involving the emperor's granddaughter.

■ **Marble Statue of Augustus from Prima Porta**

At six feet eight inches high, this statue stood a foot taller than its subject, Augustus, Rome's first emperor. Found at his wife's country villa at Prima Porta ("First Gate") just outside the capital, the statue was probably a copy of a bronze original sculpted about 20 B.C.E., when Augustus was in his early forties. The sculptor showed him as a younger man, using the idealizing techniques of Greek art of the fifth and fourth centuries B.C.E. to emphasize the emperor's dignity. The sculpture is crowded with symbols that express the image of Augustus that he wanted to communicate. His bare feet hint that he is a near-divine hero, and the statue of Cupid refers to the Julian family's descent from the goddess Venus. The carving on the breastplate shows a Parthian surrendering to a Roman soldier under the gaze of personified cosmic forces basking in the peace of Augustus's reign. **For more help analyzing this image**, *see the visual activity for this chapter in the* ONLINE STUDY GUIDE *at* bedfordstmartins.com/huntconcise.

(Scala/Art Resource, NY.)

The style of public sculpture clearly reflected the emperor's wishes. When Augustus was growing up, portraits were starkly realistic, portraying the strain of human experience. The sculpture that Augustus ordered displayed a more idealized style, recalling classical Greek portraiture. In famous works of art such as the *Prima Porta* ("First Gate") statue of himself or the sculpted frieze on his Altar of Peace (finished in 9 B.C.E.), Augustus had himself portrayed as serene and dignified, not careworn and sick as he often was. As with his monumental architecture, Augustus used sculpture to project a calm and competent image of himself as "restorer of the world" and founder of a new age for Rome.

■ **REVIEW:** *How did Augustus bring peace to Rome and transform its political system?*

Maintaining "Roman Peace"

A serious problem confronted Augustus's "restored republic": how to prevent the violent struggles for power that ruined the republic. His solution was to train an heir to take over as princeps at his death after receiving the Senate's approval and the same powers conferred on Augustus. This strategy kept the throne in his family, called the Julio-Claudians, until the death of Nero in 68, and it established the tradition that family dynasties ruled imperial Rome.

Under Augustus's system, the ruler's goals were building loyalty, preventing unrest, and financing the administration while governing a vast territory of diverse provinces. Augustus set a pattern for effective rule that some of his successors followed more successfully than others: taking special care of the army, communicating the image of the princeps as a just and generous ruler, and promoting Roman law and culture as universal standards while allowing as much local freedom in the provinces as possible. The citizens, in return for their loyalty, expected the emperors to be generous patrons, but the difficulties of long-range communication imposed practical limits on the government's intervention in the lives of the empire's residents, for better or worse.

Making Monarchy Permanent, 14–180 C.E.

Augustus wanted to make monarchy the permanent government to avoid civil war, but he needed the Senate's cooperation to give legitimacy to what he called his restoration of the republic. During the 20s B.C.E., he began looking for a male relative to name as his heir (he had no son), but one after another the young men he chose died before he did. Finally, in 4 C.E., he adopted someone who would outlive him, his stepson Tiberius (42 B.C.E.–37 C.E.). Because Tiberius had a fine record as a general, the army supported recommending him to the Senate as the next "first man." The senators approved Tiberius in this role after Augustus died in 14 C.E.; the Julio-Claudian dynasty thus began.

Tiberius's sour personality made him unpopular, but he ruled for twenty-three years (r. 14–37) because he had the most important qualification for succeeding as princeps: the army's loyalty. His long reign provided the stable transition period that the principate needed to establish the compromise between the elite and the emperor that made the monarchy workable. On the one hand, the traditional offices of consul, senator, and others continued, filled by the elite; on the other hand, the emperor decided who held office and determined law and policy. In doing this, everyone claimed that the government was still a republic.

Tiberius's reign also revealed the problems that an unhappy emperor could create. Tiberius paid a steep personal price for becoming "first man" because, to strengthen their family ties, Augustus had forced him to divorce his beloved wife Vipsania and marry Augustus's daughter, Julia. This marriage became a disaster. Tiberius's unhappiness and fear of rivals led him to spend the last decade of his rule away from Rome as a recluse on an island. His withdrawal from governing opened the way for abuses by his officials in Rome and kept him from training his successor.

Tiberius named Gaius (12–41), better known as Caligula, to be the next princeps because he was Augustus's great-grandson, despite Caligula's lack of the personal qualities and training that a worthy ruler needed. Still, the young emperor

(r. 37–41) might have been successful because he knew about soldiering. *Caligula* means "baby boots." Soldiers gave him that nickname as a child because he wore little leather shoes like theirs while growing up in the military bases his father commanded. Unfortunately, he paid attention only to his personal desires. Ruling through cruelty and violence, Caligula drained the treasury to humor his whims. Suetonius labeled him a "monster." He frequently outraged the elite by fighting mock gladiatorial combats and appearing in public in women's clothing or costumes imitating gods. Two praetorian guard commanders murdered him in 41 to avenge personal insults.

After Caligula's assassination, the Senate debated the possibility of refusing to choose a new "first man" and restoring a true republic. They gave in, however, when Claudius (r. 41–54), Augustus's grandnephew and Caligula's uncle, bought the praetorian guard's support with money and the soldiers threatened the senators. Claudius becoming princeps by threat of force made it clear that the genuine republic would never return because the soldiers would always insist on having an emperor—a patron—to promote their interests. Claudius won wider support for his rule by making men from Gaul (today France), a province outside Italy, members of the Senate. This change signaled that provincial elites would be the emperor's partners in governing. In return for their help in keeping their regions peaceful and prosperous, they received offices at Rome and the emperor as patron. Claudius also changed imperial government by employing freed slaves as top administrators. Because these men owed their positions to the emperor, they could be expected to be loyal.

Nero (r. 54–68) succeeded Claudius, whom his mother probably poisoned. Only sixteen when he became "first man," Nero loved music and theater, not governing. The spectacular public festivals he sponsored and the cash he distributed to the poor in Rome kept him popular with the masses. A giant fire in 64 (the incident that led to the legend of Nero "fiddling while Rome burned") made the elite suspect that he had ordered the blaze to clear space for an enormous new palace. Nero outraged the senators by making them attend his singing performances and by bankrupting the treasury to pay for his building project and a trip to sing all over Greece. He raised money by faking charges of treason against senators and equestrians to seize their property. When military commanders in the provinces rebelled at his abuses, he had a servant help him cut his own throat, after wailing, "To die! And such a great performer!"

A year of civil war followed in 69; four generals warred to become princeps in this "Year of the Four Emperors." Vespasian (r. 69–79) won and began the dynasty of the Flavian family. The new emperor took two steps to minimize resistance. First, he had the Senate publicly recognize him as "first man" even though he was not a Julio-Claudian. Second, he encouraged the spread of the imperial cult (worship of the emperor as a living god and sacrifices for the welfare of the emperor's household) in the provinces outside Italy, where most of the empire's population lived.

In promoting emperor worship, Vespasian was building on local traditions. In the eastern provinces, the Hellenistic kingdoms had long before established the tradition of worshiping royalty; provincials there had treated Augustus as a living god. The imperial cult communicated the same image of the emperor to people in the provinces as Rome's architecture and sculpture did to people in the city: he was larger than life, deserved loyalty, and provided aid and gifts as a patron. Because emperor worship was already well established in Greece and the ancient Near East, Vespasian concentrated on spreading it in the provinces of Spain, southern France, and North Africa. Italy, however, still had no temples to the living emperor. Traditional Romans looked down on the imperial cult as a provincial tradition. Vespasian, known for his wit, even muttered as he lay dying in 79, "Oh me! I think I'm becoming a god."

Vespasian's sons Titus (r. 79–81) and Domitian (r. 81–96) strengthened the principate with hardheaded financial policy, professional administration, and high-profile, preemptive military campaigns on the frontiers. Titus sent relief to the populations of Pompeii and Herculaneum after a giant volcanic eruption of Mount Vesuvius buried their towns in 79, and he provided a fifty-thousand seat stadium for public entertainments by finishing Rome's **Colosseum**, built on arches and out-fitted with giant awnings to shade the crowd. This multistory amphitheater was deliberately constructed on the site of the former fish pond in Nero's Golden House to demonstrate the public-spiritedness of the new Flavian dynasty. Domitian balanced the budget and led the army north to hold the line against Germanic tribes threatening the empire's frontier regions along the Rhine and Danube Rivers—an area of wars for centuries to come.

Domitian handled his success poorly, and his arrogance inspired hatred among the senators, to whom he once sent a letter announcing, "Our lord god, myself, orders you to do this." Embittered by the rebellion of a general in Germany, he executed numerous upper-class citizens as conspirators. From fear Domitian would kill them, his wife and members of his court murdered him in 96. As Domitian's murder revealed, the principate had not solved monarchy's enduring weakness: rivalry for rule that was likely to explode into murderous conspiracy and destabilize the succession. The danger of civil war always existed, whether generated by ambitious generals or by competition among the emperor's heirs. As Tacitus commented, emperors became like the weather: "We just have to wait for bad ones to pass and hope for good ones to appear."

Fortunately for Rome, politically better weather came with the next five emperors—Nerva (r. 96–98), Trajan (r. 98–117), Hadrian (r. 117–138), Antoninus Pius (r. 138–161), and Marcus Aurelius (r. 161–180). Historians call them "The Five Good Emperors" because they provided peaceful transfers of power for nearly a century (the first four of these men, lacking surviving sons, used adoption to pick capable successors). This period, however, remained full of war and strife, as Roman history always was. Trajan fought fierce campaigns expanding Roman power northward across the Danube River into Dacia (today Romania) and eastward into Mesopotamia (see Map 5.1 on page 188). Hadrian earned the hatred of the Senate by executing several senators as alleged conspirators and punished a Jewish revolt by

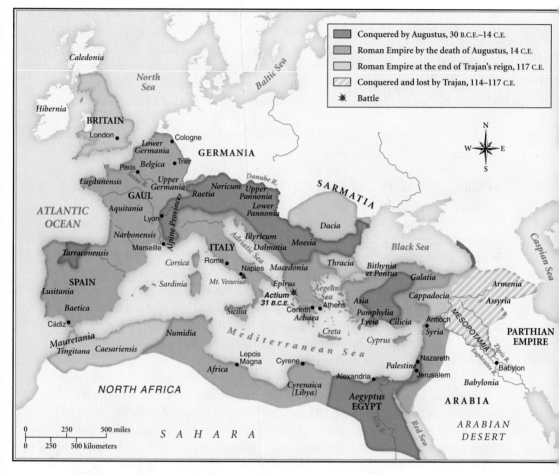

MAP 5.1 Expansion of the Roman Empire, 30 B.C.E.–117 C.E.

When Octavian (the future Augustus) captured Egypt in 30 B.C.E. after the suicides of Mark Antony and Cleopatra, he made a significant contribution to the economic strength of Rome because the land of the Nile provided huge amounts of grain and gold. Roman power now encircled the Mediterranean Sea (except for Mauretania, which remained technically under the rule of local kings with Roman approval until c. 44 C.E.). When the emperor Trajan took over the southern part of Mesopotamia in 114–117 C.E., imperial conquest reached its height: Rome's control had never before extended so far east. Hadrian, Trajan's successor, abandoned Mesopotamia, probably because it seemed too far away from Rome to defend. Egypt remained part of the empire until the Arab conquest in 642 C.E.

turning Jerusalem into a military colony. Aurelius spent many miserable years at war protecting the Danube region from outside attacks.

Still, it makes sense to speak of these five rulers as "good emperors." They succeeded one another without murder or conspiracy, the economy continued strong, and the army remained obedient. Their reigns marked the longest stretch in Roman history without a civil war since the second century B.C.E.

Life under the Five Good Emperors, 96–180 C.E.

The peace and prosperity of the second century C.E. cause historians to call it Rome's Golden Age. Imperial rule remained strong because it had a loyal military, public-spirited provincial elites, common laws and culture spreading through the provinces, and a healthy population reproducing itself.

In theory, Rome's military goal remained unlimited expansion because conquest brought glory to the emperor. Virgil in the *Aeneid* had expressed this ambition by portraying Jupiter, king of the gods, as promising "imperial rule without limit." In reality, the emperors were usually satisfied if neighboring peoples left the frontier regions undisturbed. Imperial territory never expanded permanently much beyond the area that Augustus had controlled. Stable and peaceful in the first two centuries after Augustus, most provinces had no need for garrison troops during this era; soldiers were a rare sight in many places. Even Gaul, which had bitterly resisted the Roman takeover, was now, according to a contemporary witness, "kept in order by 1,200 troops—hardly more soldiers than it has towns." Most legions (a legion was a unit of five thousand to six thousand troops) were stationed on the empire's northern and eastern frontiers, where hostile neighbors threatened and the distance from the capital weakened the provincials' loyalty.

The policy of not conquering new lands made paying for the army difficult. In the past, victories abroad had brought in huge amounts of booty, prisoners of war sold into slavery, and additional taxes from conquered peoples. These sources of money had now dried up, but the army—no longer a part-time militia—still had to be paid to maintain discipline. To fulfill their obligations as the military's patrons, emperors on their accession and on other special occasions supplemented soldiers' regular pay with large bonuses. These rewards made a legionary career desirable, and enlistment counted as a privilege restricted to free male citizens. The army, however, also included auxiliary units of noncitizens from the provinces. Serving under Roman officers, they could pick up some Latin and Roman customs, and they improved life in the provinces by constructing public works. Upon discharge, they received Roman citizenship. In this way, the army served as an instrument for spreading a common way of life.

The Roman peace guaranteed by the army allowed commerce to operate smoothly in imperial territory. The Golden Age's prosperity promoted long-distance trade for luxury goods, such as spices and silk, from as far away as India and China. Still, taxation of agricultural land in the provinces (Italy was exempt) provided the government's principal source of revenue. The administration itself cost relatively little because it was small compared with the size of the population it governed: several hundred top officials governed about fifty million people. Most taxes collected in the provinces stayed there to pay for local projects. Senatorial and equestrian governors with small staffs ran the provinces, which eventually numbered about forty. In Rome, the emperor employed a substantial palace staff, but equestrian officials called prefects managed the city itself.

The decentralized tax system required public service by the provincial elites; the government's financial well-being absolutely depended on it. Local officials called decurions (members of a municipal senate, later called curiales) collected taxes and personally guaranteed that their town's expenses were covered. If there was a shortfall in tax collection or local finances, these wealthy men had to make up the difference from their own pockets. Most emperors under the early principate attempted to keep taxes low. As Tiberius put it when refusing a request for tax increases from provincial governors, "I want you to shear my sheep, not skin them alive."

The financial obligations of civic office could make public service expensive, but the status that the positions brought made the elite willing to take the risk. Some received priesthoods in the imperial cult as a reward, an honor open to both men and women. All could hope to catch the emperor's ear for special help for their area—for example, after an earthquake or a flood. The system worked because it sprang from Roman tradition: the local social elites were the patrons of their communities but the clients of the emperors. As long as there were enough rich, public-spirited provincials participating in this system for its nonmonetary rewards, the principate could function effectively by relying on the old republic's tradition of public service.

The principate changed the Mediterranean world deeply but not evenly. Within the provinces lived a wide diversity of peoples speaking different languages, observing different customs, dressing in different styles, and worshiping different gods (Map 5.2). In the remote countryside, Roman conquest had only a modest effect on local customs. Where new cities sprang up, however, Roman influence increased. These communities sprouted around Roman forts or grew from the settlements of army veterans the emperors had sprinkled throughout the provinces. They became especially influential in western Europe, permanently rooting Latin (and the languages that would emerge from it) and Roman law and customs there. Modern cities such as Trier and Cologne in Germany started as Roman towns. As time passed, status gaps between the provinces and Italy lessened. Eventually, emperors came from the provinces; Trajan, from Spain, was the first.

Romanization, as historians call the spread of Roman culture in the provinces, raised people's standard of living as roads and bridges improved, trade increased, and agriculture flourished under the peaceful conditions provided by the army. Selling supplies to the troops brought new business to farmers and merchants. Greater prosperity under Roman rule made Romanization easier for provincials to accept. In addition, Romanization was not a one-way process of cultural change. In western areas as different from each other as Gaul, Britain, and North Africa, interactions among the local people and Romans produced new, mixed cultural traditions, especially evident in religion and art. Romanization led not to the imposition of the conquerors' way of life but to the gradual merging of Roman and local western cultures.

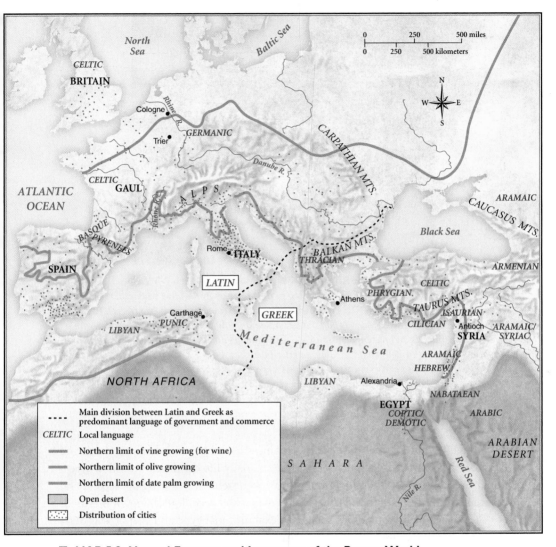

■ MAP 5.2 Natural Features and Languages of the Roman World

The Roman world had great variety in land, languages, and climate. People living there, estimated to have numbered as many as 55 million, spoke dozens of languages, many of which survived until the last years of the empire. The two predominant languages spoken by Roman citizens were Latin in the western part of the empire and Greek in the eastern. Latin remained the language of law even in the eastern empire. Fields suitable for growing grain were the most valuable land feature because wheat and barley were the basis of the ancient diet. Vineyards and olive groves also were important. Wine was regarded as an essential beverage, and olive oil was the main source of fat in the diets of most people and the principal ingredient in soap, perfume, and other products for daily life.

■ The Arch at Thamugadi, a Roman Military Colony in North Africa
The emperors fueled the process of Romanization in the provinces by building new settlements for military veterans. The best preserved such town is Thamugadi (today Timgad in Algeria). Founded by Emperor Trajan in 100 C.E., it was laid out like a Roman military camp, a perfect square with a grid of straight streets and rectangular houses. The new town's architecture imitated that of Rome. · A spacious theater provided room for public entertainments, and this mammoth arch, probably built toward the end of the second century C.E., provided a spectacular entrance to a boulevard lined with columned porches. Romanization was a two-way process: local peoples influenced the Roman settlers and vice versa. At Thamugadi, local African religious cults, lightly adapted to Roman traditions, flourished alongside ancient Roman cults and attracted worshipers of all kinds. (SEF/Art Resource, NY.)

Romanization affected the eastern provinces less; they retained their Greek and Near Eastern character. In much of this region, daily life continued to follow traditional Greek models. When the Romans took over these areas during the second and first centuries B.C.E., they found urban cultures that had been flourishing for hundreds of years. Huge Hellenistic cities such as Alexandria in Egypt and Antioch in Syria rivaled Rome in size and splendor (see Map 5.1). In fact, compared with Rome, they boasted more single-family houses, fewer blocks of high-rise apartments, and equally magnificent temples. While retaining their local languages and customs, the eastern social elites easily accepted the nature of Roman governance: the emperor was their patron, and they were his clients, with the mutual obligations this traditional relationship required. Provincial elites were long accustomed to such a system because of the paternalistic rule of Hellenistic kingdoms. Their willing cooperation in the task of governing the provinces was crucial for imperial stability and prosperity.

The continuing vitality of Greek culture and language in prosperous eastern cities contributed to the flourishing of literature. New forms of literature blossomed in Greek. Authors of the second century, such as Chariton and Achilles Tatius, wrote romantic adventure novels, making that literary form popular. Lucian (c. 117–180) composed satirical dialogues fiercely mocking both stuffy people and religious superstition. As part of his enormous literary output, the essayist and philosopher Plutarch (c. 50–120) wrote *Parallel Lives*, paired biographies of illustrious Greek and Roman men. His moral sense and taste for anecdotes made his works favorite reading for centuries; the English dramatist William Shakespeare (1564–1616) based several of his plays on Plutarch's biographies.

Latin literature thrived, too; in fact, scholars rank the late first and early second centuries C.E. as its Silver Age, second only to the masterpieces of Augustan literature. Its most famous authors wrote with acid wit, verve, and imagination. Tacitus (c. 56–120) composed his *Annals* as a biting narrative of the Julio-Claudians, laying bare the ruthlessness of Augustus and the personal weaknesses of his successors. The satiric poet Juvenal (c. 65–130) skewered pretentious Romans and greedy provincials while hilariously describing the problems of being broke in the city. Apuleius (c. 125–170) intrigued readers with *The Golden Ass*, a sex-filled novel about a man turned into a donkey who regains his body and his soul through the power of the Egyptian goddess Isis.

Unlike Augustus, later emperors never worried that sexy literature posed a threat to social order. They did, however, share his belief that law was essential. Indeed, Romans prided themselves on their ability to order their society through law. As Virgil said, their mission was "to establish law and order within a framework of peace." Even today, the influence of Roman law is still evident in most systems of law in Europe. One distinctive characteristic of Roman law was its recognition of the principle of equity, which meant accomplishing what was "good and fair" even if the letter of the law had to be disregarded. This principle led legal thinkers to insist, for example, that the intent of parties in a contract outweighed the words of their agreement and that the burden of proof lay with the accuser rather than the accused. The emperor Trajan ruled that no one should be convicted without clear evidence because it was better for a guilty person to go unpunished than for an innocent person to be condemned.

Roman notions of fairness required formal ranking of the "orders" in which it was believed people naturally belonged. As always, the elites made up a tiny portion of the population. Only about one person in fifty thousand had enough money to qualify for the senatorial order, the highest-ranking class, while about one in a thousand belonged to the equestrian order, the second-ranking class. Different purple stripes on clothing identified these orders. The third-highest order consisted of decurions, the local officials in provincial towns.

Those outside the social elite faced greater disadvantages than just snobbery. An old republican distinction between the "better people" and the "humbler people" hardened under the principate, and by the third century it spread throughout Roman law. Law protected such distinctions because social order was thought to depend on them. The "better people" included senators, equestrians, decurions, and retired army veterans. Everybody else—except slaves, who counted as property, not people—made up the vastly larger group of "humbler people." The latter faced their worst disadvantage in court: the law imposed harsher penalties on them than were imposed on the "better people" who committed the same crimes. "Humbler people" convicted of capital crimes were regularly executed by being crucified or torn apart by wild animals before a crowd of spectators. "Better people" rarely suffered the death penalty. But if they were condemned, they received a quicker and more dignified execution by the sword. "Humbler people" could also be tortured in criminal investigations, even if they were citizens. Romans regarded these differences as fair on the grounds that a person's higher status created a higher level of responsibility for the common good. As one provincial governor expressed it, "Nothing is less equitable than mere equality itself."

Law was crucial for maintaining order, but nothing mattered more to the stability and prosperity of the empire than steady population levels. Keeping up the birthrate was difficult because medicine could do little to help pregnant women or infants. The upper-class government official Pliny, for example, sent the following report to the grandfather of his third wife, Calpurnia: "You will be very sad to learn that your granddaughter has suffered a miscarriage. She is a young girl and did not realize she was pregnant. As a result she was more active than she should have been and paid a high price." Complications at birth could easily lead to the mother's death because doctors could not stop internal bleeding or cure infections. They possessed carefully made instruments for surgery and physical examinations but were seriously misinformed about reproduction. Gynecologists such as Soranus, who practiced in Rome during the reigns of Trajan and Hadrian, mistakenly recommended the days just after menstruation as the best time to become pregnant, when the woman's body was "not congested." As in Hellenistic medicine, treatments were mainly limited to potions, herbs, and bleeding; Soranus recommended treating exceptionally painful menstruation by drawing blood "from the bend of the arm." Doctors, often freedmen from Greece and other provinces, were considered of low status, unless they served the upper class.

As in earlier times, girls often wed in their early teens to have as many years as possible to bear children; their husbands would typically be around age thirty. Because so many babies died, families had to produce numerous offspring to keep from disappearing. The tombstone of Veturia, a soldier's wife married at eleven, tells a typical story: "Here I lie, having lived for twenty-seven years. I was married to the same man for sixteen years and bore six children, five of whom died before I did." Richer families usually arranged marriages between spouses who hardly knew each other, although they could grow to love each other in a partnership devoted to family.

The emphasis on childbearing in marriage brought many health hazards to women, but to remain single and childless represented social failure for Romans. Once children were born, they were cared for by their mothers and by servants. Wealthy women routinely hired "wet nurses" to attend to and breast-feed their babies. When Romans wanted to control family size, they used female contraception by obstructing the female organs or by administering drugs. Like the Greeks, they practiced exposure,

■ **Midwife's Sign Depicting Childbirth**

Childbirth was a dangerous experience for women because of the chance of dying from internal bleeding. This terra-cotta sign from Ostia, the ancient port city of Rome, probably hung outside a midwife's rooms to announce her skill in aiding women in giving birth. It shows a pregnant woman clutching the sides of her chair and supported by another woman while the midwife crouches in front to help deliver the baby. The meaning of the sign was clear to people who were illiterate; a person did not have to be able to read to understand the services that the specialist inside could provide. (Scala/Art Resource, NY.)

more frequently for infant girls than for boys because sons were considered more valuable than daughters as future supporters and protectors of families.

The emperors and some members of the social elite did their best to support reproduction. The emperors aided needy children to encourage larger families, and wealthy people often adopted children in their communities. One North African man gave enough money to support three hundred boys and three hundred girls each year until they grew up. The differing value afforded male and female children was also evident in these humanitarian programs: boys often received more aid than girls.

■ **REVIEW:** *What distinguished the rule of "bad" and "good" emperors?*

The Emergence of Christianity

Christianity began as a splinter group within Judaism in Judaea, where, as elsewhere under Roman rule, Jews were allowed to practice their ancestral religion. The new faith did not soon attract many converts; three centuries after the death of Jesus, Christians remained a small minority. Christianity grew, if only gradually, because it had an appeal based on the career of Jesus, its message of salvation, its believers' sense of mission, the democratic openness of its early congregations, and the strong bonds of community it inspired. Ultimately, the emergence of Christianity proved the most significant and enduring development during the Roman Empire.

The Teachings of Jesus

The new religion sprang from the life and teachings of Jesus (c. 4 B.C.E.–30 C.E.; see "The B.C.E./C.E. System for Dates" at the beginning of this book for an explanation of the date given for Jesus' birth). Christianity's background lay in Jewish history. By the time of Jesus' boyhood, some of his fellow Jews in Judaea were agitating for independence from Roman rule, making provincial officials fear rebellion. Jesus' career, therefore, took place in a troubled region. His execution was the typical Roman response to anyone they believed threatened peace and social order. In the two decades after his crucifixion, his devoted followers, particularly Paul of Tarsus, developed a new religion—Christianity—that expanded beyond the Jewish community in Palestine.

Christianity offered an answer to a troubling question about divine justice raised by the Jews' long history of defeat and exile: how could a just God allow the wicked to prosper and the righteous to suffer? The question had become pressing some two centuries before Jesus' birth, when persecution by the Seleucid king Antiochus IV (r. 175–164 B.C.E.) had provoked the Jews into a bloody revolt. This war gave birth to a complex of ideas called apocalypticism (from the Greek for "uncovering the future"). According to this worldview, evil powers, divine and human, controlled the present world. Their rule would soon end, however, when God and his agents revealed their plan to conquer the forces of evil by sending a **Christ** (Greek for "anointed one"; in Hebrew, *Mashia*, or in English *Messiah*) to win the great battle. A final judgment would follow, bringing eternal punishment for the wicked and eternal reward for the righteous. The apocalypticism that first inspired Jews living in Judaea under Roman rule later motivated Christians and Muslims.

Apocalyptic ideas became controversial around the time of Jesus' birth because most Judaean Jews were angry about Rome's control but disagreed about what form Judaism should take in response. Some cooperated with their overlords, while others preached rejection of the non-Jewish world and its spiritual corruption. Their local ruler, installed by the Romans, was Herod the Great (r. 37–4 B.C.E.). His Greek style of life broke Jewish law, making him unpopular with his subjects despite his magnificent rebuilding of the holiest Jewish shrine, the great temple in Jerusalem. When a decade of unrest followed Herod's death, Augustus installed a provincial government to oversee the region. The imposition of direct Roman government made many Judaeans unhappy because they were used to living under Jewish rulers.

Jesus began his career as a teacher and healer in his native Galilee, the northern region of Palestine, during the reign of Tiberius. The books that would later become the Gospels, or the first four books of the Christian New Testament, offer the earliest accounts of his life and teachings; they were composed between about 70 and 90, decades after Jesus' death. Jesus himself wrote nothing down, and others' accounts of his words and deeds do not always agree on what he said or did. He taught mostly by telling parables, stories with a moral or religious message that challenged his followers to figure out what he meant.

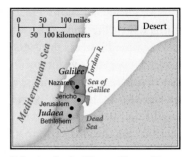

Palestine in the Time of Jesus, 30 C.E.

All of the Gospels begin the story of his career with his baptism by John the Baptist, a prophet who urged people to repent before God's final judgment, which John preached was coming soon. John was executed by the Jewish ruler Herod Antipas, a son of Herod the Great whom the Romans supported; Herod feared that John's apocalyptic preaching might set off riots. After John's death, Jesus continued his mission by traveling around Judaea's countryside warning people to prepare spiritually for the coming of God's kingdom. Many saw Jesus as the Messiah, but his apocalypticism did not preach immediate revolt against the Romans. Instead, he taught that God's true kingdom was to be sought not on earth but in heaven. He stressed that this kingdom was open to believers regardless of their social status or sinfulness. His emphasis on God's love for humanity and people's responsibility to love one another reflected Jewish religious teachings, as in the first-century scholar Hillel's interpretation of the Hebrew Bible.

An educated Jew who perhaps knew Greek as well as Aramaic, the local language, Jesus realized that he had to reach the urban crowds to make an impact. Therefore, leaving the Galilean villages where he had started, he took his message to the Jewish population of Jerusalem, the region's main city. His miraculous healings and exorcisms and his powerful preaching created a sensation. His popularity attracted the attention of the Jewish authorities, who automatically assumed he aspired to political power. Fearing he might ignite a Jewish revolt, the Roman governor Pontius Pilate (r. 26–36) ordered his crucifixion, the usual punishment for rebellion, in Jerusalem in 30.

After Jesus' death, his followers reported that they had seen him in person. They proclaimed that God had miraculously raised him from the dead, and they set about convincing other Jews that Jesus was the promised savior and would soon return to judge the world and impose God's kingdom. His closest disciples, twelve Apostles (Greek for "messengers"), still considered themselves faithful Jews and continued to follow the commandments of Jewish law.

A radical change took place with the conversion of Paul of Tarsus (c. 10–65), a pious Jew of the Diaspora and a Roman citizen who had violently opposed those who accepted Jesus as the Messiah. Around three years after Jesus' death, Paul experienced a spiritual vision on the road to Damascus in Syria, which he interpreted as a divine revelation. It inspired him to become a follower of Jesus as the Messiah or Christ—a Christian, as members of the movement came to be known. Paul taught that belief in the divinity of Jesus and that his crucifixion was the ultimate sacrifice for the sins of humanity was the only way of becoming righteous in the eyes of God. In this way alone, Paul said, could people expect to win salvation in the world to come.

Seeking to win converts outside Judaea, in about 46 Paul began to travel to preach to Jews of the Diaspora and to Gentiles (non-Jews) who had adopted some Jewish customs in Syria, Asia Minor, and Greece (see Map 5.3). Although Paul stressed the necessity of ethical behavior along traditional Jewish lines, especially the rejection of sexual immorality and polytheism, he also taught that converts did not need to obey all of Jewish law. To make conversion easier, Paul did not require men who became Christians to undergo the Jewish initiation rite of circumcision. This view, combined with his teachings that his congregations did not have to observe Jewish dietary restrictions or festivals, created great controversy and led to tensions with Jewish authorities in Jerusalem as well as with the followers of Jesus living there, who still believed that Christians had to follow Jewish law. Roman authorities then arrested Paul as a criminal troublemaker; he was executed in about 65.

Paul's mission was only one part of the unrest in the Jewish community in this period; hatred of Roman rule in Palestine finally pushed the Jews to revolt in 66. When they were defeated in 70, the Roman victors destroyed the Jerusalem temple and sold most of the city's population into slavery. This catastrophe meant that the Jewish community lost its religious center, and the separation of Christianity from Judaism begun by Paul gained momentum. In this way Christianity became a separate religion.

Paul's impact on early Christianity can be seen in the number of letters—thirteen—attributed to him in the twenty-seven writings brought together as the New Testament by around 200. Followers of Jesus came to regard the New Testament as having equal authority with the Hebrew Bible, which they then called the Old Testament. Because teachers like Paul preached mainly in the cities to reach large crowds, congregations of Christians mostly sprang up in urban areas. Originally these groups had a democratic organization without much hierarchy. Women could be leaders in this early stage of Christianity, though not without controversy; many people believed that men should teach and women only listen. Still, early Christianity was diverse enough that a woman could found a congregation, such as Lydia at Philippi in Greece, or earn respect as a "deacon," such as Phoebe at Cenchreae, also in Greece.

Growth of a New Religion

Christianity faced serious obstacles in developing as a new religion separate from Judaism. Roman officials, suspecting Christians of political disloyalty, sometimes persecuted them as traitors, especially for refusing to participate in the imperial cult (as happened to Perpetua). Christian leaders had to build an organization from scratch to administer their growing congregations. Also, they had to address the controversial question of whether women could be Christian leaders.

Most Romans found early Christians puzzling and irritating. First, in contrast to Jews, Christians proclaimed a new faith rather than a traditional religion handed down from their ancestors; they therefore enjoyed no special treatment under Roman law. Next, people feared that tolerating Christians would offend the gods of official religion; Christians' denial of the old gods and of the emperor's cult seemed sure to provoke natural catastrophes. Christians furthermore aroused contempt because they proclaimed as their divine king a man whom the imperial government had crucified as a criminal. Finally, Christians' secret rituals led to accusations of

■ Painting of a Sacred Banquet from a Roman Catacomb
This banquet scene appears on a wall of a Rome catacomb (catacombs were the underground chambers Christians used for burials and meetings before their religion was officially recognized). Such scenes seem simultaneously to represent actual meals held to remember the dead, heavenly banquets that the blessed dead were thought to have in their heavenly life, and symbolic gatherings expressing a sense of community and mutual affection among believers. Seven people were usually shown, for reasons still not clear to historians. Women are prominently depicted here in the middle and at either end of the table. The woman at the left is presenting a goblet of wine to the banqueters. As the inscription suggests, she may be a personification of agape, the shared love that such sacred banquets commemorated. (Held Collection/Bridgeman Art Library.)

cannibalism and sexual promiscuity because they symbolically ate the body and drank the blood of Jesus during communal dinners called Love Feasts, which men and women attended together. In short, Christians seemed a threat to social order and peace with the gods.

Not surprisingly, then, Romans were quick to blame Christians for disasters. When a large portion of Rome burned in 64, Nero punished them for arson. As Tacitus reports, the emperor had innocent Christians "covered with the skins of wild animals and torn to death by dogs, or fastened to crosses and set on fire to provide light at night." The cruelty of their punishment reportedly earned these Christians sympathy from Rome's population. After Nero, the government did not persecute Christians regularly or as a policy because no law specifically banned their religion. Nevertheless, Christians made easy prey for officials looking for people to blame for crimes or disruptions in public order.

In response to persecution, defenders of Christianity, such as Tertullian (c. 160–240) and Justin (c. 100–165), argued that Romans had nothing to fear from Christianity. Far from spreading disloyalty and immorality, these writers insisted, their faith taught respect for authority and a strict morality. It was not a foreign superstition but the true philosophy that combined the best features of Judaism and Greek thought and was thus a fitting religion for their diverse world. Tertullian pointed out that, although Christians could not worship the emperors, they did "pray to the true God for their [the emperors'] safety. We pray for a fortunate life for them, a secure rule, . . . a courageous army, a loyal Senate, a virtuous people, a world of peace."

Persecution did not stop Christianity. Tertullian indeed claimed that "the blood of the martyrs is the seed of the Church." Christians like Perpetua regarded public trials and executions as an opportunity to become a **martyr** (Greek for "witness") to their faith and thus to strengthen Christians' sense of identity. Their belief that their deaths would lead directly to happiness in heaven allowed them to face painful tortures with courage; some even became martyrs on purpose. For example, Ignatius (c. 35–107), bishop of Antioch, begged Rome's congregation, which was becoming the most prominent Christian group, not to ask the emperor to show him mercy after his arrest: "Let me be food for the wild animals [in the arena] through whom I can reach God," he pleaded. "I am God's wheat, to be ground up by the teeth of beasts so that I may be found pure bread of Christ." Most Christians tried their best to avoid becoming martyrs, but stories recording the martyrs' courage shaped the identity of this new religion as a faith that gave its believers the spiritual strength to endure great suffering.

Many first-century Christians expected their troubles would end during their lifetime because Jesus would return to pass judgment on the world and overturn the Roman Empire. When this expectation did not come true, believers began transforming their faith into a religion organized to survive indefinitely, instead of an apocalyptic offshoot of Judaism predicting the immediate end of the world. To make this change, they tried to achieve unity in their beliefs and created a hierarchical organization to impose order on congregations.

Unity was impossible, however, because early Christians constantly and fiercely disagreed about what they should believe, how they should live, and who had the authority to decide these questions. Some Christians believed they could observe Christ's teachings while keeping their jobs and regular lives. Others insisted that it was necessary to withdraw from the everyday world to escape its evil, even abandoning their families, sex, and reproduction. Many Christians believed they should not serve in the army because, as soldiers required to worship in the imperial cult, they would betray their faith. Controversy over such questions raged in the numerous congregations that arose in the early empire around the Mediterranean, from Gaul to Africa to the Near East (Map 5.3).

Creating bishops as religious officials with authority to specify true doctrine and proper conduct for Christian believers was the most important development in organizing the new religion to live on indefinitely. Bishops received their positions through the principle later called **apostolic succession**, which declares that

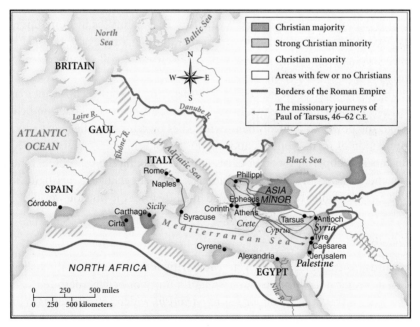

■ **MAP 5.3 Christian Populations in the Late Third Century** C.E.
Christians remained a minority in the Roman world three hundred years after the crucifixion of Jesus. Certain areas of the empire, however, especially Asia Minor (western Turkey), where Paul had preached, had a concentration of Christians. Most Christians lived in cities and towns, where missionaries had gone to spread their message to crowds of curious listeners. Paganus, a Latin word for "country person" or "rural villager," came to mean a believer in traditional polytheistic cults—hence the term pagan, *meaning "non-Christian," often found in modern works on this period.*

Jesus' Apostles appointed the first bishops as their successors, granting these new officials the powers Jesus had originally given to the Apostles. Those men named as bishops by the Apostles in turn appointed their own successors, and so on. Bishops had authority to ordain priests with the holy power to administer the sacraments, above all baptism and communion, which believers regarded as necessary for achieving eternal life. Bishops also controlled their congregations' memberships and finances (the money financing early churches came from members' gifts).

The bishops had authority to define what was true doctrine (orthodoxy) and what was false (heresy), but Christians' disagreements over doctrine were too strong for the bishops to overcome and impose unity of belief. In this early stage, the occasional meetings of the bishops of different cities constituted the church's organization. Today it is common to refer to this loose organization as the early Catholic ("universal") church, but even the bishops disagreed among themselves on what beliefs were proper.

A particularly bitter disagreement concerned women's roles in the church. In the first congregations, women sometimes held leadership positions. When bishops were established atop the hierarchy, however, women usually were kept in inferior posts. This demotion reflected the view that in Christianity, as in Roman imperial society, women should be subordinate to men. Some congregations took a long time to accept this change, however, and some women still occupied leadership positions during the second and third centuries.

When leadership roles were closed off to them, many women chose not to marry to demonstrate their devotion to Christ. This commitment to celibacy and chastity gave them the power to control their own bodies by removing their sexuality from the domination of men. Women choosing this special closeness to God were judged holy and socially superior by other Christians. By rejecting the traditional functions of wife and mother in favor of spiritual excellence, celibate Christian women achieved an independence and authority denied them in the outside world.

Competing Beliefs

Three centuries after Jesus' death, a large majority of the population still believed in polytheistic religion. Polytheists never sought a unity of beliefs (despite the implication to the contrary of the modern term *paganism*, which actually refers to diverse cults). They did agree, however, that the old gods favored and protected them and that the imperial cult added to their safety; the success and prosperity of the principate was the proof. Even people who found a more intellectually satisfying understanding of the world in philosophies, such as Stoicism, respected the traditional cults as symbols of divine protection for Rome.

Polytheistic worship therefore had as its goal gaining the favor of all the divinities who could affect human life. Its deities ranged from the traditional gods of the state cults, such as Jupiter and Minerva, to spirits thought to inhabit local groves and springs. Famous old cults, such as the initiation rituals of Demeter and Persephone at Eleusis outside Athens, remained popular; the emperor Hadrian was initiated at Eleusis in 125.

The cult of the Egyptian goddess Isis in its Hellenistic form reveals how polytheism could provide believers with a religious experience arousing strong personal emotions and demanding a moral way of life. Her cult had already attracted Romans by the time of Augustus. He tried to suppress it because it was Cleopatra's religion, but Isis's reputation as a kind, compassionate goddess who relieved her followers' suffering made her cult too popular to crush. The Egyptians believed that her tears for starving people caused the Nile to flood every year and bring them good harvests. Her image was that of a loving mother, and in art she is often shown nursing her son. A central doctrine of her cult concerned the death and resurrection of her husband, Osiris; Isis promised her followers a similar hope for life after death.

Isis required her worshipers to behave righteously. Inscriptions put up by believers declared the goddess's standards for them by quoting her on her own work for justice: "I broke down the rule of tyrants; I put an end to murders; I caused what is right to be mightier than gold and silver." The main character of Apuleius's novel *The Golden Ass*, whom Isis rescues from his mistaken transformation into a donkey, expresses his intense joy after being spiritually reborn: "O holy and eternal guardian of the human race, who always cherishes mortals and blesses them, you care for the troubles of miserable humans with a sweet mother's love. Neither day nor night, nor any moment of time, ever passes by without your blessings." Other cults also required their believers to lead just lives. Inscriptions from remote villages in Asia Minor, for example, record the confessions of peasants to sexual sins for which their local god had imposed severe penance.

Many upper-class Romans found moral guidance in philosophy. Stoicism, derived from the teachings of the Greek Zeno (335–263 B.C.E.), was the most popular. Stoics believed in self-discipline above all, and their code of personal ethics left no room for immoral conduct. As the philosopher Seneca (4 B.C.E.–65 C.E.) explained, "It is easier to prevent harmful emotions from entering the soul than it is to control them once they have entered." Stoicism taught a creative force combining reason, nature, and divinity directs the universe. Humans share in the essence of this universal force and find happiness and patience by living in harmony with it and always doing their duty. The emperor Marcus Aurelius, in his book entitled *Meditations*, emphasized the Stoic belief that people exist for each other: "Either make them better, or just put up with them," he advised.

Christian and polytheist scholars argued over the merits of Christianity compared to traditional Greek philosophy. The theologian Origen (c. 185–255), for example, argued that Christianity, because it was true, was a better guide to correct living than were Greek philosophical ideas. At about the same time, however, the

■ **Mithras Slaying the Bull**
Hundreds of shrines to the mysterious god Mithras have been found in the Roman Empire, but the cult remains poorly known because almost no texts exist to explain it. To judge from the many representations in art, such as this wall painting of about 200 C.E. from the shrine at Marino south of Rome, the story of Mithras slaying a bull was a central part of the cult's identity. Scholars debate the symbolic meaning of the bull slaying shown here, in which a snake and a dog lick the animal's blood while a scorpion pinches its testicles. Most agree, however, that Mithras was derived, perhaps as late as the early imperial period, from the ancient Persian divinity Mithra. Only men could be worshipers, and many were soldiers. Earlier scholarly claims of the cult's popularity were exaggerated; its members numbered no more than 1 or 2 percent of the population. Mithraism probably involved complex devotion to astrology, with devotees ranked in grades, each grade protected by a different celestial body. (Scala/Art Resource, NY.)

philosopher Plotinus (c. 205–270) gave Greek ideas new strength with his books on spiritual philosophy. These ideas, called **Neoplatonism** because their doctrines sprang from Plato's philosophy, influenced many educated Christians as well as polytheists. Neoplatonic religious ideas centered on a human longing to return to the universal Good from which human existence comes. By turning away from the life of the body through the study of philosophy, individual souls could rise to the level of the universal soul, becoming the whole of what as individuals they formed a potential part. This mystical union with what the Christians would call God could be achieved only through strenuous self-discipline in personal morality as well as intellectual life. Neoplatonism's stress on spiritual purity gave it a powerful appeal to educated Christians. Like the cult of Isis or Stoicism, Neoplatonism provided guidance, comfort, and hope through good times or bad.

■ **REVIEW:** *What beliefs and actions made Roman officials suspicious of Christians?*

The Crisis of the Third Century

Bad times arrived for the empire in the middle of the third century. War, money troubles, and natural disasters combined to create a crisis. Attacks by outsiders on the northern and eastern frontiers forced the emperors to expand the army for defense. The rulers' attempts to find money to pay for these wars fueled inflation and crippled the economy. The public's outrage at these developments encouraged ambitious generals to seek power by commanding personal armies, once again plunging Rome into civil war in a bloody replay of the destruction of the republic. Earthquakes and epidemics added to the crisis. By the end of the third century, this combination of troubles had shredded the "Roman peace."

Defending the Frontiers

Emperors since Domitian (r. 81–96) had been fighting wars to repel invaders from the frontier regions. The most aggressive attackers were loosely organized Germanic bands that often crossed the Danube and Rhine Rivers for raiding. Their constant fighting against Roman troops turned these raiders into powerful armies, and they launched dangerous invasions during the reign of Marcus Aurelius (r. 161–180). A major threat also emerged at the empire's eastern edge when a new dynasty, the Sassanids, defeated the Parthian Empire and reenergized the ancient Persian kingdom. By 227, Persia's military power forced the emperors to bring in legions to protect the rich eastern provinces, at the expense of the defense of the northern frontiers.

Recognizing the courage of Germanic warriors, Domitian and his successors began hiring them as auxiliary soldiers for the Roman army and settling them on the frontiers as buffers against invasion. By around 200, the army had enrolled perhaps as many as 450,000 legionary and auxiliary troops (the size of the navy remains unknown). As always, Roman military life was hard. Training constantly, soldiers had to be fit enough to carry forty-pound packs up to twenty miles in five hours, swimming rivers on the way. Since the reign of Hadrian (r. 117–138), the emperors had built many permanent bases for garrisons, but an army on the march constructed its own fort every night. Soldiers transported all the materials for a wooden-walled camp everywhere they went. As one ancient commentator noted during the republic, "Infantrymen were little different from loaded pack mules." At one camp in a frontier area, archaeologists found a supply of a million iron nails— ten tons in all. The same fort required seventeen miles of timber for its barracks walls. To outfit a legion with tents required 54,000 calves' hides.

These defensive wars strained imperial finances because they did not bring in much plunder, unlike the republic's wars of conquest. The army had become a source of negative instead of positive cash flow to the treasury, and the economy had not expanded sufficiently to make up the difference. To make matters worse, inflation had driven up prices. A main cause of inflation under the principate may have been, ironically, the long period of peace that promoted increased demand for the economy's relatively static production of goods and services.

In desperation at their financial problems, some emperors responded to rising prices by debasing imperial coinage in a vain attempt to cut government costs. **Debasement of coinage** meant putting less silver in each coin (there was no paper money) without changing its face value and therefore creating more cash with the same amount of precious metal. (See "Taking Measure," page 207.) Merchants, however, raised prices to make up for the reduced value of the debased coins. By 200, the debased coinage and inflation were ruining the imperial balance sheet and undermining public confidence in the imperial currency. As the soldiers kept demanding that their patrons, the emperors, pay them well, the situation only grew worse. The financial system fell into full collapse in the 250s and 260s.

The Severan Emperors and Catastrophe

Decisions by the emperor Septimius Severus (r. 193–211) and his sons did the most to bring on the crisis: the father drained the treasury to satisfy the army, and his sons' murderous rivalry and reckless spending destroyed the government's stability. A soldier's soldier who came from the large North African city of Leptis Magna in what is today Libya, Severus became ruler in 193 after waging a civil war to get rid of the incompetent emperor currently holding power. To restore imperial prestige and acquire money through foreign conquest, Severus fought successful campaigns beyond the frontiers of the provinces, in Mesopotamia and northern Britain.

By this time, the soldiers were angry because inflation had eroded the value of their wages to practically nothing after they bought themselves basic supplies and clothing. They therefore expected the emperors to favor them with gifts of extra money. Severus spent large sums on such gifts, but then he decided to try improve the situation by raising the soldiers' pay by one-third. The expanded size of the army made this raise more expensive than the treasury could afford and made inflation worse. The financial consequences of his policy, however, concerned Severus not at all. His deathbed advice to his sons in 211 was to "stay on good terms with each other, be generous to the soldiers, and pay no attention to anyone else."

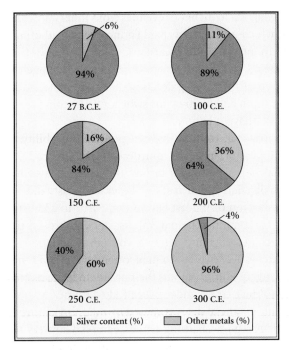

■ **TAKING MEASURE** The Falling Value of Roman Imperial Coinage,
27 B.C.E.–300 C.E.
*Ancient silver coinage derived its value from its metallic content; the less silver a coin had, the less it
was worth. Emperors facing rising government and military expenses but flat or falling revenues
tried to cut costs by debasing the coinage: they reduced the amount of silver in each coin and
increased the amount of other, cheaper metals. These pie charts reveal the gradual debasement of
the Roman imperial coinage until the third century, when military expenses apparently skyrocketed.
By 300 C.E., coins contained only trace amounts of silver. Merchants and producers had to raise
their prices for goods and services when they were being paid with currency that was increasingly
less valuable. Thus debasement fueled inflation.*

Severus's sons undermined the principate's stability by following only the last
two points of his advice. Caracalla (r. 211–217) seized the throne for himself by
murdering his brother Geta; his violent reign and limitless spending ended the
peace and prosperity of the Roman Golden Age. He increased the soldiers' pay by
another 40 to 50 percent and spent gigantic sums on building projects to display his
glory, including the largest public baths Rome had ever seen, covering blocks and
blocks of the city. The need for money to pay his out-of-control expenses put
unbearable pressure on the provincial elites responsible for collecting taxes and on
the citizens whom they squeezed for ever greater amounts.

   In 212, Caracalla took his most famous step to try to fix the budget crisis: he
granted Roman citizenship to almost every man and woman in imperial territory

except slaves. His goal was to increase revenues from inheritance taxes and from fees for freeing slaves, which only citizens paid (noncitizens paid other taxes): the more citizens, the more money (most of it earmarked for the army). Caracalla, who contemporaries whispered was insane, wrecked the imperial budget, setting in motion the ruinous inflation of the coming decades. Once when his mother criticized him for his excesses, he replied as he drew his sword, "Never mind, we shall not run out of money as long as I have this."

The empire's financial troubles created political instability. When Macrinus, commander of the praetorian guard, murdered Caracalla in 217 to make himself emperor, Caracalla's female relatives bribed the army to overthrow Macrinus in favor of a young male relative. The restored Severan dynasty did not last long, however, and the assassination of the last Severan emperor in 235 began a half-century of civil wars that, compounded by natural disasters, destroyed the principate. For the next fifty years, emperors and generals constantly fought to rule. During this period of near anarchy, over two dozen men, often several at a time, held or claimed the throne. Their only qualification was their ability to lead an army and reward the troops for loyalty to their commander instead of to Rome.

The violence and financial distress caused by the third century's civil wars made life miserable in many regions. Battling armies trampled farmers' fields searching for food, making it impossible to keep up normal agricultural production. City council members faced constantly rising demands for tax revenues from every new emperor; this financial pressure destroyed their commitment to serving their communities.

Foreign enemies took advantage of the Roman civil wars, invading from the east and north. Roman fortunes hit bottom in 260 when Shapur I, king of the Sassanid Empire of Persia, captured the emperor Valerian (r. 253–260) while attacking the province of Syria. Imperial territory was in danger of splintering into breakaway regions. Even the tough and competent emperor Aurelian (r. 270–275) could do no more to reduce the danger than to recover Egypt and Asia Minor from Zenobia, the warrior queen of Palmyra in Syria. He also had to encircle Rome with a massive wall to ward off surprise attacks by Germanic tribes smashing their way into Italy from the north.

Historians dispute how severely these troubles were worsened by natural disasters, but strong earthquakes and epidemics did strike some of the provinces around the middle of the century. The population declined significantly as food supplies became less dependable, civil war killed soldiers and civilians alike, and infection flared over large regions. The loss of population meant fewer soldiers for the army, whose efficiency as a defense and police force had already declined because of the political and financial chaos. More frontier areas became vulnerable to raids, and roving bands of robbers became increasingly common within the imperial borders.

Polytheists explained these horrible times in the traditional way: the state gods were angry. But why? The obvious answer seemed to be the presence of Christians, who denied the existence of the Roman gods and refused to participate in their worship. The emperor Decius (r. 249–251) conducted systematic persecutions to

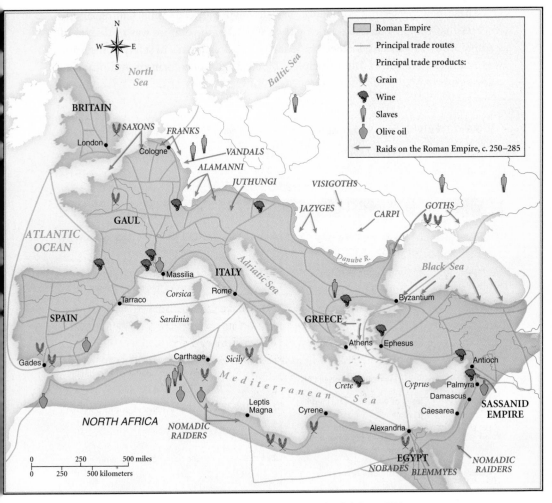

■ MAPPING THE WEST The Roman Empire in Crisis, c. 284 C.E.

By the early 280s, the principate had been torn apart by the fifty years of civil war that followed the end of the Severan dynasty. Imperial territory remained the same as in the time of Augustus (see Map 5.1), except for the loss of Dacia during the reign of Aurelian (r. 270–275). Attacks from the north and east had repeatedly penetrated the frontier regions, however. The Sassanid king Shapur I (r. c. 240–270), for example, temporarily held Antioch and captured the emperor Valerian in 260. The public humiliation and death in captivity of the elderly imperial ruler indicate the depths to which Roman fortunes sank in the third century. **For more help analyzing this map,** *see the map activity for this chapter in the* ONLINE STUDY GUIDE *at* bedfordstmartins.com/huntconcise.

eliminate Christians as a way to regain the goodwill of the gods. He justified the violence by calling himself "Restorer of the Cults," proclaiming, "I would rather see a rival to my throne than another bishop of Rome." He ordered all inhabitants of the empire to prove their loyalty to the state by participating in a sacrifice to its gods. Christians who refused to join in were killed.

These new persecutions did not end the civil war, economic failure, or the diseases that brought on the crisis. By the early 280s, the empire was in danger of fragmenting. Remarkably, in 284 Diocletian would drag it back to safety in the same way Augustus had begun the principate: by creating a new form of authoritarian leadership.

■ **REVIEW:** *What factors provoked the crisis in Roman government and society in the third century C.E.?*

IMPORTANT DATES

44 B.C.E.	Julius Caesar's assassination reignites civil war	**69 C.E.**	Civil war in the "Year of the Four Emperors"
27 B.C.E. –14 C.E.	Augustus's principate	**70 C.E.**	Titus captures Jerusalem and destroys the Jewish temple
19 B.C.E.	The poet Virgil dies, leaving the *Aeneid* unfinished	**161–180 C.E.**	Germanic bands attack northern frontiers during reign of Marcus Aurelius
2 B.C.E.	Senate proclaims Augustus "Father of his Country"	**212 C.E.**	Caracalla extends Roman citizenship to almost all free inhabitants of the provinces
8 C.E.	Augustus exiles the poet Ovid		
30 C.E.	Jesus of Nazareth crucified in Jerusalem	**250s–260s C.E.**	Imperial finances collapse from civil war, debased coinage, and inflation
c. 33 C.E.	Paul of Tarsus becomes a Christian	**284 C.E.**	Diocletian becomes emperor
64 C.E.	Nero blames Christians for great fire in Rome		

Conclusion

Augustus created the principate by installing a monarchy while insisting that he was restoring the Roman republic. He succeeded because he kept the loyalty of the army and extended the patron-client system. The principate made the emperor the patron of the army and, indeed, of everyone else. Most provincials, especially in the eastern Mediterranean, found this arrangement acceptable because it aligned with the familiar relationship between ruler and ruled in the Hellenistic kingdoms.

Stability endured as long as the emperors had enough money to keep their millions of clients satisfied. They provided food to the poor, built baths and arenas for public entertainment, and paid for a permanent army. The emperors of the first and second centuries enlarged the military to protect distant territories stretching from Britain to North Africa to Syria. By the second century, peace and prosperity had created an imperial Golden Age. Long-term money trouble set in, however, because the army, concentrating on defense rather than conquest, no longer brought money into the treasury. Severe inflation and debasement of the currency worsened the situation. The wealthy elites found they could no longer meet the demand for increased taxes without draining their personal fortunes, and they lost their public-spiritedness and avoided their communal responsibilities. Loyalty to the state became too expensive.

The emergence of Christians added to the uncertainty. Roman officials worried that some citizens placed their loyalty to their divinity ahead of their loyalty to the state. Their new religion evolved from Jewish apocalypticism to a hierarchical organization of bishops. Christians disputed with each other and with the authorities; martyrs such as Perpetua worried the imperial government with the depth of their convictions.

When financial ruin, civil war, and natural disasters struck the empire in the mid-third century, the emperors lacked the money and the popular support to end the crisis. Not even the persecution of Christians could convince the gods to restore Rome's good fortunes. The empire instead had to be transformed politically and religiously. Against all expectations, Diocletian began that process in 284.

■ **MAKING CONNECTIONS**

1. *Compare the crisis in the first century B.C.E. that undermined the republic with the crisis of the third century C.E. that undermined the principate.*

2. *If you had been a first-century emperor, what would you have done about the Christians and why? What if you had been a third-century emperor?*

■ **FOR FURTHER EXPLORATION**

For further reading and online research ideas, see the Suggested References on page SR-3 at the back of the book.

For practice quizzes, a customized study plan, and other study tools, see the ONLINE STUDY GUIDE at bedfordstmartins.com/huntconcise.

For primary-source material from this period, see Chapter 5 in *Sources of THE MAKING OF THE WEST: A CONCISE HISTORY*, Second Edition.

The Transformation of the Roman Empire

c. 284–c. 600 C.E.

A N EGYPTIAN WOMAN NAMED ISIS wrote a letter to her mother in the third century that modern archaeologists found at the site of a village near the Nile River. Written in Greek on papyrus, the letter hints at the problems and worries many people experienced during this troubled time:

> *Every day I pray to the lord Sarapis and his fellow gods to watch over you. I want you to know that I have arrived in Alexandria safely after four days. I send fond greetings to my sister and the children and Elouath and his wife and Dioscorous and her husband and children and Tamalis and her husband and son and Heron and Ammonarion and . . . Sanpat and her children. And if Aion wants to be in the army, let him come. For everybody is in the army.*

The letter leaves us with puzzling questions unanswered: What was the relationship between Isis and most of the people she mentions, with their mixture of Greek and

■ **Emperor Honorius as Christian Victor, c. 406 C.E.**
Both sides of this ivory diptych ("folding tablet") depict Honorius, emperor of the western Roman empire, as a military victor who credits Christ for his success. Petronius Probus presented this gift to the emperor to show his gratitude for being awarded the consulship, the empire's highest honor. On the left, Honorius holds a sign that says, "You will always conquer, in the name of Christ"; a statuette of Victory standing on a globe offers him a victor's wreath. On the right, he holds a shield and a scepter. His clothing and armor identify him as a military leader; the inscription above his head proclaims him "Our Master, Always Augustus," while the circle around his head testifies to his special holiness. As this carving shows, Honorius, like other emperors, believed that he had divine backing for his army. In his case, it was not enough: the Goths sacked Rome only four years later.
(© Alinari/Art Resource, NY.)

213

Semitic names? Did Isis know how to write or, as was common, had she hired a scribe? Why had she gone to Alexandria? Why did Aion want to become a soldier? Why was "everybody" in the army?

These questions relate to the crisis that had struck the Roman Empire in the third-century C.E. Perhaps financial troubles forced Isis to leave her village to seek work in the city. Perhaps Aion wanted to join the army to earn wages; the emperors, like Honorius (r. 395–423) shown in the chapter-opening illustration dressed as a general, were always looking for more soldiers. Perhaps everybody seemed to be in the army because there was continuous civil war. These answers reflect the challenge facing imperial government by the 280s, after half a century of Roman armies fighting Roman armies over who should be emperor: how to reorganize the empire to restore peace and order through military force, government administration, ancestral religion, and economic prosperity. Diocletian, emperor beginning in 284 C.E., turned out to be a leader tough enough to meet this challenge and delay the political fragmentation of the empire.

Restoring peace and order proved difficult because religious tensions were growing between Christians and followers of traditional polytheistic cults like Isis the letter writer, named after the famous Egyptian goddess. Polytheist emperors, believing that Christians angered the gods, conducted brutal persecutions. Then, unexpectedly, early in the fourth century the emperor Constantine stopped the violence by converting to Christianity and officially favoring it. By the end of the fourth century, the new faith had become the state religion. The persistence of pre-Christian traditions and Christians' fierce disputes over doctrine kept this transformed Roman world in a state of religious tension.

Ending the civil wars postponed but did not prevent the break up of imperial territory. At the end of the fourth century, Honorius's father split the empire permanently into western and eastern sections. In the west, non-Roman peoples began migrating into the region, transforming it—and themselves—socially, culturally, and politically by replacing Roman provincial government with their own new kingdoms. They lived side by side with Romans, the different groups often merging their customs. By the fifth century, the loss of Roman control had transformed western Europe politically into different states, anticipating its modern divisions. In the east, the Roman provinces remained economically vibrant and politically united, becoming (in modern terminology) the Byzantine Empire in the sixth century. Despite financial pressures and shrinking territory, the Roman Empire would endure under Christian rule for centuries, until Turkish invaders finally conquered it in 1453.

Reorganizing the Empire

During the third-century crisis, attacks by foreign enemies had weakened the Roman Empire's defenses and hurt tax collection. The emperors also faced a significant religious problem: the growing influence of the Christian church. Diocletian

■ **Miniature Portrait of Emperor Constantine**

This eight-inch-high bust of Constantine is carved from chalcedony, a crystalline mineral prized for its milky look. The first Christian emperor is shown gazing upward, imitating his hero and model Alexander the Great, who had ordered his portrait to show him in this way. Constantine does not have a beard, a style made popular by Alexander and imitated by Augustus and Trajan, successful emperors to whom Constantine also wished to be linked. The cross in the center of Constantine's breastplate makes this one of the relatively few pieces of fourth-century Roman art to display Christian symbols. The position of this unmistakable sign of the emperor's religious choice recalls the sculpture on the armor on the Prima Porta statue of Augustus (see page 184); like the founder of the principate, Constantine communicated his image through art. What do you think Constantine hoped to gain by doing this?
(Bibliothèque nationale de France.)

(r. 284–305) and Constantine (r. 306–337) met these challenges by restoring strong central authority to the empire.

Imperial Reform and Fragmentation

Diocletian was an uneducated military man from outside Italy (Dalmatia, in what is now Croatia), but his exceptional leadership and intelligence propelled him through the ranks until the army made him emperor in 284. He ended the third-century crisis by imposing the strongest form of monarchy in Roman history. With the military's support, Diocletian proclaimed himself *dominus*—"master," what slaves called their owners—to replace Augustus's republican title, *princeps* ("first man"). Roman imperial rule from Diocletian onward is therefore called the **dominate**. Senators, consuls, and other traditional republican offices continued to exist, but the emperors held all the power. They therefore reigned as autocrats—true sole rulers.

The emperors of the dominate emphasized their supremacy by placing their throne on a raised platform, wearing jeweled robes, and surrounding themselves with attendants and ceremony. Constantine wore a diadem—a purple headband sparkling with gems, a symbol of kingship that earlier emperors had avoided. To demonstrate the ruler's superiority, a series of veils separated palace waiting rooms from the inner space where the emperor listened to people's pleas for help. High-ranking officials received showy titles such as "most perfect" and wore special shoes and belts. The court of the dominate resembled the splendid court of the Great King of Persia a thousand years earlier (see photo on page 30). The emperors of the dominate abandoned the first Roman emperors' claim that the ruler was merely the princeps, the "first man" but still just a citizen. Diocletian and his successors instead believed that citizens were their subjects. The architecture of the dominate reflected its rulers' all-powerful status. Diocletian's public bath in Rome rivaled earlier emperors' buildings in the capital; its soaring vaults and domes covered a space more than three thousand feet long on each side.

The dominate also used religious language to mark the emperor's special status. The emperors added *et deus* ("and God") to *dominus* as their title. Diocletian also adopted the title *Jovius*, claiming Jupiter (Jove), the chief Roman god, as his ancestor. His titles signaled the elevated respect he now demanded from his subjects because he expected to be honored as magnificently as the gods.

The emperors alone made law and did not consider themselves bound by earlier rulers' decisions. Relying on a loyal personal staff that isolated them from the outside world, they rarely asked for advice from the elite, as the first emperors had done. Their desire to maintain order led them to impose brutal punishments for crimes. For example, Constantine punished officials who did not keep what he called their "greedy hands" off bribes by having their hands "cut off by the sword"; the guardians of a young girl who allowed a lover to seduce her were punished by having molten lead poured into their mouths. The emperors of the dominate also widened the divide between poor and rich by making punishments even more harsh for the large segment of the population legally known as "humbler people"; their laws excused the "better people" from most of the harshest penalties for the same crimes.

Diocletian decided that the empire could not be administered and defended from a single center (that is, Rome). In 293, he therefore divided imperial territory into four administrative districts, two in the west and two in the east (Map 6.1). Having no sons, he appointed three "partners" so he and they could govern cooperatively in two pairs, both consisting of a senior "Augustus" with a junior "Caesar" as his adopted son and designated successor. Each emperor controlled one of the four districts. To prevent disunity, the most senior partner—in this case Diocletian—served as supreme ruler and was supposed to receive the loyalty of the others. This **tetrarchy** ("rule by four"), as modern scholars call it, was Diocletian's attempt to keep imperial government from being isolated at the center and to prevent civil war over who should be the next emperor.

Diocletian also subdivided the provinces, nearly doubling their number to almost a hundred. He grouped them into twelve dioceses under the jurisdiction of

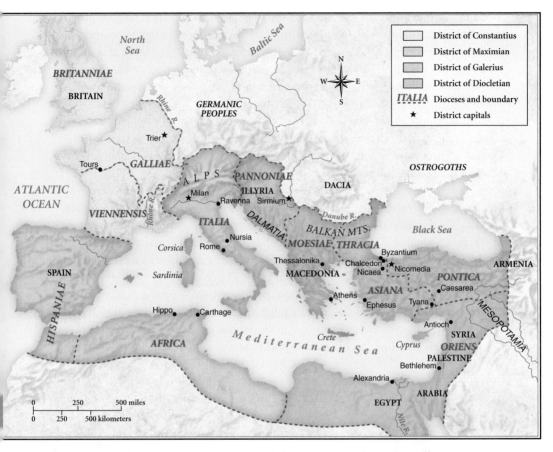

■ MAP 6.1 Diocletian's Reorganization of 293

To try to prevent civil war and tighten imperial control, Emperor Diocletian reorganized the Roman Empire. He created four administrative districts, each one governed by a different ruler. He also subdivided the preexisting provinces into smaller units and grouped them into twelve dioceses, each overseen by a regional administrator. This map shows the four districts as the imperial official Sextus Aurelius Victor described them in his book On the Caesars, *a biographically oriented history of the empire inspired by the famous biographies of Suetonius from the early second century. Victor published his book around 360.*

regional administrators, who reported to the four emperors' first assistants, the praetorian prefects. To try to keep provincial governors from becoming powerful enough to threaten the emperors, Diocletian began to separate their civil from their military authority, restricting administrators to control only of legal and financial affairs and restricting generals only to defense. Constantine completed this process.

Although later emperors abandoned the tetrarchy, Diocletian's reform of provincial administration into a hierarchy continued. He also ended Rome's thousand years as the empire's capital city. Diocletian lived in Nicomedia, in Asia Minor, and did not even visit Rome until 303, nearly twenty years after becoming emperor. He chose four new capitals for their usefulness as military command posts closer to the frontiers: Milan in northern Italy, Sirmium near the Danube River border, Trier near the Rhine River border, and Nicomedia. Italy became just another region in the empire, on an equal footing with the other provinces and subject to the same taxation system, except for the tax-free district of Rome itself—the last trace of the city's former superiority.

Despite Diocletian's reforms, civil war broke out soon after he retired in 305. It took Constantine (r. 306–337) until 324 to eliminate rivals. Near the end of his reign, he named his three sons as joint heirs, ordering them to rule as co-emperors. They failed as bloodily as had the sons of Septimius Severus a century earlier, plunging into war with one another. This civil war informally split the empire on a north-south line along the Balkan peninsula. In 395, Honorius and Arcadius divided the empire into western and eastern halves, ruling as co-emperors. The co-emperors were supposed to cooperate, but this division launched the two parts of the empire toward different fates.

Each half of the empire had its own capital. Constantinople, near the mouth of the Black Sea, was the eastern capital. Originally Byzantium (today Istanbul, Turkey), Constantinople had been reconstructed and renamed by Constantine in 324 as his "new Rome." He had chosen it for its geography, on an easily fortified peninsula controlling routes for trade and troop movements. To recall the glory of Rome, Constantine had given his refounded city a forum, an imperial palace, a hippodrome for chariot races, and huge statues of the traditional gods. The eastern emperors inherited Constantine's "new" city as their capital; from its ancient name modern historians call the eastern section of the old Roman Empire the **Byzantine Empire**.

The Division of the Empire, c. 395

Geography determined the site of the western capital as well. The western emperor Honorius (r. 395–423) wanted to keep the Alps mountains between his territory and the raiders living to the north. In 404, he made Ravenna, a port on Italy's northeastern coast, the western capital because it was a naval base and an important commercial city. Walls and marshes protected it from attack by land, while its harbor kept it from being starved out in a siege. Ravenna never rivaled Constantinople in size or riches, but the emperors did build churches gleaming with multicolored mosaics.

Financial Reform and Social Consequences

Diocletian's rescue of the empire required vast amounts of money, which the inflation of the third century had made hard to find. He tried to improve imperial finances by issuing new money, price controls, and a new taxation system. Unfortunately, Diocletian miscalculated in setting values for his new coins and set off a financial panic that increased inflation in many regions after 293. High prices caused people to hoard whatever goods they could buy, and hoarding drove prices ever higher. "Hurry and spend all my money you have; buy me any kinds of goods at whatever prices they are available," wrote one official to his servant, fearing yet another decline in the value of the currency.

In 301, Diocletian tried to stop inflation by imposing price and wage controls in the worst-hit regions. His Edict on Maximum Prices blamed high prices on profiteers' "unlimited and crazed avarice," banned hoarding, and set limits on the prices that could legally be charged for about a thousand goods and services. The edict soon became ineffective because merchants refused to cooperate and government officials were unable to enforce it despite the threat of death or exile as the penalty for violations. In his final years, Diocletian revalued the currency to restore sound money and stable prices, but the civil war under Constantine again weakened it.

With the currency losing value, the emperors began collecting taxes not only in coins but also in goods. Recent research disputes whether this form of revenue actually replaced taxes paid in coin, as previous scholars believed, or only served as a way to impose higher property taxes, which had to be paid in coin as much as possible. By the end of the fourth century, it is clear that the government expected payment in gold and silver, and that taxes rose, especially on the local elites. Taxes went mostly to support the army, which required enormous amounts of grain, meat, wine, horses, camels, and mules. The major sources of revenue were a tax on land, assessed according to its productivity, and a head tax on individuals.

The empire was too large to enforce consistency in tax rates. In some areas, both men and women from about the age of twelve to sixty-five paid the full tax; in others, women paid only one-half the tax assessment or none at all. Workers in cities probably owed taxes only on their property. They periodically paid "in kind"— laboring without pay on public works projects such as cleaning municipal drains or repairing buildings. Urban businesspeople, from shopkeepers to prostitutes, paid taxes in money. Members of the senatorial class were exempt from ordinary taxes but had to make other payments when the emperor demanded them.

The new tax system would work only if agricultural production remained stable and the government controlled the people liable for the head tax. Diocletian therefore restricted the movement of tenant farmers (*coloni*), who formed the empire's economic base. Coloni had traditionally been free to move to different farms under different landlords. Now tenant farmers were increasingly tied to a particular plot, and their children were required to remain farmers.

The government also restricted workers in other essential occupations. Bakers, for example, could not leave their jobs, and anyone who acquired a baker's property had to assume that occupation. The bakers were essential in producing free bread for Rome's poor, a tradition begun under the republic to prevent food riots. Also, from Constantine's reign on, military service became a lifetime career that sons of soldiers inherited: they had to serve in the army.

The emperors announced equally oppressive regulations for the propertied class in the empire's towns, the **curials**. Almost all men in the curial class were obliged sooner or later to serve as unsalaried city council members, who had to use their own funds if necessary to support the community. Their financial responsibilities ranged from maintaining the water supply to feeding troops, but their most expensive duty was covering shortfalls in tax collection. The emperors' demands for increased revenue made this a crushing burden, compounding the damage to the curials that the third-century crisis had begun.

For centuries, the empire's welfare had depended on a steady supply of public-spirited members of the social elite enthusiastically filling these crucial posts to win the admiration of their neighbors. Now this tradition broke down as wealthy people avoided public service to escape financial ruin. So distorted was the situation that forced service on a city council became one of the punishments for a minor crime. Eventually, to prevent curials from escaping their obligations, the emperors ordered them not to move away from the town where they had been born; they even had to ask official permission to travel. These laws made members of the elite try to win exemptions from public service by begging the emperor, bribing high-ranking officials, or taking up an occupation that freed them from such obligations (such as being a soldier, an imperial administrator, or a church official). The most desperate simply fled, abandoning home and property.

The restrictions on freedom caused by the pressure for higher taxes thus eroded wealthy Romans' long-standing commitment to public service. The emperors' attempt to stabilize the empire by increasing its revenues also hurt nonelite citizens. The tax rate on land eventually reached one-third of its gross yield. This burden crushed poor farmers. They had to eat most of what they produced just to survive, save enough seed to plant the next crop, and then pay the high tax out of what was left. A bad harvest meant starvation. Conditions became so bad in fifth-century Spain, for example, that peasants openly revolted against imperial control. Financial troubles, especially severe in the west, kept the empire from ever regaining the prosperity of its Golden Age and worsened the friction between government and citizens.

Religious Reform: From Persecution to Conversion

Traditional belief required religious explanations for disasters. Diocletian therefore concluded that the gods' anger had caused the third-century crisis. To restore divine goodwill, he instructed citizens to follow the traditional gods who had guided Rome to power and virtue: "The providence of the immortal gods has allowed superior, wise, and upright men in their wisdom to establish good and true principles. It is wrong to oppose these principles or to abandon the ancient religion for some new one." Christianity was the new religion Diocletian had in mind.

Blaming Christians for the empire's troubles, Diocletian in 303 launched the **Great Persecution**. He expelled Christians from his administration, seized their property and tore down their churches, and executed them for refusing to participate in official religious rituals. As was often true, policy was applied differently in different regions. In the western empire, the violence stopped after about a year; in the east, it continued for a decade. So gruesome were the public executions of martyrs that they aroused the sympathy of some polytheists.

Constantine changed the empire's religious history forever by converting to Christianity. He chose the new faith for the same reason that Diocletian had persecuted it: in the belief that he would receive divine protection for himself and the empire. During the civil war that he fought to succeed Diocletian, Constantine experienced a dream vision promising him the support of the Christian God. His biographer, Eusebius (c. 260–340), later reported that Constantine had also seen a vision of Jesus' cross in the sky surrounded by the words "In this sign you shall be the victor." When Constantine defeated his main rival at the Battle of the Milvian Bridge in Rome in 312, he proclaimed that God's miraculous power and goodwill had brought him the victory. He therefore declared himself a Christian emperor.

After his conversion, Constantine did not outlaw polytheism or make Christianity the official religion. Instead, he announced religious toleration. The best statement of his new policy survives in the **Edict of Milan** of 313. It proclaimed free choice of religion for everyone and referred to the empire's protection by "the highest divinity"—an imprecise term meant to satisfy both polytheists and Christians.

Constantine wanted to avoid angering polytheists because they still greatly outnumbered Christians, but he nevertheless did all he could to promote his newly chosen religion. These goals called for a careful balancing act. For example, he returned all property seized during the Great Persecution to its Christian owners, but he had the treasury pay back those who had bought the confiscated property at auction. When in 321 he made Lord's Day a holy occasion each week on which no official business or manufacturing work could be performed, he called it Sunday to blend Christian and traditional notions in honoring two divinities, God and the sun. To beautify his new capital, Constantinople, he erected numerous statues of traditional gods around the city. He also respected Roman tradition by holding the office of *pontifex maximus* ("chief priest"), which emperors had filled ever since Augustus.

■ **REVIEW:** *What changes did Diocletian and his successors make in their reorganization of the empire?*

■ **Relief Sculpture of Saturn from North Africa**

This pillar shows the god known to the Romans as Saturn and to the Carthaginians as Ba'al Hammon (one of the gods of the Phoenician founders of Carthage). This syncretism (identifying gods as the same even though they carried different names in different places) was typical of ancient polytheism and allowed Roman and non-Roman cults to merge. The smaller figure below the god is sacrificing a sheep before an altar. The inscription dates the pillar to 323, a decade later than Constantine's conversion to Christianity. Such objects testifying to the continuing existence of polytheistic cults remained common until the end of the fourth century, when the Christian emperors succeeded in suppressing most public activities of traditional religion.
(© Copyright Martha Cooper/Peter Arnold, Inc.)

Christianizing the Empire

Constantine's religious policy of toleration and compromise set the empire on the path to Christianization. The process proved to be slow and sometimes violent. Not until the end of the fourth century did the emperors close the traditional gods' temples. Even after the vast majority of people in the empire had become Christians, some polytheists long kept worshiping in private. From the perspective of later history, however, the transformation from polytheist empire into Christian state became by far the most enduring influence of Greco-Roman antiquity.

The Spread of Christianity

The empire's Christianization generated passionate disputes because ordinary people cared deeply about religion. It provided their best hope for private salvation in a dangerous world over which they had little control. On this point, polytheists and Christians held some similar beliefs. Both believed spirits and demons had powerful influences on daily life. For some, it seemed safest to believe in all religions. For example, a silver spoon used in the worship of the polytheist forest spirit Faunus has been found engraved with a fish, the common symbol whose Greek spelling (*ichthys*) was an abbreviation for the Greek words "Jesus Christ the Son of God, the Savior."

Nevertheless, the differences between polytheists' and Christians' beliefs were much greater than their similarities. People disagreed on whether there was one God or many, and about what effect God or the gods had on the human world. Polytheists still participated in festivals and sacrifices to many different gods. Why, they asked, did these joyous occasions not satisfy Christians' desires for contact with divinity?

Polytheists also could not understand why Christians believed in a savior who had not established a new kingdom on earth and been executed as a common criminal. The traditional gods, they insisted, had given a world empire to their worshipers. Moreover, they told Christians, cults such as that of the goddess Isis, after whom the worried Egyptian letter writer had been named, and philosophies such as Stoicism insisted that only the pure of heart could be their followers. Christianity, by contrast, took in sinners. Why, puzzled polytheists wondered, would any righteous person want to associate with wrongdoers? In short, as the Greek philosopher Porphyry (c. 234–305) remarked, Christians had no right to claim that only they had a true religion, for no one had ever found one single doctrine providing "a universal path to the liberation of the soul."

The slow pace of religious change revealed how strong polytheism remained in the fourth century, especially in the social elite. In fact, the emperor Julian (r. 361–363) rebelled against his family's Christianity and tried to impose his philosophical brand of polytheism as Rome's official religion. This rejection of Christianity earned him the name Julian the Apostate (someone who turns against an established faith is called an **apostate**). Deeply religious, he believed in a supreme deity corresponding to the ideas of Greek philosophers: "This divine and completely beautiful universe, from heaven's highest sky to earth's lowest limit, is tied together by the continuous providence of god, has existed forever, and will last forever." Julian's restoration of the traditional gods ended with his unexpected death while invading Persia.

The Christian emperors who followed Julian worked to end polytheism through various restrictions. In 382, Gratian (r. 375–383 in the west) removed from the Senate in Rome the Altar of Victory, which Augustus had placed there to remind senators of Rome's success under its ancestral religion; most importantly, Gratian stopped public funding for traditional sacrifices. Aurelius Symmachus (c. 340–402), a polytheist senator who served as prefect ("mayor") of Rome, objected to what he saw as an outrage against Rome's tradition of religious diversity. Protesting the emperors' moves against polytheism, he argued: "We all have our own way of life and our own way of worship. . . . So vast a mystery [as religious truth] cannot be approached by only one path."

■ **Mosaic of Christ as Sun God**
This mosaic comes from a burial cham-
ber in Rome that is now in the Vatican,
under the basilica of St. Peter built by
Constantine. It perhaps dates to the
mid-third century. Christ appears here
similar to a traditional polytheistic
representation of the Sun god, especially
the Greek Apollo: with rays of light
shining forth around his head as he
rides in a chariot pulled by horses. This
symbolism —God is light—reached
back to ancient Egypt. Christian artists
showed Jesus in this way because he had
said, "I am the light of the world" (John
8:12). The cloak flaring from Christ's
shoulder suggests the spread of his
motion across the sky. **For more help**
analyzing this image, see the visual
activity for this chapter in the ONLINE
STUDY GUIDE at bedfordstmartins.com/
huntconcise. (Scala/Art Resource, NY.)

Christianity finally replaced traditional polytheism as the state religion in 391 when the emperor Theodosius (r. 379–395 in the east) successfully banned all polytheist sacrifices, even if private individuals paid for the animals. He also made divination (predicting the future) by the inspection of animal entrails punishable as high treason and ordered that all polytheist temples be closed. Many shrines, however, such as the Parthenon in Athens, remained in use for a long time because the empire was too large for the emperors to control at the local level. Temples were only gradually converted to churches during the fifth and sixth centuries. Non-Christian schools were not forced to close—the Academy, founded by Plato in Athens in the early fourth century B.C.E., endured for 140 years after Theodosius's reign—but Christians received advantages in government careers. Over time, non-Christians became outsiders in an empire ruled by Christian emperors.

Jews posed a special problem for the Christian emperors. Like polytheists, Jews rejected the new state religion. Yet they seemed entitled to special treatment because Jesus had been a Jew and because previous emperors had allowed Jews to practice their religion, even when Hadrian refounded Jerusalem as a Roman colony after putting down a fierce revolt there (132–135). Fourth-century and later emperors placed legal restrictions on Jews. For example, they banned Jews from holding government jobs but still required them to take on the financial burdens of curials—without receiving the honor of curial status. By the late sixth century, they increased the pressure on Jews to convert to Christianity by barring them from making wills, receiving inheritances, or testifying in court.

Although these developments began the long process that made Jews into second-class citizens in later European history, they did not destroy Judaism. Synagogues continued to exist in Palestine, where a few Jews still lived (most had been dispersed throughout the cities of the empire and the lands beyond the eastern border). The study of Jewish law and traditions flourished in this period, leading to the creation of books known as the Palestinian and the Babylonian Talmuds (collections of scholars' interpretations of Jewish law) and the scriptural commentaries of the Midrash (an explanation of the meaning of the Hebrew Bible). These works of religious scholarship provided guidance on how to live according to God's will and greatly influenced later Judaism.

Christianity's status as the state religion aided its spread by encouraging new believers to adopt the emperor's religion. Soldiers, for example, now found it possible to convert to Christianity and still serve in the army. Previously, Christian soldiers had sometimes created disciplinary problems. As one senior infantryman had said in 298 at his court-martial for abandoning his duties, "A Christian serving the Lord Christ should not serve the affairs of this world." Once the emperors had become Christians, however, soldiers could more easily justify military duty as supporting Christ.

Christianity's spread also depended on the appeal of its religious and social values. Christianity offered believers a strong sense of community in this world as well as the promise of salvation in the next. Wherever they went, they could find a warm welcome in the local congregation (see Map 6.2 on page 226). The new religion also won converts by performing charitable works—in the tradition of Jews and some polytheist cults—especially for the poor, widows, and orphans. By the mid-third century, for example, Rome's congregation was supporting fifteen hundred widows and other poor people. Christianity's emphasis on taking care of others was especially important because people at that time had to depend mostly on friends and relatives for help; state-funded social services were rare.

Although scholars continue to debate the role of women in early Christianity, it is clear they were a major force in spreading the new religion. Augustine (354–430), bishop of Hippo in North Africa and perhaps the most influential theologian in Western history, recognized women's contribution to the strengthening of Christianity in a letter he wrote to the unbaptized husband of a baptized woman: "O you men, who fear all the burdens imposed by baptism. The women are far better than you. Chaste and devoted to the faith, it is their presence in large numbers that causes the church to grow." Some women earned high status by giving their property to their congregation or by refusing marriage to dedicate themselves to Christ. Life-long virgins and widows who chose not to remarry thus joined large

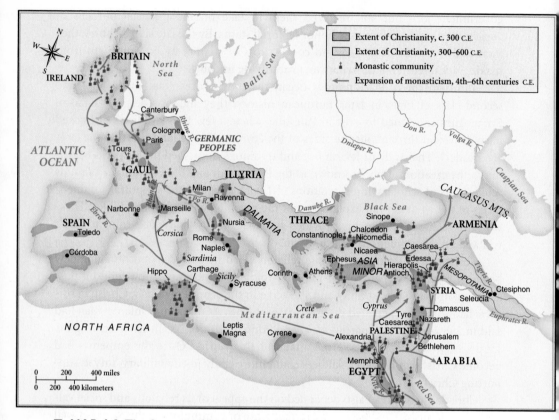

■ MAP 6.2 The Spread of Christianity, 300–600

Christians were still a minority in the population of the Roman Empire in 300, although congregations existed in many cities and towns, especially in the eastern provinces. The emperor Constantine's conversion to Christianity in the early fourth century gave a boost to the new religion; it gained further strength during that century as the Christian emperors provided financial support and eliminated payments for the polytheist cults that had previously made up the religion of the state. By 600, the preaching of the church's missionaries and the money of the emperors had spread Christianity from one end of the empire to the other.

(Adapted from Henry Chadwick and G. R. Evans, *Atlas of the Christian Church* [Oxford: Andromeda Oxford Ltd., 1987], 28. Reproduced by permission of Andromeda Oxford Limited.)

donors as especially respected women. These women rejected the traditional social order, in which women were supposed to devote themselves to raising families. But even these holy women were excluded from leadership positions once the church's organization became a hierarchy of bishops matching the male-dominated hierarchy of the Roman world.

The final development that promoted the spread of Christianity was the creation of a hierarchical organization in which male bishops became Christianity's official leaders. The bishops replaced early Christianity's more democratic organization in which women could be leaders. Bishops had the authority to certify priests to conduct the church's sacraments, above all baptism and communion—rituals guaranteeing eternal life. Bishops also controlled their congregations' memberships and finances; much of the funds came from believers' donations and gifts in their wills. Over time, bishops became the emperors' partners in local rule, replacing the curials, whose numbers had shrunk drastically from the financial pressures the government had imposed on them but not on bishops. The bishops gained power because they could influence the emperor to direct money back to their region. Regional councils of bishops appointed new bishops and tried to settle disputes over Christian doctrine. The bishops in the largest cities became the most powerful leaders in the church. The main bishop of Carthage, for example, supervised at least one hundred local bishops in the surrounding area. The bishop of Rome, however, became the church's supreme leader in the western empire. The eastern church never agreed that he controlled the entire Christian world, but his dominance in the west won him the title previously applied to many bishops: pope (from *pappas,* Greek for "father"), the name still used for the head of the Roman Catholic church.

The bishops of Rome quoted the New Testament to establish their leadership over other bishops. In the book of Matthew (16:18–19), Jesus speaks to the Apostle Peter: "You are Peter, and upon this rock I will build my church. . . . I will entrust to you the keys of the kingdom of heaven. Whatever you bind on earth shall be bound in heaven. Whatever you loose on earth shall be loosed in heaven." Because Peter's name in Greek means "rock" and because Peter was believed to have been the first bishop of Rome, later bishops in Rome, believing they inherited Peter's power, used this passage to justify their command over the church.

Competing Visions of Religious Truth

The spread of Christianity was not a calm and peaceful process because Christians had angry conflicts about what they should believe. The church's hierarchy of bishops struggled to create uniformity in belief and worship to ensure its members' spiritual purity and to maintain its authority over them. These leaders clashed over theology, however, and Christians never achieved unity on what was religious truth.

Disputes flared over what was orthodoxy (the official doctrines determined by councils of bishops, from the Greek for "correct thinking") as opposed to heresy (deviation from official doctrines, from the Greek for "private choice"). After Christianity became the state religion, the emperor became the top official responsible for enforcing orthodox creed (a summary of beliefs); he used force against believers who persisted in their heresy.

Questions about the nature of the Trinity of Father, Son, and Holy Spirit—which orthodoxy defined as a unified, co-eternal, and identical divinity—caused the worst conflict. **Arianism,** for example, generated fierce controversy for centuries. Named after its founder, Arius (c. 260–336), a priest from Alexandria in Egypt, this doctrine maintained that Jesus as God's son had not existed eternally; rather, God the Father had "begot" (created) his son from nothing and given him his special status. Thus Jesus was not co-eternal with God and not identical in nature with his father. This view implied that the Trinity was divisible and that Christianity's monotheism was not absolute. Arianism found widespread support, perhaps because it eliminated the difficulty of understanding how a son could be as old as his father and also because its making the son inferior to the father corresponded to regular family life. Arius used popular songs to make his views known, and people everywhere argued about the controversy. "When you ask for your change from a shopkeeper," one observer remarked in describing Constantinople, "he lectures you about the Begotten and the Unbegotten. If you ask how much bread costs, the reply is that 'the Father is superior and the Son inferior.' "

Many Christians became so angry about Arius's position on Jesus that Constantine had to intervene. In 325, he assembled 220 bishops at the Council of Nicaea to settle the dispute. The majority of bishops voted to crack down on Arianism: they banished Arius to the Balkan Mountains and declared that the Father and the Son were "of one substance" and co-eternal. So complicated were the issues, however, that Constantine later changed his mind twice, first recalling Arius from exile and then punishing him again not long after. The doctrine lived on: Constantine's third son, Constantius II (r. 337–361), favored Arianism, and his missionaries converted many of the immigrants who later came to live in the empire.

Nestorius, who became bishop of Constantinople in 428, disagreed with the orthodox doctrine of how Jesus' human and divine natures were related to his birth, insisting that his mother Mary gave birth to the human that became the temple for the divine. Nestorianism enraged orthodox Christians by rejecting Mary's title as *theotokos* (Greek for "bearer of God"). The bishops of Alexandria and Rome had Nestorius deposed and his doctrines officially rejected at councils held in 430 and 431; they condemned his writings in 435. Nestorian bishops in the eastern empire refused to accept these decisions, however, and they formed a separate church centered in Persia, where for centuries Nestorian Christians flourished under the tolerance of non-Christian rulers. They later became important agents of cross-cultural interaction by establishing communities that still endure in Arabia, India, and China.

No heresy better illustrates the bitterness of Christian conflicts over religious truth than Donatism. Following the Great Persecution, a dispute arose in North Africa in the fourth century over whether to readmit to their old congregations those Christians who had cooperated with imperial authorities to avoid persecution. Some

■ **Mosaic of a Family from Edessa in the Middle East**

This mosaic, found in a cave tomb, depicts an upper-class family of Edessa in the late Roman imperial period. Their names are given in Syriac, the dialect of Aramaic spoken in their region, and their colorful clothing reflects local traditions. Edessa was the capital of the small kingdom of Osrhoëne, which lay on the east bank of the Euphrates River between the Taurus Mountains and the Syrian desert. Rome took over the kingdom in 216, and it became famous in Christian history because its king, Abgar (r. 179–216), was remembered as the first ruler to convert to Christianity, well before Constantine. By the early fourth century, the story had emerged that after Jesus' death and resurrection, he sent one of his disciples to Edessa, where the disciple painted a picture of Jesus that protected the city from its enemies. The Byzantine emperors proclaimed themselves the heirs of King Abgar and of Jesus' grant to the city of special divine protection.

(Photo courtesy Thames & Hudson Ltd., London, from *Vanished Civilizations*, ed. Edward Bacon.)

North African Christians felt these lapsed members should be forgiven, but the Donatists (followers of the North African priest Donatus) insisted that the church should not be polluted with such "traitors." Most important, Donatists insisted, unfaithful priests and bishops could not administer the sacraments. So bitter was the clash that it even split Christian families. As one son threatened his mother, "I will join Donatus's followers, and I will drink your blood."

These fiery emotions made it difficult for bishops to enforce orthodoxy as religious truth. The Council of Chalcedon (an outskirt of Constantinople), at which the empress Pulcheria and her consort Marcian brought together more than five hundred bishops in 451, was the most important attempt to forge agreement. Its conclusions on correct doctrine form the basis of what many Christians still accept as doctrine: Jesus' divine and human natures were mixed within his person but nevertheless remained distinct. Monophysites (a Greek term for "single-nature believers") refused to agree, however, arguing that Jesus had only a single, divine nature. They split from the orthodox hierarchy in the sixth century to found independent churches in Egypt (the Coptic church), Ethiopia, Syria, and Armenia.

No one person had a stronger impact on the establishment of the western church's orthodoxy and therefore on later Catholicism than Augustine (354–430). Born in North Africa to a Christian mother and a polytheist father, he began his career by teaching rhetoric at Carthage, where he fathered a son by a mistress; he was later befriended by the prominent polytheist noble Aurelius Symmachus after moving to Italy. In 386, he converted to Christianity under the influence of his mother and Ambrose (c. 339–397), the powerful bishop of Milan. In 395, he himself was appointed bishop of Hippo, but his reputation rests on his writings. By around 500, Augustine and other influential theologians such as Ambrose and Jerome (c. 345–420) had earned the informal title "church fathers" because their views were quoted as authoritative in disputes over orthodoxy. Augustine became the most famous of this group of patristic (from the Greek for "father," *pater*) authors, and for the next thousand years his works would be the most influential texts in western Christianity besides the Bible. He wrote so much about religion and philosophy that a later scholar was moved to declare: "The man lies who says he has read all your works."

Augustine's most influential book on Christianity's role in the world was *City of God*, a "large and difficult work," as he called it, written between 413 and 426. In this book he knocked down the idea that Christianity, like the traditional cults it had replaced, guaranteed earthly success to Christians. Most importantly, he said, Christians were not responsible for Alaric's sacking of Rome in 410, a disaster that polytheists claimed was the gods' punishment for Romans' abandoning their traditional religion. Like other Christian thinkers, Augustine worried that Christianity would be blamed for Rome's loss of power. In addition, Augustine redefined the ideal state as a society of Christians. Not even Plato's doctrines offered a true path to purity, Augustine insisted, because the true struggle for individuals was not between their emotions and reason, but between their desire for earthly pleasures and spiritual purity. Emotions, especially love, were natural and desirable, but only when directed toward God. Humans were wrong to look for value in life on earth. Only life in God's city had meaning.

Nevertheless, Augustine wrote, earthly law and government were required because humans are by nature imperfect. God's original creation in the Garden of Eden was full of goodness, but humans lost their original perfection by inheriting a permanently sinful nature after Adam and Eve had disobeyed God. This doctrine of original sin—a subject of theological debate since at least the second century— meant that people suffered from a hereditary moral disease that turned the human will into a corrupting force. This corruption required governments to use force to combat vice. Although far inferior to the divine ideal, civil government was necessary to impose moral order on the chaos of human life after the fall from grace in the Garden of Eden. The government therefore had a right to force people to remain united to the church, by violence if necessary.

Order in society was essential, Augustine argued; it even justified the naturally evil practice of slavery because it was, in his view, a lesser evil than the violent troubles that would follow from overturning social traditions. Moreover, it was Christians' duty to obey the emperor and participate in political life. Soldiers, too, had to follow their orders. Augustine ruled out torture and capital punishment, however, because the purpose of government was to maintain a social order based on a moral order.

In *City of God*, Augustine tried to uncover a divine purpose in the events of history that humans found hard to understand, such as why God allowed Alaric to sack Rome. All that Christians could know with certainty was that history progressed toward an ultimate goal, but only God could know the meaning of each day's events. What could not be doubted was God's guiding power:

> To be truthful, I myself fail to understand why God created mice and frogs, flies and worms. Nevertheless, I recognize that each of these creatures is beautiful in its own way. For when I think about the body and limbs of any living creature, where do I not find proportion, number, and order showing the unity of concord? Where one discovers proportion, number, and order, one should look for the craftsman.

The repeated *I* in this passage reveals the intense personal commitment Augustine brought to matters of faith and doctrine.

Next to the nature of Christ, the question of how to understand and control sexual desire presented Christians with the toughest problem in the search for religious truth. Augustine became the most influential source of the doctrine that sex automatically involved human beings in evil and that they should therefore practice **asceticism**, self-denial of all pleasures (from the Greek *askesis*, meaning "training"). Augustine knew from personal experience how difficult it was to accept this doctrine. In fact, he revealed in his autobiographical work *Confessions*, written about 397, that he felt a deep conflict between his sexual desire and his religious doctrines. Only after a long period of doubt, he explained, did he find the inner strength to pledge future chastity as part of his conversion to Christianity.

He advocated no sex as the purest choice for Christians because he believed that Adam and Eve's disobedience in the Garden of Eden had forever ruined the original harmony God created between human will and human passions. According to Augustine, God punished his disobedient children by making sexual desire a corrupting force that humans could never completely control through will. Although he declared the value of marriage in God's plan, he added that sexual intercourse even between loving spouses carried the sad reminder of humanity's fall from grace. A married couple should "lie down with a certain sadness" to the task of starting a pregnancy, the only acceptable reason for sex; sexual pleasure could never be a human good.

This doctrine made virginity and avoidance of sex high virtues; in the words of Jerome, they counted as "daily martyrdom." This self-chosen holiness proved especially valuable for women in boosting their status in Christian society; their sexual abstinence earned them such respect that they could demand privileges usually reserved for men, such as more education in Hebrew and Greek to read the Bible. By the end of the fourth century, sexual purity had become so significant for Christian virtue that congregations began to expect celibate male priests and bishops.

The Beginning of Christian Monasticism

Christian asceticism reached its peak in monasticism. The word *monk* (from Greek *monos*, "single, solitary") described the basis of monasticism: men and women withdrawing from society to live a life of extreme self-denial imitating Jesus' suffering, demonstrating their devotion to God, and praying for divine mercy on the world. The earliest monks lived alone, but soon they formed communities for mutual support in the pursuit of ascetic holiness (see Map 6.2).

Polytheist and Jewish ascetics, motivated by philosophy and religion, had long existed. What made Christian monasticism different were the huge numbers of people it attracted and the high status that monks earned. Leaving their families and congregations, they gave up sex, worshiped frequently, wore the roughest clothes, and ate barely enough to survive, aiming to win an inner peace isolated from daily concerns. They reported, however, that they constantly struggled against fantasies of earthly delights, dreaming of plentiful, tasty food more often than of sex.

The earliest Christian ascetics appeared in the late third century in Egypt. Antony (c. 251–356), from a well-to-do family, was among the first. One day, he abruptly abandoned all his property after hearing a sermon based on Jesus' advice to a rich young man to sell his possessions and give the proceeds to the poor (Matt. 19:21). Putting aside his duty to see his sister married, he placed her in a home for unmarried women and spent his life alone in a barren region, demonstrating his excellence through worshiping God.

Monasticism to people appealed for many reasons, but above all because it gave ordinary people a way to achieve excellence and recognition. This opportunity seemed all the more valuable after Constantine's conversion and the end of the persecutions. Becoming a monk—a living martyrdom—served as the substitute for a martyr's death and imitated the sacrifice of Christ. Individual—or eremetic (hence "hermit")—monks went to great lengths to win fame. In Syria, for example, "holy women" and "holy men" attracted great attention by their feats of endurance. Symeon the Stylite (390–459) lived atop a tall pillar (*stylos* in

Greek) for thirty years, preaching to people gathered below his perch. Egyptian Christians believed that their monks' religious devotion made them living heroes ensuring the annual flooding of the Nile, the duty once linked to the pharaohs' divine power. Exceptionally famous ascetics had even greater influence after death. Their relics—body parts or clothing—became treasured sources of protection and healing. Relics gave believers faith in God's favor by expressing the power of saints (people receiving special honor after their deaths as reward for their special holiness).

The earliest monks followed the example of Antony in living alone. In about 323, Pachomius in Upper Egypt organized the first monastic community. In this "coenobitic" (seen-uh-BIT-ick), or "life in common," monasticism, men or women monks formed single-gender settlements to encourage one another along the hard road to holiness. Coenobitic monasticism became the primary form of Christian

■ Monastery of St. Catherine at Mount Sinai

The Byzantine emperor Justinian (r. 527–565) built a wall to enclose the building of this monastery in the desert at the foot of Mount Sinai (on the peninsula between Egypt and Arabia). Jews and Christians regarded this spot as holy because Moses had received the Ten Commandments there during the Hebrews' wanderings after their exodus from Egypt. Justinian supported the monastery to promote orthodoxy in a region dominated by Monophysite Christians. The monks at St. Catherine's gained a reputation for exceptional religious devotion: they spent much of their time repeating a simple prayer to Jesus over and over. The monastery gained its name in the ninth century from a story about angels bringing the body of Catherine of Alexandria there. Catherine was said to have been martyred in the fourth century for refusing to marry the emperor because, in her words, she was the bride of Christ. (Erich Lessing/ Art Resource, NY.)

asceticism. Monasteries were often built close together to divide their labor, with women making clothing, for example, while men farmed.

All monasteries imposed military-style discipline, but they differed in the harshness of their rules and amount of contact with the outside world. The most isolationist groups arose in the eastern empire, but the followers of Martin of Tours (c. 316–397), an ex-soldier famed for his religious deeds, founded communities in the west as harsh as any eastern ones. Basil ("the Great") of Caesarea in Asia Minor (c. 330–379) started a different tradition: monasteries serving society. He required monks to perform charitable deeds, leading to the foundation of the first hospitals attached to monasteries.

A milder, but still strict, code telling monks how to live became the standard in the west, influencing almost every area of Catholic worship. Called the Benedictine rule after its creator, Benedict of Nursia in central Italy (c. 480–553), this code prescribed a daily routine of prayer, scriptural readings, and manual labor. The rule divided the day into seven parts, each with a compulsory service of prayers and lessons, called "the office." Unlike harsher codes, Benedict's did not isolate the monks from the outside world or deprive them of sleep, adequate food, or warm clothing. Although his code gave the abbot (the head monk) full authority, it instructed him to listen to what every member of the community, even the youngest monk, had to say before he decided important matters. He was not allowed to beat them severely as punishment for breaking the rules, as sometimes happened under other, harsher systems. Communities of women, such as those founded by Basil's sister Macrina and Benedict's sister Scholastica, usually followed the rules of the male monasteries, with an emphasis on the modesty thought necessary for women.

The thousands of Christians who became monks from the fourth century onward joined monasteries for social as well as theological reasons. Some had been given as babies to monasteries by parents who could not raise them or were fulfilling religious vows, a practice called oblation. Jerome once gave this advice to a mother about her daughter:

> Let her be brought up in a monastery, let her live among virgins, let her learn to avoid swearing, let her regard lying as a sin against God, let her be ignorant of the world, let her live the angelic life, while in the flesh let her be without the flesh, and let her suppose that all human beings are like herself.

When she reaches adulthood as a virgin, he added, she should avoid the baths so she would not be seen naked or give her body pleasure by dipping in the warm pools. Jerome expressed traditional Roman values favoring males when he promised that God would reward the mother with the birth of sons to compensate for her dedicating her daughter to God. But he also said, "[As monks] we evaluate people's virtue not by their gender but by their character, and judge those to be worthy of the greatest glory who have given up both status and riches."

The monasteries' independence threatened the power of the church's hierarchy. Bishops did not like devoted members of their congregations withdrawing into monasteries, not least because they then gave their donations to their new community rather than to their local churches. Moreover, monks challenged bishops' authority because holy men and women earned their special status not by having it awarded by the church's leaders but by earning it through their own actions. Bishops and monks did share a spiritual goal—salvation and service to God. While polytheists had enjoyed immediate access to their gods, who were thought to visit the earth constantly, Christians worshiped a God outside this world. Monks bridged the gap between the human and the divine by asking God to be merciful to faithful believers.

■ **REVIEW:** *What were the major disputes among early Christians, and why were they so fierce?*

Non-Roman Kingdoms in the West

Just as western and eastern monasticism differed in the harshness of their rules, the western and eastern regions of the empire grew increasingly different in their social and political arrangements. The western part underwent the biggest changes. The migrations of non-Roman peoples into western Europe transformed politics, society, and the economy there. Two strong motives drove these diverse groups into Roman territory: to flee the brutal attacks of the Huns (nomads from the steppes of central Asia) and to benefit from the empire's prosperity. By the 370s, their presence was provoking much violence in the western empire. As the imperial government's ability to maintain order weakened, these immigrants experienced great changes themselves, transforming from vaguely defined and organized tribes into kingdoms with separate ethnic identities. By the 470s, one of their commanders ruled Italy. That political change has been said to mark the "fall of the Roman Empire." In fact, the lasting effects of the interactions of these non-Roman peoples with the diverse peoples of western Europe and North Africa are better understood as a political, social, and cultural transformation that made them the heirs of the western Roman Empire and led to the formation of medieval Europe.

Migrations into the Empire

At first, the fourth-century emperors encouraged the migrations. Like the earlier emperors, they recruited foreign warriors for the Roman army. By the late fourth century, crowds of women and children had followed these warriors into the empire

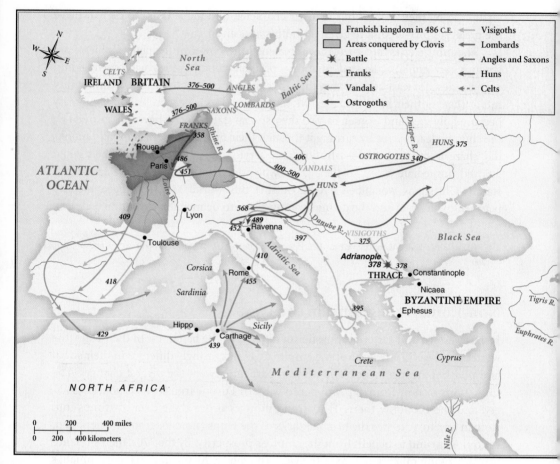

■ **MAP 6.3 Migrations and Invasions of the Fourth and Fifth Centuries**

The movements of non-Roman peoples into imperial territory transformed the Roman Empire. These migrations began as early as the reign of Domitian (r. 81–96), but in the fourth century, they became a pressing problem for the emperors when the Huns' attacks pushed many multiethnic bands from their homelands in eastern Europe into the empire's northern provinces. Maps cannot really show dynamic processes such as migrations and invasions, and the arrows on this one do not mean that the newcomers came in an unbroken stream. The map does indicate, however, the variety of peoples involved, the wide extent of imperial territory that they affected, and the concentration of their effects in the western section of the empire.

(Map 6.3). The western Roman government regarded them as barbarians; the emperors' failure either to absorb the newcomers or expel them led to the "Fall of the Roman Empire."

Economic weakness stemming from the third-century crisis hindered the emperors' ability to react to the migrations. They had demanded higher taxes during the crisis, forcing landowners to demand higher payments from their coloni.

Many of these tenants responded by illegally running away. Eventually, landowners also had to run away if they could not pay their taxes. This flight left farms deserted; as much as 20 percent of agricultural land lay unfarmed in the most seriously affected areas. The government pressed the farmers who remained to pay even more, but this only made more of them abandon their farms. In the end, the emperors' financial problems meant they could not hire enough soldiers to stop non-Roman peoples from immigrating into the empire.

Non-Roman groups crossed into Roman territory not in carefully planned invasions but often fleeing for their lives. Fourth-century raids by the Huns drove them from their homelands east of the Rhine and north of the Danube. Mostly small groups of men, women, and children crossed the Roman border as refugees. Their future looked grim because they came with no political or military unity, no clear plan, and not even a shared sense of identity.

Loosely organized in democratic groups and often warring with one another, these diverse bands or tribes originally shared only similar languages and their terror of the Huns. The migrating groups developed different ethnic identities only because the Roman government refused to accept them into Roman society. The newcomers therefore created their own kingdoms inside the imperial frontiers. Their desire for security forced them to develop a more tightly structured society to govern their new lands and gave them new identities.

Previously, these peoples lived in their homelands in small settlements as farmers, herders, and ironworkers; they had no experience running kingdoms. Most of these bands operated as chiefdoms, whose members could only be persuaded, not forced, to follow the chief. Chiefs maintained their leadership by leading warriors on successful raids to seize cattle and slaves and then giving gifts to their followers.

Family life was patriarchal: men headed households and exercised authority over women, children, and slaves. Women earned respect by bearing children, and rich men could have more than one wife and perhaps concubines as well. A clear division of labor made women responsible for agriculture, pottery making, and the production of textiles, while men worked iron and herded cattle. Fighting and raiding meant so much to the men that they packed graves with weapons, which archaeologists have found in northern European swamps. Women had some rights of inheritance and could control property, and married women received a marriage gift of one-third of their husbands' property.

Households were grouped into clans based on kinship through mothers as well as fathers. The members of a clan were supposed to keep peace among themselves, and violence against another clan member was the worst possible crime. Clans in turn grouped themselves into tribes, multiethnic coalitions that anyone could join. Different tribes identified themselves by their clothing, hairstyles, jewelry, weapons, religious cults, and oral stories.

Assemblies of free male warriors provided the tribes' only political organization. Tribal leaders' functions were mostly religious and military. Tribes tended to be unstable groupings with frequent bloody feuds between clans. Tribal law tried to set limits to the violence permitted in seeking revenge, but laws were oral, not written, and thus open to wide dispute.

Migrations into Roman territory surged when the Huns invaded eastern Europe in the fourth century. Related to the Hiung-nu people who had attacked China and Persia, these Turkish-speaking nomads arrived on the Russian plains shortly before 370. They excelled as raiders, launching cavalry attacks far and wide. With elongated skulls (from having been bound between boards in infancy), faces grooved with decorative scars, and their arms bristling with elaborate tattoos, they terrified their victims. Their skill as horsemen made them legendary. They could shoot their powerful bows while riding full speed, and they could remain on horseback for days, sleeping atop their horses and holding snacks of raw meat between their thighs and the animal's back.

The eastern emperors in Constantinople bribed the Huns not to attack their territory. The Huns then abandoned their nomadic lifestyle and became landlords, cooperating among themselves to create an empire north of the Danube that forced local farmers to support these new masters. The Huns' most ambitious leader, Attila (r. c. 440–453), extended their domains from the Caspian Sea to the Alps and even farther west. He led his forces as far as Paris in 451 and into northern Italy the next year. At Attila's death in 453, the Huns lost their unity and faded from history. By this time, however, the terror that they inspired in the people living in eastern Europe had already started the migrations that transformed the western empire.

The people who, after entering imperial territory, created a new identity as Visigoths were the first to experience what became the common pattern of the migrations: some desperate and poorly organized group would plead with the emperor for protection from the Huns, and the empire would accept them in return for military service. Shredded by constant raids by the Huns, in 376 the Visigoths begged the eastern emperor Valens (r. 364–378) to let them migrate into the Balkans. They received permission on condition that their warriors enlist in the Roman army to help drive away the Huns.

As the story of the Visigoths shows, the final part of the pattern was for these deals to fall apart. When greedy and incompetent Roman officers ordered to help the refugee Visigoths instead mistreated them, they starved; the officials forced them to sell some of their own people into slavery in return for dogs to eat. The hungry Visigoths rebelled. In 378, they defeated and killed Valens in battle at Adrianople in Thrace (see Map 6.3). The next eastern emperor, Theodosius I (r. 379–395), then had to renegotiate the deal from a position of weakness. His concessions to the Visigoths established the terms that other bands would seek for themselves and that would create new, self-conscious identities for them: permission to settle permanently inside the imperial borders, freedom to establish a kingdom under their own

■ Eagle Brooches (*Fibulae*) from Visigothic Spain

Visigothic women in their new kingdom in Spain showed their new ethnic identity by their style of dress, in particular through the tradition of fastening their clothing at the shoulders with brooches. These expensive examples, fashioned from gold inlaid with semi-precious stones, also expressed elite status. The choice of eagles as a Gothic brooch design reveals how ethnic identity can be constructed through cultural inter-action: Goths probably adopted the eagle as a symbol of power from Hunnic and Roman traditions.

(The Walters Art Museum, Baltimore.)

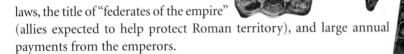

laws, the title of "federates of the empire" (allies expected to help protect Roman territory), and large annual payments from the emperors.

The eastern emperors soon realized, however, that they could not afford to keep such agreements. They therefore forced the migrating bands westward by cutting off the payments and threatening full-scale war unless the refugees left. With no army blocking them from moving westward, the Visigoths moved in that direction; neither the western empire nor they would ever be the same. In 410, they shocked the world by sacking Rome itself when the emperor Honorius in Ravenna botched negotiations. When their commander Alaric demanded all the city's gold, silver, movable property, and foreign slaves, the Romans asked, "What will be left to us?" "Your lives," he replied.

Too weak to defeat the invaders, the western emperor Honorius (r. 395–423) in 418 reluctantly agreed to settle the Visigoths in southwestern Gaul (present-day France), saving face by calling them federates. The Visigoths then completed their transition from tribal society to new kingdom by doing what no non-Roman group had done before: establishing an ethnic identity and organizing a state. They followed the model of Roman emperors by building mutually bene-ficial relations with local elites, including Romans. Romans in that elite could use time-tested ways of flattering their superiors to gain advantages. Sidonius Apollinaris, for example, a noble from Lyon (c. 430–479), once purposely lost a backgammon game to the Visigothic king as a way of gaining a favor from the ruler. Honorius tried, without much success, to limit what he saw as "barbarian" influence on Roman citizens by ordering them not to adopt Visigothic clothing styles.

How the new non-Roman kingdoms such as that of the Visigoths financed their states is a much-debated question. The older view is that the newcomers became landowners by forcing Romans to turn over some of their land, slaves, and movable property to them. Recent scholarship argues that Roman taxpayers in the kingdoms did not have to give up land but were instead made directly responsible for paying the expenses of the non-Roman soldiers, who lived mostly in city garrisons. Whatever the new arrangements were, the Visigoths found them so profitable that they later expanded into Spain.

The western emperor's deal with the Visigoths motivated other groups to enter Roman territory to create kingdoms and identities (see Map 6.4). The process was often violent. In 406, the Vandals, fleeing the Huns, fought their way all through Gaul to the Spanish coast. (The modern word *vandal*, meaning "destroyer of property," preserves their reputation for destruction.) In 429, eighty thousand Vandals crossed to North Africa, where they broke their agreement to become federates and captured the region. Their new kingdom caused tremendous hardship for local Africans by confiscating property rather than allowing owners to make regular payments to the occupiers. The Vandals further weakened the western emperors by seizing North Africa's tax payments of grain and vegetable oil and disrupting the importation of grain to Rome; they also built a navy strong enough to threaten the eastern empire. In 455, they plundered Rome, proving the western imperial government was powerless.

Other small groups also managed to break off distant pieces of the weakened western empire. The most significant small band for later history was the Anglo-Saxons. Composed of Angles from what is now Denmark and Saxons from northwestern Germany, this group invaded Britain in the 440s after the Roman army had been recalled from the province to defend Italy against the Visigoths. They established their kingdoms by taking territory away from the local Celtic peoples and the remaining Roman inhabitants. Gradually, Anglo-Saxon culture replaced the local traditions of the island's eastern regions: the Celts there lost most of their language, and Christianity survived only in Wales and Ireland.

The western empire's military weakness led to a change in leadership in 476 that has traditionally, but simplistically, been called the "fall of Rome." In that year a non-Roman commander replaced the Roman emperor in the west, and no Roman would rule there ever again. The idea of a "fall" comes from the best-selling, multivolume work that made it famous—*The Decline and Fall of the Roman Empire* by the English historian Edward Gibbon (1737–1794). The real story's details, however, reveal the complexity of the political transformation of the western empire under the pressure of the external migrations. The weakness of the imperial army in the west had forced the western emperors to employ non-Roman officers to lead the defense of Italy. By the middle of the fifth century, one general after another decided who would serve as puppet emperor under his

■ Mosaic of Upper-Class Country Life

This fourth-century mosaic, measuring fourteen-by-eighteen feet, covered a floor in a country villa at Carthage in North Africa. It shows the life of an elite couple on their estate at different seasons of the year. Their house, so large it had towers and a second-story colonnade, stands as a fortified compound at the center. The top third of the mosaic shows the lady of the house sitting in park-like surroundings while her servants and tenants tend to animals; winter activities are shown at the left, summer activities at the right. In the middle third, hunters pursue game. The bottom third shows the lady in a springtime setting (on the left) and her husband sitting (on the right) among characteristic fall activities. A servant hands the husband a roll addressed "to the master Julius." Such estates provided security and prosperity for their owners but also made desirable targets for the Vandal invaders of North Africa. (Le Musée du Bardo, Tunis.)

control. The last such unfortunate "emperor" was a usurper; his father, Orestes, a former aide to Attila, had rebelled against the emperor Julius Nepos in 475 and raised his young son to the throne. He gave the boy emperor the name Romulus Augustulus, meant to recall both Rome's founder and its first emperor. In 476, after a dispute over pay, soldiers murdered Orestes and deposed the boy; pitied as an innocent child, Romulus was given a safe home and a generous pension. The rebels' leader, Odoacer, did not choose another emperor. Instead, seeking to block Nepos's campaign to regain the throne, he had the Roman Senate ask Zeno, the eastern emperor, to recognize his leadership in return for his recognizing Zeno as sole emperor. Odoacer thereafter led Italy supposedly as the eastern emperor's assistant, but in fact, he ruled as he liked.

In 488, Zeno plotted to rid himself of Theodoric, a Germanic general living in Constantinople, by sending him to fight Odoacer, whom the emperor had found too independent. Eliminating Odoacer by 493, Theodoric (r. 493–526) established the Ostrogothic kingdom to rule Italy from the capital at Ravenna. He built legitimacy for his new state by preserving traditional Roman institutions, especially the Senate and the office of consul. An Arian Christian, Theodoric followed Constantine's example by announcing a policy of religious toleration: "No one can be forced to believe against his will." Many members of the Roman elite, such as the famous scholars Boethius and Cassiodorus, cooperated with Theodoric to try to establish stable government. Unfortunately, the Ostrogothic emperor showed that he was just as suspicious as any Roman emperor had ever been by imprisoning and executing Boethius, whom he had made a consul but later accused of disloyalty with other senators. While in prison, Boethius wrote the *Consolation of Philosophy*, a book that explained divine providence according to the ideas of Stoic and Neoplatonic philosophy as well as those of Augustine. Boethius's scholarship became vastly influential in medieval Europe.

As in the other kingdoms, the Ostrogoths took over the Roman traditions that supported their new state's legitimacy and stability. Theodoric and his Ostrogothic nobles wanted to enjoy the empire's luxury and prestige, not destroy them. For this reason, modern scholars consider it more accurate to speak of the western empire's "transformation" than its "fall" (Map 6.4), even though the process was often violent.

The Franks were the Germanic people who transformed Roman Gaul into Francia (from which the name *France* comes). They first moved into that region with the permission of the western emperor in the early fourth century. In 507, their king, Clovis (r. 485–511), overthrew the Visigothic king in southern Gaul with support from the eastern emperor. When the emperor named him an honorary Roman consul, Clovis celebrated this ancient honor by having himself crowned with a diadem in the style of the dominate's emperors. He carved out western Europe's largest new kingdom in what is today mostly France, growing larger than the neighboring and rival kingdoms of the Burgundians and Alemanni in eastern Gaul. Probably persuaded by his Christian wife Clotilda to believe that God had helped him defeat the Alemanni, Clovis proclaimed himself an orthodox Christian. To build stability, he forged good relations with Gaul's bishops, who helped him control the people in their regions.

Clovis's dynasty, called Merovingian after the legendary Frankish ancestor Merovech, lasted for another two hundred years, far longer than most other non-Roman royal families in the west. The Merovingian state anticipated the kingdom that emerged later as the forerunner of modern France. The Merovingians survived so long because their new state combined barbarian military might with Roman social and legal traditions.

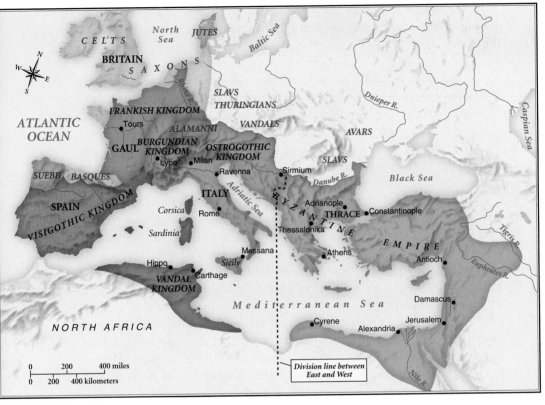

■ **MAP 6.4 Peoples and Kingdoms of the Roman World, c. 526**

The provinces of the Roman Empire had always been home to a population diverse in language and ethnicity. By the early sixth century, the territory of the western empire had fragmented into diverse political units as well. Italy and most of the former western provinces were kingdoms created and ruled by non-Roman peoples who had moved into former Roman territory over the past several centuries. The eastern empire (the Byzantine Empire) remained under the political control of the emperor in Constantinople. Justinian, who became Byzantine emperor in 527, made it his mission to try to reunite the eastern and western halves of the empire by force. How much do these states correspond to the modern boundaries of states in Europe? **For more help analyzing this map,** see the map activity for this chapter in the ONLINE STUDY GUIDE at bedfordstmartins.com/huntconcise.

Mixing Traditions

The political transformation of the western Roman empire—the replacement of imperial government by non-Roman kingdoms—fueled innovative social and cultural transformations in Europe. Newcomers and long-time Roman inhabitants combined their traditions to create new ways of life, above all law codes, but they failed to build a strong economy.

The memory of Rome's glory persisted through these changes. Visigoth king Athaulf (r. 410–415), having married a Roman noblewoman, explained his goals in this way:

> *At the start I wanted to erase the Romans' name and turn their land into a Gothic empire, myself doing what Augustus had done. But I have learned that the Goths' freewheeling wildness will never accept the rule of law, and that a state with no law is no state. Thus, I have more wisely chosen another path to glory: reviving the Roman name with Gothic strength. I pray that future generations will remember me as the founder of a Roman restoration.*

Roman law greatly influenced the new kings in their efforts to organize new states. They had never before had written laws; now that they had transformed themselves into kings ruling Romans as well as their own people, they wanted legal codes to establish justice and order. The Visigothic kings were the first non-Roman leaders to create a written law code. Composed in Latin and dependent on Roman legal tradition, it made the payment of fines and compensation the primary method for resolving disputes.

Clovis also relied on written law in his Merovingian kingdom. His code, published in Latin, supported social order by setting clear penalties for specific crimes. In particular, he established a system of payments intended to defuse feuds between individuals and between clans. This system of penalties included **wergild**, the payment a murderer had to make as compensation for his crime. Most of the money was paid to the victim's kin, but the king received perhaps one-third of the amount.

Because law codes correspond to social values, the differing payments offer a glimpse of the relative social value of different categories of people in Clovis's kingdom. The penalty for murdering a woman of childbearing age, a boy under twelve, or a man in the king's service was a massive fine of six hundred gold coins, enough to buy six hundred cattle. The fine for murdering a woman past childbearing age (specified as sixty years), a young girl, or a freeborn man was two hundred gold coins; for murdering ordinary slaves, thirty-five.

The migrations that transformed the west harmed its already weak economy. The Vandals damaged many towns in Gaul. In the countryside, now outside the control of any central government, wealthy Romans from the social elite built villas on large estates staffed by tenants bound to the land like slaves. The owners of these estates operated them as self-sufficient units by producing all they needed, defending themselves against raids, and keeping their distance from any authorities. Craving isolation, the owners shunned membership on city councils and tax collection—the public services that had supplied the lifeblood of Roman administration—although the wealthiest boasted an annual income rivaling that of an entire region in the old western empire. The elites' withdrawal from public service withered Roman provincial government, and the new kingdoms never matured sufficiently to replace its services to the population.

A few provincial Romans helped transmit ancient learning to later ages. Cassiodorus, one of the scholars who had worked for Theodoric, founded a monastery on his ancestral estate in Italy in the 550s following his career in imperial administration. He gave the monks the task of copying manuscripts to keep their contents alive as old texts disintegrated. His own book *Institutions*, composed in the 550s to guide his monks, explained the respect for tradition that kept classical traditions alive: in prescribing the works a person of superior education should read, it included ancient secular texts as well as Scripture and Christian literature. The most energetic effort to perpetuate the Roman past, however, came from the eastern empire.

■ **REVIEW:** *What societal changes took place among non-Romans who came to the Roman Empire from around 370 to the 550s?*

The Byzantine Empire in the East

The eastern Roman Empire avoided the transformations that reshaped western Europe. Trade routes and diverse agriculture kept the east richer than the west, and the eastern emperors minimized the effect of the foreign migrations on their territory and blunted the aggression of the Sassanid kingdom in Persia with force, diplomacy, and bribery. By the early sixth century, the empire's eastern half had achieved such power, riches, and ambition that historians have given it a new name, the Byzantine Empire; its emperors held power until 1453.

The Byzantine emperors saw themselves as continuing the Roman Empire and guarding its culture against barbarians. Justinian (r. 527–565), the most famous of the early Byzantine emperors, took this mission so seriously that he nearly bankrupted his treasury with wars to recover the western empire; he tried to impose religious orthodoxy to win God's will for his projects. One especially significant contribution of the early Byzantine Empire to later history was its crucial role in preserving classical literature and learning, which nearly disappeared in the west.

Byzantine Society

The sixth-century Byzantine Empire enjoyed a prosperity that western Europe had lost. Members of the elite spent freely on luxury goods imported from China and India: silk, precious stones, and expensive spices such as pepper. People of all kinds flocked to the empire's largest cities—Constantinople, Damascus, and Alexandria. There, churches with soaring domes testified to the Byzantines' confidence in God's power and favor.

■ Justinian and His Court in Ravenna

This mosaic scene centered on the Byzantine emperor Justinian (r. 527–565) is opposite Theodora's mosaic in San Vitale's Church in Ravenna. Justinian and Theodora had finished building the church, which the Ostrogothic king Theodoric had started, to celebrate their successful campaign to restore Italy to the Roman Empire and retake control of the western capital, Ravenna. The soldiers at left remind viewers of the rulers' aggressive military policy in service of imperial unity. The presence of Maximianus, bishop of Ravenna, standing on Justinian's left and identified by name, stresses the theme of cooperation between bishops and emperors in ruling the world. (Scala/Art Resource, NY.)

Continuing a Roman imperial tradition, the Byzantine emperors sponsored costly religious festivals and entertainments to rally public support. Rich and poor alike crowded city squares, theaters, and racetracks on these spirited occasions; chariot racing aroused the hottest passions. Constantinople's residents, for example, divided themselves into competitive factions—called Blues and Greens after the racing colors of their favorite charioteers—that combined religious and sports rivalries: orthodox Christians became Blues, Monophysites Greens. They clashed as frequently over theological arguments as over race results.

The eastern emperors did everything they could to preserve "Romanness." They feared that contact with non-Roman peoples would make their empire "barbarian,"

■ Theodora and Her Court in Ravenna

This mosaic shows the empress Theodora (c. 500–548) and her court. It was placed on one wall of the church of San Vitale in Ravenna, facing the matching scene of her husband, Justinian, and his attendants. Theodora wears the jewels, pearls, and rich robes characteristic of Byzantine rulers. She extends in her hands a gem-encrusted bowl, evidently a present to the church; her gesture imitates the gift-giving of the Magi to the baby Jesus, the scene illustrated on the hem of her garment. Like Honorius on page 212, a circle around her head indicates special holiness. (Scala/Art Resource, NY.)

as in the west. Like the western emperors, they employed foreign mercenaries, but they tried to keep foreign customs from influencing the empire's residents. They paid special attention to clothing styles. Like the western emperor Honorius in the early fifth century, eastern emperors banned Constantinople's residents from wearing barbarian-style outfits (especially heavy boots and clothing made from animal furs) instead of traditional Roman clothes (sandals or light shoes and robes).

The Byzantines referred to themselves as "the Romans" because they saw themselves as the heirs and protectors of ancient Roman culture. At the same time, they spoke Greek as their native language and used Latin only for government and military communication. (The Latin-speaking western empire referred to them as

"Greeks.") Since Byzantine society was deeply multilingual and multiethnic, preserving an unchanging Roman identity was a hopeless goal. Many people spoke their traditional languages, such as Phrygian and Cappadocian in western Asia Minor, Armenian farther east, and Syriac and other Aramaic dialects in the Levant. Travelers around the empire heard countless languages, saw varying styles of dress, and encountered numerous ethnic groups.

For the Byzantines, Romanness included Christianity, but their theological diversity rivaled their ethnic variety. Bitter controversies over doctrine divided eastern Christians, and emperors joined forces with bishops to impose orthodoxy. They generally preferred words to swords to pressure heretics to accept orthodox theology, but they used violence when persuasion failed. Resorting to such extreme measures against fellow Christians was necessary, they believed, to save lost souls and preserve God's goodwill toward the empire. The persecution of nonorthodox Christian subjects by Christian emperors demonstrated the depth of passion created by the desire for a unitary identity.

In patriarchal Byzantine society, most women followed ancient Mediterranean tradition by focusing their lives on their households and minimizing contact with men outside that circle. Law barred women from fulfilling many public functions, such as witnessing wills. Subject to the authority of their fathers and husbands, women veiled their heads (though not their faces) to show modesty. Christian theology made divorce more difficult than under Roman law and discouraged remarriage, even for widows. Stiffer legal penalties for sexual offenses also developed. Female prostitution remained legal, but emperors raised the penalties for people forcing women (children or slaves) to become prostitutes.

As always, women in the imperial family lived by different rules than ordinary women and could directly influence government. Theodora (c. 500–548), wife of the emperor Justinian, became the most influential and talked about of all Byzantine empresses. Using her brains and beauty to overcome her low social status (she was the daughter of a bear trainer and then an actress accused of performing pornographic scenes), she married Justinian and advised him in every part of his rule. She helped him make personnel choices for his administration, strongly pushed her religious views in the continuing disputes over Christian doctrine, and rallied her husband's courage in time of crisis. John Lydus, a high-ranking administrator, judged her "superior in intelligence to any man."

Byzantine government made the social hierarchy more rigid than ever because it provided services according to people's wealth. It required piles of paperwork and fees for official transactions, from commercial permits to legal complaints. Without bribery, nothing got done. This arrangement benefited people with status and money: they used their social connections to get a hearing from the right official and used their wealth to pay bribes to get fast action.

The poor, by contrast, could not afford the large bribes that government officials expected. Since interest rates were high, they had to take on backbreaking debt to raise the cash to pay officials to help them. This system saved the emperors money: they paid civil servants small salaries because bribes from the public supplemented their incomes. John Lydus, for example, reported that he earned thirty times his annual salary in bribes during his first year in office. To keep unlimited extortion from destroying the system, the emperors published an official list of the maximum bribes that employees could demand. Overall, however, this kind of government generated enormous hostility among poorer subjects and did nothing to encourage public support for the emperors' plans for glory and conquest.

The Reign of Justinian, 527–565

Justinian dreamed of reuniting the empire as it had been under Augustus. Born to a Latin-speaking family in a small Balkan town, he rose rapidly in imperial service until 527, when he succeeded his uncle as emperor. During his reign, he launched military expeditions to try to win back western Europe and North Africa from the non-Roman kingdoms. His desire to build imperial glory led him to decorate Constantinople with magnificent and costly buildings. He was also an intellectual—the first on the throne since Julian in the 360s—whose passion for the law and theology drove him to push reforms with the same goals cherished by all previous emperors, whether Christian or polytheist: to preserve social order based on hierarchy and maintain divine favor for himself and his subjects.

Unfortunately for Justinian's dream, the huge expense of his plans created social unrest. His taxes became so heavy and his chief tax collector so violent that they provoked a major riot in 532. Known as the "Nika Riot," it erupted when the Blue and Green factions gathering in Constantinople's hippodrome to watch chariot races united against the emperor, shouting "Nika! Nika!" ("Win! Win!"). After nine days of violence that left much of the capital in ashes, a panicky Justinian prepared to abandon his throne and flee. Theodora, however, showed the steel in her soul by telling him: "Once born, no one can escape dying, but for one who has held imperial power it would be unbearable to be a fugitive. May I never take off my imperial robes of purple, nor live to see the day when those who meet me will not greet me as their ruler." Shamed, Justinian called out his guard, who crushed the rebellion by slaughtering thirty thousand rioters trapped in the racetrack.

Justinian's most ambitious plan was to reunite the eastern and western empires. His generals defeated the Vandals and Ostrogoths after campaigns that in some cases took decades to complete. At enormous expense, imperial armies reoccupied Italy, the Dalmatian coast, Sicily, Sardinia, Corsica, part of southern Spain, and western North Africa by 562. These successes temporarily restored the old empire's geography: Justinian's territory stretched from the Atlantic to the western edge of Mesopotamia (see "Mapping the West," page 254).

These triumphs carried a tragic price: inflicting horrible damage on Europe and emptying Justinian's treasury. Italy endured the greatest damage; the war there against the Goths inflicted death and destruction on a massive scale. The east suffered as Justinian squeezed ever more taxes out of his already overburdened population to finance the western wars and bribe the Sassanids in Mesopotamia not to attack while his eastern defenses were weak. The tax burden crippled the economy, leading to constant banditry in the countryside. Crowds poured into the capital from rural areas, seeking relief from poverty and robbers.

Natural disasters added to Justinian's troubles. In the 540s, an epidemic killed a third of the empire's inhabitants; a quarter of a million died in Constantinople alone, half the capital's population. This was only the first in a long series of diseases that erased millions of people in the eastern empire over the next two centuries. The loss of so many people created a shortage of army recruits, forced the emperors to hire expensive mercenaries, and left many farms vacant, thus hurting tax revenues.

The wars and the resulting financial pressures made Justinian crave stability; to strengthen his authority, he emphasized the emperor's closeness to God and his authority over the people. He had his artists portray the symbols of rule in a Christian context. A gleaming mosaic in his church at San Vitale in Ravenna, for example, displayed a dramatic vision of the emperor's role: Justinian standing at the center of the universe shoulder to shoulder with both the ancient Hebrew leader Abraham and Christ. In legal matters, Justinian proclaimed the emperor the "living law," reviving a Hellenistic royal doctrine.

Justinian's building program in Constantinople expressed his religious devotion and worldly power. Most spectacular of all was his magnificent reconstruction of Constantine's Church of the Holy Wisdom (Hagia Sophia). Its location facing the palace matched Justinian's emphasis on combining imperial and Christian authority. Creating a new design for churches, his architects erected a huge building on a square plan capped by a dome 107 feet across and soaring 160 feet above the floor. Its interior walls glowed like the sun from the light reflecting off their four acres of gold mosaics. Imported marble of every color added to the sparkling effect. When he first entered his masterpiece, dedicated in 538, Justinian exclaimed, "Solomon, I have outdone you," boasting that he had bested the glorious temple the ancient king built for the Hebrews.

Justinian's building up of the emperor's power made Constantinople still more important and reduced the local independence of the empire's other cities. Their councils ceased to govern; imperial officials took over instead. Provincial elites still had to ensure full payment of their area's taxes, but they lost the compensating reward of deciding local matters. Now the imperial government made all decisions and determined people's social status. Men of property from the provinces who wanted a public career knew they could satisfy their ambitions only by joining the imperial administration.

■ **The Soaring Architecture of Hagia Sophia**
Golden mosaics originally reflected a dazzling light from the interior of Hagia Sophia ("Holy Wisdom"), the enormous church that the Byzantine emperor Justinian built in the 530s c.e. near his palace in Constantinople. A central dome, 184 feet high and supported by four arches resting on massive piers, capped the church's vast interior; the ring of windows at the base of the dome is just visible at the top of the picture. Hagia Sophia became a mosque after the Turks captured the city in 1453; the large medallions contain religious quotations in Arabic. Now a museum, Hagia Sophia continues to host people offering prayers. (© Adam Woolfitt/Corbis.)

To strengthen his control, Justinian had the empire's laws codified to bring uniformity to the inconsistent decisions of earlier emperors; the final edition of his *Codex* (set of laws) appeared in 534. A team of scholars also condensed millions of words to produce the *Digest* in 533, a collection of past decisions intended to make legal cases go faster and provide class materials for law schools. This collection, written like the others in Latin and therefore readable in the western empire, influenced legal scholars for centuries. Justinian's experts also wrote a textbook for students in 533, the *Institutes*, which proclaimed the principles of a just life: "live honorably, harm no one else, and give to each his own"; it remained on law school reading lists until modern times.

To fulfill his sacred duty to protect the empire, Justinian enacted reforms to guarantee religious orthodoxy. Like the emperors before him, he believed his world would suffer if its divine protector became angered by the presence of religious offenders. Harshly enforcing laws against polytheists, he ordered them to be baptized or else lose their lands and official positions. Three times he purged Christians whom he could not convince to accept his version of orthodoxy. In pursuit of sexual purity, his laws made sex between men illegal for the first time in Roman history. Homosexual marriage, apparently not uncommon earlier, had been officially prohibited in 342, but penalties had never before been imposed on men engaging in homosexual activity. All the previous emperors, for example, had simply taxed male prostitutes. The legal status of homosexual activity between women is unclear; it probably counted as criminal adultery for married women.

A brilliant theologian, Justinian tried to unite orthodox and Monophysite Christians by revising the creed of the Council of Chalcedon. But church leaders in Rome and Constantinople had become too bitterly divided to agree on a unified church. The church's eastern and western divisions were by now launched on the diverging courses that would climax in a formal schism five hundred years later. Perhaps no emperor could have done better, but Justinian's drive for religious orthodoxy only drove Christians further apart and worked against his dream of a reunited Roman world.

Preserving Classical Literature

The empire's Christianization endangered classical literature—from plays and histories to speeches and novels—because these works were polytheist, and therefore many Christians thought they were the work of the devil. The real danger to the survival of pre-Christian literature, however, stemmed less from active censorship than from simple neglect. As Christians became authors in great numbers, their works displaced the ancient texts of Greece and Rome as the most important literature of the age. Fortunately for later times, however, the Byzantine Empire helped preserve at least part of the famous works of the past.

Classical texts survived because elite Christian culture was rooted in traditional polytheist learning, both Greek and Roman. Latin literature continued to be read in the eastern empire because the administration was bilingual; official documents were published in Rome's original language along with Greek translations. Latin scholarship in the east received a boost when Justinian's wars sent Latin-speaking scholars fleeing from Italy for safety to Constantinople. Their work there helped conserve many works that might otherwise have disappeared in the destruction in the west.

Byzantine scholars valued classical literature because they regarded it as the basis of a high-level education. Many of the classical works available today survived because they served as school texts in the eastern empire. A basic knowledge of famous pre-Christian classics was a requirement for a good career in government service, the goal of most ambitious students. In the words of an imperial decree from 360, "No person shall obtain a post of the first rank unless it shall be shown that he excels in long practice of liberal studies, and that he is so polished in literary matters that words flow from his pen faultlessly."

IMPORTANT DATES

284	Diocletian becomes Roman emperor	c. 413–426	Augustine writes *City of God*
303	Diocletian begins Great Persecution of Christians	418	Western emperor settles Visigoths in southwestern Gaul
312	Constantine wins the Battle of the Milvian Bridge in Rome and converts to Christianity	429	Vandals capture Roman North Africa after invading Spain
		440s	Anglo-Saxons take over Roman Britain
c. 323	Pachomius in Upper Egypt establishes the first monasteries for men and women	451	Council of Chalcedon
		476	"Fall of the Roman Empire" when German commander Odoacer deposes the final western emperor, Romulus Augustulus
324	Constantine refounds Byzantium as Constantinople, the "new Rome"		
325	Council of Nicaea	c. 480–553	Life of Benedict of Nursia, who devises the Benedictine rule
361–363	Julian attempts to restore polytheism as the state religion	493–526	Theodoric establishes Ostrogothic kingdom in Italy
391	Theodosius bans polytheist sacrifice and closes the temples of traditional Roman religion	507	Clovis establishes Frankish kingdom in Gaul
395	Roman Empire is split into western and eastern sections	c. 530	Plato's Academy in Athens closes
410	Visigoths sack Rome	538	Justinian dedicates Church of the Holy Wisdom

What also helped classical literature survive was the use of the principles of ancient rhetoric for effective presentation of Christian theology. When Ambrose, bishop of Milan from 374 to 397, composed the first systematic description of Christian ethics for young priests, he imitated the great classical orator Cicero. Theologians employed the dialogue form pioneered by Plato to refute Christian heresies, and polytheist traditions in writing biography influenced the hugely popular Christian literature of saints' lives. Similarly, Christian artists used polytheist traditions to communicate their beliefs in paintings, mosaics, and carved reliefs. Artists showing Christ with a sunburst surrounding his head, for example, took their inspiration from polytheist depictions of the radiant Sun as a god (see page 224).

Ironically, a technological innovation related to the growth of Christian literature also helped preserve classical polytheist texts. Previously, scribes had written

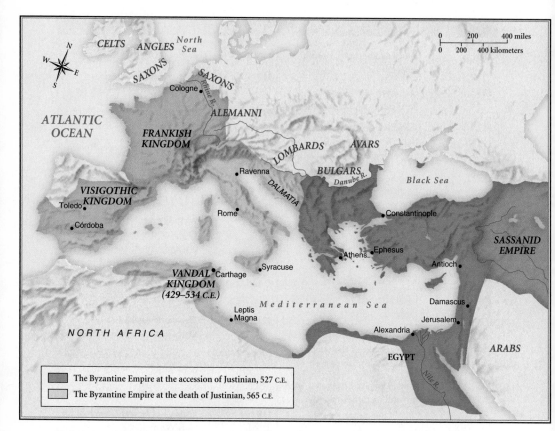

■ **MAPPING THE WEST The Byzantine Empire and Western Europe, c. 600**
Justinian employed brilliant generals and spent huge sums of money to reconquer Italy, North Africa, and part of Spain to reunite the western and eastern halves of the old Roman Empire. His wars to regain Italy and North Africa eliminated the Ostrogothic and Vandal kingdoms, respectively, but at a huge cost in effort, time—the war in Italy took twenty years—and expense. The resources of the eastern empire were so exhausted that following emperors could not maintain the reunification. By the early seventh century, the Visigoths had taken back all of Spain. Africa, despite serious revolts by local Berber tribes, remained under imperial control until the Arab conquest of the seventh century, but within five years of Justinian's death, the Lombards set up a new kingdom that controlled a large section of Italy. Never again would anyone attempt to reestablish a universal Roman Empire. Compare the political divisions on this map with the one at the end of Chapter 5 (page 209) showing Roman territory more than two centuries earlier.

books on sheets made from thin animal skin or paper made from papyrus, gluing the sheets together and attaching rods at both ends to form a scroll. Readers had to unroll the books to read them. For ease of use, Christians produced their literature in the form of the codex—a book with bound pages. Eventually the codex became the standard form of book production in the Byzantine world. Because the codex was less subject to damage from rolling and unrolling and could contain text more efficiently than scrolls, which were inefficient for long works, this invention aided the preservation of all forms of literature.

Despite the continuing importance of classical Greek and Latin literature in Byzantine education and rhetoric, its survival remained uncertain in a war-torn world governed by Christians. Knowledge of Greek in the transformed west faded so drastically that almost no one could read the original versions of Homer's *Iliad* and *Odyssey*, the traditional foundations of a polytheist literary education. Latin fared better, and scholars such as Augustine and Jerome knew Rome's ancient literature extremely well. But they also saw its classics as too seductive because the pleasure of reading them could distract Christians from worshiping God. Jerome once had a nightmare of being condemned on Judgment Day for having been a Ciceronian instead of a Christian.

The closing around 530 of Plato's Academy, founded in Athens more than nine hundred years earlier, demonstrated the dangers for classical learning in the Byzantine world. This most famous of classical schools finally shut its doors when many of its scholars moved to Persia to escape restrictions on polytheists and its revenues dwindled because the Athenian elite, its traditional supporters, were increasingly Christianized. The Neoplatonist school at Alexandria, by contrast, continued; its leader John Philoponus (c. 490–570) was a Christian. In addition to Christian theology, Philoponus wrote commentaries on Aristotle's works; some of his ideas anticipated those of Galileo a thousand years later. John's work achieved the kind of blending of old and new that was one fruitful possibility of the transformation of the late Roman world—that is, he was a Christian subject of the Byzantine Empire in Egypt, heading a school founded long before by polytheists, studying the works of an ancient Greek philosopher as the inspiration for his innovative scholarship. The strong possibility that the present could learn from the past would continue as Western civilization once again remade itself in medieval times.

■ **REVIEW:** *What role did the emperor Justinian see himself playing in Roman history?*

Conclusion

Tension between unity and division characterized the late Roman Empire. Diocletian's reorganization delayed the empire's fragmentation but opened the way to its eventual separation in 395 into western and eastern halves. From then on, Roman history increasingly divided into two regional streams, even though emperors as late as Justinian in the sixth century clung to the dream of reuniting the empire and restoring the glory of Rome's Golden Age.

Multiple causes interacted to destroy the Roman Empire's unity, beginning with the catastrophic losses of property and people during the third-century crisis, which hit the west harder than the east. The late-fourth-century migrations of non-Roman peoples fleeing the Huns further weakened centralized rule. When Roman authorities failed to absorb these tribes peacefully, the newcomers violently created kingdoms that replaced imperial government in the west. This change transformed not only the west's politics, society, and economy but also the tribes themselves, who developed ethnic identities while organizing themselves into new political states. The economic troubles accompanying these transformations destroyed the elite's commitment to public office and public service, which had been essential to imperial government. Wealthy nobles in the west retreated to self-sufficient country estates and avoided local politics.

The eastern empire fared better economically and avoided the worst of the violent effects from the foreign migrations, as the Byzantine emperors sought to preserve an idealized "Romanness" that they believed would strengthen their rule. The financial drain of pursuing unity through war against the new kingdoms, however, fueled social unrest by raising tax rates to punishing levels, while the concentration of power in the capital weakened other cities, the traditional centers for collecting taxes and maintaining social order.

In religion, the emperor Constantine's conversion to Christianity in 312 marked a turning point in Western civilization. Nevertheless, Christianization of the Roman world proceeded slowly because many polytheists were reluctant to abandon their traditional religion. Christians fiercely disagreed among themselves over doctrine, to the point of violence. Some of them abandoned everyday society to live as monks, to come closer to God personally and to pray for mercy for the world. Monastic life redefined the meaning of holiness by creating communities of God's heroes who withdrew from this world to devote their service to glorifying the next.

In the end, the emperor's dream of political and religious unity faded before the divisive forces of the human spirit combined with the unpredictable effects, especially economic, of political and social transformation. Nevertheless, the memory of Roman power, culture, and glory remained potent and present, providing an influential inheritance to the peoples and states that would become Rome's heirs.

■ **MAKING CONNECTIONS**

1. *What similarities existed between traditional Roman religion and Christianity as official state religion?*

2. *Compare the fates of the eastern and western empires after they split apart.*

■ **FOR FURTHER EXPLORATION**

For further reading and online research ideas, see the Suggested References on page SR-3 at the back of the book.

For practice quizzes, a customized study plan, and other study tools, see the ONLINE STUDY GUIDE at bedfordstmartins.com/huntconcise.

For primary-source material from this period, see Chapter 6 in *Sources of THE MAKING OF THE WEST: A CONCISE HISTORY*, Second Edition.

7

The Heirs of the Roman Empire

600–750

A CCORDING TO A WRITER who was not very sympathetic to the Byzantines, one night Emperor Heraclius (r. 610–641) had a dream: "Verily [he was told] there shall come against thee a circumcised nation, and they shall vanquish thee and take possession of the land." Heraclius thought the vision foretold an uprising of the Jews, and he ordered mass baptisms into the Christian faith in all his provinces. "But," continued the story,

> after a few days there appeared a man of the Arabs, from the southern dis-
> tricts, that is to say, from Mecca or its neighborhood, whose name was
> Muhammad; and he brought back the worshipers of idols to the knowledge of
> the One God. . . . And he took possession of Damascus and Syria, and crossed
> the Jordan and dammed it up. And the Lord abandoned the army of the
> Romans before him.

This tale, however fanciful, recalls the most astonishing development of the sev-enth century: the Arabs conquered much of the Roman Empire and became one of its heirs. The western and eastern parts of the empire, both diminished, were now joined by yet a third power—Arab and Muslim. The resulting triad has endured in

■ **Mosque at Damascus (detail)**
Islam conquered the Byzantines; then Islam was "conquered" in turn by Byzantine culture. For the grand mosque at Damascus, his capital city, the Umayyad caliph al-Walid employed Byzantine-trained mosaicists, who depicted classical motifs—buildings, animals, vegetation—in a style that harked back to the classical past. However, the artists scrupulously avoided depicting human beings, in this way conforming to one strain of Islamic thought that argued against figural representations.
(The Bridgeman Art Library.)

259

various forms to the present day: the western third of the old Roman Empire became western Europe; the eastern third, occupying what is now Turkey, Greece, and some of the Balkans, became part of eastern Europe and helped to create Russia; and North Africa, together with the ancient Near East (now called the Middle East), remains the Arab world.

As diverse as these cultures are today, they share many of the same roots. All were heirs of Hellenistic and Roman traditions. All adhered to monotheism. The western and eastern halves of the empire had Christianity in common, although they differed at times in interpreting it. The Arab world's religion, Islam, accepted the same one God that Christians did but considered Jesus a prophet of God rather than his son.

The history of the seventh and eighth centuries is a story of adaptation and transformation. Historians consider the changes important enough to signal the end of one era—antiquity—and the beginning of another—the Middle Ages.* During this period, all three heirs of the Roman Empire combined elements of their heritage with new values, interests, and conditions. The divergences among them resulted from disparities in geographical and climatic conditions, material and human resources, skills, and local traditions. But these differences should not obscure the fact that the Byzantine, Muslim, and western European worlds were sibling cultures.

Byzantium: A Christian Empire under Siege

Emperor Justinian (r. 527–565) had tried to re-create the old Roman Empire. On the surface he succeeded. His empire once again included Italy, North Africa, and the Balkans. Vestiges of old Roman society persisted: an educated elite maintained its prestige, town governments continued to function, and old myths and legends were retold in poetry and depicted on silver plates and chests. By 600, however, the eastern empire began to undergo a transformation as striking as the one that had earlier remade the western half. Historians call this reorganized empire the Byzantine Empire, or Byzantium, after the Greek name for the city of Constantinople. From the last third of the sixth century, Byzantium was almost constantly at war, and its territory shrank drastically. Cultural and political change came as well. Cities—except for a few such as Constantinople—decayed, and the countryside became the focus of government and military administration. Following these shifts, the old elite largely disappeared, and classical learning gave way to new forms of education, mainly religious in content. The traditional styles of urban life, dependent on public gathering places and community spirit, faded away.

---

*The term *Middle Ages* was coined in the sixteenth century to refer to the period "in between"—in the middle of—the ancient and modern periods.

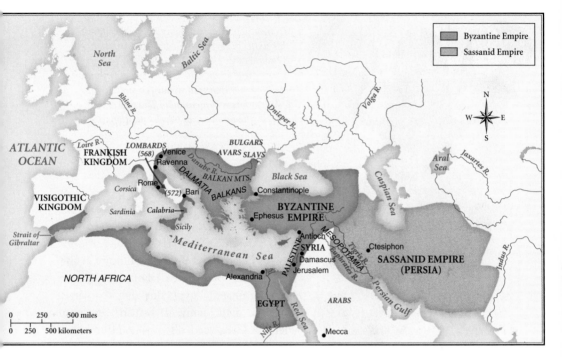

■ **MAP 7.1 Byzantine and Sassanid Empires, c. 600**
Justinian hoped to re-create the old Roman Empire, but just a century after his death Italy was largely conquered by the Lombards. Meanwhile, the Byzantine Empire had to contend with the Sassanid Empire to its east. In 600, these two major powers faced each other uneasily. Three years later, the Sassanid king attacked Byzantine territory. The resulting wars, which lasted until 627, exhausted both empires and left them open to invasion by the Arabs.

Wars on the Frontiers, c. 570–750

From about 570 to 750, the Byzantine Empire waged war against invaders on all fronts. Its first major challenge came from the east, from the **Sassanid Empire** of Persia. Its second came from new groups—Lombards, Slavs, Avars, Bulgars, and Muslims—who pushed into the empire. In the wake of these onslaughts, Byzantium was transformed.

The Persian challenge was the most predictable: since the third century, the Sassanid kings and Roman emperors had fought sporadically but never with decisive effect on either side. But in the middle of the sixth century, the Sassanids chose to concentrate their activities on their western half, Mesopotamia (today Iraq), nearer the Byzantine border (Map 7.1). Reforming the army, which previously had depended on nobles who could provide their own arms, the Sassanid kings began to pay and arm new warriors drawn from the lower nobility. With the army more fully their

■ A Sassanid King

His head topped by a mighty horned headdress, this sixth- or seventh-century representation of a Sassanid ruler evokes the full majesty of a king of kings. A glance at "The Great King of Persia" on page 30 shows that traditional Persian sculpture was not, as here, three dimensional. The new style is explained by the influence of Greek and Roman sculpture, despite the enmity between Sassanid Persia and Byzantium (heir of Greece and Rome) at the time.
(Réunion des Musées Nationaux/Art Resource, NY.)

own, the Sassanid kings tried to re-create the Persian Empire of Xerxes and Darius (see page 104). Under Chosroes II (r. 591–628), the Persians invaded the Byzantine Empire in 603. By 613, they had taken Damascus; by 619, they dominated Egypt. But after reorganizing his own army, Byzantine emperor Heraclius regained all of Byzantium's lost territory by 627. The chief outcome of these confrontations was the exhaustion of both sides.

The Byzantines could ill afford this weakness. From every side, new groups were pushing into their empire. The Lombards, a Germanic people, arrived in northern Italy in 568 and by 572 were masters of the Po valley and some inland regions in Italy's south, leaving the Byzantines only Bari, Calabria, and Sicily as well as Rome and a narrow swath of land through Italy's middle called the Exarchate of Ravenna.

The Byzantines were equally weak in the face of the Slavs, Bulgars, and Avars just beyond the Danube River. The Slavs conducted lightning raids on the Balkan countryside (part of Byzantium at the time) and, joined by the Avars—nomadic pastoralists and warriors—they attacked Byzantine cities as well. The Bulgars, entering what is now Bulgaria in the 670s, defeated the Byzantine army and in 681 forced the emperor to recognize the state they carved out of formerly Byzantine territory. This Bulgar state crippled Byzantine influence in the Balkans and helped isolate them from western Europe. Avar and Slavic control of the Balkans effectively cut off trade and travel between Constantinople and the cities of the Dalmatian coast, and the Bulgar state threw a political barrier across the Danube River. Perhaps as a result of this physical separation, Byzantine historians ceased to be interested in the West, and eastern scholars no longer bothered to learn Latin. The two halves of the Roman Empire, once united, communicated very little in the seventh century.

While fighting these groups on their northern frontier, the Byzantines at the same time had to contend with the Arabs, whose military prowess was creating a new empire and spreading a new religion, Islam. In the hundred years between 630 and 730, the Muslim Arabs succeeded in conquering much of the Byzantine Empire, at times attacking the walls of Constantinople itself. No wonder the patriarch of Jerusalem, chief bishop of the entire Levant, saw in the Arab onslaught the impending end of the world: "Behold," he said, "the Abomination of Desolation, spoken of by the Prophet Daniel, that standeth in the Holy Place."

From an Urban to a Rural Way of Life

As Byzantine borders shrank, Byzantines confronted new rulers and learned to accommodate them. Slavs and Avars settling in the Balkans intermingled with the indigenous population, gradually absorbing local agricultural techniques and burial practices while contributing the Slavic language and religious cults. When Byzantine subjects in Syria and Egypt found themselves under Arab rule, they learned to adjust, paying a special tax to their conquerors but continuing to practice their Christian and Jewish religions in peace. In the countryside they were permitted to keep and farm their lands, and their cities remained centers of government, scholarship, and business. For these former Byzantines, daily life remained essentially unchanged.

Ironically, the most radical transformations in seventh- and eighth-century Byzantine life occurred not in the territories conquered but in the shrunken empire itself. Under the ceaseless barrage of invaders, many towns, formerly bustling hubs of trade and centers of the imperial bureaucratic network, vanished or became unrecognizable in their changed way of life. The public activity of marketplaces, theaters, and town squares gave way to the private pursuits of table and hearth. City baths, once places where people gossiped, made deals, and talked politics and philosophy, disappeared in most Byzantine towns—with the significant exception of Constantinople. Warfare reduced some cities to rubble, and when they were rebuilt, the limited resources available went to construct thick city walls and solid churches instead of large open marketplaces and baths. Markets moved to overcrowded streets that looked much like the open-air bazaars of the modern Middle East. People under siege sought protection rather than community pastimes. In the Byzantine city of Ephesus, for example, the citizens who built the new walls in the seventh century enclosed not the old public edifices but rather their homes and churches. Despite the new emphasis on church buildings, many cities were too impoverished even to repair their churches.

The Byzantine Empire, c. 700

■ The Walls of Constantinople

The thick walls and stone forts built by Emperor Theodosius II (r. 408–450) are still visible at Istanbul. The walls enclosed not only the urban center but rural fields and gardens as well, ensuring that the city could support and feed itself even when under siege. For over a thousand years, the walls helped protect Constantinople from the onslaughts of invaders. (Sonia Halliday Photographs.)

The pressures of war against the Arabs brought a change in Byzantine society parallel to the change in the West a few centuries before, spelling the end of the class of *curiales* (town councilors), the elite that for centuries had mediated between the emperor and the people. But an upper class nevertheless remained: as in the West, bishops and their clergy continued to form a rich and powerful upper stratum even within the declining cities.

In spite of the general urban decay, Constantinople and a few other urban centers retained much of their old vitality. Some industry and trade continued, particularly the manufacture of silk textiles. These were the prestige items of the time, and their production and distribution were monitored by the government. State-controlled factories produced the finest fabrics, which legally could be worn only by the emperor, his court, and his friends. In private factories, merchants, spinners, and weavers turned raw silk into slightly less luxurious cloth for both internal consumption and foreign trade. Even though Byzantium's economic life became increasingly rural and barter-based in the seventh and eighth centuries, the skills, knowledge, and institutions of urban workers made possible long-distance trade and the domestic manufacture of luxury goods.

As urban life declined, agriculture, always the basis of the Byzantine economy, became the center of its social life as well. But unlike the West, where an extremely rich and powerful elite dominated the agricultural economy, the Byzantine Empire of the seventh century was principally a realm of free and semi-free peasant farmers who grew food, herded cattle, and tended vineyards on small plots of land. In the shadow of decaying urban centers, the social world of the farmer was narrow. Two or three neighbors were enough to witness a land transfer. Farmers interacted mostly with their families or with local monasteries. The buffer once provided by the curial class was gone; these families now felt directly the impact of imperial rule.

Eager to strengthen these social developments, the emperors of the seventh and eighth centuries tried to give ordinary family life new institutional importance. Imperial legislation narrowed the grounds for divorce and set new punishments for marital infidelity. Husbands and wives who committed adultery were whipped and fined, and their noses were slit. Abortion was prohibited, and new protections were set in place against incest with children. Mothers were given equal power with fathers over their offspring and, if widowed, became the legal guardians of their minor children and controlled the household property.

The transformations of the countryside went hand in hand with military, political, and cultural changes. On the military front, the Byzantine navy found a potent weapon in "Greek fire," a combustible oil that floated on water and burst into flames upon hitting its target. Determined to win wars on land as well, the imperial government exercised greater autocratic control, hastening the decline of the curial class, wresting power from other elite families, and encouraging the formation of a middle class of farmer-soldiers.

In the seventh century, an emperor, possibly Heraclius, divided the army into region-based regiments called *themes*. Soon the regions (also called *themes*) came to be dominated by the army general, a *strategos* (plural, *strategoi*), who took over civilian as well as military administration. Landless men were lured to join the army with the promise of land and low taxes; they fought side by side with local farmers, who provided their own weapons and horses. The new organization effectively countered frontier attacks.

Military reorganization was matched by a new educational curriculum emphasizing piety over the classics. The old curial elite had studied classical literature and sent their children (above all, their sons) to city schools or tutors to learn to read the works of Greek poets and philosophers. In the face of Islam's challenge, however, eighth-century parents wanted to give their children, both sons and daughters, a Christian religious education. Even with the decay of urban centers, cities and villages often retained an elementary school. There teachers used the Book of Psalms (the Psalter) as their primer. Throughout the seventh and eighth centuries, secular, classical learning remained decidedly out of favor, while dogmatic writings, saints' lives, and devotional works took center stage.

Religion, Politics, and Iconoclasm

The importance placed on religious learning and piety complemented both the autocratic imperial ideal and the powers of the bishops in the seventh century. Since the spiritual and secular realms were understood to be inseparable, the bishops wielded political power in their cities, while Byzantine emperors ruled as religious as well as political figures. In theory, imperial and church power were separate but interdependent. In fact, the emperor exercised considerable power over the church: he influenced the appointment of the chief religious official, the patriarch of Constantinople; he called church councils to determine dogma; and he regularly used bishops as local governors.

Because of this, bishops functioned as administrators, acting as judges and tax collectors in their cities. They distributed food in times of famine or siege, provisioned troops, and set up military fortifications. As part of their charitable work, they cared for the sick and the needy. In theory, they controlled the monasteries in their region (diocese) as well. However, in fact, monasteries were enormously powerful institutions that often defied the authority of bishops and even emperors. Monks commanded immense prestige as the holiest of God's faithful, and they were the chief sponsors of icons.

Icons were (and are) images of holy people—Christ, the Virgin, and the saints. To many Byzantine Christians, they were far more than mere representations: they were believed to possess holy power that directly affected people's daily lives as well as their chances for salvation. Many seventh-century Byzantines followed the monks in making icons the focus of their religious devotion. To them, icons were like the incarnation of Christ; they turned

■ **Icon of Virgin and Child**
With two angels behind them and a saint at either side, the Virgin Mary and the Christ Child display a still, otherworldly dignity. Working with hot pigmented beeswax, the sixth-century artist gave the angels transparent halos to emphasize their spiritual natures but depicted the saints as earthly men, with hair and beard, feet planted firmly on the ground. Icons such as this were used in private worship as well as in the religious life of Byzantine monasteries. **For more help analyzing this image,** see the visual activity for this chapter in the ONLINE STUDY GUIDE at bedfordstmartins.com/ huntconcise.

spirit into material substance. Thus an icon manifested in physical form the holy person it depicted. As the monk St. John of Damascus put it, in his vigorous defense of holy images, "I do not worship matter, I worship the God of matter, who became matter for my sake, and deigned to inhabit matter, who worked out my salvation through matter."

Other Byzantines, however, abhorred icons. Most numerous of these were soldiers on the frontiers. Shocked by Arab triumphs, they thought that the cause of their misfortunes was the biblical injunction against graven images. When they compared their defeats to Muslim successes, they could not help but notice that Islam prohibited all representations of the divine. To these soldiers and others who shared their view, icons revived pagan idolatry and desecrated Christian divinity. As iconoclastic ("anti-icon" or, literally, "icon-breaking") feeling grew, some churchmen became outspoken in their opposition to icons.

Byzantine emperors shared these religious objections, and they also had important political reasons for opposing icons. In fact, the issue of icons became a test of their authority. Icons represented intermediaries between worshipers and God; they undermined the emperor's exclusive place in the divine and temporal order. In addition, the emphasis on icons in monastic communities made the monks potential threats to imperial power; the emperors hoped to use this issue to break the power of the monasteries. Above all, though, the emperors opposed icons because the army did, and they needed the support of their troops.

The controversy climaxed in 726, after Emperor Leo III the Isaurian (r. 717–741) had defeated the Arabs besieging Constantinople in 718 and turned his attention to consolidating his political position. In the wake of the victory, officers of the imperial court tore down the great golden icon of Christ at the gateway of the palace and replaced it with a cross. In protest, a crowd of women went on a furious rampage in support of icons. This event marked the beginning of the period of **iconoclasm**; soon afterward, Leo ordered all icons destroyed, a ban that remained in effect, despite much opposition, until 787. A modified ban would be revived in 815 and last until 843. Thereafter, icons again became an important part of Byzantine Christianity.

Iconoclasm had an enormous impact on daily life. At home, where people had their own portable icons, it forced changes in private worship: the devout had to destroy their icons or venerate them in secret. Many women were devoted to icons—it was an empress who overturned the ban (temporarily, however) in 787. Iconoclasm also meant ferocious attacks on the monasteries: splendid collections of holy images were destroyed, vast properties were confiscated, and monasteries were disbanded. With their power now consolidated, Byzantine rulers were able to maintain themselves against the onslaught of the Arabs, who attacked under the banner of Islam.

■ **REVIEW:** *What stresses did the Byzantine Empire endure in the seventh and eighth centuries, and how was iconoclasm a response to those pressures?*

Islam: A New Religion and a New Empire

Islam, which means "submission to God" in Arabic, called for all to submit to the will of one God. It demanded a revolutionary change—the conversion to one community—of the many tribes who lived on the Arabian peninsula. The first to teach Islam was Muhammad, a merchant turned holy man from the Arabian city of Mecca, a major oasis near the Red Sea. He recognized only one God, that of the Jews and the Christians. He saw himself as God's last prophet, receiving and in turn repeating God's final words to humans. Invited by the city of Medina to come and mediate disputes there, Muhammad exercised the powers of both a religious and a secular leader. This dual role became the model for his successors (the caliphs) as well. Through a combination of persuasion and force, Muhammad and his coreligionists, the Muslims, converted most of the Arabian peninsula. By the time he died in 632, Islamic conquest and conversion had begun to move northward, into Byzantine and Persian territories. In the next generation, the Muslims took over most of Persia and all of Egypt and were on their way across North Africa to Spain. Yet within the territories they conquered with such lightning speed, daily life went on much as before.

The Rise and Development of Islam, c. 610–632

In the seventh century, the Arabian peninsula was populated by both sedentary and nomadic peoples. By far the largest group was made up of those who lived in one place (the sedentary), some making a living by farming, others living in oases, where they raised dates (a highly prized food). Some oases were prosperous enough to support merchants and artisans. By contrast, the nomads and seminomads (called Bedouins) lived in the desert. They herded goats, sheep, or camels, surviving largely from the products (leather, milk, meat) of their animals. Warriors, the Bedouins raided one another, valuing their honor highly and prizing bravery and generosity as well. Lacking written literature, they were proud of their oral culture of storytelling and poetry.

Islam began as a religion of the sedentary, but it soon found support and military strength among the nomads. It began in Mecca, a major oasis and commercial center. More important, Mecca was a religious center because it contained a shrine, the Ka'ba, which served as a sacred place within which war and violence among all tribes were prohibited. The tribe that dominated Mecca, the Quraysh, controlled access to the shrine and was able to tax the pilgrims who flocked there as well as sell them food and drink. Plunder from raids was transformed into trade as the visitors bartered on the sacred grounds, assured of their security.

Mecca was the birthplace of Muhammad (c. 570–632). His early years were unpromising: orphaned at the age of six, he spent two years with his grandfather and then came under the care of his uncle, a leader of the Quraysh tribe. Eventually, Muhammad became a trader. At the age of twenty-five, he married Khadija, a rich widow who had once employed him. They had at least four daughters and lived (to all appearances) happily and comfortably. Yet Muhammad sometimes left home and spent a few days in a nearby cave in prayer and contemplation, practicing a type of piety similar to that of early Christians.

In about 610, on one such retreat, Muhammad heard a voice calling on him to worship Allah, the God of the Jews and Christians. (*Allah* means "the God" in Arabic.) He accepted the call as coming from God. Over the next years he received mes-

Arabia in Muhammad's Lifetime

sages that he understood to be divine revelation. Later, when they had been written down and arranged—a process that was completed in the seventh century, but after Muhammad's death—these messages became the Qur'an, the holy book of Islam. The Qur'an, which means "recitation," is understood to be God's revelation as told to Muhammad by the angel Gabriel, then recited in turn by Muhammad to others. Its first chapter—or *sura*—is the Fatihah, which begins: "In the name of Allah, most benevolent, ever-merciful. All praise be to Allah." The Qur'an continues with 114 suras that are vaguely equivalent to (but generally much shorter than) books of the Bible. For Muslims (literally, "those who submit to Islam") the Qur'an addresses all of human experience—the sum total of history, prophecy, and the legal and moral code by which men and women should live—and the life to come.

The Qur'an emphasizes the nuclear family—a man, his wife, and children—as the basic unit of Muslim society. With the family given new importance, larger tribal affiliations were downgraded. However, all Muslims did have a wider identity as part of the ***ummah***, the community of believers, who shared both a belief in one God and a set of religious practices. Islam stresses individual belief and adherence to the Qur'an. Thus Muslims have no priests, no mass, and no intermediaries between the divine and the individual. However, Islam does recognize authorities whose interpretations of the Qur'an and related texts are considered decisive. The Ka'ba, with its many idols, had attracted tribes from the surrounding vicinity. Muhammad, with his beliefs in one God, forged an even more universal religion.

■ **Qur'an**

More than a "holy book," the Qur'an represents the very words of God. Usually the text appeared on pages wider than they were long, perhaps to differentiate the Qur'an from other books. This particular example dates from the seventh or eighth century. It is written in Kufic script, a formal and majestic form of Arabic that scribes used for the Qur'an until the eleventh century. The round floral decoration on the right-hand page marks a new section of the text.

(Property of the Ambrosian Library. All rights reserved.)

First to convert to Muhammad's faith were his wife, Khadija, and a few friends and members of his immediate family. However, Muhammad's insistence that all polytheistic cults be abandoned in favor of his one faith brought him into conflict with leading members of the Quraysh tribe, whose positions of leadership and livelihood were tied to the Ka'ba. Lacking political means to expel him, they insulted Muhammad and harassed his adherents.

Disillusioned and angry with his own tribe and with Mecca, where he had failed to make much of an impact, Muhammad tried to find a place and a population receptive to his message. Most important, he expected support from Jews, whose monotheism, in Muhammad's view, prepared them for his own faith. When a few of Muhammad's converts from Medina promised to protect him if he would join them there, he eagerly accepted the invitation, in part because Medina had a significant Jewish population. In 622, Muhammad emigrated to Medina, an oasis about two hundred miles north of Mecca. This journey, known as the Hijra, proved a crucial event for the fledgling movement. At Medina, Muhammad found followers ready to listen to his religious message and to regard him as the leader of their community. They expected him to act as a neutral and impartial judge in their interclan disputes. Muhammad's political position in the community set the pattern by which Islamic society would be governed afterward; rather than add a church to political and cultural life, Muslim political and religious institutions were inseparable. After Muhammad's death, the year of the Hijra was named the first year of the Islamic calendar; it marked the beginning of the new Islamic era.*

Although successful at Medina, the Muslims felt threatened by the Quraysh at Mecca, who actively opposed the public practice of Islam. For this reason, Muhammad led raids against them. At the battle of Badr in 624, Muhammad and his followers killed forty-nine of the Meccan enemy, took numerous prisoners, and confiscated rich booty. Thus traditional Bedouin plundering was grafted onto the Muslim duty of jihad.†

The battle of Badr was a great triumph for Muhammad, who was now able to consolidate his position at Medina, gaining new adherents and silencing all doubters. When Jews at Medina remained unreceptive to his message, Muhammad attacked them, expelling, executing, or enslaving many. At the same time Muhammad instituted new practices to define Islam as a unique religion. Among these were the *zakat*, a tax on possessions to be used for alms; the fast of Ramadan, which took place during the ninth month of the Islamic year, the month in which the battle of Badr had been fought; the *hajj*, an annual pilgrimage to Mecca that each Muslim was to try to accomplish at least once in his or her lifetime; and the *salat*, formal worship at least three times a day (later increased to five), which could include the *shahadah*, or profession of faith—"There is no god but God, and Muhammad is his Messenger." Soon Muhammad had Muslims direct their prayer away from Jerusalem, the center of Jewish worship, toward Mecca and the Ka'ba. Detailed regulations for these practices, sometimes called the "five pillars of Islam," were worked out in the eighth and early ninth centuries.

Meanwhile, the fierce rivalry between Mecca's tribes and Medina's Muslims began to spill over into the rest of the Arabian peninsula as both sides strove to win converts. Muhammad sent troops to subdue Arabs north and south. In 630, he entered Mecca with ten thousand men and took over the city, assuring the Quraysh of leniency and offering alliances with tribal leaders. By this time the prestige of Islam was enough to convince tribes elsewhere to convert. Through a combination of force, conversion, and negotiation, Muhammad was able to unite many, though

---

*Thus 1 A.H. (1 *anno Hegirae*, "year of the Hijra") on the Muslim calendar is equivalent to A.D. 622 (*anno Domini*, "year of the Lord," 622) on the Christian calendar.

†*Jihad* means "striving" and is used in particular in the context of striving against unbelievers. In that sense, it is often translated as "holy war." But it can also mean striving against one's own worst impulses.

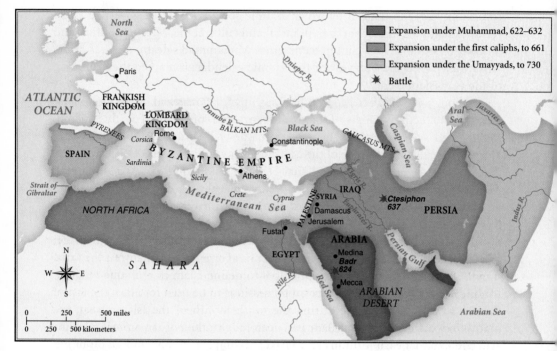

■ MAP 7.2 Expansion of Islam to 730
*In little more than a century, Islamic armies conquered a vast region that included numerous differ-
ent peoples, cultures, climates, and living conditions. Under the Umayyads, these disparate territories were administered by one ruler from his capital city at Damascus. The uniting force was the
religion of Islam itself, which gathered all believers into one community, the ummah.*

by no means all, Arabic-speaking tribes under his leadership by the time of his death
two years later (Map 7.2).

In so doing, Muhammad transformed Arab society. As Muhammad's converts
"submitted" to Islam, they formed not a tribe but rather a community bound
together by the worship of God. Women were accepted into this community, and
their status was enhanced. Islam prohibited all infanticide, a practice that had long
been used largely against female infants. Men were allowed to have up to four wives
at one time, but they were obliged to treat them equally; wives received dowries and
had certain inheritance rights. At first, Muslim women joined men during the salat,
the prayer periods that punctuated the day. Beginning in the eighth century, however, women began to pray apart from the men. Like Judaism and Christianity,
Islam retained the practices of a patriarchal society in which women's participation
in community life was circumscribed.

Even though Islamic society was a new sort of community, in many ways it functioned as a tribe, or rather a "supertribe," obligated to fight common enemies, share
plunder, and resolve peacefully any internal disputes. Muslims participated in group

rituals, such as the salat and public recitation. The Qur'an was soon publicly sung by professional reciters, much as the old tribal poetry had been. Most significant for the eventual spread of Islam, Muslim men were warriors, and their armies reaped profits at the point of a sword. But this differed from intertribal fighting; it was the "striving" (jihad) of people who were carrying out the injunction of God against unbelievers. "Strive, O Prophet," says the Qur'an, "against the unbelievers and the hypocrites, and deal with them firmly. Their final abode is Hell: And what a wretched destination!"

Muhammad's Successors, 632–750

Following his death, Muhammad's successors, the caliphs, conquered much of the Roman and Persian world. To the west, the Muslims attacked Byzantine territory in Syria with ease and moved into Egypt in the 640s (see Map 7.2). To the east, they invaded the Sassanid Empire, defeating the Persians at the gates of their capital, Ctesiphon, in 637. All of Persia was in Muslim hands by 661. During the last half of the seventh and the beginning of the eighth century, Islamic rule extended from Spain to India.

How were such conquests possible, especially in so short a time? First, the Islamic forces came up against weakened empires. The Byzantine and Sassanid states were exhausted from fighting each other. The cities of the Middle East that had been taken by the Persians and retaken by the Byzantines were depopulated, their few survivors burdened with heavy taxes. Second, the Muslims were welcomed into both Byzantine and Sassanid territories by discontented groups. Many Monophysite Christians in Syria and Egypt, for example, had suffered persecution by the Byzantines and were glad to have new, Islamic overlords.

These were the external reasons for Islamic success. There were also internal reasons. Arabs had long been used to intertribal warfare; now, under the banner of jihad, Muslims exercised their skills as warriors not against one another but rather against unbelievers. Fully armed, on horseback, and employing camels in convoys, they seemed almost a force of nature. Where they conquered, the Muslims built garrison cities from which soldiers requisitioned taxes and goods. Sometimes whole Arab tribes, including women and children, were imported to settle conquered territory, as happened in parts of Syria. In other regions, such as Egypt, a small Muslim settlement at Fustat sufficed to gather the spoils of conquest.

These successes hid tensions that developed within the Muslim leadership. Muhammad's death in 632 marked a crisis in the government of the new Islamic state, as different groups sought to promote their own successor. The first caliphs came not from the traditional tribal elite but rather from a new inner circle of men close to Muhammad and participants in the Hijra. The first two caliphs ruled without serious opposition, but the third, Uthman (r. 644–656), a member of the Umayyad family and one of Muhammad's sons-in-law, aroused discontent among other clan members of the inner circle and soldiers unhappy with his distribution of high offices and revenues. Accusing Uthman of favoritism, they supported his rival,

■ **Arab Coin**

The Arabs learned coinage and minting from peoples whom they conquered—the Persians and the Byzantines. Although one branch of Islam barred depicting the human form, others were less condemning. Thus the Umayyads saw nothing wrong with imitating traditional coinage. The ruler depicted on this silver coin is wearing a headdress that echoes the one worn by the Sassanid ruler depicted on page 262. But dirham, *the word for this type of coin, was not Persian but rather Greek, from* drachma. *The Umayyad Islamic fiscal system retained the old Roman land tax and was administered by Syrians who had served Byzantine rulers in the same capacity.* (© Copyright The Trustees of the British Museum.)

Ali, a member of the Hashim clan (to which Muhammad had belonged) and the husband of Muhammad's only surviving child, Fatimah. After a group of discontented soldiers murdered Uthman, civil war broke out between the Umayyads and Ali's faction. It ended in 661 when Ali was killed by one of his own former supporters, and the caliphate remained in Umayyad hands from 661 to 750.

Nevertheless, the *Shi'at Ali*, the faction of Ali, did not fade away. Ali's memory lived on among groups of Muslims, Shi'ites, who saw in him a symbol of justice and righteousness. For them, Ali's death was the martyrdom of the only true successor to Muhammad. They remained faithful to his dynasty, shunning the caliphs of the other Muslims (Sunni Muslims, from Arabic *sunna*, "custom" or "the way"). The Shi'ites awaited the arrival of the true leader—the imam—who in their view could come only from the house of Ali. The Sunni–Shi'ite split remains a political fact even today.

Under the **Umayyad caliphate**, the Muslim world became a state with its capital at Damascus. Borrowing from the institutions well known to the civilizations they had just conquered, the Muslims issued coins and hired former Byzantine and Persian officials. They made Arabic a tool of centralization, imposing it as the language of government on regions not previously united linguistically. For Byzantium this period was one of unparalleled military crisis, the prelude to iconoclasm. For the Islamic world, now a diverse society of Muslim Arabs, Syrians, Egyptians, Iraqis, and other peoples, it was a period of settlement, new urbanism, and literary and artistic flowering.

Peace and Prosperity in Islamic Lands

Ironically, the Islamic warriors brought peace. While the conquerors stayed within their fortified cities or built magnificent hunting lodges in the deserts of Syria, the conquered went back to work, to study, to play, and—in the case of Christians and

Jews, who were considered "protected subjects"—to worship as they pleased in return for the payment of a special tax. At Damascus, local artists and craftspeople worked on the lavish decorations for a mosque in a neoclassical style at the very moment Muslim armies were storming the walls of Constantinople (see page 264). Leaving the Byzantine institutions in place, the Muslim conquerors allowed Christians and Jews to retain their posts and even protected dissidents.

During the seventh and eighth centuries, Muslim scholars wrote down the hitherto largely oral Arabic literature. They determined the definitive form for the Qur'an and compiled pious narratives about Muhammad (hadith literature). Scribes composed these works in exquisite calligraphy, handwriting that was also an art form. A literate class, composed mainly of the old Persian and Syrian elite now converted to Islam, created new forms of prose writing in Arabic—official documents as well as essays on topics ranging from hunting to ruling. Umayyad poetry explored new worlds of thought and feeling. Patronized by the caliphs, who found in written poetry an important source of propaganda and a buttress for their power, the poets also reached a wider audience that delighted in their clever use of words, their satire, and their invocations of courage, piety, and sometimes erotic love:

> *I spent the night as her bed-companion, each enamored of the other,*
> *And I made her laugh and cry, and stripped her of her clothes.*
> *I played with her and she vanquished me;*
> *I made her happy and I angered her.*
> *That was a night we spent, in my sleep, playing and joyful,*
> *But the caller to prayer woke me up.*

Such poetry scandalized conservative Muslims, brought up on the ascetic tenets of the Qur'an. But this love poetry was a product of the new urban civilization of the Umayyad period, where wealth, cultural mix, and the confidence born of conquest inspired diverse and experimental literary forms. By the close of the Umayyad era in 750, Islamic civilization was multiethnic, urban, and sophisticated—a true heir of Roman and Persian traditions.

■ **REVIEW:** *How and why did the Muslims conquer so many lands in the relatively short period from 632 to 750?*

The Western Kingdoms

With the demise of Roman imperial government in the West, the primary foundations of power and stability in Europe were kinship networks, church patronage, royal courts, and wealth derived from land and plunder. In contrast to Byzantium, where an emperor still ruled as the successor to Augustus and Constantine, drawing

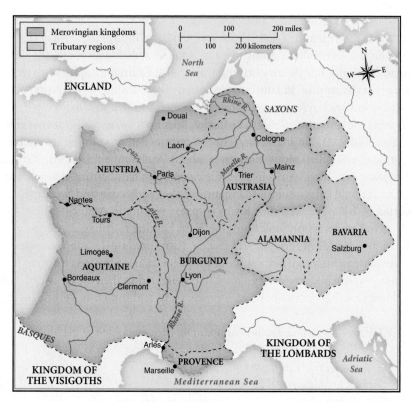

■ **MAP 7.3 The Merovingian Kingdoms in the Seventh Century**
By the seventh century, there were three powerful Merovingian kingdoms: Neustria, Austrasia, and Burgundy. The important cities of Aquitaine were assigned to one or another of these major kingdoms, while Aquitaine as a whole was assigned to a duke or other governor. Kings did not establish capital cities; they did not even stay in one place. Rather, they continually traveled throughout their kingdoms, making their power felt in person.

upon an unbroken chain of Roman legal and administrative traditions, political power in the West was more diffuse. Churchmen and rich magnates, sometimes one and the same person, held sway. Power derived as well from membership in royal dynasties, such as that of the Merovingian kings of the Franks. In addition, people believed that power lodged in the tombs and relics of saints, who represented and wielded the divine forces of God. Although the patterns of daily life and the procedures of government in the West remained recognizably Roman, they were undergoing change, borrowing from and adapting local traditions.

Frankish Kingdoms with Roman Roots

The core of the Frankish kingdoms was Roman Gaul. During the sixth century, the Franks had established themselves as dominant in Gaul, and by the seventh century

■ Stadium and Amphitheater at Arles

In what is today the south of France, the ruins of an amphitheater built by the Romans still dwarf the surrounding buildings of the modern city of Arles. This huge stadium was even more striking in the seventh century, when the city was impoverished and depopulated. Plague, war, and the dislocation of Roman trade networks forced most people to abandon the cities to live on the land. Only the bishop and his clergy—and individuals who could make a living servicing them—stayed in the cities. At Arles there were monasteries as well, and some of them were thriving. In the mid-sixth century there were perhaps two hundred nuns at one of the female convents there.

(Bridgeman-Giraudon/Art Resource, NY.)

the limits of their kingdoms roughly approximated the eastern borders of present-day France, Belgium, Switzerland, and Luxembourg (Map 7.3). Moreover, their kings, the Merovingians (c. 485–751), had conquered many of the peoples beyond the Rhine, foreshadowing the contours of modern Germany. These northern and eastern regions were little Romanized, but the inhabitants of the rest of the Frankish kingdoms lived with bits and pieces of the ancient Roman Empire at their front door.

Travel was difficult in this world of decaying roads and few amenities. Yet there were many travelers, such as pilgrims on their way to Rome and traders with slaves—precious human cargo captured on the borders of the Christian world and sold to wealthy aristocrats within. Most seventh-century voyagers would have relied on river routes, for land travel was very slow, and even large groups of travelers on the roads were vulnerable to attacks by robbers. Such travelers would have seen a very diverse landscape. Imagine pilgrims returning north from a pious trip to Rome. They might take the Rhône River, in which case they would pass Roman amphitheaters and farmland neatly and squarely laid out by Roman land surveyors. The great stone palaces of villas still dotted the countryside of southern Gaul. All this would have seemed quite classical and Roman. But if the travelers had been very observant, they would have noticed what was missing: thriving cities. By the seventh century, Roman cities were mere shells, serving as the centers of church administration but no longer boasting commercial or cultural vitality. Depopulated, many survived as mere skeletons, with the exception of such busy commercial centers as Arles and Marseille.

Continuing their journey north along the Moselle River, our travelers would pass through dense, nearly untouched forests and land more often used as pasture for animals than for cereal cultivation. Not much influenced by the Romans, these areas represented far more the farming and village settlement patterns of the Germans. Yet even here some structures of the Roman Empire remained. Fortresses were still standing at Trier, and large stone villas, such as the one excavated by archaeologists near Douai, loomed over the humble wooden dwellings of the countryside.

In the south, gangs of slaves still might occasionally be found cultivating the extensive lands of wealthy estate owners, as they had done since the days of the late Roman Republic. Scattered here and there, independent peasants worked their own small plots as they had for centuries. But for the most part, seventh-century travelers would find semifree peasant families settled on small holdings, their manse—including a house, a garden, and cultivable land—for which they paid dues and owed labor services to a landowner. Some of these peasants were descendants of the *coloni* (tenant farmers) of the late Roman Empire; others were the sons and daughters of slaves, now provided with a small parcel of land; and a few were people of free Germanic origin who for various reasons had come down in the world. At the lower end of the social scale, the status of Germans and Romans had become identical.

At the upper end of the social scale, Romans (or, more precisely, Gallo-Romans) and Germans had also merged. Although people south of the Loire River continued to be called "Romans" and people to the north "Franks," their cultures were strikingly similar: they shared languages, settlement patterns, and religious sensibilities. Many dialects were spoken in the western kingdoms in the seventh century, many deriving from Latin, though no longer the Latin of Cicero. "Though my speech is rude," Gregory, bishop of Tours (r. 573–c. 594), wrote at the end of the sixth century,

> I have been unable to be silent as to the struggles between the wicked and the upright; and I have been especially encouraged because, to my surprise, it has often been said by men of our day, that few understand the learned words of the rhetorician but many the rude language of the common people.

Thus Gregory began his *Histories*, a valuable source for the Merovingian period (c. 485–751). He was trying to evoke the sympathies of his readers, a traditional Roman rhetorical device; but he also expected that his "rude" Latin—the plain Latin of everyday speech—would be understood and welcomed by the general public.

In the fourth and fifth centuries Gallo-Roman aristocrats had lived in isolated villas with their *familia*—family members, slaves, and servants. In the seventh century, aristocrats lived in more populous settlements: in small villages surrounded by the huts of peasants, shepherds, and artisans. The early medieval village, constructed mostly out of wood or baked clay, was generally built near a waterway or forest or around a church for protection.

The cities, too, were transformed. At Tours, Bishop Gregory and his household and clerics still lived in the old Roman city center. But Tours's main focus was now outside the city walls, where a church had been built. The population of the surrounding countryside was pulled to this church as if to a magnet, for it housed the remains of the most important and venerated person in the locale: St. Martin. This saint, a fourth-century soldier-turned-monk, was long dead, but his relics—his bones, teeth, hair, and clothes—could be found at Tours, where he had served as bishop. There, in succeeding centuries, he remained a supernatural force: a protector, healer, and avenger through whom God manifested divine power. In Gregory's view, for example, Martin's relics (or rather God *through* Martin's relics) had prevented armies from plundering local peasants. Martin was not the only human thought to have great supernatural power; all of God's saints were miracle workers.

In the classical world, the dead had been banished from the presence of the living; in the medieval world, the holy dead held the place of highest esteem. The church had no formal procedures for proclaiming saints in the early Middle Ages, but influential

■ **Reliquary**

The cult of relics necessitated housing the precious parts of the saints in equally precious containers. This reliquary, made of cloisonné enamel (bits of enamel framed by metal), garnets, glass gems, and a cameo, is in the shape of a miniature sarcophagus. On the back is the inscription "Theuderic the priest had this made in honor of Saint Maurice." Theuderic must have given the reliquary to the monastery of Saint-Maurice d'Agaune (today in Switzerland), which was renowned for its long and elaborate liturgy—its daily schedule of prayer—in the late seventh century.
(Photo courtesy Thames and Hudson Ltd., London, from *The Dark Ages*, ed. David Talbot Rice.)

community leaders, including the local bishop, "recognized" holiness. When, for example, miracles were observed at the site of a tomb in Dijon, the common people went there regularly to ask for help. The nearby bishop, however, was convinced that St. Benignus inhabited the tomb only after the martyr himself visited the bishop in a vision. At St. Illidius's tomb in Clermont, it was reported that "the blind are given light, demons are chased away, the deaf receive hearing, and the lame the use of their limbs." Even a few women were so esteemed: "[Our Savior] gave us as models [of sanctity] not only men, who fight [against sinfulness] as they should, but also women, who exert themselves in the struggle with success," wrote Gregory as a preface to his story of the nun Monegund, who lived with a few other ascetic women and whose miracles included curing tumors and prompting paralyzed limbs to work again. No one at Tours doubted that Martin was a saint, and to tap into the power of his relics one of Gregory's predecessors as bishop had constructed his church in the cemetery directly over Martin's tomb. For a man like Gregory of Tours and his flock, the church building was above all a home for the relics of the saints.

Economic Activity in a Peasant Society

As a bishop, Gregory was aware of some of the sophisticated forms of economic activity in seventh- and eighth-century Europe, such as long-distance trade. Yet most people lived on the edge of survival. Studies of Alpine peat bogs show that from the fifth to the mid–eighth century glaciers advanced and the average temperature in Europe dropped. This climatic change spelled shortages in crops. Chronicles, histories, and saints' lives also describe crop shortages, famines, and diseases as a normal part of life. For the year 591 alone, Gregory reported that

> a terrible epidemic killed off the people in Tours and in Nantes. . . . In the town of Limoges a number of people were consumed by fire from heaven for having profaned the Lord's day by transacting business. . . . There was a terrible drought which destroyed all the green pasture. As a result there were great losses of flocks and herds.

An underlying reason for these calamities was the weakness of the agricultural economy. The dry, light soil of the Mediterranean region was easy to till, and wooden implements were no liability there. But in the north of Europe, where the soil was heavy, wet, and difficult to turn, the limitations of wooden implements meant a meager food supply. At the same time, agricultural work was not equitably or efficiently allocated and managed. A leisure class of landowning warriors and churchmen lived off the work of peasant men, who tilled the fields, and peasant women, who gardened, brewed, baked, and wove cloth.

Occasionally surpluses developed, either from peaceful agriculture or plunder in warfare, and these were traded, though rarely in an impersonal, commercial manner. Most economic transactions of the seventh and eighth centuries were part of a **gift economy**, a system of give-and-take: booty was taken, tribute was demanded, harvests were hoarded, and coins were minted, all to be redistributed to friends, followers, and dependents. Kings and other rich and powerful men and women amassed gold, silver, ornaments, and jewelry in their treasuries and grain in their storehouses to mark their power, add to their prestige, and demonstrate their generosity. Those benefiting from this bounty included religious people and institutions: monks, nuns, and bishops, monasteries and churches. We still have a partial gift economy today. At holidays, for example, goods change hands for social purposes: to consecrate a holy event, to express love and friendship, to show off wealth and status. In the Merovingian world, the gift economy was the dynamic behind most of the moments when goods and money changed hands.

Some economic activity in the seventh century was purely commercial and impersonal. In the north of Europe, a thriving North Sea trade was beginning. Older networks still tied the West—which supplied slaves and raw materials such as furs and honey—to the East, which provided luxuries and manufactured goods such as silks and papyrus. Trade was a way for the Byzantine, Islamic, and western European descendants of the Roman Empire to keep in tenuous contact with one another. Seventh- and eighth-century sources speak of Byzantines, Syrians, and Jews as the chief intermediaries, many of them living in the still-thriving port cities of the Mediterranean. Gregory of Tours associated Jews with commerce, complaining that they sold things "at a higher price than they were worth."

Contrary to Gregory's view, Jews were not involved only, or even primarily, in trade but were almost entirely integrated into every aspect of secular life in many regions of Europe. They used Hebrew in worship, but otherwise they spoke the same languages as Christians and used Latin in their legal documents. Their children were often given the same names as Christians (and, in turn, Christians often took Old Testament biblical names); they dressed like everyone else; and they engaged in the same occupations. Many Jews planted and tended vineyards, in part because of the importance of wine in synagogue services, in part because the surplus could easily be sold. Some Jews were rich landowners, with slaves and dependent peasants working for them; others were independent peasants of modest means. Some Jews lived in towns with a small Jewish quarter where their homes and synagogues were located. However, most Jews, like their Christian neighbors, lived on the land. Only much later, in the tenth century, would their status change as they were driven off of the land.

Women were also more fully integrated into the society of Merovingian Gaul than had been the case in the ancient world. Like Islamic women, those of the West received dowries and could inherit property. In the West, they could be entrepreneurs as well: documents reveal at least one enterprising peasant woman who sold wine at Tours to earn additional money.

The Powerful in Merovingian Society

Monarchs and aristocrats were the powerful people in Merovingian society. Aristocrats included monks and bishops as well as laypeople. Holding power through hereditary wealth, status, and political influence, they lived in leisurely abundance. At the end of the sixth century, for example, one of them, Bishop Nicetius, inhabited a palace that commanded a view of his estates overlooking the Moselle River:

> *From the top [of the palace] you can see boats gliding by on the surface of the river in summertime; orchards with fruit-trees growing here and there fill the air with the perfume of their flowers.*

Besides tending their estates, male aristocrats of the period spent their time honing their skills as warriors. To be a great warrior in Merovingian society, as in the otherwise very different world of the Bedouin, meant more than just fighting: it meant perfecting the virtues necessary for leading armed men. Aristocrats affirmed their skills and comradeship in the hunt; they proved their worth in the regular taking of booty; and they rewarded their followers afterward at generous banquets. At these feasts, following the dictates of the gift economy, the lords combined fellowship with the redistribution of wealth, as they gave abundantly to their retainers.

Merovingian aristocrats also spent a good deal of time in bed. The bed—and the production of children—was the focus of their marriage. Because of its importance to the survival of aristocratic families and to the transmission of their property and power, marriage was an expensive institution, especially the most formal kind, in which the husband paid a dowry to his bride—a generous gift of livestock and land—and gave her a smaller morning gift after the marriage was consummated. Very wealthy men might also support "lesser wives," to whom they gave a morning gift but no dowry. In this period, churchmen had many ideas about the value of marriages, but in practice they had little to do with the matter: no one was married in a church.

Sixth-century aristocrats with wealth and schooling like Nicetius patterned their lives on those of Romans, teaching their children Latin poetry and writing to one another in phrases borrowed from the classical poet Virgil. Less than a century later, however, aristocrats no longer adhered to the traditions of the classical past. Some still learned Latin, but they cultivated it mainly to read the Psalms. A religious culture emphasizing Christian piety over the classics was developing in the West at the same time as in Byzantium.

The new religious sensibility was given powerful impetus by the arrival (c. 591) on the European continent of the Irish monk St. Columbanus (d. 615). The Merovingian aristocracy, by now highly Christianized and anxious about the afterlife, was much taken by Columbanus's brand of monasticism, which stressed prayer, penance, and discipline. The numerous monasteries that St. Columbanus established from Gaul to Italy attracted local recruits from the aristocracy, some of them grown men and women. Others were young children, given to the monastery by their parents. This practice, called oblation, was not only accepted but also often considered essential for the spiritual well-being of both the children and their families. Irish monasticism introduced aristocrats on the continent to a deepened religious devotion. Those aristocrats who did not join or patronize a monastery still often read (or listened to others read) books about penitence, and they chanted the Psalms.

Bishops, generally aristocrats, ranked among the most powerful men in Merovingian society. Gregory of Tours, for example, considered himself the protector of "his citizens" at Tours. When representatives of the king came to collect taxes, Gregory stopped them in their tracks, warning them that St. Martin would punish anyone who tried to tax his people. "That very day," Gregory reported, "the man who had produced the tax rolls caught a fever and died." Gregory then obtained a letter from the king, "confirming the immunity from taxation of the people of Tours, out of respect for Saint Martin."

Like other aristocrats, many bishops were married. Church councils demanded celibacy, however, and as the overseers of priests, bishops were expected to be moral supervisors and refrain from sexual relations with their wives. Since bishops were ordinarily appointed late in life, long after they had raised a family, this restriction did not get in the way of their founding a family and fathering heirs.

Because unions bound together extended families rather than simply husbands and wives, noble parents determined whom their daughters were to marry. But women had some control over their lives. If they were widowed without children, they were allowed to sell, give away, exchange, or rent out their dowry estates as they wished. Moreover, men could give their women kinfolk property outright in written testaments. Fathers so often wanted to share their property with their daughters that an enterprising author created a formula for scribes to follow when drawing up such wills. It began:

> For a long time an ungodly custom has been observed among us that forbids sisters to share with their brothers the paternal land. I reject this impious law: I make you, my beloved daughter, an equal and legitimate heir in all my patrimony [inheritance].

Because of such bequests, dowries, and other gifts, many aristocratic women were very rich. Childless widows frequently gave grand and generous gifts to the church from their vast possessions. But a woman need not have been a widow to control enormous wealth: in 632, for example, the nun Burgundofara, who had never married, drew up a will giving her monastery the land, slaves, vineyards, pastures, and forests she

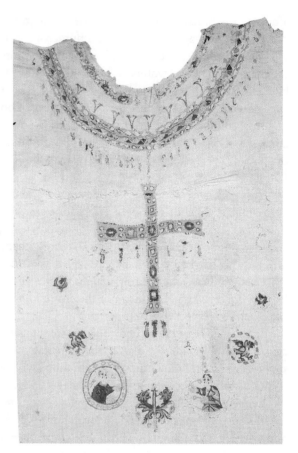

■ **Relic of Queen Balthild**
The slave Balthild, purchased in England by a Frankish mayor of the palace, caught the eye of the Frankish king himself, who made her his queen. This seventh-century Cinderella story did not end with marriage. When her husband died, Balthild played an important role as regent (caretaker ruler) for her young son. Later, she retired to a monastery, where she was revered as a saint. This shirt is one of her relics. Tradition has it that instead of wearing real jewels, Balthild distributed them to the poor and contented herself with their images in embroidery.
(Musée Alfred Bonno, Chelles, France. Photographers: E. Mittard and N. Georgieff.)

had received from her two brothers and her father. In the same will, she gave other properties near Paris to her brothers and sister. Aristocratic women maintained close ties with their relatives. They tried to find powerful husbands for their sisters and prestigious careers for their brothers; in turn, they relied on their relatives for support.

Though legally under the authority of her husband, a Merovingian woman often found ways to assert control over her life and her husband's life as well. Tetradia, wife of Count Eulalius, left her husband, taking all his gold and silver, because

> *he was in the habit of sleeping with the women-servants in his household . . .*
> *[and] neglected his wife. . . . As a result of his excesses, he ran into serious debt,*
> *and to meet this he stole his wife's jewelry and money.*

In a court of law, Tetradia was sentenced to repay Eulalius four times the amount she had taken from him, but she was allowed to keep and live on her own property. Other women were able to exercise behind-the-scenes control through their sons. Nicetius's mother, Artemia, used the prophecy that her son would become a bishop to prevent her husband from taking the bishopric himself. The prophecy took some time to be fulfilled, so Nicetius remained at home with his mother well into his thirties, working alongside the servants and teaching the younger children of the household to read the Psalms.

Occasionally women exercised direct power. Some women were abbesses, rulers in their own right over female monasteries and sometimes over "double monasteries," with separate facilities for men and women. These could be very substantial centers of population: the convent at Laon, for example, had three hundred nuns in the seventh century. Because women lived in populous convents or were monopolized by rich men able to support several wives or mistresses at one time, unattached aristocratic women were scarce in society and therefore valuable.

Atop this aristocracy of men and women were the Merovingian kings, rulers of the Frankish kingdoms from about 485 to 751. The **Merovingian dynasty** owed its longevity to good political sense: it had allied itself with local lay aristocrats and ecclesiastical authorities. The kings relied on these men to bolster their power, which was largely based on their tribal war leadership and access to the lion's share of plunder as well as their takeover of the taxation system, public lands, and the legal framework of Roman administration. The kings' courts functioned as schools for the sons of the aristocracy, tightening the bonds between royal and aristocratic families and loyalties. And when kings sent officials—counts and dukes—to rule in their name in various regions of their kingdoms, these regional governors worked with and married into the aristocratic families who had long controlled local affairs.

Aristocrats as well as kings had good reason to want a powerful royal authority. The king acted as arbitrator and intermediary for the competing interests of the aristocrats while taking advantage of local opportunities to appoint favorites and garner prestige by giving out land and privileges to supporters and religious institutions. Gregory of Tours's history of the sixth century is filled with stories of bitter battles between Merovingian kings, as royal brothers fought continuously over territories, wives, and revenues. Yet what seemed like royal weakness and violent chaos to the bishop was in fact one way the kings focused local aristocratic enmities, preventing them from spinning out of royal control. By the beginning of the seventh century, three relatively stable kingdoms had emerged: Austrasia to the northeast; Neustria to the west, with its capital city at Paris; and Burgundy, incorporating the southeast (see Map 7.3). These divisions were so useful to local aristocrats and to the Merovingian dynasty alike that even when royal power was united in the hands of one king, Clothar II (r. 584–629), he made his son the independent king of Austrasia.

The very power of the kings in the seventh century, however, gave greater might to their chief court official, the mayor of the palace. In the following century, allied with the Austrasian aristocracy, one mayoral family would displace the Merovingian dynasty and establish a new royal line, the Carolingians.

Christianity and Classical Culture in the British Isles

The Frankish kingdoms exemplify some of the ways in which Roman and non-Roman traditions combined. **Anglo-Saxon England** shows still another blending in its formation of a learned monastic culture. The impetus for this culture came not from native traditions but from Rome and Ireland. After the Anglo-Saxon conquest (440–600), England gradually emerged politically as a mosaic of about a dozen kingdoms ruled by separate kings. They were surrounded by Christian cultures in the rest of the British Isles (Wales, Scotland, and Ireland), and slowly the quadrant conquered by the Anglo-Saxons became Christian as well.

In the north of England, Irish monks brought their own brand of Christianity. Converted in the fifth century by St. Patrick and other missionaries, the Irish had rapidly evolved a church organization that corresponded to its rural clan organization. Abbots and abbesses, generally from powerful dynasties, headed monastic *familiae*, communities composed of blood relatives, servants, and slaves as well as monks or nuns. Bishops were often under the authority of abbots, and the monasteries rather than cities were the centers of population settlement in Ireland. The Irish missionaries to England were monks, and they set up monasteries on the model of those at home.

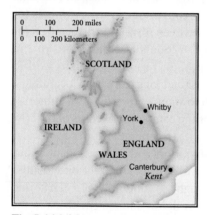

The British Isles

In the south of England, Christianity came by way of missionaries sent by Pope Gregory the Great (r. 590–604) in 596 to 597. The missionaries, under the leadership of Augustine (not the same Augustine as the bishop of Hippo), intended to convert the king and people of Kent, the southernmost kingdom, and then work their way northward. But Augustine and his party brought with them Roman practices at odds with those of Irish Christianity, stressing ties to the pope and the organization of the church under bishops rather than abbots. Using the Roman model, they divided England into dioceses, territorial units headed by an archbishop and bishops. Augustine, for example, became archbishop of Canterbury. Because he was a monk, he set up a monastery right next to his cathedral, and it became a unique characteristic of the English church to have a community of monks attached to the bishop's church.

A major bone of contention between the Roman and Irish churches involved the calculation of the date of Easter. The Roman church insisted that Easter fall on the first Sunday following the first full moon after the spring equinox. The Irish had a different method of determining Easter's date, and therefore they celebrated on a different day. As everyone agreed that believers could not be saved unless they observed Christ's resurrection properly and on the right day, the conflict over dates was bitter. It was resolved by Oswy, king of Northumbria. In 664, he organized a meeting of churchmen, the Synod of Whitby, which chose the Roman calculation. Oswy was convinced that Rome spoke with the voice of St. Peter, who, according to the New Testament, held the keys of the Kingdom of Heaven. Oswy's decision paved the way for the triumph of the Roman brand of Christianity in England.

St. Peter was not the only reason the Anglo-Saxons favored Rome. To many English churchmen, Rome had great prestige because it was a treasure trove of knowledge, piety, and holy objects. Benedict Biscop (c. 630–690), the founder of two important English monasteries, made many arduous trips to Rome, bringing back relics, liturgical vestments, and even a cantor to teach his monks the proper melodies in a time before written musical notation. Above all, he went to Rome to get books. At his monasteries in the north of England, he built up a grand library. In Anglo-Saxon England as in Ireland, both of which lacked a strong classical tradition from Roman times, a book was considered a precious object, to be decorated as finely as a garnet-studded brooch.

The Anglo-Saxons and Irish Celts had a thriving oral culture but extremely limited uses for writing. The ability to write and read became valuable only when these societies converted to Christianity. Just as Islamic reliance on the Qur'an made possible a literary culture under the Umayyads, so Christian dependence on the Bible, written liturgy, and the ideas of "church fathers" such as Jerome and Augustine helped make England and Ireland centers of literature and learning in the seventh and eighth centuries. Archbishop Theodore (r. 669–690), who had

■ Page from the Lindisfarne Gospels

The lavishly illuminated manuscript known as the Lindisfarne Gospels, of which this is one page, was probably produced in the first third of the eighth century. For the monks at Lindisfarne and elsewhere in the British Isles, books were precious objects, to be decorated much like pieces of jewelry. To introduce each of the four Gospels of the New Testament, the artist—who was also the scribe—produced three elaborate pages: the first was a "portrait" of the evangelist, the second a decorative "carpet" page, and the third the beginning of the text itself. The page depicted here is the beginning of the Gospel according to St. Matthew, which opens with the words "Liber generationis." Note how elaborately the first letter, L, is treated and how the decoration gradually recedes, so that the last line, though still very embellished, is quite plain in comparison with the others. In this way, the very layout of the book led the reader slowly and reverently into the text of the Gospels itself. (By permission of the British Library.)

studied at Constantinople and was one of the most learned men of his day, founded a school at Canterbury where students mined Latin and even some Greek manuscripts to comment on biblical texts. Men like Benedict Biscop soon sponsored other centers of learning, using texts from the classical past. Although women did not establish famous schools, many abbesses ruled over monasteries that stressed Christian learning. Here as elsewhere, Latin writings, even pagan texts, were studied diligently, in part because Latin was so foreign a language that mastering it required systematic and formal study. One of Benedict Biscop's pupils was Bede (673–735), an Anglo-Saxon monk and a historian of extraordinary breadth. Bede in turn taught a new generation of monks who became advisers to eighth-century rulers.

Unity in Spain, Division in Italy

In contrast to England, southern Gaul, Spain, and Italy had long been part of the Roman Empire and preserved many of its traditions. Nevertheless, as new peoples settled and fought over them, their histories diverged dramatically. When the Merovingian king Clovis defeated the Visigoths in 507, their vast kingdom, which had sprawled across southern Gaul and into Spain, was dismembered. By mid-century, the Franks came into possession of most of the Visigothic kingdom in southern Gaul.

In Spain the Visigothic king Leovigild (r. 569–586) established territorial control by military might. But no ruler could hope to maintain power there without the support of the Hispano-Roman population, which included both the great landowners and the leading bishops. Their backing was unattainable while the Visigoths remained Arian Christians, but in 587 Leovigild's son Reccared (r. 586–601) took the necessary step, converting to Catholic Christianity. Two years later, at the Third Council of Toledo, most of the Arian bishops followed their king by announcing their conversion to Catholicism, and the assembled churchmen enacted decrees for a united church in Spain.

Thereafter the bishops and kings of Spain cooperated to a degree unprecedented in other regions. The king gave the churchmen free rein to set up their own hierarchy (with the bishop of Toledo at the top) and to meet regularly at synods to regulate and reform the church. The bishops in turn supported their Visigothic king, who ruled as a minister of the Christian people. Rebellion against him was considered equivalent to rebellion against Christ. The Spanish bishops reinforced this idea by anointing the king, daubing him with holy oil in a ritual that paralleled the ordination of priests and demonstrated divine favor. Toledo, the city where the highest bishop presided, was also where the kings were "made" through anointment. While the bishops in this way adopted the king's cause as their own, their lay counterparts, the great landowners, helped supply the king with troops, allowing him to maintain internal order and repel his external enemies.

Ironically, it was precisely the centralization and unification of the Visigothic kingdom that proved its undoing. When the Arabs arrived in 711, they needed only to kill the king, defeat his army, and capture Toledo to deal it a crushing blow.

By contrast, in Italy the Lombard king constantly faced a hostile papacy in the center of the peninsula and virtually independent dukes in the south. Theoretically royal officers, in fact the dukes of Benevento and Spoleto ruled on their own behalf.

Although many Lombards were Catholics, others, including important kings and dukes, were Arian. The official religion varied with the ruler in power. Rather than signal a major political event, the conversion of the Lombards to Catholic Christianity occurred gradually, ending only around the mid-seventh century. Partly as a

Lombard Italy, Early Eighth Century

result of this slow development, the Lombard kings, unlike the Visigoths, Franks, or even the Anglo-Saxons, never enlisted the wholehearted support of any particular group of churchmen.

Lacking a strong and united church to back them up, Lombard kings still had important sources of power. Chief among these were the traditions of leadership associated with the royal dynasty and the kings' military role. In addition, the crown controlled large estates in northern Italy and made use of surviving Roman urban institutions. Although the Italian peninsula had been devastated by the wars between the Ostrogoths and the Byzantine Empire, the Lombard kings took advantage of the still-urban organization of Italian society and economy, assigning dukes to city bases and setting up a royal capital at Pavia. Recalling emperors like Constantine and Justinian, the kings built churches, monasteries, and other places of worship in the royal capital, maintained the walls, and minted coins.

Revenues from tolls, sales taxes, port duties, and court fines filled their coffers. Like other Germanic kings, the Lombards issued law codes that revealed a great debt to Roman legal collections, such as those commissioned by Justinian. While individual provisions of the law code promulgated by King Rothari (r. 636–652), for example, reflected Lombard traditions, the code also suggested the Roman idea that the law should apply to all under his rule, not just Lombards. "We desire," Rothari wrote,

> *that these laws be brought together in one volume so that everyone may lead a secure life in accordance with the law and justice, and in confidence thereof will willingly set himself against his enemies and defend himself and his homeland.*

Unfortunately for the Lombard kings, the "homeland" that they hoped to rule was fractured, not only by the duchies of Spoleto and Benevento but, more importantly, by the papacy, which dominated central Italy.

By 600, the pope's position was ambiguous: he was both a ruler and a subordinate. On the one hand, believing he was the successor of St. Peter and head of the church, he wielded real secular power. Pope Gregory the Great (r. 590–604) in many ways laid the foundations for the papacy's later spiritual and temporal ascendancy. During his tenure, the pope became the greatest landowner in Italy; he organized the defenses of Rome and paid for its army; he heard court cases, made treaties, and provided welfare services. The missionary expedition he sent to England was only a small part of his involvement in the rest of Europe. For example, Gregory maintained close ties with the churchmen in Spain who were working to convert the Visigoths from Arianism to Catholicism. A prolific author of spiritual works and biblical commentaries, Gregory digested and simplified the ideas of church fathers like St. Augustine of Hippo, making them accessible to a wider audience. His practical handbook for the clergy, *Pastoral Rule*, was matched by practical reforms within the church: in Italy, he tried to impose regular elections of bishops and to enforce clerical celibacy.

On the other hand, the pope was not independent. He was only one of many bishops in the Roman Empire, which was now ruled from Constantinople; and he was therefore subordinate to the emperor and Byzantium. Imperial authority did not begin to unravel in Rome until the late seventh century. In 691, Emperor Justinian II convened a council that determined 102 rules for the church, and he sent them to Rome for papal endorsement. Most of the rules were unobjectionable, but Pope Sergius I (r. 687–701) was unwilling to agree to the whole because it permitted priestly marriages (which the Roman church did not want to allow) and it prohibited fasting on Saturdays in Lent (which the Roman church required). Outraged by Sergius's refusal, Justinian tried to arrest the pope, but Italian armies (theoretically under the emperor) came to the pontiff's aid, while Justinian's arresting officer cowered under the pope's bed. The incident reveals that some local forces were already willing to rally to the side of the pope against the emperor. By now Constantinople's influence and authority over Rome was tenuous at best. Sheer distance, as well as diminishing imperial power in Italy, meant the popes were in effect the leaders of the parts of Italy not controlled by the Lombards.

The gap between Byzantium and the papacy widened in the early eighth century as Emperor Leo III tried to increase the taxes on papal property to pay for his all-consuming war against the Arab invaders. The pope responded by leading a general tax revolt. Meanwhile, Leo's fierce policy of iconoclasm collided with the pope's tolerance of images. In the West, Christian piety focused not so much on icons as on relics, but the papacy was not willing to allow sacred images and icons to be destroyed. The pope argued that holy images could and should be venerated—but not worshiped. His support of images reflected popular opinion as well. A later

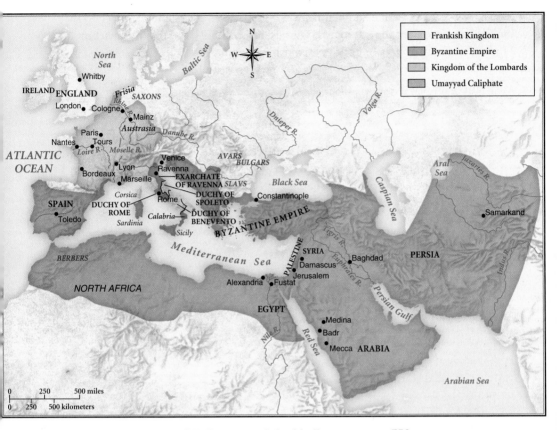

■ **MAPPING THE WEST** Europe and the Mediterranean, c. 750

The major political event of the period 600–750 was the emergence of Islam and the conquest of an Islamic state that reached from Spain to the Indus River. The Byzantine Empire, once a great power, was dwarfed—and half swallowed up—by its Islamic neighbor. To the west were fledgling barbarian kingdoms, mere trifles on the world stage. The next centuries, however, would prove their resourcefulness and durability. **For more help analyzing this map,** see the map activity for this chapter in the ONLINE STUDY GUIDE at bedfordstmartins.com/huntconcise.

commentator wrote that iconoclasm so infuriated the inhabitants of Ravenna and Venice that "if the pope had not prohibited the people, they would have attempted to set up a [different] emperor over themselves."

These difficulties with the emperor were matched by increasing friction between the pope and the Lombards. The Lombard kings had gradually managed to bring under their control the duchies of Spoleto and Benevento as well as part of the Exarchate of Ravenna. By the mid-eighth century, the popes feared that Rome would fall to the Lombards, and Pope Zachary (r. 741–752) looked northward for friends. He created an ally by sanctioning the deposition of the last Merovingian king and his replacement by the first Carolingian king, Pippin III the Short (r. 751–768). In 753,

Zachary's successor, Pope Stephen II (r. 752–757), called on Pippin to march to Italy with an army to fight the Lombards. Thus events at Rome had a major impact on the history not only of Italy but of the Frankish kingdom as well.

■ **REVIEW:** *How important was the papacy in early medieval Europe?*

IMPORTANT DATES			
c. 570–632	Life of Muhammad, prophet of Islam	630–730	Period of Islamic conquests
590–604	Papacy of Gregory the Great	661	Death of Ali; origins of Sunni–Shi'ite split
c. 591	Columbanus, an Irish monk, arrives on the European continent	661–750	Umayyad caliphate
		664	Synod of Whitby; English king opts for Roman Christianity
596–597	Augustine sent to England by Pope Gregory the Great to convert the Anglo-Saxons	718	Major Arab attack on Constantinople repulsed
610–641	Reign of Emperor Heraclius	726–843	Period of iconoclasm at Byzantium
622	Muhammad's Hijra to Medina and beginning of Islamic calendar		

Conclusion

The three heirs of the Roman Empire—Byzantines, Muslims, and the peoples of western Europe—built upon three distinct legacies. Byzantium directly inherited the central political institutions of Rome; its people called themselves Romans; its emperor was the Roman emperor; and its capital, Constantinople, was the new Rome. Sixth-century Byzantium also inherited the cities, laws, and religion of Rome. The changes of the seventh and eighth centuries—contraction of territory, urban decline, disappearance of the old elite, a ban on sacred images—whittled away at this Roman character. By 750, Byzantium was less Roman than it was a new, resilient political and cultural entity, a Christian community on the borders of the new Muslim Empire.

Muslims were the newcomers to the Roman world, with Islam influenced by Jewish monotheism and only indirectly by Roman Christianity. Under the guidance of the Prophet Muhammad, Islam became both a coherent theology and a tightly structured way of life with customs based on Bedouin tribal traditions and defined in the Qur'an. But once the Muslim Arabs embarked on military conquests, they, too, became heirs of Rome, preserving its cities, hiring its civil servants, and adopting its artistic styles. Drawing upon Roman and Persian traditions, the Muslims created a powerful Islamic state, with a capital city in Syria, regional urban centers elsewhere,

and a culture that tolerated a wide variety of economic, religious, and social institutions so long as the conquered paid taxes to their Muslim overlords.

Western Europe also inherited Roman institutions but changed them in many
diverse ways. Merovingian Gaul built on Roman traditions that had long been
transformed by provincial and Germanic customs. In Italy and at Rome itself, the
traditions of the classical past remained living parts of the fabric of life. The roads
remained, the cities of Italy (though depopulated) survived, and both the popes and
the Lombard kings ruled in the traditions of Roman government. In Spain, the
Visigothic kings allied themselves with a Hispano-Roman elite that maintained elements of the organization and vigorous intellectual traditions of the late empire.
However, in England, once the far-flung northern summit of the Roman Empire,
the Roman legacy had to be "re-imported" in the seventh century by Anglo-Saxon
churchmen seeking what they took to be a more authentic Christianity.

All three heirs to Rome suffered the ravages of war. In all three societies the social
hierarchy became simpler, with the loss of "middle" groups like the *curiales* at
Byzantium, the decline of city dwellers in western Europe, and the near suppression of
tribal affiliations among Muslims. As each of the three heirs shaped Roman institutions
to its own uses and advantages, each also strove to create a state founded on religion.
In Byzantium, the emperor was a religious force, presiding over the destruction of
images. In the Islamic world, the caliph was the successor to Muhammad, a religious
and political leader. In the West, the kings allied with churchmen in order to rule.
Despite their many differences, all these leaders had a common understanding of their
place in a divine scheme: they were God's agents on earth, ruling over God's people.

■ MAKING CONNECTIONS

1. *What were the similarities and what were the differences between the three
   heirs of the Roman Empire?*

2. *Which of the heirs seemed best poised for economic, political, and cultural success around the year 750 and why?*

■ FOR FURTHER EXPLORATION

For further reading and online research ideas, see the Suggested References on
page SR-4 at the back of the book.

For practice quizzes, a customized study plan, and other study tools, see the
ONLINE STUDY GUIDE at bedfordstmartins.com/huntconcise.

For primary-source material from this period, see Chapter 7 in *Sources of THE
MAKING OF THE WEST: A CONCISE HISTORY*, Second Edition.

Unity and Diversity in Three Societies

750–1050

I N 841, A FIFTEEN-YEAR-OLD BOY NAMED WILLIAM went to serve at the court of Charles the Bald, king of the Franks. William's father was Bernard, an extremely powerful noble. His mother was Dhuoda, a well-educated, pious, and able woman who administered the family's estates in the south of France while her husband occupied himself in court politics and royal administration. In 841, however, politics had become a dangerous business. King Charles, named after his grandfather Charlemagne, was fighting with his brothers over his portion of the Carolingian Empire, and Bernard (who had been a supporter of Charles's father, Louis the Pious) held a precarious position at the young king's court. In fact, William was sent to Charles's court as a kind of hostage, to ensure Bernard's loyalty. Anxious about her son, Dhuoda wanted to educate and counsel him, so she wrote a handbook of advice for William, outlining what he ought to believe about God, about politics and society, about obligations to his family, and, above all, about his duties to his father, which she emphasized even over loyalty to the king:

> In the human understanding of things, royal and imperial appearance and power seem preeminent in the world, and the custom of men is to account those men's actions and their names ahead of all others. . . . But despite all

■ **Carolingian Mother**
This depiction of a nursing mother is a detail from a full-page illustration of the biblical story of the Creation and Fall in a Carolingian Bible manuscript made in the ninth century. The mother is Eve, cast out of the Garden of Eden and suckling her firstborn, Cain. Christian mothers had an important model in Mary, the mother of Jesus, and Eve's dignified placement within a bower of garlands may reflect this association. (By permission of the British Library.)

this . . . I caution you to render first to him whose son you are special, faithful, steadfast loyalty as long as you shall live.

William heeded his mother's words, with tragic results: when Bernard ran afoul of Charles and was executed, William died in a failed attempt to avenge his father.

Dhuoda's handbook reveals the volatile political atmosphere of the mid-ninth century, and her advice to her son points to one of its causes: a crisis of loyalty. Loyalty to emperors, caliphs, and kings—all of whom were symbols of unity cutting across regional and family ties—competed with allegiances to local authorities; those, in turn, vied with family loyalties. The period 600–750 had seen the startling rise of Islam, the whittling away of Byzantium, and the emergence of stable political and economic institutions in an impoverished West. The period 750–1050 would see all three societies contend with internal issues of diversity even as they became increasingly conscious of their unity and uniqueness. At the beginning of this period, rulers built up and dominated strong and united polities. By the end, these realms had fragmented into smaller, more local units. Although men and women continued to feel some loyalty toward faraway kings, caliphs, or emperors, their most powerful allegiances often focused on authorities closer to home.

At Byzantium, military triumphs brought the emperors enormous prestige. A renaissance of culture and art took place at Constantinople. Yet at the same time newly powerful families began to dominate the Byzantine countryside. In the Islamic world, a dynastic revolution in 750 ousted the Umayyads from the caliphate and replaced them with a new family, the **Abbasids**. The new caliphs moved their capital eastward—shifting from Damascus to Baghdad—and adopted some elements of the persona of the Sassanid king of kings of Persia. Yet their power, too, began to ebb as regional Islamic rulers came to the fore. In the West, Charlemagne—a Frankish king from a new dynasty, the Carolingians—forged an empire that embraced most of Europe. But this new state, like the others, turned out to be fragile, disintegrating within a generation of Charlemagne's death. Indeed, in the West even more than in the Byzantine and Islamic worlds, power fell into the hands of local strongmen.

All along the fringes of these realms, new political entities began to develop, conditioned by the religion and culture of their more dominant neighbors. Russia grew up in the shadow of Byzantium, as did Bulgaria and Serbia. The West was more crucial in the development of central Europe. By the year 1050, the contours of modern Europe and the Middle East were dimly visible.

Byzantium: Renewed Strength and Influence

In the hundred years between 750 and 850, Byzantium staved off Muslim attacks in Asia Minor and began to rebuild itself. After 850 it went on the attack, and by 900 it had reconquered some of the territory it had lost. Military victory brought new wealth and power to the imperial court, and the emperors supported a vast program of literary and artistic revival—the Macedonian renaissance—at Constantinople. But while the emperor dominated at the capital, a new landowning elite began to control the countryside. On its northern front, Byzantium helped create new Slavic realms.

Imperial Might

The seventh-century imperial reorganization of the Byzantine army into *themes*—regiments based in particular regions—proved effective against Islamic armies. Avoiding battles in the field, the Byzantines allowed Muslim warriors to enter their territory, but they evacuated the local populations and burned any extra food. Then they waited in their fortified strongholds for the Muslims to attack. In this way they fought from a position of strength. If the Muslims decided to withdraw, other Byzantine troops were ready at the border to ambush them.

Beginning around 850 and lasting until 1025, the Byzantines turned the tables. They began advancing on all fronts, employing new mobile forces along with the theme soldiers. By the 1020s, they had regained Antioch, Crete, and Bulgaria (see Map 8.1 on page 298). They had not controlled so much territory since their wars with the Sassanid Persians four hundred years earlier.

Victories such as these gave new prestige to the army and the imperial court. New wealth matched this prestige. The emperors drew revenues from vast and growing imperial estates. They could tax and demand services from the general population at will—requiring them to build bridges and roads, to offer lodging to the imperial retinue, and to pay taxes in cash. These taxes increased over time, partly because of fiscal reforms and partly because of population increases (the approximately seven million people who lived in the empire in 780 had swelled to about eight million less than a century later).

The emperor's power extended over both civil administration and military command. Fearing potential rivals, whether from the court or in the army, emperors surrounded themselves with eunuchs—castrated men who were believed unfit to rule as emperors themselves and who were unable to have sons to challenge the imperial dynasty. Eunuchs were employed in the civil service; they held high positions in the army; and they were important palace officials.

Supported by their wealth and power, emperors negotiated with other rulers from a position of strength. Ambassadors were exchanged, and the Byzantine court received and entertained diplomats with elaborate ceremonies. One such diplomat, Liutprand, bishop of the northern Italian city of Cremona, reported on his audience with Emperor Constantine VII Porphyrogenitos (r. 913–959):

> *Leaning upon the shoulders of two eunuchs I was brought into the emperor's presence. At my approach [mechanical] lions began to roar and birds to cry out, each according to its kind. . . . After I had three times made obeisance to*

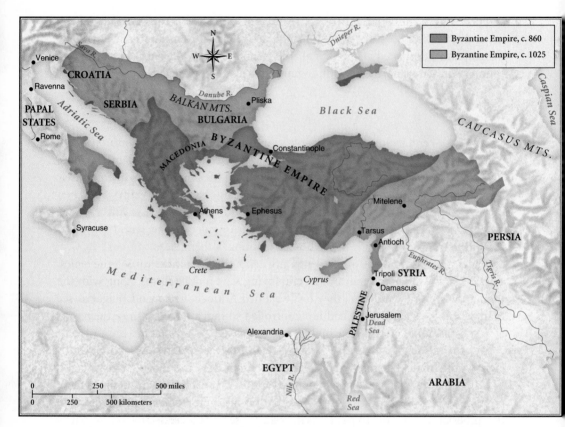

■ MAP 8.1 The Expansion of Byzantium, 860–1025

In 860, the Byzantine Empire was only a fraction of its former size. To the west, it had lost most of Italy; to the east, it held only part of Asia Minor. On its northern flank, the Bulgarians had set up an independent state. By 1025, however, it had ballooned, its western half embracing all of the Balkans, its eastern arm reaching around the Black Sea, and its southeastern fringe reaching nearly to Tripoli. The year 1025 marked the Byzantine Empire's greatest size after the rise of Islam.

> *the emperor with my face upon the ground, I lifted my head, and behold! the man whom just before I had seen sitting on a moderately elevated seat had now changed his raiment and was sitting on the level of the ceiling. How it was done I could not imagine, unless perhaps he was lifted up by some such sort of device as we use for raising the timbers of a wine press.*

Although this elaborate court ceremonial clearly amused Liutprand, its real function was to express the serious, sacred, concentrated power of imperial majesty. Liutprand missed the point because he was a westerner unaccustomed to such displays.

The emperor's wealth relied on the prosperity of an agricultural economy organized for trade. State regulation and entrepreneurial enterprise were delicately balanced in Byzantine commerce. Although the emperor controlled craft and commercial guilds (such as those of the silk industry) to ensure imperial revenues and a stable supply of valuable and useful commodities, entrepreneurs organized most of the fairs held throughout the empire. Foreign merchants traded within the empire, either at Constantinople or in some border cities. Because this international trade intertwined with foreign policy, the Byzantine government considered trade a political as well as an economic matter. Emperors issued privileges to certain "nations" (as such groups as the Venetians, Russians, and Jews were called), regulating the fees they were obliged to pay and the services they had to render. At the end of the tenth century, for example, the Venetians bargained to reduce their customs dues per ship from thirty *solidi* (coins) to two; in return they promised to transport Byzantine soldiers to Italy whenever the emperor wished.

Imperial authority was not absolute, however. In the countryside, particularly in Anatolia, powerful families—often army generals but also members of the civil service and the church—bought and dominated huge tracts of land. Many peasants became dependents of these great landlords, tilling the soil without owning it. Although the new magnates were a potential counterweight to imperial power, they ordinarily considered their interests to coincide with that of the emperor. They were glad to profit from imperial victories and the expansion of Byzantine territory.

The Macedonian Renaissance, c. 870–c. 1025

Flush with victory, which reminded them of Rome's glory, the emperors revived classical intellectual pursuits. Basil I (r. 867–886) from Macedonia founded the imperial dynasty that presided over the so-called Macedonian renaissance (c. 870–c. 1025). The *renaissance* (French for "rebirth")* was made possible by an intellectual elite, members of families who, even in the anxious years of the eighth century, had persisted in studying the classics despite the trend toward a simple religious education.

Now, with the empire slowly regaining its military eminence and with icons permanently restored in 843, this scholarly elite thrived again. Emperors and other members of the new court society, liberated from sober taboos, sponsored sumptuous artistic productions. Emperor Constantine Porphyrogenitos wrote books of geography and history and financed the work of other scholars and artists. He even supervised the details of his craftspeople's products, insisting on

---

*The word *renaissance* is commonly used in connection with a revival of classical art, languages, and culture in Italy during the period c. 1350–1500. However, it is also used for *any* artistic, intellectual, or cultural flowering nourished by classical traditions. It has both meanings in this book.

■ The Crowning of Constantine Porphyrogenitos

This ivory plaque was carved at Constantinople in the middle of the tenth century. The artist wanted to emphasize hierarchy and symbolism, not nature. Christ is shown placing the imperial crown on the head of Emperor Constantine Porphyrogenitos (r. 913–959). What message do you suppose the artist wanted to convey by placing Christ higher than the emperor and by having the emperor slightly incline his head to receive the crown? **For more help analyzing this image**, see the visual activity for this chapter in the ONLINE STUDY GUIDE at bedfordstmartins. com/huntconcise.

(Hirmer Fotoarchiv, Munich, Germany.)

exacting standards: "Who could enumerate how many artisans the Porphyrogenitos corrected? He corrected the stonemasons, the carpenters, the goldsmiths, the silversmiths, and the blacksmiths," wrote a historian supported by the same emperor's patronage.

Other members of the imperial court also sponsored writers, philosophers, and historians. Scholars wrote summaries of classical literature, encyclopedias of ancient knowledge, and commentaries on classical authors. Others copied manuscripts of religious and theological commentaries, such as homilies, liturgical texts, Bibles, and Psalters. They hoped to revive the intellectual and artistic achievements of the heyday of imperial Roman rule. But the Macedonian renaissance could not possibly succeed in this endeavor: too much had changed since the time of Justinian. Nevertheless, the renaissance permanently integrated classical forms into Byzantine political and religious life.

■ The Macedonian Renaissance

This manuscript illumination, made at Constantinople in the mid-ninth century, combines Christian and classical elements in a harmonious composition. David, author of the Psalms, sits in the center. Like the classical Orpheus, he plays music that attracts and tames the beasts. In the right-hand corner a figure labeled "Bethlehem" is modeled on a lounging river or mountain god. Compare this image with the crowning of Constantine Porphyrogenitos on page 300 and describe, using these two objects, the various styles and subject matters of the Macedonian renaissance.

(Bibliothèque nationale de France.)

New States under the Influence of Byzantium

The shape of modern eastern Europe—formed around Bulgaria, Serbia, and Russia—grew out of the Slavic states created during the period 850–950. By 800, Slavic settlements dotted the area from the Danube River down to Greece and from the Black Sea to Croatia. The Bulgar khagan ruled over the largest realm, populated mostly by Slavic peoples and situated northwest of Constantinople. Under Khagan Krum (r. c. 803–814) and his son, Slavic rule stretched west all the way to the Tisza River in modern Hungary. At about the same time as Krum's triumphant expansion, however, the Byzantine Empire began its own campaigns to conquer, convert, and control these Slavic regions.

The Byzantine offensive began under Emperor Nicephorus I (r. 802–811), who waged war against the Slavs of Greece in the Peloponnese, set up a new Christian diocese there, organized it as a new military theme, and forcibly resettled Christians in the area to counteract Slavic paganism. The Byzantines followed this pattern of conquest as they pushed northward. By 900, Byzantium ruled all of Greece.

Still under Nicephorus, the Byzantines launched a massive attack against the Bulgarians, took the chief city of Pliska, plundered it, burned it to the ground, and then marched against Krum's encampment in the Balkan mountains. Krum took advantage of his position, however, attacked the imperial troops, killed Nicephorus,

The Balkans, c. 850–950

and brought home the emperor's skull in triumph. Cleaned out and lined with silver, the skull served as the victorious Krum's drinking goblet. In 816, the two sides agreed to a peace that lasted for thirty years. But hostility remained, and wars between the Bulgarians and Byzantines broke out with increasing intensity. Intermittent skirmishes gave way to longer wars throughout the tenth century. The Byzantines advanced, at first taking Bulgaria's eastern territory. Then, in a slow and methodical conquest (1001–1018) led by Emperor Basil II (r. 963–1025), aptly called the "Bulgar-Slayer" (Bulgaroctonos), they subjected the entire region to Byzantine rule and forced its ruler to accept the Byzantine form of Christianity. Similarly the Serbs, encouraged by Byzantium to oppose the Bulgarians, began to form the state that would become Serbia, in the shadow of Byzantine interest and religion.

Religion played an important role in the Byzantine offensive. In 863, two brothers, Cyril and Methodius, were sent as missionaries from Byzantium to the Slavs. Well-educated Greeks, they spoke one Slavic dialect fluently and devised an alphabet for Slavic (until then an oral language) based on Greek forms. It was the ancestor of the modern Cyrillic alphabet used in Bulgaria, Serbia, and Russia.

Russia in the ninth and tenth centuries lay outside the sphere of direct Byzantine rule, but like Serbia and Bulgaria, it came under increasingly strong Byzantine cultural and religious influence. Vikings—Scandinavian adventurers who ranged over vast stretches of ninth-century Europe seeking trade, booty, and land—had penetrated Russia from the north and imposed their rule over the Slavs inhabiting the broad river valleys connecting the Baltic Sea with the Black Sea and thence with Constantinople. Like the Bulgars in Bulgaria, the Scandinavian Vikings gradually blended into the larger Slavic population. At the end of the ninth century, one Dnieper valley chief, Oleg, established control over most of the tribes in southwestern Russia and forced peoples farther away to pay tribute. The tribal association he created formed the nucleus of Kievan Russia, named for the city that had become the commercial center of the region and is today the capital of Ukraine (see "Mapping the West," page 335).

Kievan Russia and Byzantium began their relationship with war, developed it through trade agreements, and finally sustained it by religion. Around 905, Oleg launched a military expedition to Constantinople, forcing the Byzantines to pay a large fee and open their doors to Russian traders in exchange for peace. At the time only a few Christians lived in Russia, along with Jews and probably some Muslims. The Russians' conversion to Christianity was spearheaded by a Russian ruler later in the century. Vladimir (r. c. 980–1015), the grand prince of Kiev and all Russia, saw great military, cultural, and economic advantages in allying with the Byzantines. He and the Byzantine emperor Basil II agreed that Vladimir should adopt the Byzantine form of Christianity. Vladimir took a variant of the name Basil in honor of the emperor and married the emperor's sister Anne; then he reportedly had all the people of his state baptized in the Dnieper River.

Vladimir's conversion represented a wider pattern. Along with the Christianization of Slavic realms such as Old Moravia, Serbia, and Bulgaria under the Byzantine church, the rulers and peoples of Poland, Hungary, Denmark, and Norway were converted under the auspices of the Roman church. Russia's conversion to Christianity was especially significant, however, because Russia was geographically as close to the Islamic world as to the Christian and could conceivably have become an Islamic land. By converting to Byzantine Christianity, Russians made themselves heirs to Byzantium and its church, customs, art, and political ideology. Adopting Christianity linked Russia to the Christian world, but choosing Byzantine rather than Roman Christianity served to isolate Russia later from western Europe because in time the Greek and Roman churches would become estranged.

Under Prince Iaroslav the Wise (r. 1019–1054), Russia forged links through Iaroslav's own marriage and the marriages of his sons and daughters to rulers and princely families in France, Hungary, and Scandinavia. His ideal of rulership came directly from Roman traditions; he encouraged intellectual and artistic developments that would connect Russian culture to the classical past. But after his death, civil wars broke out, shredding what unity Russia had known. Massive invasions by outsiders, particularly from the east, further weakened Kievan rulers, who were eventually displaced by princes from northern Russia. At the crossroads of East and West, Russia could meet and adopt a great variety of traditions; but its situation also opened it to unremitting military pressures.

■ **REVIEW:** *How did Byzantium's expansion affect the power of its emperor?*

From Unity to Fragmentation in the Islamic World

A new dynasty of caliphs—the Abbasids—first brought unity and then, in their decline, fragmentation to the Islamic world. Caliphs continued to rule in name only, while regional rulers took over the real business of governing Islamic lands. Local traditions based on religious and political differences played an increasingly important role in people's lives. Yet even in the eleventh century, the Islamic world had a clear sense of its own unity, based on language, commercial life, and vigorous intellectual give-and-take across regional boundaries.

The Abbasid Caliphate, 750–c. 950

In 750, a civil war ousted the Umayyads and raised the Abbasids to the caliphate. The Abbasids found support in an uneasy coalition of Shi'ites (the faction loyal to Ali's memory) and non-Arabs who had been excluded from Umayyad government and now demanded a place in political life. The new regime signaled a revolution. The center of the Islamic state shifted from Damascus, with its roots in the Roman tradition, east to Baghdad, a new capital city built by the Abbasids right next to Ctesiphon, which had been the Sassanid capital. At first the caliphs were powerful: commanding a large centralized civil service, they also controlled the appointment of regional governors.

The Abbasid caliph Harun al-Rashid (r. 786–809), for example, presided over a flourishing empire from Baghdad. (He and his court are immortalized in some of the stories of *A Thousand and One Nights*, as for example "Sindbad the Sailor," in which a merchant's seagoing adventures bring him fabulous wealth.) Charlemagne, Harun's contemporary, was very impressed with the elephant Harun sent him as a gift, along with monkeys, spices, and medicines. But these items were mainstays of everyday commerce in Harun's Iraq. For example, a mid-ninth-century list of imports inventoried "tigers, panthers, elephants, panther skins, rubies, white sandal, ebony, and coconuts" from India and "silk, chinaware, paper, ink, peacocks, racing horses, saddles, felts, [and] cinnamon" from China.

■ **Minaret of the Great Mosque at Samarra**
From 836 to 892, the Abbasid caliphs had their capital at Samarra, about seventy miles north of Baghdad. In part, the choice of this location was a response to the very tensions that eventually produced the separate Islamic states of the tenth century. At Samarra itself, the Abbasid court created a cultural center. The Great Mosque, begun in 847, is the largest mosque ever built. Shown here is its minaret (the tower from which Muslims are summoned to prayer), which looms over the mosque some distance from its outer wall. Scholars still debate the reasons for its spiral shape.
(Bildarchiv Preußischer Kulturbesitz/Art Resource, NY.)

The Abbasid dynasty began to decline after Harun's death, mostly due to economic problems. Obliged to support a huge army and an increasingly complex civil service, the Abbasids found their tax base inadequate. They needed to collect revenues from their provinces, such as Syria and Egypt, but the governors of those regions often refused to send the revenues. After Harun's caliphate, ex-soldiers, seeking better salaries, recognized different caliphs and fought for power in savage civil wars. The caliphs tried to bypass the regular army, made up largely of free Muslim foot soldiers, by turning to Turkish slaves—Mamluks—bought and armed to serve as mounted cavalry. But the caliphate's dwindling revenues could not sustain a loyal or powerful military force, and in the tenth century the caliphs became figureheads only, as independent rulers established themselves in the various Islamic regions. To support themselves militarily, many of these new rulers turned to independent military commanders who led Mamluk troops. Well paid to maintain their mounts and arms, many Mamluks gained renown and, after being freed by their masters, high positions at the courts of regional rulers. In the thirteenth century, some of them became rulers themselves.

Regional Diversity

A faraway caliph could not command sufficient allegiance from local leaders once he demanded more in taxes than he gave back in favors. The forces of fragmentation were strong in the Islamic world: it was, after all, based on the conquest of many diverse regions, each with its own deeply rooted traditions and culture. The Islamic religion, with its Sunni–Shi'ite split, also became a source of polarization. Western Europeans knew almost nothing about Muslims and ordinarily called them all Saracens (from the Latin for "Arabs") without distinction. But, in fact, Muslims were of different ethnicities, practiced different customs, and identified with different regions. With the fragmentation of political and religious unity, each of the tenth- and early-eleventh-century Islamic states built on local traditions under local rulers (see Map 8.2 on page 306).

The most important and successful of these new states was formed by the Fatimids, a group of Shi'ites who took their name after Fatimah, wife of Ali and Muhammad's only surviving child. Allying with the Berbers in North Africa, the Fatimids established themselves in 909 as rulers in the region now called Tunisia. The Fatimid Ubayd Allah claimed to be not only the true imam, descendant of Ali, but also the *mahdi*, the "divinely guided" messiah, come to bring justice on earth. In 969, the Fatimids declared themselves rulers of Egypt, and eventually they controlled North Africa, Arabia, and even southern Syria. Their dynasty lasted for about two hundred years.

While the Shi'ite Fatimids were dominating Egypt, Sunni Muslims ruled al-Andalus, the Islamic central and southern heart of Spain. Unlike the other independent Islamic states forged during the ninth and tenth centuries, the Spanish

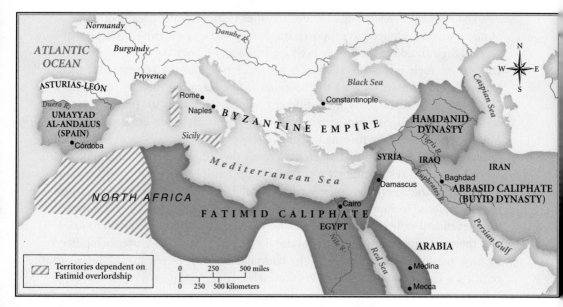

■ MAP 8.2 Islamic States, c. 1000

A glance back at Map 7.2 (see page 272) quickly demonstrates the fragmentation of the once united Islamic caliphate. In 750, one caliph ruled territory stretching from Spain to India. In 1000, there was more than one caliphate as well as several other ruling dynasties. The most important were the Fatimids, who began as organizers of a movement to overthrow the Abbasids. By 1000, they had conquered Egypt and controlled all of North Africa and even Sicily.

emirate of Córdoba (so called because its ruler took the secular title *emir*, "commander," and fixed his capital at Córdoba) was created near the start of the Abbasid caliphate, in 756. During the Abbasid revolution, Abd al-Rahman—a member of the Umayyad family—fled to North Africa, gathered an army, invaded Spain, and was declared emir after only one battle. He and his Umayyad successors ruled a broad range of peoples, including many Jews and Christians. After the initial Islamic conquest of Spain, the Christians adopted so much of the new language and so many of the customs that they were called Mozarabs, "would-be Arabs," by Christians elsewhere. Their rulers allowed them freedom of worship and let them live according to their own laws. Some Mozarabs were content with their status; others converted to Islam; still others intermarried—most commonly, Christian women married Muslim men and raised their children as Muslims.

Under Abd al-Rahman III (r. 912–961), who took the title caliph ("successor" to Muhammad) in 929, members of all religious groups in al-Andalus were given absolute freedom of worship and equal opportunity to rise in the civil service. Abd al-Rahman initiated important diplomatic contacts with Byzantine and European rulers. He felt strong enough not to worry much about the weak and tiny Christian kingdoms squeezed into northern Spain. Yet al-Andalus, too, experienced the same political fragmentation that was occurring everywhere else. In 1031, the caliphate of Córdoba broke up, as rulers of small, independent regions, called *taifas*, took power.

The regional diversity exemplified by the Fatimids and rulers of Islamic Spain did not prevent a measure of unity through trade networks and language. The principal bond of all Islamic lands was Arabic, the language of the Qur'an. At once poetic and sacred, Arabic was also the language of commerce and government from Baghdad to Córdoba. Moreover, despite political differences, borders were open: an artisan could move from Córdoba to Cairo; a landowner in North Africa might very well own property in al-Andalus; a young man from North Africa would think nothing of going to Iran to find a wife; a young girl purchased as a slave in Mecca might become part of a prince's harem in Baghdad. With no national barriers to trade and few regulations (though every city and town had its own customs dues), traders regularly dealt in far-flung, various, and often exotic goods.

Although the primary reason for this internationalism was Islam itself, open borders extended to non-Muslims as well. The Tustari brothers, Jewish merchants from southern Iran, typified the commercial activity in the Arabic-speaking world. By 1026, they had established a flourishing business in Egypt. The Tustaris did not have "branch offices," but informal contacts allowed them many of the same advantages and much flexibility: friends and family in Iran shipped them fine textiles to sell in Egypt, and the Tustaris exported Egyptian fabrics to sell in Iran. But the sophisticated Islamic society of the tenth and eleventh centuries supported networks even more vast than those represented by the Tustari family. Muslim merchants brought tin from England; salt and gold from Timbuktu in west-central Africa; amber, gold, and copper from Russia; and slaves from every region.

The Islamic Renaissance, c. 790–c. 1050

The dissolution of the caliphate into separate political entities multiplied the centers of learning and intellectual productivity. Unlike the Macedonian renaissance of Byzantium, which was concentrated in Constantinople, a "renaissance of Islam" occurred throughout the Islamic world. It was particularly dazzling in urban court centers such as Córdoba, where tenth-century rulers presided over a brilliant court culture. They patronized scholars, poets, and artists, and their library at Córdoba contained the largest collection of books in Europe.

Elsewhere, already in the eighth century, the Abbasid caliphs endowed research libraries and set up centers for translation where scholars culled the writings of the ancients, including the classics of Persia, India, and Greece. Scholars read, translated, and commented on the works of Neoplatonists and Aristotle. Others worked on mathematical matters. Al-Khwarizmi wrote a book on equation theory in about 825 that became so well known in the West that the word *al-jabr* in the title of his book became the English word *algebra*. Other scholars, such as Ali al-Hasan

■ Andromeda

The study of medicine, physics, astronomy, and other sciences flourished in the tenth and eleventh centuries in the cosmopolitan Islamic world. This whimsical depiction of Andromeda, a constellation visible in the Northern Hemisphere, illustrates the Book of Images of the Fixed Stars *(c. 965), an astronomical treatise written by al-Sufi at the request of his "pupil," the ruler of Iran. Knowledge of astronomy was important for both secular and religious reasons: the Muslim calendar was lunar, and the times of Muslim prayer were calculated from the movement of the sun. Al-Sufi drew from classical treatises, particularly the* Almagest *by Ptolemy. This copy of the* Book of Images, *probably made by al-Sufi's son in 1009, also draws on classical models for the illustrations, although instead of Greek clothing, Andromeda wears the pantaloons and skirt of an Islamic dancer.* (Bodleian Library, University of Oxford.)

(d. 1038) (known as "Alhazen" in the West), wrote studies on cubic and quadratic equations. Muhammad ibn Musa (d. 850) used a numeral system devised in India in his treatise on arithmetical calculations, introducing as well the crucial number zero. No wonder that the numbers 1, 2, 3, and so on were known as "Arabic numerals" when they were introduced into western Europe in the twelfth century.

The newly independent Islamic rulers supported science as well as mathematics. Unusual because she was a woman was al-Asturlabi, who followed her father's profession as a maker of astrolabes for the Syrian court. Astrolabes measured the altitude of the sun and stars to calculate time and latitude. More typical were men like Ibn Sina (980–1037), known in the West as Avicenna, who wrote books on logic, the natural sciences, and physics. His *Canon of Medicine* systematized earlier treatises and reconciled them with his own experience as a physician. Active in the centers of power, he served as vizier (prime minister) to various rulers.

Long before there were universities in the West, there were important institutions of higher learning in the Islamic world. In Islam all law and literature was understood to derive from God's commands as contained in the Qur'an or as revealed to the ummah, the community of believers. For this reason, the study of the Qur'an and related texts held a central place in Islamic life. In the tenth and eleventh centuries, rich Muslims, generally of the ruling elite, demonstrated their piety and charity by establishing schools for professors and their students. Each school, or **madrasa**, was located within or attached to a mosque. Visiting scholars often arrived at the madrasas to dispute, in a formal and rational way, with the professors there. Such events of intellectual sparring attracted huge audiences. On ordinary days, though, the professors held regular classes. A professor might begin his day with a class interpreting the Qur'an, following it with a class on other interpretations, and ending with a class on literary or legal texts. Students, all male, attended the classes that suited their achievement level and interest. Most students paid a fee for learning, but there were also scholarship students, such as one group of lucky students who were given annual funds by a vizier. This official was so solicitous for the welfare of all scholars that each day he set out for them iced refreshments, candles, and paper in his own kitchen.

The use of paper, made from flax and hemp or rags and vegetable fiber, points to a major difference among the Islamic, Byzantine, and (as we shall see) Carolingian renaissances. Byzantine scholars worked to enhance the prestige of the ruling classes. Using expensive parchment, their manuscripts could serve only the very rich. This was true of scholarship in the West as well. By contrast, Islamic scholars had goals that cut across all classes: to be physicians to the rich, teachers to the young, and contributors to passionate religious debates. Their writings, on less expensive paper, were widely available.

> ■ **REVIEW:** *What forces led to the fragmentation of the Islamic world in the tenth and eleventh centuries?*

The Creation and Division of a New Western Empire

Just as in the Byzantine and Islamic worlds, so, too, in the West, the period 750–1050 saw first the formation of a strong empire, ruled by one man, and then its fragmentation, as local rulers took power into their own hands. A new dynasty, the Carolingians, came to rule in the Frankish kingdom at almost the very moment that the Abbasids gained the caliphate. Charlemagne, the most powerful Carolingian monarch, conquered new territory, took the title of emperor, and initiated the revival of Christian classical culture known as the "Carolingian renaissance" (c. 790–c. 900). He ruled at the local level through counts and other military men who were faithful to him—he called them his *fideles*, or "loyal men." Nevertheless, the unity of this empire, based largely on conquest, a measure of prosperity, and personal allegiance to Charlemagne, was shaky. Its weaknesses were exacerbated by attacks from invaders—Vikings, Muslims, and Magyars. Charlemagne's successors divided his empire among themselves and saw it divided further as local strongmen took over the defense—and rule—of the land.

The Rise of the Carolingians

The Carolingians were among many aristocratic families on the rise during the Merovingian period. Like the others, they were important landowners, but unlike the others they gained exceptional power by monopolizing the position of "palace mayor" in the kingdom of Austrasia and, after 687, the kingdom of Neustria as well (see Map 7.3 on page 276). As mayors, the Carolingians traveled with the Merovingian kings, signed their documents, and helped them formulate and carry out policies. They also cemented alliances with other aristocrats on their own behalf and, by patronizing monasteries and supporting churchmen in key positions, they garnered additional prestige and influence. In the first half of the eighth century, many of the Merovingian kings were children, and the mayors took over much of the responsibility and power of kings themselves.

Charles Martel gave the name "Carolingian" (from *Carolus*, Latin for "Charles") to the dynasty. As palace mayor from 714 to 741, Charles Martel spent most of his time fighting vigorously against opposing aristocratic groups, although later generations would recall with nostalgia his defeat of a contingent of Muslims between Poitiers and Tours in 732. In contending against regional aristocrats who were trying to carve out independent lordships for themselves, Charles Martel and his successors turned aristocratic factions against one another, rewarded supporters while crushing enemies, and brought both lay and clerical aristocrats into alliance with him.

The Carolingians chose their allies well. One was the Anglo-Saxon monk Boniface (680–754), who wanted the continental church to have the same close relations with Rome as the English church had had with the papacy since the time of Gregory the Great. With Carolingian support Boniface went as a missionary to Frisia (today the Netherlands) and Germany, converting the population as a prelude to conquest. Many of the areas he reached had long been Christian, but the churches there had followed local or Irish models rather than Roman. Boniface, who came to Germany from England as the pope's ambassador, set up a hierarchical church organization and founded monasteries dedicated to the rule of St. Benedict. His newly appointed bishops were loyal to Rome and the Carolingians, not to regional aristocracies. They knew that their power came from papal and royal fiat rather than from local power centers.

Charles Martel's son Pippin III (d. 768) and his supporters cemented the Carolingian partnership with the pope by deposing the Merovingian king in 751 and petitioning Pope Zachary to legitimize their actions. He agreed. The Carolingians readily returned the favor a few years later when the pope asked for their help in defense against hostile Lombards. The request signaled a major shift. Before 754, the papacy had been part of the Byzantine Empire; after that it turned to the West. Pippin launched a successful campaign against the Lombard king that ended in 756 with the so-called Donation of Pippin, a peace accord between the

Lombards and the pope. The treaty gave back to the pope cities that had been ruled by the Lombard king. The new arrangement recognized what the papacy had long ago created: a territorial "republic of St. Peter" ruled by the pope, not by the Byzantine emperor. Henceforth the fate of Italy would be tied largely to the policies of the pope and the Frankish kings to the north, not to the emperors of the East.

The Carolingian partnership with the Roman church gave the dynasty a Christian aura, expressed in symbolic form by anointment. Carolingian kings, as Visigothic kings had been, were rubbed with holy oil on their foreheads and on their shoulders in a ceremony that to contemporaries harked back to the Old Testament kings who had been anointed by God.

Charlemagne and His Kingdom, 768–814

The most famous Carolingian king was Charles (r. 768–814), called "the Great" (*le Magne* in Old French) by his contemporaries. Epic poems portrayed Charlemagne as a just, brave, wise, and warlike king. In a biography written by Einhard, his friend and younger contemporary, Charlemagne was the model of a Roman emperor. Some scholars at his court described him as another David, the anointed Old Testament king. Modern historians are less dazzled than his contemporaries were, noting that he was complex, contradictory, and sometimes brutal. He loved listening to St. Augustine's *City of God* and supported major scholarly enterprises, yet he never learned to write. He was devout, building a beautiful chapel at his major residence at Aachen in Austrasia, yet he flouted the advice of churchmen when they told him to convert pagans rather than force baptism on them. He waged many successful wars, yet he thereby destroyed the buffer states surrounding the Frankish kingdoms, unleashing a new round of invasions even before his death.

Behind these contradictions, however, lay a unifying vision. Charlemagne dreamed of an empire that would unite the military and learned traditions of the Roman and Germanic worlds with the legacy of Christianity. In the early years of his reign, he emphasized the military tradition, conquering lands in all directions and subjugating the conquered peoples (see Map 8.3 on page 312). He invaded Italy, seizing the crown of the Lombard kings and annexing northern Italy in 774. He then moved northward and began a long and difficult war against the Saxons, concluded only after more than thirty years of fighting, during which he forcibly annexed Saxon territory and converted the Saxon people to Christianity through mass baptisms at the point of the sword. To the southeast, Charlemagne waged a campaign against the Avars, the people who had fought the Byzantines almost two centuries before. To the southwest, Charlemagne led an expedition to Spain, setting up a march, or military buffer region, between al-Andalus and his own realm. By the 790s, Charlemagne's kingdom stretched eastward to the Saale River (today in eastern Germany), southeast to what is today Austria, and south to Spain and Italy.

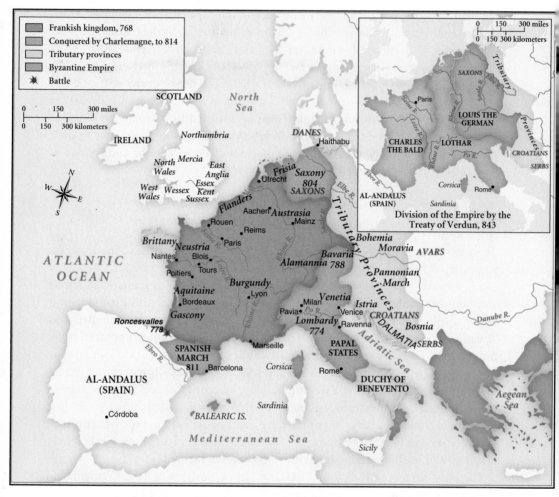

■ **MAP 8.3 Expansion of the Carolingian Empire under Charlemagne**
*The conquests of Charlemagne temporarily united almost all of western Europe under one govern-
ment. Although this great empire broke apart (the inset shows the divisions resulting from the
Treaty of Verdun), the legacy of that unity remained, even serving as one of the inspirations behind
today's European Union.*

Such hegemony in the West was unheard of since the time of the Roman
Empire, and Charlemagne began to act according to the old Roman imperial
model. He sponsored building programs to symbolize his authority, standardized
weights and measures, and became a patron of intellectual and artistic efforts,
building at Aachen a capital city that included a church patterned on one built
by Justinian at Ravenna. To discourage corruption, Charlemagne appointed special officials, called *missi dominici* (meaning "those sent out by the lord king"), to
oversee his regional governors—the counts—on the king's behalf. The missi—lay

aristocrats or bishops—traveled in pairs to make a circuit of regions of the kingdom. As one of Charlemagne's capitularies (summaries of royal decisions) put it, the missi "are to make diligent inquiry wherever people claim that someone has done them an injustice, so that the missi fully carry out the law and do justice for everyone everywhere, whether in the holy churches of God or among the poor, orphans, or widows."

While Charlemagne was busy imitating Roman emperors through his conquests, his building programs, his legislation, and his efforts at church reform, the papacy was beginning to claim imperial power for itself. At some point, perhaps in the 760s, members of the papal chancery, or writing office, forged a document, called the Donation of Constantine, that declared the pope the recipient of the fourth-century emperor Constantine's crown, cloak, and military rank along with "all provinces, palaces, and districts of the city of Rome and Italy and of the regions of the West." The tension between the imperial claims of the Carolingians and those of the pope was heightened by the existence of an emperor at Constantinople who also had rights in the West.

Pope Hadrian I (r. 772–795) maintained a balance among these three powers. But Hadrian's successor, Leo III (r. 795–816), tipped the balance. In 799, accused of adultery and perjury by a faction of the Roman aristocracy, Leo narrowly escaped being blinded and having his tongue cut out. He fled northward to seek Charlemagne's protection. Charlemagne had him escorted back to Rome and arrived there himself in late November 800 to an imperial welcome orchestrated by Leo. On Christmas Day of that year, Leo put an imperial crown on Charlemagne's head, and the clergy and nobles who were present acclaimed the king *Augustus*, the title of the first Roman emperor. The pope hoped in this way to exalt the king of the Franks, to downgrade the Byzantine ruler, and to enjoy the role of "emperor maker" himself.

About twenty years later, when Einhard wrote about this coronation, he said that the imperial title at first so displeased Charlemagne "that he stated that, if he had known in advance of the pope's plan, he would not have entered the church that day." In fact, Charlemagne did not use any title but king for more than a year afterward. But it is unlikely that he was completely surprised by the imperial title; his advisers certainly had been thinking about claiming it. He might have hesitated adopting it because he feared the reaction of the Byzantines, as Einhard went on to suggest, or he might well have objected to the papal role in his crowning rather than to the crown itself. When he finally did call himself emperor, after establishing a peace with the Byzantines, he used a long and revealing title: "Charles, the most serene Augustus, crowned by God, great and peaceful Emperor who governs the Roman Empire and who is, by the mercy of God, king of the Franks and the Lombards." According to this title, Charlemagne was not the Roman emperor crowned by the pope but rather God's emperor, who governed the Roman Empire along with his many other duties.

The Carolingian Renaissance

Charlemagne inaugurated—and his successors continued to support—a revival of learning designed to enhance the glory of the kings, educate their officials, reform the liturgy, and purify the faith. Like the renaissances of the Byzantine and Islamic worlds, the Carolingian renaissance resuscitated the learning of the past. Scholars studied Roman imperial writers such as Suetonius and Virgil; they read and commented on the works of the church fathers; and they worked to establish complete and accurate texts of everything they read and prized.

The English scholar Alcuin (c. 732–804), a member of the circle of scholars whom Charlemagne recruited to form a center of study, brought with him the traditions of Anglo-Saxon scholarship that had been developed by men such as Benedict Biscop and Bede. Invited to Aachen, Alcuin became Charlemagne's chief adviser, writing letters on the king's behalf, counseling him on royal policy, and tutoring the king's household, including the women. Charlemagne's sister and daughter, for example, often asked Alcuin to explain passages from the Gospel to them. Charlemagne entrusted Alcuin with the task of preparing an improved edition of the Vulgate, the Latin Bible read in all church services.

■ **St. Matthew**

The Carolingian renaissance produced art of extraordinary originality. Although the artist of this picture was inspired by classical models, his frenetic, emotional lines and uncanny colors are something new. This illustration, a depiction of St. Matthew writing (with an ink horn in his left hand and a quill in his right hand), precedes the text of St. Matthew's Gospel in a book of Gospels made around 820. Compare it to the Psalter illumination from Constantinople on page 301. What does this comparison tell you about the similarities and differences between the Macedonian and Carolingian renaissances? (La Médiathèque, Ville d'Epernay.)

The Carolingian renaissance depended on an elite staff of scholars such as Alcuin, yet its educational program had broader appeal. In one of his capitularies, Charlemagne ordered that the cathedrals and monasteries of his kingdom teach reading and writing to all who were able to learn. Some churchmen expressed the hope that schools for children (perhaps they were thinking of girls as well as boys) would be established even in small villages and hamlets. Although this dream was never realized, it shows that even before the Islamic world was organizing the madrasa system of schools, the Carolingians were thinking about the importance of religious education for more than a small elite.

Scholarship complemented the alliance between the church and the king symbolized by Charlemagne's anointment. In the Carolingian world, much as in the Islamic and Byzantine, there was little distinction between politics and religion: kings considered themselves appointed by the grace of God, often based their laws on biblical passages, involved themselves in church reform, appointed churchmen on their own initiative, and believed their personal piety a source of power.

Art, like scholarship, served Carolingian political and religious goals. Just as in the Byzantine renaissance, Carolingian artists illuminated texts—often lavish Gospels meant for the royal family or liturgical books commissioned by bishops and abbots—using earlier pictures as models. But their imitation was not slavish. To their models Carolingian artists added exuberant decoration and design, often rendering architectural elements as bands of color and portraying human figures with great liveliness. Some models came from Byzantium, and perhaps some Carolingian artists themselves came from there, refugees from Byzantium during its iconoclastic period. Pictorial models from Italy provided the kings' artists with examples of the sturdy style of the late Roman Empire.

The Carolingian program was ambitious and lasting, even after the Carolingian dynasty had faded to a memory. The work of locating, understanding, and transmitting models of the past continued in a number of monastic schools. In the materials they studied, the questions they asked, and the answers they suggested, the Carolingians offered a mode of inquiry fruitful for subsequent generations. In the twelfth century, scholars would build on the foundations laid by the Carolingian renaissance. The very print of this textbook depends on one achievement of the period: modern letter fonts are based on the clear and beautiful letter forms, called Caroline minuscule, invented in the ninth century to standardize manuscript handwriting and make it more readable.

Charlemagne's Successors, 814–911

Charlemagne's son Louis the Pious (r. 814–840) was also crowned emperor, and he took his role as guarantor of the Christian empire even more seriously. He brought the monastic reformer Benedict of Aniane to court and issued a capitulary in 817 imposing on all the monasteries of the empire a uniform way of life based on the rule of St. Benedict. Although some monasteries opposed this legislation, and in the years to come the king was unable to impose his will directly, this moment marked the effective adoption of the Benedictine rule as the monastic standard in the West. Louis also standardized the practices of his notaries, who issued his documents and privileges, and he continued to use missi to administer justice throughout the realm.

In a new development of the coronation ritual, Louis's first wife, Ermengard, was crowned empress by the pope in 816. In 817, their firstborn son, Lothar, was given the title emperor and made coruler with his father. Their other sons, Pippin and Louis (later called "the German"), were made subkings under imperial rule. Louis the Pious hoped in this way to ensure the unity of the empire while satisfying the claims of his and Ermengard's three sons. But Louis's plans were thwarted by events.

Ermengard died, and Louis married Judith, the daughter of one of the most powerful families in the kingdom. In 823, Judith and Louis had a son, Charles (later known as "the Bald," to whose court Dhuoda's son William was sent). The three sons of Ermengard, bitter over the birth of another royal heir, rebelled against their father and fought one another. A chronicle written during this period suggests that nearly every year was filled with family tragedies. In 830, for example, Pippin and his brother Lothar plotted to depose their father and shut Judith up in a convent. Louis the Pious regained control, but three years later his sons by Ermengard once again banded together and imprisoned him. Louis was lucky that the brothers began quarreling among themselves. Their alliance broke apart, and he was released.

Family battles such as these continued, both during Louis's lifetime and, with great vigor, after his death in 840. In 843, the Treaty of Verdun divided the empire among the three remaining brothers (Pippin had died in 838) in an arrangement that would roughly define the future political contours of western Europe (see Map 8.3, inset). The western third, bequeathed to Charles the Bald (r. 840–877), would eventually become France; the eastern third, handed to Louis the German (r. 840–876), would become Germany. The "Middle Kingdom," which was given to Lothar (r. 817–855) along with the imperial title, had a different fate: parts of it were absorbed by France and Germany, and the rest eventually formed the modern states of the Netherlands, Belgium, Luxembourg, Switzerland, and Italy.

In 843, the European-wide empire of Charlemagne dissolved. Forged by conquest, it had been supported by a small group of privileged aristocrats with lands and offices stretching across the entire realm. Their loyalty, based on shared values, real friendship, expectations of gain, and sometimes formal ties of vassalage and fealty (see pages 324–25), was crucial to the success of the Carolingians. The empire had also been supported by an ideal, shared by educated laymen and churchmen alike, of Christian belief and imperialism working together to bring good order to the earthly state. But powerful forces operated against the Carolingian Empire. Once the empire stopped expanding, the aristocrats could no longer hope for new lands and offices. They put down roots in particular regions and began to gather their own followings. Powerful local traditions such as different languages also undermined imperial unity. Finally, as Dhuoda revealed, some people disagreed with the imperial ideal. Asking her son to put his father before the emperor, she demonstrated her belief in the primacy of the family and the intimate and personal ties that bound it together. Dhuoda's ideal did not eliminate the emperor (European emperors would continue to reign until World War I), but it represented a new sensibility that saw real value in the breaking apart of Charlemagne's empire into smaller, more intimate local units.

Land and Power

The Carolingian economy, based on trade and agriculture, contributed to both the rise and the dissolution of the Carolingian Empire. At the onset, its wealth came from land and plunder. After the booty from war ceased to pour in, the Carolingians still had access to money and goods. To the north, in Viking trading stations such as Haithabu (today Hedeby, in northern Germany), archaeologists have found Carolingian glass and pots alongside Islamic coins and cloth, which tells us that the Carolingian economy intermingled with that of the Abbasid caliphate. Silver from the Islamic world probably came north up the Volga River through Russia to the Baltic Sea. There the coins were melted down, the silver traded to the Carolingians in return for wine, jugs, glasses, and other manufactured goods. The Carolingians turned the silver into coins of their own, to be used throughout the empire for small-scale local trade. The weakening of the Abbasid caliphate in the mid-ninth century, however, disrupted this far-flung trade network and contributed to the weakening of the Carolingians at about the same time.

Land provided the most important source of Carolingian wealth and power. Like the landholders of the late Roman Empire and the Merovingian period, Carolingian aristocrats held many estates, scattered throughout the Frankish Empire. But in the Carolingian period these estates were reorganized, and their productivity was carefully calculated. Modern historians often call these estates **manors.**

Typical was the manor called Villeneuve St.-Georges, which belonged to the monastery of St.-Germain-des-Prés (today in Paris) in the ninth century. Villeneuve consisted of arable fields, vineyards, meadows where animals could roam, and woodland, all scattered about the countryside rather than connected in a compact unit. The land was not tilled by slave gangs, as had been the custom on great estates of the Roman Empire, but rather by peasant families, each one settled on its own manse, consisting of a house, a garden, and small pieces of the arable land. The peasants farmed the land that belonged to them and also worked the demesne, the very large manse of the lord (in this case, the abbey of St.-Germain). These peasant farms marked a major social and economic development. Slaves had not been allowed to live in family units. By contrast, the peasants on Villeneuve and on other Carolingian estates could not be displaced from their manses or separated involuntarily from their families. In this sense, the peasant household of the Carolingian period was the precursor of the modern nuclear family.

Peasants at Villeneuve practiced the most progressive sort of plowing, known as the three-field system. At any one time, they farmed two-thirds of the arable land. They plowed one-third and planted winter wheat; they plowed another third and planted summer crops; and they plowed the final third but left the land fallow, to restore its fertility. The fields sown with crops and the field left fallow were then rotated so that land use was repeated only every three years. Because two-thirds of the arable land was cultivated each year, this system produced larger yields than did the still prevalent two-field system, in which only one-half of the arable land was cultivated in any one year.

All the peasants at Villeneuve were dependents of the monastery and owed dues and services to St.-Germain. Peasants' obligations varied enormously, depending on their status and on the manse they held. One family, for example, owed four silver coins, wine, wood, three hens, and fifteen eggs every year, and the men had to plow the fields of the demesne land. Another family owed the intensive labor of working the vineyards. One woman was required to weave cloth and feed the chickens. Peasant women spent much time at the lord's house in the *gynaeceum*—the women's workshop, where they made and dyed cloth and sewed garments—or in the kitchens as cooks. Peasant men spent most of their time in the fields.

Like other lords, the Carolingians benefited from their extensive estates. Nevertheless, farming was still too primitive to return great surpluses. Further, as the lands belonging to the king were divided up in the wake of the partitioning of the empire and new invasions, Carolingian dependence on manors scattered throughout the kingdom proved to be a source of weakness.

Vikings, Muslims, and Magyars Invade

Like the Roman emperors they emulated, Carolingian kings and counts confronted new groups along their borders (Map 8.4). The new peoples—Vikings to the north, Muslims to the south, and Magyars to the east—were feared and hated; but like the Germanic tribes that had entered the Roman Empire earlier, they also served as military allies. As royal sons fought one another and as counts and other powerful men sought to carve out their own principalities, their alliances with the newcomers helped integrate the outsiders swiftly into European politics. The impact of these foreign groups hastened, but did not cause, the dissolution of the empire. The Carolingian kings could not muster troops quickly or efficiently enough to counter

■ **MAP 8.4 Viking, Muslim, and Magyar Invasions of the Ninth and Tenth Centuries**

Bristling with multicolored arrows, this map suggests that western Europe was continually and thoroughly pillaged by outside invaders for almost two centuries. That impression is only partially true; it must be offset by several factors. First, not all the invaders came at once. The Viking raids were about over when the Magyar attacks began. Second, the invaders were not entirely unwelcome. The Magyars were for a time enlisted as mercenaries by the king of Italy, and some Muslims were allied to local lords in Provence. Third, the invasions, though widespread, were local in effect. Note, for example, that the Viking raids were largely limited to rivers and coastal areas.

the lightning attacks of the raiders. Defense fell into the hands of local authorities who, building on their new prestige and the weakness of the king, became increasingly independent rulers themselves.

The first of the new groups to attack the Carolingian Empire was the Vikings. The Franks called them "Northmen"; the English called them "Danes." They were, in fact, much less united than their victims thought. When they began their voyages at the end of the eighth century, they did so in independent bands. Merchants and pirates at the same time, Vikings followed a chief, seeking profit, prestige, and land. Many traveled as families: husbands, wives, children, and slaves.

The Vikings perfected the art of navigation. In their longships they crossed the Atlantic, settling Iceland and Greenland and (about 1000 C.E.) landing on the coast of North America. Other Viking bands navigated the rivers of Europe. The Vikings were pagans, and to them monasteries and churches—with their reliquaries, chalices, and crosses—were storehouses of booty. "Never before," wrote Alcuin, who experienced one attack, "has such terror appeared in Britain as we have now suffered from a pagan race. . . . Behold the church of St. Cuthbert spattered with the blood of the priests of God, despoiled of all its ornaments."

The British Isles confronted sporadic invasions by the Vikings from the eighth to the tenth century. From their fortified bases along the coast of Ireland the Vikings attacked and plundered churches and monasteries. But they also established Dublin as a commercial center and, in the tenth century, began to intermarry with the Irish and convert to Christianity. In Scotland, the Scandinavians settled on the west coast. Meanwhile, by the 870s, they had settled the east coast of England, plowing the land and preparing to live on it. The

■ **Viking Picture Stone**

Picture stones, some very elaborate, others with simple incisions, were made on the island of Gotland, today part of Sweden, from the fifth to the twelfth century. This one, dating from the eighth or ninth century, has four interrelated scenes. At the bottom is a battle between people defending a farm (note the cattle tied to the walls of the enclosure) and archers outside. Above is another enclosure with a woman at its wall. She is either Gudrun mourning her brother Gunnar, who was thrown into a snake pit, or Sigyn, the faithful wife of the god Loke, catching in a bowl the venom that a snake pours down on her chained husband. Next comes a ship, a typical picture stone motif; it is the ship of death that takes heroes to heaven. At the very top is heaven, or Valhalla, itself, where the heroes hunt and feast for all eternity. (Photo: Raymond Hejdstrom.)

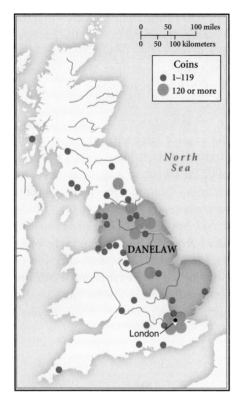

■ TAKING MEASURE Viking Coin Hoards, c. 865–895

From chronicles and other texts, we know that the Vikings invaded and settled in England. But from such sources it is very hard to know exactly where they settled and how many Vikings there were. Counting buried coins from the period can help answer these questions. Before safe-deposit boxes and banks, people buried their money in times of trouble. Archaeologists counting Viking coin hoards in England believe that the area called Danelaw was fairly thickly populated by Vikings, with a scattering in other regions as well. The Viking impact on England was not so much political—no Viking king took it over—as demographic. After 900, England was as much Scandinavian as it was Anglo-Saxon.

region where they settled and imposed their own laws was later called the *Danelaw.* (See "Taking Measure," above.)

In Wessex, the southernmost kingdom of England, King Alfred the Great (r. 871–899) bought time and peace by paying tribute and giving hostages. Such tribute, later called *Danegeld,* was collected as a tax that eventually became the basis of a relatively lucrative taxation system in England. Then in 878, Alfred led an army that, as his biographer put it, "gained the victory through God's will. He destroyed the Vikings with great slaughter and pursued those who fled . . . hacking them down." Thereafter, the pressures of invasion eased as Alfred reorganized his army, set up strongholds, and deployed new warships.

On the continent of Europe, too, the invaders set up trading emporia and settled where originally they had raided. Beginning about 850, their attacks became well-organized expeditions for regional control. At the end of the ninth century, one contingent settled in the region of France that soon took the name Normandy, land of the Northmen. The new inhabitants converted to Christianity during the tenth century. Rollo, the Viking leader in Normandy, accepted Christianity in 911 when the Frankish king Charles the Simple (or Straightforward) formally ceded Normandy to him.

Normandy was not the only new Christian state formed in the north during the tenth and eleventh centuries. Scandinavia itself was transformed with the creation of the powerful kingdom of Denmark. There had been kings in Scandinavia before the tenth century, but they had been weak, their power challenged by nearby chieftains. The Vikings had been led by these chieftains, each competing for booty to win prestige, land, and power back home. During the course of their raids, they and their followers came into contact with new cultures and learned from them. Meanwhile the Carolingians and the English supported missionaries in Scandinavia. By the middle of the tenth century, the Danish kings and their people had become Christian. Following the model of the Christian kings to their south, the Danish kings built up an effective monarchy, with a royal mint and local agents who depended on them. By about 1000, the Danes had extended their control to parts of Sweden, Norway, and even, under King Cnut (r. 1017–1035), England.

Far from Denmark, Muslims were taking advantage of Byzantium's early weakness. In 827 one group unconnected to the caliphate began the slow conquest of Sicily, which took nearly one hundred years. During the same century, Muslim pirates set up bases on Mediterranean islands and strongholds in Provence (in southern France) and near Naples (in southern Italy). Liutprand of Cremona reported on the activities of one such group:

> [*Muslim pirates from al-Andalus*], *disembarking under cover of night, entered the manor house unobserved and murdered—O grievous tale!—the Christian inhabitants. They then took the place as their own ... [fortified it, and] started stealthy raids on all the neighboring country.*

The Muslims at this base, set up in 891, robbed, took prisoners, and collected ransoms. But they were so useful to their Christian neighbors, who called on them to support their own feuds, that they were not ousted until 972. Only then, when they caused a scandal by capturing the holiest man of his era, Abbot Maieul of Cluny, did the count of Provence launch a successful attack against their lair.

Farther to the east, the Magyars, latecomers to the West, arrived around 899 in the Danube basin. Until then, the region had been predominantly Slavic, but the Magyars came from the East and spoke a language unrelated to any other in Europe (except Finnish). Their entry drove a wedge between the Slavs near the Frankish kingdom and those bordering on Byzantium; those near Byzantium, such as the Bulgarians, Serbs, and Russians, were driven into the Byzantine orbit, while those nearer the Frankish kingdom came under the influence of Germany.

From their bases in present-day Hungary, the Magyars raided far to the west, attacking Germany, Italy, and even southern Gaul frequently between 899 and 955. Then in the summer of 955, one marauding party of Magyars was met at the Lech River by the German king Otto I (r. 936–973), whose army decimated them in the battle of Lechfeld. Otto's victory, his subsequent military reorganization of his eastern frontiers, and the cessation of Magyar raids around this time made Otto a great hero to his contemporaries. Today, however, historians think the containment of the Magyars had more to do with their internal transformation from nomads to farmers than with their military defeat.

The Viking, Muslim, and Magyar invasions were the final onslaught western Europe experienced from outsiders. In some ways they were a continuation of the invasions that had rocked the Roman Empire in the fourth and fifth centuries. Loosely organized in warbands, the new groups entered western Europe looking for wealth but, apart from the Muslims, stayed on to become absorbed in its new post-invasion society.

■ **REVIEW:** *What were the strengths and weaknesses of the Carolingian institutions of government, warfare, and defense?*

The Emergence of Local Rule in the Post-Carolingian Age

The Carolingian Empire was too diverse to cohere. Latin was a universal language, but few people spoke it; instead they used a wide variety of languages and dialects. The king demanded loyalty from everyone, but most people knew only his representative, the local count. As the empire ceased to expand and was instead attacked by outsiders, the counts and other powerful men stopped looking to the king for new lands and offices and began to develop and exploit what they already had. They became powerful lords, commanding warriors and peasants, building castles, setting up markets, collecting revenues, keeping the peace, and seeing themselves as independent regional rulers. In this way, a new warrior class of lords and vassals came to dominate post-Carolingian society.

Yet it would be wrong to imagine that all of Europe came under the control of rural warlords. In Italy, where cities had never lost their importance, urban elites ruled over the surrounding countryside. Everywhere, kings retained a certain amount of power; indeed, in some places, such as Germany and England, they were extremely effective. Central European monarchies formed under the influence of Germany.*

Public Power and Private Relationships

The key way in which both kings and less powerful men commanded others was by ensuring personal loyalty. In the ninth century, the Carolingian kings had their

---

*Terms such as *Germany, France,* and *Italy* are used here for the sake of convenience. They refer to regions, not to the nation-states that would eventually become associated with those names.

fideles, their "faithful men." Among these were the counts. In addition to a share in the revenues of their administrative district, the county, the counts received benefices, later also called fiefs, which were temporary grants of land given in return for service. These short-term arrangements often became permanent, however, once a count's son inherited the job and the fiefs of his father. By the end of the ninth century, fiefs were often properties that could be passed on to heirs.

In the wake of the invasions, more and more warriors were drawn into similar networks of dependency, but not with the king: they became the faithful men—the **vassals**—of local lords. From the Latin word for fief comes the word *feudal*, and historians often use the term *feudalism* to describe the social and economic system created by the relationship among vassals, lords, and fiefs.*

It was frequently said by medieval people that their society consisted of three groups: those who prayed, those who fought, and those who worked. All of these people were involved in hierarchies of dependency and were linked by personal bonds, but the upper classes—the prayers (monks) and the fighters (the knights)— were free. Their brand of dependency was honorable, whether they were vassals, lords, or both. In fact, a typical warrior was lord of several vassals and the vassal of another lord. Monasteries normally had vassals to fight for them, and their abbots in turn were likely to be vassals of a king or other powerful lord.

Vassalage grew up as an alternative to public power and at the same time as a way to strengthen what little public power there was. Given the impoverished economic conditions of the West, its primitive methods of communication, and its lack of unifying traditions, kings came to rely on vassals personally loyal to them to muster troops, collect taxes, and administer justice. When in the ninth century the Frankish Empire broke up politically and power fell into the hands of local lords, they, too, needed "faithful men" to protect them and carry out their orders. And vassals needed lords. At the low end of the social scale, poor vassals looked to their lords to feed, clothe, house, and arm them. They hoped that they would be rewarded for their service with a fief of their own, with which they could support themselves and a family. At the upper end of the social scale, vassals looked to lords to enrich them further.

A few women were vassals and some were lords (or, rather, "ladies," the female counterpart); many upper-class laywomen participated in the society of fighters and prayers as wives and mothers of vassals and lords. Other aristocratic women entered convents and became members of the social group that prayed. Through its abbess or a man standing in for her, a convent was likely to have vassals as well.

---

*Many historians, however, regard *feudalism* as a problematic term. Does it mean "anarchy"? Some historians have used it that way. Does it mean "a hierarchical scheme of lords and knights"? This is another common definition. And there are others as well. This imprecision has led some historians to drop the word altogether. Moreover, feudalism implies that one way of life dominated the Middle Ages, when in fact, there were numerous social, political, and economic arrangements. For these reasons, *feudalism* rarely appears in *The Making of the West*.

Becoming the vassal of a lord often involved both ritual gestures and verbal promises. In a ceremony witnessed by others, the vassal-to-be knelt and, placing his hands between the hands of his lord, said, "I promise to be your man." This act, known as homage, was followed by the promise of **fealty**—fidelity, trust, and service—which the vassal swore with his hand on relics or a Bible. Then the vassal and the lord kissed. In an age when many people could not read, a public ceremony such as this represented a visual and verbal contract. Vassalage bound the lord and vassal to one another with reciprocal obligations, usually military. Knights, as the premier fighters of the day, were the most desirable vassals.

At the bottom of the social scale were those who worked—the peasants. In the Carolingian period, many peasants were free; they did not live on a manor, or if they did, they owed very little to its lord. But as power fell into the hands of local rulers, fewer and fewer peasants remained free. Rather, they were made dependent on lords, not as vassals but as **serfs**. Serfdom was a dependency separate from and completely unlike that of a vassal. It was not voluntary but inherited. No serf did homage or fealty to his lord; no serf kissed his lord as an equal. And the serf's work as a laborer was not considered honorable. Unlike knights, who were celebrated in songs and stories, peasants, who constituted the majority of the population, were nevertheless barely noticed by the upper classes—except as a source of revenue.

New methods of cultivation and a burgeoning population helped transform the rural landscape and make it more productive. With a growing number of men and women to work the land, the lower classes now had more mouths to feed and faced the hardship of food shortage. Landlords began reorganizing their estates to run more efficiently. In the tenth century, the three-field system became more prevalent; heavy plows that could turn the heavy northern soils came into wider use; and horses (more effective than oxen) were harnessed to pull the plows. The result was surplus food and a better standard of living for nearly everyone.

In search of greater profits, some lords lightened the dues and services of peasants temporarily to allow them to open up new lands by draining marshes and cutting down forests. Some landlords converted dues and labor services into money payments, a boon for both lords and peasants. Lords now had money to spend on what they wanted rather than hens and eggs they might not need or want. Peasants benefited because their tax was fixed despite inflation. Thus, as the prices of their hens and eggs went up, they could sell them, reaping a profit in spite of the dues they owed their lords.

By the tenth century, many peasants lived in populous rural settlements, true villages. In the midst of a sea of arable land, meadow, wood, and wasteland, these villages developed a sense of community. Boundaries—sometimes real fortifications, sometimes simple markers—told nonresidents to keep out and to find shelter in huts located outside the village limits.

The church often formed the focal point of local activity. There people met, received the sacraments, drew up contracts, and buried their parents and children.

Religious feasts and festivals joined the rituals of farming to mark the seasons. The church dominated the village in another way: men and women owed it a tax called a **tithe** (equivalent to one-tenth of their crops or income, paid in money or in kind), which was first instituted on a regular basis by the Carolingians.

Village peasants' sense of common purpose grew out of their practical interdependence, as they shared oxen or horses for the teams that pulled the plow or turned to village craftsmen to fix their wheels or shoe their horses. Their feeling of solidarity sometimes encouraged villagers to band together to ask for privileges as a group. Near Verona, in northern Italy, for example, twenty-five men living around the castle of Nogara in 920 joined together to ask their lord, the abbot of Nonantola, to allow them to lease plots of land, houses, and pasturage there in return for a small yearly rent and the promise to defend the castle. The abbot granted their request.

Village solidarity could be compromised, however, by conflicting loyalties and obligations. A peasant in one village might very well have one piece of land connected with a certain manor and another bit of arable field on a different estate, and he or she might owe several lords different kinds of dues. Even peasants of one village working for one lord might owe him varied services and taxes.

Layers of obligations were even more striking across the regions of Europe than in particular villages. The principal distinction was between free peasants, such as small landowners in Saxony and other parts of Germany, and unfree peasants, who were especially common in France and England. In Italy, peasants ranged from small independent landowners to leaseholders (like the tenants at Nogara); most were both, owning a parcel in one place and leasing another nearby.

Once the power of kings began to weaken, this system of peasant obligations became part of a larger system of local rule. As landlords consolidated their power over their manors, they collected not only dues and services but also fees for the use of their flour mills, bake houses, and breweries. Some built castles, fortified strongholds, and imposed the even wider powers of the **ban**: the rights to collect taxes, hear court cases, levy fines, and muster men for defense.

The Fragmentation of France, c. 1000

In France, for example, as the king's power waned, political control fell into the hands of counts and other princes. By 1000, castles had become the key to their power. In the south of France, power was so fragmented that each man who controlled a castle—a **castellan**—was a virtual ruler, although often with a very limited reach. In northwestern France, territorial princes, basing their rule on the control of *many* castles, dominated much broader regions. For example, Fulk Nera, count of Anjou (r. 987–1040), built more than thirteen castles and captured others from rival counts. By the end of his life, he controlled a region extending from Blois to Nantes along the Loire valley.

Castellans extended their authority by subjecting everyone near their castle to their ban. Peasants, whether or not they worked on a castellan's estates, had to pay him a variety of dues for his "protection" and judicial rights over them. Castellans also established links with the better-off landholders in the region, tempting or coercing them to become vassals. Lay castellans often supported local monasteries and controlled the appointment of local priests. But churchmen themselves sometimes held the position of territorial lord: a good example is the archbishop of Milan in the eleventh century.

The development of nearly independent local political units, dominated by a castle and controlled by a military elite, marked an important turning point for western Europe. Although this development did not occur everywhere simultaneously (and in some places it hardly occurred at all), the social, political, and cultural life of the West was now dominated by landowners who saw themselves as military men and regional leaders.

War and Peace

All warriors were not alike. At the top of the elite were the kings, counts, and dukes. Below them, but "on the rise," were ordinary castellans. Still farther down the social scale were knights. Yet all shared in a common lifestyle.

Knights and their lords fought on horseback. High astride his steed, wearing a shirt of chain mail and a helmet of flat metal plates riveted together, the knight marked a military revolution. The war season started in May, when the grasses were high enough for horses to forage. Horseshoes allowed armies to move faster than ever before and to negotiate rough terrain previously unsuitable for battle. Stirrups, probably invented by Asiatic nomadic tribes, allowed the mounted warrior to hold his seat. This made it possible for knights to thrust at their enemy with heavy lances. The light javelin of ancient warfare was abandoned.

Lords and their vassals often lived together. In the lord's great hall they ate, listened to entertainment, and bedded down for the night. They went out hunting together and went off to the battlefield as a group as well. More powerful vassals—counts, for example—lived on their own fiefs and hardly ever saw their lord (probably the king), except when doing homage and fealty—once in their lifetime—or serving him in battles, for perhaps forty days a year. But they themselves were lords of knightly vassals who were not married and who lived and ate and hunted with them.

No matter how old they might be, unmarried knights who lived with their lords were called youths by their contemporaries. Such perpetual bachelors were something new, the result of a profound transformation in the organization of families and inheritance. Before the eleventh century, noble families had recognized all their children as heirs and had divided their estates accordingly. In the mid-ninth century, Count Everard and his wife, for example, willed their large estates, scattered from Belgium to Italy, to their four sons and three daughters (although they gave the boys far more than they gave the girls, and the oldest boy far more than the others).

By around the year 1000, however, adapting to diminished opportunities for land and office and wary of fragmenting the estates they had, French nobles changed both their conception of their families and the way property passed to the next generation. Recognizing the overriding claims of one son, often the eldest, they handed down their entire inheritance to him. In cases where the heir is indeed the eldest son, this system of inheritance is called **primogeniture**. The heir, in turn, traced his lineage only through the male line, backward through his father and forward through his own eldest son. Such patrilineal families left many younger sons without an inheritance and therefore without the prospect of marrying and founding families; instead, the younger sons lived at the courts of the great as youths or they joined the church as clerics or monks. The development of territorial rule and patrilineal families went hand in hand, as fathers passed down to one son undiminished not only manors but titles, castles, and the authority of the ban.

Patrilineal inheritance tended to bypass daughters and so tended to work against the interests of aristocratic women. In families without sons, however, widows and daughters did inherit property. And wives often acted as lords of estates when their husbands were at war. Moreover, all aristocratic women played an important role in this warrior society, whether in the monastery (where they prayed for the souls of their families) or through their marriages (where they helped forge alliances between their own families and the families of their husbands).

This highly militarized society was almost constantly at war. Warfare benefited territorial rulers in the short term, but in the long run their revenues suffered as armies plundered the countryside and sacked walled cities. Bishops, who were themselves from the class of lords and warriors, worried about the dangers to church property. Peasants cried out against wars that destroyed their crops or forced them to join regional infantries. Monks and religious thinkers were appalled at violence that was not in the service of an anointed king. By the end of the tenth century, all classes clamored for peace.

Sentiment against local violence was united in a movement called the **Peace of God**, which began in the south of France and by 1050 had spread over a wide region. Meetings of bishops, counts, and lords and often crowds of lower-class men and women set forth the provisions of this peace: "No man in the counties or bishoprics shall seize a horse, colt, ox, cow, ass, or the burdens which it carries. . . . No one shall seize a peasant, man or woman," ran the decree of one council held in 990. Anyone who violated this peace was to be excommunicated: cut off from the community of the faithful, denied the services of the church and the hope of salvation.

The peace proclaimed at local councils like this limited some violence but did not address the problem of conflict between armed men. A second set of agreements, the Truce of God, soon supplemented the Peace of God. The truce prohibited fighting between warriors at certain times: on Sunday because it was the Lord's Day, on Saturday because it was a reminder of Holy Saturday, on Friday because it symbolized Good Friday, and on Thursday because it stood for Holy Thursday. Enforcement of the truce fell to the local knights and nobles, who swore over saints' relics to uphold it and to fight anyone who broke it.

The Peace of God and Truce of God were only two of the mechanisms that attempted to contain or defuse violent confrontations in the tenth and eleventh centuries. At times, lords and their vassals mediated wars and feuds in assemblies called *placita*. In other instances, monks or laymen tried to find solutions to disputes that would leave the honor of both parties intact. Rather than try to establish guilt or innocence, winners or losers, these methods of adjudication often resulted in compromises on both sides.

Political Communities in Italy, England, and France

The political systems that emerged in the wake of the breakup of the Carolingian Empire were as varied as the regions of Europe. In Italy, cities were the centers of power, still reflecting, though feebly, the political organization of ancient Rome. In England, strong kings came to the fore. In France, as we have seen, great lords dominated the countryside; there the king was relatively weak.

Whereas in France great landlords built their castles in the countryside, in Italy they often constructed their family seats within the walls of cities such as Milan and Lucca. Churches, as many as fifty or sixty, were also built within the city walls, the proud work of rich laymen and laywomen or of bishops. From their perches within the cities, the great landholders of Italy, both lay and religious, dominated the countryside.

Italian cities also functioned as important marketplaces. Peasants sold their surplus goods there; artisans and merchants lived within the walls; foreign traders offered their wares. These members of the lower classes were supported by the noble rich, who in Italy even more than elsewhere depended on cash to satisfy their desires. In the course of the ninth and tenth centuries, both servile and free tenants became renters who paid in currency.

Social and political life in Italy favored a familial organization somewhat different from the patrilineal families of France. To stave off the partitioning of their properties among heirs, families organized themselves by formal contract into *consorteria*, in which all male members shared the profits of the family's inheritance and all women were excluded. The consorterial family became a kind of blood-related corporation, a social unit on which early Italian businesses and banks would later be modeled.

Where Italy was urban, England was rural. In the face of the Viking invasions in England, King Alfred of Wessex (r. 871–899) developed new mechanisms of royal government, instituting reforms that his successors continued. He fortified settlements throughout Wessex and divided the army into two parts. The duty of one was to defend the fortifications (or *burhs*); the other operated as a mobile unit. Alfred also started a navy. These military innovations cost money, and the assessments fell on peasants' holdings.

England in the Age of King Alfred, r. 871–899

Alfred sought to strengthen his kingdom's religious integrity as well as its regional fortifications. In the ninth century, people interpreted invasions as God's punishment for sin, which therefore was the real culprit. Thus Alfred began a program of religious reform by bringing scholars to his court to write and to educate others. Above all, Alfred wanted to translate key religious works from Latin into Anglo-Saxon (or Old English). He was determined to "turn into the language that we can all understand certain books which are the most necessary for all men to know." Alfred and scholars under his guidance translated works by church fathers such as Gregory the Great and St. Augustine. Even the Psalms, until now sung only in Hebrew, Greek, and Latin, were rendered into Anglo-Saxon. In most of ninth- and tenth-century Europe, Latin remained the language of scholarship and writing, separate from the language people spoke. In England, however, the vernacular—the common spoken language—was also a literary language. With Alfred's work giving it greater legitimacy, Anglo-Saxon came to be used alongside Latin for both literature and royal administration.

Alfred's reforms strengthened not only defense, education, and religion but also royal power. He consolidated his control over Wessex and fought the Danish kings, who by the mid-870s had taken Northumbria, northeastern Mercia, and East Anglia. Eventually, as he harried the Danes who were pushing south and westward, he was recognized as king of all the English not under Danish rule. He issued a law code, the first by an English king since 695. Unlike earlier codes, drawn up for each separate kingdom of England, Alfred drew up his laws from and for all of the English kingdoms. In this way, Alfred became the first king of all the English.

Alfred's successors rolled back Danish rule in England. "Then the Norsemen departed in their nailed ships, bloodstained survivors of spears," wrote one poet about a battle the Vikings lost in 937. But many Vikings remained. Converted to Christianity, their great men joined Anglo-Saxons in attending the English king at court. As peace returned, new administrative subdivisions—shires (counties) and

■ The Alfred Jewel

About two and a half inches long, this jewel consists of a gold drop-shaped frame surrounding an enamel plaque that depicts a man enthroned and holding two flowering rods. Rock crystal encloses the plaque within the frame. Along the side of the frame are gold letters in Anglo-Saxon that say: "Alfred had me made." The snout of the beast at the bottom was hollowed out, probably to hold a wooden or ivory pointer. If this jewel belonged to King Alfred, as is likely, it may be like the pointers that Alfred wanted distributed to all the bishops in his kingdom along with the Anglo-Saxon translation of Gregory the Great's Pastoral Care. *Such pointers were used to point to passages in manuscripts. Why did Alfred have the* Pastoral Care *translated? Why did he want copies sent to the bishops? And why did he want the bishops to have pointers?*
(Ashmolean Museum, Oxford.)

hundreds (districts)—were established throughout England for judicial and taxation purposes. The powerful men of the kingdom swore fealty to the king, promising to be enemies of his enemies, friends of his friends. England was united and organized to support a strong ruler.

Alfred's grandson Edgar (r. c. 959–975) commanded all the possibilities early medieval kingship offered. He was the sworn lord of all the great men of the kingdom. He controlled appointments to the English church and sponsored monastic reform. In 973, following the continental fashion, he was anointed. The fortifications of the kingdom were in his hands, as was the army, and he took responsibility for keeping the peace by proclaiming certain crimes—arson and theft—to be under his special jurisdiction and mobilizing the machinery of the shire and the hundred to find and punish thieves.

Despite its apparent centralization, England was not a unified state in the modern sense, and the king's control was often tenuous. Many royal officials were great landowners who (as on the continent) worked for the king because doing so was in their best interest. When it was not, they allied with different claimants to the throne. This political fragility may have helped the Danish king Cnut (or Canute) to conquer England. King there from 1017 to 1035, Cnut reinforced the already strong connections between England and Scandinavia while keeping intact much of the administrative, ecclesiastical, and military apparatus already established in England by the Anglo-Saxons. By Cnut's time Scandinavian traditions had largely merged with those of the rest of Europe, and the Vikings were no longer an alien culture.

French kings had a harder time than the English coping with the invasions because their realm was much larger. They had no chance to build up their defenses slowly from one powerful base. During most of the tenth century, Carolingian kings alternated on the throne with kings from a family that would later be called "Capetian." As the Carolingian dynasty waned, the most powerful men of the kingdom—dukes, counts, and important bishops—came together to elect as king Hugh Capet (r. 987–996), a lord of considerable prestige yet relatively little power. His choice marked the end of Carolingian rule and the beginning of the new Capetian dynasty, which would hand down the royal title from father to son until the fourteenth century.

In the eleventh century, the reach of the Capetian kings was limited by territorial lordships in the vicinity. The king's scattered but substantial estates lay in the north of France, in the region around Paris—the Île-de-France (literally, "island of France"). His castles and his vassals were there. Independent castellans, however, controlled areas nearby. In the sense that he was a neighbor of castellans and not much more powerful militarily than they, the king of the Franks—who would only later take the territorial title of king of France—was just another local strongman. Yet the Capetian kings enjoyed considerable prestige. They were anointed with holy oil, and they represented the idea of unity inherited from Charlemagne. Most of the counts, at least in the north of France, became their vassals. They did not promise to obey the king, but they did vow not to try to kill or depose him.

Emperors and Kings in Central and Eastern Europe

In contrast with the development of territorial lordships in France, Germany's fragmentation hardly began before it was reversed. Five duchies (regions dominated by dukes) emerged in Germany in the late Carolingian period, each much larger than the counties and castellanies of France. With the death in 911 of the last Carolingian king in Germany, Louis the Child, the dukes elected one of themselves as king. Then, as the Magyar invasions increased, the dukes gave the royal title to the duke of Saxony, Henry I (r. 919–936), who proceeded to set up fortifications and reorganize his army, crowning his efforts with a major defeat of a Magyar army in 933.

Otto I (r. 936–973), the son of Henry I, was an even greater military hero. His defeat of the Magyar forces in 955 gave him prestige and helped solidify his dynasty. In 951, he marched into Italy and took the Lombard crown. Against the Slavs, with whom the Germans shared a border, Otto set up marches from which he could make expeditions and stave off counterattacks.

The Ottonian Empire, 936–1002

After the pope crowned him emperor in 962, he claimed the Middle Kingdom carved out by the Treaty of Verdun and cast himself as the agent of Roman imperial renewal.

Otto's victories brought tribute, plunder, plum positions to disburse, and lands to give away, ensuring him a following among the great men of the realm. His successors, Otto II (r. 961–983), Otto III (r. 983–1002)—not surprisingly, the dynasty is called the "Ottonian"—and Henry II (r. 1002–1024), built on his achievements. Granted power by the magnates, they gave back in turn: they gave away lands and appointed their aristocratic supporters to duchies, counties, and bishoprics. Always, however, their decisions were tempered by hereditary claims and plenty of lobbying by influential men at court and at the great assemblies that met with the king to hammer out policies. The role of kings in appointing bishops and archbishops was particularly important because these positions, unlike counties and duchies, could not be inherited. Otto I created new eastern bishoprics, endowing them with extensive lands and subjecting the local peasantry to their overlordship. In some areas of Germany, bishops gained the power of the ban: they collected revenues, gained rights of justice, and called men to arms. Answering to the king and furnishing him with troops, the bishops became royal officials while also carrying out their pastoral and religious duties. German kings claimed the right to select bishops (usually with the consent of the cathedral clergy) and to "invest" them by participating in the ceremony that installed them in office. The higher clergy joined the king at court, gaining their schooling there in their youth and, in their more mature years, teaching the kings, princes, and noblewomen there.

Like all the strong rulers of the day, whether in the West or in the Byzantine and Islamic worlds, the Ottonians presided over a renaissance of learning. For example, the tutor of Otto III was Gerbert (d. 1003) (later Pope Sylvester II), the best-educated man of his time. Gerbert knew how to use the abacus and to calculate with Arabic numerals. He spent "large sums of money to pay copyists and to acquire copies of authors," as he put it. He studied the classics as models of rhetoric and argument, and he reveled in logic and debate. Not only did churchmen and kings support Ottonian scholarship, but to an unprecedented extent, noblewomen in Germany also acquired an education and participated in the intellectual revival. Aristocratic women spent much of their wealth on learning. Living at home with their kinfolk and servants or in convents that provided them with comfortable private apartments, noblewomen wrote books and occasionally even Roman-style plays. They also supported other artists and scholars.

The German kings' policies played a crucial role in the political communities on its eastern border. Hand in hand with the papacy, the Ottonians fostered the emergence of Christian monarchies aligned with the Roman church in the regions that today constitute the Czech and Slovak Republics, Poland, and Hungary.

The Czechs, who lived in the region of Bohemia, converted under the rule of Václav (r. 920–929), who thereby gained recognition in Germany as the duke of Bohemia. He and his successors did not become kings, remaining politically within

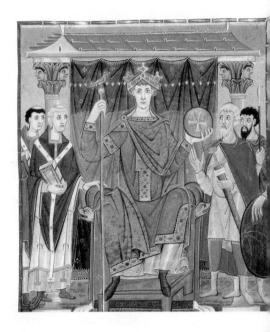

■ **Otto III Receiving Gifts**
This triumphal image is in a book of Gospels made for Otto III. The crowned women on the left are personifications of the four "parts" of Otto's empire: Sclavinia (the Slavic lands), Germania (Germany), Gallia (Gaul), and Roma (Rome). Each holds a gift in tribute and homage to the emperor, who sits on a throne, holding the symbols of his power (orb and scepter) and flanked by representatives of the church (on his right) and of the army (on his left). Why do you suppose the artist separated the image of the emperor from that of the women? What does the body language of the women tell you about the relations that Otto wanted to portray between himself and the parts of his empire? Can you relate this manuscript, which was made in 997–1000, to Otto's conquest over the Slavs in 997? (Bayerische Staatsbibliothek, Munich.)

the German sphere. Václav's murder by his younger brother made him a martyr and the patron saint of Bohemia, a symbol around which later movements for independence rallied.

The Poles gained a greater measure of independence than the Czechs. In 966, Mieszko I (r. 963–992), the leader of the Slavic tribe known as the Polanians, accepted baptism to forestall the attack that the Germans were already mounting against pagan Slavic peoples along the Baltic coast and east of the Elbe River. Busily engaged in bringing the other Slavic tribes of Poland under his control, he adroitly shifted his alliances with various German princes to suit his needs. In 991, Mieszko placed his realm under the protection of the pope, establishing a tradition of Polish loyalty to the Roman church. Mieszko's son Boleslaw the Brave (r. 992–1025) greatly extended Poland's boundaries, at one time or another holding sway from the Bohemian border to Kiev. In 1000, he gained a royal crown with papal blessing.

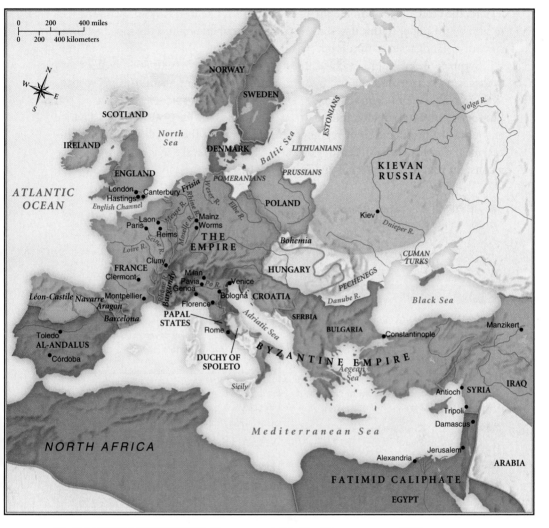

■ **MAPPING THE WEST** Europe and the Mediterranean, c. 1050

The clear borders and bright colors of the "states" on this map distort an essential truth: none of them had centralized governments that controlled whole territories, as in modern states. Instead, there were numerous regional rulers within each, and there were numerous overlapping claims of jurisdiction. The next centuries would show both the weaknesses and surprising strengths of this fragmentation. **For more help analyzing this map,** see the map activity for this chapter in the ONLINE STUDY GUIDE at bedfordstmartins.com/huntconcise.

Hungary's case was similar to that of Poland. The Magyars settled in the region known today as Hungary. They became landowners, using the native Slavs to till the soil and imposing their language. At the end of the tenth century, the Magyar ruler Stephen I (r. 997–1038) accepted Christianity. In return, German knights and monks helped him consolidate his power and convert his people. According to legend, the crown placed on Stephen's head in 1001, like Boleslaw's crown, was sent to him by the pope. To this day, the crown of St. Stephen remains the most hallowed symbol of Hungarian nationhood.

Symbols of rulership such as crowns, consecrated by Christian priests and accorded a prestige almost akin to saints' relics, were among the most vital institutions of royal rule in central Europe. The economic basis for the power of central European rulers gradually shifted from slave raids to agriculture. This change encouraged a proliferation of regional centers of power that challenged monarchical rule. From the eleventh century onward, all the medieval Slavic states would face a constant problem of internal division.

■ **REVIEW:** *How did power over people and land shift from kings and emperors to local rulers between 800 and 1050?*

IMPORTANT DATES			
750	Abbasid caliphate begins	843	End of iconoclasm at Byzantium; Treaty of Verdun divides Frankish kingdom
751	Pippin III deposes the last Merovingian king; Carolingian monarchy begins		
		c. 870–c. 1025	Macedonian renaissance at Byzantium
756	Spanish emirate at Córdoba begins	871–899	Reign of King Alfred the Great in England
768–814	Charlemagne rules as king of the Franks		
		955	Otto I defeats Magyars
786–809	Caliphate of Harun al-Rashid	969–1171	Fatimid dynasty in Egypt
c. 790–c. 900	Carolingian renaissance	963–1025	Reign of Byzantine emperor Basil II Bulgaroctonos
c. 790–c. 1050	Islamic renaissance		
800	Charlemagne crowned emperor by Pope Leo III	c. 1000	Age of the castellans in France

Conclusion

In 800, the three heirs of the Roman Empire all appeared to be organized like their "parent": centralized, monarchical, imperial. Byzantine emperors writing their learned books, Abbasid caliphs holding court in their resplendent new palace at Baghdad, and Carolingian emperors issuing their directives for reform to the *missi dominici* all mimicked the Roman emperors. Yet they confronted tensions and regional pressures that tended to decentralize political power. Byzantium felt this fragmentation least, yet even there the emergence of a new elite led to decentralization and the emperor's loss of control over the countryside. In the Islamic world, economic crisis, religious tension, and the ambitions of powerful local rulers decisively weakened the caliphate and opened the way to separate successor states. In the West, powerful independent landowners strove with greater or lesser success (depending on the region) to establish themselves as effective rulers. By 1050, the states that would become those of modern Europe began to form.

In Europe, local conditions determined political and economic organizations. Between 900 and 1000, for example, French society was transformed by the development of territorial lordships, patrilineal families, and ties of vassalage. These factors figured less prominently in Germany, where a central monarchy remained, buttressed by churchmen and conquests to the east. We shall see in the next chapter, however, how fragile this centralization was to be.

■ **MAKING CONNECTIONS**

1. *How were the Byzantine, Islamic, and European economies similar? How did they differ? How did these economies interact?*

2. *Compare the effects of the barbarian invasions into the Roman Empire with the effects of the Viking, Muslim, and Magyar invasions into the Carolingian Empire.*

■ **FOR FURTHER EXPLORATION**

For further reading and online research ideas, see the Suggested References on page SR-4 at the back of the book.

For practice quizzes, a customized study plan, and other study tools, see the ONLINE STUDY GUIDE at bedfordstmartins.com/huntconcise.

For primary-source material from this period, see Chapter 8 in *Sources of THE MAKING OF THE WEST: A CONCISE HISTORY*, Second Edition.

Renewal and Reform

1050–1200

B RUNO OF COLOGNE WAS AN ESTEEMED TEACHER at the prominent French cathedral school of Reims and the likely choice for promotion to bishop or even
archbishop. But around 1084, outraged by a new archbishop of Reims who had
purchased his office and cared nothing about religion, Bruno abandoned his
promising career and left the city. He did not do what ethical and morally outraged men of the time were expected to do—join a monastery. Instead, he set up
a hermitage—an isolated retreat—in an Alpine valley. The hermits who gathered
there lived in poverty. One of Bruno's contemporaries marveled: "They do not take
gold, silver, or ornaments for their church from anyone." This unworldliness was
matched, however, by keen interest in learning: for all its poverty, Bruno's community had a rich library.

Thus began La Chartreuse, the chief house of the Carthusian order, an order
still in existence. The Carthusian monks lived as hermits, rejected material wealth,
and emphasized learning. In some ways their style of life was a reaction against
the monumental changes rumbling through their age: their solitude countered
newly bustling cities, and their austerity contrasted sharply with the opulence and
power of princely courts. Their reverence for the written word, however, reflected
the growing interest in scholarship and learning.

The most salient feature of the period 1050–1200 was increasing wealth. Cities,
trade, and agricultural production swelled. The resulting worldliness met with a

■ **La Chartreuse**
*The impulse behind the foundation of La Chartreuse was withdrawal from the world. Yet the
world came to the Carthusians' high perch. One of the abbots of the Cluny made it his custom
to visit every year. He said that the new monks reminded him of the desert hermits. He did not
mean that the Alps looked liked Egypt but rather that the monks, living in separate cells,
practiced the heroically ascetic life of the first monks.* (Bridgeman Art Library.)

wide variety of responses. Some people, like Bruno, fled the world; others tried to reform it; and still others embraced, enjoyed, or tried to understand it. Within one century, the development of a profit economy transformed western European communities. Many villages and fortifications became cities where traders, merchants, and artisans conducted business. Although most people still lived in less-populated, rural areas, their lives were touched in many ways by the new cash economy. Economic concerns drove changes within the church, where a movement for reform gathered steam. Money helped redefine the role of the clergy, while popes, kings, and princes came to exercise new forms of power. At the same time, city dwellers began to demand their own governments. Monks and clerics reformulated the nature of their communities and, like Bruno of Cologne, sought intense spiritual lives. All of these developments inspired (and in turn were inspired by) new ideas, new forms of scholarship, and new methods of inquiry. The rapid pace of religious, political, and economic change was matched by new developments in thought, learning, and artistic expression.

The Commercial Revolution

As the population of Europe continued to expand in the eleventh century, cities, long-distance trade networks, local markets, and new business arrangements meshed to create a profit-based economy. With improvements in agriculture and more land in cultivation, the great estates of the eleventh century produced surpluses that helped feed—and therefore made possible—a new urban population. The result was the **commercial revolution** of the Middle Ages, which produced the institutions that would be the direct ancestors of modern business and commerce.

Centers of Commerce and Commercial Life

The new commercial centers developed around castles and monasteries and within the walls of ancient towns. Great lords in the countryside—including monasteries—were eager to take advantage of the profits generated by their estates. In the late tenth century, they had reorganized their lands for greater productivity, encouraged their peasants to cultivate new land, and converted services and dues to money payments. Now with ready cash, they not only fostered the development of temporary markets where they could sell their surpluses and buy luxury goods, but even encouraged traders and craftspeople to settle down near them. The lords gained at each step: their purchases brought them an enhanced lifestyle and greater prestige, while they charged merchants tolls and sales taxes, in this way profiting even more from trade. At Besalú (Spain), for example, the count's castle was a magnet for artisans and food purveyers. Sometimes markets formed just outside the walls of older cities; these gradually merged into new and enlarged urban communities as town walls were built around them to protect the inhabitants. At other times informal country markets came to be

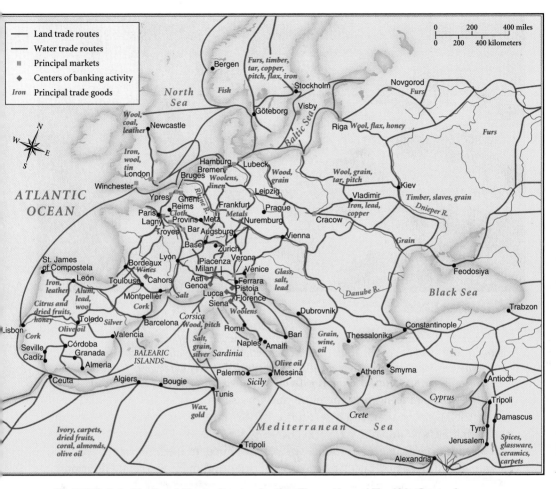

■ MAP 9.1 Medieval Trade Routes in the Eleventh and Twelfth Centuries

In the medieval world, bulk goods from the north (furs, fish, and wood) were traded for luxury goods from the south (ivory, spices, medicines, perfumes, and dyes). Already regions were beginning to specialize. England, for example, supplied raw wool, and Flanders (Ypres, Ghent) specialized in turning that wool into cloth and shipping it farther south, to the fairs of Champagne (whose capital was Troyes) or Germany. Italian cities channeled goods from the Muslim and Byzantine worlds northward and exported European goods south and eastward.

housed in permanent structures. Along the Rhine and in other river valleys, cities sprang up to service the merchants who traversed the route between Italy and the north (Map 9.1).

By the mid-twelfth century even rural life was increasingly organized for the marketplace in many regions of western Europe. The commercialization of the countryside opened up opportunities for both peasants and lords, but it also burdened

■ **Medieval Besalú**

The bridge leading to Besalú, a town in Catalonia (Spain), was constructed, like the town's walls and many of its other buildings, during the eleventh and twelfth centuries. The high fortified entrance was added in the fourteenth century. Already in the ninth century, Besalú was the center of a county, and in the eleventh century, it briefly became the seat of a bishopric. At the same time, it was home to a thriving Jewish population, whose mikvah, or ritual bath house, still stands today. (AKG Images/Schütze/Rodemann.)

some with unwelcome obligations. Great lords hired trained, literate agents to administer their estates, calculate profits and losses, and make marketing decisions. Aristocrats needed money not only because they relished luxuries such as fine wines, spices, and soft, glowing fabrics, but also because their honor and authority continued to depend on their personal generosity, patronage, and displays of wealth. In the late twelfth century, when some townsmen could boast fortunes that rivaled the riches of the landed aristocracy, economic pressures on the nobles increased as their extravagance exceeded their income. Many went into debt.

The lord's need for money changed peasant life, as peasants, too, became more integrated into the developing commercial economy. The population continued to increase in the twelfth century, and the greater demand for food required more farmland. By the middle of the century, isolated and sporadic attempts to cultivate new land had become a regular and coordinated activity. Great lords offered special privileges to peasants who would do the backbreaking work of plowing marginal land. In Flanders, where land was regularly inundated by seawater, the great monasteries sponsored drainage projects, and newly dug canals linking the cities to the agricultural regions let boats ply the waters to nearly every nook and cranny of the region.

On old estates the rise in population strained the manse organization that had developed in Carolingian Europe, where each household was settled on the land that supported it. In the twelfth century, twenty peasant families might live on what had been, in the tenth century, the manse of one family. With the manse supporting so many more people, labor services and dues had to be recalculated, and peasants and their lords often turned services and dues into money rents, payable once a year. With this change, peasant men gained more control over their plots— they could sell them, will them to their sons, or even designate a small portion for their daughters. However, for these privileges, they had to pay high fees. In addition, the revived monarchies of the twelfth century required taxes that were passed along to the lowest classes either directly or indirectly. In Italy the cities themselves often imposed and enforced dues on the peasants, normally tenant farmers who leased their plots in the *contado*, the countryside surrounding each city. Thus peasants' gains from rising prices, access to markets, greater productivity, and increased personal freedom were partially canceled out by their cash burdens.

Business Arrangements

The development of commercial centers reflected changing attitudes toward money. The new mode of commerce transformed the social relations involved in economic transactions. In the gift economy, exchanges of coins, gold, and silver were components of ongoing relationships. Kings offered treasures to their followers, peasants gave dues to their lords, and pious donors presented land to the saintly patrons of churches, all in the expectation of long-term relationships. In the new market economy, which thrived on the profit motive, arrangements were less personal. They often relied on written contracts and calculations of the profitability of a particular business venture.

Although the new business agreements took many forms, they had the common purpose of bringing people together to pool their resources and finance larger enterprises. The *commenda*, for example, an Italian invention, was a partnership established for commerce by sea. In a common arrangement, one or more investors furnished the money, and the other partners undertook the risks of the actual voyage. If a trip proved successful, the investors received three-quarters of the profit and the travelers the rest. But if the voyage failed, the investors lost their outlay, and the travelers expended their time and labor for no profit. The impermanence of such partnerships (they lasted for only one voyage) meant that capital could be shifted easily from one venture to another and could therefore be used to support a variety of enterprises.

Land trade often involved a more enduring partnership. In Italy this took the form of a *compagnia*, formed when family property was invested in trade. Unlike the *commenda*, in which the partners could lose no more than they had put into the enterprise, the compagnia left its members with joint and unlimited liability for all losses and debts. This provision enhanced family solidarity, as each member was responsible for the debts of all the others; but it also risked bankrupting entire households.

The commercial revolution also fostered the development of contracts for sales, exchanges, and loans. Loans were the most problematic. In the Middle Ages, as now, interest payments were the chief inducement for an investor to supply money. To circumvent the church's ban on usury (profiting from loans), interest was often disguised as a penalty for "late payment" under the rules of a contract. The new willingness to finance business enterprises with loans signaled a changed attitude toward credit: risk was acceptable if it brought profit.

Contracts and partnerships made large-scale productive enterprises possible. In fact, light industry began in the eleventh century. Just as in the Industrial Revolution of the eighteenth and nineteenth centuries, one of the earliest products to benefit from new industrial technologies was cloth. Water mills powered machines such as flails to clean and thicken cloth and presses to extract oil from fibers. Machines were also used to exploit raw materials more efficiently: new deep-mining technology provided Europeans with hitherto untapped sources of metals. At the same time, forging techniques improved, and iron was for the first time regularly used for agricultural tools and plows. This, in turn, made for better farming, and better farming fed the commercial revolution. Metals were also used for weapons, armor, and coins.

Whether fashioned by machines or handworkers, production relied on the expertise of artisans able to finish the cloth, mint the coins, and forge the weapons. To regulate and protect their products and trades, craftspeople and others involved in commerce formed **guilds**: local social, religious, and economic associations whose members plied the same trade. By the late twelfth century, they had become corporations defined by statutes and rules. They controlled their membership and determined dues, working hours, wages, and standards for materials and products.

Guilds often had to cooperate with one another. Producing wool cloth involved numerous guilds—shearers, weavers, fullers (people who beat the cloth to make it bulkier), dyers—generally working under the supervision of the merchant guild that imported the raw wool. Some guilds were more prestigious than others: in Florence, for example, professional guilds of notaries and judges ranked above craft guilds.

Within each guild of artisans or merchants existed another kind of hierarchy. Apprentices were at the bottom, journeymen and -women in the middle, and masters at the top. Apprentices were boys and occasionally girls placed under the tutelage of a master for a number of years to learn a trade. For example, in Paris a baker's apprenticeship took four years, while it took eleven years to train a harness maker. Once trained, the worker became a journeyman or -woman—a simple day laborer working for a wage. Only a few would become masters, the men (but almost never women) who dominated the offices and policies of the guild, hired journeymen, and recruited and educated apprentices. The masters drew up the guild regulations and served as chief overseers, inspectors, and treasurers.

During the late twelfth century, women's labor in some trades gradually declined in importance. In Flanders, for example, as the manufacture of woolen cloth shifted from rural areas to cities, women participated less in the process. In cities like Ypres and Ghent, men working in pairs ran new-style large looms, producing a heavy-weight cloth superior to the fabric that women could make on lighter looms. Similarly, water mills and animal-powered mills gradually took over the grinding of grain, formerly women's work. Most millers who ran the new machinery were male. Some women were certainly artisans and traders, and their names occasionally appeared in guild memberships. But they did not become guild officers, and they played no official role in town government.

Self-Government for the Towns

Guilds were one way townspeople expressed their mutual concerns and harnessed their collective energies. Movements for self-government were another. Townspeople banded together for protection and freedom.

Both to themselves and to outsiders, townspeople seemed different. Tradespeople, artisans, ship captains, innkeepers, and moneychangers did not fit into the old categories of medieval types—those who pray, those who fight, and those who labor. Just knowing they were different gave townspeople a sense of solidarity with one another. But practical reasons also contributed to their feeling of common purpose: they lived in close quarters with one another, and they shared a mutual interest in reliable coinage, laws to facilitate commerce, freedom from servile dues and services, and independence to buy and sell as the market dictated. Already in the early twelfth century, the king of England granted to the citizens of Newcastle-upon-Tyne the privilege that any unfree peasant who lived there unclaimed by his lord for a year and a day would thereafter be a free person. To townspeople, freedom meant having their own officials and law courts. They petitioned the political powers that ruled them—bishops, kings, counts, castellans—for the right to govern themselves. Often they formed **communes**, sworn associations of townspeople that generally cut across the boundaries of rich and poor, merchants and craftspeople, clergy and laity.

Collective movements for urban self-government emerged especially in Italy, France, and Germany. Italian cities were centers of regional political power even before the commercial revolution. Castellans constructed their fortifications, and bishops ruled the countryside from such cities. The commercial revolution swelled the Italian cities with tradespeople, whose interest in self-government was often fueled by religious as well as economic concerns. At Milan in the second half of the eleventh century, popular discontent with the archbishop, who effectively ruled the city, led to numerous armed clashes. In 1097, the Milanese succeeded in transferring political power from the archbishop and his clergy to a government of leading men of the city who called themselves "consuls." The title recalled the government of the ancient Roman republic, affirming the consuls' status as representatives of the people. Like the archbishops' power before, the consuls' rule extended beyond the town walls, into the contado, the outlying countryside.

Outside of Italy, movements for city independence took place within the framework of larger kingdoms or principalities. Such movements were sometimes violent, as at Milan, but at other times they were peaceful. For example, William Clito, who claimed the county of Flanders (today in Belgium), willingly granted the citizens of Saint-Omer the rights they asked for in 1127 in return for their support of his claims: he recognized them as legally free, gave them the right to mint coins, allowed them their own laws and courts, and lifted certain tolls and taxes.

▪ **REVIEW:** *What new professions and institutions arose as a result of the commercial revolution?*

Church Reform and Its Aftermath

The commercial revolution affected the church because the church, too, was part of the world. Bishops ruled over many cities. Kings appointed many bishops. Local lords installed priests in their parish churches. Churchmen gave gifts and money to these secular powers for their offices. The impulse to free the church from "the world" was as old as the origins of monasticism, but, beginning in the tenth century and increasingly insistent in the eleventh, reformers demanded that the church as a whole remodel itself and become free of secular entanglements.

This freedom was from the start as much a matter of power as of religion. Most people had long believed that their ruler—whether king, duke, count, or castellan—reigned by the grace of God and had the right to control the churches in his territory. But by the second half of the eleventh century, more and more people saw a great deal wrong with secular power over the church. They looked to the papacy to lead the movement of church reform. The most important moment came in 1075, when Pope Gregory VII called on the emperor, Henry IV, to end his appointment of churchmen. This request brought about a major civil war in Germany and a great upheaval in the distribution of power everywhere. By the early 1100s, a reformed church—with the pope at its head—had become institutionalized, penetrating into areas of life never before touched by churchmen. Church reform began as a way to free the church from the world; but in the end, the church was equally involved in the new world it had helped to create.

Beginnings of the Reform Movement

The idea of freeing the church from the world began in the tenth century with no particular program and only a vague idea of what it might mean. At the Benedictine monastery of Cluny, for example, which was founded in 910, there was no organized program of reform. Nevertheless, the founders of the monastery, the duke and duchess of Aquitaine, wanted to "free" it from the world. They achieved this goal by endowing the monastery with property but then giving it and its worldly possessions to Saints Peter and Paul. In this way, they put control of the monastery into the hands of the two most powerful heavenly saints. They designated the pope, as the successor of St. Peter, to be the monastery's worldly protector if anyone should bother or threaten it. The whole notion of "freedom" at this point was very vague. But Cluny's prestige was great because of its status as St. Peter's property and because of the elaborate round of prayers that its monks carried out with scrupulous devotion. The Cluniac monks fulfilled the role of "those who pray" in a way that dazzled their contemporaries. Through their prayers they seemed to guarantee the salvation of all Christians. Rulers, bishops, rich landowners, and even serfs (if they could) gave Cluny donations of land, joining their contributions to the land of St. Peter. Powerful men and women called on the Cluniac monks to reform new monasteries along the Cluniac model.

The abbots of Cluny came to see themselves as reformers of the world as well. They believed in clerical celibacy, preaching against the prevailing norm that let parish priests and even bishops marry. They also thought that the laity could be reformed, become more virtuous, and cease its oppression of the poor. In the eleventh century, the Cluniacs began to link their program of internal monastic and external worldly reform to the papacy. They asked the popes to help them when Cluniac lands were encroached upon by bishops and laypeople at the same time as the papacy itself was becoming interested in reform.

Around the time when the Cluniacs were joining their fate to that of the popes, a small group of clerics and monks in the empire began calling for systematic reform within the church. They buttressed their arguments with new interpretations of canon law—the laws decreed over the centuries at church councils and by bishops and popes. They concentrated on two breaches of those laws: nicolaitism (clerical marriage) and **simony** (buying church offices). Most of the men who promoted these ideas lived in the most commercialized regions of the empire: the Rhineland (the region along the northern half of the Rhine River) and Italy. Their familiarity with the impersonal practices of a profit economy led them to interpret as crass purchases the gifts that churchmen were used to giving in return for their offices.

Emperor Henry III (r. 1039–1056) supported the reformers. Taking seriously his position as the anointed of God, Henry felt responsible for the well-being of the church in his empire. He denounced simony and personally refused to accept money or gifts when he appointed bishops to their posts. When in 1046 three men, each representing a different faction of the Roman aristocracy, claimed to be pope, Henry, as ruler of Rome, traveled to Italy to settle the matter. The Synod of Sutri (1046), over which he presided, deposed all three popes and elected another. In 1049, Henry appointed Leo IX (r. 1049–1054), a bishop from the Rhineland, to the papacy. This appointment marked an unanticipated turning point for the emperor when Leo set out to reform the church under papal, rather than imperial, control. He traveled to France and Germany, holding councils to condemn simoniac bishops. He sponsored the creation of a canon law textbook—the *Collection in 74 Titles*—that emphasized the pope's power. To the papal court, Leo brought the most zealous reformers of his day: Humbert of Silva Candida, Peter Damian, and Hildebrand (later Pope Gregory VII).

At first, Leo's claims to new power over the church hierarchy were complacently ignored by clergy and secular rulers alike. The Council of Reims, which he called in 1049, for example, was attended by only a few bishops and boycotted by the king of France. Nevertheless, Leo made it into a forum for exercising his authority. Placing the relics of St. Remegius (the patron saint of Reims) on the altar of the church, he demanded that the attending bishops and abbots say whether or not they had purchased their offices. A few confessed that they had; some did not respond; others gave excuses. The new and extraordinary development was that all present felt accountable to the pope and accepted his verdicts.

In 1054, Leo sent Humbert of Silva Candida to Constantinople on a diplomatic mission to argue against the patriarch of Constantinople on behalf of the new, lofty claims of the pope. Furious at the contemptuous way he was treated by the patriarch, Humbert ended his mission by excommunicating the patriarch. In retaliation, the Byzantine emperor and his bishops excommunicated Humbert and his party, threatening them with eternal damnation. Clashes between the two churches had occurred before and had been patched up, but this one, called the **Great Schism** (1054), proved insurmountable.* Thereafter, the Roman Catholic and the Greek Orthodox churches were largely separate.

The popes who followed Leo continued his program to expand papal power. When military adventurers from Normandy began carving out states for themselves in southern Italy, the popes in nearby Rome felt threatened. After waging unsuccessful war against the interlopers, the papacy made the best of a bad situation by granting the Normans Sicily and parts of southern Italy as a fief, turning its former enemies into vassals. Similarly, the papacy participated in wars in Spain, where it supported Christians against the dominant Muslims. The political fragmentation of al-Andalus into small and weak *taifas* (see page 307) made it seem fair game to the Christians to the north. Slowly the idea of the *reconquista*, the Christian reconquest of Spain, took shape, fed by religious fervor as well as worldly ambition.

---

*Despite occasional thaws and liftings of the sentences, the mutual excommunications of pope and patriarch largely remained in effect until 1965, when Pope Paul VI and the Greek Orthodox patriarch, Athenagoras I, publicly deplored them.

Gregorian Reform and the Investiture Conflict, 1073–1085

The papal reform movement is above all associated with Pope Gregory VII ↳ (r. 1073–1085) and is therefore often called the **Gregorian reform**. Gregory began as a lowly Roman cleric—Hildebrand—with the job of administering the papal estates and rose slowly in the hierarchy. A passionate advocate of papal primacy (the theory that the pope was head of the church), he was not afraid to clash with Emperor Henry IV (r. 1056–1106) over leadership of the church. In his view—and it was astonishing at the time, given the religious and spiritual roles associated with rulers—the emperor was just a layman who had no right to meddle in church affairs.

Gregory was and remains an extraordinarily controversial figure. He certainly thought that he was acting as the vicar, or representative, of St. Peter on earth. Describing himself, he declared, "I have labored with all my power that Holy Church, the bride of God, our Lady Mother, might come again to her own splendor and might remain free, pure, and Catholic." He thought the reforms he advocated and the upheavals he precipitated were necessary to free the church from the Satanic rulers of the world. His great nemesis, Henry IV, had a very different view. He considered Gregory an ambitious and evil man who "seduced the world far and wide and stained the Church with the blood of her

The World of the Investiture Conflict, c. 1070–1122

sons." Not surprisingly, modern historians are only a bit less divided in their assessment of Gregory. Few deny his sincerity and deep religious devotion, but many speak of his pride, ambition, and single-mindedness. He was not an easy man.

Henry IV was less complex. He was brought up in the traditions of his father, Henry III, a pious church reformer who considered it part of his duty to appoint bishops and even popes to ensure the well-being of church and state together. The emperor believed that he and his bishops—who were, at the same time, his most valuable supporters and administrators—were the rightful leaders of the church. He had no intention of allowing the pope to become head of the church.

The great confrontation between Gregory and Henry began over the appointment of the archbishop of Milan. Gregory disputed Henry's right to "invest" the archbishop (put him into office). In the investiture ritual, the emperor or his representative symbolically gave the church and the land that went with it to the priest or bishop or archbishop chosen for the job. When, in 1075, Henry invested his own candidate as archbishop of Milan, Gregory called on Henry to "give more respectful attention to the master of the Church"; he meant St. Peter and his living representative, Gregory himself. In reply, Henry and the German bishops called on Gregory to resign from the papacy. This was the beginning of what historians delicately call the **Investiture Conflict** or "Investiture Controversy." In fact, it was war. In February 1076, Gregory called a synod that both excommunicated and suspended Henry from office, authorizing anyone in Henry's kingdom to rebel against him. Henry's enemies, mostly German princes (as German aristocrats were called), now threatened to elect another king.

His fortunes low, Henry traveled to intercept Gregory, who was journeying northward to visit the rebellious princes. In early 1077, the king and pope met at Canossa, high in central Italy's Apennine Mountains. Gregory was inside a fortress there; Henry stood outside as a penitent—barefoot in the cold and snow. The gesture was an astute move by Henry because no priest could refuse absolution to a penitent; Gregory had to lift the excommunication and receive Henry back into the church. But Gregory had the advantage of making the king humble himself before the majesty of the pope.

Although Henry was technically back in the fold, nothing of substance had been resolved, and civil war began. The princes elected an antiking (a king chosen illegally), and Henry and his supporters elected an antipope. From 1077 until 1122, papal and imperial armies waged intermittent war. Long after the original antagonists Gregory and Henry had died, the Concordat of Worms of 1122 ended the fighting with a compromise that relied on a conceptual distinction between two parts of the investiture ceremony—the spiritual (in which a man received the symbols of his clerical office) and the secular (in which he received the symbols of the material goods that would allow him to function). Under the terms of the concordat, the ring and staff, the symbols of church office, would be given by a churchman in the first part of the ceremony. In the second part, the emperor or his representative would touch the bishop with a scepter, a symbolic gesture that stood for the land and other possessions that went with his office. Elections of bishops in Germany would take place "in the presence" of the emperor—that is, under his influence. In Italy, the pope would have a comparable role.

Superficially, nothing much had changed; secular rulers would continue to have a part in choosing and investing churchmen. In fact, however, almost no one any longer would claim that the king was head of the church. Just as the new investiture ceremony broke the ritual into spiritual and secular parts, so too, it implied a new notion of kingship that separated it from priesthood. The Investiture Conflict did not produce the modern distinction between church and state—that would develop only very slowly—but it set the wheels in motion.

The most important changes brought about by the Investiture Conflict, however, were on the ground: the political landscape in both Italy and Germany was irrevocably transformed. In Germany, the princes consolidated their lands and their positions at the expense of royal power. They gradually became virtual monarchs within their own principalities; the emperor, though retaining his title, eventually became a figurehead. In Italy, the emperor lost power to the cities. The Italian communes were formed in the crucible of the war between the pope and the emperor. In fierce communal struggles, city factions, motivated in part by local grievances but often claiming to fight on behalf of the papal or the imperial cause, created their own governing bodies. In the course of the twelfth century, northern Italian cities became used to self-government.

The Sweep of Reform

Church reform involved much more than the clash of popes, emperors, and their supporters. It penetrated deeply into the daily lives of ordinary Christians, in part through the church's new emphasis on the sacraments—the regular means (according to the Catholic church) by which God's heavenly grace infused mundane existence. But this did not mean that Christians were clear about how many sacraments there were, how they worked, or even their significance. Eleventh-century church reformers began the process—which continued into the thirteenth century—of emphasizing the importance of the sacraments and the special nature of the priest, whose chief role was to administer them.

In the sacrament of marriage, for example, the effective involvement of the church in the wedding of man and woman came only after the Gregorian reform. Not until the twelfth century did people regularly come to be married by a priest, and only then did churchmen assume jurisdiction over marital disputes, not simply in cases involving royalty but also in those of lesser aristocrats. At the same time, churchmen began to stress the sanctity of marriage. Hugh of St. Victor, a twelfth-century scholar, dwelled on the sacramental meaning of marriage:

> Can you find anything else in marriage except conjugal society which makes it sacred and by which you can assert that it is holy? . . . Each shall be to the other as a same self in all sincere love, all careful solicitude, every kindness of affection, in constant compassion, unflagging consolation, and faithful devotedness.

Hugh saw marriage as a matter of love.

The reformers also proclaimed the special importance of the sacrament of the Mass, holy communion through the body and blood of Christ. Gregory VII called the Mass "the greatest thing in the Christian religion." No layman, no matter how powerful, and no woman of any sort at all could perform anything equal to it, for the Mass was the key to salvation.

The new emphasis on the difference between the priest (who could celebrate Mass) and the laity (who could not) led to vigorous enforcement of an old element of church discipline: the celibacy of priests. The demand for a celibate clergy had far-reaching significance for the history of the church. It distanced western clerics even further from their eastern Orthodox counterparts (whose priests did not practice celibacy), exacerbating the Great Schism of 1054. It also broke with traditional local practices, for clerical marriage was customary in many places in the West. Gregorian reformers exhorted every cleric in higher orders, from the humble parish priest to the exalted bishop, to refrain from marriage or to abandon his wife. In 1123 the pope proclaimed all clerical marriages invalid.

The rule about clerical marriages was only one in a veritable explosion of canon law. Canon law had begun simply as rules determined at church councils. These were then coupled with papal declarations. Some attempts to gather together and organize these laws had been made before the eleventh century. But the proliferation of rules during that century, along with the desire of Gregorians to clarify church law as they saw it, made a systematic collection even more necessary. This was supplied in about 1140 by a landmark work in canon law: the *Concordance of Discordant Canons*, also known as the *Decretum*, by Gratian, a monk who taught law at Bologna in northern Italy. Gratian gathered thousands of passages from the decrees of popes and councils with the intention of showing their harmony. If he found any "discord," he strove to show how they applied to different situations. A bit later a different legal scholar revised and expanded the *Decretum*, adding Roman law to the mix. Meanwhile the papacy itself was gradually developing its own court of law to hear cases and rule on petitions. These services were expensive, and the papacy made the petitioners and litigants pay. Before the Gregorian reform the papacy had been relatively powerless and much loved; afterward, it was very powerful and often resented. A satire written about 1100, in the style of the Gospels, made bitter fun of papal greed:

> There came to the court a certain wealthy clerk, fat and thick, and gross, who in the sedition [rebellion] had committed murder. He first gave to the dispenser, second to the treasurer, third to the cardinals. But they thought among themselves that they should receive more. The Lord Pope, hearing that his cardinals had received many gifts, was sick, nigh unto death. But the rich man sent to him a couch of gold and silver and immediately he was made whole.

With his law courts, bureaucracy, and financial apparatus, the pope had become a monarch.

Early Crusades and Crusader States

Asserting itself as head of the Christian church and leader of its reform movement, the papacy sometimes supported and proclaimed holy wars to advance the cause of Christianity. The most important of these were the crusades. Combinations of war and pilgrimage—the popular practice of making a pious voyage to a sacred shrine to petition for help or cure—the early crusades sent armed European Christians into

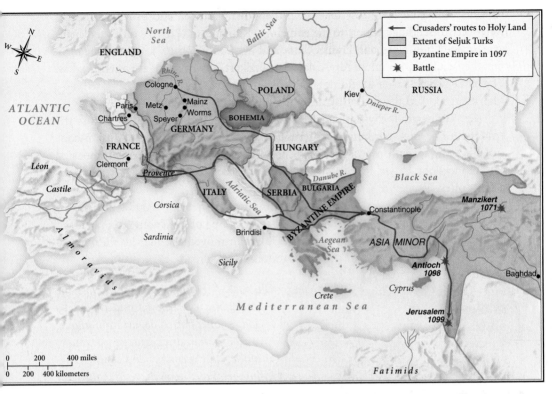

■ MAP 9.2 The First Crusade, 1096–1098

The First Crusade was a major military undertaking that required organization, movement over both land and sea, and enormous resources. Four main groups were responsible for the conquest of Jerusalem. One set out from Cologne, in northern Germany; a second group started from Blois, in France; the third originated to the west of Provence; and the fourth launched ships from Brindisi, at the heel of Italy. All joined up at Constantinople, where their leaders negotiated with Alexius for help and supplies in return for a pledge of vassalage to the emperor.

battle against Muslims in the Holy Land, the place where Christ had lived and died. The crusaders established several tiny states in the Levant, holding on to them precariously until 1291. Although the crusades ultimately "failed," in the sense that the crusaders did not succeed in permanently retaining the Holy Land for Christendom, they were a pivotal episode in Western civilization. They marked the first stage of European overseas expansion, of what later would become imperialism.

The First Crusade began with the entry of the **Seljuk Turks** in Asia Minor (Map 9.2). In the 1050s, taking advantage of the political fragmentation of the Muslim world, the Seljuks, converts to Sunni Islam, captured Baghdad, subjugated the caliphate, and began to threaten Byzantium. The difficulties the Byzantine emperor Romanus IV had in pulling together an army to attack the Turks in 1071 reveal how weak his position had become. Unable to muster Byzantine troops—the generals (*strategoi*) were busy defending their own districts, and provincial nobles were wary of sending support to the emperor—Romanus had to rely on a mercenary army made up of Normans, Franks, Slavs, and even Turks. In 1071, this motley force met the Seljuks under Sultan Alp Arslan at Manzikert, in what is today eastern Turkey. The battle was a disaster for Romanus: the Seljuks routed his army and captured him. Manzikert marked the end of Byzantine domination in the region.

The Turks, gradually settling in Asia Minor, extended their control across the empire and beyond, all the way to Jerusalem, which had been under Muslim control since the seventh century. In 1095, the Byzantine emperor Alexius I appealed for help to Pope Urban II (r. 1088–1099), hoping to get new mercenary troops for a fresh offensive.

Urban II chose to interpret the request in his own way. At the Council of Clermont (in France) in 1095, Urban moved outside the church and addressed an already excited throng:

> Oh, race of Franks, race from across the mountains, race beloved and chosen by God. . . . Let hatred depart from among you, let your quarrels end, let wars cease, and let all dissensions and controversies slumber. Enter upon the road to the Holy Sepulcher; wrest that land from the wicked race, and subject it to yourselves.

The crowd reportedly responded with one voice: "God wills it." Urban's call placed the papacy in a new position of leadership, one that complemented in a military arena the position the popes had gained in the church hierarchy.

■ A Crusader and His Wife

How do we know that the man on the left is a crusader? On his shirt is a cross, the sign worn by all men going on the crusades. In his right hand is a pilgrim's staff, a useful reminder that the crusades were sometimes considered less a matter of war than of penance and piety. What does the embrace of the crusader's wife imply about marital love in the twelfth century?

(© Musée Lorrain, Nancy/Photo: P. Mignot.)

Men and women, rich and poor, young and old, heeded Urban's call. They abandoned their homes and braved the rough journey to the Holy Land to fight for their God. They also went—especially younger sons of aristocrats, who could not expect an inheritance because of the practice of primogeniture—because they wanted land and booty. Some knights went on the expedition because in addition to their pious duty, they were obligated to follow their lord. Although women were discouraged from going on the crusades, some crusaders were accompanied by their wives. Other women went as servants; a few may have been fighters. Children, old men, and women, not able to fight, made the cords for siege engines—giant machines used to hurl stones at enemy fortifications. As more crusades were undertaken during the twelfth century, the transport and supply of these armies became a lucrative business for the commercial classes of maritime Italian cities such as Venice.

The main objective of the First Crusade—to wrest the Holy Land from the Muslims and subject it to Christian rule—was accomplished largely because of Muslim disunity. After nearly a year of ineffectual attacks, the crusaders took Antioch on June 28, 1098; on July 15, 1099, they seized Jerusalem. By 1109 they had carved out several tiny states in the Holy Land.

Because the crusader states were created by conquest, they were treated as lordships. The rulers granted fiefs to their own vassals, and some of these men in turn gave portions of their holdings as fiefs to some of their own vassals. Since most Europeans went home after the First Crusade, the rulers who remained learned to coexist with the indigenous population, which included Muslims, Jews, and Greek Orthodox Christians. They encouraged a lively trade at their ports, which received merchants from Italy, Byzantium, and Islamic cities.

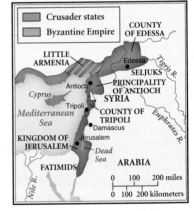

The Crusader States in 1109

The main concern of these rulers, however, was military. They set up castles and recruited knights from Europe. So organized for war was this society that it produced a new and militant kind of monasticism: the Knights Templar. Like Bruno's Carthusians, the Templars vowed themselves to poverty and chastity. But rather than withdraw to a hermitage on a mountaintop, the Templars, whose name came from their living quarters in the area of the former Jewish Temple at Jerusalem, devoted themselves to warfare. Their first mission—to protect the pilgrimage routes from Palestine to Jerusalem—soon diversified. They manned the town garrisons of the crusader states, and they transported money from Europe to the Holy Land. In this way the Templars became enormously wealthy, with branch "banks" in major cities across Europe.

The presence of the Templars did not prevent a new Seljuk chieftain, Zengi, from taking the city of Edessa in 1144. The event marked the slow but steady

■ Krak-des-Chevaliers

The Hospitallers, a religious military order much like the Templars, built this imposing castle in 1142 on the site of a Muslim fortification in Syria. A large community of perhaps fifty monk-knights and their hired mercenaries lived there. To the northeast (in back of the complex seen here) was a fortified village that served the needs of the castle. Peasants raised grain, which was ground by a windmill on one wall of the castle. For water, there were reservoirs to catch the rain, wells, and an aqueduct (visible on the right). Twelve toilets connected to a common drain. The monks worshiped in a chapel within the inner walls. The outer walls, built of masonry, completely enclosed the inner buildings, making Krak one of the most important places for refuge and defense in the crusader states.
(Maynard Owen Williams/National Geographic Image Collection.)

shrinking of the crusader states. New crusades were called, but none was successful. The Second Crusade (1147–1149) came to a disastrous end. After besieging the walls of Damascus for only four days, the crusaders, whose leaders could not keep the peace among themselves, gave up and went home. Soon the Muslim hero Nur al-Din united Syria under his command and presided over a renewal of Sunni Islam. His successor, Saladin (1138–1193), took Jerusalem in 1187, galvanizing the pope to call the Third Crusade (1189–1192). Led by the greatest rulers of Europe—Emperor Frederick I Barbarossa, Philip II of France, Leopold of Austria, and Richard I of England—the Third Crusade nevertheless accomplished little, and the crusader states were reduced to a few tiny outposts.

The Jews as Strangers

The same militant piety that inspired the crusades was turned against the Jews. Sentiment against Jews grew over time. Ever since the Roman Empire had become Christian, Jews had been seen as separate from Christians. Imperial law, for example, prohibited them from owning Christian slaves or marrying Christian women. Church laws added to these restrictions. Socially isolated and branded as outcasts,

Jews served as scapegoats who helped define the larger society as orthodox. But only at the end of the eleventh century did severe persecution begin.

Forced out of the countryside during the eleventh century by castellans and other regional rulers, most Jews ended up in the cities as craftsmen or merchants. But they were not allowed into guilds, and many were thus pushed into the one profession that Christians could not have: moneylending. Jews thus provided capital for the developing commercial society, whose Christian members were prohibited from charging interest by the Bible's constraints against usury. Many Jews lived in the flourishing commercial region of the Rhineland. Under Henry IV, the Jews in Speyer and elsewhere in the empire gained a place within the government system by receiving protection from the local bishop (an imperial appointee) in return for paying a tax. Within these cities, the Jews lived in their own neighborhoods, their tightly knit communities focused on local synagogues, which served as schools and community centers as well as places of worship. Nevertheless, Jews also participated in the life of the larger Christian community. Archbishop Anno of Cologne dealt with Jewish moneylenders, and other Jews in Cologne were allowed to trade their wares at the fairs there.

It was against these Rhineland Jews that some of the earliest anti-Jewish attacks were directed. Some of the crusaders of the First Crusade declared it ridiculous to attack Muslims when other infidels lived in their own backyards: "That's doing our work backward," they said, as they moved into the Rhineland to force conversions or to kill. Some Jews found refuge with bishops or in the houses of Christian friends, but in many cities—Metz, Speyer, Worms, Mainz, and Cologne—they were massacred.

In the course of the twelfth century, Jews were attacked elsewhere as well. European rulers claimed the Jews as their serfs and Jewish property as their own. King Henry II of England (r. 1154–1189) imposed new and arbitrary taxes on the Jewish community. In France, persecuting Jews and confiscating

■ **The Jew as the Other**
Medieval artists often portrayed people not as individuals but rather as "types" that could be identified by physical markers. In the second half of the twelfth century, Jews were increasingly portrayed as looking different from Christians. This illustration shows clerics borrowing money from a Jew. What physical features do all the clerics have in common? (Be sure to look at the clothes as well as the hairstyle.) What distinguishes the layman from the clerics? How do you know who is meant to be the Jew? In fact, Jews did not regularly wear this type of pointed hat until they were forced to do so in some regions of Europe in the late thirteenth century.
(Bayerische Staatsbibliothek, Munich.)

their property benefited both the treasury and the authoritative image of the king. Early in the reign of the French king Philip II—known as Philip Augustus (r. 1180–1223)—royal agents surprised Jews at Sabbath worship in their synagogues and seized their goods, demanding that they redeem their own property for a large sum of money. Shortly thereafter, Philip canceled 80 percent of all debts owed to Jews; the remaining 20 percent was to be paid directly to the king. About a year later, in 1182, Philip expelled the Jews from the Île-de-France. When he allowed them to return in 1198, he permitted them to be moneylenders or moneychangers only, taxed and monitored by royal officials.

Limiting Jews to moneylending in an increasingly commercial economy, then persecuting them, served the interests of lords in debt to Jewish creditors. For example, in 1190, local nobles orchestrated a brutal attack on the Jews of York (in England). Their purpose was to rid themselves of their debts—and of the Jews to whom they owed money. Churchmen, too, used credit in a money economy but resented the fiscal obligations it imposed. With their drive to create centralized territorial states and their desire to make their authority known and felt, powerful rulers of Europe—churchmen and laymen alike—exploited and coerced the Jews while drawing upon and encouraging widespread anti-Jewish feeling. Although Jews must have looked exactly like Christians in reality, Jews now became clearly identified in sculpture and in drawings by markers such as conical hats and, increasingly, by demeaning features.

Attacks against Jews were inspired by more than resentment against Jewish money and the desire for power and control. They also grew out of the codification of Christian religious doctrine and Christians' anxiety about their own institutions. For example, in the twelfth century, church leaders promulgated a newly rigorous definition of the Eucharist, declaring that when the bread and wine were blessed by the priest during Mass, they became the true body and blood of Christ. For some believers this meant that Christ, wounded and bleeding, lay on the altar. Miracle tales sometimes reported that the elements of the Eucharist bled. Reflecting Christian anxieties about the presence of real flesh on the altar, sensational stories—originating in clerical circles but soon widely circulated—told of Jews who secretly sacrificed Christian children in a morbid revisiting of the crucifixion of Jesus. This charge, called "blood libel" by historians, led to massacres of Jews in cities in England, France, Spain, and Germany. Jews had no rituals involving blood sacrifice at all, but they were convenient and vulnerable scapegoats for Christian guilt and anxiety.

■ **REVIEW:** *What were the causes and consequences of the Gregorian reform?*

The Revival of Monarchies

Attacks on the Jews reveal the ugly side of a wider development: kings and other rulers were enhancing and consolidating their power. They created new and revived old ideologies to justify their power; they hired officials to work for them;

and they found vassals and churchmen to support them. The money that flowed into their treasuries from the new urban economy increased their effectiveness.

Byzantium in Its Prime

The First Crusade was an unanticipated result of a monarchical revival at Byzantium. In 1081, ten years after the disastrous battle at Manzikert, the energetic soldier Alexius Comnenus (r. 1081–1118) seized the throne. He faced considerable unrest in Constantinople, whose populace suffered from a combination of high taxes and rising living costs. In addition, the empire was under attack on every side—by Normans in southern Italy, Seljuk Turks in Asia Minor, and new groups in the Balkans. But, Alexius managed to turn actual and potential enemies against one another, staving off immediate defeat.

When Alexius asked Pope Urban II to supply him with some western troops to fight his enemies, he was shocked and disappointed to learn that crusaders rather than mercenaries were on the way. His daughter Anna Comnena (1083–c. 1148) later wrote an account of the crusades from the Byzantine perspective in a book about her father, the *Alexiad*. To her, the crusaders were barbarians and her father the consummate statesman and diplomat:

> *The emperor sent envoys to greet them as a mark of friendship. . . . It was typical of Alexius: he had an uncanny prevision [foresight] and knew how to seize a point of vantage before his rivals. Officers appointed for this particular task were ordered to provide victuals on the journey—the pilgrims must have no excuse for complaint for any reason whatever.*

To wage all the wars he had to fight, Alexius relied less on the peasant farmers and the *theme* system than on mercenaries and great magnates armed and mounted like western knights and accompanied by their own troops. In return for their services he gave these nobles *pronoia* grants, lifetime possession of large imperial estates and their dependent peasants. The theme system, under which peasant soldiers in earlier centuries had been settled on imperial lands, gradually disappeared. Alexius conciliated the great families by giving the provincial nobility pronoia grants and satisfied members of the urban elite by granting them new offices. The emperor normally got on well with the patriarch and Byzantine clergy, for emperor and church depended on each other to suppress heresy and foster orthodoxy. The emperors of the Comnenian dynasty (1081–1185) thus gained a measure of increased imperial power, but at the price of important concessions to the nobility.

In the eleventh and twelfth centuries, Constantinople remained a rich, sophisticated, and highly cultured city. Sculptors and other artists strove to depict ideals of human beauty and elegance. Churches built during the period were decorated with elaborate depictions of the cosmos. Significant innovations occurred in Byzantine scholarship and literature. The Neoplatonic tradition of late antiquity had always influenced Byzantine religious and philosophical thought, but now scholars renewed their interest in the wellsprings of classical Greek philosophy, particularly Plato and Aristotle. The rediscovery of ancient culture inspired Byzantine writers to reintroduce old forms into the grammar, vocabulary, and rhetorical style of Greek literature. Anna Comnena wrote her *Alexiad* in this newly learned Greek and prided herself on "having read thoroughly the treatises of Aristotle and the dialogues of Plato." The revival of ancient Greek writings, especially those of Plato, in eleventh- and twelfth-century Byzantium would have profound consequences for both eastern and western European civilization in centuries to come as their ideas slowly penetrated European culture.

The Anglo-Norman realm
← William
← Harold

0   100   200 miles
0   100   200 kilometers

SCOTLAND

North Sea

York

ENGLAND

Hastings   Canterbury
Wessex   1066   Flanders

Normandy

Norman Conquest of England, 1066

Norman and Angevin England

In Europe, the twelfth-century kings of England were the most powerful monarchs before 1200 because they ruled the whole kingdom by right of conquest. When the Anglo-Saxon king Edward the Confessor (r. 1042–1066) died childless in 1066, the duke of Normandy, William (1027–1087), claimed the throne of England. Gathering a force recruited from many parts of France, he launched an invasion. His armies clashed with those of another claimant to the throne, Harold, at Hastings on October 14, 1066. In one of history's rare decisive battles, William won and took over the realm.

Some people in England gladly supported William, considering his victory a verdict from God and hoping to be granted a place in the new order themselves. But William—known to posterity by the epithet "the Conqueror"—wanted to replace, not assimilate, the Anglo-Saxons. In the course of William's reign, families from continental Europe almost totally supplanted the English aristocracy. And although the English peasantry remained—now with new lords—the peasants were severely shaken. A twelfth-century historian claimed to record William's deathbed confession:

> I have persecuted [England's] native inhabitants beyond all reason. Whether gentle or simple, I have cruelly oppressed them; many I unjustly disinherited; innumerable multitudes, especially in the county of York, perished through me by famine or the sword.

Modern historians estimate that one out of five people in England died as a result of the Norman conquest and its immediate aftermath.

Although the Normans destroyed a generation of English men and women, they preserved and extended some Anglo-Saxon institutions, retaining the old

■ **Bayeux "Tapestry"**
This famous "tapestry" is misnamed; it is really an embroidery, 231 feet long and 20 inches wide, created to tell the story of William's conquest of England from his point of view. In this detail, Norman archers are lined up at the bottom. Above them, Norman knights on horseback attack English foot soldiers wielding long battle-axes. Who seems to be winning? **For more help analyzing this image,** see the visual activity for this chapter in the ONLINE STUDY GUIDE at bedfordstmartins.com/huntconcise. (Tapisserie de Bayeux. By special permission of the City of Bayeux, France.)

administrative divisions and legal system of shires (counties) and hundreds (see pages 330–31). The Normans also, of course, drew from continental institutions. They set up a political hierarchy, culminating in the king and buttressed by his castles, just as French kings were trying to do at about the same time (see page 366). But because all of England was the king's by conquest, he could treat it as his booty; William kept about 20 percent of the land for himself and divided the rest, distributing it in large but scattered fiefs to a relatively small number of his barons and family members, lay and ecclesiastical, as well as to some lesser men, such as personal servants and soldiers. In turn, these men and their vassals owed the king military service along with certain dues, such as reliefs (money paid upon inheriting a fief) and aids (payments made on important occasions).

Those were the revenues expected from the nobles, but the king of England commanded the peasantry as well. In 1086, twenty years after his conquest, William ordered a survey and census of England, popularly called "Domesday" because, like the records of people judged at doomsday, it provided facts that could not be appealed. It was the most extensive inventory of land, livestock, taxes, and population that had ever been compiled in Europe. The king

> *sent his men over all England into every shire and had them find out how many hundred hides [a measure of land] there were in the shire, or what land and cattle the king himself had in the country, or what dues he ought*

to receive every year from the shire. . . . So very narrowly did he have the survey to be made that there was not a single hide or yard of land, nor indeed . . . an ox or a cow or a pig left out.

The Norman conquest tied England to the languages, politics, institutions, and culture of France and Flanders. Modern English is an amalgam of Anglo-Saxon and Norman French, the language spoken by the Normans. English commerce was linked to the wool industry in Flanders. St. Anselm (1033–1109), the archbishop of Canterbury (England), was born in Italy and was the abbot of a monastery in Normandy before crossing the Channel. The barons of England retained their estates in Normandy and elsewhere, and the kings of England often spent more time on the continent than they did on the island. When William's son Henry I (r. 1100–1135) died without male heirs, civil war soon erupted: the throne of England was fought over by two French counts—one married to Henry's daughter, the other to his sister.

The outcome of that civil war was the accession to the English throne of Henry II (r. 1154–1189).* He was not only count of Anjou but also, by an astute marriage to Eleanor of Aquitaine in 1152, duke of Aquitaine. His father, who had conquered Normandy, named him duke there, and he also exercised hegemony over Poitou and Brittany. Although technically a vassal of the king of France for his continental lands, in effect, Henry ruled a territory that stretched from England to the south of France (Map 9.3).

The marriage to Eleanor brought Henry both a huge duchy and a feisty queen, who, however, bore him the sons he needed to maintain his dynasty. Before her marriage to Henry, Eleanor was married to King Louis VII of France. Louis had the marriage annulled because she bore him only daughters. Nevertheless, as queen of France, Eleanor enjoyed an important position: she disputed with St. Bernard, the Cistercian abbot who was the most renowned churchman of the day; and she accompanied her husband on the Second Crusade, bringing more troops than he did. She determined to separate from Louis even before he considered leaving her. Married to Henry, she had much less power, for he dominated her as he dominated his barons. Turning to her offspring in 1173, Eleanor, disguised as a man, tried to join her eldest son, Henry the Younger, in a plot against his father. But the rebellion was put down, and she spent most of her years thereafter, until her husband's death in 1189, confined under guard at Winchester Castle.

As king of England, Henry immediately set to work to undo the damage to the monarchy caused by the civil war of 1139–1153, during which the English barons and high churchmen had gained new privileges and powers, building

---

*Henry II is known as the first Angevin (from *Anjou*) king of England because by inheritance, he was count of Anjou. But he also has another name: his father, Count Geoffrey of Anjou, was nicknamed *Plantagenet*, from *genet*, a shrub that he liked, and historians sometimes use that name to refer to the entire dynasty. Thus Henry II was the first Plantagenet as well as the first Angevin king of England.

■ MAP 9.3 Europe in the Age of Frederick Barbarossa and Henry II, 1150–1190

The second half of the twelfth century was dominated by two men, Emperor Frederick Barbarossa and King Henry II. Not just king of England, Henry also held northwestern France by inheritance and southwestern France through his wife, Eleanor of Aquitaine. A few hundred miles to the east were the borders of Frederick Barbarossa's empire, a huge territory—much of it held by him only weakly. Only the Staufen lands were directly under his control.

private castles as symbols of their strength. Henry destroyed or confiscated the new castles and regained crown lands. Then he proceeded to further extend monarchical power, above all by imposing royal justice.

Henry's judicial reforms built on an already well-developed English system. The Anglo-Saxon kings had established royal district courts and appointed sheriffs to police the shires, call up men to fight, and haul criminals into court. The

Norman kings retained these courts, which all the free men of the shire were summoned to attend. To these already well-developed institutions, Henry II added a system of judicial visitations called eyres (from the Latin *iter*, "journey"). Under this system, royal justices made regular trips to every locality in England. Henry declared that some crimes, such as murder, arson, and rape, were so heinous as to violate the "king's peace," no matter where they were committed. The king required local representatives of the knightly class to meet during each eyre and either give the sheriff the names of those suspected of committing crimes in the vicinity or arrest the suspects and hand them over to the royal justices.

During the eyres, the justices also heard cases between individuals, now called civil cases. Free men and women (that is, people of the knightly class or above) could bring their disputes over such matters as inheritance, dowries, and property claims to the king's justices. Earlier courts had generally relied on duels between litigants to determine verdicts. Henry's new system offered a different option, an inquest under royal supervision.

The new system was praised for its efficiency, speed, and conclusiveness by a contemporary legal treatise known as *Glanvill* (after its presumed author): "This legal institution emanates from perfect equity. For justice, which after many and long delays is scarcely ever demonstrated by the duel, is advantageously and speedily attained through this institution." *Glanvill* might have added that the king also speedily gained a large treasury. The exchequer, as the financial bureau of England was called, recorded all the fines paid for judgments and the sums collected for writs. The amounts, entered on parchment sewn together and stored as rolls, became the Receipt Rolls and Pipe Rolls, the first of many such records of the

■ **Hanging Thieves**

The development of common law in England meant mobilizing royal agents to bring charges and make arrests. In 1124, the royal justice Ralph Basset hanged forty-four thieves. This miniature from around 1130 shows the hanging of eight thieves for breaking into the shrine of St. Edmund. Under Henry II, all cases of murder, arson, and rape were considered crimes against the king himself. The result, in addition to the enhancement of the king's power, was new definitions of crime, more thorough policing, and more systematic punishments.

(Pierpont Morgan Library/Art Resource, NY.)

English monarchy and an indication that writing had become a mechanism for institutionalizing royal power in England.

The stiffest opposition to Henry's extension of royal courts came from the church, where a separate system of trial and punishment had long been available to the clergy and to others who enjoyed church protection. The punishments that these courts meted out were generally quite mild. Jealous of their prerogatives, churchmen refused to submit to the jurisdiction of Henry's courts, and the ensuing contest between Henry II and his appointed archbishop, Thomas Becket (1118–1170), became the greatest battle between the church and the state in the twelfth century. The conflict over jurisdiction simmered for six years, until Henry's henchmen murdered Thomas, unintentionally turning him into a martyr. Although Henry's role in the murder remained ambiguous, he had to do public penance for the deed largely because of the general outcry. In the end, both church courts and royal courts expanded to address the concerns of an increasingly litigious society.

Praising the King of France

The twelfth-century kings of France were much less obviously powerful than their English and Byzantine counterparts. Yet they too took part in the monarchical revival. Louis VI the Fat (r. 1108–1137), so heavy that he had to be hoisted onto his horse by a crane, was a tireless defender of royal power. We know a good deal about him because a contemporary and close associate, Suger (1081–1152), abbot of St. Denis, wrote Louis's biography. When Louis set himself the task of consolidating his rule in the Île-de-France, Suger portrayed the king as a righteous hero. He thought of the king as the head of a political hierarchy in which Louis had rights over the French nobles because they were his vassals or because they broke the peace.

Suger also believed that Louis had a religious role: to protect the church and the poor. He viewed Louis as another Charlemagne, a ruler for all society, not merely an overlord of the nobility. Louis waged war to keep God's peace. Of course, the Gregorian reform had made its mark: Suger did not claim Louis was head of the church. Nevertheless, he emphasized the royal dignity and its importance to the papacy. When a pope happened to arrive in France, Louis, not yet king, and his father, Philip I (r. 1052–1108), bowed low, but (recalled Suger) "the pope lifted them up and made them sit before him like devout sons of the apostles. In the manner of a wise man acting wisely, he conferred with them privately on the present condition of the church." Here, the pope was shown needing royal advice. Meanwhile, Suger stressed Louis's piety and active defense of the faith:

> Helped by his powerful band of armed men, or rather by the hand of God, he abruptly seized the castle [of Crécy] and captured its very strong tower as if it were simply the hut of a peasant. Having startled those criminals, he piously slaughtered the impious.

When Louis VI died in 1137, Suger's notion of the might and right of the king of France reflected reality in an extremely small area. Nevertheless, Louis laid the groundwork for the gradual extension of royal power in France. As the lord of vassals, the king could call upon his men to aid him in times of war (though the great ones sometimes disregarded his wishes and chose not to help). As a king and landlord, he could obtain many dues and taxes. He also drew revenues from Paris, a thriving city not only of commerce but also of scholarship. Officials enforced his royal laws and collected taxes. With money and land, Louis could dispense the favors and give the gifts that added to his prestige and his power. Louis VI and Suger together created the territorial core and royal ideal of the future French monarchy. Louis's grandson Philip Augustus would build on this foundation, greatly expanding the territory of the French monarchy in the thirteenth century.

Remaking the Empire

The Investiture Conflict and the civil war it generated (1075–1122) strengthened the German princes and weakened the emperors. For decades, the princes enjoyed near independence, building castles on their properties and establishing control over whole territories. To ensure that the emperors who succeeded Henry V (r. 1106–1125) would be weak, the princes supported only rulers who agreed to give them new lands and powers. A ruler's success depended on his ability to juggle the many conflicting interests of his own royal and imperial offices, his family, and the German princes. He also had to contend with the increasing influence of the papacy and the Italian communes, which were forging alliances with one another and with the German princes, preventing the consolidation of power under a strong German monarch during the first half of the twelfth century.

Weakness at the top, however, meant constant warfare among princely factions. Eventually the German princes became exhausted by conflict and in 1152 elected Frederick I Barbarossa (r. 1152–1190) as the first Hohenstaufen king of Germany. He was an impressive man with a striking red-blond beard (hence *Barbarossa*, or "red-beard") and a firm sense of his position. Frederick affirmed royal rights even when he handed out duchies and allowed others to name bishops, because in return for these political powers he required the princes to concede formally and publicly that they held their rights and territories from him as their lord. By making them his vassals, though with nearly royal rights within their principalities, Frederick defined the princes' relationship to the German king: they were powerful yet personally subordinate to him. In this way, Frederick hoped to save the monarchy and to coordinate royal and princely rule, thus ending Germany's chronic civil wars. Frederick used the lord–vassal relationship to give himself a free hand to rule while placating the princes.

Since the Investiture Conflict, the emperor had ruled Italy in name only. The communes of the northern cities guarded their liberties jealously, and the pope considered Italy his own sphere of influence. Frederick's territorial base north of Italy (in Swabia) and his designs on northern Italy threatened those interests (see Map 9.3). Some historians have criticized Frederick for "entangling" himself in Italy, but Frederick's title was *emperor*, a position that demanded he intervene there. To fault him for not concentrating on Germany is to blame him for lacking modern wisdom, which knows from hindsight that European polities developed into nation-states, such as France, Germany, and Italy. There was nothing inevitable about the development of nation-states, however, and Frederick should not be condemned for failing to see into the future. In addition, control of Italy made sense even for Frederick's effectiveness in Germany. His base in Swabia together with northern Italy would give him a compact and central territory. Moreover, the flourishing commercial cities of Italy would make him rich. Taxes on agricultural production there alone would yield thirty thousand silver talents annually, an incredible sum.

By alternately negotiating with and fighting against the great cities of northern Italy, especially Milan, Frederick achieved military control there in 1158. No longer able to make Italian bishops royal governors, as German kings had done earlier—the Investiture Conflict had effectively ended that practice—Frederick insisted that the communes be governed by magistrates (called *podestà*) from outside the commune who were appointed (or at least authorized) by the emperor and who would collect revenues on his behalf. Here is where Frederick made his mistake: the heavy hand of these officials, many of them from Germany, created enormous resentment. By 1167, most of the cities of northern Italy had joined with Pope Alexander III (r. 1159–1181) to form the Lombard League against Frederick. Defeated at the battle of Legnano (near Milan) in 1176, Frederick made peace with Alexander and withdrew most of his forces from Italy. The battle marked the triumph of the city over the crown in Italy, which would not have a centralized government until the nineteenth century; Italy's political history would instead be that of its various regions and their dominant cities.

The Courtly Culture of Europe

With the consolidation of territory, wealth, and power in the last half of the twelfth century, kings, barons, princes, and their wives and daughters created a newly opulent court culture. For the first time on the European continent, poems and songs were written in the vernacular, the spoken language, rather than in Latin. They celebrated the lives of the nobility and were meant to be read aloud or sung as entertainment. Already at the beginning of the twelfth century, Duke William IX of Aquitaine (1071–1126), the grandfather of Eleanor of Aquitaine, had written lyric poems in Occitan, the vernacular spoken in southern France. Perhaps influenced by love poetry in Arabic and Hebrew from al-Andalus, his own poetry in

■ Troubadour Song

Raimon de Miraval flourished between 1191 and 1229, very late for a troubadour. He was a petty knight who became a poet and was welcomed at the courts of rulers such as those of Toulouse, Aragon, and Castile. More than forty of his poems have survived, twenty-two with written music. The song here, beginning "A penas," is set to music with a five-line staff. Notice that some of the notes (called neumes) are single and others are in groups. The grouped notes are to be sung, one right after the other, on the same syllable or word.

turn provided a model for poetic forms that gained great popularity. The final four-line stanza of one such poem demonstrates the composer's skill with words:

Per aquesta fri e tremble,	*For this one I shiver and tremble,*
quar de tan bon' amor l'am;	*I love her with such a good love;*
qu'anc no cug qu'en nasques semble	*I do not think the like of her was ever born*
en semblan de gran linh n'Adam.	*in the long line of Lord Adam.*

The rhyme scheme of this poem appears to be simple—*tremble* rhymes with *semble, l'am* with *n'Adam.* But the poem has five earlier verses, all six lines long and all containing the *-am, -am* rhyme in the fourth and sixth lines, while every other line within each verse rhymes as well. The whole scheme is dazzlingly complex.

William was followed by other troubadours—lyric poets who wrote in Occitan. Whether male or female, their subject was love. The Contessa de Dia, probably the wife of the lord of Die in France, wrote about her unrequited love for a man:

> So bitter do I feel toward him
> whom I love more than anything.
> With him my mercy and fine manners [*cortesia*] are in vain.

The key to troubadour verse was the notion of *cortesia*—courtesy—which referred to the refinement of people living at court and to their struggle to achieve an ideal of virtue.

Historians and literary critics used to use the term *courtly love* to emphasize one of the themes of courtly literature: the poet expresses overwhelming love for a beautiful married noblewoman who is far above him in status and utterly unattainable. But this was only one of many aspects of love that the troubadours sang about. Some boasted of sexual conquests; others played with the notion of equality between lovers; still others preached that love was the source of virtue. The real overall theme of this literature was not courtly love but the power of women. No wonder Eleanor of Aquitaine and other aristocratic women patronized the troubadours: they enjoyed the image that the poetry gave them of themselves. Nor was that image a delusion. There were many powerful female lords in southern France. They owned property, had vassals, led battles, decided disputes, and entered into and broke political alliances as their advantage dictated. Both men and women appreciated troubadour poetry, which recognized and praised women's power even as it eroticized it.

From southern France the lyric love song spread to Italy, northern France, England, and Germany—regions where Occitan was a foreign language. Similar poetry appeared in other vernacular languages: the *minnesingers* (literally, "love singers") sang in German; the *trouvères* sang in the Old French of northern France.

Some poets wrote much longer works—long heroic poems focused on war (later called epics) or equally long romantic poems about love (later called romances). Romances, often inspired by the legend of King Arthur, reached the zenith of their popularity during the late twelfth and early thirteenth centuries. A good example is *Lancelot* by Chrétien de Troyes (c. 1150–1190). The hero, in love with Queen Guinevere, the wife of his lord, King Arthur, will do anything for her. When she sees him—the greatest knight in Christendom—fighting in a tournament, she tests his love for her by asking him to do his "worst." The poor knight is obliged to lose all his battles until she changes her mind.

Lancelot was the perfect chivalric knight. The word **chivalry** derives from the French word *cheval* ("horse"); the fact that the knight was a horseman marked him as a warrior of the most prestigious sort. Perched high on his mount, his heavy lance couched in his right arm, the knight was an imposing and menacing figure. Chivalry made him gentle—except to his enemies on the battlefield. The chivalric hero was a knight constrained by a code of refinement, fair play, piety, and devotion to an ideal. Historians debate whether real knights lived up to the codes implicit in epics and romances. But there is no doubt that real knights liked to imagine themselves that way.

■ **REVIEW:** *What new sources and institutions of power became available to rulers in the twelfth century?*

New Forms of Scholarship and Religious Experience

The commercial revolution, the newly organized church, and the revived monarchies of the twelfth century set the stage for the growth of schools and for new forms of scholarship. Money and career opportunities attracted unheard-of numbers of young men to city schools. Worldly motivations, however, were equaled by spiritual ones. The movement for church reform stressed the importance of the church and its beliefs. Many students and teachers in the twelfth century sought knowledge to make their faith clearer and deeper. "Nothing can be believed unless it is first understood," said one of the period's greatest scholars, Peter Abelard (1079–1142).

Other people in the twelfth century, however, sought to avoid the cities and the schools. Some found refuge in the measured ceremonies and artistic splendor of Benedictine monasteries such as Cluny. Others considered these vast monastic complexes to be ostentatious and worldly. Rejecting the opulence of cities and the splendor of well-endowed monasteries alike, some pursued a monastic life of poverty, while others, like St. Francis, rejected even the shelter of the cloister.

Schools, Scholars, and the New Learning

Schools had been connected to monasteries and cathedrals since the Carolingian period. They served to train new recruits to become either monks or priests. Some were better endowed with books and masters (or teachers) than others; a few developed a reputation for a certain theological approach or specialized in a certain branch of learning, such as literature, medicine, or law. By the end of the eleventh century, the best schools were generally in the larger cities: Reims, Paris, Bologna, Montpellier.

Eager students sampled nearly all of them. The young monk Gilbert of Liège was typical: "Instilled with an insatiable thirst for learning, whenever he heard of somebody excelling in the arts, he rushed immediately to that place and drank whatever delightful potion he could draw from the master there." For Gilbert and other students, a good lecture had the excitement of theater. Teachers at cathedral schools found themselves forced to find larger halls to accommodate the crush of students. Other teachers simply declared themselves "masters" and set up shop by renting a room. If they could prove their mettle in the classroom, they had no trouble finding paying students.

"Wandering scholars" like Gilbert were probably all male, and because schools had hitherto been the training ground for clergymen, all students were considered clerics, whether or not they had been ordained. Wandering became a way of life as the consolidation of castellanies, counties, and kingdoms made violence against travelers less frequent. Urban centers soon responded to the needs of transients with markets, taverns, and lodgings. Using Latin, Europe's common language, students could drift from, say, Italy to Spain, Germany, England, and France, wherever a noted master had settled. Along with crusaders, pilgrims, and merchants, students made the roads of Europe very crowded indeed.

What the students sought, above all, was knowledge of the seven liberal arts. Grammar, rhetoric, and logic (or dialectic) belonged to the "beginning" arts, the so-called trivium. Logic, involving the technical analysis of texts as well as the application and manipulation of mental constructs, was a transitional

■ A Teacher and His Students

*This miniature expresses the hierarchical relation-
ship between students and teachers in the twelfth
century. But there is more. The miniature
appears in a late-twelfth-century manuscript of a
commentary written by Gilbert (d. 1154), bishop
of Poitiers. Gilbert's ideas in this commentary provoked the ire of St. Bernard, who accused Gilbert
of heresy. But Gilbert escaped condemnation.
Here, in pictorial form, the artist asserts Gilbert's
orthodoxy by depicting him with a halo, in the
full dress of a bishop, speaking from his throne.
Below Gilbert are three of his disciples, also with
halos. The artist's positive view of Gilbert is
echoed by modern historians, who recognize
Gilbert as a pioneer in his approach to scriptural
commentary.* (Bibliothèque municipale de Valenciennes.)

subject leading to the second, higher part of the liberal arts, the quadrivium. This comprised four areas of study that we might call theoretical math and science: arithmetic, geometry, music (theory rather than practice), and astronomy. Of all these subjects, logic excited the most intense interest. Medieval students and masters were convinced that logic clarified every issue, even questions about the nature of God. With logic, they thought, one could prove that what one believed on faith was in fact true. At the end of the twelfth century, some western scholars took advantage of Islamic achievements; they traveled to Islamic centers in Spain and Sicily, where the Greek texts of Aristotle, with their sophisticated logic, had already been translated into Arabic and closely commented on. Translating these Arabic texts into Latin, western scholars made Aristotle their own.

After studying the liberal arts, students went on to study medicine, theology, or law. At Bologna, for example, students studied Lombard, Roman, and canon law. Men skilled in canon law served popes and bishops; popes, kings, princes, and communes all found that Roman law, which claimed the emperor as its fount, justified their claims to power. The University of Paris, established at the very end of the twelfth century, concentrated on theology. Montpellier, in the south of France, was noted for its medical education. With books expensive and hard to find, lectures were the chief method of communication. These were centered on important texts: the master read an excerpt aloud, delivered his commentary on it, and disputed any contrary commentaries that rival masters might have proposed. Student committed the lectures to memory.

Universities functioned as guilds, with the teachers in the role of the masters and the students the apprentices (except at Bologna, where the students, usually older men experienced in administration, had their own guild). Like guilds, they set prices (in this case, fees), determined standards (in this case, the knowledge that had to be learned), and regulated discipline. Given generous privileges by both popes and kings, who valued the services of scholars, the universities were sometimes at odds with the townspeople. It is common to speak of "town against gown"—the "gown" referring to the garb worn by the students and masters (and imitated by the American graduation gown). Students could be rowdy and worse; and townspeople resented a self-governing body of transients—the university—in their midst. On the other hand, pub owners, innkeepers, food purveyors, and landlords benefited from the patronage of students and masters, and generally town–gown relations were good.

The remarkable renewal of scholarship in the twelfth century had an unexpected benefit: we know a great deal about the men involved in it—and a few of the women—because they wrote so much, often about themselves. Three important figures typify the scholars of the period: Abelard and Heloise, who embraced the new learning wholeheartedly and retired to monasteries only when forced to do so, and Hildegard of Bingen, who spent most of her life happily in a cloister yet wrote knowingly about the world.

Peter Abelard (1079–1142) was one of the twelfth century's greatest thinkers. Turning his back on an expected career as a warrior and lord, he studied in Paris and soon began to write influential works on ethics, logic, and theology. Around 1122–1123, he prepared a textbook for his students, the *Sic et Non* (*Yes and No*), unusual because it arranged side-by-side opposing positions on various subjects without reconciling them. Instead, Abelard challenged his students to make sense of the conflicts and resolve the contradictions themselves. In Abelard's view, the inquiring student would follow the model of Christ himself, who as a boy sat among the rabbis, questioning them.

Abelard's fame as a teacher was such that a Parisian cleric named Fulbert gave him room and board and engaged him as tutor for Heloise (c. 1100–c. 1163/1164), Fulbert's niece. Brought up under her uncle's guardianship, Heloise had been sent as a young girl to a convent school, where she received a thorough grounding in literary skills. Her uncle hoped to continue her education at home by hiring Abelard. Abelard, however, became her secret lover as well as her tutor. "Our desires left no stage of love-making untried," wrote Abelard in his *Historia calamitatum* (*Story of My Calamities*), his autobiographical account. When Heloise became pregnant, Abelard insisted they marry. They did so clandestinely, informing only a very few, such as Fulbert, for the new emphasis on clerical celibacy meant that Abelard's professional success and prestige would have been compromised if news of his marriage were made public. After they were married, Heloise and Abelard rarely saw one another. Suspecting that Abelard had abandoned his niece, Fulbert plotted a cruel punishment: he paid a servant to castrate Abelard. Soon after, husband and wife entered separate monasteries.

For Heloise, separation from Abelard was a lasting misfortune. For Abelard, however, the loss of Heloise and even his castration were not the worst disasters of his life. The cruelest blow came later, and it was directed at his intellect. He wrote a book that applied "human and logical reasons" (as he put it) to the Trinity; the book was condemned at the Council of Soissons in 1121, and he was forced to throw it, page by page, into the flames. Bitterly weeping at the injustice, Abelard lamented, "This open violence had come upon me only because of the purity of my intentions and love of our Faith which had compelled me to write."

Abelard had written the treatise on the Trinity for his students, maintaining that "words were useless if the intelligence could not follow them, [and] that nothing could be believed unless it was first understood." For Abelard, logic was the key to knowledge, and knowledge the key to faith.

Unlike Abelard and Heloise, Hildegard of Bingen (1098–1179) did not attend the city schools or learn under one of their scholars. Placed in a German convent at age eight, she received her schooling there and took vows as a nun. In 1136, she was elected abbess of the convent. Shortly thereafter, very abruptly, she began to write and to preach. She was probably the only woman authorized by the church to preach in her day.

Writing and preaching were the sudden external manifestations of an inner life that had been extraordinary from the beginning. Even as a child, Hildegard had experienced visions—of invisible things, of the future, and (always) of a special kind of light. These visions were intermingled with pain and sickness. Only in her forties did Hildegard interpret her sickness and her visions as gifts from God. In her *Scivias* ("Know the Ways of the Lord," 1151), Hildegard described some of her visions and explained their meaning. She interpreted them as containing nothing less than the full story of creation and redemption, a summa, or compendium, of church doctrine.

Benedictine Monks and Artistic Splendor

Hildegard's contentment within the confines of her cloister was characteristic of many. Known as "black monks"—so called because they dyed their robes black—the Benedictines reached the height of their popularity in the eleventh century. Monasteries often housed hundreds of monks; convents for nuns were usually less populated. Cluny was one of the largest monasteries, with some four hundred brothers in the mid-eleventh century.

The chief occupation of the monks, as befitted (in their view) citizens of heaven, was prayer. The black monks and nuns devoted themselves to singing Psalms and other prayers specified in the rule of St. Benedict, adding to them still more Psalms. The rule called for chanting the entire Psalter—150 psalms—over the course of a week, but some monks, like those at Cluny, chanted that number in a day. Such prayer was neither private nor silent. Black monks had to know not only the words but also the music that went with their prayers; they had to be

■ **Eve**

The Romanesque sculptor of this depiction of Eve delighted in her sinuous curves, which he portrayed as a continuation of the snake from which Eve accepted the apple. Compare this seductive view of Eve with the motherly Eve on page 294. Sculptural figures such as this one, which once adorned the church at Autun, France, were typical of the inventive variety of the Romanesque style. (© Musée Rolin, Autun, France/Peter Willi/SuperStock.)

musicians. The music of the Benedictine monastery was plainchant, also known as Gregorian chant, which consisted of melodies, each sung in unison, without accompaniment. Although chant was rhythmically free, lacking a regular beat, its melodies ranged from extremely simple to highly ornate and embellished. By the twelfth century, a large repertoire of melodies had grown up—at first through oral composition and transmission and then in written notation, which was first invented in the ninth century.

The **Romanesque** church (so called because its round arches and other architectural elements reminded modern art historians of Roman buildings) was the place in which black monks spent most of their day chanting the psalms. It was ideally quite large, finely decorated with inventive sculpture and wall paintings, and built of stone. The various parts of the church—the chapels in the *chevet*, or apse (at the east end of the building), for example—were treated as discrete units, retaining the forms of cubes, cones, and cylinders (Figure 9.1).

In such a setting, gilded reliquaries and altars made of silver, precious gems, and pearls were the fitting accoutrements of worship. Prayer, liturgy, and music in this way complemented the gift economy: richly clad in vestments of the finest materials, intoning the liturgy in the most splendid of churches, monks and priests offered up the gift of prayer to God; in return they begged for the gift of salvation of their souls and the souls of all the faithful.

New Monastic Orders of Poverty

Not everyone agreed that such opulence pleased God. At the end of the eleventh century, the new commercial economy and the profit motive that fueled it led many to reject wealth and to embrace poverty as a key element of religious life. The Carthusian order founded by Bruno of Cologne was one such group. Each monk took a vow of silence and lived as a hermit in his own small hut. Monks occasionally joined others for prayer in a common prayer room, or oratory. When not engaged in prayer or meditation, the Carthusians copied manuscripts. They considered this task part of their religious vocation, a way to preach God's word with their hands rather than their mouths. The Carthusian order grew slowly. Each monastery was limited to only twelve monks, the number of the Apostles.

The Cistercians, by contrast, expanded rapidly. Rejecting even the conceit of blackening their robes, they left them the original color of wool (hence their nickname, "white monks"). The Cistercian order began as a single monastery, Cîteaux (in Latin, *Cistercium*) in France, founded in 1098. It grew rapidly under the leadership of St. Bernard (c. 1090–1153), abbot of the important Cistercian monastery Clairvaux. Despite the Cistercian order's official repudiation of female houses,

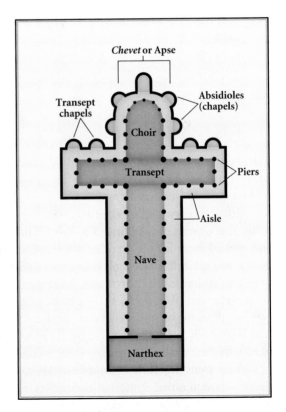

■ FIGURE 9.1 Floor Plan of a Romanesque Church
As churchgoers entered a Romanesque church, they passed through the narthex, an anteroom decorated with sculptured depictions of important scenes from the Bible. Walking through the portal of the narthex, they entered the church's nave, at the east end of which—just after the crossing of the transept and in front of the choir—was the altar, the focus of the Mass. Walking down the nave, they passed massive and tall piers leading up to the vaulting (the roof) of the nave. Each of these piers was decorated with sculpture, and the walls were brightly painted. Romanesque churches were both lively and colorful (because of their decoration) and solemn and somber (because of their heavy stones and massive scale).

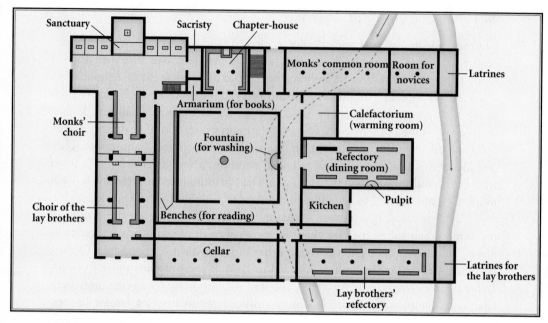

■ FIGURE 9.2 Floor Plan of a Cistercian Monastery
Cistercian monasteries seldom deviated much from this standard plan, which perfectly suited their double lifestyle: one half for the lay brothers, who worked in the fields, the other half for the monks, who performed the prayers. This plan shows the first floor. Above were dormitories: the lay brothers slept above their cellar and refectory; the monks slept above their chapter-house (where the rule of St. Benedict was read to them), common room, and room for novices. No one had a private bedroom, just as the rule prescribed.

many convents followed its lead and adopted its customs. Women were as eager as men to live the life of simplicity and poverty that they believed the Apostles had enjoyed and endured.

Although they held up the rule of St. Benedict as the foundation of their customs, the Cistercians elaborated a style of life all their own, largely governed by the goal of simplicity. Cistercian churches, though built of stone, were initially unlike the great Romanesque churches of the Benedictines. They were remarkably standardized; the church and the rest of the buildings of any one Cistercian monastery were almost exactly like those of any other (Figure 9.2). The churches were small, made of smoothly hewn, undecorated stone. Wall paintings and sculpture were prohibited. Illuminated by the pure white light that came through clear glass windows, Cistercian houses were luminous, cool, and serene.

There were two sorts of white monks: *conversi* or "lay brothers" toiled in the fields; "choir monks" dedicated themselves to private prayer and contemplation and to monastic administration. By the end of the twelfth century, the Cistercians had a closely monitored network of houses, and each year the Cistercian abbots met to hammer out legislation for all of them. The abbot of the mother house (or founding house) visited the daughter houses annually to make sure the legislation was being followed. Each house, whether mother or daughter, had large and highly organized farms and grazing lands called granges. Cistercian monks spent much of their time managing their estates and flocks, both of which were yielding handsome profits by the end of the twelfth century. Clearly part of the agricultural and commercial revolutions of the Middle Ages, the Cistercian order made managerial expertise a part of the monastic life.

At the same time, the Cistercians elaborated a spirituality of intense personal emotion. As Bernard said:

> *Often enough when we approach the altar to pray our hearts are dry and luke-warm. But if we persevere, there comes an unexpected infusion of grace, our breast expands as it were, and our interior is filled with an overflowing love.*

The Cistercians emphasized not only human emotion but also Christ's and Mary's humanity. While pilgrims continued to stream to the tombs and reliquaries of saints, the Cistercians dedicated all their churches to the Virgin Mary (for whom they had no relics) because for them she signified the model of a loving mother. Indeed, the Cistercians regularly used maternal imagery (as Bernard's description invoking the metaphor of a flowing breast illustrates) to describe the nurturing care provided to humans by Jesus himself. The Cistercians' God was approachable, human, protective, even mothering.

Similar views of God were held by many who were not members of the Cistercian order; their spirituality signaled wider changes. For example, around 1099, St. Anselm wrote a theological treatise entitled *Why God Became Man*, in which he argued that since man had sinned, only a sinless man could redeem him. St. Anselm's work represented a new theological focus on the redemptive power of human charity, including that of Jesus as a human being.

Religious Fervor and Dissent

The emphasis on a common humanity in Christ beckoned to men and women of every age and every walk of life. Fervent piety spread beyond the convent, punctuating the routines of daily life with scriptural reading, fasting, and charity. The new religious groups of the late twelfth century embraced urban populations. Rich and poor, male and female joined these movements. Many criticized the existing church as too wealthy, ritualistic, and impersonal. Intensely and personally focused on the life of Christ, men and women in the late twelfth century made his childhood, agony, death, and presence in the Eucharist—the bread and wine that became the body and blood of Christ in the Mass—the most important experiences of their own lives. Some of this intense religious response developed into official, orthodox movements within

■ **St.-Savin-sur-Gartempe**

The nave of the church of St.-Savin was built between 1095 and 1115. Its barrel (or tunnel) vault is typical of Romanesque churches, as is its sense of liveliness, variety, and color. The columns, decorated with striped or wavy patterns, are topped by carved capitals, each one different from the next. The entire vault is covered with frescoes painted in shades of brown, ocher, and yellow depicting scenes from the Old Testament. What were the purposes of such decorations?

(Bridgeman-Giraudon/Art Resource, NY.)

■ **Eberbech**

Compare the nave of Eberbech, a Cistercian church built between 1170 and 1186, with the nave of St.-Savin. What at St.-Savin appears full of variety and color is here subdued by order and calm. There are no wall paintings in a Cistercian church, no variegated columns— nothing that might distract the worshiper. Yet a close look reveals subtle points of interest. How has the architect played with angles, planes, and light in the vaulting? Are the walls utterly smooth? What decorative elements can you see on the massive piers between the arches?

(AKG London/Stefan Drechsel.)

the church; other religious movements so threatened established doctrine that church leaders declared them heretical.

St. Francis (c. 1182–1226) founded the most famous orthodox religious movement—the Franciscans. Francis was a child of the commercial revolution. Expected to follow his well-to-do father in the cloth trade at Assisi in Italy, Francis experienced doubts, dreams, and illnesses, which spurred him to religious self-examination. In time, he renounced his family's wealth, dramatically marking the decision by casting off all his clothes and standing naked before his father, a crowd of spectators, and the bishop of Assisi. Francis then put on a simple robe and went about preaching penance to anyone who would listen. Adopting the life of a mendicant (one who begs for his livelihood), he accepted no money (only hospitality), walked without shoes, wore only one coarse tunic, and refused to be cloistered. Intending to follow the model of Christ, he received, as his biographers put it, a miraculous gift of grace: the stigmata, bleeding sores corresponding to the wounds Christ suffered on the cross.

By all accounts Francis was a spellbinding speaker, and he attracted many followers. Recognized as a religious order by the pope, the Brothers of St. Francis (or **friars**, from the Latin term for "brothers") spent their time preaching, ministering to lepers, and doing manual labor. Eventually they dispersed, setting up fraternal groups throughout Italy and then in France, Spain, the Holy Land, Germany, and England. Unlike Bruno of Cologne and the Cistercians, who had rejected cities, the friars sought town life, preaching to urban crowds and begging for their daily bread. St. Francis converted both men and women. In 1212, a young noblewoman named Clare formed the nucleus of a community of pious women, which became the Order of the Sisters of St. Francis. At first the women worked alongside the friars; but the church disapproved of their activities in the world, and soon Franciscan sisters were confined to cloisters under the rule of St. Benedict.

Clare was one of many women who sought a new kind of religious expression. In northern Europe at the end of the twelfth century, laywomen who lived together in informal pious communities were called Beguines. Without permanent vows or an established rule, the Beguines chose to be celibate (though they were free to leave and marry) and often made their living by weaving cloth or working with the sick and old. Although their daily occupations were ordinary, the Beguines' private, internal lives were often emotional and ecstatic, infused with the combined imagery of love and religion so pervasive in both monasteries and courts. One renowned Beguine, Mary of Oignies (1177–1213), who like St. Francis was said to have received the very wounds of Christ (the stigmata), felt herself to be a pious mother entrusted with the Christ child. As her biographer, Jacques de Vitry, wrote:

> *Sometimes it seemed to her that for three or more days she held [Christ] close to her so that He nestled between her breasts like a baby, and she hid Him there lest He be seen by others.*

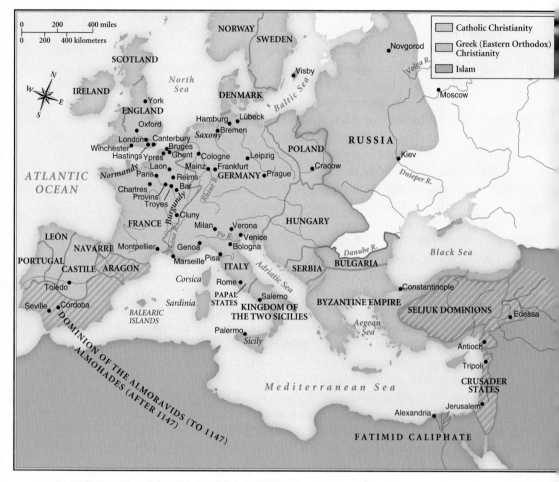

■ MAPPING THE WEST Major Religions in the West, c. 1200

The broad washes of color on this map tell a striking story: by 1150, there were three major religions, each corresponding to a broad region. To the west, north of the Mediterranean Sea, Catholic Christianity held sway; to the east, the Greek Orthodox church was ascendent; all along the southern Mediterranean, Islam triumphed. Only a few places defied this logic: one was the crusader states, a tiny outpost of Catholics who ruled over a largely Muslim population. What this map does not show, however, are the details: Jewish communities in many cities; lively varieties of Islamic beliefs within the Muslim world; communities of Coptic Christians in Egypt; and scattered groups of heretics in Catholic lands. **For more help analyzing this map,** see the map activity for this chapter in the ONLINE STUDY GUIDE at bedfordstmartins.com/huntconcise.

More hardheaded was St. Dominic (1170–1221), founder of an order of friars—the Dominicans—that was patterned very closely on the Franciscans. Like Francis, Dominic and his followers rejected material riches and instead went about on foot, preaching and begging. Their initial audience was not the men and women of the Italian cities, however, but rather the people of southern France, where new doctrines that contradicted those officially accepted by the church—and were therefore labeled "heretical"—had become very popular.

Dominic and his friars were responding to an unprecedented explosion of heresies, part of the ferment of ideas and experiments in social life that were characteristic of medieval city growth. Among the most visible of the heretics were dualists, who saw the world torn between two great forces—one good, the other evil. Dualism became a prominent ingredient in religious life in Italy and the Rhineland by the end of the twelfth century. Another center of dualism was Languedoc, an area of southern France; there the dualists were called Albigensians, a name derived from the Languedoc town of Albi.

Described collectively as Cathars, or "Pure Ones," these dualists believed that the devil had created the material world. Therefore they renounced the world, abjuring wealth, sex, and meat. Their repudiation of sex reflected some of the attitudes of eleventh-century church reformers (whose orthodoxy, however, was never in doubt); their rejection of wealth echoed the same concerns that moved Bruno of Cologne to abandon city life and St. Francis to embrace poverty. In many ways the dualists simply took these attitudes to an extreme; but unlike orthodox reformers, they also challenged the efficacy and value of the church hierarchy. Cathars considered themselves followers of Christ's original message. But the church called them heretics.

The church also condemned other, nondualist groups as heretical, not on doctrinal grounds but because these groups allowed their lay members to preach, challenging the authority of the church hierarchy. In Lyon (in southeastern France) in the 1170s, for example, a rich merchant named Waldo decided to take literally the Gospel message "If you wish to be perfect, then go and sell everything you have, and give to the poor" (Matt. 19:21). The same message had inspired countless monks and would worry the church far less several decades later, when St. Francis established his new order. But when Waldo went into the street and gave away his belongings, announcing, "I am not really insane, as you think," he scandalized not only the bystanders but the church as well. Refusing to retire to a monastery, Waldo and his followers, men and women called Waldensians, lived in poverty and went about preaching, quoting the Gospel in the vernacular so that everyone would understand. But the papacy rebuffed Waldo's bid to preach freely, and the Waldensians—denounced, excommunicated, and expelled from Lyon—wandered to Languedoc, Italy, northern Spain, and the Moselle valley (in Germany).

■ **REVIEW:** *How and to what degree was religious life and thought influenced by the new learning of the schools?*

IMPORTANT DATES			
1054	Great Schism between Roman Catholic and Greek Orthodox churches	c. 1122	Abelard writes *Sic et Non*
		1139–1153	Civil war in England
1066	Norman conquest of England; battle of Hastings	c. 1140	Gratian's *Decretum* published
		1151	Hildegard of Bingen's *Scivias* published
1077	Emperor Henry IV does penance before Pope Gregory VII at Canossa		
		1152–1190	Reign of Emperor Frederick Barbarossa
1086	Domesday survey commissioned by William I of England	1154–1189	Reign of Henry II of England
		1176	Battle of Legnano; Frederick Barbarossa defeated in northern Italy
c. 1090–1153	Life of St. Bernard, leader of Cistercian order		
1095	Urban II preaches the First Crusade at Clermont	1182–1226	Life of St. Francis
1122	Concordat of Worms ends the Investiture Conflict		

Conclusion

The commercial revolution and the building boom it spurred profoundly changed the look of Europe. Thriving cities of merchants and artisans brought trade, new wealth, and new institutions to the West. Mutual and fraternal organizations like the commune, the compagnia, and the guilds expressed and reinforced the solidarity and economic interest of city dwellers.

Political consolidation accompanied economic growth, as kings and popes exerted their authority and tested its limits. The Gregorian reform pitted the emperor against the pope, and two separate political hierarchies emerged: the secular and the ecclesiastical. The two might cooperate, as Suger and Louis VI showed in their mutual respect, admiration, and dependence. But they might also clash, as Becket did with Henry II. Secular and religious leaders developed new and largely separate systems of administration, reflecting in political life the new distinctions that separated clergy from laity, such as clerical celibacy and allegiance to the pope. Although in some ways growing apart, the two groups never worked together so closely as in the crusades, military pilgrimages inspired by the pope and led by lay lords.

The commercial economy, political stability, and ecclesiastical needs fostered the growth of schools and the achievements of new scholarship. Young men sought learning to enhance their careers and bring personal fulfillment; women gained excellent educations in convents. Logic fascinated some students because it seemed to clarify the nature of both the world and God. But others, such as St. Bernard, felt that faith could not be analyzed.

While Benedictine monks added to their hours of worship, built lavish churches, and devoted themselves to the music of the plainchant, the white monks insisted on an intense, interior spiritual life in a monastery shorn of decoration. Other reformers, such as Bruno of Cologne, sought isolation and hardship. These reformers repudiated urban society yet unintentionally reflected it: the Cistercians were as anxious as any tradesman about the success of their granges, and the Carthusians were dedicated to their books. With the Franciscans and Dominicans—as well as heretical groups such as the Cathars—laypeople were drawn to participate actively in a deeply felt imitation of Christ's life and sufferings. Yet this new piety, paired with new power, contributed to the persecution of Jews and the periodic call for Crusades against the Muslims.

■ MAKING CONNECTIONS

1. *What were the similarities and differences between the powers wielded by the Carolingian kings and those wielded by twelfth-century rulers?*

2. *Contrast the purposes and the institutions of the gift economy discussed in Chapter 8 with those of the new profit economy.*

■ FOR FURTHER EXPLORATION

For further reading and online research ideas, see the Suggested References on page SR-5 at the back of the book.

For practice quizzes, a customized study plan, and other study tools, see the ONLINE STUDY GUIDE at bedfordstmartins.com/huntconcise.

For primary-source material from this period, see Chapter 9 in *Sources of THE MAKING OF THE WEST: A CONCISE HISTORY*, Second Edition.

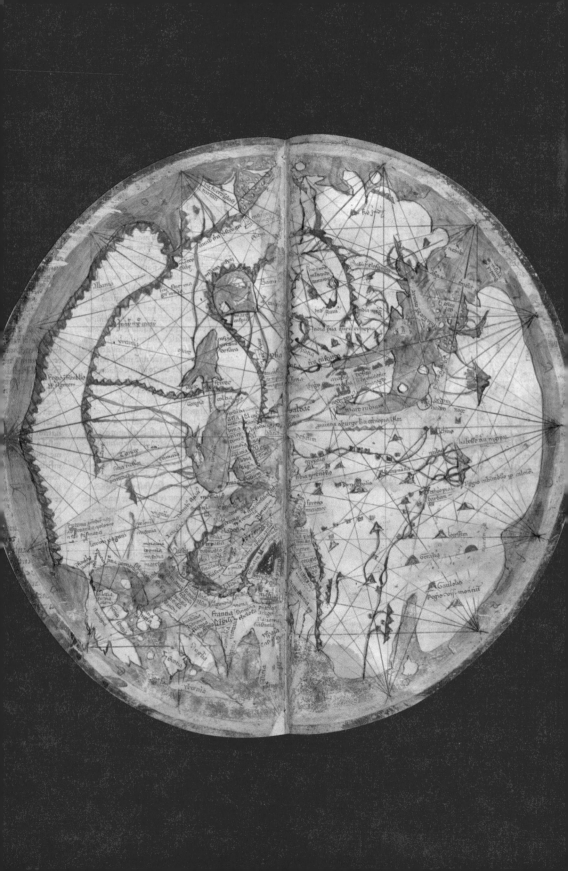

10

An Age of Confidence

1200–1340

I N ABOUT 1220, CHINGIZ KHAN (c. 1162–1227), leader of a confederation of horseback warriors in Mongolia, conquered northern China. By 1240, his successors had conquered Russia and were attacking Poland and Hungary. Europeans were galvanized. Some considered the Mongols a new incarnation of the Devil. Others looked forward to converting the newcomers to Christianity and hoped for new ports of call for their ships, caravans, and traders. The brothers Niccolò and Maffeo Polo, merchants from Venice, were among the first Western adventurers who saw an opportunity to make a profit. According to Niccolò's son Marco, early in their travels the brothers met the Mongol ruler of the Volga region in Russia, "gave him all the jewels they had brought; and [the ruler] took [the jewels] willingly . . . and gave them goods of fully twice the value in return." After making a tidy profit, the brothers moved on, eventually finding their way to China. On a second trip, they brought with them the young Marco, whose later account of his travels dazzled his contemporaries.

Niccolò and Maffeo's fearless self-confidence in the face of the "inhuman Tartars," as Pope Alexander IV called the Mongols in 1260, was characteristic of an age in which participants in emerging institutions of government, commerce, and religion were unafraid to assert themselves, their rights, and their interests. In the

■ **Pietro Vesconte's World Map (c. 1320)**
The Polo brothers knew perfectly well how to travel from Venice to China, but not because they were guided by maps. Most of the maps available in their day were symbolic rather than accurate. Pietro Vesconte's world map is partly in that old style. But it also shows a growing interest in precision. Note, for example, the "rhumb lines" that crisscross the map. These were carefully constructed as a series of equidistant spokes radiating from a point, each indicating a wind direction. Vesconte was here copying "portolan charts"—the most scientific maps of his day—which gave accurate indications of land and water shapes to help sailors navigate. (By permission of the British Library.)

thirteenth century, merchants, kings, princes, popes, city dwellers, and even heretics were acutely conscious of themselves as individuals and as members of like-minded groups with identifiable objectives and plans to promote and perpetuate their aims. Staffs of literate government officials now preserved official documents and other important papers; lords calculated their profits with the help of accountants; craft guilds and religious associations defined and regulated their membership with increased precision.

The period 1200–1340 was characterized by confidence bolstered by new organizations and institutions. Well-prepared rulers exercised control over whole territories through organs of government that could—if need be—function without them. As monarchs gained power, so, too, did the popes, and this period witnessed the height of the medieval church. In the cultural arena, vernacular poets wrote literature of astonishing beauty and increasing complexity and sophistication. Musicians, like poets, developed forms that bridged sacred and secular subjects, and Gothic churches sprang up in cities throughout Europe, dazzling observers with their light-filled expression of a universe of order and harmony.

With greater confidence and more clearly defined group and individual identities came conflict as well as unity. Kings and popes disputed about the limits of their power, while theologians fought over the place of reason in matters of faith. The church created tribunals of inquisition to root out religious dissidents, and kings and other rulers extended their influence over their subjects. Yet these tribunals did not end heresy, and kings did not gain all the power that they wanted. Diversity and opposition continually threatened expectations of harmony and order.

War, Conquest, and Settlement

In the thirteenth and early fourteenth centuries, Europeans aggressively moved outward in nearly all directions. While one group of armies pushed north and east on the Baltic coast, another was attacking Constantinople itself, while still a third was pursuing the *reconquista* of Spain. In the south of France and in Sicily, crusaders, with the pope's blessing, waged war against people whom the church declared to be heretics, including a Christian king. Far beyond Europe's eastern fringes, merchants like Marco Polo traveled to and settled in lands ruled by the Mongols.

 The Northern Crusades

Long before the twelfth century, the peoples living along the Baltic coast—partly pagan, mostly Slavic- or Baltic-speaking—had learned to glean a living and a profit from the inhospitable soil and climate. Through fishing and trading, they supplied the rest of Europe and Russia with slaves, furs, amber, wax, and dried fish. Like the Vikings, they combined commercial competition with outright raiding. The Danes and the Saxons (that is, the Germans in Saxony) both benefited and suffered from their presence.

When St. Bernard began to preach the Second Crusade in Germany, he discovered that the Germans were indeed eager to attack the infidels—the ones right next door to them. St. Bernard pressed the pope to add these northern heathens to the list of those against whom holy war should be launched, and he urged their conversion or extermination. Thus began the Northern Crusades, which continued intermittently until the early fifteenth century.

The king of Denmark and the duke of Saxony launched the first phase of the Northern Crusades. Their initial attacks were uncoordinated—in some instances they even fought each other. Then, in key raids in the 1160s and 1170s, the two leaders worked together briefly to bring much of the region west of the Oder River under their control. They took some land outright—the Saxon duke apportioned conquered territory to his followers, for example—but more often the Slavic princes surrendered and had their territories reinstated once they became vassals of the Christian rulers.

In 1198, Pope Innocent III (r. 1198–1216) declared a crusade against the Livs, even farther to the north and east. A military order—the Order of Sword Brothers, later supplanted by the Teutonic Knights—was set up to lead crusading armies, and a bishopric, the "see of Riga," was established at the mouth of the Dvina River. The native populations were obliged to submit, whether by material inducements (the crusaders helped the Livs raid the Estonians, for example) or by sheer force. Repeatedly they agreed to truce and baptism, and just as repeatedly they rebelled. In some areas, the crusaders resorted to scorched-earth tactics. By 1300, they had secured Livonia, Prussia, Estonia, and Finland. Only Lithuania managed to resist conquest and conversion (see Map 10.1 on page 388).

Though less well known than the crusades to the Holy Land, the Northern Crusades had far more lasting effects: they settled the Baltic region with German-speaking lords and peasants, and they forged a permanent relationship between the very north of Europe and its neighbors to the south and west. With the Baltic dotted with churches and monasteries and its peoples dipped into baptismal waters, the region would gradually adopt the institutions of western medieval society—cities, guilds, universities, castles, and manors.

The Capture of Constantinople

Four years after calling for the crusade against the Livs, Pope Innocent III declared the Fourth Crusade (1202–1204) to the Holy Land. He hoped to reverse the failures of the Second and Third Crusades, but attitudes and circumstances beyond his control took over the new enterprise. Prejudices, religious zeal, and self-confidence had become characteristic of western European dealings with the Byzantine Greeks.

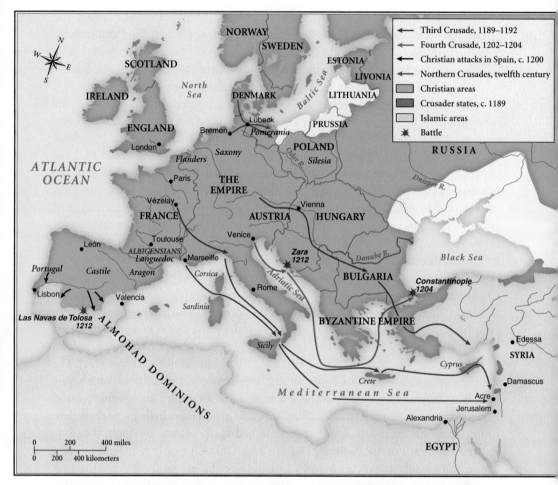

■ **MAP 10.1 Crusades and Anti-Heretic Campaigns, 1150–1204**
Europeans aggressively expanded their territory during the second half of the twelfth century. To the north, German knights pushed into the lands bordering the Baltic Sea; to the south, Spanish warriors moved into most of Islamic Iberia; to the east, new crusades were undertaken to shore up the tiny European outpost in the Holy Land. Although most of these aggressive activities had the establishment of Christianity as at least one motive, the conquest of Constantinople in 1204 had no such justification. It occurred in part because of general European hostility toward Byzantium but mainly because of Venice's commercial ambitions.

These attitudes help explain what happened from 1202 to 1204. The crusading army turned out to be far smaller than had been expected. Its leaders could not pay the Venetians, who had fitted out a large fleet of ships in anticipation of carrying multitudes of warriors across the Mediterranean to Jerusalem. The Venetians seized the opportunity to exact a different form of payment by convincing the crusade's

■ Innocent III

Pope Innocent III appears young, aristocratic, and impassive in this thirteenth-century fresco in the lower church of Sacro Speco, Subiaco, about thirty miles east of Rome and not far from Innocent's birthplace. Innocent claimed full power over the whole church, in any region. Moreover, he thought the pope had the right to intervene in any issue where sin might be involved—and that meant most matters. Although these were only theoretical claims, difficult to put into practice given his meager resources and inefficient staff, Innocent was a major force through his calls for crusade and through the Fourth Lateran Council, which set the standard for Catholic belief and worship. (Scala/Art Resource, NY.)

leaders to attack Zara, a Christian city that was Venice's competitor in the Adriatic (see Map 10.1). The Venetians then turned their sights toward Constantinople, hoping to control it and gain a commercial monopoly there. They persuaded the crusaders to join them on behalf of Alexius, a member of the ousted imperial family. Alexius claimed the Byzantine throne and promised the crusaders that he would reunite the eastern with the western church and fund the expedition to the Holy Land. Most of the crusaders convinced themselves that the cause was noble. "Never," wrote a contemporary, "was so great an enterprise undertaken by any people since the creation of the world."

The siege of Constantinople lasted nearly a year. Finally, on April 12, 1204, the city fell to the crusaders. Their deal with Alexius had broken down, and the crusaders brutally sacked Constantinople, killing residents and plundering treasure and relics. When one crusader discovered a cache of relics, a chronicler recalled, "he plunged both hands in and, girding up his loins, he filled the folds of his gown with the holy booty of the Church." The loss of that "holy booty" was, for the Byzantines, a great tragedy. The bishop of Ephesus wrote:

> *And so the streets, squares, houses of two and three stories, sacred places, nunneries, houses for nuns and monks, sacred churches, even the Great Church of God and the imperial palace, were filled with men of the enemy, all of them*

*maddened by war and murderous in spirit. . . . [T]hey tore children from their
mothers and mothers from their children, and they defiled the virgins in the
holy chapels, fearing neither God's anger nor man's vengeance.*

Pope Innocent decried the looting of Constantinople but also took advantage
of it, ordering the crusaders to stay there for a year to consolidate their gains.
The crusade leaders chose one of themselves—Baldwin of Flanders—to be
Byzantine emperor, and he, the other princes, and the Venetians parceled out the
empire among themselves. This new Latin empire of Constantinople lasted until
1261, when the Byzantines recaptured the city and some of its outlying territory. No
longer a strong heir to the Roman Empire, Byzantium in 1204 became overshadowed and hemmed in by the military might of the Muslims and the Europeans.

Popes continued to call crusades to the Holy Land until the mid-fifteenth century,
but the Fourth Crusade marked the last major mobilization of men and leaders.
Working against these expeditions were the new values of the late twelfth century,
which placed a premium on the *interior* pilgrimage of the soul and valued rulers who
stayed home to care for their people. The crusades to the Holy Land served as an outlet for religious fervor, self-confidence, ambition, prejudice, and aggression. But they
had very little lasting positive effect. They managed to stimulate the European economy slightly, and they inspired a vast literature of songs and chronicles. Such achievements must be weighed against the lives lost on both sides and the religious polarization and prejudices that the crusades fed upon and fortified. The bitterest fruit of the
crusades was the destruction of Byzantium. The Latin conquest of Constantinople in
1204 irrevocably weakened the one buffer state standing between Europe and Islam.

The Spanish Reconquista Advances

By 1200, Christian Spain had achieved the political configuration that would last
for centuries: to the east was the kingdom of Aragon; to the west was Portugal;
and in between was Castile, which in 1230 merged with León (see Map 10.2). The
leaders of these kingdoms competed for territory and power, but above all, they
sought an advantage against the Muslims who still ruled a strip of southern Spain.

The reconquista, which had begun against the Muslim *taifas* (small, independent
Muslim states) continued in full force, aided by Muslim disunity. The taifas not only
were in competition with one another but were beset from the south by the Almoravids
and, after 1147, the Almohades, Muslims from North Africa. Claiming religious purity, these Berber groups declared their own holy war against the Andalusians. These
simultaneous threats caused alliances within Spain to be based on political as well as
religious considerations. The Muslim ruler of Valencia, for example, declared himself a
vassal of the king of Castile and bitterly opposed the Berber expansion.

The crusading ideal, however, held no room for such subtleties. During the 1140s,
armies under the command of the Christian kings of Portugal, Castile, and Aragon
scored resounding victories against Muslim cities. Enlisting the aid of crusaders on

■ **MAP 10.2 The Reconquista Triumphs, 1212–1275**

A major turning point in the reconquista *was the battle of Las Navas de Tolosa (1212). This marked not only the defeat of the Muslims but also the triumph of Castile, which had originally been a tributary of León. In the course of the twelfth century, Castile became a power in its own right; in 1230, León and Castile merged into one kingdom. During the thirteenth century, Castile-León (and, to a lesser extent, Portugal and Aragon) conquered most of the rest of the Iberian peninsula, leaving only Granada under Islamic rule.*

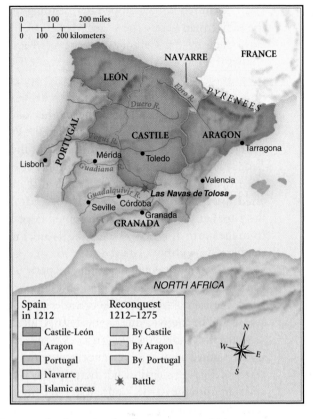

their way to the Holy Land in 1147, the king of Portugal promised land, plunder, and protection to all who would help him attack Muslim-controlled Lisbon. His efforts succeeded, and Lisbon's Muslim inhabitants fled or were slain, its Mozarabic bishop (the bishop of the Christians living under Muslim rule) was killed, and a crusader from England was set up as bishop.

In the 1170s, the Almohades conquered the Muslim south and advanced toward the cities taken by the Christians, but their exertions had no lasting effect. In 1212, a Christian crusading army of Spaniards led by the kings of Aragon and Castile defeated the Almohades decisively at Las Navas de Tolosa. "On their side 100,000 armed men or more fell in the battle," the king of Castile wrote afterward, "but of the army of the Lord . . . incredible though it may be, unless it be a miracle, hardly 25 or 30 Christians of our whole army fell. O what happiness! O what thanksgiving!" The turning point in the reconquista had been reached (Map 10.2). The Almohades continued to lose strength, and Christian armies marched from victory to victory. Mérida fell in 1230. Córdoba was taken six years later, Seville in 1248. All that remained of Muslim-controlled Spain was a thin wedge of territory around Granada.

Putting Down the Heretics in Their Midst

In the thirteenth century, the church and secular powers combined not only to conquer pagans and Muslims on the borders of Europe but also to stamp out heresy in their midst. The papacy declared crusades against the dualist Albigensians of southern France and even against a reigning emperor, Frederick II.

The church initially hoped that sending missionaries to Languedoc would end the Albigensian heresy there (see Map 10.1). But it did not bargain for the impression made by the Catholic preachers, who arrived on horseback, wearing fine clothes and followed by a crowd of servants. These men had no moral leverage with their audience. This was immediately apparent to St. Dominic (1170–1221), founder of the Dominican order. Like his adversaries the Albigensians, Dominic rejected material riches. Instead he and his followers went about on foot, preaching and begging. The Dominicans resembled the Franciscans both organizationally and spiritually; they, too, were called friars. But their first calling was to the heretics of Languedoc rather than to the city dwellers of Italy.

Even with St. Dominic's preachers at the forefront, missionary work was slow and frustrating. In 1208, the murder of a papal legate (an official representative of the pope) in southern France prompted Pope Innocent III to demand that princes from the north of France take up the sword, invade Languedoc, wrest the land from the heretics, and populate it with orthodox Christians. This Albigensian Crusade (1209–1229) marked the first time the pope offered warriors fighting an enemy in Christian Europe all the spiritual and temporal benefits of a crusade to the Holy Land. Innocent suspended the crusaders' monetary debts and promised that their sins would be forgiven after forty days' service.

Like all crusades, the Albigensian Crusade had political as well as religious dimensions. It pitted southern French princes with Cathar connections, like Raymond VI, count of Toulouse, against northern leaders like Simon IV de Montfort l'Amaury, a castellan from the Île-de-France eager to demonstrate his piety and win new possessions. After twenty years of fighting, leadership of the crusade was taken over in 1229 by the Capetian kings of France. Southern resistance was broken, and Languedoc was brought under the French crown.

Meanwhile, the papacy set up the Inquisition in southern France to discover undetected heretics. The **Inquisition** was a legal proceeding. First the inquisitors typically called the people of a district to a "preaching," where they gave a sermon and promised clemency to those who confessed their heresy promptly. Then, at a general inquest, they questioned each man and woman who seemed to know something about heresy: "Have you ever seen any heretics . . . ? Have you heard them preach? Attended any of their ceremonies? Adored heretics?" The judges assigned relatively lenient penalties to those who were not aware that they held heretical beliefs and to heretics who quickly recanted. But unrepentant heretics were punished, because the church believed that such people threatened the salvation of all. Anyone who died while still a heretic could not be buried in consecrated ground. Raymond VII, count of Toulouse, saw the body of his father—who died excommunicated—rot in its coffin as the pope denied all requests for its burial. Houses where heretics had resided or even simply entered were burned, and the sites were turned into garbage dumps. Children of heretics could not inherit any property or become priests, even if they adopted orthodox views.

In the thirteenth century, for the first time, long-term imprisonment became a tool to repress heresy, even if the heretic confessed. "It is our will," wrote one tribunal, "that [Raymond Maurin and Arnalda, his wife,] because they have rashly transgressed against God and holy church . . . be thrust into perpetual prison to do [appropriate] penance, and we command them to remain there in perpetuity." The inquisitors also used imprisonment to force people to recant, to give the names of other heretics, or to admit a plot. Guillaume Agasse, for example, confessed to participating in a wicked (and imaginary) meeting of lepers who planned to poison all the wells. As the quest for religious control spawned wild fantasies of conspiracy, the inquisitors pinned their paranoia on real people.

The Inquisition also created a new group—penitent heretics—who lived on the margins of Christian society. Forced to wear huge yellow fabric crosses sewn on the front and back of their shirts, they were publicly disgraced. Moreover, every Sunday and every feast day penitent heretics had to attend church twice; and during religious processions these men and women were required to join with the clergy and the faithful, carrying large branches in their hands as a sign of their penance. (See "Taking Measure," below.)

One "heretic" was an emperor. Innocent III—the pope who called the Fourth Crusade, the crusade against the Livs, and the Albigensian Crusade—had given the imperial crown to Frederick II (r. 1212–1250). Innocent's successors would rue the day. Like his grandfather Frederick Barbarossa, Frederick II, who was king of Sicily as well as Germany, sought to control Italy. This policy was intolerable to the papacy, which had its own ambitions on the peninsula.

■ TAKING MEASURE
Sentences Imposed by an Inquisitor, 1308–1323

How harsh was the Inquisition? Did its agents regularly burn people alive? How frequently did they imprison people or order them to wear crosses on their clothing? Statistical data to answer these sorts of questions are normally lacking for the medieval period. But there are exceptions. One comes from a register of offenses and punishments kept by the Languedocian inquisitor Bernard Gui from 1308 to 1323. Of 633 punishments handed down by Gui's tribunal, only a relatively small number of people were burned alive. (Those "burned posthumously" would have been burned alive, but they died before that could happen.) Nearly half of

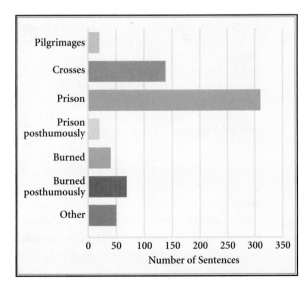

the guilty were sentenced to prison, usually for life. (Some were sent to prison posthumously—that is, they would have gone to prison had they not died in the meantime.) Many historians conclude that the Inquisition was not particularly harsh, for capital punishment at the time was regularly meted out to criminals under secular law.

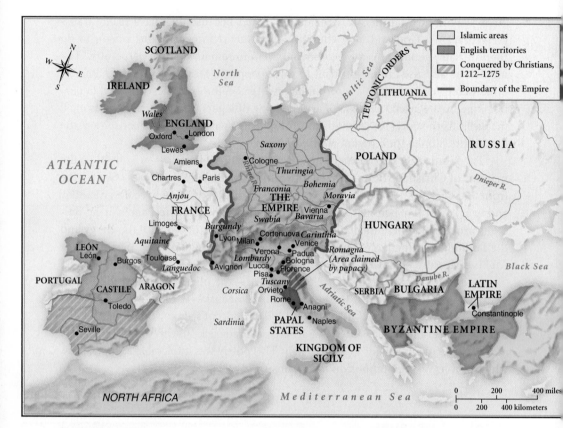

■ MAP 10.3 Europe in the Time of Frederick II, r. 1212–1250

King of Sicily and Germany and emperor as well, Frederick ruled over territory that encircled—and threatened—the papacy. Excommunicated several times, Frederick spent much of his career fighting the pope's forces. In the process, he conceded so many powers to the German princes that the emperor thenceforth had little power in Germany. Meanwhile, rulers of smaller states, such as England, France, and Castile-León, were increasing their power and authority. **For more help analyzing this map,** see the map activity for this chapter in the ONLINE STUDY GUIDE at bedfordstmartins.com/huntconcise.

Frederick was an amazing ruler: *stupor mundisli* —"wonder of the world"—his contemporaries called him. Heir to two cultures, Sicilian on his mother's side and German on his father's, he cut a worldly and sophisticated figure. In Sicily, he moved easily within a diverse culture of Jews, Muslims, and Christians. There he could play the role of all-powerful ruler. In Germany, where Christian princes—often churchmen with military retinues—were acutely aware of their rights and privileges, he was less at home.

Frederick had a three-pronged imperial strategy. First, to ensure that opponents in Germany would not hound him, he granted the princes important concessions, finalized in 1232. These privileges allowed the German princes to turn their principalities into virtually independent states. Second, Frederick revamped the government of Sicily to give himself more control and yield greater profits. His *Constitutions of Melfi* (1231), an eclectic body of laws, called for nearly all court cases to be heard by royal courts, regularized commercial privileges, and set up a system of taxation. Third, Frederick sought to enter Italy through Lombardy, as his grandfather had done (Map 10.3).

The papacy followed Frederick's every move, excommunicating the emperor a number of times. The most serious of these came in 1245, when the pope and other churchmen, assembled at the Council of Lyon, excommunicated and deposed Frederick, absolving his vassals and subjects of their fealty to him and, indeed, forbidding anyone to support him. "He has deservedly become suspect of heresy," the council intoned, explaining that "he has despised and continues to despise the keys of the church [the symbol of St. Peter and thus of the pope], causing the sacred rites to be celebrated or rather . . . to be profaned. . . . Besides, he is joined in odious friendship with the Saracens [Muslims]." By 1248, papal legates were preaching a crusade against Frederick and all his followers. Two years later, Frederick died.

The fact that Frederick's vision of the empire failed is of less long-term importance than the way it failed. His concessions to the German princes meant that Germany would remain divided under numerous regional princes until the nineteenth century. Between 1254 and 1273, the princes kept the German throne empty. Splintered into factions, they elected two different foreigners, who spent their time fighting each other. In one of history's strange twists, it was during this low point of the German monarchy that the term *Holy Roman Empire* was coined. In 1273, the princes at last united and elected a German, Rudolph (r. 1273–1291), whose family, the Habsburgs, was new to imperial power. Rudolf used the imperial title to help him gain Austria for his dynasty, but he did not try to fulfill the meaning of the imperial title in Italy. For the first time, the word *emperor* was freed from its association with Italy and Rome. For the Habsburgs, the title Holy Roman Emperor was prestigious but otherwise meaningless. In 1356 the reigning emperor published the Golden Bull—so called because of its golden seal—which delared the seven German princes who henceforth were to be the electors of the emperor. They included three churchmen (the archbishop of Mainz was one) and four laymen (for example, the duke of Saxony). The office of "king of the Romans"—

Italy at the End of the Thirteenth Century

as the Bull called the emperor—was completely divorced from papal power, and Germany was henceforth to be ruled by the princes.

As for Italy, Frederick's failure meant that the cities of northern Italy would continue their independent course, while the papacy ensured that the heirs of Frederick would not continue to rule in Sicily. The popes called successively on other rulers to take over the island—first Henry III of England and then Charles of Anjou. Forces loyal to Frederick's family turned to the king of Aragon (Spain). That move left two enduring claimants to Sicily's crown: the kings of Aragon and the house of Anjou. And it spawned a long war impoverishing the region.

In the struggle between pope and emperor, the pope had clearly won. The moment marked a high point in the political power of the medieval papacy. Nevertheless, some agreed with Frederick II's view that by tampering with secular matters the popes had demeaned and sullied their office: "These men who feign holiness," Frederick sneered, referring to the popes, are "drunk with the pleasures of the world." Scattered throughout Germany were people who believed that Frederick was a divine scourge sent to overpower a materialistic papacy. The papacy won the war against Frederick, but at a cost. Even the king of France criticized the popes for doing "new and unheard of things." By making its war against Frederick part of its crusade against heresy, the papacy came under attack for using religion as a political tool.

The Mongol Takeover

Europeans were not the only warring society in the thirteenth century: to the east, the Mongols (sometimes called Tatars or Tartars) created an aggressive army under the leadership of Chingiz Khan and his sons. In part, economic necessity impelled them out of Mongolia: climatic change had reduced the grasslands that sustained their animals and their nomadic way of life. But they were also inspired by Chingiz's hope of conquering the world. In the 1230s, the Mongols began concerted attacks in Europe—in Russia, Poland, and Hungary—where weak native princes were no match for the Mongols' formidable armies and tactics. Only the death of their Great Khan, Chingiz's son Ogodei (1186–1241)—styled the *khagan*, or khan of khans—and disputes over his succession prevented a concentrated assault on Germany. In the 1250s, the Mongols took Iran, Baghdad, and Damascus.

The Mongols' sophisticated and devastating military tactics contributed to their overwhelming success. Organizing their campaigns at meetings held far in advance of a planned attack, they devised two- and three-flank operations. The invasion of Hungary, for example, was two-pronged: one division of the Mongol army arrived from Russia while the other moved through Poland and Germany. Many Hungarians perished in the assault as the Mongols, fighting mainly on horseback and wielding heavy lances and powerful bows whose arrows traveled far and penetrated deeply, crushed the Hungarian force of mixed infantry and cavalry (Map 10.4).

The Mongols' attacks on Russia had the most lasting impact. At Vladimir, in the north, they broke through the walls of the city and burned the people huddled for protection in the cathedral. The Mongols' most important victory in Russia was the capture of Kiev in 1240. Making the mouth of the Volga River the seat of their power in Russia, the Mongols dominated Russia's principalities for about two hundred years.

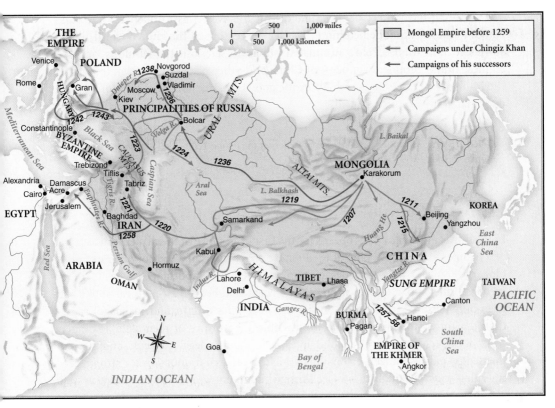

■ **MAP 10.4 The Mongol Invasions to 1259**

The Mongols were the first people to tie the eastern world to the west. Their conquest of China, which took place at about the same time as their invasions of Russia and Iran, opened up trade relations across regions formerly separated by language, religion, and political regimes.

The Mongol Empire in Russia, later called the **Golden Horde** (*golden* probably from the color of their leader's tent; *horde* from a Turkish word meaning "camp"), adopted much of the local government apparatus. The Mongols standardized the collection of taxes and the recruitment of troops by basing them on a population census, and they allowed Russian princes to continue ruling as long as they paid homage and tribute to the khan. Mongol overlords even exempted the Russian church from taxes.

The Mongol invasion changed the political configuration of Europe and Asia. Because the Mongols were willing to deal with westerners such as the Polo family, one effect of their conquests was to open China to Europeans for the first time. For example, an entire community of Venetian traders—women, men, and children—lived in the city of Yangzhou in the mid-fourteenth century. Some missionaries, diplomats, and merchants traveled overland to China; others made the difficult journey from the Persian Gulf (controlled by the Mongols), rounding India before arriving in China.

The long-term effect of the Mongols on the West was to open up new land routes to the East that helped bind together the regions of the known world. Travel stories such as Marco Polo's stimulated others to seek out the fabulous riches— textiles, ginger, ceramics, copper—of China and other places in the East. In a sense, the Mongols initiated the search for exotic goods and missionary opportunities that culminated in the European "discovery" of a new world, the Americas.

■ **REVIEW:** *In what ways did the secular rulers of the period 1200–1340 cooperate with the church? In what ways did they not—and why?*

Politics of Control

In the thirteenth century, Europeans for the first time spoke of their rulers not as kings of a people (for example, king of the Franks) but as kings of a territory (for example, king of France). This new designation reflected an important new element in medieval rulership. However strong earlier rulers had been, their political power had been only personal (depending on ties of kinship, friendship, and vassalage) rather than territorial (touching all who lived within the borders of their state). The new conception, reinforced by renewed interest in Roman legal concepts and supplemented by old-fashioned personal networks, served as a foundation for strong, central rule—most strikingly in western Europe but in central and eastern Europe as well.

France: From Acorn to Oak

Even with the achievements of Louis VI, the French monarchy remained weak, a realm surrounded by powerful neighbors. This changed under Philip Augustus (r. 1180–1223), whose acquisitive policies toward the Jews (see page 358) were matched by his territorial ambitions. When Philip first came to the throne, the royal domain, the Île-de-France, was sandwiched between territory controlled by the counts of Flanders, Champagne, and Anjou. By far the most powerful ruler on the European continent was King Henry II of England, who was both count of Anjou and duke of Normandy and also held the duchy of Aquitaine through his wife while exercising hegemony over Poitou and Brittany.

Henry and the counts of Flanders and Champagne vied to control the young king of

Consolidation of France under Philip Augustus, r. 1180–1223

France. Philip, however, quickly learned to play them off against one another. Contemporaries were astounded when Philip successfully gained territory: he wrested Vermandois and Artois from Flanders in the 1190s and Normandy, Anjou, Maine, Touraine, and Poitou from Henry II's son King John of England in 1204, making good his claim at the decisive battle of Bouvines in 1214.

Pivotal forces led to the extension of the French king's power and the territorial integrity of France. The Second Crusade (1147–1149) had brought together many French lords as vassals of the king and united them against a common foe. The language they spoke was becoming increasingly uniform and "French." Nevertheless, this in itself did not create a larger French kingdom. That came about through royal strategy. Rather than give his new territories out as fiefs, Philip determined to govern them himself.* In Normandy, for example, he demanded that the aristocrats become his vassals, and he sent his officials to collect taxes and hear cases. Philip also instituted a new kind of French administration, based on writing. Before his day, most royal arrangements were committed to memory rather than to parchment. If decrees were written at all, they were saved by the recipient, not by the government. For example, when a monastery wanted a confirmation of its privileges from the king, its own scribes wrote the document for its archives to preserve the monastery against possible future challenges. The king did keep some documents, which generally followed him in his travels like personal possessions. But in 1194, in a battle with the king of England, Philip lost his meager cache of documents along with much treasure when he had to abandon his baggage train. After 1194, the king had all his decrees written down, and he established permanent repositories in which to keep them.

To do the daily work of government, Philip relied on members of the lesser nobility—knights and clerics, many of whom were "masters" educated in the city schools of France. They served as officers of his court; as *prévôts* (provosts), who oversaw the king's estates and collected his taxes; and as *baillis* (bailiffs; *sénéchaux* in the south), who supervised the provosts and functioned as regional judges, presiding over courts that met monthly and making the king's power felt locally as never before.

Under Philip's grandson, Louis IX (r. 1226–1270), the Capetian monarchy reached the height of its prestige if not its power. Louis was revered, not because he was a military leader but because he was an administrator, judge, and "just father" of his people. On warm summer days, he would sit under a tree in the woods near his castle at Vincennes on the outskirts of Paris, hearing disputes and dispensing justice personally. He used his administrators to impose royal law and justice throughout his kingdom. Over the city of Paris he appointed a salaried officer who could be supervised and fired if necessary. During his reign, the influence of the parlement of Paris, the royal court of justice, increased significantly. Originally a changeable and movable body, part of the king's personal entourage when he dealt

---

*Philip was particularly successful in imposing royal control in Normandy; later French kings gave most of the other territories to collateral members of the royal family.

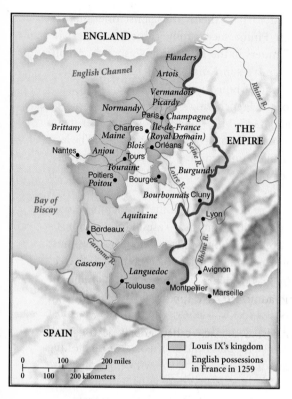

■ **MAP 10.5 France under Louis IX, r. 1226–1270**

Louis IX did not expand his kingdom as dramatically as his grandfather Philip Augustus had done. He was greatly admired nevertheless, for he was seen by contemporaries as a model of Christian charity, piety, and justice. After his death, Louis IX was recognized as a saint and thus posthumously enhanced the prestige of the French monarchy in a new way.

with litigation, it was now permanently housed in Paris and staffed by professional judges who heard cases and recorded their decisions.

Unlike his grandfather Philip Augustus, Louis did not try to expand his territory. He inherited a large kingdom that included Poitou and Languedoc (Map 10.5), and he was content. Although the king of England attacked him continually to try to regain territory lost under Philip Augustus, Louis remained unprovoked. Rather than prolong the fighting, he conceded a bit and made peace in 1259. At the same time, Louis was a zealous crusader. He took seriously the need to defend the Holy Land when most of his contemporaries were weary of the idea.

Louis was respectful of the church and the pope; he accepted limits on his authority in relation to the church and never claimed power over spiritual matters. Nevertheless, Louis vigorously maintained the dignity of the king and his rights. He expected royal and ecclesiastical power to work in harmony, and he refused to let the church dictate how he should use his temporal authority. For example, French bishops wanted royal officers to support the church's sentences of excommunication. But Louis declared that he would authorize his officials to do so only if he were able to judge each case for himself, to see whether the excommunication had been justly pronounced. The bishops refused, but Louis held his ground. Royal and ecclesiastical power would work side by side, neither subservient to the other.

Many modern historians fault Louis for his policies toward the Jews. His hatred of them was well known. He did not exactly advocate violence against them, but he sometimes subjected them to arrest, canceling debts owed to them (but collecting part into the royal treasury) and confiscating their belongings. In 1253, he ordered them to live "by the labor of their hands" or leave France. He meant that they should no longer lend money, in effect taking away their one means of livelihood. Louis's contemporaries did not criticize him for his Jewish policies. If anything, his hatred of Jews enhanced his reputation.

In fact, many of Louis's contemporaries considered him a saint, praising his care for the poor and sick, the pains and penances he inflicted on himself, and his regular participation in church services. In 1297, Pope Boniface VIII canonized him as St. Louis. The result was enormous prestige for the French monarchy. This prestige, joined with the renown of Paris as the center of scholarship and the repute of French courts as the hubs of chivalry, made France the cultural model of Europe.

England: Crisis and Consolidation

What the French king gained the English king lost. Henry II had been very strong, and his son Richard I (r. 1189–1199) was called "Lion-Hearted" for his boldness. Under these men, the English monarchy was omnipresent and rich. Its omnipresence derived largely from its judicial and administrative apparatus. Its wealth came from court fees, income from numerous royal estates both in England and on the continent, taxes from cities, and customary feudal dues (called aids) collected from barons and knights. These aids were paid on such occasions as the knighting of the king's eldest son and the marriage of the king's eldest daughter. Enriched by the commercial economy of the late twelfth century, the English kings encouraged their knights and barons not to serve them personally in battle but instead to pay the king a tax called scutage in lieu of service. The monarchs preferred to hire mercenaries both as troops to fight external enemies and as policemen to enforce the king's will at home.

But Richard died young, and his brother and heir, John (r. 1199–1216), lost badly to Philip Augustus. John was widely disliked by his contemporaries, who accused him of asserting his will in a high-handed way. But to understand John, it is necessary to appreciate how desperate he was to keep his continental possessions. After he lost his northern French territories to Philip, John did everything he could to add to the crown revenues so he could pay for an army to fight the French. He forced his vassals to pay ever-increasing scutages and extorted money in the form of new feudal aids. He compelled the widows of his vassals to marry men of his choosing or pay him a hefty fee if they refused. John's heavy investment in this war effort, however, could not prevent defeat of his army in 1214 at the battle of Bouvines, and this defeat caused discontented English barons to rebel openly against the king. At Runnymede in June 1215, John was forced to agree to the charter of baronial liberties that has come to be called Magna Carta, "Great Charter."

The English barons intended Magna Carta (so named to distinguish it from a smaller charter issued around the same time concerning the royal forests) to be a conservative document defining the "customary" obligations and rights of the

■ John's Seal on Magna Carta

When the rebels at Runnymede got John to assent to their charter, later known as Magna Carta, he did not sign it; he sealed it. From the thirteenth through the fifteenth century, kings, queens, aristocrats, guilds, communes, and many other people at all levels of society used seals to authenticate their charters, or legal documents. The seal itself was made of melted wax or lead, which was dropped onto the document and pressed with a gold or brass matrix carved with an image in the negative. These images reminded the public of the status as well as the name of the sealer. Notice the image that John chose to place on his seal. (© Copyright The Trustees of The British Museum.)

nobility and forbidding the king to break from these customs without consulting his barons. "No widow shall be forced to marry so long as she wishes to live without a husband," it declares, continuing:

> *No scutage or aid shall be imposed in our kingdom unless by common counsel of our kingdom, except for [the customary purposes:] ransoming our person, for making our eldest son a knight, and for once marrying our eldest daughter.*

In its most famous clause, Magna Carta provided that

> *No free man shall be arrested or imprisoned or disseised [deprived of his property] or outlawed or exiled or in any way victimized, neither will we attack him or send anyone to attack him, except by the lawful judgment of his peers or by the law of the land.*

Thus Magna Carta established that all free men in the land had certain customs and rights in common and that the king had to uphold those customs and rights. In this way, it documented the subordination of the king to custom; it implied that the king was not above the law. Magna Carta shows that the growth of royal power was matched by the self-confidence of the English barons, certain of their rights and eager to articulate them. Although in the thirteenth century the "free men" of the realm were a tiny elite, in time, as the definition of *free men* expanded to include all the king's subjects, Magna Carta came to be seen as a guarantee of the rights of Englishmen in general.

Papal Monarchy

As the kings of France and England were gaining newly precise roles, so, too, were the popes. Innocent III was the most powerful, respected, and prestigious of the medieval popes. The first pope to be trained at the city schools, Innocent had studied theology at Paris and law at Bologna. From theology, he learned to tease new meaning out of the pope's position: he thought of himself as ruling in the place of Christ the King. In his view, secular kings and emperors existed to help the pope. From law, Innocent gained his conception of the pope as lawmaker and of law as an instrument of moral reformation.

Utilizing the traditional method of declaring church law, Innocent convened and presided over a council in 1215 at the pope's Lateran Palace in Rome. Known as the Fourth Lateran Council, it aimed to reform not only the clergy but also the laity. Innocent and the other assembled churchmen hoped to create a society united under the authority of the church.

For laymen and laywomen, perhaps the most important canons of the Fourth Lateran concerned the sacraments, the rites the church believed Jesus had instituted to confer sanctifying grace. One canon required Christians to attend Mass and confess their sins to a priest at least once a year. At the same time, the council explained with new precision the transformation of bread and wine (the Eucharist) in the Mass. In the twelfth century, a newly rigorous understanding of this transformation had already been publicized, according to which Christ's body and blood were truly contained in the sacrament that looked like bread and wine on the altar. The Fourth Lateran Council not only declared this to be dogma (authoritative) but also explained it by using a technical term coined by twelfth-century scholars. The bread and wine were *transubstantiated*: although the Eucharist continued to *look* like bread and wine, with its consecration during the Mass the bread became the actual flesh and the wine the real blood of Christ. The council's emphasis on this potent event strengthened the role of the priesthood, for only a priest could celebrate this mystery (that is, transform the bread and wine into Christ's body and blood) through which God's grace was transmitted to the faithful.

Innocent III wanted the council to condemn Christian men who had intercourse with Jewish women and then claimed "ignorance" as their excuse. But the council went even further, requiring all Jews to advertise their religion by some outward sign: "We decree that [Jews] of either sex in every Christian province at all times shall be distinguished from other people by the character of their dress in public." Like all church rules, this canon took effect only when local rulers enforced it. In many instances, they did so with zeal, not so much because they were eager to humiliate Jews but rather because they could make money selling exemptions to Jews who were willing to pay to avoid the requirements. Nonetheless, sooner or later Jews almost everywhere had to wear a badge as a sign of their second-class status. In southern France and in a few places in Spain, Jews were supposed to wear round badges. In England, the city of Salisbury demanded that they wear special clothing. In Vienna, they were told to put on pointed hats.

The Fourth Lateran Council's longest decree blasted heretics: "Those condemned as heretics shall be handed over to the secular authorities for punishment." If the secular authority did not "purge his or her land of heretical filth," the heretic was to be excommunicated. If he had vassals, they were to be released from their oaths of fealty, and the heretic's land was to be taken over by orthodox Christians. Rulers heeded these rules. Already some had taken up arms against heretics in the Albigensian Crusade (1209–1229). The Fourth Lateran Council was also responsible for setting up the Inquisition.

The Fourth Lateran was the high-water mark of the medieval papacy. However, the growing prestige and actual jurisdiction of secular rulers changed the balance of power between church and state in the course of the thirteenth century. At the end of that century, when the pope clashed with the kings of France and England, the kings were the clear winners, and the papacy lost both prestige and power.

The clash began over taxing the clergy. The French king Philip IV (r. 1285–1314), known as Philip the Fair, and the English king Edward I (r. 1272–1307) financed their wars (mainly against one another) by taxing the clergy along with everyone else. The new principle of national sovereignty that they were claiming led them to assert jurisdiction over all people, even churchmen, who lived within their borders. For the pope, however, the principle at stake was his role as head of the clergy. In response to clerical taxation, Boniface VIII (r. 1294–1303) declared that only the pope could authorize such taxes. Threatening to excommunicate kings who taxed prelates without papal permission, he called upon clerics to disobey any such royal orders.

Edward and Philip reacted swiftly. Taking advantage of the important role that English courts played in protecting the peace, Edward

■ Boniface VIII

For the sculptor who depicted Pope Boniface VIII, Arnolfo di Cambio (d. 1302), not much had changed since the time of Innocent III. Look at the picture of Innocent on page 389 and compare the two popes: both are depicted as young, majestic, authoritative, sober, and calm. Yet Boniface could not have been very calm, for his authority was challenged at every turn. He was forced to withdraw his opposition to royal taxation of the clergy. He tried to placate the French king, Philip the Fair, by canonizing Philip's grandfather, Louis IX. Even so, Philip arrested the bishop of Pamiers and brought him to trial. When Boniface protested, he was proclaimed a heretic by the French. A few months later he was dead. (Scala/Art Resource, NY.)

declared that all clerics who refused to pay their taxes would be considered outlaws—literally, "outside the law." Clergymen who were robbed, for example, would have no recourse against their attackers; if accused of crimes, they would have no defense in court. Relying on a different strategy, Philip forbade the exportation of precious metals, money, or jewels, effectively sealing the French borders. Immediately the English clergy cried out for legal protection, while the papacy itself clamored for the revenues it had long enjoyed from French pilgrims, litigants, and travelers. Boniface was forced to back down, conceding in 1297 that kings had the right to tax the clergy of their kingdoms in emergencies.

But the crisis was not over. In 1301, Philip the Fair tested his jurisdiction in southern France by arresting Bernard Saisset, the bishop of Pamiers, on a charge of treason for slandering the king by comparing him with an owl, "the handsomest of birds which is worth absolutely nothing." Saisset's imprisonment violated the principle, maintained both by the pope and by French law, that a clergyman was not subject to lay justice. Boniface reacted angrily, and Philip seized the opportunity to deride and humiliate the pope, orchestrating a public relations campaign against him. Boniface's reply, the bull* *Unam Sanctam* (1302), intensified the situation by declaring bluntly "that it is altogether necessary to salvation for every human creature to be subject to the Roman Pontiff." At meetings of the king's inner circle, Philip's agents declared Boniface a false pope, accusing him of sexual perversion, various crimes, and heresy. In 1303, royal agents, acting under Philip's orders, invaded Boniface's palace at Anagni (southeast of Rome) to capture the pope, bring him to France, and try him. Fearing for the pope's life, however, the people of Anagni joined forces and drove the French agents out of town. Yet even after such public support for the pope, the king made his power felt. Boniface died shortly thereafter, and the next two popes quickly pardoned Philip and his agents for their actions.

Just as Frederick II's defeat showed the weakness of the empire, so Boniface's humiliation showed the limits of papal control. The two powers that claimed "universal" authority had little weight in the face of the new, limited, but tightly controlled national states. After 1303, popes continued to criticize kings, but their words had less and less impact. In the face of newly powerful medieval states such as France, Spain, and England—supported by vast revenues, judicial apparatuses, representative institutions, and even the loyalty of churchmen—the papacy could make little headway. The delicate balance between church and state, a hallmark of the years of Louis IX, broke down by the end of the thirteenth century.

In 1309, forced from Rome by civil strife, the papacy settled at Avignon, a city technically in the Holy Roman Empire but very close to, and influenced by, France (see Map 10.5). Here the popes remained until 1378. The period from 1309 to 1378 came to be called the "Babylonian Captivity" by Europeans sensitive to having the popes live far from Rome, on the Rhône River. The Avignon popes, many of them

---

*An official papal document is called a *bull*, from the *bulla*, or seal, that was used to authenticate it.

French, established a sober and efficient organization that took in regular revenues and gave the papacy more say than ever before in the appointment of churchmen. They would, however, slowly abandon the idea of leading all of Christendom and would tacitly recognize the growing power of the secular states to regulate their internal affairs.

Power Shifts in the Italian Communes

During the thirteenth century, the Italian communes continued to extend their control over the surrounding countryside as independent city-states. While generally presenting a united front to outsiders, factions within the communes fought for control and its spoils. In the early thirteenth century, these factions represented noble families. However, in the course of the century, newer groups, generally—though not exclusively—from the non-noble classes, attempted to take over the reins of power in the communes. The *popolo* ("people"), as such groups were called, incorporated members of city associations such as craft and merchant guilds, parishes, and the commune itself. In fact, the popolo was a kind of alternative commune, a sworn association in each city that dedicated itself to upholding the interests of its members. Armed and militant, the popolo demanded a share in city government, particularly to gain a voice in matters of taxation. In 1222 at Piacenza, for example (see Mapping the West, page 420), the popolo's members won half the government offices; a year later, they and the nobles worked out a plan to share the election of their city's *podestà*, or chief executive. Such power sharing often resulted from the popolo's struggle, though in some cities, nobles overcame and dissolved the popolo, while in others, the popolo virtually excluded the nobles from government. Constantly confronting one another, quarreling, feuding, and compromising, such factions turned Italian cities into centers of civil discord.

Weakened by this constant friction, the communes were tempting prey for great regional nobles who, allying with one or another faction, established themselves as *signori* (singular *signore*, "lord") of the cities, keeping the peace at the price of repression. In these circumstances, the commune gave way to the *signoria* (a state ruled by a signore), and one family began to dominate the government. The communes ceased to exist, and many Italian cities fell under control of despots. The fate of Piacenza over the course of the thirteenth century was typical. First dominated by nobles, its commune granted the popolo a voice by 1225; but then by mid-century the signore's power eclipsed both the nobles and the popolo.

New-Style Associations amid the Monarchies

Although the thirteenth century was the age of newly strong signori or monarchs, there were some exceptions. Under the leadership of the city of Lübeck, the cities of northern Germany trading between the Baltic and the North Seas banded together to form the Hanseatic League (or Hanse). It was one fruit of the Northern Crusades: even the Teutonic Knights were members. Merchants in these cities dominated the northern grain trade, and their control over this commodity gave them power. They were able to declare embargoes against enemies and monopolies for themselves. Throughout the thirteenth and fourteenth centuries, the Hanse dominated the Baltic region.

Similarly independent were the self-governing peasant and town communes in the high Alpine valleys that became a united Swiss Confederation. In 1291, the peasants of Uri, Schwyz, and Unterwalden swore a perpetual alliance against their oppressive Habsburg overlord. After defeating a Habsburg army in 1315, these free peasants took the name "Confederates" and developed a new alliance that would become Switzerland. In the process, the Swiss enshrined their freedom in the legend of William Tell, their national hero, who was forced by a Habsburg official to prove his archery skills by shooting an apple placed on the head of his own son. This act so outraged the

Growth of the Swiss Confederation to 1353

citizens that they rose up in arms against Habsburg rule. By 1353, the important cantons of Lucerne, Zurich, and Bern had joined the confederation. The Swiss Confederation continued to acquire new members into the sixteenth century, defeating armies sent by different princes to undermine its liberties.

The Birth of Representative Institutions

Even monarchies found it useful to embrace groups beyond the narrow elite of the aristocracy. One of the ways in which Philip the Fair orchestrated his public relations campaign against Pope Boniface was to convene representatives of the clergy, nobles, and townspeople to explain, justify, and propagandize his position. This new assembly, which met at Paris in 1302, was the ancestor of the Estates General, which would meet sporadically for centuries thereafter—for the last time in 1789, at the beginning of the French Revolution. (In France, the various orders—clergy, nobles, and commoners—were called estates.) After Philip's agents declared Boniface a false pope, the king sent his commissioners to the various provinces of France to convene local meetings to popularize his charges against Boniface and gain support. Clergy, local nobles, townspeople, and even villagers attending these meetings almost unanimously denounced the pope.

As in France, representative institutions elsewhere began as political tools with which rulers hoped to broaden their support. All across Europe—from Spain to Poland, from England to Hungary—rulers summoned parliaments. These assemblies grew out of the ad hoc advisory sessions kings customarily held with their nobles and clergy, men who informally represented the two most powerful classes, or "orders," of medieval society. Although these bodies differed from place to place, the impulse behind their creation was similar. They began (as in France) as assemblies where kings celebrated their royal power and prestige and where the "orders" simply assented to royal policy. In the thirteenth century, the advisory sessions became solemn, formal meetings of representatives of the "orders" to the kings' chief councils—the precursor of parliamentary sessions. Eventually these bodies became organs through which people not ordinarily at court could articulate their wishes.

In practice, thirteenth-century kings did not so much command representatives of the orders to come to court as they simply summoned the most powerful members of their realm—whether clerics, nobles, or important townsmen—to support their policies. In thirteenth-century León (part of present-day Spain), for example, the king sometimes called only the clergy and nobles; sometimes he sent for representatives of the towns, especially when he wanted the help of town militias. As townsmen gradually began to participate regularly in advisory sessions, kings came to depend on them and their support. In turn, commoners became more fully integrated into the work of royal government.

The *cortes* of Castile-León were among the earliest representative assemblies called to the king's court and the first to include townsmen. Enriched by plunder from the reconquista, fledgling villages soon turned into major commercial centers. Like the cities of Italy, Spanish towns dominated the countryside. Their leaders—called *caballeros villanos*, or "city horsemen," because they were rich enough to fight on horseback—monopolized municipal offices. In 1188, when King Alfonso IX (r. 1188–1230) summoned townsmen to the cortes, the city caballeros served as their representatives, agreeing to Alfonso's plea for military and financial support and for help in consolidating his rule. Once convened at court, these wealthy townsmen joined bishops and noblemen in formally counseling the king and assenting to royal decisions. Beginning with Alfonso X (r. 1252–1284), Castilian monarchs regularly called on the cortes to participate in major political and military decisions and to assent to new taxes to finance them.

The English Parliament* also developed as a new tool of royal government. In this case, however, the king's control was complicated by the power of the barons, manifested, for example, in Magna Carta. In the twelfth century, King Henry II had consulted prelates and barons at Great Councils, using these parliaments as his tool to ratify and gain support for his policies. Although Magna Carta had nothing to do with such councils, the barons thought the document gave them an important and permanent role in royal government as the king's advisers and a solid guarantee of their customary rights and privileges. When Henry III (r. 1216–1272) was crowned at the age of nine, he was king in name only for the first sixteen years of his reign. During that period, England was governed by a council consisting of a few barons, professional administrators, and a papal legate. Though not quite "government by Parliament," this council set a precedent for baronial participation in government.

---

*Although *Parliament* and *Parlement* are very similar words, both deriving from the French word *parler* ("to speak"), the institutions they named were very different. The Parlement of France was a law court, whereas the English Parliament, although beginning as a court to redress grievances, had by 1327 become above all a representative institution. The major French representative assembly, the Estates General, first convened at the beginning of the fourteenth century.

An English parliament that included commoners came into being in the midst of war and as a result of political weakness. Henry so alienated nobles and commoners alike by his wars, debts, choice of advisers, and demands for money that the barons threatened to rebel. At a meeting at Oxford in 1258, they forced Henry to dismiss his foreign advisers; to rule with the advice of a Council of Fifteen chosen jointly by the barons and the king; and to limit the terms of his chief officers. However, this new government itself was riven by strife among the barons, and civil war erupted in 1264. At the battle of Lewes in the same year, the leader of the baronial opposition, Simon de Montfort (c. 1208–1265), routed the king's forces, captured the king, and became England's de facto ruler. Because only a minority of the barons followed Simon, he sought new support by convening a parliament in 1265. He summoned not only the earls, barons, and churchmen who backed him but also representatives from the towns—the "commons"—and he appealed for their help. Thus, for the first time, the commons were given a voice in government. Simon's brief rule ended that very year, and Henry's son Edward I (r. 1272–1307) became a rallying point for royalists (backers of the king). Yet the idea of representative government in England had emerged, born out of the interplay between royal initiatives and baronial revolts. Edward's constant need for new revenues led him to call regular sessions of Parliament. Without meaning to do so, he solidified its role as a regular institution of royal government in England.

■ **REVIEW:** *Compare the institutions of papal monarchy with those of secular monarchies in France and England.*

Religious and Cultural Life in an Age of Expansion

In the course of the thirteenth century, the religious life, originally associated with monks, nuns, priests, and bishops, became possible—and officially recognized—for laypeople as well. There was a clear connection between this development and the rise of universities, for the ethical teachings of "scholastics" (the scholars of medieval universities) were preached to the people. But the scholastics were also occupied with subjects that ranged far beyond ethics. Outside of the schools, poets well aware of scholastic teachings wrote vernacular works of great sophistication. And architects and artists elaborated the soaring structures of "Gothic" style in which much of this activity took place.

Lay Religious Fervor

The Fourth Lateran's mission to regulate and Christianize lay behavior was carried forward by the friars. Both the Dominican and Franciscan orders insisted on travel, preaching, and poverty—vocations that brought friars into cities and towns. Soon

■ **A Lady and Her Loving Falcon**

This sumptuous velvet-and-silk pouch, made by an embroideress in about 1320, shows a lady in the position of falconer. The falcon—a bird ordinarily used as an aid in hunting—is here depicted as her lover. He is flying toward her to place a crown of greenery on her head while she touches him tenderly on the shoulder. In her other hand she holds the leash with which she trained him. (© Musée de Tissus, Lyon.)

their members dominated the fledgling city universities and were sending into the community friar-preachers trained by the scholastics. Townspeople flocked to such preachers because they wanted to know how the Christian message applied to their daily lives. They were concerned, for example, about the ethics of moneymaking, sex in marriage, and family life. In turn, the preachers represented the front line of the church. They met the laity on their own turf and taught them to bend their activities to church teachings.

The friars further tied their members to the lay community through **tertiaries**, affiliated laymen and -women who adopted many Franciscan practices—prayer and works of charity, for example—while continuing to live in the world, raising families and tending to the normal tasks of daily life, whatever their occupation. Even kings became tertiaries.

All across Europe, women, too, sought outlets for their piety. As in previous centuries, powerful families founded new nunneries, especially within towns and cities. On the whole, these were set up for the daughters of the wealthy, while ordinary women found different modes of religious expression. Some sought the lives of quiet activity and rapturous mysticism of the Beguines; others found comfort in the lives of charity and service of women's mendicant orders, such as those connected to the Franciscans; and still others lived happily as wives and mothers, punctuating their domestic duties with religious devotions. Elisabeth of Hungary, who married a German prince at the age of fourteen, raised three children. At the same time, she devoted her life to fasting, prayer, and service to the poor.

Of course, many women were not as devout as Elisabeth. In the countryside, they cooked their porridge, brewed their ale, and raised their children. They attended church regularly, on major feast days or for churching—the ritual of purification after a pregnancy—but not extravagantly. In the cities, workingwomen scratched out a meager living. They sometimes made pilgrimages to relic shrines to seek help or cures.

■ Friars and Usurers

As the illustration on page 357 indicates, clerics sometimes borrowed money. The friars had a different attitude. St. Francis, son of a merchant, refused to touch money altogether. Franciscans begged for food and shelter. Even when their numbers grew and they began forming communities and living in monasteries, the friars still insisted on personal poverty while ministering to city dwellers, who had to deal with money in some way to make a living. In this illumination from about 1250, a Franciscan (in light-colored robes) and a Dominican (in black) reject offers from two usurers, whose profession they are thus shown to condemn. Other friars, including Thomas Aquinas, worked out justifications for some kinds of moneymaking professions. (Bibliothèque nationale de France.)

Religion was part of these women's lives but did not dominate them.

For some women, however, religion was the focus of life, and the church's attempt to define and control the Eucharist had some unintended results. The new emphasis on the holiness of the transformed wine and bread induced some of these pious women to eat nothing but the Eucharist. One such woman, Angela of Foligno, reported that the consecrated bread swelled in her mouth, tasting sweeter than any other food. In the minds of these holy women, Christ's crucifixion was the literal sacrifice of his body, to be eaten by sinful men and women as the way to redeem themselves. Renouncing all other foods became part of a life of service to others, because many of these devout women gave to the poor the food that they refused to eat. Even if not engaged in community service, holy women felt their suffering itself was a work of charity, helping to release souls from purgatory, the place where (the church taught) souls were cleansed of their sins.

Scholastics and Scholasticism

Purgatory was a doctrine first elaborated in the universites by "scholastics"—scholars who used a form of inquiry and exposition called **scholasticism**. It was a method based on the logical analysis of contradictory points, pioneered by Abelard in his *Sic et Non* and extended by other twelfth-century teachers. In the thirteenth century, the method was used to summarize and reconcile all knowledge. Many of the thirteenth-century scholastics were members of the Dominican and Franciscan orders, who dominated some of the faculties of the universities. Most were sure that knowledge obtained through the senses and by logical reasoning was compatible with the knowledge known through faith and revelation. One of their goals was to

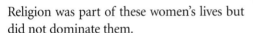

demonstrate this harmony. The scholastic *summa*, or summary of knowledge, was a systematic exposition of the answer to every possible question about human morality, the physical world, society, belief, action, and theology.

The summa was an orderly presentation of various positions that were then "reconciled" by the author. Both the presentation and the arguments borrowed much of the vocabulary and rules of logic long ago outlined by Aristotle. Even though Aristotle was a pagan, scholastics considered his coherent and rational body of thought the most perfect that human reason alone could devise. Because they had the benefit of Christ's revelations, the scholastics considered themselves able to take Aristotle's philosophy one necessary step further and reconcile human reason with Christian faith. Full of confidence in their method and conclusions, scholastics embraced the world and its issues.

Some scholastics considered questions about the natural world. Albertus Magnus (c. 1200–1280), a major theologian, also contributed to the fields of biology, botany, astronomy, and physics. His reconsideration of Aristotle's views on motion led the way to distinctions that helped scientists in the sixteenth and seventeenth centuries arrive at the modern notion of inertia.

One of Albertus's students was St. Thomas Aquinas (c. 1225–1274), perhaps the most famous scholastic. Huge of build, renowned for his composure in debate, Thomas came from a noble Neapolitan family that had hoped to see him become a powerful bishop rather than a poor university professor. When he was about eighteen years old, he thwarted his family's wishes and joined the Dominicans. Soon he was studying at Cologne with Albertus. At thirty-two he became a master at the University of Paris.

Like many other scholastics, Thomas considered Aristotle "the Philosopher," the authoritative voice of human reason, which he sought to reconcile with divine revelation in a universal and harmonious scheme. In 1273, he published his monumental *Summa Theologiae* (sometimes called the *Summa Theologica*), which covered all important topics, human and divine. He divided these topics into questions, exploring each one thoroughly and systematically, and concluding each question with a decisive position and a refutation of opposing views.

Many of Thomas's questions spoke to the keenest concerns of his day. He asked, for example, whether it was lawful to sell something for more than its worth. Thomas arranged his argument systematically, quoting first authorities that seemed to declare every sort of selling practice, even deceptive ones, to be lawful. This was the *sic* (or "yes") position. Then he quoted an authority who opposed selling something for more than its worth. This was the *non*. Following that, he gave his own argument, prefaced by the words *I answer that*. Unlike Abelard, whose method left differences unresolved, Thomas wanted to harmonize the two points of view, so he pointed out that price and worth depended on the circumstances of the buyer and seller, and he concluded that charging more than a seller had originally paid could be legitimate at times.

For townspeople engaged in commerce and worried about biblical prohibitions on moneymaking, Thomas's ideas about selling practices addressed burning questions. Hoping to go to heaven as well as reap the profits of their business ventures, laypeople listened eagerly to preachers who delivered their sermons in the vernacular but who based their ideas on the Latin *summae* of Thomas and other scholastics. Thomas's conclusions aided townspeople in justifying their worldly activities.

In his own day, Thomas Aquinas was a controversial figure, and his ideas, emphasizing reason, were by no means universally accepted. In Thomas's view, God, nature, and reason were in harmony, so Aristotle's arguments could be used to explore both the human and the divine orders. The work of the thirteenth-century scholastics to unite the secular with the sacred continued for another generation after Thomas. Yet at the beginning of the fourteenth century, fissures began to appear. In the summae of John Duns Scotus (c. 1266–1308), for example, the world and God were less compatible. John, whose name "Duns Scotus" betrays his Scottish origin, was a Franciscan who taught at both Oxford and Paris. For John, human reason could know truth only through the "special illumination of the uncreated light"—that is, by divine illumination. But unlike his predecessors, John believed that this illumination came not as a matter of course but only when God chose to intervene. John—and others—now sometimes experienced God as willful rather than reasonable. Human reason could not soar to God; God's will alone determined whether a person could know God. In this way, John separated the divine and secular realms.

Like John, William of Ockham (c. 1285–1349), an English Franciscan who was one of the most eminent theologians of his age, rejected any confident synthesis of Christian doctrine and Aristotelian philosophy. Ockham believed that universal concepts had no reality in nature but instead existed only as mere representations, names in the mind—a philosophy that came to be called nominalism. Perceiving and analyzing such concepts as "man" or "papal infallibility" offered no assurance that the concepts expressed truth. Observation and human reason were limited as the means to understand the universe and to know God. Ockham's insistence that the simplest explanation is the best came to be known as "Ockham's razor." Where human reason left off, God's covenant with his faithful took over.

New Syntheses in Writing and Music

Thirteenth-century writers and musicians, as confident in their powers as any king or scholastic, presented complicated ideas and feelings as harmonious and unified syntheses. Writers explored the relations between this world and the next; musicians found ways to bridge sacred and secular forms of music.

Dante Alighieri (1265–1321), perhaps the greatest vernacular poet of the Middle Ages, harmonized the scholastic universe with the mysteries of faith and the poetry of love. Born in Florence in a time of political turmoil, Dante incorporated the heroes and villains of his day into his most famous poem, the *Commedia*, written between 1313 and 1321. Later known as the *Divine Comedy*, Dante's poem describes the poet taking an imaginary journey from Hell to Purgatory and finally to Paradise.

The poem is an allegory in which every person and object must be read at more than one level. At the most literal level, the poem is about Dante's travels. At a deeper level, it is about the soul's search for meaning and enlightenment and its ultimate discovery of God in the light of divine love. Just as Thomas Aquinas thought that Aristotle's logic could lead to important truths, so Dante used the pagan poet Virgil as his guide through Hell and Purgatory. And just as Thomas believed that faith went beyond reason to even higher truths, so Dante found a new guide representing earthly love to lead him through most of Paradise. This guide was Beatrice, a Florentine girl with whom Dante had fallen in love as a boy and whom he never forgot. But only the Virgin Mary, representing faith and divine love, could bring Dante to the culmination of his journey—a blinding and inexpressibly awesome vision of God:

> *What I then saw is more than tongue can say.*
> *Our human speech is dark before the vision.*
> *The ravished memory swoons and falls away.*

Dante's poem electrified a wide audience. By elevating one dialect of Italian—the language that ordinary Florentines used in their everyday life—to a language of exquisite poetry, Dante was able to communicate the scholastics' harmonious and optimistic vision of the universe in an even more exciting and accessible way. So influential was his work that it is no exaggeration to say that modern Italian is based on Dante's Florentine dialect.

Other writers of the period used different methods to express the harmony of heaven and earth. The anonymous author of *Quest of the Holy Grail* (c. 1225), for example, wrote about the adventures of the knights of King Arthur's Round Table to convey the doctrine of transubstantiation and the wonder of the vision of God.

In *The Romance of the Rose*, begun by one author (Guillaume de Lorris, a poet in the romantic tradition) and finished by another (Jean de Meun, a poet in the

■ French Gothic: Ste.-Chapelle

Gothic architecture opened up the walls of the church to windows. Filled with "stained" glass—actually, the colors were added to the ingredients of the glass before they were heated, melted, and blown—the windows glowed like jewels. Moreover, each had a story to tell: the life of Christ, major events from the Old Testament, the lives of saints. Ste.-Chapelle, commissioned by King Louis IX (St. Louis) and consecrated in 1248, was built to house Christ's crown of thorns and other relics of the Passion. Compare the use of windows, walls, vault, and piers here with that of a Romanesque church such as St.-Savin (see page 378).

(Bridgeman-Giraudon/Art Resource, NY.)

scholastic tradition), a lover seeks the rose, his true love. In the long dream that the poem describes, the narrator's search for the rose is thwarted by personifications of love, shame, reason, abstinence, and so on. They present him with arguments for and against love, not incidentally commenting on people of the poets' own day. In the end, sexual love is made part of the divine scheme—and the lover plucks the rose.

Musicians, like poets, developed new forms that bridged sacred and secular subjects in the thirteenth and fourteenth centuries. This connection appears in the most distinctive musical form of the thirteenth century, the **motet** (from the French *mot*, meaning "word"). The motet is an example of **polyphony**, music that consists of two or more melodies performed simultaneously. Before about 1215, most polyphony was sacred; purely secular polyphony was not common before the fourteenth century. The motet, a unique merging of the sacred and the secular, evidently originated in Paris, the center of scholastic culture as well.

The typical thirteenth-century motet has three melody lines (or "voices"). The lowest, usually from a liturgical chant melody, has no words and may have been played on an instrument rather than sung. The remaining melodies have different texts, either Latin or French (or one of each), which are sung simultaneously. Latin texts are usually sacred, whereas French ones are secular, dealing with themes such as love and springtime. In one example, the top voice chirps in quick rhythm about a lady's charms ("Fair maiden, lovely and comely; pretty maiden, courteous and pleasing, delicious one"); the middle voice slowly and mournfully laments the "malady" of love; and the lowest voice sings a liturgical melody. The motet thus weaves the sacred (the chant melody in the lowest voice) and the secular (the French texts in the upper voices) into a sophisticated tapestry of music. Like the scholastic summae, the motets were written by and for a clerical elite. Yet, they incorporated the music of ordinary people, such as the calls of street vendors and the boisterous songs of students. In turn, they touched the lives of everyone, for polyphony influenced every form of music, from the Mass to popular songs that entertained and diverted laypeople and churchmen alike.

Complementing the motet's complexity was the development of a new notation for rhythm. Until the thirteenth century, musical notation could indicate pitch but had no way to denote the duration of the notes. In that century, music theorists developed increasingly precise methods to indicate rhythm. Franco of Cologne, for example, in his *Art of Measurable Song* (c. 1280), used different shapes to mark the number of beats each note should be held. His system became the basis of modern musical notation. Because each note could now be allotted a specific duration, written music could express new and complicated rhythms. The music of the thirteenth century reflected both the melding of the secular and the sacred and the possibilities for greater order and control.

The Order of High Gothic

Just as polyphonic music united the sacred with the secular, so Gothic architecture, sculpture, and painting expressed the order and harmony of the universe. The term

Gothic was originally used to belittle medieval art and architecture, but it now refers with admiration to a particular syle used in the twelfth to fifteenth centuries. Its chief characteristic is the use of pointed arches, which began as architectural motifs but were soon adopted in every art form. Gothic churches appealed to the senses the way that scholastic argument appealed to human reason: both were designed to lead people to knowledge that touched the divine. Being in a Gothic church was a foretaste of heaven.

Gothic architecture began around 1135, with the project of Abbot Suger, the close associate of King Louis the Fat (see page 365), to remodel portions of the church of St. Denis. Suger's rebuilding of St. Denis was part of the fruitful melding of royal and ecclesiastical interests and ideals in the north of France. At the west end of his church, the point where the faithful entered, Suger decorated the portals with figures of Old Testament kings, queens, and patriarchs, signaling the links between the present king and his illustrious predecessors. Within the church, Suger rebuilt the *chevet*, or choir area, using pointed arches and stained glass to let in light, which Suger believed would transport the worshiper from the "slime of earth" to the "purity of Heaven." Suger thought that the Father of lights, God himself, "illuminated" the minds of the beholders via the light that filtered through the stained-glass windows.

Soon the style that Suger pioneered was taken up across northern France and then, in the 1250s, as French culture gained enormous prestige under Louis IX, all across Europe. Gothic was an urban architecture, reflecting—in its towering heights, jewel-like windows, and bright ornaments—the aspirations, pride, and confidence of rich and powerful merchants, artisans, and bishops. A Gothic church, usually a cathedral (the bishop's principal church), was the focal point of a city.

Building Gothic cathedrals was a community project, enlisting the labor and support of an entire urban center. New cathedrals required a small army of quarrymen, builders, carpenters, and glass cutters. Bishops, papal legates, and clerics planned and helped pay for these grand churches, but townspeople also generously financed them and filled them to attend Mass and visit relics. Guilds raised money to pay for stained-glass windows that depicted and celebrated their own patron saints. In turn, towns made money when pilgrims came to visit relics, and sightseers arrived to marvel at their great churches. At Chartres, near Paris, for example, which had the relic of the Virgin's robe, crowds thronged the streets, the poor buying small lead figures of the Virgin, the rich purchasing wearable replicas of her robe. Churches were centers of commercial activity. In their basements, wine merchants plied their trade, while other vendors sold goods outside.

The technologies that made Gothic churches possible were all known before the twelfth century. But Suger's church showed how they could be used together to achieve a particularly dazzling effect. Gothic techniques included ribbed vaulting, which gave a sense of precision and order; pointed arches, which produced a feeling of soaring height; and flying buttresses, which took the weight of the vault off the walls (Figure 10.1). The buttresses permitted much of the wall to be cut away and the open spaces to be filled with glass.

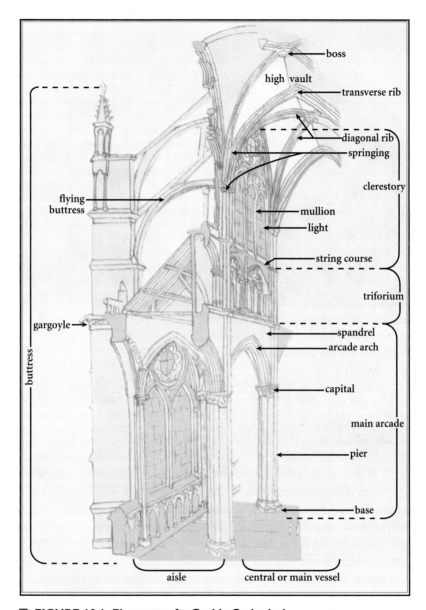

boss

high vault

transverse rib

diagonal rib

springing

clerestory

flying buttress

mullion

light

string course

triforium

gargoyle

spandrel

arcade arch

buttress

capital

main arcade

pier

base

aisle   central or main vessel

■ **FIGURE 10.1 Elements of a Gothic Cathedral**

Bristling on the outside with stone flying buttresses, Gothic cathedrals were lofty and serene on the inside. The buttresses, which held the weight of the vault, allowed Gothic architects to pierce the walls with windows running the full length of the church. Within, thick piers anchored on sturdy bases became thin columns as they mounted over the triforium and clerestory, blossoming into ribs at the top. Whether plain or ornate, the ribs gave definition and drew attention to the high pointed vault.

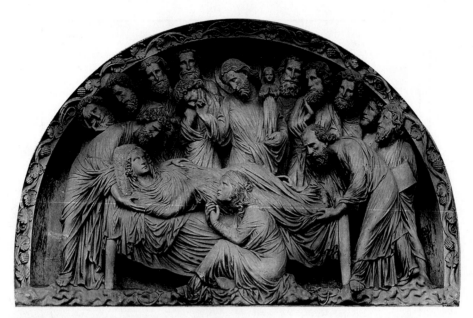

■ German Gothic: Strasbourg

The Virgin is mourned in this tympanum over the portal of the Strasbourg cathedral's south transept (the arm that crosses the church from north to south). Here, in German Gothic, the emphasis is on emotion and expressivity. Notice the depiction of Mary, with her bedclothes agitated and her body contorted. Why do you suppose that Christ stands in the center of the tympanum, as if he is one of the mourners? What is he holding in the crook of his arm? (Hint: The souls of the dead are often shown as miniature people.) **For more help analyzing this image**, see the visual activity for this chapter in the ONLINE STUDY GUIDE at bedfordstmartins.com/huntconcise.

(Foto Marburg/Art Resource, NY.)

Unlike Romanesque churches, whose exteriors prepare visitors for what they will see within, Gothic cathedrals surprise. The exterior of a Gothic church has an opaque, bristling, and forbidding look owing to the dark surface of its stained glass and its flying buttresses. The interior, however, is just the opposite. It is all soaring lightness, harmony, and order. Just as a scholastic presented his argument with utter clarity, so the interior of a Gothic church revealed its structure through its skeleton of ribbed vaults and piers. And just as a scholastic bridged the earthly and celestial realms, so the cathedral elicited a response beyond reason, evoking a sense of awe.

By the mid-thirteenth century, Gothic architecture had spread from France to other European countries. Yet the style varied by region, most dramatically in Italy. The outer walls of the cathedral at Orvieto, for example, alternate bricks of light and dark color, providing texture instead of glass and light; and the vault over the large nave is round rather than pointed, recalling the Roman aqueducts that could still be seen in Italy when the builders were designing the cathedral. With no flying buttresses and relatively little portal sculpture, Italian Gothic churches convey a spirit of austerity.

Gothic art, both painting and sculpture, echoed and decorated the Gothic cathedral. Gothic sculpture differed from earlier church sculpture by its naturalism and monumentality. Romanesque sculpture played upon a flat surface; Gothic figures were liberated from their background. Sculpted in the round, they turned,

■ Mocking of Christ

Like the artist who portrayed "A Teacher and His Students" on page 371, Giotto, too, used decorative bands to frame his subject. But, within the frame, the conception of the human body and the human interaction is entirely different. On page 371, the four figures are elongated to express their elegance and unworldliness; they interact via scrolls. Gilbert is clearly the oldest: he wears a beard. But the three students look almost exactly the same. By contrast, in the "Mocking of Christ" the figures are heavy and fleshy, emphasizing their presence in a real world. They poke and stare and converse with one another. Each torturer around Christ takes individual delight in his particular cruelty, while a group of elders a bit apart shows weighty concern. Giotto was here portraying factions as well as individuals. (Scala/Art Resource, NY.)

■ MAPPING THE WEST Europe, c. 1340

The empire, now called the Holy Roman Empire, still dominated the map of Europe in 1340, but the emperor himself had power only in his own principality. Each region—and sometimes each city—was ruled separately and independently. To the east, the Ottoman Turks were beginning to make themselves felt. In the course of the next century, they would disrupt Mongol hegemony and become a great power.

moved, and interacted with one another. The positions of the figures, the people they represented, and the ways in which they interacted were meant to be "read" like a scholastic *summa*, for Gothic sculpture often depicted complex stories or scenes. The south portal complex of Chartres cathedral is a good example. Each massive doorway tells a separate story through sculpture: the left depicts the martyrs, the right the confessors, and the center the Last Judgment. Like Dante's *Divine Comedy*, these portals taken together show the soul's pilgrimage from the suffering of this world to eternal life.

Gothic sculpture began in France and was adopted, with many variations, elsewhere in Europe during the thirteenth century. The German sculptor who carved the tympanum (the half-circle form over the portal) over the south portal of

Strasbourg's cathedral was particularly interested in emotional expression. As the Virgin Mary dies, the figures around her bend and gesture, showing their grief with their hands and faces. The Italian sculptor Nicola Pisano (c. 1220–1278?), by contrast, was very interested in classical forms.

By the early fourteenth century, the expressive sculptures so prominent in architecture were reflected in painting as well. This new style is evident in the work of Giotto (1266–1337), a Florentine artist who helped change the emphasis of painting, which had been predominantly symbolic, decorative, and intellectual. For example, Giotto filled the walls of a private chapel at Padua with paintings depicting scenes of Christ's life. Here he experimented with the illusion of depth. Giotto's figures, appearing weighty and voluminous, express a range of emotions as they seem to move across interior and exterior spaces. In bringing sculptural realism to a flat surface, Giotto stressed three-dimensionality, illusional space, and human emotion. By melding earthly sensibilities with religious themes, Giotto found yet another way to bring together the natural and divine realms.

■ **REVIEW:** *How did artists, architects, musicians, and scholastics try to link this world with the divine?*

IMPORTANT DATES

1180–1223	Reign of Philip II ("Philip Augustus") of France	1265	English Parliament called by Simon de Montfort includes representatives of the commons
1198–1216	Papacy of Innocent III	1265–1321	Life of Dante Alighieri
1202–1204	Fourth Crusade; sack of Constantinople	1273	*Summa Theologiae* of Thomas Aquinas
1209–1229	Albigensian Crusade	1285–1314	Reign of Philip IV ("the Fair") of France
1212–1250	Reign of Frederick II		
1215	Magna Carta; Fourth Lateran Council	1294–1303	Papacy of Boniface VIII
1216–1272	Reign of Henry III of England	1302	Meeting of the Estates at Paris; Boniface issues *Unam Sanctam*
c. 1225–1274	Life of Thomas Aquinas	1309–1378	Avignon papacy ("Babylonian Captivity")
1226–1270	Reign of Louis IX ("St. Louis") of France		
		1313–1321	Dante's *Divine Comedy*
1230s	Mongols begin attacks on the West		
1250s	Gothic becomes a European-wide style		

Conclusion

In the thirteenth and early fourteenth centuries, western Europeans aggressively expanded outward, from the Baltic to the Strait of Gibraltar. When they sacked Constantinople in 1204, they joined the Muslims as the dominant political forces in the West. They treated the Mongol hegemony in the East as an opportunity for trade and missionary work.

Powerful territorial kings and princes expressed their new self-confidence through bureaucratic institutions. They hired staffs to handle their accounts, record acts, collect taxes, issue writs, and preside over courts. Flourishing cities, a growing money economy, and trade and manufacturing provided the finances necessary to support the personnel now used by medieval governments. The universities became the training grounds for the new administrators as well as for urban preachers.

Both the church and the state became more assertive. The Fourth Lateran Council was an attempt to regulate intimate aspects of the lives of all, even lay-people and non-Christians. The conflict between Boniface and Philip showed how the French king could galvanize his subjects—even his clergy—on behalf of the interests of the state. In England, where John agreed to Magna Carta, it was the barons who helped forge a notion of government that transcended the king. On the other hand, the artists and architects of the time sought to bring together two separate entities—the worldly and the divine.

New power, new piety, and new exclusivity arose in a society both more confident and less tolerant. Crusaders fought against an increasing variety of foes, not only in the Holy Land but in Spain, in southern France, and on Europe's northern frontiers. With heretics voicing criticisms and maintaining their beliefs, the church, led by the papacy, now defined orthodoxy and declared dissenters its enemies. The Jews, who had once been fairly well integrated into the Christian community, were treated ambivalently, alternately used and abused. Balts became targets for new evangelical and armed zeal; the Greeks became the butt of envy, hostility, and finally enmity.

Confident and aggressive, the leaders of Christian Europe in the thirteenth and early fourteenth centuries attempted to impose their rule, legislate morality, and create a unified worldview impregnable to attack. But their drive for order would be countered by economic and political crises and epidemic disease.

■ **MAKING CONNECTIONS**

1. *Why was Innocent III more successful than Boniface VIII in carrying out his objectives?*

2. *What impact did the Mongolian invasion have on the medieval economy?*

■ FOR FURTHER EXPLORATION

For further reading and online research ideas, see the Suggested References on page SR-5 at the back of the book.

For practice quizzes, a customized study plan, and other study tools, see the ONLINE STUDY GUIDE at **bedfordstmartins.com/huntconcise**.

For primary-source material from this period, see Chapter 10 in *Sources of THE MAKING OF THE WEST: A CONCISE HISTORY*, Second Edition.

11

Crisis and Renaissance
1340–1500

W HEN, IN 1453, THE CANNONS OF OTTOMAN RULER MEHMED II breached the walls of Constantinople, the whole Christian world shuddered. Yet a very few years later, Mehmed was writing to the lord of the Renaissance Italian city of Rimini, asking for the Rimini court painter and architect Matteo de Pasti to come help him build a new palace. The Ottoman sultan considered himself a Renaissance prince and expected cooperation from his European counterparts. Pasti's lord accepted the invitation, but on his way to Istanbul, Pasti was waylaid by the Venetians, who wanted no city but theirs to have relations with the sultan. Mehmed didn't give up; he simply called upon several Venetian painters to come instead. The palace came to be called the Topkapi Saray and still stands today looking across the Bosporus, the strait that divides European and Asian Turkey.

Mehmed sums up in one personage the twin themes of the period 1340–1500. His conquest of Constantinople was one of many crises that rocked the West from the Bosporus to the Atlantic: his age saw disease, war, economic contraction, and religious upheaval. At the same time, his tastes and culture aligned him with the Renaissance, a movement that was rediscovering the arts and worldview of classical antiquity. His interest in Italian art reflected the connection between power and

■ **The Siege of Constantinople**

Bertrandon de la Broquiere wrote his Overseas Voyage *in the 1430s for the Duke of Burgundy, who was contemplating a new crusade against the Turks. "I will discuss the means and the men necessary to break their power and defeat them in battle and gain their territory," he wrote, adding: "I don't think it would be very hard to break and defeat them, given their lack of arms." Within two decades, however, the Turks had taken Constantinople. When an artist was commissioned around 1455 to illustrate Bertrandon's work, he or she chose to show the siege. In this picture, you can see the tents of the Turkish captains, their cannons and cannonballs just behind them, and, across the water, the city of Constantinople with its doomed defenders.*
(Bibliothèque Nationale, Paris/Bridgeman Art Library.)

culture characteristic of his era. In the fourteenth and fifteenth centuries, much new artistic, architectural, and musical work was created in praise of personal and public lives. Portraits, palaces, and poetry commemorated the glory of the rich and powerful, while a new cultural movement called humanism advocated classical learning and argued for the active participation of the individual in civic affairs. Family, honor, social status, and individual distinction—these were the goals that fueled the ambitions of Renaissance men and women.

Their quest for glory duplicated on a smaller scale the enhanced power of the state, shored up by new military technologies—firearms, siege equipment, fortifications, and well-equipped soldiers. Commoners, criminals, and adventurers often joined the ranks of the fighters. To maintain their social eminence, many nobles were forced to take on new roles as officials or officers in the service of the state. By appointing nobles to the royal household, as military commanders and councilors, kings and princes consolidated their power.

Like individuals, these states, too, competed for wealth, glory, and honor. While warfare and diplomacy channeled the restless energy of the Italian states, monarchies and empires outside of Italy also expanded their power through conquests and institutional reforms. The European world changed dramatically as new powers such as the Ottoman Empire and Muscovy rose to prominence in the east, while the Iberian kingdoms of Portugal and Spain expanded European domination to Africa, Asia, and the Americas.

A Multitude of Crises

Beginning in the fourteenth century and extending to the middle of the fifteenth, Europeans confronted crises of both nature and human design. The plague wracked the cities and hurt the countryside. The Hundred Years' War devastated France. To the east, the rise of the Ottomans had a cataclysmic impact on the politics of eastern and central Europe. Everywhere, economic contraction made for material hard times, while spiritual well-being seemed threatened by a long papal schism. Minorities—religious dissenters, heretics, Jews, and Muslims in Spain—suffered the effects of pent-up anxieties.

Economic Contraction and the Black Death

Bad weather and overpopulation contributed to a series of famines at the beginning of the fourteenth century. Having cleared forests and drained swamps, peasants divided their plots into ever smaller parcels and farmed marginal land; their income and the quality of their diet eroded. In the great urban centers, where thousands depended on steady employment and cheap bread, a bad harvest, always followed by sharply rising food prices, meant hunger and eventual famine. A cooling of the European climate also contributed to the crisis in the food supply.

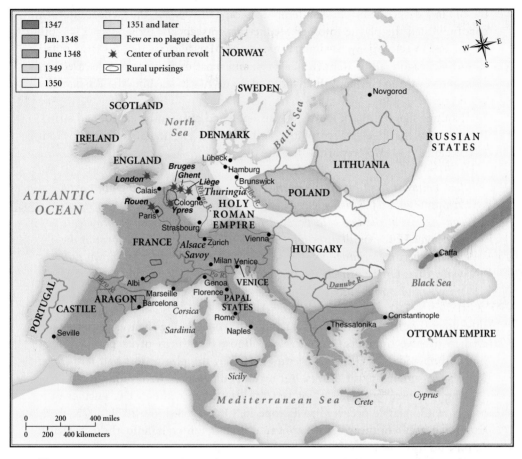

■ MAP 11.1 Advance of the Plague

The gradual but deadly spread of the plague followed the roads and rivers of Europe. Note the earlier transmission by sea from the Crimea to the ports of the Mediterranean before the general spread to northern Europe.

Modern studies of tree rings (dendrochronology) indicate that fourteenth-century Europe entered a colder period, with a succession of severe winters beginning in 1315 and extending to 1317. Crop failures were widespread. In many cities of northwestern Europe, the price of bread tripled, and thousands starved to death. Some Flemish cities, for example, lost 10 percent of their population. Many who survived were badly weakened and vulnerable to disease.

In midcentury, the bubonic plague passed from its breeding ground in central Asia eastward into China, where it decimated the population and wiped out the remnants of the tiny Italian merchant community in Yangzhou. Bacteria-carrying fleas living on black rats transmitted the disease. They traveled back to Europe alongside valuable cargoes of silk, porcelain, and spices. In 1347, the Genoese colony in Caffa in the Crimea contracted the plague (Map 11.1). Fleeing by ship in a desperate but futile attempt to escape the disease, the Genoese in turn communicated the plague to other Mediterranean seaports. By January 1348, the plague had infected Sicily, Sardinia, Corsica, and Marseille. Six months later, it had spread to Aragon, all of Italy, the Balkans, and most of France. The disease then crept northward to Germany, England, and Scandinavia, reaching the Russian city of Novgorod in 1351.

Nothing like the Black Death, as this epidemic came to be called, had struck Europe since the great plague of the sixth century. The Italian writer Giovanni Boccaccio (1313–1375) reported that the plague

> *first betrayed itself by the emergence of certain tumors in the groin or the armpits, some of which grew as large as a common apple, others as an egg. . . . From the two said parts of the body this . . . began to propagate and spread itself in all directions indifferently; after which the form of the malady began to change, black spots or livid making their appearance in many cases on the arm or the thigh or elsewhere, now few and large, now minute and numerous.*

Inhabitants of cities, where crowding and filth increased the chances of contagion, died in massive numbers. Florence lost almost two-thirds of its population of ninety thousand; Siena, like most cities visited by the plague, lost half its people. Rural areas suffered fewer deaths, but regional differences were pronounced. (See "Taking Measure," page 429.) Nor was the danger over after 1350. Further outbreaks of the plague occurred in Europe in 1361, 1368–1369, 1371, 1375, 1390, and 1405; they continued, with longer dormant intervals, into the eighteenth century.

Although the Black Death took a horrible human toll, the disaster actually profited some people. In an overpopulated society with limited resources, massive death opened the ranks for advancement. For example, after 1350, landlords had difficulty acquiring new tenant farmers without making concessions in land contracts, fewer priests competed for the same number of benefices (ecclesiastical offices funded by an endowment), and workers received much higher wages because the supply of laborers had plummeted. The Black Death and the resulting decline in urban population meant there was less demand for grain relative to the supply and thus brought about a drop in cereal prices.

All across Europe noble landlords, whose revenues fell as prices dropped, had to adjust to these new circumstances. Some revived seigneurial demands for labor services. Others looked to their central government for legislation to regulate wages. Still others granted favorable terms to peasant proprietors, often after bloody peasant revolts. Many noblemen lost a portion of their wealth and a measure of their autonomy and political influence. Consequently, European nobles

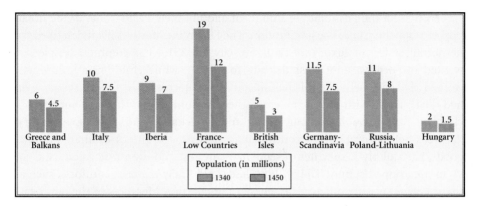

■ TAKING MEASURE Population Losses and the Plague, 1340–1450

The bar chart represents dramatically the impact of the Black Death and the recurrent plagues between 1340 and 1450. More than a century after the Black Death, none of the regions of Europe had made up for the losses of population. The population of 1450 stood at between 75 and 80 percent of the preplague population. The hardest-hit areas were France and the Low Countries, which also suffered from the devastations of the Hundred Years' War.

became more dependent on their monarchs and on war to supplement their incomes and enhance their power.

For the peasantry and the urban working population, higher wages generally meant an improvement in living standards. To compensate for the lower demand and price for grain, many peasants and landlords turned to stock breeding and grape and barley cultivation. As European agriculture diversified, peasants and artisans consumed more beer, wine, meat, cheese, and vegetables, a better and more varied diet than their thirteenth-century forebears had eaten.

Because of the shrinking population and decreased demand for food, cultivating marginal fields was no longer profitable, and many settlements were simply abandoned. By 1450, for example, some 450 large English villages and many small hamlets had disappeared. In central Europe east of the Elbe River, where German peasants had migrated, large tracts of cultivated land reverted to forest. Estimates suggest that some 80 percent of all villages in parts of Thuringia (Germany) vanished.

In the cities, production shifted from manufacturing for a mass market to a highly lucrative, though small, luxury market. The drastic loss in urban population had reduced the demand for such mass-manufactured goods as cloth. Fewer people now possessed proportionately greater concentrations of wealth. In the southern French city of Albi, for example, the proportion of citizens possessing more than 100 livres in per capita income doubled between 1343 and 1357, while the number of poor people, those with less than 10 livres, declined by half.

Faced with the possibility of imminent and untimely death, some of the urban populace sought immediate gratification. The Florentine Matteo Villani described the newfound desire for luxury in his native city in 1351. "The common people . . . wanted the dearest and most delicate foods . . . while children and common women clad themselves in all the fair and costly garments of the illustrious who had died." Those with means increased their consumption of luxuries such as silk clothing, hats, doublets (snug-fitting men's jackets), and expensive jewelry. Whereas agricultural prices continued to decline, the prices of manufactured goods, particularly luxury items, remained constant and even rose as demand for them outstripped supply. The middle class sought new material comforts, such as fireplaces and private toilets, beds, chests, and curtains. Members of the new peasant elite must have lived in simpler style, but perhaps they no longer shared their house with animals, as they had in the thirteenth century.

The long-term consequences of this new consumption pattern spelled the end for the traditional woolen industry that had produced for a mass market. Diminishing demand for wool caused hardships for woolworkers, and social and political unrest shook many older industrial centers dependent on the cloth industry, such as Flanders. At Ypres, for example, production figures fell from a high of ninety thousand pieces of cloth in 1320 to fewer than twenty-five thousand by 1390. In Ghent, where 44 percent of all households were woolworkers and where some 60 percent of the working population depended on the textile industry, the woolen market's slump meant constant labor unrest.

The new labor market tended to undermine women's economic position. In the German city of Cologne, for example, more and more artisan guilds excluded women from their ranks. Everywhere, fathers favored sons and sons-in-law to succeed them in their crafts. Daughters and widows resisted this patriarchal regime in the urban economy, but they were most successful in industries with the least regulations, such as beer brewing.

The Hundred Years' War, 1337–1453

In France, the misery wrought by the plague was compounded by the devastation of war. The English and French kings had long sparred over control of territories in France. In 1337, as part of the French royal policy to centralize its jurisdiction, Philip VI confiscated the southwestern province of Aquitaine, which had been held by the English monarchs as a fief of the French crown. To recover his lands, Edward III of England in turn laid claim to the French throne. Thus the Hundred Years' War began. It satisfied the interests of many groups, especially on the English side: nobles and knights hoped to demonstrate their chivalric valor on the battlefield; English yeomen (free farmers) were eager for booty, hostages, and amorous conquests. Mercenary companies hired by the English were glad to make money; when not employed in war, they remained to wreak havoc on the French countryside.

Ruling over a more populous realm and commanding far larger armies than the English, the French kings were nevertheless hindered in the war by the independent actions of their powerful barons. Against the accurate and deadly English freemen archers, the French knights met repeated defeats. Yet the French nobility despised their own peasants, perhaps fearing them and the urban middle classes more than they feared their noble English adversaries.

The war may be divided into three periods: the first was marked by English triumphs, the second saw France slowly gaining the upper hand, and the third ended in the English expulsion from France (see Map 11.2 on page 432). The final, most important phase saw two key developments: the rise of Burgundy, a hodgepodge of territories held together only by the political machinations of its dukes; and the rise of France as a distinct nation. This phase began when the English king Henry V (r. 1413–1422) launched a full-scale invasion of France and crushed the French at Agincourt (1415). Three parties then struggled for domination in France. Henry occupied Normandy and claimed the French throne; the dauphin (heir apparent to the French throne), Charles VII of France (r. 1422–1461),* ruled central France; and the duke of Burgundy held a vast territory in the northeast that included the Low Countries. Burgundy was thus able to broker war or peace by shifting support first to the English and then to the French. But even with Burgundian support, the English could not establish firm control. In Normandy, a savage guerrilla war harassed the English army. Driven from their villages by pillaging and murdering soldiers, Norman peasants retreated into forests, formed armed bands, and attacked the English. The miseries of war inspired prophecies of miraculous salvation; among the predictions was that a virgin would deliver France from the English invaders.

At the court of the dauphin, in 1429, a sixteen-year-old peasant girl presented herself and her vision to save France. Born in a village in Lorraine, Joan of Arc, La Pucelle ("the Maid"), as she always referred to herself, grew up in a war-ravaged country that longed for divine deliverance. She had first presented herself as God's messenger to the local noble, who was sufficiently impressed to equip Joan with horse, armor, and a retinue to send her to the dauphin's court. Joan of Arc's extraordinary appearance inspired the beleaguered French to trust in divine providence. In 1429, she accompanied the French army that laid a prolonged but successful siege on Orlèans, was wounded, and showed great courage in battle. Upon her urging, the dauphin traveled deep into hostile Burgundian territory to be anointed King Charles VII of France at Reims cathedral, thus strengthening his legitimacy by following the traditional ritual of coronation.

---

*Although the dauphin was not crowned until 1429, he assumed the title Charles VII in 1422, after the death of his father.

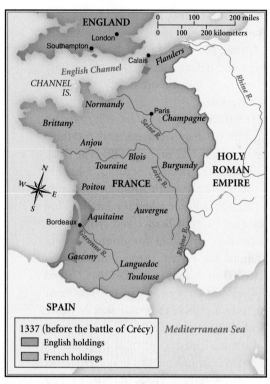

1337 (before the battle of Crécy)
- English holdings
- French holdings

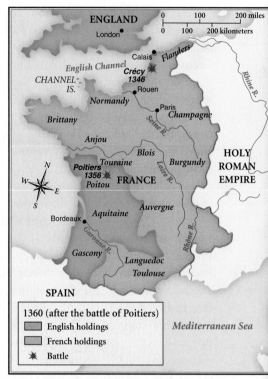

1360 (after the battle of Poitiers)
- English holdings
- French holdings
- ✳ Battle

c. 1429 (after the Siege of Orléans)
- English holdings
- French holdings
- Burgundian lands allied with England to 1435
- ✳ Battle
- ← Route taken by Joan of Arc, 1429–1431

1453 (end of war)
- English holdings
- French holdings
- Burgundian lands reconciled with France after 1435

■ **The Spoils of War**
This illustration from Jean Froissart's Chronicles *depicts soldiers pillaging a conquered city. During the Hundred Years' War, looting became the main source of income for mercenary troops and contributed to the general misery of late-medieval society. Food, furniture, and even everyday household items were taken.* (Bibliothèque nationale de France.)

Although Joan's fortunes declined after Reims and she was burned as a heretic by the English in 1431, she had helped undermine the English position, which slowly crumbled thereafter. The duke of Burgundy recognized Charles VII as king of France, and Charles entered Paris in 1437. Skirmish by skirmish, the English were driven from French soil.

The Hundred Years' War profoundly altered the economic and political landscape of western Europe. It aggravated the demographic and economic crises of the fourteenth century by further ravaging the countryside. Constant insecurity

■ **MAP 11.2 The Hundred Years' War, 1337–1453**
As rulers of Aquitaine and claimants to the throne of France, English kings contested the French monarchy for domination of France. Squeezed between England and Burgundy, the holdings of the French kings were vastly reduced after the battle of Poitiers in 1356. Then the fortune of war changed, and slowly France emerged as an intact nation.

■ **Joan of Arc, c. 1430**

Painted in the style of the French-Flemish school, this manuscript illustration contrasts the metallic hardness of Joan's armor and sword with the soft fluttering banner depicting God and two angels. With her right hand upturned clasping a sword and her left turned down to support the banner, Joan strikes a perfect pose as a messenger of God, similar to the angels depicted above. **For more help analyzing this image,** see the visual activity for this chapter in the ONLINE STUDY GUIDE at bedfordstmartins.com/huntconcise. (© AKG-Images, London.)

caused by marauding bands of soldiers prevented the cultivation of fields even in times of truce. City and countryside united in 1358, unhappy with the heavy war taxes and the incompetence of the warrior nobility. The movement, called the Jacquerie, began when the townspeople of Paris, led by Étienne Marcel, the provost of the merchants there, sought to take over control of the city. His rebellion was put down and Marcel was killed, but meanwhile rebels in the countryside began their own revolt, destroying manor houses and castles near Paris and massacring entire noble families in a savage class war. The chronicler Jean Froissart, sympathetic to the nobility, reflected the views of the ruling class in describing the rebels as "small, dark, and very poorly armed." Repression by nobles was swift, as thousands of rebels died in battles or were executed.

In England, the war brought discontent to the rural and urban classes as well. The trigger for outright rebellion by the peasantry was the imposition of a poll tax passed by Parliament in 1377 to raise money for the war against France, a war that peasants believed benefited only the king and the nobility. Unlike traditional subsidies to the king, the poll tax was levied on everyone. In May 1381, a revolt broke out to protest the taxes. Rebels in Essex and Kent joined bands in London to confront the king. The famous couplet of the radical preacher John Ball, who was executed after the revolt, expresses the rebels' egalitarian, antinoble sentiment:

When Adam delved [dug] and Eve span [spun]
Who was then the gentleman?

Forced to address the rebels, young King Richard II (r. 1377–1399) agreed to abolish serfdom and impose a ceiling on land rent, but he immediately rescinded these concessions after the rebels' defeat.

Richard was not the only monarch to pay little attention to the pains of the war. In France, the ruler benefited from it: under Charles VII, a standing army was established to supplement the feudal noble levies, an army financed by increased taxation and expanded royal judicial claims. Steadily increasing in power and pretensions, in the 1470s the French monarchy dismantled and absorbed Burgundy, and in the 1490s it entered Italy with conquest in mind. By 1500, it was clear that the French monarchy was one of the leading powers of Europe.

Defeated in war, the English monarchy suffered more. From the 1460s to 1485, England was torn by civil war—the War of the Roses between the red rose of Lancaster and the rival white rose of York. A deposed king (Henry VI), a short reign (Edward IV), and the murder of two princes by their uncle (Richard III) followed in quick succession in a series of conflicts that decimated the leading noble families of England. When Henry Tudor succeeded to the throne as Henry VII in 1485, England was tired of civil war. Henry ended the fighting and united the houses of Lancaster and York. By the early sixteenth century, the English monarchy was poised to take advantage of the general prosperity and war-weariness to enhance its position and power.

When the Hundred Years' War began, there were still knights who thought they could achieve valorous deeds of chivalry for their own glory and on behalf of their lord. By its end, chivalry was clearly a dreamy fantasy: cannons and gunpower had been added to the arsenal of European weapons, and many soldiers were mercenaries who hired themselves out to whichever ruler would pay. Equipment and fortifications counted more than valor in the outcome of battles.

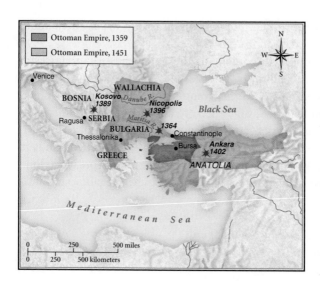

■ MAP 11.3 Ottoman Expansion in the Fourteenth and Fifteenth Centuries

The Balkans were the major theater of expansion for the Ottoman Empire, whose conquests also included Egypt and the North African coast. The Byzantine Empire was long reduced to the city of Constantinople and surrounded by the Ottomans before its final fall in 1453.

Ottoman Conquest and New Political Configurations in Eastern Europe

The rise of the Ottoman Turks was the most astonishing development of the late thirteenth century, when the Islamic Ottomans began a holy war against Byzantium. Under Osman I (r. 1280–1324), who gave the dynasty its name, and his successors, the Ottomans became a formidable force in Anatolia and the Balkans, where political disunity opened the door for their advances (Map 11.3). By the end of the fourteenth century, they had reduced the Byzantine Empire to the city of Constantinople, Thessalonika, and a narrow strip of land in modern-day Greece. Further to the west, the Ottomans defeated a joint Hungarian-Serbian army at the Maritsa River (1364), alerting Europe for the first time to the threat of an Islamic invasion. Pope Urban V called vainly for a crusade. In the Balkans, the Ottomans skillfully exploited Christian disunity, playing local interests against one another. An Ottoman army allied with the Bulgarians and some Serbian princes won the battle of Kosovo (1389), destroying the last organized Christian resistance south of the Danube. Even today the battle remains a rallying cry for Serbian nationalists. The Ottomans secured control of southeastern Europe after 1396, when at Nicopolis they crushed a crusading army summoned by Pope Boniface IX.

When Mehmed II (r. 1451–1481) ascended the Ottoman throne, he proclaimed a holy war and laid siege to Constantinople in 1453. A city of 100,000, the Byzantine capital could muster only 6,000 defenders (including a small contingent of Genoese) against an Ottoman force estimated at between 200,000 and 400,000 men. The city's fortifications, many of which dated from Emperor

Justinian's rule in the sixth century, were no match for fifteenth-century cannons. The defenders held out for fifty-three days. While the Christians confessed their sins and prayed for divine deliverance in desperate anticipation of the Second Coming, the Muslim besiegers pressed forward, urged on by the certainty of rich spoils and Allah's promise of a final victory over the infidel Rome. Finally the defenders were overwhelmed, and the last Byzantine emperor, Constantine XI Palaeologos, died in battle. Some 60,000 residents were carried off into slavery, and the city was sacked. Mehmed entered Constantinople in triumph and rendered thanks to God in Justinian's Church of the Holy Wisdom (Hagia Sophia), which became a mosque.

Mehmed wanted to be the new ruler of the Roman Empire—a Muslim Roman Empire. We have seen that he asked Italian court painter Matteo de Pasti to help create his Topkapi palace, intended to communicate Ottoman power. The Ottoman conquest was more than a continuation of the struggle between Christendom and Islam. The battle for territory transcended the boundaries of faith. Christian princes also served the Ottoman Empire as vassals to the sultan. The Janissaries, Christian slave children raised by the sultan as Muslims, constituted the fundamental backbone of the Ottoman army. They formed a service class that was both dependent on and loyal to the ruler. At the sultan's court, Christian women were prominent in the harem; thus many Ottoman princes had Greek or Serbian mothers. In addition to the Janissaries, Christian princes and converts to Islam served in the emerging Ottoman administration. In areas conquered, existing religious and social structures remained intact when local people accepted Ottoman overlordship and paid taxes. Only in areas of persistent resistance did the Ottomans drive out or massacre the inhabitants, settling Turkish tribes in their place. A distinctive pattern of Balkan history was therefore established at the beginning of the Ottoman conquest: the extremely diverse ethnic and religious communities were woven together into the fabric of an efficient central state.

The rise of strong, new monarchies—represented by France, England, and the Ottoman sultanate—contrasted sharply with the weakness of state authority in central and eastern Europe, where Hungary, Bohemia, and Poland were held together, like Burgundy, by personal dynastic authority alone (see Map 11.4 on page 438). Under Matthias Corvinus (r. 1456–1490), the Hungarian king who briefly united the Bohemian and Hungarian crowns, a central-eastern European empire seemed to be emerging. A patron of the arts and a humanist, Matthias created a great library in Hungary. He repeatedly defeated the encroaching Austrian Habsburgs and even occupied Vienna in 1485. However, his empire did not outlast his death in 1490. The powerful Hungarian magnates, who enjoyed the constitutional right to elect the king, ended it by refusing to acknowledge his son's claim to the throne.

In the mid-fourteenth century, two large monarchies—Poland and Lithuania— began to take shape in northeastern Europe. King Casimir III (r. 1333–1370)

☐	Ottoman conquests, 1451–1500
▨	Polish dependencies

0   200   400 miles
0   200   400 kilometers

SWEDEN

MUSCOVY

Baltic Sea

Novgorod
1471

LIVONIA

Moscow

Volga R.

East
Prussia

Mazovia

MONGOL
KHANATES

Bohemia

POLAND-
LITHUANIA

Vienna
AUSTRIA

HUNGARY

Black Sea

Danube R.

BALKAN MTNS.

Constantinople
1453

OTTOMAN EMPIRE

Mediterranean   Sea

■ **MAP 11.4 Eastern Europe in the Fifteenth Century**

The rise of Muscovy and the Ottomans shaped the map of eastern Europe. Some Christian monarchies, such as Serbia, lost their independence. Others, such as Hungary, held off the Ottomans until the early sixteenth century.

won recognition in most of Poland's regions. A problem that persisted throughout his reign, however, was conflict with the neighboring princes of Lithuania, Europe's last pagan rulers, who for centuries had fiercely resisted the Christianization demanded by the German crusading order, the Teutonic Knights. After the Mongols conquered Russia, Lithuania extended its rule southward, offering western Russian princes protection against Mongol and Muscovite rule. By the late fourteenth century, a vast Lithuanian principality had arisen, embracing modern Lithuania, Belarus, and Ukraine.

Casimir III died in 1370 without a son; the failure of a new dynasty to take hold opened the way for the unification of Poland and Lithuania. In 1386, the Lithuanian prince Jogaila (Jagiellon) accepted Roman Catholicism, married the young queen of Poland, and assumed the Polish crown as Wladyslaw II. Under the Jagiellonian dynasty, Poland and Lithuania kept separate legal systems. Catholicism and Polish culture prevailed among the principality's upper class, while most native Lithuanian village folk remained pagan for several centuries. With only a few interruptions, the Polish-Lithuanian federation would last for five centuries.

North of the Black Sea and east of Poland-Lithuania, a different polity was taking shape. In the second half of the fifteenth century, the princes of Muscovy embarked on a spectacular path of success that would make their state the largest on earth. Subservient to the Mongols in the fourteenth century, the Muscovite princes began to assert their independence with the collapse of Mongol power. Ivan III (r. 1462–1505) was the first Muscovite prince to claim an imperial title, referring to himself as **tsar** (or "czar," from the name *Caesar*). Expanding his power to Novgorod in 1471, Ivan then moved to the south and east, pushing back the Mongols to the Volga River. Unlike monarchies in western and central-eastern Europe, whose powers were bound by collective rights and laws, Ivan's Russian monarchy claimed absolute property rights over all lands and subjects.

The expansionist Muscovite state was shaped by two traditions: religion and service. After the fall of the Byzantine Empire, the tsar was the Russian Orthodox church's only defender of the faith against Islam and Catholicism. Orthodox propaganda thus legitimized the tsar's rule by proclaiming Moscow the "Third Rome" (the first two being Rome and Constantinople) and praising the tsar's autocratic power as essential to protect the faith. The Mongol system of service to rulers also deeply informed Muscovite statecraft. Ivan III and his descendants considered themselves heirs to the empire of the Mongols. In their conception of the state as private dominion, their emphasis on autocratic power, and their division of the populace into a landholding elite in service to the tsar and a vast majority of taxpaying subjects, the Muscovite princes created a state more in the despotic political tradition of the central Asian steppes and the Ottoman Empire than of western Europe.

Hard Times

The wars of the fourteenth and fifteenth centuries brought hard times to many members of the commercial classes. During the Hundred Years' War, the English king Edward III borrowed heavily from the largest Italian banking houses, the Bardi and Peruzzi of Florence. With many of their assets tied up in loans to the English monarchy, the Italian bankers had no choice but to extend new credits, hoping vainly to recover their initial investments. In the early 1340s, however, Edward defaulted, and the once-illustrious houses went bankrupt. Meanwhile, diminished production and trade eventually caused turmoil in northern Europe and a crisis for financiers in the Low Countries. Bruges, the financial center for northwestern Europe, saw its power fade during the fifteenth century when a succession of its money changers went bankrupt.

This breakdown in the most advanced economic sector reflected the general recession in the European economy. Merchants were less likely to take risks and more willing to invest their money in government bonds than in production and commerce. Fewer merchants traveled to Asia, partly because of the danger of attack by Ottoman Turks on the overland routes that had once been protected by the Mongols. Italians, while still exporting luxuries north and obtaining raw materials and silver in return, now tended to invest in the arts rather than in trade and industry. The Medici, who dominated Florence in the fifteenth century, are good examples. They stayed close to home, investing part of their banking profits in art and politics and relying on business agents to conduct their affairs in other European cities.

At the lower end of the economic ladder, this war-torn society rested on a broad base of underclass—poor peasants and laborers in the countryside, workers and servants in the cities. Lower still were the marginal elements of society. Organized gangs prowled the larger cities, their members mostly artisans vacillating between work and crime. Paris, for example, teemed with thieves, thugs, beggars, prostitutes, and vagabonds. Some disguised themselves as clerics to escape the law, and others were bona fide clerics who turned to crime to make ends meet during an age of steadily declining clerical income.

Often the underclass served as soldiers as well. War was no longer mainly for knights; it absorbed young men from poor backgrounds. Initiated into a life of plunder and killing, soldiers adjusted poorly to civilian life after discharge; between wars, these men turned to crime, adding to the misery.

Women featured prominently in the underclass, reflecting the unequal distribution of power between the sexes. Urban domestic service was the major employment for girls from the countryside, who worked to save money for their dowries. In addition to the usual household chores, women also worked as wet nurses (women hired to nurse other people's children). Some women, unable to find other means of support, became prostitutes. In Mediterranean Europe, some 90 percent of slaves were women in domestic servitude. They came from Muslim or Greek Orthodox countries and usually served in upper-class households in the great commercial city republics of Venice, Florence, and Ragusa. Their actual numbers were small—several hundred in fourteenth-century Florence, for example—because only rich households could afford slaves.

The Crisis of the Papacy

In the early years of the fourteenth century, the papacy moved from Rome to Avignon, just outside the borders of France. It had a markedly French character: all five popes elected between 1305 and 1378 were natives of southern France. Subjected to pressure from the French monarchy and turning increasingly secular in its opulence and splendor, the papacy was lambasted by the Italian poet Francesco Petrarch as being "in Babylonian Captivity," like the Jews of ancient Israel who were exiled by their Babylonian conquerors.

The popes did not see themselves as captives. Lawyers by training, they concentrated on consolidating the financial and legal powers of the church, mainly through appointments and taxes. Claiming the right to assign all benefices (the properties or income that supported clerical positions), the popes gradually secured authority over the clergy throughout western and central Europe. Under the skillful guidance of John XXII (r. 1316–1334), papal rights increased incrementally without causing much protest. By 1350, the popes had secured the right to grant all major benefices and many minor ones. To gain these lucrative positions, potential candidates often made gifts to the papal court. The imposition of papal taxes on all benefice holders originated in taxes to finance the crusades. Out of these precedents, the papacy instituted a regular system of papal taxation that produced the money it needed to consolidate papal government.

That government—the curia—consisted of the pope's personal household, the College of Cardinals, and the church's financial and judicial apparatuses. Combining elements of monarchy and oligarchy, the curia developed a bureaucracy that paralleled the organization of secular government. The pope's relatives often played a major role in his household; many popes came from extended noble lineages, and they often gave their family members preferential treatment.

After the pope, the cardinals as a collective body were the most elevated entity in the church. Like great nobles in royal courts, the cardinals, many of them nobles themselves, advised and aided the pope. They maintained their own households, employing scores of scribes, servants, and retainers. The papal army also expanded at the same time, as the popes sought to restore and control the Papal States in the region around Rome.

This growing papal monarchy was sharply criticized by some members of the Franciscan and Dominican orders, who denounced the papal pretension to worldly power and wealth. The scholastic William of Ockham, for example, believed that church power derived from the congregation of the faithful, both laity and clergy, not from the pope or church councils. Imprisoned by Pope John XXII for heresy, Ockham escaped in 1328 and found refuge with Emperor Louis of Bavaria.

Another antipapal refugee at the imperial court was Marsilius of Padua, a citizen of an Italian commune, a physician and lawyer by training, and rector of the University of Paris. Marsilius attacked the very basis of papal power in *The Defender of the Peace* (1324). The true church, Marsilius argued, was constituted by the people, who had the right to select the head of the church, either through the body of the faithful or through a "human legislator." Papal power, Marsilius asserted, was the result of historical usurpation, and its exercise represented tyranny. In 1327, John XXII, the living target of the treatise, decreed the work heretical.

Greater stability in Italy emboldened Gregory XI, elected pope in 1371, to return to Rome. When he died in 1378, sixteen cardinals—one Spanish, four Italian, and eleven French—met in Rome to elect the new pope. Although many in the curia were homesick for Avignon, the Roman people, determined to keep the papacy and its revenues in Rome, clamored for the election of a Roman. An unruly crowd rioted outside the conclave, drowning out the cardinals' discussions. Fearing for their lives, the cardinals elected the archbishop of Bari, an Italian, who took the title Urban VI. If the cardinals thought they had elected a weak man who

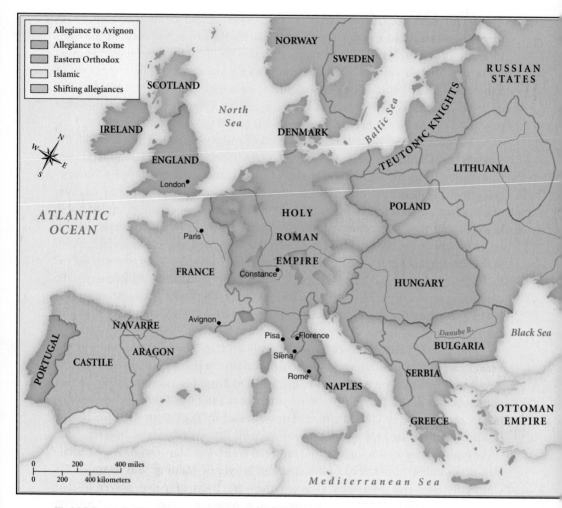

■ **MAP 11.5 The Great Schism, 1378–1417**
*Allegiance to Roman and Avignon popes followed the political divisions among the European
monarchs. The Great Schism weakened the Latin West during a period of Islamic expansion
through the Ottoman Empire.*

would do their bidding and satisfy the Romans, they were wrong: Urban immediately tried to curb the cardinals' power. In response, thirteen cardinals elected
another pope, Clement VII, and returned to Avignon.

Thus began the **Great Schism** of the papacy, which was perpetuated by political divisions in Europe (Map 11.5). Charles V of France, who did not want the
papacy to return to Rome, immediately recognized Clement, his cousin, as did several other rulers, including those of Sicily, Scotland, and Castile. An enemy of

Charles V, Richard II of England professed allegiance to Urban, as did the rulers of other areas, including most of the Holy Roman Empire, central and northern Italy, and Hungary and Poland. Faithful Christians were equally divided in their loyalties. Even the greatest mystic of the age—Catherine of Siena (1347–1380), who told of her mystical unions with God and spiritual ecstasies in more than 350 letters and was later canonized a saint—found herself forced to take sides. Catherine supported Urban. But another holy man, Vincent Ferrer (1350–1419), a popular Dominican preacher, supported Clement. All Christians theoretically found themselves deprived of the means of salvation, as bans from Rome and Avignon each placed part of Christian Europe under interdict, which deprived them of most sacraments and Christian burial.

Because neither pope would step down willingly, the leading intellectuals in the church tried to end the schism another way. Many of them became "conciliarists." According to canon law, only a pope could summon a general council of the church—a sort of parliament of all Christians. But given the state of confusion in Christendom, many intellectuals argued that the crisis justified calling a general council to represent the body of the faithful, over and against the head of the church. Jean Gerson, chancellor of the University of Paris, asserted that "the pope can be removed by a general council celebrated without his consent and against his will."

In 1409 the Council of Pisa asserted its supremacy and declared both popes deposed. It then elected a new pontiff, Alexander V. When the popes at Rome and Avignon refused to yield to the authority of the council, Christian Europe found itself in the embarrassing position of having three popes. Pressure to hold another council then came from central Europe, where a new heretical movement, ultimately known as Hussitism, undermined orthodoxy from Bohemia to central Germany. Threatened politically by challenges to church authority, Emperor Sigismund pressed Pope John XXIII, the successor to Alexander (who had died ten months after being elected), to convene a church council at Constance in 1414.

The cardinals, bishops, and theologians assembled in Constance felt compelled to combat heresy, heal the schism, and reform the church. They ordered Jan Hus, the Prague professor and inspiration behind the Hussite movement, burned at the stake despite an imperial safe conduct he had been promised, but this act failed to suppress dissent. They deposed John XXIII, the "Pisan pope," because of tyrannical behavior, condemning him as an antipope. The Roman pope, Gregory XII, accepted the council's authority and resigned in 1415 (having been elected in 1406). At its closing in 1417, the council also deposed Benedict XIII (Clement's successor), the "Spanish mule," who refused to abdicate the Avignon papacy and lived out his life in a fortress in Spain, still regarding himself as pope and surrounded by his own curia. The rest of Christendom, however, hailed Martin V, the council's appointment, as the new pope, thus ending the Great Schism. The council had taken a stand against heresy and had achieved unity under one pope. But the papacy's prestige had suffered a lasting blow.

■ **The Burning of Jews**

While knights and noblewomen watch, an executioner carries more firewood to the pyre of Jews, an example of the horrible persecutions against Jewish communities during the plague years from 1348 to 1350. This religious violence, arising out of the confrontation between Christianity and Judaism, had the opposite effect to that intended by Christians. Instead of converting, most Jews honored their martyrs and felt less incentive to accept the faith of their oppressors.

(Copyright, Bibliothèque royale de Belgique, Brussels.)

Stamping Out Dissenters, Heretics, Jews, and Muslims

The Council's burning of Hus was part of a wider movement. Everywhere church and state moved to stamp out groups that, in their view, did not fit within the established church. The church condemned the Free Spirits, for example. These groups, found mostly in northern Europe, practiced an extreme form of mysticism, asserting that humans and God were of the same essence and that individual believers could attain salvation, even sanctity, without the church and its sacraments. In the 1360s, Emperor Charles IV and Pope Urban V extended the Inquisition to Germany in a move to crush this heresy. In the cities of the Rhineland, fifteen mass trials took place, most around the turn of the fifteenth century.

In England, intellectual dissent, social unrest, and nationalist sentiment combined to create a powerful movement that the church hierarchy labeled Lollardy (from *lollar*, meaning "idler"). It was inspired by John Wycliffe (c. 1330–1384), an Oxford professor who challenged the very foundations of the Roman church. His treatise *On the Church*, composed in 1378, advanced the view that the true church was a community of believers rather than a clerical hierarchy. In other writings, Wycliffe repudiated monasticism, excommunication, the Mass, and the priesthood, substituting reliance on Bible reading and individual conscience in place of the official church as the path to salvation. Responsibility for church reform, Wycliffe believed, rested with the king, whose authority (in his view) exceeded that of the pope. Despite persistent persecutions, Lollardy survived underground during the fifteenth century, to resurface during the convulsive religious conflict of the early sixteenth century known as the Reformation.

The most profound challenge to papal authority in the later Middle Ages came from Bohemia. Here the spiritual, intellectual, political, and economic criticisms of the papacy that sprang up in other countries fused in one explosive spark. Religious dissent quickly became the vehicle for a nationalist uprising and a social revolution: the Hussite movement.

Under Emperor Charles IV, the pace of economic development and social change in the Holy Roman Empire had quickened in the mid-fourteenth century. Prague, the capital of Bohemia, became one of Europe's great cities: the new silver mine at Kutnà Hora boosted Prague's economic growth, and the first university in the empire was founded there in 1348. Bohemia, a part of the Holy Roman Empire, had been settled by a Slavic people, the Czechs, since the early Middle Ages. Later, many German merchants and artisans migrated to Bohemian cities, and Czech peasants, uprooted from the land, flocked to the cities in search of employment. This diverse society became a potentially explosive mass when heightened expectations of commercial and intellectual growth collided with the grim realities of the plague and economic problems in the late fourteenth century. Tax protests, urban riots, and ethnic conflicts signaled growing unrest, but it was religious discontent that became the focus for popular revolt.

Critics of the clergy, often clergy themselves, decried the moral conduct of priests and bishops, accusing them of holding multiple benefices, leading dissolute lives, and ignoring their pastoral duties. How could the clergy, living in a state of mortal sin, legitimately perform the sacraments? critics asked. Advocating greater lay participation in the Mass and in the reading of Scripture, religious dissenters drew some of their ideas from the writings of Wycliffe. Among those influenced by Wycliffe's ideas were Jan Hus (d. 1415) and his follower Jerome of Prague (d. 1416), both Prague professors, ethnic Czechs, and leaders of a reform party in Bohemia. Although the reform party attracted adherents from all Czech-speaking social groups, the German minority, who dominated the university and urban elites in Prague, opposed it out of ethnic rivalry. The Bohemian nobility protected Hus; the common clergy rebelled against the bishops; and the artisans and workers in Prague were ready to back the reform party by force. These disparate social interests all focused on one symbolic but passionately felt religious demand: the right to receive the Eucharist as both bread and wine at Mass. In traditional Roman liturgy, the chalice was reserved for the clergy; the Utraquists, as their opponents called them (from *utraque*, Latin for "both"), wanted to drink wine from the chalice as well, to achieve a measure of equality between laity and clergy.

When Hus was burned at the stake by the Council of Constance in 1415, his death caused a national uproar. The reform movement, which had thus far focused only on religious issues, burst forth as a national revolution. Sigismund's initial repression of the revolt in the provinces was brutal, and many dissenters were massacred. To organize their defense, the Hussites gathered at a mountain in southern Bohemia, which they called Mount Tabor after the mountain in the New Testament where the transfiguration of Christ took place. Now called Taborites, they began to restructure their community according to biblical injunctions. Like the first Christian church, they initially practiced communal ownership of goods and thought of themselves as the only true Christians awaiting the return of Christ and the end of the world. As their influence spread, the Taborites compromised with the surrounding social order, collecting tithes from peasants and retaining magistrates in towns under their control. Taborite leaders were radical priests who ministered to the community in the Czech language, exercised moral and judicial leadership, and even led the people into battle. Resisting all attempts to crush them, the Czech revolutionaries eventually gained the right from the papacy to receive the Eucharist as both bread and wine, a practice that continued until the sixteenth century.

A still different group of heretics grew out of the anguish of the Black Death. Believing that the plague was God's way of chastising a sinful world, bands of men and women sought to save themselves by repenting their sins in a dramatic manner: wearing tattered clothes, they visited local churches and sang hymns while publicly whipping themselves until blood flowed. The **flagellants**, as they soon came to be called, cried out to God for mercy and called upon the congregation to repent their sins. But the clergy distrusted this lay movement that did not originate within the church hierarchy.

In some communities, the religious fervor aroused by the flagellants spawned violence against Jews. From 1348 to 1350, anti-Semitic persecutions, beginning in southern France and spreading through Savoy to the Holy Roman Empire, destroyed many Jewish communities in central and western Europe. Sometimes the clergy incited the attacks against the Jews, calling them Christ-killers, accusing them of poisoning wells and kidnapping and ritually slaughtering Christian children. In towns throughout Europe, economic resentment fueled anti-Semitism as those in debt turned on creditors, often Jews who had become rich from the commercial expansion of the thirteenth century.

Many anti-Semitic incidents were spontaneous, with mobs plundering Jewish quarters and killing anyone who refused baptism. But it is equally true that at times civic authorities orchestrated the violence. For example, the magistrates of Nuremberg obtained approval from Emperor Charles IV before organizing the 1349 persecution directed by the city government. Thousands of German Jews were slaughtered. Many fled to Poland, where the incidence of plague was low and where the authorities welcomed Jews as productive taxpayers. In western and central Europe, however, the persecutions destroyed the financial power of the Jews.

End of the Reconquista and Expulsion of the Jews from Spain, 1492

Like France and England, war wracked Spain as dynasties fought over the royal succession in the various kingdoms. But again, as in France and England, the result was a strengthened monarchy. In 1469, Queen Isabella of Castile and King Ferdinand of Aragon married. Retaining their separate titles, the two monarchs ruled jointly over their dominions, each of which adhered to its traditional laws and privileges. Their union represented the first step toward the creation of a unified Spain out of two medieval kingdoms. Isabella and Ferdinand limited the privileges of the nobility and allied themselves with the cities, relying on urban militias to enforce justice and on professional lawyers to staff the royal council.

Unification of Spain, Late Fifteenth Century

The reconquista, the slow "reconquest" of Muslim Spain by the Christian north, came to a close under the united strength of Castile and Aragon. In 1478 war broke out between Granada, the last Iberian Muslim state, and Catholic royal forces. Weakened by internal strife, Granada finally fell in 1492. Two years later, in recognition of that crusade, Pope Alexander VI bestowed the title "Catholic monarchs" on Isabella and Ferdinand.

In this climate, it no longer seemed possible for Iberian Muslims, Jews, and Christians to live side by side. The practice of Catholicism became a test of one's loyalty to the church and to the Spanish monarchy. In 1478, the king and queen introduced the Inquisition into Spain, primarily as a means to control the **conversos** (Jewish converts to Christianity), whose elevated positions in the economy and the government aroused widespread resentment from the so-called Old Christians. Conversos often were suspected of practicing Judaism, their ancestral religion, in secret while pretending to adhere to their new Christian faith. Appointed by the monarchs, the inquisitors presided over tribunals set up to investigate those suspected of religious deviancy. The accused, who were arrested on charges often based on anonymous denunciations and information gathered by the inquisitors, could defend themselves but not confront their accusers. The wide spectrum of punishments ranged from monetary fines to the **auto da fé** (a ritual of public confession) to burning at the stake. After the fall of Granada, many Muslims were forced to convert or resettle. At the same time, Ferdinand and

Isabella ordered all Jews in their kingdoms to choose between exile and conversion. Many chose exile.

The expulsion of the Jews from Spain had far greater consequences than their earlier banishments from France and England. Spain had had the largest and most vibrant Jewish communities of Europe. On the eve of the expulsion, approximately 200,000 Jews and 300,000 conversos were living in Castile and Aragon. Faced with the choice to convert or leave, well over 100,000 Jews dispersed, some settling in North Africa, more in Italy, and many in the Ottoman Empire, Greek-speaking Thessalonika, and Palestine. Conversant in two or three languages, these Jews often served as intermediaries between the Christian West and Muslim East.

■ **REVIEW:** *What central factors contributed to the crises of the fourteenth and mid-fifteenth centuries?*

New Forms of Thought and Expression: The Renaissance

The Renaissance had its medieval roots in vernacular literature like Dante's *Divine Comedy* and the humanism of the Gothic sculptors who portrayed figures in the round. But it grew far beyond those roots, to discover and embrace the classical past and to use classical themes to celebrate human glory. Fostered by the printing press, Renaissance writings spread far and wide to a literate middle class eager to absorb every sort of text. Meanwhile, Renaissance artists celebrated the newly powerful republics, principalities, and kingdoms of their age. Flush with power, these states intruded into the most intimate personal matters, such as sexuality, marriage, and childbirth.

Renaissance Humanism

From the epics and romances of the twelfth and thirteenth centuries, vernacular writings blossomed into a full-blown literature in the fourteenth. Poetry, stories, and chronicles composed in Italian, French, English, and other national languages helped redefine style and beauty. The great writers of late medieval Europe were of urban middle-class origins, from families that had done well in government, church service, or commercial enterprises. Unlike the medieval troubadours, with their aristocratic backgrounds, the men and women who wrote vernacular literature in this age typically came from the cities, and their audience was the literate laity. Francesco Petrarch (1304–1374), the poet laureate of Italy's vernacular literature, and his younger contemporary and friend Giovanni Boccaccio (1313–1375) were both from the Florentine professional classes. Geoffrey Chaucer (c. 1342–1400), an important vernacular poet of medieval England, came from a family of wine

■ **Poet and Queen**

Christine de Pisan, kneeling, presents a manuscript of her poems to Isabella of Bavaria, the queen of France. Isabella's royal status is indicated by the royal French emblem, the fleur-de-lis, which decorates the bedroom walls. The sumptuous interior (chairs, cushions, tapestry, paneled ceiling, glazed and shuttered windows) was typical of aristocratic domestic architecture. Even in the intimacy of her bedroom, Queen Isabella, like all royal personages, was constantly attended and almost never alone (notice her ladies-in-waiting).
(The British Library.)

merchants. Even writers who celebrated the life of the nobility were children of commoners. Though born in Valenciennes to a family of moneylenders and merchants, Jean Froissart (c. 1333–c. 1405), whose chronicle vividly describes the events of the Hundred Years' War, was an ardent admirer of chivalry. Christine de Pisan (1364–c. 1430), a poet and prose writer of great range, was the daughter of a Venetian municipal counselor who spent most of her life in France. Widowed early in life, she made a living and supported her children by writing books.

Life in all its facets found expression in the new vernacular literature, as writers told of love, greed, and salvation. Boccaccio's *Decameron* popularized the short story, as the characters in this novella tell sensual and bizarre tales in the shadow of the Black Death. Members of different social orders parade themselves in Chaucer's *Canterbury Tales*, journeying together on a pilgrimage. Christine de Pisan celebrated womanhood—and refuted misogynists (women-haters)—in *The Book of the City of Ladies* (1405); she populated her city with all the heroines of the past, present, and future. At the end of her book she turned to her readers, inviting them into the city:

> My most honored ladies, may God be praised, for now our City is entirely finished and completed, where all of you who love glory, virtue, and praise may be lodged in great honor . . . for it has been built and established for every honorable lady.

Noble patronage was crucial to the growth of vernacular literature. Christine often found wealthy female patrons within the royal French household. Even

Petrarch, perhaps closest to the model of an independent man of letters, relied on powerful patrons at various times. His early career began at the papal court in Avignon, where his father worked as a notary; during the 1350s, Petrarch enjoyed the protection and patronage of the Visconti duke of Milan. Boccaccio started out in the Neapolitan world of commerce. The court of King Robert of Naples initiated him into the realm of letters. Chaucer served in administrative posts and on many diplomatic missions. Noble patronage also shaped the literary creations of Froissart.

Vernacular literature blossomed not at the expense of Latin but alongside a classical revival. Despite the renown of their Italian writings, Petrarch and Boccaccio, for example, took great pride in their Latin works. In the second half of the fourteenth century, writers began to imitate the antiquated "classical" Latin of Roman literature. In the forefront of this literary and intellectual movement, Petrarch traveled to many monasteries in search of long-ignored Latin manuscripts. Writers like Petrarch considered medieval church Latin an artificial, awkward language, whereas classical Latin and classical Greek they believed the mother tongues of the ancients, even more authentic, vivid, and glorious than the poetry and prose written in Italian and other contemporary European languages. Classical allusions and literary influences abound in the works of Boccaccio, Chaucer, Christine de Pisan, and others. The new intellectual fascination with the ancient past also stimulated translations of classical works into the vernacular.

The attempt to emulate the virtues and learning of the ancients gave impetus to an intellectual movement: **humanism**. Humanists believed that a person could develop his or her full human potential only by studying the "humanities"—the liberal arts, and in particular literature and its subgenre history. They absorbed the eloquence of a Cicero with gusto, finding in it a source of virtue as well as style. "For what," the humanist Poggio Bracciolini asked his friend Guarino of Verona,

> is there that could be more delightful, more pleasant, and more agreeable to you and the rest of the learned world than the knowledge of those things whose acquaintance makes us more learned and, what seems even more important, stylistically more polished? . . . For it is speech alone which we use to express the power of our mind and which separates us from the other beings.

Gradually the imitation of ancient style led to the adoption of ancient ideas. In the writings of Roman historians such as Livy and Tacitus, fifteenth-century Italian civic elites (many of them lawyers) found echoes of their own devout patriotism. Between 1400 and 1430 in Florence, a time of war and crisis, the study of the humanities evolved into a republican ideology that historians call "civic humanism." In the early fifteenth century, the Florentines waged a highly successful propaganda war on behalf of virtuous republican Florence against tyrannical

Milan, invoking the memory of the overthrow of Etruscan tyrants by the first Romans. Thus, the study of ancient civilization was not only an antiquarian quest but also a call to public service and political action.

The fall of Constantinople in 1453 sent Greek scholars to Italy for refuge, giving extra impetus to the revival of Greek learning in the West. Venice and Florence assumed leadership in this new field—the former by virtue of its commercial and political ties to the eastern Mediterranean, the latter thanks to the patronage of Cosimo de' Medici, who sponsored the Platonic Academy, a discussion group dedicated to the study of Plato and his followers under the intellectual leadership of Marsilio Ficino (1433–1499).

Humanists did not consider the study of ancient cultures to be in conflict with their Christian faith. In "returning to the sources"—a famous slogan of the time— philosophers attempted to harmonize the disciplines of Christian faith and ancient learning. Ficino, the foremost Platonic scholar of the Renaissance, was also a priest. He argued that the immortality of the soul, a Platonic idea, was perfectly compatible with Christian doctrine and that much of ancient wisdom actually foreshadowed later Christian teachings.

Through their activities as educators and civil servants, professional humanists gave new vigor to the humanist curriculum of grammar, rhetoric, poetry, history, and moral philosophy. By the end of the fifteenth century, European intellectuals considered a good command of classical Latin, with perhaps some knowledge of Greek, as one of the requirements of an educated person.

The invention of mechanical printing aided greatly in making the classical texts widely available. Printing from movable type—a revolutionary departure from the old practice of copying by hand—was invented in the 1440s by Johannes Gutenberg, a German goldsmith. Mass production of identical books and pamphlets made the world of letters more accessible to a literate audience.

The advent of mass-printed books depended on paper production. The art of papermaking came to Europe from China via Arab intermediaries. By the fourteenth century, paper mills were operating in Italy, producing paper that was more fragile but much cheaper than parchment or vellum, the animal skins that Europeans had previously used for writing. To produce paper, old rags were soaked in a chemical solution, beaten by mallets into a pulp, washed with water, treated, and dried in sheets—a method that still produces good-quality paper today.

Even before the printing press, a brisk industry in manuscript books had been flourishing in Europe's university towns and major cities. Production was in the hands of stationers, who organized workshops known as *scriptoria*, where the manuscripts were copied, and acted as retail booksellers. Demand was high. The stationer for Cosimo de' Medici, for example, employed forty-five copyists to complete two hundred volumes in twenty-two months.

Nonetheless, bookmaking in scriptoria was slow and expensive, and the invention of movable type was an enormous technological breakthrough. It took bookmaking out of the hands of human copyists. Movable type consisted of reusable metal molds of letters, numbers, and various other characters. The typesetter arranged the characters by hand, page by page, to create a printable text. The surface of the type was inked, and sheets of paper pressed against the type picked up an impression of the text. Numerous copies could be made with only a small amount of human labor.

After the 1440s, printing spread rapidly from Germany to other European countries. In Germany, Cologne, Strasbourg, Nuremberg, and Augsburg all had major presses. In 1467, two German printers established the first press in Rome and produced twelve thousand volumes in five years, a feat that in the past would have required a thousand scribes working full-time. By 1480, many Italian cities had established their own presses. In the 1490s, the German city of Frankfurt-am-Main became an international meeting place for printers and booksellers. The Frankfurt Book Fair, where printers from different nations exhibited their newest titles, represented a major international cultural event and remains an unbroken tradition to this day.

The invention of mechanical printing gave rise to a "communications revolution" as significant as the widespread use of the personal computer today. The multiplication of standardized texts altered the thinking habits of Europeans by freeing individuals from having to memorize everything they learned; it made possible the relatively speedy and inexpensive dissemination of knowledge; and it created a wider community of scholars, no longer dependent on personal patronage or church sponsorship for texts. Printing facilitated the free expression and exchange of ideas, and its disruptive potential did not go unnoticed by political and ecclesiastical authorities. Emperors and bishops in Germany, the homeland of the printing industry, moved quickly to issue censorship regulations.

New Perspectives in Art and Music

New techniques in painting, architecture, and musical performance fostered original styles and subjects. Artists paid close attention to the human figure and strove to depict the world from nature rather than from pictorial models. Musicians enhanced polyphony with new harmonies and more versatile instruments.

As individual talent and genius were recognized by a society hungry for culture, artists themselves gained prestige. In exalting the status of the artist, Leonardo da Vinci (1452–1519), painter, architect, and inventor, described himself as a creative genius. He was not alone; Renaissance artists intended to convince society that their works were unique and their talents priceless. They exalted the artist above the "mere artisan," claiming to be independent of the blueprints of a patron. During the fifteenth century, as artists began to claim the respect and recognition of society, however, the reality was that most relied on wealthy patrons for support. And although they wished to create as their genius dictated, not all patrons of the arts allowed artists to work without restrictions. While the duke of Milan appreciated Leonardo's genius, the duke of Ferrara paid for his art by the square foot.

A successful artist who did fit the new vision of unfettered genius was the Florentine sculptor Donatello (1386–1466). Not only did Donatello's sculptures evoke classical Greek and Roman models, but the grace and movement of his work inspired Cosimo de' Medici, the ruler of Florence, to excavate antique works of art and put them on display. Donatello was one artist who enjoyed the long-term, high-status patronage of a prince. Others, like Andrea Mantegna (1431–1506), worked more precariously. Treated more as a skilled worker in service to the prince than as an independent artist, he was once even required to adorn his majestic Gonzaga tapestries with life sketches of farm animals.

The workshop—the normal place of production in Renaissance Italy and in northern European cities such as Nuremberg and Antwerp—afforded the artist greater autonomy. As heads of workshops, artists trained apprentices and negotiated contracts with clients. The most famous artists fetched good prices for their work. These artists developed followings, and wealthy consumers were willing to pay a premium for work done by a master instead of apprentices. Studies of art contracts show that in the course of the fifteenth century artists gained greater control over their work. Early in the century, clients routinely stipulated detailed conditions for works of art—specifying, for instance, gold paint or "ultramarine blue," which were among the most expensive pigments. Clients might also determine the arrangement of figures in a picture, leaving to the artist little more than the execution. After midcentury, such specific directions became less common. In 1487, for example, the Florentine painter Filippo Lippi (1457–1504), in his contract to paint frescoes in the Strozzi chapel, specified that the work should be "all from his own hand and particularly the figures." The shift underscores the increasing recognition of the unique skills of individual artists.

A market system for the visual arts emerged during the Renaissance, initially in the Low Countries. In the fifteenth century, most large-scale work was commissioned by specific patrons, but the art market, for which artists produced works without prior arrangement for sale, was to develop into the major force for artistic creativity, a force that prevails in contemporary society. The commercialization of art celebrated the new context of artistic creation itself: artists working in an open, competitive, urban civilization.

If the individual artist was a man of genius, what greater subject for the expression of beauty was there than the human body itself? Taking their cue from fourteenth-century painters such as Giotto (see page 421), Renaissance artists learned to depict ever more expressive human emotions and movements. The work of the short-lived but brilliant painter Masaccio (1401–1428) exemplifies this development. His painting *St. Peter Baptizing* shows the recipient of the baptism trembling in the cold water. In addition to rendering homage to classical and

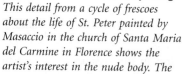

■ **Masaccio's *St. Peter Baptizing***
*This detail from a cycle of frescoes
about the life of St. Peter painted by
Masaccio in the church of Santa Maria
del Carmine in Florence shows the
artist's interest in the nude body. The
man receiving baptism is portrayed in
the round, light playing on his flesh and
revealing its contours. This emphasis on
human nakedness may have reflected
an egalitarian strain in republican
Florence. It also echoes what Masaccio
found in ancient art and sculpture.*
(Erich Lessing/Art Resource, NY.)

biblical figures, Renaissance artists painted their contemporaries as well. For the
first time after classical antiquity, sculptors again cast the human body in bronze,
in life-size or bigger freestanding statues. Free from fabric and armor, the human
body was idealized in the eighteen-foot marble sculpture *David*, the work of the
great Michelangelo Buonarroti (1475–1564).

The increasing number of portraits in Renaissance painting illustrates the new,
elevated view of human existence. Portraiture initially was limited to representations of pontiffs, monarchs, princes, and patricians, but soon portraits of middle-
class people became more widespread. Painters from the Low Countries such as
Rogier van der Weyden (c. 1400–1464) distinguished themselves in this genre; their
portraits achieved a sense of detail and reality unsurpassed until the advent of
photography.

All of this art was distinguished from its predecessors by its depiction of the
world as the eye perceives it. The use of *visual perspective*—an illusory three-
dimensional space on a two-dimensional surface and the ordered arrangement of
painted objects from one viewpoint—became one of the distinctive features of
Western art. Underlying the idea of perspective was a new Renaissance worldview:
humans asserting themselves over nature in painting and design by controlling
space. Optics became the organizing principle of the natural world in that it

detected the "objective" order in nature. The Italian painters were keenly aware of their new technique, and they criticized the Byzantine and the northern Gothic stylists for "flat" depictions of the human body and the natural world. The highest accolade for a Renaissance artist was to be described as an "imitator of nature": this epithet meant that the artist's teacher was nature, not design books or master painters. For the frescoes of the bridal chamber of the Gonzaga palace (executed 1465–1474), Mantegna created an illusory extension of reality: the actual living space in the chamber "opened out" to the painted landscape on the walls.

Perhaps even more than visual artists, fifteenth-century architects fulfilled the Renaissance ideals of uniting artistic creativity and scientific knowledge. The Florentine architect Leon Battista Alberti (1404–1472) made such ideas explicit in *On Architecture* (1415). Alberti argued for large-scale urban planning, with monumental buildings set on open squares, harmonious and beautiful in their proportions. His ideas were put into action by Pope Sixtus IV (r. 1471–1484) and his successors in the urban renewal of Rome, and they served to transform the city into a geometrically constructed monument to architectural brilliance by recalling the grandeur of its ancient origins.

Musicians and composers, too, worked for wealthy patrons at court. Developments in polyphony were led by Guillaume Dufay (1400–1474), whose musical training began in the cathedral choir of his hometown, Cambrai, in the Low Countries. His successful career took him to all the cultural centers of the Renaissance, where nobles sponsored new compositions and maintained a corps of

■ **Michelangelo's *David***

Michelangelo realized a synthesis of the ancient nude statue and the biblical figure of David in this larger-than-life sculpture of the young David, his body poised for action against the giant Goliath. The figure's easy slouch recalls depictions of Greek athletes, but this sculpture was commissioned by the administrators of the cathedral at Florence and was placed in front of the Florentine town hall. Both church and state thus garnered prestige from the artist and his work.
(Nimatallah/Art Resource, NY.)

■ **St. Ivo by**
Rogier van der Weyden
This painting of St. Ivo of
Chartres (c. 1040–1116) by
Rogier van der Weyden
(c. 1400–1464) exemplifies the
Flemish School style of detailed
realistic human portraits shown
against the backdrop of a land-
scape or city scene. Born in
Tournai, Weyden spent most of
his life as the official city painter
of Brussels. The Flemish School
exerted a significant influence on
painting in France, Portugal, and
Castile in the fifteenth century.
(© National Gallery Collection; by kind
permission of the Trustees of the
National Gallery/CORBIS.)

musicians for court and religious functions. In 1438, Dufay composed festive music to celebrate the completion of the cathedral dome in Florence designed by Filippo Brunelleschi (1377–1446). Dufay expressed the harmonic relationship among four voices in ratios that matched the mathematically precise dimensions of Brunelleschi's architecture. After a period of employment at the papal court, Dufay returned to his native north and composed music for the Burgundian and French courts.

Josquin des Prez (1440–1521), another Netherlander, wrote music in Milan, Ferrara, Florence, Paris, and at the papal court. Music was an integral part of courtly life: Lorenzo de' Medici sent Dufay a love poem to set to music, and the great composer maintained a lifelong relationship with the Medici family. Composers often adapted familiar folk melodies for sacred music, expressing religious feeling primarily through human voices instead of instruments. The tambourine and the lute were indispensable for dances, however, and small ensembles of wind and string instruments with contrasting sounds performed with singers in the fashionable courts of Europe. Also in use in the fifteenth century were new keyboard instruments—the harpsichord and clavichord—which could play several harmonic lines at once.

Republics and Principalities in Italy

In his book *The Prince*, the Florentine political theorist Niccolò Machiavelli (1469–1527) argued that the state was an artifice of human creation to be conquered, shaped, and administered by princes according to the principles of power politics. Whether a republic—which preserved the traditional institutions of the medieval commune by allowing a civic elite to control political and economic life—or a principality, ruled by one dynasty, each Italian Renaissance state was as centralized and controlling as the new monarchies of France and England.

Venice and Florence were republics. Venice, built on a lagoon, ruled an extensive colonial empire that extended from the Adriatic to the Aegean Sea. Venetian merchant ships sailed the Mediterranean, the Black Sea, and, increasingly, the Atlantic coast. Whether threatened by competing Italian states or by the Turks, Venice drew strength from its internal social cohesion. Under the rule of an oligarchy of aristocratic merchants, Venice enjoyed stability. Its maritime empire benefited citizens of all social classes, who joined efforts to defend the interests of the "Most Serene Republic," a contemporary name that reflected Venice's lack of social strife.

Compared with serene Venice, the republic of Florence was in constant agitation, as social classes and political factions engaged in ongoing conflict. By 1434, a single family had emerged dominant in this fractious city: the Medici. Cosimo de' Medici (1388–1464), head of the family, "disposed of his rivals, proceeded to administer the state at his pleasure and amassed wealth. . . . In Florence he built a palace fit for a king," as Pope Pius II put it. Head of one of the largest banks of Europe, Cosimo de' Medici used his immense wealth to influence politics. Even though he did not hold any formal political office, he wielded influence in government through business associates and clients indebted to him for loans, political appointments, and other favors. Cosimo became the arbiter of war and peace, the regulator of law, more master than citizen. Yet the prosperity and security that Florence enjoyed made him popular as well. At his death, Cosimo was lauded as "father of his country."

Cosimo's grandson Lorenzo (called "the Magnificent"), who assumed power in 1467, bolstered the regime's legitimacy with his lavish patronage of the arts. But opponents were not lacking. In 1478, Lorenzo narrowly escaped an assassination attempt. Two years after Lorenzo's death in 1494, partisans who opposed the Medici drove them from Florence. The Medici returned to power in 1512, only to be driven out again in 1527. In 1530, the republic fell and the Medici once again seized control, declaring themselves dukes of Florence.

Milan had been a principality long before then. Since the fourteenth century, it had been a military state, relatively uninterested in supporting the arts but with first-class armaments and textile industries in the capital city and rich farmlands in Lombardy. Until 1447, the duchy was ruled by the Visconti dynasty, a group of powerful lords whose plans to unify all of northern and central Italy failed from the combined opposition of Venice, Florence, and other Italian powers. After a brief republican interlude (1447–1450) during which Milan fought against its neighbors, its ruling nobility appointed Francesco Sforza, who had married the illegitimate daughter of the last Visconti duke, to the post of general. Sforza promptly turned against his employers, claiming the duchy as his own. A bitter struggle between the nobility and the townspeople in Milan further undermined the republican cause, and in 1450 Sforza entered Milan in triumph.

The power of the Sforza dynasty reached its height during the 1490s. In 1493, Duke Ludovico married his niece Bianca Maria to Maximilian, the newly elected Holy Roman Emperor, promising an immense dowry in exchange for the emperor's legitimization of his rule. But the newfound Milanese glory was soon swept aside by France's invasion of Italy in 1494, and the duchy itself eventually came under Spanish rule.

In the violent arena of Italian politics, the papacy, an uneasy mixture of worldly splendor and religious authority, was a player like the other states. The popes' concern with politics stemmed from their desire to restore papal authority, greatly undermined by the Great Schism and the conciliar movement. To that end, the popes used both politics and culture. Politically, they curbed local power, expanded papal government, increased taxation, enlarged the papal army and navy, and cultivated diplomacy. Culturally, the popes renovated churches, created the Vatican Library, sponsored artists, and patronized writers to glorify their role and power. In undertaking these measures, the Renaissance papacy merely exemplified the larger trend toward the centralization of power evident everywhere else.

Concentrated power, competition between states, and the extension of warfare all raised the practice of diplomacy to nearly an art form. The first diplomatic handbook, composed in 1436, emphasized ceremonies, elegance, and eloquence. These masked the complex game of diplomatic intrigue and spying. In the fifteenth century, a resident ambassador was expected to keep a continuous stream of foreign political news flowing to the home government, not just to conduct temporary diplomatic missions, as earlier ambassadors had done. In some cases, the presence of semiofficial agents developed into full-fledged ambassadorships: the Venetian embassy to the sultan's court in Constantinople developed out of the merchant-consulate that had represented all Venetian merchants, and Medici Bank branch managers eventually acted as political agents for the Florentine republic.

Foremost in the development of diplomacy was Milan. Under the Visconti dukes, Milan sent ambassadors to Aragon, Burgundy, the Holy Roman Empire, and the Ottoman Empire. Under the Sforza dynasty, Milanese diplomacy continued to function as a cherished form of statecraft. For generations, Milanese diplomats at the French court sent home an incessant flow of information on the rivalry between France and Burgundy. Francesco Sforza, founder of the dynasty, also used his diplomatic corps to extend his political patronage. In letters of recommendation to the papacy, Francesco commented on the political desirability of potential ecclesiastical candidates by using code words, sometimes supplemented with instructions to his ambassador to indicate his true intent regardless of the coded letter of recommendation. Ciphers were used in more sensitive diplomatic reports to hide their real meaning from hostile powers.

The most outstanding achievement of Italy's Renaissance diplomacy was the negotiation of a general peace treaty that settled the decades of warfare engendered by Milanese expansion and civil war. The Treaty of Lodi (1454) established a complex balance of power among the major Italian states and maintained relative stability on the peninsula for half a century. Renaissance diplomacy eventually failed, however, when more powerful northern European neighbors invaded in 1494, bringing on the collapse of the whole Italian state system.

The Intersection of Private and Public Lives

To deal with a mounting fiscal crisis, in 1427 the government of Florence ordered that a comprehensive tax record of households in the city and territory be compiled. Completed in 1430, this survey (called a *catasto*) represented the most detailed population census then taken in European history. From the resulting mass of fiscal and demographic data, historians have been able to reconstruct a picture of Florentine society.

The state of Florence, roughly the size of Massachusetts, had a population of more than 260,000. Tuscany, the area in which the Florentine state was located, was one of the most urbanized regions of Europe. With 38,000 inhabitants, the capital city of Florence claimed 14 percent of the total population and an enormous 67 percent of the state's wealth. Straddling the Arno River, Florence was a beautiful, thriving city with a defined social hierarchy. In describing class divisions, the Florentines themselves referred to the "little people" and the "fat people." Some 60 percent of all households belonged to the "little people"—workers, artisans, small merchants. The "fat people" (roughly our middle class) made up 30 percent of the urban population and included the wealthier merchants, the leading artisans, notaries, doctors, and other professionals. At the very bottom of the hierarchy were slaves and servants, most of them women employed in domestic service. Whereas the small number of slaves were of Balkan origin, the much larger population of domestic servants came to the city from the surrounding countryside as contracted wage earners. At the top, a tiny elite of patricians, bankers, and wool merchants controlled the state with their enormous wealth. In fact, the richest 1 percent of urban households (approximately one hundred families) owned more than one-quarter of the city's wealth and one-sixth of Tuscany's total wealth. The patricians in particular owned almost all government bonds, a lucrative investment guaranteed by a state they dominated.

Surprisingly, men seem to have outnumbered women in the 1427 survey. For every 100 women there were 110 men, unlike most past and present populations, in which women are the majority. In addition to female infanticide, which was occasionally practiced, the survey itself reflected the society's bias against women: persistent underreporting on women probably explained the statistical abnormality; and married daughters, young girls, and elderly widows frequently disappeared from the memories of householders. Most people, men and women alike, lived in households with at least six inhabitants, although the form of family unit—nuclear or extended—varied, depending mainly on wealth. Poor people rarely were able to support extended families. Among the urban rich and landowning peasants, the extended family held sway. The number of children in a family, it seems, reflected class differences as well. Wealthier families had more children; childless couples existed almost exclusively among the poor.

▪ Renaissance "Birth Tray" (c. 1450)

Scenes from the story of David and Goliath decorate this round tray, which was used to bring sweets to a well-to-do Florentine mother who had just given birth. Such trays were relatively common in fifteenth-century Florence. They were commissioned by husbands, and after their initial presentation, they were hung on a wall in the family's home. This one shows David (in red) flinging a stone at Goliath with his slingshot; cutting off Goliath's head; and, in the center, holding up Goliath's head as a trophy. Such scenes were meant to inspire the young child to be brave, like David.

(Courtesy of The Loyola University Museum of Art, Martin D'Arcy Collection, Chicago.)

Wealth and class clearly determined family structure and the pattern of marriage and childbearing. In a letter to her eldest son, Filippo, dated 1447, Alessandra Strozzi announced the marriage of her daughter Caterina to the son of Parente Parenti. She described the young groom, Marco Parenti, as "a worthy and virtuous young man, and . . . the only son, and rich, 25 years old, and keeps a silk workshop; and they have a little political standing." The dowry was set at one thousand florins, a substantial sum—but for four to five hundred florins more, Alessandra admitted to Filippo, Caterina would have fetched a husband from a more prominent family.

The Strozzi belonged to one of Florence's most distinguished traditional families, but at the time of Caterina's betrothal the family had fallen into political disgrace. Alessandra's husband, an enemy of the Medici, was exiled in 1434; Filippo, a rich merchant in Naples, lived under the same political ban. Although Caterina was clearly marrying beneath her social station, the marriage represented an alliance in which money, political status, and family standing all balanced out. More an alliance between families than the consummation of love, an Italian Renaissance marriage was usually orchestrated by the male head of a household. In this case, Alessandra, as a widow, shared the matchmaking responsibility with her eldest son and other male relatives. Eighteen years later, when it came time to find a wife for Filippo, who had by then accumulated enough wealth to start his own household, Marco Parenti, his brother-in-law, would serve as matchmaker.

The upper-class Florentine family was patrilineal, tracing descent and determining inheritance through the male line. Because the distribution of wealth depended on this patriarchal system, women occupied an ambivalent position in the household. A daughter could claim inheritance only through her dowry, and she often disappeared from family records after her marriage. A wife seldom emerged from the shadow of her husband, and consequently the lives of many women have been lost to history.

Women's subordination in marriages often reflected the age differences between spouses. The Italian marriage pattern, in which young women married older men, contrasted sharply with the northern European model, in which partners were much closer in age. Significant age disparity also left many women widowed in their twenties and thirties, and remarriage often proved a hard choice. A widow's father and brothers frequently pressed her to remarry to form a new family alliance. A widow, however, could not bring her children into her new marriage because they belonged to her first husband's family. Faced with the choice between her children and her paternal family, not to mention the question of her own happiness, a widow could hope to gain greater autonomy only in her old age, when, like Alessandra, she might assume matchmaking responsibilities to advance her family's fortunes.

In northern Europe, however, women enjoyed a relatively more autonomous position. In England, the Low Countries, and Germany, for example, women played a significant role in the economy—not only in the peasant household, in which everyone worked, but especially in the town, serving as peddlers, weavers, seam-stresses, shopkeepers, midwives, and brewers. In Munich, for example, they ranked among some of the richest brewers. Women in northern Europe shared inheritances with their brothers, retained control of their dowries, and had the right to repre-sent themselves before the law. Italian men who traveled to the north were appalled at the differences in gender relations, criticizing English women as violent and brazen and disapproving of the mixing of the sexes in German public baths.

Child care and attitudes toward sexuality also reflected class differences in Renaissance life. Florentine middle- and upper-class fathers arranged business con-tracts with wet nurses to breast-feed their infants; babies thus spent prolonged peri-ods of time away from their families. Such elaborate child care was beyond the reach of the poor, who often abandoned their children to strangers or to public charity.

By the beginning of the fifteenth century, Florence's two hospitals were accept-ing large numbers of abandoned children in addition to the sick and infirm. In 1445, the government opened the Ospedale degli Innocenti to deal with the large number of abandoned children from poor families or from women who had given birth out of wedlock. Many of the latter were domestic slaves or servants impreg-nated by their masters; in 1445, one-third of the first hundred foundlings at the new hospital were children of the unequal liaisons between masters and women slaves. For some women, the foundling hospital provided an alternative to infanti-cide. Over two-thirds of abandoned infants were girls. Although Florence's government employed wet nurses to care for the foundlings, the large number of abandoned infants overtaxed the hospital's limited resources. The hospital's death rate for infants was much higher than the already high infant mortality rate of the time.

Illegitimacy in itself did not necessarily carry a social stigma in fifteenth-century Europe. Most upper-class men acknowledged and supported their illegitimate chil-dren as a sign of virility, and illegitimate children of noble lineage often rose to social and political prominence. Any social stigma was borne primarily by the woman, whose ability to marry became compromised. Shame and guilt drove some poor sin-gle mothers to kill their infants, a crime for which they paid with their own lives.

In addition to prosecuting infanticide, the public regulation of sexuality focused on prostitution and homosexuality. Intended "to eliminate a worse evil by a lesser one," a 1415 statute established government brothels in Florence. Concurrent with its higher tolerance of prostitution, the Renaissance state had a low tolerance of homosexuality. In 1432, the Florentine state appointed magistrates "to discover—whether by means of secret denunciation, accusations, notification, or any other method—those who commit the vice of sodomy, whether actively or passively." The government set fines for homosexual acts and carried out death sentences against pederasts (men who have sex with boys).

Fifteenth-century European magistrates took violence against women less seri-ously than illegal male sexual behavior, as the different punishments indicate. In Renaissance Venice, for example, the typical jail sentence for rape and attempted rape was only six months. Magistrates often treated noblemen with great leniency and handled rape cases according to class distinctions. For example, Agneta, a young girl living with a government official, was abducted and raped by two millers, who were sentenced to five years in prison; several servants who abducted and raped a slave woman were sentenced to three to four months in jail; and a nobleman who abducted and raped Anna, a slave woman, was freed. Whether in marriage, inheritance, illicit sex, or sexual crime, the Renaissance state regulated the behavior of men and women according to differing concepts of gender. The brilliant civilization of the Renaissance was experienced quite differently by men and women.

■ **REVIEW:** *How did the Renaissance encompass both arts and conceptions of the state?*

On the Threshold of World History

The fifteenth century constituted the first time that Europe was a major player in world history. Before the maritime explorations of Portugal and Spain, Europe had remained at the periphery of world events. Fourteenth-century Mongols had been more interested in conquering China and Persia—lands with sophisticated cultures—than in invading Europe; Persian historians of the early fifteenth century dismissed Europeans as "barbaric Franks"; and China's Ming dynasty rulers, who sent maritime expeditions to Southeast Asia and East Africa around 1400, seemed unaware of the Europeans, even though Marco Polo and other Italian merchants had appeared at the court of the preceding Mongol Yuan dynasty. In the fifteenth century, Portuguese and Spanish vessels, followed a century later by English, French, and Dutch ships, sailed across the Atlantic, Indian, and Pacific Oceans, bringing with them people, merchandise, crops, and diseases in a global exchange that would shape the modern world. For the first time, the people of the Americas were brought into contact with a larger historical force that threatened to destroy not only their culture but their existence. European exploitation and conquest defined this historical era of transition from the medieval to the modern world, as Europeans left the Baltic and the Mediterranean for wider oceans.

The Divided Mediterranean

In the second half of the fifteenth century, the Mediterranean Sea, which had dominated medieval maritime trade, began to lose its preeminence to the Atlantic Ocean. To win control over the Mediterranean, the Ottomans embarked on an ambitious naval program to transform their empire into a major maritime power. War and piracy disrupted the flow of Christian trade: the Venetians mobilized all their resources to fight off Turkish advances, and the Genoese largely abandoned the eastern Mediterranean for trade opportunities presented by the Atlantic.

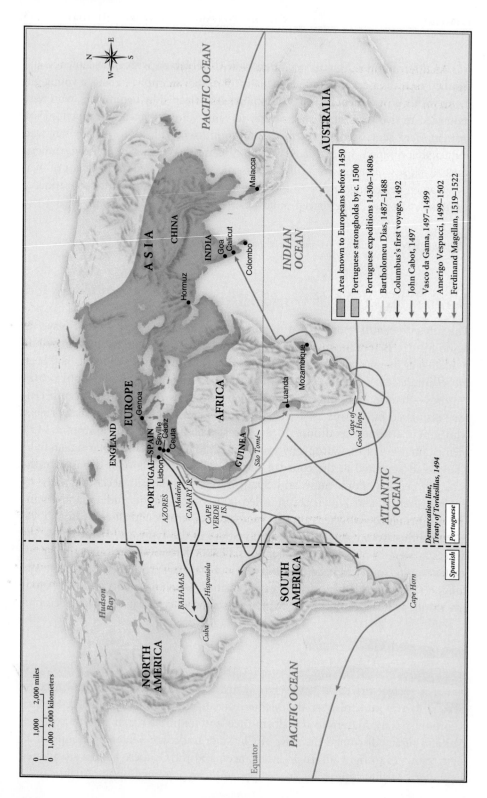

PACIFIC OCEAN

AUSTRALIA

ASIA

CHINA

Malacca

INDIA

Goa

Calicut

Colombo

INDIAN
OCEAN

Hormuz

EUROPE

Genoa

AFRICA

Mozambique

Luanda

ENGLAND

PORTUGAL—SPAIN

Seville
Cadiz
Lisbon
Ceuta

Cape of
Good Hope

GUINEA

São Tomé

AZORES

Madeira

CANARY IS.

CAPE
VERDE
IS.

ATLANTIC
OCEAN

BAHAMAS

Hispaniola

Cuba

Hudson
Bay

SOUTH
AMERICA

Cape Horn

NORTH
AMERICA

PACIFIC OCEAN

Equator

Demarcation line,
Treaty of Tordesillas, 1494

Spanish | Portuguese

| Area known to Europeans before 1450 |
| Portuguese strongholds by c. 1500 |
| Bartholomeu Dias, 1487–1488 |
| Columbus's first voyage, 1492 |
| John Cabot, 1497 |
| Vasco da Gama, 1497–1499 |
| Amerigo Vespucci, 1499–1502 |
| Ferdinand Magellan, 1519–1522 |

Portuguese expeditions 1430s–1480s

0   1,000   2,000 miles
0   1,000 2,000 kilometers

Mediterranean trade used ships made with relatively backward naval technology. The most common ship, the galley—a flat-bottom vessel propelled mainly by oarsmen with the help of a sail—dated from the time of ancient Rome. Most galleys could not withstand open-ocean voyages, although Florentine and Genoese galleys did make long journeys to Flanders and England, hugging the coast for protection. The galley's dependence on human labor was a more serious handicap. Because prisoners of war and convicted criminals toiled as oarsmen in both Christian and Muslim ships, victory in war or the enforcement of criminal penalties was crucial to a state's ability to float large numbers of galleys. Slaves, too, sometimes provided the necessary labor.

Portuguese Confrontations

The exploration of the Atlantic began with the Portuguese (Map 11.6). By 1415, they had captured Ceuta on the Moroccan coast, establishing a foothold in Africa. Thereafter, Portuguese voyages sailed farther still down the West African coast. By midcentury, a chain of Portuguese forts reached Guinea, protecting the trade in gold and slaves. At home, the royal house of Portugal financed the fleets, with crucial roles played by Prince Peter, regent between 1440 and 1448; his more famous younger brother Prince Henry the Navigator; and King John II (r. 1481–1495). As a governor of the noble crusading Order of Christ, Henry financed many voyages out of the order's revenues. Private monies also helped, as leading Lisbon merchants participated in financing the gold and slave trades off the Guinea coast.

In 1455, Pope Nicholas V (r. 1447–1455) sanctioned Portuguese overseas expansion, commending King John II's crusading spirit and granting him and his successors the monopoly on trade with inhabitants of the newly "discovered" regions. In 1478–1488, Bartholomeu Dias took advantage of the prevailing winds in the South Atlantic to reach the Cape of Good Hope. A mere ten years later (1497–1499), under the captainship of Vasco da Gama, a Portuguese fleet rounded the cape and reached Calicut, India, center of the spice trade. By 1517, a chain of Portuguese forts dotted the Indian Ocean. In 1519, Ferdinand Magellan, a Portuguese sailor in Spanish service, led the first expedition to circumnavigate the globe.

■ **MAP 11.6 Exploitation and Exploration in the Sixteenth Century**
At the end of the fifteenth century, Europeans began moving aggressively across the globe. Beginning with initial forays along the African coast, their voyages soon widened out to transatlantic crossings and, by 1522, the circumnavigation of the world. The web of arrows on this map suggests an earth bound together by many threads, and this is partly true, for never again would the two halves of the globe be isolated. At the same time, the threads pulled in one direction only—toward the Europeans. Africa was exploited for gold and slaves, while the discovery of precious metals fueled the explorations and settlements of Central and South America. **For more help analyzing this map,** *see the map activity for this chapter in the* ONLINE STUDY GUIDE *at* bedfordstmartins.com/huntconcise.

In many ways a continuation of the struggle against Muslims on the Iberian peninsula, Portugal's maritime voyages displayed that country's mixed motives of piety, glory, and greed. The sailors dreamed of finding gold mines in West Africa and a mysterious Christian kingdom established by a mythical Prester John. The Portuguese hoped to reach the spice-producing lands of South and Southeast Asia by sea to bypass the Ottoman Turks, who controlled the traditional land routes between Europe and Asia.

The new voyages depended for their success on several technological break-throughs. The lateen (triangular) sail permitted ships to tack against headwinds. Light caravels and heavy galleons, however different in size, were alike in using more than one mast and sail, harnessing wind—rather than human—power to move them. Better charts, maps, and instruments made long-distance voyages less risky.

After the voyages of Christopher Columbus, Portugal's interests clashed with those of Spain. Mediated by Pope Alexander VI, the 1494 Treaty of Tordesillas rec-onciled Portugal and Spain by dividing the Atlantic world between the two royal houses. A demarcation 370 leagues west of the Cape Verde Islands divided the Atlantic Ocean, reserving for Portugal the western coast of Africa and the route to India and giving Spain the oceans and lands to the west (see Map 11.6). Unwittingly, this agreement also allowed Portugal to claim Brazil in 1500, which Pedro Álvares Cabral (1467–1520) accidentally "discovered" on his voyage to India.

The Voyages of Columbus

Historians agree that Christopher Columbus (1451–1506) was born of Genoese parents; beyond that, we have little accurate information about this man who brought together the history of Europe and the Americas. In 1476, he arrived in Portugal, apparently a survivor in a naval battle between a Franco-Portuguese and a Genoese fleet; in 1479, he married a Portuguese noblewoman. He spent the next few years mostly in Portuguese service, gaining valuable experience in regular voy-ages down the west coast of Africa. In 1485, after the death of his wife, Columbus settled in Spain.

Fifteenth-century Europeans already knew that Asia lay beyond the vast Atlantic Ocean, and *The Travels of Marco Polo*, written more than a century ear-lier, still exerted a powerful hold on European images of the East. Columbus read it many times, along with other travel books, and proposed to sail west across the Atlantic to reach the lands of the khan, unaware that the Mongol Empire had already collapsed in eastern Asia. Vastly underestimating the distances, he dreamed of finding a new route to the East's gold and spices and partook of the larger European vision that had inspired the Portuguese voyages. (His critics had a much more accurate idea of the globe's size and of the difficulty of the venture, but no one believed that the world was flat!) But after the Portuguese and French monarchs rejected his proposal, Columbus found royal patronage with the recently proclaimed Catholic monarchs Isabella of Castile and Ferdinand of Aragon.

In August 1492, equipped with a modest fleet of three ships and about ninety men, Columbus set sail across the Atlantic. His contract stipulated that he would claim Castilian sovereignty over any new land and inhabitants and share any profits with the crown. Reaching what is today the Bahamas on October 12, Columbus mistook the islands to be part of the East Indies, not far from Japan and "the lands of the Great Khan." As the Castilians explored the Caribbean islands, they encountered communities of peaceful Indians, the Arawaks, who were awed by the Europeans' military technology, not to mention their appearance. Exchanging gifts of beads and broken glass for Arawak gold—an exchange that convinced Columbus of the trusting nature of the Indians—the crew established peaceful relationships with many communities. Yet despite many positive entries in the ship's log referring to Columbus's personal goodwill toward the Indians, the Europeans' objectives were clear: find gold, subjugate the Indians, and propagate Christianity.

Excited by the prospect of easy riches, many flocked to join Columbus's second voyage. When Columbus departed Cádiz in September 1493, he commanded seventeen ships that carried between 1,200 and 1,500 men, many believing all they had to do was "to load the gold into the ships." Failing to find the imaginary gold mines and spices, however, the colonial enterprise quickly switched its focus to finding slaves. Columbus and his crew first enslaved the Caribs, enemies of the Arawaks; in 1494, Columbus proposed a regular slave trade based in Hispaniola. The Spaniards exported enslaved Indians to Spain, and slave traders sold them in Seville. Soon the Spaniards began importing sugarcane from the Portuguese island of Madeira, forcing large numbers of Indians to work on plantations to produce enough sugar for export to Europe. Columbus himself was edged out of this new enterprise. When the Spanish monarchs realized the vast potential for material gain that lay in their new dominions, they asserted direct royal authority by sending officials and priests to the Americas, which were later named after the Italian Amerigo Vespucci, who led a voyage across the Atlantic in 1499–1502.

Columbus's place in history embodies the fundamental transformations of his age. A Genoese in the service of Portuguese and Spanish employers, Columbus had a career illustrating the changing balance between the Mediterranean and the Atlantic. The voyages of 1492–1493 would eventually draw a triangle of exchange among Europe, the Americas, and Africa, an exchange gigantic in its historical impact and its human cost.

A New Era in Slavery

During the Middle Ages and Renaissance, female slaves served as domestic servants in wealthy Mediterranean homes, and male slaves toiled in the galleys of Ottoman and Christian fleets. Some were captured in war or by piracy; others—Africans—were

■ **Dürer's Engraving of Katharina, an African Woman**
Like other artists in early-sixteenth-century Europe, Albrecht Dürer would have seen in person Africans who went to Portugal and Spain as students, servants, and slaves. Notice Katharina's noble expression and dignified attire. Before the rise of the slave trade in the seventeenth century, most Africans in Europe were household servants of the aristocracy. Considered symbols of prestige, such servants generally were not used for economic production.
(Foto Marburg/Art Resource, NY.)

sold by other Africans and Bedouin traders to Christian buyers. In western Asia, parents sold their children into servitude out of poverty. Many people in the Balkans became slaves when their land was devastated by Ottoman invasions. Slaves were Greek, Slav, European, African, and Turk.

The Portuguese maritime voyages changed this picture. From the fifteenth century, Africans increasingly filled the ranks of slaves. Exploiting warfare in West Africa, the Portuguese traded in gold and "pieces," as African slaves were called, a practice condemned at home by some conscientious clergy. Critical voices, however, could not deny the enormous profits that the slave trade brought to Portugal. Most slaves toiled in the sugar plantations of the Portuguese Atlantic islands and in Brazil. A fortunate few labored as domestic servants in Portugal, where African freedmen and slaves, some 35,000 in the early sixteenth century, constituted almost 3 percent of the population, a percentage that was much higher than in other European countries. In the Americas, slavery would truly flourish as an institution of exploitation.

Europeans in a New World

In 1500, on the eve of European invasion, the native peoples of the Americas were divided into many sedentary and nomadic societies. Among the settled peoples,

■ **MAPPING THE WEST** Renaissance Europe, c. 1500

By 1500, the shape of early modern Europe was largely set. It would remain stable until the eighteenth century, except for the disappearance of an independent Hungarian kingdom, which was conquered by the Ottomans in 1529.

the largest political and social organizations centered in the Mexican and Peruvian highlands. The Aztecs and the Incas ruled over subjugated Indian populations in their respective empires. With an elaborate religious culture and a rigid social and political hierarchy, the Aztecs and Incas based their civilizations in large urban capitals.

The Spanish explorers organized their expeditions to the mainland from a base in the Caribbean (see Map 11.6). Two prominent leaders, Hernán Cortés (1485–1547) and Francisco Pizarro (c. 1475–1541), gathered men and arms and set off in search of gold. Catholic priests accompanied the fortune hunters to bring

Christianity to allegedly uncivilized peoples and thus to justify brutal conquests. His small band swelled by peoples who had been subjugated by the Aztecs, Cortés captured the Aztec capital, Tenochtitlán, in 1519. To the south, Pizarro conquered the Andean highlands, exploiting a civil war between rival Incan kings.

By the mid-sixteenth century, the Spanish Empire stretched unbroken from Mexico to Chile. Not to be outdone by the Spaniards, other European powers joined the scramble for gold in the New World. In 1500, a Portuguese fleet led by Pedro Álvares Cabral landed at Brazil, but Portugal did not begin colonizing there until 1532, when it established a permanent fort on the coast. In North America, the French went in search of a "northwest passage" to China. By 1504, French fishermen had appeared in Newfoundland. Thirty years later, Jacques Cartier led three voyages that explored the St. Lawrence River as far as Montreal. An early attempt in 1541 to settle Canada failed because of the harsh winter and Indian hostility, and John Cabot's 1497 voyage to find a northern route to Asia also failed. More permanent settlements in Canada and the present-day United States would succeed only in the seventeenth century.

■ **REVIEW:** *Which European countries led the way in maritime expansion, and what were their motives?*

IMPORTANT DATES

1337–1453	Hundred Years' War	1440s	Gutenberg introduces the printing press
1347–1350	First outbreak of the Black Death in Europe; anti-Jewish persecutions in the empire	c. 1450–1500	Height of the Florentine Renaissance
1358	Jacquerie uprising in France	1453	Fall of Constantinople; end of the Byzantine Empire
1378	Beginning of the Great Schism; John Wycliffe's treatise *On the Church*	1460s–1485	Wars of the Roses in England
1381	English peasant uprising	1462	Ivan III of Muscovy claims imperial title "tsar"
1389	Ottomans defeat Serbs at Kosovo	1478	Inquisition established in Spain
1414–1417	Council of Constance ends the Great Schism	1492	Columbus's first voyage; Christians conquer Muslim Granada and expel Jews from Spain
1415	Execution of Jan Hus; Portugal captures Ceuta, establishing foothold in Africa	1499	Vasco da Gama reaches India
		1500	Portugal claims Brazil

Conclusion

Confronted by war, plague, peasant uprisings, turbulence in the cities, anti-Jewish pogroms, and a disgraced papacy, Europe's ruling classes grasped the reins of power ever more tightly, creating more centralized and institutionalized states. Surrounding themselves with artists, musicians, and humanists, these new-style rulers supported the "Renaissance"—an attempt to resuscitate the classical past for the purposes of the present. The Renaissance, which emphasized human potential and achievement, was one of Europe's most brilliant periods in artistic activity, one that glorified both God and humanity. Overwhelming confidence spurred Renaissance artists to a new appreciation for the human body and a new visual perspective in art and to apply mathematics and science to architecture, music, and artistic composition.

This intense cultural production both resulted from and fueled the competition among the burgeoning Renaissance states and between Christian Europe and the Muslim Ottoman Empire. The competition also fostered an expansion of the frontiers of Europe first to Africa and then across the Atlantic Ocean to the Americas, ushering in the first period of global history. Few at the time would have guessed that Europe would soon enter yet another period of turmoil, one brought about not by demographic and economic collapse but by a profound crisis of conscience that the brilliance of Renaissance civilization had tended to obscure.

■ MAKING CONNECTIONS

1. *How did Renaissance states differ from medieval monarchies?*

2. *How did the impact of the Ottomans on Europe differ from the impact of the Mongols?*

■ FOR FURTHER EXPLORATION

For further reading and online research ideas, see the Suggested References on page SR-6 at the back of the book.

For practice quizzes, a customized study plan, and other study tools, see the ONLINE STUDY GUIDE at bedfordstmartins.com/huntconcise.

For primary-source material from this period, see Chapter 11 in *Sources of THE MAKING OF THE WEST: A CONCISE HISTORY*, Second Edition.

Struggles over Beliefs

1500–1648

H ILLE FEIKEN LEFT THE NORTHERN GERMAN CITY of Münster on June 16, 1534, elegantly dressed, bedecked with jewels, and determined to kill. Münster, which religious radicals had declared a holy city, lay under siege by armies loyal to the local Catholic bishop—her intended victim. Hille crossed enemy lines and tried to persuade the commander of the besieging troops to take her to the bishop, promising to reveal a secret means of recapturing the city. When a defector from her camp recognized Hille and betrayed her, she was beheaded.

Hille Feiken belonged to the religious group known as Anabaptists, who wanted to form a holy community separate from the rest of society. Anabaptists organized in response to the Protestant Reformation, which was set in motion by the German friar Martin Luther in 1517 and quickly became a sweeping movement to uproot church abuses and restore early Christian teachings. Supporters of Luther were called **Protestants**, those who protested. Inspired by Luther and then by other reformers, ordinary men and women across much of Europe attempted to remake their heaven and earth. Their stories intertwined with bloody struggles among princes for domination in Europe, an age-old conflict now complicated by the clash of rival faiths.

Struggles over religious beliefs frequently erupted into armed confrontation, culminating in the Thirty Years' War of 1618–1648, which devastated the lands of

■ **Vincenzo Catena, *Judith***
The Book of Judith tells the story of a beautiful young Israelite who presents herself to Holofernes, the general of an army besieging Jerusalem. His guard lowered by wine and Judith's charms, Judith assassinates Holofernes and cuts off his head, thus frightening off the enemy and saving her people. In this painting from the 1520s, Venetian artist Vincenzo Catena conveys Judith's strength, beauty, and commitment to her task—one that Hille Feiken sought to reenact so that she might free her own besieged city of Münster. (AKG Images/Cameraphoto.)

473

central Europe. The orgy of mutual destruction in the Thirty Years' War left no winners in the religious struggle, and the cynical manipulation of religious issues by both Catholic and Protestant leaders showed that political interests eventually outweighed those of religion. The extreme violence of religious conflict pushed rulers and political thinkers to seek other, nonreligious grounds for governmental authority. Few would argue for genuine toleration of religious differences, but many began to insist that the interests of states had to take priority over the desire for religious conformity.

Although particularly dramatic and deadly, the church-state crisis was only one of a series of upheavals that shaped this era. After decades of rapid economic and population growth in the sixteenth century, a major economic downturn led to food shortages, famine, and disease in the first half of the seventeenth century. An upheaval in worldviews was also in the making, catalyzed by increasing knowledge of the new worlds discovered overseas and in the heavens. The development of new scientific methods of research would ultimately reshape Western attitudes toward religion and state power, as Europeans desperately sought alternatives to wars over religious beliefs.

The Protestant Reformation

Since the mid-fifteenth century, many clerics had tried to reform the church from within, criticizing clerical abuses and calling for moral renewal, but their efforts came up against the church's inertia and resistance. At the beginning of the sixteenth century, widespread popular piety and anticlericalism existed side by side, fomenting a volatile mixture of need and resentment. A young German friar, tormented by his own religious doubts, was to become the spokesman for a generation. From its origins as a theological dispute, Martin Luther's reform movement sparked explosive protests. By the time he died in 1546, half of western Europe had renounced allegiance to the Roman Catholic church. Christian unity fractured, opening the way not only to widespread turmoil but also to a host of new attitudes about the nature of religious and political authority.

Popular Piety and Christian Humanism

Numerous signs pointed to an intense spiritual anxiety among the laity. New shrines sprang up, reports of miracles multiplied, and prayer books sold briskly. Critics complained that the church gave external behavior more weight than spiritual intentions. In receiving the sacrament of penance—one of the central pillars of the Roman church—sinners were expected to examine their consciences, sincerely confess their sins to a priest, and receive forgiveness. In practice, however, some priests abused their authority by demanding sexual or monetary favors in return for forgiveness. Priests also sold **indulgences**, which according to doctrine could alleviate suffering in purgatory after death. The faithful were supposed to earn indulgences by performing certain religious tasks—going on pilgrimage, attending mass, doing holy works. The sale of indulgences as a substitution for performing good works suggested that the church was more interested in making money than in saving souls.

Dissatisfaction with the official church prompted some Christian intellectuals to link their scholarship to the cause of social reform and to dream of ideal societies based on peace and morality. The Dutch scholar Desiderius Erasmus (c. 1466–1536) and the English lawyer Thomas More (1478–1535) stood out as representatives of these Christian humanists, who, unlike Italian humanists, placed their primary emphasis on Christian piety. Each established close links to the powerful. Erasmus was on intimate terms with kings and popes, and his fame spread across all Europe. More became lord chancellor to England's king Henry VIII.

Erasmus advocated a simple piety devoid of greed and the lust for power, but he also promoted the new humanist learning. To this end he devoted years to translating a new Latin edition of the New Testament from the original Greek. He argued ironically in *The Praise of Folly* (1509) that the wise appeared foolish, because modesty, humility, and poverty had few adherents in this world. Although Erasmus mocked the clergy's corruption and Christian princes' bloody ambitions, he emphasized the role of education in reforming individuals and through them society as a whole. Even ordinary table manners drew his attention. In the *Colloquies* (1523), a compilation of Latin dialogues intended as language-learning exercises, he advised his cultivated readers not to pick their noses at meals and not to speak while stuffing their mouths. He also advocated an end to wet nursing. Challenged by angry younger men and radical ideas once the Reformation took hold, Erasmus chose Christian unity over reform and schism. He died in the Swiss city of Basel, isolated from the Protestant community and condemned by many in the Catholic church, who found his writings too critical of the church's authority.

Erasmus's good friend Thomas More, to whom *The Praise of Folly* was dedicated,* met with even greater suffering for his beliefs. He would later pay with his life for upholding conscience over political expediency. Inspired by the recent voyages of discovery, More's best-known work, *Utopia* (1516), describes an imaginary ideal place that offered a stark contrast to his own society. Because Utopians enjoyed public schools, communal kitchens, hospitals, and nurseries, they had no need for money. Greed and private property disappeared in this world. Dedicated to the pursuit of knowledge and natural religion, with equal distribution of goods and few laws, Utopia knew neither crime nor war (*Utopia* means both "no place" and "best place" in Greek). More believed that politics,

---

*The Latin title *Encomium Moriae* ("The Praise of Folly") was a pun on More's name and the Latin word for *folly*.

property, and war fueled human misery, whereas for his Utopians, "fighting was a thing they absolutely loathe. They say it's a quite subhuman form of activity, although human beings are more addicted to it than any of the lower animals." Despite a few oddities—voluntary slavery, for instance, and strictly controlled travel—Utopia seemed a paradise compared with the increasing violence in a Europe divided by religion.

Martin Luther and the German Nation

Like Erasmus and More, Martin Luther (1483–1546) pursued a life of scholarship, but a personal crisis of faith led him to break with the Roman church and establish a competing one. The son of a miner, Luther abandoned his studies in the law to enter the Augustinian order. The choice of a monastic life did not resolve Luther's doubts about his own salvation. Appalled at his own sense of sinfulness and the weakness of human nature, he lived in terror of God's justice despite frequent confessions and penance. A pilgrimage to Rome only deepened his unease with the institutional church. Sent to study theology by a sympathetic superior, Luther gradually came to new insights through his study of Scripture. He later described his breakthrough experience:

> At last, by the mercy of God, meditating day and night, I gave heed to the context of the words [in Romans 1:17], namely, "In [the gospel] the righteousness of God is revealed, as it is written, 'He who through faith is righteous shall live.'" There I began to understand that the righteousness of God is that by which the righteous live by a gift of God, namely by faith.

Luther soon came into conflict with the church authorities. In 1516, the new archbishop ordered the sale of indulgences to help cover the cost of constructing St. Peter's Basilica in Rome and also to defray his expenses in pursuing his election. Such blatant profiteering outraged many, including Luther, who now served as professor of theology at the University of Wittenberg. In 1517, Luther composed ninety-five theses—propositions for an academic debate—that questioned indulgence peddling and the purchase of church offices. Once they became public, the theses unleashed a torrent of pent-up resentment and frustration among the laypeople. This apparently ordinary academic dispute soon engulfed the Holy Roman Empire in conflict.

As Luther developed his ideas more fully, rupture became inevitable. In 1520, he published three treatises that laid out his theological position, attacked the papacy in Rome as the embodiment of the Antichrist, and called upon the German princes to reform the church themselves. Luther insisted that faith alone, not good works or penance, could save sinners from damnation. Faith came from the believer's personal relationship with God, which he or she cultivated through

■ Luther as Monk, Doctor, Man of the Bible, and Saint, 1521
This woodcut by an anonymous artist appeared in a volume that the Strasbourg printer Johann Schott published in 1521. In addition to being one of the major centers of printing, Strasbourg was also a stronghold of the reform movement. Notice the use of traditional symbols to signify Luther's holiness: the Bible in his hands, the halo, the Holy Spirit in the form of a dove, and his friar's robes. Although monasticism and the cult of saints came under severe criticism during the Reformation, the representation of Luther with traditional symbols of sanctity stressed his conservative values instead of his radical challenge to church authorities.
(The Granger Collection, NY.)

individual study of Scripture. Ordinary laypeople thus made up "the priesthood of all believers," who had no need of a professional caste of clerics to show them the way to salvation. The attack on the church's authority could not have been more dramatic.

From Rome's perspective, the "Luther Affair," as church officials called it, was essentially a matter of clerical discipline. Rome ordered Luther to obey his superiors and keep quiet. But the church establishment had seriously misjudged the extent of Luther's influence. Luther's ideas, published in numerous German and Latin editions, spread rapidly throughout the Holy Roman Empire, unleashing forces that Luther himself could not control. Social, nationalist, and religious protests fused into an explosive mass very similar to the Czech revolution that Jan Hus had inspired a century earlier. Like Hus, Luther appeared before an emperor: in 1521, he defended his faith before Charles V (r. 1520–1558), the newly elected Holy Roman Emperor who at the age of nineteen was the ruler of the Low Countries, Spain, Spain's Italian and New World dominions, and the Austrian Habsburg lands. At the Imperial Diet of Worms, the formal assembly presided over by this powerful ruler, Luther shocked Germans by declaring his admiration for the Czech heretic. But unlike Hus, Luther did not suffer martyrdom because he enjoyed the protection of Frederick the Wise, the elector of Saxony (one of the seven German princes entitled to elect the Holy Roman Emperor) and Luther's lord.

Luther also had the support of many literate townspeople who were eager to read the Scriptures for themselves.

What began as an urban movement turned into a war in the countryside in 1525. Lutheran propaganda radiated outward from the German towns, where local officials had appointed clerics sympathetic to reform. Luther's anticlerical message struck home with merchants and artisans who resented the clergy's tax-exempt status, but peasants had even more reason for discontent because they paid taxes to both their lord and the church. The church was the largest landowner in the Holy Roman Empire: about one-seventh of the empire's territory consisted of ecclesiastical principalities in which bishops and abbots exercised both secular and churchly power. In the spring of 1525, many peasants in southern and central Germany rose in rebellion, sometimes inspired by wandering preachers. Urban workers and artisans joined the peasant bands, plundering monasteries, refusing to pay church taxes, and demanding village autonomy, the abolition of serfdom, and the right to appoint their own pastors. In Thuringia, the rebels were led by an ex-priest, Thomas Müntzer (1468?–1525), who promised to chastise the wicked and thus clear the way for the Last Judgment.

The uprising of 1525, known as the Peasants' War, split the reform movement. In Thuringia, Catholics and reformers joined hands to crush Müntzer and his supporters. All over the empire, princes rallied their troops to defeat the peasants and hunt down their leaders. By the end of 1525, more than 100,000 rebels had been killed and others maimed, imprisoned, or exiled. Luther had tried to mediate, criticizing the princes for their brutality toward the peasants but also warning the rebels against mixing religion and social protest. Luther believed that rulers were ordained by God and thus must be obeyed even if they were tyrants. The Kingdom of God belonged not to this world but to the next. When the rebels ignored Luther's appeal and continued to follow radical preachers like Müntzer, Luther called on the princes to destroy "the devil's work" and slaughter the rebels. Fundamentally conservative in its political philosophy, the Lutheran church would henceforth depend on established political authority for its protection.

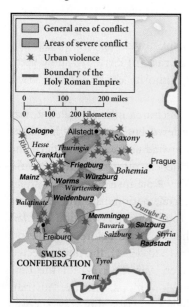

The Peasants' War of 1525

Emerging as the champions of an orderly religious reform, many German princes eventually confronted Emperor Charles V, who supported Rome. In 1529, Charles declared the Roman Catholic faith the empire's only legitimate religion.

Proclaiming their allegiance to the reform cause, the Lutheran German princes protested and thus came to be called Protestants.

Huldrych Zwingli and John Calvin

While Luther provided the religious leadership for northern Germany, the south soon came under the influence of reformers based in Switzerland. In 1520, Huldrych Zwingli (1484–1531), the son of a Swiss village leader, broke with Rome and established his reform headquarters in German-speaking Zurich. In 1541, the Frenchman John Calvin (1509–1564) made French-speaking Geneva his center for reform campaigns in western Europe (see Map 12.1). Like Luther, Zwingli and Calvin began their careers as priests, but in contrast to their predecessor, they demanded an even more radical break with the Roman Catholic church.

Zwingli served as an army chaplain before declaring himself a reformer, and he brought to his version of church reform a stern disciplinarian's emphasis on a theocratic (church-directed) society in which religious values infused every aspect of politics and social life. Zwingli differed from Luther in his view of the role of the Eucharist, or holy communion. According to Catholic doctrine, during the mass officiated by a priest the bread and wine of holy communion changed into the body and blood of Christ. Luther believed that the body and blood were actually present in the bread and wine, but only because of the faith of the believer, not because a priest officiated. Zwingli took Luther's argument a step further and insisted that the bread and wine simply symbolized Christ's union with believers; the bread and wine did not change in substance. Efforts to mediate between Luther and Zwingli in this critical element of doctrine failed. The German and Swiss reform movements continued on separate paths.

In Zurich, Zwingli tolerated no dissent. When laypeople secretly set up their own new sect, called Anabaptists, Zwingli immediately attacked them. The **Anabaptists** believed that only adults had the free will to truly understand and accept baptism and therefore had to be rebaptized (*anabaptism* means "rebaptism"). How could a baby knowingly choose Christ? Rebaptism symbolized the Anabaptists' determination to withdraw from a social order corrupted, as they saw it, by power and evil. They therefore rejected the authority of courts and magistrates and refused to bear arms or swear oaths of allegiance. When persuasion failed to convince them, Zwingli urged Zurich magistrates to impose the death sentence.

Anabaptism spread quickly from Zurich to many cities in southern Germany, despite the Holy Roman Empire's general condemnation of the movement in 1529. In 1534, one incendiary Anabaptist group, believing that the end of the world was imminent, seized control of the northwestern German town of Münster. Proclaiming themselves a community of saints and imitating the ancient Israelites, they were initially governed by twelve elders and later by Jan of Leiden, a Dutch Anabaptist tailor who claimed to be the prophesied leader—a second "King David."

The Münster Anabaptists abolished private property and dissolved traditional marriages, allowing men, like Old Testament patriarchs, to have multiple wives, to the chagrin of many women. In 1535, Münster fell to a combined Protestant and Catholic army. Many Anabaptists died in battle or—like Hille Feiken—were executed. The remnants of the Anabaptist movement survived under the determined pacifist leadership of the Dutch reformer Menno Simons (1469–1561), whose followers were eventually named Mennonites.

Yet another wave of reform surged forward under the leadership of John Calvin. As a young priest, Calvin believed it might be possible to reform the Roman Catholic church from within, but gradually he came to share Luther and Zwingli's conviction that only fundamental change could reestablish the true religion. While Calvin moved toward the Protestant position, his homeland of France experienced increasing turmoil over religion. On Sunday, October 18, 1534, in the so-called Affair of the Placards, Parisians found church doors posted with ribald broadsheets denouncing the Catholic Mass. The government arrested hundreds of French Protestants and executed scores of them, precipitating the flight into exile of many others, including Calvin.

Calvin did not intend to settle in Geneva, but when he stopped there, a local reformer threatened him with God's curse if he did not stay and help organize reform in the city. After intense conflict between the supporters of reform, many of whom were French refugees, and the opposition, led by the traditional elite families, the Calvinists triumphed in 1541. Geneva soon followed the precepts laid out in Calvin's great work, *The Institutes of the Christian Religion*, first published in 1536. Calvin took the reform doctrines to their logical conclusion. If God is almighty and humans cannot earn their salvation by good works, as all Protestants argued, then no Christian can be certain of salvation. Developing the doctrine of **predestination**, Calvin insisted that God had foreordained every man, woman, and child to

The Progress of the Reformation	
1517	Martin Luther disseminates ninety-five theses attacking the sale of indulgences and other church practices
1520	Reformer Huldrych Zwingli breaks with Rome
1525	Radical reformer Thomas Müntzer killed in Peasants' War
1529	Lutheran German princes protest the condemnation of religious reform by Charles V; genesis of the term *Protestants*
1529	The English Parliament establishes King Henry VIII as head of the Anglican church, severing ties to Rome
1534–1535	Anabaptists control the city of Münster, Germany, in a failed experiment to create a holy community
1541	John Calvin and his followers take control in Geneva, making that city the center for Calvinist reforms

salvation or damnation—even before the creation of the world. Only God knew who was among the "elect."

In practice, however, Calvinist doctrine demanded rigorous discipline: the knowledge that a small group of "elect" would be saved should guide the actions of the godly in an uncertain world. Fusing church and society into what followers named the "Reformed church," Geneva became a single theocratic community, in which dissent was not tolerated. The Genevan magistrates arrested the Spanish physician Michael Servetus when he passed through in 1553 because he had published books attacking Calvin and questioning the doctrine of the Trinity, the belief shared by virtually all Christians that God exists in three persons—the Father, Son (Christ), and Holy Spirit. Calvin urged the authorities to execute him. Geneva quickly became the new center of the Reformation, sending out pastors trained for mission work and exporting books that taught Calvinist doctrines. The Calvinist movement spread to France, the Netherlands, England, Scotland, the German states, Poland, Hungary, and eventually New England, becoming the established form of the Reformation in many of these countries (Map 12.1).

Reshaping Society through Religion

For all their differences over doctrine and church organization, the Protestant reformers shared a desire to instill greater discipline in Christian worship and in social behavior. As a consequence, they advocated changes in education and marriage to create a God-fearing, pious, and orderly Christian society. Some of these efforts grew out of developments that stretched back to the Middle Ages, but others, such as an emphasis on literacy, appeared first in Protestant Europe.

Prior to the Reformation, the Latin Vulgate was the only Bible authorized by the church; as a result, priests interpreted the Bible for their parishoners. In 1522, Martin Luther translated Erasmus's Greek New Testament into German because he believed that everyone should read the Bible for him- or herself. Within twelve years, printers published more than 200,000 copies of it, an immense number for the time. In 1534, Luther completed a German translation of the Old Testament. In the same year that Luther's German New Testament appeared in print, the French humanist Jacques Lefèvre d'Étaples (c. 1455–1536) translated the Vulgate New Testament into French. Sponsored by the bishop of Meaux, who wanted to distribute free copies of the New Testament to the poor of the region, Lefèvre's translation represented an early attempt to reform the French church without breaking with Rome. By contrast, England's church hierarchy reacted swiftly against English-language Bibles, sensing in them the threat of heresy. Inspired by Luther's example during a visit to Wittenberg, the Englishman William Tyndale (1495–1536) translated the Bible into English. After he had his translation printed in Germany and the Low Countries, Tyndale smuggled copies into England. He paid for his boldness by being burned at the stake as a heretic.

The map legend reads:

- Reformed faith dominant, c. 1560
- Reformed faith growing, c. 1560
- Considerable local reformed faith, c. 1560
- Calvinist influenced
- Some penetration of reform, c. 1560
- Boundary of the Holy Roman Empire

■ **MAP 12.1 Spread of Protestantism in the Sixteenth Century**

The Protestant Reformation divided northern and southern Europe. From its heartland in the Holy Roman Empire, the Reformation won the allegiance of Scandinavia, England, and Scotland and made considerable inroads in the Low Countries, France, eastern Europe, the Swiss Confederation, and even parts of northern Italy. While the Mediterranean countries remained loyal to Rome, a vast zone of confessional divisions and strife characterized the religious landscape of Europe from Britain in the west to Poland in the east.

■ The Disciplined Home
Proper table manners reflected discipline and morality in the godly household, an ideal of the religious reformers of the sixteenth century. The householder, the father-patriarch, leads his wife and children in prayer before a meal. The orderly behavior parallels the comfort (oven, smoked glass windows, chandeliers, timber ceiling, and cabinets) of a well-off patrician family. **For more help analyzing this image**, see the visual activity for this chapter in the ONLINE STUDY GUIDE at bedfordstmartins.com/huntconcise.
(Staatsbibliothek Bamberg, Germany.)

Although the vernacular Bible was a prized possession in many Protestant households, Bible reading did not become widespread until the 1600s. To educate children in the new religious principles, and replace the late medieval church schools, the Protestant reformers set up state school systems. Luther urged the German princes to use the proceeds of confiscated church properties to establish primary schools in every parish for boys and girls between six and twelve. The Protestant churches also developed a secondary system of higher schools for boys, called gymnasia (from the Greek *gymnasion*), in which the study of Greek and Latin classics and religious instruction prepared future pastors, scholars, and officials for university study.

Like the reforms of education, Protestant efforts to reshape marriage reflected their concern to discipline individual behavior and institute an orderly Christian society. Protestant magistrates established marital courts, passed new marriage laws, closed brothels, and inflicted harsher punishments for sexual deviance. Under canon law, the Catholic church recognized any promise made between two consenting adults (with the legal age of twelve for females, fourteen for males) as a valid marriage. In rural areas and among the urban poor, most couples simply lived together as common-law husband and wife, and some couples never even registered with the church. Sometimes young men promised marriage in a moment of passion only to renege later. Protestant governments declared a marriage illegitimate if the partners failed to register their marriage with a local official and a pastor. They usually also required parental consent, thus giving parents immense power in regulating marriage and the transmission of family property.

Taught to become obedient spouses and affectionate companions in Christ, women approached this new sexual regime with ambivalence. The new laws stipulated that women could seek divorce for desertion, impotence, and flagrant abuse, although in practice the marital courts encouraged reconciliation. These improvements came at a price, however: Protestant women were expected to be obedient wives, helpful companions, and loving mothers, but they could no longer join the convent and pursue their own religious paths outside the family. Luther's wife, Katharina von Bora, typified the new ideal Protestant woman. A former nun, she accepted her prescribed role in a patriarchal household: once married, Katharina ran the couple's household, feeding their children, relatives, and student boarders. Although she deferred to Luther—she addressed him as "Herr Doktor"—she nonetheless defended a woman's right as an equal in marriage. Other Protestant women spoke out even more decisively. Katharina Zell, wife of the reformer Matthew Zell, wrote hymns, fed the sick and imprisoned, and denounced the intolerance of the new Protestant clergy. Rebuking one for his persecution of dissenters, she wrote, "You young fellows tread on the graves of the first fathers of this church in Strasbourg and punish all who disagree with you, but faith cannot be forced." She also insisted that women should have a voice in religious affairs.

Catholic Renewal and Missionary Zeal

Reacting to the waves of Protestant challenge, the Catholic church mobilized for defense in a movement that is called by some the Counter-Reformation and by others Catholic Reform. Pope Paul III (r. 1534–1549) convened a general church council to codify church doctrine, and he personally approved the founding of new religious orders to undertake aggressive missionary efforts. The Council of Trent (Trent sat on the border between the Holy Roman Empire and Italy) met intermittently between 1545 and 1563, when it concluded its work. Its decisions shaped the essential character of Catholicism until the 1960s. Emphatically rejecting the major Protestant positions, the council reasserted the supremacy of clerical authority over the laity and reaffirmed that the bread and wine of communion actually becomes Christ's body and blood. It required that all weddings take place in churches and be registered by the parish clergy and explicitly refused to allow for divorce. All hopes of reconciliation between Protestants and Catholics faded.

Most important of the new Catholic religious orders was the Society of Jesus. Its founder was Ignatius of Loyola (1491–1556), a Spanish nobleman and charismatic former military officer, who abandoned his quest for military glory in favor of serving the church. Ignatius soon attracted other young men to his side, and in 1540 the pope recognized his small band of "Jesuits." Over time, the Jesuits founded hundreds of colleges in Spain, Portugal, France, Italy, the German states, Hungary, Bohemia, and Poland. Among their alumni would be princes, philosophers, lawyers, churchmen, and officials—the elite of Catholic Europe. In 1544 the

■ **The Portuguese in Japan**
In this sixteenth-century Japanese black-lacquer screen painting of Portuguese missionaries, the Jesuits are dressed in black and the Franciscans in brown. At the lower right corner is a Portuguese nobleman depicted with exaggerated "Western" features. The Japanese considered themselves lighter in skin color than the Portuguese, whom they classified as "barbarians." In turn, the Portuguese classified Japanese (and Chinese) as "whites." The perception of ethnic differences in the sixteenth century depended less on skin color than on clothing, eating habits, and other cultural signals. Color classifications were unstable and changed over time: by the late seventeenth century, Europeans no longer regarded Asians as "white." (Laurie Platt Winfrey, Inc.)

pope recognized a new order for women, the Company of Saint Ursula, known as the "Ursulines," who devoted themselves to the education of girls. Together these new religious orders restored the confidence of the faithful in the dedication and power of the Catholic church.

Catholic missionaries set sail throughout the globe in order to bring Roman Catholicism to Africans, Asians, and native Americans. They saw their effort as proof of the truth of Roman Catholicism and the success of their missions as a sign of divine favor, both particularly important in the face of Protestant

challenge. To ensure rapid Christianization, European missionaries focused initially on winning over local elites. A number of young African nobles went to
Portugal to be trained in theology. Catholic missionaries preached the Gospel
to Confucian scholar officials in China and to the samurai (the warrior aristocracy) in Japan. Measured in numbers alone, the missionary enterprise
seemed highly successful: by the second half of the sixteenth century, vast multitudes of native Americans had become Christians at least in name, and thirty
years after Francis Xavier's 1549 landing in Japan the Jesuits could claim over
100,000 Japanese converts.

After an initial period of relatively little racial discrimination, the Catholic
church in the Americas and Africa adopted strict rules based on color. For example,
the first Mexican Ecclesiastical Provincial Council in 1555 declared that holy orders
were not to be conferred on Indians, mestizos (people of mixed European-Indian
parentage), or mulattoes (people of mixed European-African heritage), groups
deemed "inherently unworthy of the sacerdotal [priestly] office." Europeans
reinforced their sense of racial superiority with their perception of the "treachery"
that native Americans and Africans exhibited whenever they resisted domination.
Frustrated in his efforts to convert Brazilian Indians, a Jesuit missionary wrote to
his superior in Rome in 1563 that "for this kind of people it is better to be preaching with the sword and rod of iron." The Dominican Bartolomé de Las Casas
(1474–1566) criticized the treatment of the Indians in Spanish America, yet even
he argued that Africans should be imported in order to relieve the indigenous
peoples, who were being worked to death.

■ **REVIEW:** *In what ways did Luther, Zwingli, and Calvin challenge the Roman Catholic church?*

State Power and Religious Conflict, 1500–1618

Even as religious disputes heightened the potential for conflict within Europe, the
European powers continued to fight their traditional dynastic wars and still faced
the military threat posed by the Muslim Ottoman Turks in the east. But these wars
did not long deflect attention from increasing divisions within European countries. Rulers viewed religious divisions as a dangerous challenge to the unity of
their realms and the stability of their regimes; a subject could very well swear
greater allegiance to God than to his lord. Yet rulers often proved powerless to
stem the rising tide of religious strife. Lutheranism flourished in the northern
German states and Scandinavia; Calvinism spread from its headquarters in the
Swiss city of Geneva all the way to England and Poland-Lithuania. The rapid
expansion of Lutheranism and Calvinism created deadly political conflicts between
Protestants and Catholics.

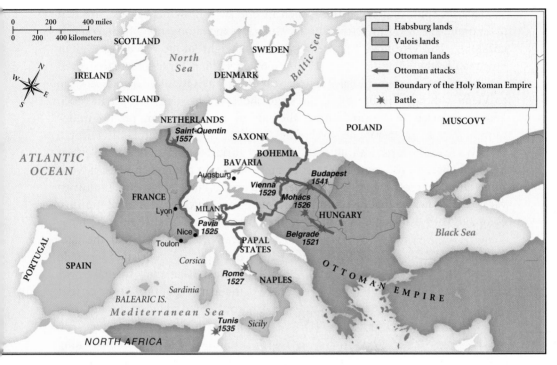

■ **MAP 12.2 Habsburg-Valois-Ottoman Wars, 1494–1559**

As the dominant European power, the Habsburg dynasty fought on two fronts: a religious war against the Islamic Ottoman Empire and a political war against the French Valois, who challenged Habsburg hegemony. The Mediterranean, the Balkans, and the Low Countries all became theaters of war.

Wars among Habsburgs, Valois, and Ottomans

While the Reformation was taking hold in the German states, the great powers of Spain and France fought each other for the domination of Europe (Map 12.2). French claims over Italian territories sparked conflict in 1494, but the ensuing Italian Wars soon involved most Christian monarchs and the Muslim Ottoman sultan as well. Despite some spectacular and bloody turns of fortune, no one power ultimately emerged victorious. In 1525, the troops of Habsburg Emperor Charles V crushed the French army at Pavia, Italy, and captured the French king, Francis I (r. 1515–1547). Charles treated Francis as an honored guest but held him in Spain until he agreed to renounce his claims to Italy. Furious at this humiliation, Francis repudiated the agreement the moment he returned to France, reigniting the conflict. In 1527, Charles's troops invaded and then pillaged Rome to punish the pope for allying with the French. Among the imperial troops were German Protestant mercenaries, who pillaged Catholic churches. The sack of Rome shocked the Catholic church hierarchy and helped turn it toward renewal.

Charles could not crush the French in one swift blow because he also had to counter the Muslim Ottomans in Hungary and along the Mediterranean coastline. The Ottoman Empire reached its height of power under Sultan Suleiman I, "the Magnificent" (r. 1520–1566). In 1526, a Turkish force destroyed the Hungarian army at Mohács. Three years later, the Ottoman army laid siege to Vienna; though unsuccessful, the siege shocked Christian Europe. In 1535, Charles V tried to capture Tunis, the lair of North African pirates under Ottoman rule. Desperate to overcome Charles's superior forces in Europe, Francis I eagerly forged an alliance with the Turkish sultan. The Turkish fleet besieged Nice, on the southern coast of France, to help the French wrest it from imperial occupiers. Francis even ordered all inhabitants of nearby Toulon to vacate their town so that he could turn it into a Muslim colony for eight months, complete with a mosque and slave market. The Franco-Turkish alliance, however brief, showed that the age-old idea of Christian crusade against Islam had to make way for a new political strategy that considered religion as but one factor in power politics.

In 1559, the French king finally acknowledged defeat and signed the peace treaty of Cateau-Cambrésis. By then, years of conflict had drained the treasuries of all monarchs. Fueled by warfare, all armies grew in size, firepower

■ **The Battle at Mohács**
This Ottoman painting shows the 1529 victory of the sultan's army over the Hungarians at Mohács. The battle resulted in the end of the Hungarian kingdom, which would be divided into three realms under Ottoman, Habsburg, and Transylvanian rule. Notice the prominence of artillery and the Ottoman fighting force (the Janissaries) with muskets. The Ottomans commanded a vast army with modern equipment, a key to their military prowess in the sixteenth century.
(Topkapi Palace Museum.)

became ever more deadly, and costs soared. For example, heavier artillery pieces meant that the rectangular walls of medieval cities had to be transformed into fortresses with jutting forts and gun emplacements. Charles V boasted the largest army in Europe—but he could not make ends meet with the proceeds from taxation, the sale of offices, and even outright confiscation.

Like other rulers, Charles V looked to private bankers for funds. Charles relied on the Fugger bank, based in the southern German imperial city of Augsburg. Jakob Fugger (1459–1525) had loaned money to Charles V's grandfather, Maximilian I, in exchange for mining and minting concessions as well as hefty interest payments. In 1519, Fugger assembled a consortium of German and Italian bankers to secure the election of Charles V as Holy Roman Emperor. The assets of the Fuggers more than doubled between 1527 and 1547; Charles V's debts nearly doubled, too. The French kings fared no better. On his death in 1547, Francis owed the bankers of Lyon nearly 7 million pounds—approximately the entire royal income for that year. As a result, the Valois and the Habsburgs had to pay 14 to 18 percent interest on their loans.

French Wars of Religion

During the 1540s and 1550s, one-third of the French nobles converted to Calvinism, usually influenced by noblewomen who protected pastors, provided money and advice, and helped found schools and establish relief for the poor. With this noble backing, the Reformed church organized openly and held synods (church meetings), especially in southern and western France. The Catholic Valois monarchy tried to maintain a balance of power between Catholics and Calvinists. Francis I and his successor, Henry II (r. 1547–1559), both succeeded to a degree. But when Henry was accidentally killed during a jousting tournament, the weakened monarchy could no longer hold together the fragile realm. Henry was succeeded first by his fifteen-year-old son Francis II, who died in 1560, and then by his ten-year-old son, Charles IX (r. 1560–1574).

Catherine de Medicis (1519–1589), the Italian wife of Henry II, acted as regent for her young son. She first urged limited toleration for the Calvinists—called **Huguenots** in France—in an attempt to maintain political stability, but she could not prevent the eruption of civil war between Catholics and Huguenots in 1562. Although a Catholic herself, Catherine desperately tried to play the Catholic and Huguenot factions off each other so that neither would dominate. To this end, she arranged the marriage of her daughter Marguerite to Henry of Navarre, head of the Bourbon family, which had converted to Calvinism. Just four days after the wedding in August 1572, assassins tried but failed to kill one of the Huguenot nobles allied with the Bourbons, Gaspard de Coligny. Panicked at the thought of Huguenot revenge and perhaps herself implicated in the botched plot, Catherine convinced her son to order the killing

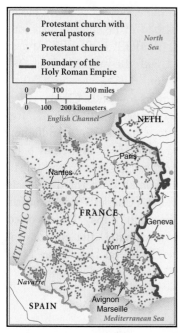

Protestant Churches in
France, 1562

of leading Huguenots. On St. Bartholomew's Day, August 24, a bloodbath began, fueled by years of growing animosity between Catholics and Protestants. In three days, Catholic mobs murdered three thousand Huguenots in Paris. Ten thousand died in the provinces over the next six weeks. The pope joyfully ordered the church bells rung throughout Catholic Europe; Spain's Philip II wrote Catherine that it was "the best and most cheerful news which at present could come to me." Protestants and Catholics alike now saw the conflict as an international struggle for survival that required aid to coreligionists in other countries. In this way, the French Wars of Religion paved the way for wider international conflicts over religion in the future.

The religious division in France grew even more dangerous when Charles IX died and his brother Henry III (r. 1574–1589) became king. Like his brothers before him, Henry III failed to produce an heir. Next in line to succeed the throne was none other than the Calvinist Bourbon leader Henry of Navarre. Because Henry III saw an even greater threat to his authority in a newly formed Catholic League, which had requested Spain's help in rooting out Protestantism in France, he took action against the league. In 1588, he summoned two prominent league leaders to a meeting and had his men kill them. A few months later a fanatical monk stabbed Henry III to death, and Henry of Navarre became Henry IV (r. 1589–1610), despite Spain's attempt to block his way with military intervention.

The new king soon concluded that to establish control over the war-weary country he had to place the interests of the French state ahead of his Protestant faith. In 1593, Henry IV publicly embraced Catholicism, reputedly explaining his conversion with the phrase "Paris is worth a Mass." In 1598, he made peace with Spain and issued the Edict of Nantes, in which he granted the Huguenots a large measure of religious toleration. The approximately 1.25 million Huguenots became a legally protected minority within an officially Catholic kingdom of some 20 million people. Protestants were free to worship in specified towns and were allowed their own troops, fortresses, and even courts. Few believed in religious toleration, but Henry IV followed the advice of those neutral Catholics and Calvinists called **politiques** who urged him to give priority to the development of a durable state. Although their opponents hated them for their compromising spirit, the politiques believed that religious disputes could be resolved only in the peace provided by strong government.

The Edict of Nantes ended the French Wars of Religion, but Henry still needed to reestablish monarchical authority. He used court festivities and royal processions to rally subjects around him, and he developed a new class of royal officials to counterbalance the fractious nobility. In exchange for an annual payment, officials who had purchased their offices could pass them on to heirs or sell them to someone else. By buying offices that eventually ennobled their holders, rich middle-class merchants and lawyers could become part of a new social elite known as the "nobility of the robe" (named after the robes that magistrates wore, much like those judges wear today). New income raised by the increased sale of offices reduced the state debt and helped Henry build the base for a strong monarchy. His efforts did not, however, prevent his own assassination in 1610 after nineteen unsuccessful attempts.

Challenges to Habsburg Power and the Rise of the Dutch Republic

Charles V proved more successful at fending off the Turks and subduing the French than he did at resolving growing religious conflicts inside his empire. After an Imperial Diet at Regensburg in 1541 failed to patch up the theological differences between Protestants and Catholics, Charles secured papal support for a war against the Schmalkaldic League, a powerful alliance of Lutheran princes and cities. Charles's army occupied the German imperial cities in the south, restoring Catholic patricians and suppressing the Reformation wherever they triumphed. In 1547, Charles defeated the Schmalkaldic League armies at Mühlberg and captured the leading Lutheran princes. Jubilant, Charles proclaimed a decree, the "Interim," which restored Catholics' right to worship in Protestant lands while still permitting Lutherans to celebrate their own services. Riots broke out in many cities as resistance to the Interim spread. Charles's victory proved ephemeral, for after one of his former allies, Duke Maurice of Saxony, joined the other side, the princes revived the war in 1552 and chased a surprised, unprepared, and practically bankrupt emperor back to Italy.

Forced to negotiate, Charles V agreed to the Peace of Augsburg in 1555. The settlement recognized the Lutheran church in the empire, accepted the secularization of church lands but kept the remaining ecclesiastical territories (mainly the bishoprics) for Catholics, and, most important, established the principle that all princes, whether Catholic or Lutheran, enjoyed the sole right to determine the religion of their lands and subjects. Significantly, the Peace excluded Calvinist, Anabaptist, and other dissenting groups from the settlement. The Peace of Augsburg preserved a fragile peace in central Europe until 1618, but the exclusion of Calvinists would plant the seeds for future conflict.

Exhausted by constant war and depressed by the disunity in Christian Europe, Charles V resigned his many thrones in 1555 and 1556, leaving his Netherlandish-Burgundian and Spanish dominions to his son, Philip II, and his Austrian lands to his brother, Ferdinand, who was also elected Holy Roman Emperor to succeed Charles. Retiring to a monastery in southern Spain, the once powerful Christian monarch spent his last years quietly seeking salvation. Although Philip II of Spain (r. 1556–1598) ruled over fewer territories than his father, his inheritance still left him the most powerful ruler in Europe (Map 12.3). In addition to the western Habsburg lands in Spain and the Netherlands, he had inherited all the Spanish colonies recently settled in the New World of the Americas. In 1580, when the king of Portugal died without a direct heir, Philip took over this neighboring realm with its rich empire in Africa, India, and the Americas. Gold and silver funneled from the colonies supported his campaigns against the Ottoman Turks and French and English Protestants.

A deeply devout Catholic, Philip II came to the Spanish throne at age twenty-eight determined to restore Catholic unity in Europe and lead the Christian defense against the Muslims. His brief marriage to Mary Tudor (Mary I of England) did not produce an heir, but it and his subsequent marriage to Elisabeth de Valois, the sister of Charles IX and Henry III of France, gave him reason enough to oppose the spread of Protestantism in England and France. In 1571, Philip

joined with Venice and the papacy to defeat the Turks in a great sea battle off the Greek coast at Lepanto. But Philip could not rest on his laurels. Between 1568 and 1570, the Moriscos—Muslim converts to Christianity who remained secretly faithful to Islam—had revolted in the south of Spain, killing 90 priests and 1,500 Christians.

■ **Titian, *Gloria* (detail)**
All military glory and earthly power is doomed to fade away, as the Venetian painter Titian (1477–1576) vividly depicted in Gloria. Among the multitude turning to the Trinity in the heavens is the Emperor Charles V, dressed in a white robe. Painted after his abdication in 1556, Gloria is a reminder to Charles of the transience of earthly glory, for white is both the color of newborn innocence and that of the burial shroud. (Institut Amatller d'Art Hispanic.)

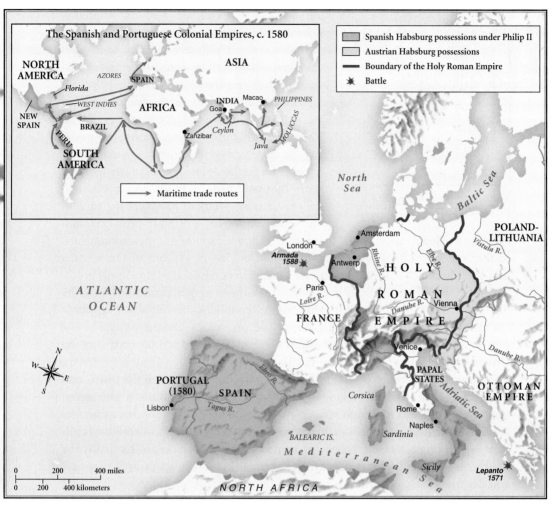

The Spanish and Portuguese Colonial Empires, c. 1580

NORTH AMERICA

ASIA

AZORES   SPAIN

Florida

WEST INDIES   AFRICA   INDIA   Macao   PHILIPPINES

NEW SPAIN   BRAZIL   Goa

PERU   Zanzibar   Ceylon   MOLUCCAS

SOUTH AMERICA   Java

Maritime trade routes

Spanish Habsburg possessions under Philip II
Austrian Habsburg possessions
Boundary of the Holy Roman Empire
Battle

North Sea

Baltic Sea

POLAND-LITHUANIA
Vistula R.

Amsterdam

London   Antwerp   Rhine R.   Elbe R.   H O L Y

Armada 1588

ATLANTIC OCEAN

Paris   R O M A N

Loire R.   Danube R.   Vienna

FRANCE   E M P I R E

Venice   Danube R.

PORTUGAL (1580)   SPAIN   Ebro R.   PAPAL STATES   OTTOMAN EMPIRE

Lisbon   Tagus R.   Corsica   Rome   Adriatic Sea

BALEARIC IS.   Sardinia   Naples

Mediterranean Sea   Sicily   Lepanto 1571

NORTH AFRICA

0   200   400 miles
0   200   400 kilometers

N W E S

■ **MAP 12.3 The Empire of Philip II, r. 1556–1598**
Spanish king Philip II drew revenues from a truly worldwide empire. In 1580, he was the richest European ruler, but the demands of governing such far-flung territories eventually drained many of his resources. **For more help analyzing this map,** *see the map activity for this chapter in the* ONLINE STUDY GUIDE *at* bedfordstmartins.com/huntconcise.

The victory at Lepanto destroyed any prospect that the Turks might come to their aid, yet Philip nonetheless forced 50,000 Moriscos to leave their villages and resettle in other regions. In 1609, his successor, Philip III, ordered their expulsion, and by 1614 some 300,000 Moriscos had been forced to relocate to North Africa.

The Calvinists of the Netherlands were less easily intimidated than the Moriscos: they were far from Spain and accustomed to being left alone. In 1566, Calvinists in

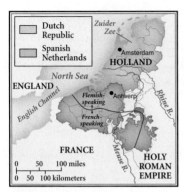

The Netherlands during the Revolt, c. 1580

the Netherlands attacked Catholic churches, smashing stained-glass windows and statues of the Virgin Mary. Philip sent an army, which executed more than 1,100 people during the next six years. When resistance revived, the Spanish responded with more force, culminating in November 1576 when Philip's armies sacked Antwerp, then Europe's wealthiest commercial city. In eleven days of horror known as the Spanish Fury, the Spanish soldiers slaughtered seven thousand people. Shocked into response, the ten Catholic southern provinces joined with the seven Protestant northern provinces and expelled the Spaniards. In 1579, however, the Catholic southern provinces returned to the Spanish fold. Despite the assassination in 1584 of William of Orange, the leader of the anti-Spanish forces, Spanish troops never regained control in the north.

Spain would not formally recognize Dutch independence until 1648, but by the end of the sixteenth century the Dutch Republic was a self-governing state sheltering a variety of religious groups. The princes of Orange (whose name came from family lands in southern France) resembled a ruling family in the Dutch Republic, but their powers paled next to those of local interests. Urban merchant and professional families known as "regents" controlled the towns and provinces. Each province (Holland was the most populous of the seven provinces) governed itself and sent delegates to the one common institution, the States General. Well situated for maritime commerce, the Dutch Republic developed a thriving economy based on shipping and shipbuilding. By 1670, the Dutch commercial fleet was larger than the English, French, Spanish, Portuguese, and Austrian fleets combined.

Dutch society tolerated more religious diversity than the other European states. One-third of the Dutch population remained Catholic, and the secular authorities allowed Catholics to worship as they chose in private. Because Protestant sects could generally count on toleration from local regents, they remained peaceful. The Dutch Republic also had a relatively large Jewish population because many Jews had settled there after being driven out of Spain and Portugal; from 1597, Jews could worship openly in their synagogues. This openness to various religions helped make the Dutch Republic one of Europe's chief intellectual and scientific centers in the seventeenth and eighteenth centuries.

England Goes Protestant

Until 1527, England's king Henry VIII (r. 1509–1547) firmly opposed the Reformation, even receiving the title "Defender of the Faith" from Pope Leo X for a treatise Henry wrote against Luther. Henry's family problems changed his mind. Henry had married Catherine of Aragon (d. 1536), the daughter of Ferdinand and Isabella of Spain and the aunt of Charles V, and the marriage had produced a daughter, Princess Mary (known as Mary Tudor). Henry wanted a male heir to consolidate the rule of his Tudor dynasty, and he had fallen in love with Anne Boleyn, a lady-in-waiting at court and a strong supporter of the Reformation. In 1527, Henry asked the reigning pope, Clement VII, to declare his eighteen-year marriage to Catherine invalid on the grounds that she was the widow of his older brother, Arthur. Arthur and Catherine's marriage, which apparently was never consummated, had been annulled by Pope Julius II. When Henry failed to secure a papal dispensation for his divorce, he chose two Protestants as his new loyal servants: Thomas Cromwell (1485–1540) as chancellor and Thomas Cranmer (1489–1556) as archbishop of Canterbury. Under their leadership the English Parliament passed a number of acts that severed ties between the English church and Rome. The Act of Supremacy of 1529 established Henry as the head of the Anglican church (the Church of England), invalidated the claims of Catherine and Princess Mary to the throne, recognized Henry's marriage to Anne Boleyn, and allowed the English crown to confiscate the properties of the monasteries.

By 1536, Henry had grown tired of Anne Boleyn, who had given birth to the future Queen Elizabeth I but had produced no sons. The king, who would go on to marry four other wives but father only one son, Edward (by his third wife, Jane Seymour), had Anne beheaded on the charge of adultery, an act that he defined as treason. Thomas More, once Henry's chancellor, had been executed in 1535 for treason—in his case, for refusing to recognize Henry as "the only supreme head on earth of the Church of England"—and Cromwell suffered the same fate in 1540 when he lost favor. After Henry's death in 1547, the Anglican church, nominally Protestant, still retained much traditional Catholic doctrine and ritual. But the principle of royal supremacy in religious matters would remain a lasting feature of Henry's reforms.

When Henry's Protestant son Edward VI (r. 1547–1553) died at age 16, his half-sister Mary Tudor (r. 1553–1558) succeeded him. She restored Catholicism and executed three hundred Protestants. Hundreds more fled. Finally, after Anne Boleyn's daughter, Elizabeth, came to the throne in 1558, the Anglican cause again gained momentum. As Elizabeth I (r. 1558–1603) moved to solidify her personal power and the authority of the Anglican church, she had to squash uprisings by Catholics in the north and at least two serious plots against her life. She also had to hold off Calvinist Puritans who pushed for more reform and Spain's Philip II, who first wanted to be her husband then, failing that, planned to invade her country to restore Catholicism.

The **Puritans** were strict Calvinists who opposed all vestiges of Catholic ritual in the Church of England. After Elizabeth became queen, many Puritans returned

Elizabeth Regina.

2. PARALIPOM. 6.

*Domine Deus Ifrael, non eft fimilis tui Deus in cœlo & in ter-
ra, qui pacta cuftodis & mifericordiam cum feruis tuis, qui
ambulant coram te in toto corde fuo.*

■ **Queen Elizabeth I of England**
*The Anglican (Church of England)
Prayerbook of 1569 included a hand-
colored print of Queen Elizabeth saying her prayers. As queen, Elizabeth
was also official head of the Church of
England (the scepter or sword at her
feet symbolizes her power). She named
bishops and made final decisions
about every aspect of church
governance.* **For more help analyzing
this image,** see the visual activity for
this chapter in the ONLINE STUDY
GUIDE at **bedfordstmartins.com/
huntconcise.** (Bridgeman Art Library.)

from exile abroad, but Elizabeth
resisted their demands for drastic
changes in Anglican ritual and
governance. She had assumed
control as "supreme governor"
of the Church of England,
replacing the pope as the ultimate religious authority, and
she appointed all bishops. The
Church of England's Thirty-Nine
Articles of Religion, issued in
1563, incorporated elements of
Catholic ritual along with
Calvinist doctrines. Puritan ministers angrily denounced the Church of England's
"popish attire and foolish disguising, . . . tithings, holy days, and a thousand more
abominations." Puritans tried to undercut the bishops' authority by placing control
of church administration in the hands of the local congregation. Elizabeth rejected
this Calvinist "presbyterianism." The Puritans nonetheless steadily gained influence.
Known for their emphasis on strict moral lives, the Puritans tried to close the theaters and Sunday fairs and insisted that every father "make his house a little church"
by teaching the children to read the Bible. At Puritan urging, a new translation of
the Bible, known as the King James Bible after Elizabeth's successor, James I, was
authorized in 1604. Believing themselves God's elect and England an "elect nation,"
the Puritans also urged Elizabeth to help Protestants in Europe.

Spain's Philip II had been married to Elizabeth's half-sister Mary Tudor and
had enthusiastically seconded Mary's efforts to return England to Catholicism.
When Mary died, Elizabeth rejected Philip's proposal of marriage and eventually
provided funds and troops to the Dutch rebels. Philip II bided his time as long as

she remained unmarried and her Catholic cousin Mary Stuart—better known as Mary, Queen of Scots—stood next in line to inherit the English throne. In 1568, Scottish Calvinists forced Mary to abdicate the throne of Scotland in favor of her year-old son James (eventually James I of England), who was then raised as a Protestant. The Scottish Calvinists feared Mary's connections to Catholic France; her mother was French and devoutly Catholic, and Mary Stuart had earlier been married to France's Francis II (he died in 1560). After her abdication, Mary spent nearly twenty years under house arrest in England, fomenting plots against Elizabeth. In 1587, when Mary's letter offering her succession rights to Philip was discovered, Elizabeth overcame her reluctance to execute a fellow monarch and ordered Mary's beheading.

In response, Pope Sixtus V decided to subsidize a Catholic crusade under Philip's leadership against the heretical queen. At the end of May 1588, Philip II sent his armada (Spanish for "fleet") of 130 ships from Lisbon toward the English Channel. The English scattered the Spanish Armada by sending blazing fire ships into its midst. A great gale then forced the Spanish to flee around Scotland. When the Armada limped home in September, half the ships had been lost and thousands of sailors were dead or starving. Protestants throughout Europe rejoiced. A Spanish monk lamented, "Almost the whole of Spain went into mourning."

By the time Philip II died in 1598, his great empire had begun to lose its luster. The costs of fighting the Dutch, the English, and the French mounted, and an overburdened peasantry could no longer pay the taxes required to meet rising expenses. In his novel *Don Quixote* (1605), the Spanish writer Miguel de Cervantes captured the sadness of Spain's loss of grandeur. Cervantes himself had been wounded at Lepanto, held captive in Algiers, and then served as a royal tax collector. His hero, a minor nobleman, reads so many romances and books of chivalry that he loses his wits and wanders the countryside hoping to re-create the heroic deeds of times past. He refuses to believe that these books are only fantasies: "Books which are printed under license from the king . . . can such be lies?" Don Quixote's futile adventures incarnated the thwarted ambitions of a declining military aristocracy.

England could never have defeated Spain in a head-to-head battle on land, but Elizabeth made the most of her limited means and consolidated the country's position as a Protestant power. In her early years, she held out the prospect of marriage to many political suitors but never married. She cajoled Parliament with references to her female weaknesses, but she showed steely-eyed determination in protecting the monarchy's interests. Her chosen successor, James I (r. 1603–1625), came to the throne as king of both Scotland and England. Elizabeth left James secure in a kingdom of growing weight in world politics.

■ **REVIEW:** *How did the power of states depend on unity in religion?*

The Thirty Years' War and the Balance of Power, 1618–1648

In 1618, a new series of violent conflicts between Catholics and Protestants erupted in the Holy Roman Empire. The final and most deadly of the wars of religion, the Thirty Years' War eventually drew in most European states. By the end of the war in 1648, many central European lands lay in ruins and many rulers were bankrupt. Reformation and Counter-Reformation had shattered the Christian humanist dream of peace and unity. The Thirty Years' War brought the preceding religious conflicts to a head and by its very violence effectively removed religion from future European disputes. Although religion still divided people *within* various states, after 1648 religion no longer provided the rationale for wars *between* European states. Out of the carnage would emerge centralized and powerful states that made increasing demands on ordinary people.

Origins and Course of the War

The fighting that devastated central Europe had its origins in religious, political, and ethnic divisions within the Holy Roman Empire. The Austrian Habsburg emperor and four of the seven electors who chose him were Catholic; the other three electors were Protestants. The Peace of Augsburg of 1555 was supposed to maintain the balance between Catholics and Lutherans, but it had no mechanism for resolving conflicts. Tensions rose as the Jesuits won many Lutheran cities back to Catholicism and as Calvinism, unrecognized under the Peace, made inroads into Lutheran areas. By 1613, two of the three Protestant electors had become Calvinists. When the Catholic Habsburg heir Archduke Ferdinand was crowned king of Bohemia in 1617, he began to curtail the religious freedom previously granted to Protestants. Protestants wanted to build new churches; Ferdinand wanted to stop them. Tensions boiled over when two Catholic deputy-governors tried to dissolve the meetings of Protestants.

On May 23, 1618, a crowd of angry Protestants surged up the stairs of the royal castle in Prague, trapped the two Catholic deputies, dragged them screaming for mercy to the windows, and hurled them to the pavement below. Because they landed in a dung heap, the Catholic deputies survived. Although no one died, this "defenestration" (from the French for "window," *la fenêtre*) of Prague touched off a new cycle of conflict. The Czechs, the largest ethnic group in Bohemia, established a Protestant assembly to spearhead resistance. A year later, when Ferdinand was elected emperor (as Ferdinand II, r. 1619–1637), the rebellious Bohemians deposed him and chose in his place the young Calvinist Frederick V of the Palatinate (r. 1616–1623). A quick series of clashes ended in 1620 when the imperial armies defeated the outmanned Czechs at the Battle of White Mountain, near Prague (see Map 12.4). Like the martyrdom of the religious reformer Jan Hus in 1415, White Mountain became an enduring symbol of the Czechs' desire for self-determination. They would not gain their independence until 1918.

White Mountain did not end the war. Private mercenary armies (armies for hire) began to form during the fighting, and the emperor had virtually no control over them. In 1625, a Czech Protestant, Albrecht von Wallenstein (1583–1634), offered to raise an army for the Catholic emperor and soon had in his employ 125,000 soldiers, who occupied and plundered much of Protestant Germany with the emperor's approval. In response, the Lutheran king of Denmark Christian IV (r. 1596–1648) invaded to protect the Protestants and to extend his own influence. Wallenstein's forces defeated him. Emboldened by his general's victories, Ferdinand issued the Edict of Restitution in 1629, which outlawed Calvinism in the empire and reclaimed Catholic church properties confiscated by the Lutherans.

With Protestant interests in serious jeopardy, Gustavus Adolphus (r. 1611–1632) of Sweden marched into Germany in 1630. A Lutheran by religion, he also hoped to gain control over trade in northern Europe, where he had already ejected the Poles from present-day Latvia and Estonia. Poland and Lithuania had joined in a commonwealth (common state) in 1569, and many Polish and Lithuanian nobles converted to Lutheranism or Calvinism, but this did not ensure common cause with Sweden. Gustavus's highly trained army of some 100,000 soldiers made Sweden, with a population of only one million, the supreme power of northern Europe, even more powerful than Russia, which had barely recovered from the "Time of Troubles" that followed on the rule of Tsar Ivan IV (r. 1533–1584). Ivan "the Terrible" initiated Russian expansion eastward into Siberia, but his moves westward ran up against the Poles and the Swedes.

Although Gustavus had religious motives for intervention in German affairs, events soon showed that power politics trumped religious interests. The Catholic French government under the leadership of Louis XIII (r. 1610–1643) and his chief minister Cardinal Richelieu (1585–1642) offered to subsidize Gustavus—and the Lutheran ruler accepted. The French hoped to counter Spanish involvement in the war and win influence and perhaps territory in the Holy Roman Empire. Gustavus defeated the imperial army and occupied the Catholic parts of southern Germany before he was killed at the battle of Lützen in 1632 (see Map 12.4). Once again the tide turned, but this time it swept Wallenstein with it. Because Wallenstein was rumored to be negotiating with Protestant powers, Ferdinand dismissed his general and had his henchmen assassinate him.

France openly joined the fray in 1635 by declaring war on Spain and soon after forged an alliance with the Calvinist Dutch to aid them in their struggle for independence from Spain. The two Catholic powers, France and Spain, pummeled each other. The Swedes kept up their pressure in Germany, the Dutch attacked the Spanish fleet, and a series of internal revolts shook the cash-strapped Spanish

Ifrael ex . Cum privil. Reg.

Icy par vn effort facrilege et barbaro   *Pillent, et bruflent tout, abattent les Autels ;*   *Et tirent des fainctes lieux les Vierges defolees*
Car Demons enragez, et d'vne humeur auare   *Se mocquent du refpect qu'on doit aux Immortels,*   *Quils ofent enleuer pour eftres violeer .   6*

■ The Horrors of the Thirty Years' War

The French artist Jacques Callot produced this engraving of the Thirty Years' War as part of a series called The Miseries and Misfortunes of War (1633). It shows soldiers burning down a church, pillaging the goods of local residents, and carrying off girls to rape them.
(Grosjean Collection, Paris/The Bridgeman Art Library.)

crown. In 1640, peasants in the rich northeastern province of Catalonia rebelled, overrunning Barcelona and killing the viceroy; the Catalans resented government confiscation of their crops and demands that they house and feed soldiers on their way to the French frontier. The Portuguese revolted in 1640 and proclaimed independence like the Dutch. In 1643, the Spanish suffered their first major defeat at French hands. Although the Spanish were forced to concede independence to Portugal (part of Spain only since 1580), they eventually suppressed the Catalan revolt.

France, too, faced exhaustion after years of rising taxes and recurrent revolts. In 1642, Richelieu died. Louis XIII followed him a few months later and was succeeded by his five-year-old son Louis XIV. With the queen mother, Anne of Austria, serving as regent and depending on the Italian cardinal, Mazarin, for advice, French politics once again moved into a period of instability, rumor, and crisis. All sides were ready for peace.

The Effects of Constant Fighting

When peace negotiations began in the 1640s, they did not come a moment too soon for the ordinary people of Europe. Some towns faced up to ten or eleven prolonged sieges during the fighting. In 1648, as negotiations dragged on, a

late sixteenth century had hoped, state interests now outweighed motivations of faith in political affairs.

Growth of State Authority

Warfare increased the reach of states: as the size of armies increased, governments needed more men, more money, and more supervisory officials. Most armies in the 1550s had fewer than 50,000 men, but Gustavus Adolphus had 100,000 men under arms in 1631. In France, the rate of land tax paid by peasants doubled in the eight years after France joined the Thirty Years' War. In addition to raising taxes, governments deliberately depreciated the value of the currency, which often resulted in inflation and soaring prices; sold new offices; and manipulated the embryonic stock and bond markets. When all else failed, they declared bankruptcy. The Spanish government, for example, did so three times in the first half of the seventeenth century.

As the demand for soldiers and for the money to supply them rose, the number of state employees multiplied, paperwork proliferated, and appointment to office began to depend on university education in the law. Monarchs relied on advisers who began to take on the role of modern prime ministers. As French king Louis XIII's chief minister, Richelieu arranged support for the Lutheran Gustavus even though Richelieu was a cardinal of the Catholic church. His priority was **raison d'état** ("reason of state")—that is, the state's interest above all else. Richelieu silenced Protestants within France because they had become too independent, and he crushed noble and popular resistance to Louis's policies. He set up intendants— delegates from the king's council dispatched to the provinces—to oversee police, army, and financial affairs. Richelieu and his intendants still had to contend with the thousands of officials who had bought their offices and therefore owned them as personal property.

To justify the growth of state authority and the expansion of government bureaucracies, rulers carefully cultivated their royal images. James I of England explicitly argued that he ruled by divine right and was accountable only to God: "kings are not only God's lieutenant on earth, but even by God himself they are called gods." But words rarely sufficed to make the point, and rulers used displays at court to overawe their subjects. Already in the 1530s, the French court of Francis I numbered 1,600 people. Included were officials to handle finances, guard duty, clothing, and food as well as physicians, librarians, musicians, dwarfs, animal trainers, and a multitude of hangers-on. When the court changed residence, which it did frequently, no fewer than 18,000 horses were required to transport the people, furniture, and documents—not to mention the dogs and falcons for the royal hunt. Hunting and mock battles honed the military skills of the male courtiers. Francis once staged a mock combat at court involving 1,200 "warriors," and he led a party to lay siege to a model town during which several players were accidentally killed.

Just as soldiers had to learn new drills for combat, courtiers had to learn to follow precise rituals. In his influential treatise, *The Courtier* (1528), the Italian diplomat Baldassare Castiglione (1478–1529) depicted the ideal courtier as a gentleman who speaks in a refined language and carries himself with nobility and dignity in the service of his prince and his lady. Spain's king Philip IV (r. 1621–1665) translated this notion of courtesy into detailed regulations that set the wages, duties, and ceremonial functions of every courtier. State funerals, public festivities, and court display, like the acquisition of art and the building of sumptuous palaces, served to underline the power and glory of the ruler.

■ **REVIEW:** *Why did a war fought over religious disputes result in stronger states?*

From Growth to Recession

A major economic shift occurred alongside the struggles over beliefs. The Protestant Reformation started in a period of economic growth, but by the time of the Thirty Years' War recession had set in. In the sixteenth century, despite religious and political turbulence, population grew, doubling in Spain and increasing 70 percent in England. The supply of precious metals swelled, too. In the 1540s new silver mines had been discovered in Mexico and Peru. Spanish gold imports peaked in the 1550s, silver in the 1590s. (See "Taking Measure," below.) The flood of gold and silver fueled an astounding inflation in food

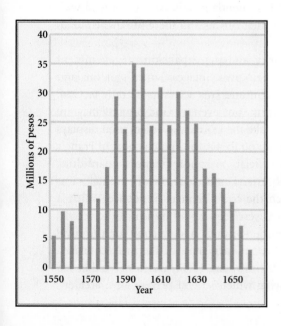

■ **TAKING MEASURE The Rise and Fall of Silver Imports to Spain, 1550–1660**
Gold and silver from the New World enabled the king of Spain to pursue aggressive policies in Europe and around the world. At what point did silver imports reach their highest level? Was the fall in silver imports precipitous or gradual? What can we conclude about the resources available to the Spanish king?

prices in western Europe—400 percent in the sixteenth century—and a more moderate rise in the cost of manufactured goods. When recession struck after 1600, all the economic indicators slumped. Silver imports to Spain declined. Textile production collapsed. Agricultural prices dropped. Overall, Europe's population may actually have declined, from 85 million in 1550 to 80 million in 1650.

Causes and Consequences of Economic Crisis

Historians have long disagreed about the causes of the early-seventeenth century recession. Some cite the inability of agriculture to support a growing population by the end of the sixteenth century; others blame the Thirty Years' War, the states' demands for more taxes, the irregularities in money supply resulting from rudimentary banking practices, or the waste caused by middle-class expenditures in the desire to emulate the nobility. To this list of causes, recent researchers have added climate change. Global cooling translated into advancing glaciers, falling temperatures, and great storms, like the one that blocked the escape of the Spanish Armada. Bad harvests, food shortages, and famine followed in short order.

Economic crisis dramatically altered the rural landscape. As prices began to stagnate and population growth slowed, farmers converted grain-growing land to pasture or vineyards. Interest in improvement of the land diminished. In some places, peasants abandoned their villages and left land to waste, as had happened during the plague epidemic of the late fourteenth century. The only country that emerged relatively unscathed from this downturn was the Dutch Republic, principally because it had long excelled in agricultural innovation. Inhabiting Europe's most densely populated area, the Dutch developed systems of field drainage, crop rotation, and animal husbandry that provided high yields of grain for both people and animals. After the Dutch, the English fared best; unlike the Spanish, the English never depended on New World gold and silver, and unlike most continental European countries, England escaped the direct impact of the Thirty Years' War.

When grain harvests fell short, peasants immediately suffered because outside of England and the Dutch Republic, grain had replaced more expensive meat as the essential staple of most Europeans' diets. Peasants lived on bread, soup with a little fat or oil, peas or lentils, garden vegetables in season, and only occasionally a piece of meat or fish. Usually the adverse years differed from place to place, but from 1594 to 1597 most of Europe suffered from shortages that triggered revolts from Ireland to Muscovy. To head off social disorder, the English government drew up a new Poor Law in 1597 that required each community to support its poor. Many other governments also increased relief efforts.

Most people, however, did not respond to their dismal circumstances by rebelling or mounting insurrections. They simply left their huts and hovels and took to the road in search of food and charity. Overwhelmed officials recorded pitiful tales of suffering. Women and children died while waiting in line for food at convents or churches. Husbands left their wives and families to search for better conditions in other parishes or even other countries. Those left behind might be reduced to eating chestnuts, roots, bark, and grass. In eastern France in 1637, a witness reported, "The roads were paved with people. . . . Finally it came to cannibalism." Eventually compassion gave way to fear as these hungry vagabonds, who sometimes banded together to beg for bread, became more aggressive, occasionally threatening to burn a barn if they were not given food.

Successive bad harvests led to malnutrition, which weakened people and made them more susceptible to such epidemic diseases as the plague, typhoid fever, typhus, dysentery, smallpox, and influenza. Disease did not spare the rich, although many epidemics hit the poor hardest. The plague was feared most: in one year it could cause the death of up to half of a town or village's population, and it struck with no discernible pattern. Nearly 5 percent of France's entire population died in the plague of 1628–1632.

Economic crisis heightened the contrast between prosperity and poverty. In England, the Dutch Republic, northern France, and northwestern Germany, the peasantry was disappearing: improvements gave some peasants the means to become farmers who rented substantial holdings, produced for the market, and in good times enjoyed relative comfort and higher status. Those who could not afford to plant new crops such as buckwheat or to use techniques that ensured higher yields became simple laborers with little or no land of their own. One-half to four-fifths of the peasants in Europe did not have enough land to support a family. They descended deeper into debt during difficult times and often lost their land to wealthier farmers or to city officials intent on developing rural estates.

Families reacted almost immediately to economic crisis. During bad harvests, they postponed marriages and had fewer children. When hard times passed, more people married and had more children. But even in the best of times, one-fifth to one-quarter of all children died in their first year, and half died before age twenty. Ten percent of women died in childbirth, and even in the richest homes childbirth often occasioned an atmosphere of panic. It might be assumed that families would have more children to compensate for high death rates, but from around 1600 to 1800, families in all ranks of society started to limit the number of children. Because methods of contraception were not widely known, they did this for the most part by marrying later; the average age at marriage during the seventeenth century rose from the early twenties to the late twenties. The average family had about four children. Poorer families seem to have had fewer children, wealthier ones more. Peasant couples, especially in eastern and southeastern Europe, had more children than urban couples because cultivation still required intensive manual labor.

The consequences of late marriage were profound. Young men and women were expected to put off marriage (*and* sexual intercourse) until their mid to late

■ The Life of the Poor
This mid-seventeenth-century painting by the Dutch artist Adriaen Pietersz van de Venne depicts the poor peasant weighed down by his wife and child. An empty food bowl signifies their hunger. In retrospect, this painting seems unfair to the wife of the family; she is shown in clothes that are not nearly as tattered as her husband's and is portrayed entirely as a burden, rather than as a help in getting by in hard times. In reality, many poor men abandoned their homes in search of work, leaving their wives behind to cope with hungry children and what remained of the family farm.
(Allen Memorial Art Museum, Oberlin College, Oberlin, Ohio, Mrs. F. F. Prentiss Fund, 1960. Inv. #1960.94.)

twenties—if they were among the lucky 50 percent who lived that long and not among the 10 percent who never married. Because both the Reformation and the Counter-Reformation stressed sexual fidelity and abstinence before marriage, the number of births out of wedlock was relatively small (2–5 percent of births); premarital intercourse was generally tolerated only after a couple had announced their engagement.

The Economic Balance of Power

Just as the recession produced winners and losers among ordinary people, so, too, it created winners and losers among the competing states of Europe. The seventeenth-century downturn ended the dominance of Mediterranean economies, which had endured since the time of the Greeks and Romans, and ushered in the new powers of northwestern Europe with their growing Atlantic economies. With expanding populations and geographical positions that promoted Atlantic trade, England and the Dutch Republic vied with France to become the leading mercantile powers. Northern Italian industries were eclipsed; Spanish commerce with the New World dropped. Amsterdam replaced Seville, Venice, Genoa, and Antwerp as the center of European trade and commerce. The plague also had differing effects. Whereas central Europe and the Mediterranean countries took generations to recover from its ravages, northwestern Europe quickly replaced its lost population, no doubt because this area's people had suffered less from the effects of the Thirty Years' War and from the malnutrition related to the economic crisis.

All but the remnants of serfdom had disappeared in western Europe, but in eastern Europe nobles reinforced their dominance over peasants, and the burden of serfdom increased. The price rise of the sixteenth century had prompted Polish and eastern German nobles to expand their holdings and step up their production of grain for western markets. Although noble landlords lost income in the economic downturn of the first half of the seventeenth century, their peasants gained nothing. Those who were already dependent became serfs—completely tied to the land. In Muscovy, the complete enserfment of the peasantry would eventually be recognized in the Code of Laws in 1649. Although enserfment produced short-term profits for landlords, in the long run it retarded economic development in eastern Europe and kept most of the population in a stranglehold of illiteracy and hardship.

Competition for colonies overseas intensified because many European states, including Sweden and Denmark, considered it a branch of mercantilist policy. According to the doctrine of mercantilism, governments should sponsor policies to increase national wealth. To this end, they chartered private joint-stock companies to enrich investors by importing fish, furs, tobacco, and precious metals, if they could be found, and to develop new markets for European products. Because Spain and Portugal had divided among themselves the rich spoils of South America, other prospective colonizers had to carve niches in seemingly less hospitable places, especially North America and the Caribbean. Eventually the English, French, and Dutch would dominate commerce with these colonies (see Map 14.1, page 570).

In establishing permanent colonies, the Europeans created whole new communities across the Atlantic. Originally, the warm climate of Virginia made it an attractive destination for the Pilgrims, a small English sect that, unlike the Puritans, attempted to separate from the Church of England. But the *Mayflower*, which sailed for Virginia with Pilgrim emigrants, landed far to the north in Massachusetts, where in 1620 the settlers founded New Plymouth Colony. As the religious situation for English Puritans worsened, wealthier people became willing to emigrate, and in 1629 a prominent group of Puritans incorporated themselves as the Massachusetts Bay Company. They founded a virtually self-governing colony headquartered in Boston.

Colonization gradually spread. Migrating settlers, including dissident Puritans, soon founded new settlements in Connecticut and Rhode Island. Catholic refugees from England established a much smaller colony in Maryland. By the 1640s, the British North American colonies had more than fifty thousand people—not including the Indians, whose numbers had been decimated in epidemics and wars—and the foundations of representative government in locally chosen colonial assemblies. By contrast, French Canada had only about three thousand European inhabitants by 1640. Because the French government refused to let Protestants emigrate from France and establish a foothold in the New World, it denied itself a ready population for the settling of permanent colonies abroad. Both England and France turned their attention to the Caribbean in the 1620s and 1630s when they occupied the islands of the West Indies after driving off the native Caribs. These islands would prove ideal for a plantation economy of tobacco and sugarcane.

■ **REVIEW:** *What were the consequences of economic recession in the early 1600s?*

A Clash of Worldviews

The countries that moved ahead economically in this period—England, the Dutch Republic, and to some extent France—turned out to be the most receptive to new secular worldviews. Although secularization did not entail a loss of religious faith, it did prompt a search for nonreligious explanations for political authority and natural phenomena. During the late sixteenth and early seventeenth centuries, art, political theory, and science all began to break some of their bonds with religion. A "scientific revolution" was in the making. Yet traditional attitudes such as belief in magic and witchcraft did not disappear. People of all classes accepted supernatural explanations for natural phenomena, a view only gradually and partially undermined by new ideas.

The Arts in an Age of Religious Conflict

A new form of artistic expression—professional theater—developed to express secular values in this age of conflict over religious beliefs. In previous centuries, traveling companies made their living by playing at major religious festivals. In London, Seville, and Madrid, the first professional acting companies performed before paying audiences in the 1570s. A huge outpouring of playwriting followed. The Spanish playwright Lope de Vega (1562–1635) alone wrote more than fifteen hundred plays. Between 1580 and 1640, three hundred English playwrights produced works for a hundred different acting companies. Theaters did a banner business despite Puritan opposition in England and Catholic objections in Spain. Shopkeepers, apprentices, lawyers, and court nobles crowded into open-air theaters to see everything from bawdy farces to profound tragedies.

The most enduring and influential playwright of the time was the Englishman William Shakespeare (1564–1616), son of a glovemaker, who wrote three dozen plays and acted in one of the chief troupes. Shakespeare never referred to religious disputes in his plays and did not set the action in contemporary England. Yet his works clearly reflected the political concerns of his age: the nature of power and the crisis of authority. Three of his greatest tragedies—*Hamlet* (1601), *King Lear* (1605), and *Macbeth* (1606)—show the uncertainty and even chaos that result when power is misappropriated or misused. In each play, family relationships are linked to questions about the legitimacy of government, just as they were for Elizabeth I herself. Hamlet's mother marries the man who murdered his royal father and usurped the crown; two of Lear's daughters betray him when he tries to divide his kingdom; Macbeth's wife persuades him to murder the king and seize the throne. One character in the final act describes the tragic story of Prince Hamlet as one "Of carnal, bloody, and unnatural acts; / Of accidental judgments, casual slaughters; / Of deaths put on by cunning and forced cause." Like many real-life people, Shakespeare's tragic characters found little peace in the turmoil of their times.

Although many rulers commissioned paintings on secular subjects for their own uses, religion still played an important role in painting, especially in Catholic Europe. The popes competed with secular rulers to hire the most talented painters and sculptors. Pope Julius II, for example, engaged the Florentine Michelangelo Buonarroti (1475–1564) to paint the walls and ceiling of the Sistine Chapel and to prepare a tomb and sculpture for himself. Michelangelo's talents served to glorify a papacy under siege, just as other artists burnished the image of secular rulers.

In the late sixteenth century, the artistic style known as mannerism departed abruptly from the Renaissance perspective of painters like Michelangelo. An almost theatrical style, **mannerism** allowed painters to distort perspective to convey a message or emphasize a theme. The most famous mannerist painter, El Greco, created new and often strange visual effects. The religious intensity of his pictures shows that faith still motivated many artists, as it did much political conflict.

The most important new style was the **baroque**, which featured exaggerated lighting, intense emotions, release from restraint, and even a kind of artistic sensationalism. Baroque was not used as a label by people living at the time; in the eighteenth century, art critics coined the word to mean shockingly bizarre, confused, and extravagant, and until the late nineteenth century, art historians and collectors largely disdained the baroque. Closely tied to the Counter-Reformation, the baroque melodramatically reaffirmed the emotional depths of the Catholic faith and glorified both church and monarchy. The first great baroque painter was Peter Paul Rubens (1577–1640). Born in the Spanish Netherlands and trained in Italy, Rubens painted vivid, exuberant pictures on religious themes. The style spread from Rome to other Italian states and then into central Europe, Spain, and the Spanish Netherlands. The Spanish built baroque churches in their American colonies as part of their massive conversion campaign. The great Dutch Protestant painters of the next generation, such as Rembrandt van Rijn (1606–1669), sometimes used biblical subjects, but their pictures were more realistic and focused on everyday scenes. Many of them suggested the Protestant concern for an inner life and personal faith rather than the public expression of religiosity.

Differences in musical style also reflected religious divisions. The new Protestant churches developed their own distinct music, which differentiated their worship from the Catholic Mass. Unlike Catholic services, for which professional musicians sang in Latin, Protestant services invited the entire congregation to sing, thereby encouraging participation. Martin Luther, an accomplished lute player, composed many hymns in German, including "Ein' feste Burg" ("A Mighty Fortress"). Protestants sang hymns before going into battle, and Protestant martyrs sang before their executions.

A new secular musical form, the opera, grew up parallel to the baroque style in the visual arts. First influential in the Italian states, opera combined music, drama, dance, and scenery in a grand sensual display, often with themes chosen to please the ruler and the aristocracy. Like Shakespeare, opera composers often turned to familiar

■ **Mannerist Painting**

With its distortion of perspective, crowding of figures, and mysterious allusions, El Greco's painting The Dream of Philip II *(1577) is a typical mannerist painting. Philip II can be seen in his usual black clothing with a lace ruffle as his only decoration. The painter Domenikos Theotokopoulos was called El Greco because he was of Greek origin. He trained in Venice and Rome before he moved to Spain in the 1570s.*

(© National Gallery, London.)

■ Baroque Painting

The baroque painter Peter Paul Rubens used monumental canvases like this one from the Antwerp cathedral to celebrate the Catholic religion. Known as The Elevation of the Cross, *this painting from 1610 to 1611 shows one of the most important moments in the story of the crucifixion of Jesus.*
(The Bridgeman Art Library.)

stories their audiences would recognize and readily follow. One of the most innovative composers of opera was Claudio Monteverdi (1567–1643), whose work contributed to the development of both opera and the orchestra. His earliest operatic production, *Orfeo* (1607), was the first to require an orchestra of about forty instruments and to include instrumental as well as vocal sections.

The Natural Laws of Politics

In reaction to the wars over religious beliefs, jurists and scholars not only began to defend the primacy of state interests over those of religious conformity but also insisted on secular explanations for politics. Machiavelli had pointed in this direction with his prescriptions for Renaissance princes in the early sixteenth century, but the intellectual movement gathered steam in the aftermath of the religious violence unleashed by the Reformation. Religious toleration could not take hold until government could be organized on some principle other than one king, one faith. The French *politiques* Michel de Montaigne and Jean Bodin and the Dutch jurist Hugo Grotius started the search for those principles.

Michel de Montaigne (1533–1592) was a French magistrate who resigned his office in the midst of the wars of religion to write about the need for tolerance and open-mindedness. Although himself a Catholic, Montaigne painted on the beams of his study the words "All that is certain is that nothing is certain." To capture this need for personal reflection in an age of religious turmoil, he invented the essay as a short and thoughtful form of expression. He revived the ancient doctrine of skepticism, which held that total certainty is never attainable—a doctrine, like toleration of religious differences, that was repugnant to Protestants and Catholics alike, both of whom were certain that their religion was the right one. Montaigne also questioned the common European habit of calling newly discovered peoples in the New World barbarous and savage: "Everyone gives the title of barbarism to everything that is not in use in his own country."

The French Catholic lawyer Jean Bodin (1530–1596) sought systematic secular answers to the problem of disorder in *The Six Books of the Republic* (1576). Comparing the different forms of government throughout history, he identified three basic types of sovereignty: monarchy, aristocracy, and democracy. Only strong monarchical power offered hope for maintaining order, he insisted. Bodin rejected any doctrine of the right to resist tyrannical authority: "I denied that it was the function of a good man or of a good citizen to offer violence to his prince for any reason, however great a tyrant he might be" (and, it might be added, whatever his ideas on religion). Bodin's ideas helped lay the foundation for absolutism, the idea that the monarch should be the sole and uncontested source of power. Nonetheless, the very discussion of types of governments in the abstract implied that they might be subject to choice rather than simply being God-given, as most rulers maintained.

During the Dutch revolt against Spain, the jurist Hugo Grotius (1583–1645) gave new meaning to the notion of "natural law"—laws of nature that give legitimacy to government and stand above the actions of any particular ruler or religious group. Grotius argued that natural law stood beyond the reach of either secular or divine authority; it would be valid even if God did not exist. Natural law should govern politics, by this account, not Scripture, religious authority, or tradition. Such ideas got Grotius into trouble with both Catholics and Protestants. When the Dutch Protestant government arrested him, his wife helped him escape prison by hiding him in a chest of books. Grotius was one of the first to argue that international conventions should govern the treatment of prisoners of war and the making of peace treaties.

At the same time that Grotius expanded the principles of natural law, many jurists worked on codifying the huge amount of legislation and jurisprudence devoted to legal forms of torture. Most states and the courts of the Catholic church used torture when the crime was serious and the evidence seemed to point to a particular defendant but no definitive proof had been established. The judges ordered torture—hanging the accused by the hands with a rope thrown over a beam, pressing the legs in a leg screw, or just tying the hands very tightly—to extract a confession, which had to be given with a medical expert and notary present and had to be repeated without torture. Children, pregnant women, the elderly, aristocrats, kings, and even professors were exempt.

Grotius's conception of natural law directly challenged the use of torture. To be in accord with natural law, Grotius argued, governments had to defend natural rights, which he defined as life, body, freedom, and honor. Grotius's ideas would influence John Locke and the American revolutionaries of the eighteenth century:

although Grotius did not encourage rebellion in the name of natural law or rights, he did hope that someday all governments would adhere to these principles and stop killing their own and one another's subjects in the name of religion. Natural law and natural rights would play an important role in the founding of constitutional governments from the 1640s forward and in the establishment of various charters of human rights in our own time.

Origins of the Scientific Revolution

Although the Catholic and Protestant churches encouraged the study of science and many prominent scientists were themselves clerics, the search for a secular, scientific method of determining the laws of nature eventually challenged the traditional accounts of natural phenomena. Christian doctrine had incorporated the scientific teachings of ancient philosophers, especially Ptolemy and Aristotle; now these came into question. A revolution in astronomy challenged the Ptolemaic view, endorsed by the Catholic church, which held that the sun revolved around the earth. Remarkable advances took place in medicine, too, which laid the foundations for modern anatomy and pharmacology. Conflicts between the new science and religion followed almost immediately.

The "new science" began with the first subject ever studied by scientists, astronomy. The traditional account of the movement of the heavens derived from the second-century Greek astronomer Ptolemy, who put the earth at the center of the cosmos. Above the earth were fixed the moon, the stars, and the planets in concentric crystalline spheres; beyond these fixed spheres dwelt God and the angels. The planets revolved around the earth at the command of God. In this view, the sun revolved around the earth; the heavens were perfect and unchanging, and the earth was "corrupted." Ptolemy insisted that the planets revolved in perfectly circular orbits (because circles were more "perfect" than other figures). To explain the actual elliptical paths that could be observed and calculated, he posited orbits within orbits, or epicycles.

In 1543, the Polish clergyman Nicolaus Copernicus (1473–1543) attacked the Ptolemaic account in his treatise *On the Revolution of the Celestial Spheres.* He argued that the earth and planets revolved around the sun, a view known as **heliocentrism** (a sun-centered universe). Copernicus discovered that by placing the sun instead of the earth at the center of the system of spheres, he could eliminate many epicycles from the calculations. In other words, he claimed that the heliocentric view simplified the mathematics.

Copernicus's views began to attract widespread attention in the early seventeenth century, when astronomers systematically collected evidence that undermined the Ptolemaic view. A leader among them was the Danish astronomer Tycho Brahe (1546–1601), whose observations of a new star in 1572 and a comet in 1577 called into question the Aristotelian view that the universe was unchanging. Brahe still rejected heliocentrism, but the assistant he employed when he moved to Prague in 1599, Johannes Kepler (1571–1630), was converted to the Copernican view. Kepler continued Brahe's collection of planetary observations and used the evidence to develop his three laws of planetary motion, published between 1609 and 1619. Kepler's laws provided mathematical backing for heliocentrism and directly challenged the claim long held, even by Copernicus, that planetary motion was circular. Kepler's first law stated that the orbits of the planets are ellipses, with the sun always at one focus of the ellipse.

The Italian Galileo Galilei (1564–1642) provided more evidence to support the heliocentric view and also challenged the doctrine that the heavens were perfect and unchanging. In 1609, he developed an improved telescope and then observed the earth's moon, four satellites of Jupiter, the phases of Venus (a cycle of changing physical appearances like that of the moon), and sunspots. The moon, the planets, and the sun were no more perfect than the earth, he insisted, and the shadows he could see on the moon could only be the product of hills and valleys like those on earth. Galileo portrayed the earth as a moving part of a larger system, only one of many planets revolving around the sun, not as the fixed center of a single, closed universe. Because he recognized the utility of the new science for everyday projects and hoped to appeal to a lay audience of merchants and aristocrats, Galileo was the first scientist to publish his studies in the vernacular (Italian) rather than in Latin.

Since his discoveries challenged the Bible as well as the commonsensical view that the sun rises and sets while the earth stands still, Galileo's work alarmed the Catholic church. In 1616, the church forbade Galileo to teach that the earth moves and in 1633 accused him of not obeying the earlier order. Forced to appear before the Inquisition, he agreed to publicly recant his assertion that the earth moves to save himself from torture and death. Afterward he lived under house arrest and could publish his work only in the Dutch Republic, which had become a haven for iconoclastic scientists and thinkers.

Startling breakthroughs took place in medicine, too. Until the mid-sixteenth century, medical knowledge in Europe had been based on the writings of the second-century Greek physician Galen, a contemporary of Ptolemy. In the same year that Copernicus challenged the traditions of astronomy (1543), the Flemish scientist Andreas Vesalius (1514–1564) did the same for anatomy. He published a new illustrated anatomical text, *On the Construction of the Human Body*, that revised Galen's work by drawing on public dissections in the medical faculties of European universities. Theophrastus Bombastus von Hohenheim, better known as Paracelsus (1493–1541), went even further than Vesalius. He burned Galen's text at the University of Basel, where he was a professor of medicine.

Paracelsus experimented with new drugs, performed operations (at the time most academic physicians taught medical theory, not practice), and pursued his interests in magic, alchemy, and astrology. He helped establish the modern science of pharmacology.

The Englishman William Harvey (1578–1657) also used dissection to examine the circulation of blood within the body, demonstrating how the heart worked as a pump. The heart and its valves were "a piece of machinery," Harvey claimed. They obeyed mechanical laws just as the planets and earth revolved around the sun in a mechanical universe. Nature could be understood by experiment and rational deduction, not by following traditional authorities.

In the 1630s, the European intellectual elite began to accept the new scientific views. Ancient learning, the churches and their theologians, and even cherished popular beliefs seemed to be undermined by a new standard of truth—**scientific method**, which was based on systematic experiments and rational deduction. Two men were chiefly responsible for spreading the prestige of scientific method, the English politician Sir Francis Bacon (1561–1626) and the French mathematician and philosopher René Descartes (1596–1650). Respectively, they represented the two essential processes of scientific method: (1) inductive reasoning through observation and experimental research and (2) deductive reasoning from self-evident principles.

In *The Advancement of Learning* (1605), Bacon attacked reliance on ancient writers and optimistically predicted that scientific method would lead to social progress. The minds of the medieval scholars, he said, had been "shut up in the cells of a few authors (chiefly Aristotle, their dictator) as their persons were shut up in the cells of monasteries and colleges." Knowledge, in Bacon's view, must be empirically based—that is, gained by observation and experiment. Bacon ardently supported the scientific method over popular beliefs, which he rejected as "fables and popular errors." Claiming that God had called the Catholic church "to account for their degenerate manners and ceremonies," Bacon looked to the Protestant English state, which he served as lord chancellor, for leadership on the road to scientific advancement.

Although Descartes agreed with Bacon's denunciation of traditional learning, he saw that the attack on tradition might only replace the dogmatism of the churches with the skepticism of Montaigne—that nothing at all was certain. A Catholic who served in the Thirty Years' War, Descartes insisted that human reason could not only unravel the secrets of nature but also prove the existence of God. He aimed to establish the new science on more secure philosophical foundations, those of mathematics and logic. Not coincidentally, Descartes invented analytic geometry. In his *Discourse on Method* (1637), he argued that mathematical and mechanical principles provided the key to understanding all of nature, including the actions of people and states. All prior assumptions must be repudiated in favor of one elementary principle: "I think, therefore I am." Everything else

■ Persecution of Witches
This engraving from a pamphlet account of witch trials in England in 1589 shows three women hanged as accused witches. At their feet are frogs and toads, which were supposed to be the witches' "familiars," sent by the devil to help them ruin the lives of their neighbors by causing disease or untimely deaths among people and live-stock. The ferret on the woman's lap was reported to be the devil himself in disguise. (Lambeth Palace Library.)

could—and should—be doubted, but even doubt showed the certain existence of someone thinking. Begin with the simple and go on to the complex, he asserted, and believe only those ideas that present themselves "clearly and distinctly." Although Descartes hoped to secure the authority of both church and state, his reliance on human reason alone irritated authorities, and his books were banned in many places. He moved to the Dutch Republic to work in peace. Scientific research, like economic growth, became centered in the northern, Protestant coun-tries, where it was less constrained by church control.

Magic and Witchcraft

Despite the new emphasis on clear reasoning, observation, and independence from past authorities, science had not yet become separate from magic. Paracelsus and other scholars studied alchemy alongside other scientific pursuits: magic and science were still closely linked. In a world in which most people believed in astrology, magical healing, prophecy, and ghosts, it is hardly surprising that many of Europe's learned people also firmly believed in witchcraft, the exercise of mag-ical powers gained by a pact with the devil. The same Jean Bodin who argued against religious fanaticism insisted on death for witches—and for those magis-trates who would not prosecute them. In France alone, 345 books and pamphlets on witchcraft appeared between 1550 and 1650. Trials of witches peaked in

Europe between 1560 and 1640, the very time of the celebrated breakthroughs of the new science. Montaigne was one of the few to speak out against executing accused witches: "It is taking one's conjectures rather seriously to roast someone alive for them," he wrote in 1580.

Belief in witches was not new in the sixteenth century. Witches had long been thought capable of almost anything: passing through walls, flying through the air, destroying crops, and causing personal catastrophes from miscarriage to demonic possession. What was new was the official persecution, justified by the notion that witches were agents of Satan whom the righteous must oppose. In a time of economic crisis, plague, warfare, and the clash of religious differences, witchcraft trials provided an outlet for social stress and anxiety, legitimated by state power. At the same time, the trials seem to have been part of the religious-reform movement itself. Denunciation and persecution of witches coincided with the spread of reform, both Protestant and Catholic. The trials concentrated especially in the German lands of the Holy Roman Empire, the boiling cauldron of the Thirty Years' War.

The victims of the persecution were overwhelmingly female: women accounted for 80 percent of the accused witches in about 100,000 trials in Europe and North America during the sixteenth and seventeenth centuries. About one-third were sentenced to death. Before 1400, when witchcraft trials were rare, nearly one-half of those accused had been men. Two Catholic clergymen compiled a guide for detecting witches, the *Malleus maleficarum* [Hammer of Witches], which was published in 1486 and reissued countless times in the sixteenth and seventeenth

---

IMPORTANT DATES

1517	Martin Luther criticizes sale of indulgences and other church practices, igniting the Reformation	1598	French Wars of Religion end with Edict of Nantes
		1618	Thirty Years' War begins
1529	Henry VIII is declared head of the Anglican church	1629	English Puritans set up the Massachusetts Bay Company and begin to colonize New England
1545–1563	Council of Trent		
1555	Peace of Augsburg	1633	Galileo Galilei is forced to recant his support of heliocentrism
1571	Battle of Lepanto marks victory of West over Ottomans at sea		
1572	St. Bartholomew's Day Massacre (August 24)	1648	Peace of Westphalia ends the Thirty Years' War
1588	Defeat of the Spanish Armada by England		

centuries. Official descriptions of witchcraft oozed lurid details of sexual orgies, incest, homosexuality, and cannibalism, in which women acted as the devil's sexual slaves. Social factors help explain the prominence of women among the accused. The poorest and most socially marginal people in most communities were elderly spinsters and widows. Because they were thought likely to hanker after revenge on those more fortunate, they were singled out as witches.

Witchcraft trials declined when scientific thinking about causes and effects raised questions about the evidence used in court: how could judges or jurors be

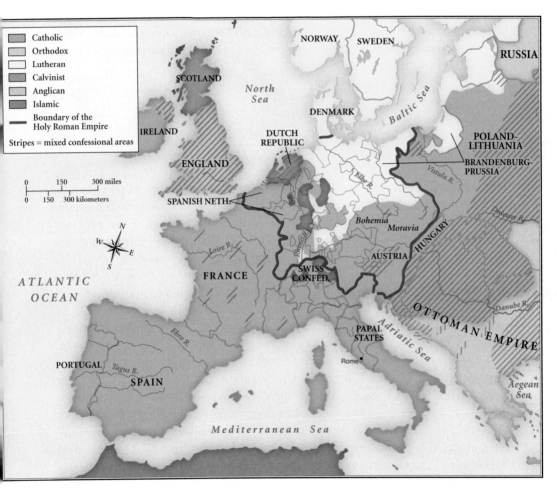

■ MAPPING THE WEST The Religious Divisions of Europe, c. 1648

The Peace of Westphalia recognized major religious divisions within Europe that have endured for the most part to the present day. Catholicism dominated in southern Europe, Lutheranism had its stronghold in northern Europe, and Calvinism flourished along the Rhine River. In southeastern Europe, the Islamic Ottoman Turks accommodated the Greek Orthodox Christians under their rule but bitterly fought the Catholic Austrian Habsburgs for control of Hungary.

certain that someone was a witch? The tide turned everywhere at about the same time, as physicians, lawyers, judges, and even clergy came to suspect that accusations were based on popular superstition and peasant untrustworthiness. In 1682, a French royal decree treated witchcraft as fraud and imposture, meaning that the law did not recognize anyone as a witch. In 1693, the jurors who had convicted twenty witches in Salem, Massachusetts, recanted, claiming: "We confess that we ourselves were not capable to understand. . . . We justly fear that we were sadly deluded and mistaken." The Salem jurors had not stopped believing in witches; they had simply lost confidence in their ability to identify them. When physicians and judges had believed in witches and persecuted them officially, with torture, witches had gone to their deaths in record numbers. But when the same groups distanced themselves from popular beliefs, the trials and the executions stopped.

■ **REVIEW:** *How could belief in witchcraft and the rising prestige of the scientific method coexist?*

Conclusion

The witchcraft persecutions reflected the traumas of these times of religious war and economic decline. Marauding armies combined with economic depression, disease, and the threat of starvation to shatter the lives of many ordinary Europeans, while religious conflicts shaped the destinies of every European power in this period. These conflicts began with the Protestant Reformation, which dispelled forever the Christian humanist dream of peace and unity, and came to a head from 1618 to 1648 in the Thirty Years' War, which cut a path of destruction through central Europe and involved most of the European powers. Shocked by the effects of religious violence, European rulers agreed to a peace that effectively removed disputes between Catholics and Protestants from the international arena.

The growing separation of political motives from religious ones did not mean that violence or conflict had ended, however. Struggles for religious uniformity within states would continue, though on a smaller scale. Bigger armies required more state involvement, and almost everywhere rulers emerged from these decades of conflict with expanded powers. The growth of state power directly changed the lives of ordinary people: more men went into the armies, and most families paid higher taxes. The constant extension of state power is one of the defining themes of modern history; religious warfare gave it a jump-start.

For all their increased power, rulers could not control economic, social, or intellectual trends, much as they often tried. The economic downturn of the seventeenth century produced unexpected consequences for European states even while it made life miserable for many ordinary people. Economic power and vibrancy shifted from the Mediterranean world to the northwest because the countries of northwestern Europe—England, France, and the Dutch Republic especially—suffered less from the fighting of the Thirty Years' War and recovered more quickly from the loss of population and production during bad times.

In the face of violence and uncertainty, some began to look for secular alternatives in art, politics, and science. Although it would be foolish to claim that everyone's mental universe changed because of the clash between religious and secular worldviews, a truly monumental shift in attitudes had begun. Secularization combined a growing interest in nonreligious forms of art, such as theater and opera, the search for nonreligious foundations of political authority, and the establishment of scientific method as the standard of truth. Proponents of these changes did not renounce their religious beliefs or even hold them less fervently, but they did insist that attention to state interests and scientific knowledge could serve as a brake on religious violence and popular superstitions. The search for order in the aftermath of religious warfare would continue in the decades to come.

■ **MAKING CONNECTIONS**

1. *How did the balance of power in Europe shift between 1500 and 1648? What were the main reasons for the shift?*

2. *Relate the new developments in the arts and sciences to the political and economic changes in this period of crisis.*

■ **FOR FURTHER EXPLORATION**

For further reading and online research ideas, see the Suggested References on page SR-6 at the back of the book.

For practice quizzes, a customized study plan, and other study tools, see the ONLINE STUDY GUIDE at bedfordstmartins.com/huntconcise.

For additional primary-source material from this period, see Chapter 12 in *Sources of THE MAKING OF THE WEST: A CONCISE HISTORY*, Second Edition.

A.F. VANDER. MEULEN. FE.

13

State Building and the Search for Order

1648–1690

I N ONE OF HER HUNDREDS OF LETTERS TO HER DAUGHTER, the French noblewoman
Marie de Sévigné (1626–1696) told a disturbing story about a well-known cook.
The cook got upset when he did not have enough roast for several unexpected
guests at a dinner for King Louis XIV. Early the next morning, when the fish he had
ordered did not arrive, the cook rushed up to his room, put his sword against the
door, and, on the third try, ran it through his heart. The fish arrived soon after. The
king regretted the trouble his visit had caused, but others soon filled in for the dead
cook. That evening, Sévigné wrote, there was "a very good dinner, light refreshments
later, and then supper, a walk, cards, hunting, everything scented with daffodils,
everything magical."

It is difficult now for us to comprehend how anyone could care that much
about a shipment of fish. The story nonetheless reveals an important aspect of state
building in the seventeenth century: to extend state authority, which had been challenged during the wars over religion and threatened by economic recession, many
rulers created an aura of overwhelming power and brilliance around themselves.
Louis XIV, like many rulers, believed that he reigned by divine right. He served as
God's lieutenant on earth and even claimed certain godlike qualities. The great gap
between the ruler and ordinary subjects accounts for the extreme reaction of Louis's

■ **Louis XIV and His Bodyguards**
*One of Louis XIV's court painters, Adam Frans van der Meulen, depicted the king arriving at the
Palace of Versailles, still under construction (the painting dates from 1669). None of the gardens,
pools, or statues had yet been installed. Louis is the only figure facing the viewer, and his dress is
much more colorful than that of anyone else in the painting.*
(Réunion des Musées Nationaux/Art Resource, NY.)

cook, and even leading nobles such as Sévigné came to see the king and his court as somehow "magical."

Louis XIV's model of state building was known as **absolutism**, a system of government in which the ruler claimed sole and uncontestable power. Although absolutism exerted great influence, especially in central and eastern Europe, it faced competition from **constitutionalism**, a system in which the ruler had to share power with parliaments made up of elected representatives. Constitutionalism led to weakness in Poland-Lithuania, but it provided a strong foundation for state power in England, the English North American colonies, and the Dutch Republic. Constitutionalism triumphed in England, however, only after one king had been executed as a traitor and another had been deposed.

Whether absolutist or constitutionalist, seventeenth-century states faced similar challenges to state building in the mid-seventeenth century. Competition in the international arena required resources, and all states raised taxes, provoking popular protests and even rebellions. The wars over religion that had culminated in the Thirty Years' War (1618–1648) left many economies in dire straits, and, even more significant, they created a need for new explanations of political authority. Monarchs still relied on religion to justify their divine right to rule, but they increasingly sought secular defenses of their powers, too. Absolutism and constitutionalism were the two main responses to the threat of disorder and breakdown left as a legacy of the wars over religion.

The search for order took place not only at the level of states and rulers but also in intellectual, cultural, and social life. In science, the Englishman Isaac Newton explained the regular movement of the universe with the law of gravitation and thereby consolidated the scientific revolution. Artists sought means of glorifying power and expressing order and symmetry in new fashion. As states consolidated their power, elites endeavored to distinguish themselves more clearly from the lower orders. The upper classes emulated the manners developed at court and tried in every way to distance themselves from anything viewed as vulgar or lower class. Officials, clergy, and laypeople all worked to reform the poor, now seen as a major source of disorder.

Louis XIV: Model of Absolutism

French king Louis XIV (r. 1643–1715) personified the absolutist ruler who in theory shared his power with no one. Louis personally made all important state decisions and left no room for dissent. In 1651, he reputedly told the Paris high court of justice, "*L'état, c'est moi*" ("I am the state"), emphasizing that state authority rested in him personally. Louis cleverly manipulated the affections and ambitions of his courtiers, chose as his ministers middle-class men who owed everything to him, built up Europe's largest army, and snuffed out every hint of religious or political opposition. Yet the absoluteness of his power should not be exaggerated.

Like all other rulers of his time, Louis depended on the cooperation of many others: local officials who enforced his decrees, peasants and artisans who joined his armies and paid his taxes, creditors who loaned crucial funds, and nobles who joined court festivities organized to glorify the king rather than stay home and cause trouble.

The Fronde, 1648–1653

Louis XIV built on a long French tradition of increasing centralization of state authority, but before he could extend it, he had to weather a series of revolts known as the **Fronde**. Derived from the French word for a child's slingshot, the term was used by critics to signify that the revolts were mere child's play. In fact, they posed an unprecedented threat to the French crown. Louis was only five when he came to the throne in 1643 upon the death of his father, Louis XIII. Louis XIV's mother, Anne of Austria, and her Italian-born adviser and rumored lover Cardinal Mazarin (1602–1661) ruled in the young monarch's name. To meet the financial pressure of fighting the Thirty Years' War and then even after the peace to keep up a draining war against Spain, Mazarin sold new offices, raised taxes, and forced creditors to extend loans to the government. In 1648, a coalition of his opponents presented him with a charter of demands that, if granted, would have given

The Fronde, 1648–1653

the **parlements** (high courts) a form of constitutional power with the right to approve new taxes. Mazarin responded by arresting the coalition's leaders. He soon faced a series of revolts that at one time or another involved nearly every social group in France.

Faced with barricades in the streets of Paris, Anne took Louis and fled Paris. As civil war threatened, Mazarin and Anne agreed to compromise with the parlements. The nobles then tried to reassert their own claims to power by raising private armies. The middle and lower classes chafed at the constant tax increases and in some places organized revolts. Conflicts erupted throughout the kingdom, and rampaging soldiers devastated rural areas and disrupted commerce.

Neither the nobles nor the judges of the parlements really wanted to overthrow the king; they simply wanted a greater share in power. But Louis XIV never forgot the humiliation and uncertainty that marred his childhood. Years later he recalled an incident in which a band of Parisians invaded his bedchamber to determine whether he had fled the city, and he declared the event an affront not only to himself but also to the state. His own policies as ruler would be designed to prevent the repetition of any such revolts.

Court Culture as an Element of Absolutism

When Cardinal Mazarin died in 1661, Louis XIV decided to rule without a first minister. He described the dangers of his situation in memoirs he wrote later for his son's instruction: "Everywhere was disorder. My Court as a whole was still very far removed from the sentiments in which I trust you will find it." Typically quarrelsome, the French nobles had long exercised local authority by maintaining their own fighting forces, meting out justice on their estates, arranging jobs for underlings, and resolving their own conflicts through dueling.

Louis set out to domesticate the warrior nobles by replacing violence with court ritual. Using a systematic policy of bestowing pensions, offices, honors, gifts, and the threat of disfavor or punishment, he made himself the center of French power and culture. The aristocracy soon vied for his favor, attended the ballets and theatricals he put on, and learned the rules of etiquette he supervised. Great nobles competed for the honor of holding his shirt when he dressed; foreign ambassadors squabbled for places near him; and royal mistresses basked in the glow of his personal favor. In a typically acerbic comment, Louis de Rouvroy, duke of Saint-Simon (1675–1755), complained, "There was nothing he [Louis XIV] liked so much as flattery . . . the coarser and clumsier it was, the more he relished it." Madame de Lafayette described the effects on court life in her novel *The Princess of Clèves* (1678): "The Court gravitated around ambition. Nobody was tranquil or indifferent—everybody was busily trying to better his or her position by pleasing, by helping, or by hindering somebody else." Occasionally the results were tragic, as in the suicide of the cook recounted by Marie de Sévigné.

Louis XIV appreciated the political uses of every form of art. Mock battles, extravaganzas, theatrical performances, even the king's dinner—Louis's daily life was a public performance designed to enhance his prestige. Calling himself the Sun King, Louis adorned his court with statues of Apollo, Greek god of the sun, and emulated the style of ancient Roman emperors. Sculpture and paintings adorned his palace, commissioned histories vaunted his achievements, and coins and medals spread his likeness throughout the realm.

The king's officials treated the arts as a branch of government. Louis's ministers set up royal academies of dance, painting, architecture, and music and took control of the Académie Française (French Academy), which to this day decides on correct usage of the French language. A royal furniture workshop at the Gobelins tapestry works on the outskirts of Paris turned out the delicate and ornate pieces whose style bore the king's name. Louis's government also regulated the number and locations of theaters and closely censored all forms of publication.

■ **The Palace of Versailles**
This 1675 painting shows the central section of the newly reconstructed palace. The entire building was still not complete at this date, but some sense of King Louis XIV's emphasis on majesty and order is already apparent. (Réunion des Musées Nationaux/Art Resource, NY. Photo: Gérard Blot.)

Music and theater enjoyed special prominence. Louis commissioned operas to celebrate royal marriages, baptisms, and military victories. The king himself danced in ballets if a role seemed especially important. Playwrights presented their new plays directly to the court. Pierre Corneille and Jean-Baptiste Racine wrote tragedies set in Greece or Rome that celebrated the new aristocratic virtues that Louis aimed to inculcate: a reverence for order and self-control.

Louis glorified his image as well through massive public works projects. Military facilities, such as veterans' hospitals and new fortified towns on the frontiers, represented his military might. Urban improvements, such as the reconstruction of the Louvre palace in Paris, proved his wealth. But his most ambitious project was the construction of a new palace at Versailles, twelve miles from the turbulent capital. Building began in the 1660s, and by 1685, the frenzied effort engaged 36,000 workers, not including the thousands of troops who diverted a local river to supply water for pools and fountains. Even the gardens reflected the spirit of Louis XIV's rule: their geometrical arrangements and clear lines showed that art and design could tame nature and that order and control defined the exercise of power.

Versailles symbolized Louis's success in reining in the nobility and dominating Europe, and other monarchs eagerly mimicked French fashion and often conducted their business in French.

By the time Louis actually moved from the Louvre to Versailles in 1682, he had reigned as monarch for thirty-nine years. Fifteen thousand people crowded into the palace's apartments, including all the highest military officers, the ministers of state, and the separate households of each member of the royal family. After the death of his queen in 1683, Louis secretly married his mistress, Françoise d'Aubigné, marquise de Maintenon, and conducted most state affairs from her apartments at the palace. De Maintenon's opponents at court complained that she controlled all the appointments, but her efforts focused on her own projects, including her favorite: the founding in 1686 of a royal school for girls from impoverished noble families. She also inspired one of Louis XIV's most critical decisions—to pursue his devotion to Catholicism.

Enforcing Religious Orthodoxy

Louis believed that he ruled by divine right. As Bishop Jacques-Benigne Bossuet (1627–1704) explained, "We have seen that kings take the place of God, who is the true father of the human species. We have also seen that the first idea of power which exists among men is that of the paternal power; and that kings are modeled on fathers." The king, like a father, should instruct his subjects in the true religion, or at least make sure that others did so.

Louis's campaign for religious conformity first focused on the Jansenists, Catholics whose doctrines and practices resembled some aspects of Protestantism. Following the posthumous publication of the book *Augustinus* (1640) by the Flemish theologian Cornelius Jansen (1585–1638), the Jansenists stressed the need for God's grace in achieving salvation. They emphasized the importance of original sin and insisted on an austere religious practice. Prominent among the Jansenists was Blaise Pascal (1623–1662), a mathematician of genius, who wrote his *Provincial Letters* (1656–1657) to defend Jansenism against charges of heresy. Many judges in the parlements likewise endorsed Jansenist doctrine.

Some questioned Louis's understanding of the finer points of doctrine: according to his German-born sister-in-law, Louis himself "has never read anything about religion, nor the Bible either, and just goes along believing whatever he is told." But Louis rejected any doctrine that gave priority to considerations of individual conscience over the demands of the official church hierarchy. He preferred teachings that stressed obedience to authority. Therefore, in 1660 he began enforcing various papal bulls (decrees) against Jansenism and closed down Jansenist theological centers. Jansenists were forced underground for the rest of his reign.

After many years of escalating pressure on the Calvinist Huguenots, Louis revoked the Edict of Nantes in 1685 and eliminated all of the Calvinists' rights. Louis considered the edict (1598), by which his grandfather Henry IV granted the Protestants religious freedom and a degree of political independence, a temporary measure, and he fervently hoped to reconvert the Huguenots to Catholicism. He closed their churches and schools, banned all their public activities, and exiled those who refused to embrace the state religion. Thousands of Huguenots emigrated to England, Brandenburg-Prussia, or the Dutch Republic. Many now wrote for publications attacking Louis XIV's absolutism. Protestant European countries were shocked by this crackdown on religious dissent and would cite it when they went to war against Louis.

Extending State Authority at Home and Abroad

Louis XIV could not have enforced his religious policies without the services of a nationwide bureaucracy. **Bureaucracy**—a network of state officials carrying out orders according to a regular and routine line of authority—comes from *bureau*, the French word for "desk," which came to mean "office," in the sense of both a physical space and a position of authority. Louis extended the bureaucratic forms his predecessors had developed, especially the use of intendants, officials who held their positions directly from the king rather than owning their offices. Louis handpicked them to represent his will against entrenched local interests such as the parlements, provincial estates, and noble governors. The intendants reduced local powers over finances and insisted on more efficient tax collection. Despite the doubling of taxes in Louis's reign, the local rebellions that had so beset the crown from the 1620s to the 1640s subsided in the face of these better-organized state forces.

Louis's success in consolidating his authority depended on hard work, an eye for detail, and an ear to the ground. In his memoirs he explained his priorities:

> to be well-informed on an infinite number of matters about which we are supposed to know nothing; to elicit from our subjects what they hide from us with the greatest care; to discover the most remote opinions of our courtiers and the most hidden interests of those who come to us with quite contrary professions [claims].

To gather all this information, Louis relied on a series of talented ministers, usually of modest origins, who gained fame, fortune, and even noble status from serving the king. Most important among them was Jean-Baptiste Colbert (1619–1683), the son of a wool merchant turned royal official. Colbert had managed Mazarin's personal finances and worked his way up under Louis XIV to become controller general, the head of royal finances, public works, and the navy. He founded a family dynasty that eventually produced five ministers of state, an archbishop, two bishops, and three generals.

Colbert used the bureaucracy to establish a new economic doctrine, **mercantilism**. According to mercantilist policy, governments must intervene to increase national wealth by whatever means possible. Such government intervention inevitably increased the role and eventually the number of bureaucrats needed. Under Colbert, the French government established overseas trading companies, granted manufacturing monopolies, and standardized production methods for textiles, paper, and soap. A government inspection system regulated the quality of finished goods and compelled all craftsmen to organize into guilds, in which masters could supervise the work of the journeymen and apprentices. To protect French production, Colbert rescinded many internal customs fees while enacting high foreign tariffs, which effectively cut imports of competing goods. To compete more effectively with England and the Dutch Republic, Colbert also subsidized shipbuilding, a policy that dramatically expanded the number of seaworthy vessels. Such mercantilist measures aimed to ensure France's prominence in world markets and to provide the resources needed to fight wars against the increasingly long list of enemies. Although later economists questioned the value of this state intervention in the economy, nearly every government in Europe embraced mercantilism.

Colbert's mercantilist projects extended to Canada, where in 1663 he took control of the trading company that had founded New France. He transplanted several thousand peasants from western France to the present-day province of Quebec, which France had claimed since 1608, and he sent fifteen hundred soldiers to fend off the Iroquois, who regularly raided French fur-trading convoys. Shows of French military force, including the burning of Indian villages and winter food supplies, forced the Iroquois to make peace, and from 1666 to 1680 French traders moved westward with minimal interference. In 1672, fur trader Louis Jolliet and Jesuit missionary Jacques Marquette reached the upper Mississippi River and traveled downstream as far as Arkansas. In 1684, French explorer Sieur de La Salle ventured all the way down to the Gulf of Mexico, claiming a vast territory for Louis XIV and calling it Louisiana after him. Louis and Colbert encouraged colonial settlement as part of their rivalry with the English and the Dutch in the New World.

Colonial settlement occupied only a small portion of Louis XIV's attention, however, for his main foreign policy goal was to extend French power in Europe. In pursuing this purpose, he inevitably came up against the Spanish and Austrian Habsburgs, whose lands encircled his. To expand French power, Louis needed the biggest possible army. The ministry of war centralized the organization of French troops. Barracks built in major towns received supplies from a central distribution system. The state began to provide uniforms for the soldiers and to offer veterans some hospital care. A militia draft instituted in 1688 supplemented the army in times of war and enrolled 100,000 men. Louis's wartime army could field a force as large as that of all his enemies combined.

Louis gained new enemies as he tried to expand the territory under his rule. In 1667–1668, in the first of his major wars after assuming personal direction of French affairs, Louis defeated the Spanish armies but had to make peace when England, Sweden, and the Dutch Republic joined the war. In the Treaty of Aix-la-Chapelle in 1668, he gained control of towns on the border of the Spanish

■ **MAP 13.1 Louis XIV's Acquisitions, 1668–1697**

Every ruler in Europe hoped to extend his or her territorial control, and war was often the result. Louis XIV steadily encroached on the Spanish Netherlands to the north and the lands of the Holy Roman Empire to the east. Although coalitions of European powers reined in Louis's grander ambitions, he incorporated many neighboring territories into the French crown.

Netherlands. Pamphlets sponsored by the Habsburgs accused Louis of aiming for "universal monarchy," or domination of Europe.

In 1672, Louis XIV opened hostilities against the Dutch because they stood in the way of his acquisition of more territory in the Spanish Netherlands. He declared war again on Spain in 1673. By now the Dutch had allied themselves with their former Spanish masters to hold off the French. Louis also marched his troops into territories of the Holy Roman Empire, provoking many of the German princes to join with the emperor, the Spanish, and the Dutch in an alliance against Louis, now denounced as a "Christian Turk" for his imperialist ambitions. But the French armies more than held their own. Faced with bloody yet inconclusive results on the battlefield, the parties agreed to the Treaty of Nijmegen of 1678–1679, which ceded several Flemish towns and Franche-Comté to Louis (Map 13.1). These territorial additions were costly: French government deficits soared, and increases in taxes touched off the most serious antitax revolt of Louis's reign, in 1675.

Louis had no intention of standing still. Heartened by the Habsburgs' seeming weakness, he pushed eastward, seizing the city of Strasbourg in 1681 and invading the province of Lorraine in 1684. Lorraine would remain a subject of contention between France and its neighbors for nearly three centuries. In 1688, Louis attacked some of the small German cities of the Holy Roman Empire and was soon involved again in a long war against a Europe-wide coalition. Between 1689 and 1697, a coalition made up of England, Spain, Sweden, the Dutch Republic, the Austrian emperor, and various German princes fought Louis XIV to a stalemate. When hostilities ended in the Peace of Rijswijk in 1697, Louis returned many of his conquests made since 1678 with the exception of Strasbourg (see Map 13.1). Louis never lost his taste for war, but his enemies learned how to set limits on his ambitions.

Louis was the last French ruler before Napoleon to accompany his troops to the battlefield. In later generations, as the military became more professional, French rulers left the fighting to their generals. Although Louis had managed to suppress the private armies of his noble courtiers, he constantly promoted his own military prowess in order to keep his noble officers under his sway. He had miniature battle scenes painted on his high heels and commissioned tapestries showing his military processions into cities, even those he did not take by force. He seized every occasion to assert his supremacy, insisting that other fleets salute his ships first.

War required money and men, which Louis obtained by expanding state control over finances, conscription into the army, and military supply. Thus absolutism and warfare fed each other, as the bureaucracy created new ways to raise and maintain an army and the army's success in war justified the expansion of state power. But constant warfare also eroded the state's resources. Further administrative and legal reform, the elimination of the buying and selling of offices, and the lowering of taxes—all were made impossible by the need for more money.

The playwright Corneille wrote, no doubt optimistically, "The people are very happy when they die for their kings." What is certain is that the wars touched many peasant and urban families. The people who lived on the routes leading to the battlefields had to house and feed soldiers; only nobles were exempt from this requirement. Everyone, moreover, paid the higher taxes that were necessary to support the army. By the end of Louis's reign, one in six Frenchmen had served in the military.

■ **REVIEW:** *How "absolute" was the power of Louis XIV?*

Absolutism in Central and Eastern Europe

Central and eastern European rulers saw in Louis XIV a powerful model of absolutist state building. Yet they did not blindly emulate the Sun King, in part because they confronted conditions peculiar to their regions. The ruler of Brandenburg-Prussia had to rebuild lands ravaged by the Thirty Years' War and unite far-flung territories. The Austrian Habsburgs needed to govern a mosaic of ethnic and religious groups while fighting off the Ottoman Turks. The Russian tsars wanted to extend their power over a large but relatively impoverished empire. The great exception to absolutism in eastern Europe was Poland-Lithuania, where a long crisis virtually destroyed central authority and sucked much of eastern Europe into its turbulent wake.

Brandenburg-Prussia and Sweden: Militaristic Absolutism

Brandenburg-Prussia began as a puny state on the Elbe River, but it would have a remarkable future. In the nineteenth century, it would unify the disparate German states into modern-day Germany. The ruler of Brandenburg was an elector, one of the seven German princes entitled to select the Holy Roman Emperor. Since the sixteenth century, the ruler of Brandenburg had also controlled the duchy of East Prussia; after 1618, the state was called Brandenburg-Prussia. Despite meager resources, Frederick William of Hohenzollern, the Great Elector of Brandenburg-Prussia (r. 1640–1688), succeeded in welding his scattered lands into an absolutist state.

Pressured first by the necessities of fighting the Thirty Years' War and then by the demands of reconstruction, Frederick William determined to force his territories' estates (representative institutions) to grant him a dependable income. The Great Elector struck a deal with the Junkers (nobles) of each land: in exchange for allowing him to collect taxes, he gave them complete control over their enserfed peasants and exempted them from taxation. The tactic worked. By the end of his reign the estates met only on ceremonial occasions.

Supplied with a steady income, Frederick William could devote his attention to military and bureaucratic consolidation. Over forty years he expanded his army from eight thousand to thirty thousand men. (See "Taking Measure," page 534.) The army mirrored the rigid domination of nobles over peasants that characterized Brandenburg-Prussian society: peasants filled the ranks, and Junkers became officers. Nobles also took positions as bureaucratic officials, but military needs always had priority. The elector named special war commissars to take charge not only of military affairs but also of tax collection. To hasten military dispatches, he also established one of Europe's first state postal systems.

As a Calvinist ruler, Frederick William disdained the ostentation of the French court, even while following the absolutist model of centralizing state power. He boldly rebuffed Louis XIV by welcoming twenty thousand French Huguenot refugees after Louis's revocation of the Edict of Nantes. In pursuing policies that promoted state power, Frederick William adroitly switched sides in Louis's wars and would stop at almost nothing to crush resistance at home. In 1701, his son Frederick I (r. 1688–1713) persuaded Holy Roman Emperor Leopold I

State	Soldiers	Population	Ratio of soldiers/ total population
France	300,000	20 million	1:66
Russia	220,000	14 million	1:64
Austria	100,000	8 million	1:80
Sweden	40,000	1 million	1:25
Brandenburg-Prussia	30,000	2 million	1:66
England	24,000	10 million	1:410

*Figures for the end of the seventeenth century, ranging from 1688 for Prussia to 1710 for France

■ **TAKING MEASURE** The Seventeenth-Century Army
The figures in this chart are only approximate, but they tell an important story. What conclusions can be drawn about the relative weight of the military in the different European states? Why would England have such a smaller army than the others? Is the absolute or the relative size of the military the more important indicator?

to grant him the title "king in Prussia." Prussia had arrived as an important power (Map 13.2).

Across the Baltic, Sweden also stood out as an example of absolutist consolidation. In the Thirty Years' War, King Gustavus Adolphus's superb generalship and highly trained army had made Sweden the supreme power of northern Europe. The huge but sparsely populated state included not only most of present-day Sweden but also Finland, Estonia, half of Latvia, and much of the Baltic coastline of modern Poland and Germany. The Baltic, in short, was a Swedish lake. After Gustavus Adolphus died, his daughter Queen Christina (r. 1632–1654) conceded much authority to the estates. Absorbed by religion and philosophy, Christina eventually abdicated and converted to Catholicism. Her successors temporarily made Sweden an absolute monarchy.

In Sweden (as in neighboring Denmark-Norway), absolutism meant simply the estates standing aside while the king led the army on lucrative foreign campaigns. The aristocracy went along because it staffed the bureaucracy and reaped war profits. Intrigued by French culture, Sweden also gleamed with national pride. In 1668, the nobility demanded the introduction of a distinctive national costume: should Swedes, they asked, "who are so glorious and renowned a nation . . . let ourselves be led by the nose by a parcel of French dancing-masters"? Sweden spent the forty years after 1654 continuously warring with its neighbors. By the 1690s, war expenses

■ MAP 13.2 State Building in Central and Eastern Europe, 1648–1699

Brandenburg-Prussia emerged from relative obscurity after the Thirty Years' War to begin an aggressive program of expanding its military and its territorial base. The Austrian Habsburgs had long contested the Ottoman Turks for dominance of eastern Europe, and by 1699, they had pushed the Turks out of Hungary.

began to outrun the small Swedish population's ability to pay, threatening the continuation of absolutism.

An Uneasy Balance: Austrian Habsburgs and Ottoman Turks

Holy Roman Emperor Leopold I (r. 1658–1705) ruled over a variety of territories of different ethnicities, languages, and religions, yet in ways similar to his French and Prussian counterparts, he gradually consolidated his power. Like all the Holy Roman emperors since 1438, Leopold was an Austrian Habsburg. He was simultaneously duke of Upper and Lower Silesia, count of Tyrol, archduke of Upper and Lower Austria, king of Bohemia, king of Hungary and Croatia, and ruler of Styria and Moravia (see Map 13.2). Some of these territories were provinces in the Holy Roman Empire; others were simply ruled from Vienna as Habsburg family holdings.

■ The Siege of Vienna, 1683

This detail from a painting by Franz Geffels shows the camp of the Ottoman Turks. The Turkish armies had surrounded Vienna since July 14, 1683. Jan Sobieski led an army of Poles that joined with Austrians and Germans to beat back the Turks on September 12, 1683.

(© Archivo Iconografico, S.A. / CORBIS.)

Leopold needed to build up his armies and state authority in order to defend the Holy Roman Empire's international position, which had been weakened by the Thirty Years' War, and to push back the Ottoman Turks who steadily encroached from the southeast. The emperor and his closest officials took control over recruiting, provisioning, and strategic planning and worked to replace the mercenaries hired during the Thirty Years' War with a permanent standing army that promoted professional discipline. To pay for the army and to staff his growing bureaucracy, Leopold had to gain the support of local aristocrats and chip away at provincial institutions' powers. Intent on replacing Bohemian nobles who had supported the 1618 revolt against Austrian authority, the Habsburgs promoted a new nobility made up of Czechs, Germans, Italians, Spaniards, and even Irish, who used German as their common tongue, professed Catholicism, and loyally served the Austrian dynasty. Bohemia became a virtual Austrian colony. "You have utterly destroyed our home, our ancient kingdom," lamented a Czech Jesuit in 1670, addressing Leopold. "Woe to you! . . . The nobles you have oppressed, great cities made small. Of smiling towns you have made straggling villages." Austrian censors prohibited publication of this protest for over a century.

In addition to holding Louis XIV in check on his western frontiers, Leopold confronted the ever-present challenge of the Ottoman Turks to his east. In 1683, the

Turks pushed all the way to the gates of Vienna and laid siege to the Austrian capital; after reaching this high-water mark, however, Turkish power ebbed. With the help of Polish cavalry, the Austrians finally broke the siege and turned the tide in a major counteroffensive. By the Treaty of Karlowitz of 1699, the Ottoman Turks surrendered almost all of Hungary to the Austrians.

Hungary's "liberation" from the Turks came at a high price. The fighting laid waste vast stretches of Hungary's central plain, and the population may have declined as much as 65 percent since 1600. To repopulate the land, the Austrians settled large communities of foreigners: Romanians, Croats, Serbs, and Germans. Magyar (Hungarian) speakers became a minority, and the seeds were sown for the poisonous nationality conflicts in nineteenth- and twentieth-century Hungary, Romania, and Yugoslavia.

Once the Turks had been beaten back, Austrian rule over Hungary tightened. In 1687, the Habsburg dynasty's hereditary right to the Hungarian crown was acknowledged by the Hungarian diet, a parliament revived by Leopold in 1681 to gain the support of Hungarian nobles. The diet was dominated by nobles who had amassed huge holdings in the liberated territories. They formed the core of a pro-Habsburg Hungarian aristocracy that would buttress the dynasty until it fell in 1918. As the Turks retreated from Hungary, Leopold systematically rebuilt churches, monasteries, roadside shrines, and monuments in the flamboyant Austrian baroque style.

The Ottoman Turks also pursued state consolidation but in a very different fashion from the Europeans. The Ottoman state extended its authority through a combination of settlement and military control. Hundreds of thousands of Turkish families moved with Turkish soldiers into the Balkan peninsula in the 1400s and 1500s. As locals converted to Islam, administration passed gradually into their hands. In the Ottoman homeland of Anatolia, the sultans, the Ottoman rulers, were often challenged by mutinous army officers. Despite frequent palace coups and assassinations, the Ottoman state survived by hiring restive peasants as mercenaries and by playing bureaucratic elites off each other. This constantly shifting social and political system explains how the coup-ridden Ottoman state could appear "weak" in Western eyes and still pose a massive military threat on Europe's southeastern borders. In the end, the Ottoman state lasted longer than Louis XIV's absolute monarchy.

Russia: Foundations of Bureaucratic Absolutism

Seventeenth-century Russia seemed a world apart from the Europe of Louis XIV. Straddling Europe and Asia, it stretched across Siberia to the Pacific Ocean. Western visitors either sneered or shuddered at the "barbarism" of Russian life, and Russians reciprocated by nursing deep suspicions of everything foreign. But under the surface, Russia was evolving along paths much like the rest of absolutist Europe; the tsars increased their powers by surmounting internal disorder and coming to an accommodation with noble landlords.

When Tsar Alexei (r. 1645–1676) tried to extend state authority by imposing new administrative structures and taxes in 1648, Moscow and other cities erupted in bloody rioting. The government immediately doused the fire. In 1649, Alexei convoked the Assembly of the Land (consisting of noble delegates from the provinces) to consult on a sweeping law code to organize Russian society in a strict social hierarchy that would last for nearly two centuries. The code of 1649 assigned all subjects to a hereditary class according to their current occupation or state needs. Slaves and free peasants were merged into a serf class. As serfs they could not change occupations or move; they were tightly tied to the soil and to their noble masters. To prevent tax evasion, the code also forbade townspeople to move from the community where they resided. Nobles owed absolute obedience to the tsar and were required to serve in the army, but in return no other group could own estates worked by serfs. Serfs became the chattel of their lord, who could sell them like horses or land. Their conditions of life differed little from those of the slaves on the plantations in the Americas.

Some peasants resisted enserfment. In 1667, Stenka Razin led a huge rebellion in southern Russia that promised liberation from "the traitors and bloodsuckers of the peasant communes"—the great noble landowners, local governors, and Moscow courtiers. Razin was a Cossack, the name given to bandit gangs formed of runaway serfs and poor nobles in southern Russia and Ukraine. Captured four years later by the tsar's army, Razin was dismembered, his head and limbs publicly displayed, and his body thrown to the dogs. Thousands of his followers also suffered grisly deaths, but his memory lived on in folk songs and legends. Landlords successfully petitioned for the abolition of the statute of limitations on runaway serfs and for harsh penalties against those who harbored runaways. The increase in Russian state authority went hand in hand with the enforcement of serfdom.

To extend his power and emulate his western rivals, Tsar Alexei wanted a bigger army, exclusive control over state policy, and a greater say in religious matters. The size of the army increased dramatically from 35,000 in the 1630s to 220,000 by the end of the century (see "Taking Measure" on page 534). The Assembly of the Land, once an important source of noble consultation, never met again after 1653. In 1666, the Russian Orthodox church reaffirmed the tsar's role as God's direct representative on earth and took action against a religious group called the Old Believers, who rejected church efforts to bring Russian worship in line with Byzantine tradition. Whole communities of Old Believers starved or burned themselves to death rather than submit. Religious schism opened a gulf between the Russian people and the crown.

The tsar's emulation of western rivals extended to culture too. Alexei set up the first Western-style theater in the Kremlin, and his daughter Sophia

■ **Stenka Razin in Captivity**
After leading a revolt of thousands of serfs, peasants, and members of non-Russian tribes of the middle and lower Volga region, Razin was captured by Russian forces and led off to Moscow, as shown here, where he was executed in 1671. He has been the subject of songs, legends, and poems ever since.
(Novosti Photo Library, London.)

translated French plays. Nobles and ordinary citizens commissioned portraits of themselves instead of buying only religious icons. The most adventurous nobles began to wear German-style clothing. A long struggle over Western influences had begun.

Poland-Lithuania Overwhelmed

Unlike the other eastern European powers, Poland-Lithuania did not follow the absolutist model. Decades of war weakened the monarchy and made the great nobles into practically autonomous warlords. They used the parliament and demands for constitutionalism to stymie monarchical power. The result was a precipitous slide into political disarray and weakness.

In 1648, Ukrainian Cossack warriors revolted against the king of Poland-Lithuania, inaugurating two decades of tumult known as the Deluge. In 1654, the Cossacks offered Ukraine to Russian rule, provoking a Russo-Polish war that ended in 1667 when the tsar annexed eastern Ukraine and Kiev. To profit from the chaos in Poland-Lithuania, Sweden, Brandenburg-Prussia, and Transylvania sent armies to seize territory. As much as a third of the Polish population eventually perished in the fighting. The once prosperous Jewish and Protestant minorities suffered great losses: some fifty-six thousand Jews were killed either by the Cossacks, Polish peasants, or Russian troops. One rabbi wrote, "We were slaughtered each day, in a more agonizing way than cattle: they are butchered quickly, while we were being executed slowly." Surviving Jews moved from towns to *shtetls* (Jewish villages), where they could survive only by petty trading, moneylending, tax gathering, and tavern leasing—activities that fanned peasant anti-Semitism. Desperate for protection amid the war, most Protestants backed the violently anti-Catholic Swedes, and the victorious Catholic majority branded them as traitors, forcing some Protestants to seek refuge as far away as the Dutch Republic and England. In Poland-Lithuania— once an outpost of religious toleration—it came to be assumed that a good Pole was a Catholic.

The commonwealth revived briefly when Jan Sobieski (r. 1674–1696) was elected king. He gained a reputation throughout Europe when he led twenty-five thousand Polish cavalrymen into battle in the siege of Vienna in 1683. His cavalry helped rout the Turks and turned the tide against the Ottomans. Married to a politically shrewd French princess, Sobieski openly admired Louis XIV's France. Despite his efforts to rebuild the monarchy, he could not halt Poland-Lithuania's decline into powerlessness.

Elsewhere the ravages of war had created opportunities for kings to increase their power, but in Poland-Lithuania the great nobles gained all the advantage. They dominated the Sejm (parliament), and to maintain an equilibrium among themselves, they each wielded an absolute veto power. This "free veto" constitutional system soon deadlocked parliamentary government. The monarchy lost its room to maneuver, and with it much of its remaining power. An appalled Croat visitor in 1658 commented, "Among the Poles there is no order in the state. . . . Everybody who is stronger thinks to have the right to oppress the weaker, just as the wolves and bears are free to capture and kill cattle. . . . Such abominable depravity is called by the Poles 'aristocratic freedom.'" The Polish version of constitutionalism fatally weakened the state and made it prey to its neighbors.

■ **REVIEW:** *Why did absolutism succeed everywhere in eastern Europe except Poland-Lithuania?*

Constitutionalism in England

In the second half of the seventeenth century, western and eastern Europe began to move in different directions. In general, the farther east one traveled, the more absolutist the style of government (with the exception of Poland-Lithuania) and the greater the gulf between landlord and peasant. In eastern Europe, nobles lorded over their serfs but owed almost slavish obedience in turn to their rulers. In western Europe, even in absolutist France, serfdom had almost entirely disappeared and nobles and rulers alike faced greater challenges to their control. The greatest challenges of all would come in England.

This outcome might seem surprising, for the English monarchs enjoyed many advantages compared with their continental rivals: they needed less money for their armies because they had stayed out of the Thirty Years' War, and their island kingdom was in theory easier to rule because they governed a relatively homogeneous population only one-fourth the size of France's with few regional institutions to block the ruler's will. Yet the English rulers failed in their efforts to install absolutist policies. The English revolutions of 1642–1660 and 1688–1689 overturned two kings, confirmed the constitutional powers of an elected parliament, and laid the foundation for the idea that government must guarantee certain rights under the law.

England Turned Upside Down, 1642–1660

Disputes about the right to levy taxes and the nature of authority in the Church of England had long troubled the relationship between the English crown and Parliament. For over a hundred years, wealthy English landowners had been accustomed to participating in government through Parliament and expected to be consulted on royal policy. Although England had no one constitutional document, a variety of laws, judicial decisions, charters, and petitions granted by the king, and customary procedures all regulated relations between king and Parliament. When Charles I tried to assert his authority over Parliament, a civil war broke out. It set in motion an unpredictable chain of events, which included an extraordinary ferment of religious and political ideas. Some historians view the English civil war of 1642–1646 as the last great war of religion because it pitted Puritans against those trying to push the Anglican church toward Catholicism, but it should be considered the first modern revolution because it gave birth to democratic political and religious movements.

Charles I (r. 1625–1649) inherited the problems that had been left by his father, James I, and James's predecessor, Elizabeth I. Elizabeth had defended the crown's right to regulate religion, but neither she nor James definitively reined in the Puritans. In addition, James antagonized Parliament by selling monopolies and titles to raise money and by relying increasingly on the advice of his personal favorite, George Villiers, on whom he bestowed the title of duke of Buckingham. Charles consequently faced an increasingly aggressive Parliament when he inherited the throne. In 1628, Parliament forced Charles to agree to a Petition of Right by which he promised not to levy taxes without its consent. Charles hoped to avoid further interference with his plans by simply refusing to call Parliament into session between 1629 and 1640.

Religious tensions brought conflicts over the king's authority to a head. The Puritans had long agitated for the removal of any vestiges of Catholicism, but

Charles, married to a French Catholic, moved in the opposite direction. With Charles's encouragement, the archbishop of Canterbury, William Laud (1573–1645), imposed increasingly elaborate ceremonies on the Anglican church. Angered by these moves toward "popery," the Puritans poured forth vituperative pamphlets and sermons. In response Laud hauled them before the feared Court of Star Chamber, which the king personally controlled. The court ordered harsh sentences for Laud's Puritan critics; they were whipped, pilloried, and branded, and even had their ears cut off and their noses split. When Laud tried to apply his policies to Scotland, however, they backfired completely: the stubborn Presbyterian Scots rioted against the imposition of the Anglican prayer book—the Book of Common Prayer—and in 1640 they invaded the north of England. To raise money to fight the war, Charles called Parliament into session and unwittingly opened the door to a constitutional and religious crisis.

England during the Civil War

Reformers in the House of Commons (the lower house of Parliament) seized the opportunity to undo what they saw as the royal tyranny of the 1630s. Parliament removed Laud from office, ordered the execution of an unpopular royal commander, abolished the Court of Star Chamber, repealed recently levied taxes, and provided for a parliamentary assembly at least once every three years, thus establishing a constitutional check on royal authority. Moderate reformers expected to stop there and resisted Puritan pressure to abolish bishops and eliminate the Anglican prayer book. But their hand was forced in January 1642, when Charles and his soldiers invaded Parliament and tried unsuccessfully to arrest those leaders who had moved to curb his power. Faced with mounting opposition within London, Charles withdrew from the city and organized an army.

The ensuing civil war between king and Parliament lasted four years (1642–1646) and divided the country. The king's army of royalists, known as Cavaliers, enjoyed the most support in northern and western England. The parliamentary forces, called Roundheads because they cut their hair short, had their stronghold in the southeast, including London. Although Puritans dominated on the parliamentary side, they were divided among themselves about the proper form of church government: the Presbyterians wanted a Calvinist church with some central authority, whereas the Independents favored entirely autonomous congregations free from other church government (hence the term *congregationalism*, often associated with the Independents). Putting aside their differences for the sake of military unity, the

Puritans united under an obscure member of the House of Commons, the country gentleman Oliver Cromwell (1599–1658), who sympathized with the Independents. After Cromwell skillfully reorganized the parliamentary troops, his New Model Army defeated the Cavaliers at the battle of Naseby in 1645. Charles surrendered in 1646.

Although the civil war between king and Parliament had ended in victory for Parliament, divisions within the Puritan ranks now came to the fore: the Presbyterians dominated Parliament, but the Independents controlled the army. The disputes between elites drew lower-class groups into the debate. When Parliament tried to disband the New Model Army in 1647, disgruntled soldiers protested. Called Levellers because of their insistence on leveling social differences, the soldiers took on their officers in a series of debates about the nature of political authority. The Levellers demanded that Parliament meet annually, that members be paid so as to allow common people to participate, and that all male heads of households be allowed to vote. Their ideal of political participation excluded servants, the propertyless, and women but offered access to artisans, shopkeepers, and modest farmers. Cromwell and other army leaders rejected the Levellers' demands as threatening to property owners. Cromwell insisted, "You have no other way to deal with these men but to break them in pieces. . . . If you do not break them they will break you."

Just as political differences between Presbyterians and Independents helped spark new political movements, so, too, their conflicts over church organization fostered the emergence of new religious doctrines. The new sects had in common only their emphasis on the "inner light" of individual religious inspiration and a disdain for hierarchical authority. Their emphasis on equality before God and greater participation in church governance appealed to the middle and lower classes. The Baptists, for example, insisted on adult baptism because they believed that Christians should choose their own church and that every child should not automatically become a member of the Church of England. The Quakers demonstrated their beliefs in equality and the inner light by refusing to doff their hats to men in authority. Manifesting their religious experience by trembling, or "quaking," the Quakers believed that anyone—man or woman—inspired by a direct experience of God could preach.

Parliamentary leaders feared that the new sects would overturn the whole social hierarchy. Rumors abounded, for example, of naked Quakers running through the streets waiting "for a sign." Some sects did advocate sweeping change. The Diggers promoted rural communism—collective ownership of all property. Seekers and Ranters questioned just about everything. A few men advocated free love. In keeping with their notions of equality and individual inspiration, many of the new sects provided opportunities for women to become preachers and prophets. Women also presented petitions, participated prominently in street demonstrations, distributed tracts, and occasionally even dressed as men, wearing swords and joining armies. The outspoken women in new sects like the Quakers underscored the threat of a social order turning upside down. These developments convinced the political elite that tolerating the new sects would lead to skepticism, anarchism, and debauchery.

At the heart of the continuing political struggle was the question of what to do with the king, who tried to negotiate with the Presbyterians in Parliament. In late 1648, Independents in the army purged the Presbyterians from Parliament, leaving a "rump" of about seventy members. This Rump Parliament then created a high court to try Charles I. The court found him guilty of attempting to establish "an unlimited and tyrannical power" and pronounced a death sentence. On January 30, 1649, Charles was beheaded before an enormous crowd, which reportedly groaned as one when the axe fell. Although many had objected to Charles's autocratic rule, few had wanted him killed. For royalists, Charles immediately became a martyr, and reports of miracles, such as the curing of blindness by the touch of a handkerchief soaked in his blood, soon circulated.

The Rump Parliament abolished the monarchy and the House of Lords (the upper house of Parliament) and set up a Puritan republic with Oliver Cromwell as chairman of the Council of State. Cromwell did not tolerate dissent from his policies. He saw the hand of God in events and himself as God's agent. Pamphleteers and songwriters ridiculed his red nose and accused him of wanting to be king, but few challenged his leadership. When his agents discovered plans for mutiny within the army, they executed the perpetrators; new decrees silenced the Levellers. Although Cromwell allowed the various Puritan sects to worship rather freely and permitted Jews with needed skills to return to England for the first time since the thirteenth century, Catholics could not worship publicly, nor could Anglicans use the Book of Common Prayer. The elites—many of whom were still Anglican—were troubled by Cromwell's religious policies but pleased to see some social order reestablished.

The new regime aimed to extend state power just as Charles I had before. Cromwell laid the foundation for a Great Britain made up of England, Wales, Ireland, and Scotland by reconquering Scotland and subduing Ireland. Anti-English rebels in Ireland had seized the occasion of troubles between king and Parliament to revolt in 1641. When Cromwell's position was secured in 1649, he went to Ireland with a large force and easily defeated the rebels, massacring whole garrisons and their priests. He encouraged expropriating the lands of the Irish "barbarous wretches," and Scottish immigrants resettled the northern county of Ulster. This seventeenth-century English conquest left a legacy of bitterness that the Irish even today call "the curse of Cromwell." In 1651, Parliament turned its attention overseas, putting mercantilist ideas into practice in the first Navigation Act, which allowed imports only if they were carried on English ships or came directly from the producers of goods. The Navigation Act was aimed at the Dutch, who dominated world trade; Cromwell tried to carry the policy further by waging naval war on the Dutch from 1652 to 1654.

■ Oliver Cromwell
In this painting of 1649, Robert Walker deliberately evokes previous portraits of English kings. Cromwell is shown preparing for battle in Ireland (note the shore and sea on Cromwell's left); he holds the baton of military command, and a young page is tying on a sash, symbol of his rank. Cromwell lived an austere life, and he is depicted here without any sign of luxury. When he died, he was buried in Westminster Abbey, but in 1661 his body was exhumed and hanged in its shroud. His head was cut off and displayed outside Westminster Hall for nearly twenty years.
(Courtesy of the National Portrait Gallery, London.)

At home, however, Cromwell faced growing resistance. His wars required a budget twice the size of Charles I's, and his increases in property taxes and customs duties alienated landowners and merchants. The conflict reached a crisis in 1653: Parliament considered disbanding the army, whereupon Cromwell abolished the Rump Parliament in a military coup and made himself Lord Protector. He now silenced his critics by banning newspapers and using networks of spies and mail readers to keep tabs on his enemies. Cromwell's death in 1658 revived the prospect of civil war and political chaos. In 1660, a newly elected, staunchly Anglican Parliament invited Charles II, the son of the executed king, to return from exile.

The "Glorious Revolution" of 1688

The traditional monarchical form of government was reinstated in 1660, restoring the king to full partnership with Parliament. Charles II (r. 1660–1685) promised to extend religious toleration, especially to Catholics, with whom he sympathized. Yet in the first years of his reign more than a thousand Puritan ministers lost their positions, and after 1664, attending a service other than one conforming with the Anglican prayer book was illegal. Natural disasters also marred the early years of Charles II's reign. The plague stalked London's rat-infested streets in May 1665 and claimed more than thirty thousand victims by September. Then in 1666, the Great Fire swept the city, causing cataclysmic destruction. The crown now had a city as well as a monarchy to rebuild.

■ Great Fire of London, 1666

This painting shows the three-day fire at its height. The writer John Evelyn described the scene in his diary: "All the sky was of a fiery aspect, like the top of a burning oven, and the light seen above 40 miles round about for many nights. God grant mine eyes may never behold the like, who now saw above 10,000 houses all in one flame; the noise and cracking and thunder of people, the fall of towers, houses, and churches, was like an hideous storm." Everyone in London at the time felt overwhelmed by the catastrophe, and many attributed it to God's punishment for the upheavals of the 1640s and 1650s. (Museum of London Photographic Library.)

The restoration of monarchy made some in Parliament fear that the English government would come to resemble French absolutism. This fear was not unfounded. In 1670, Charles II made a secret agreement, soon leaked, with Louis XIV in which he promised to announce his conversion to Catholicism in exchange for money for a war against the Dutch. Charles never proclaimed himself a Catholic, but in his Declaration of Indulgence (1673) he did suspend all laws against Catholics and Protestant dissenters. Parliament refused to continue funding the Dutch war unless Charles rescinded his Declaration of Indulgence. Asserting its authority further, Parliament passed the Test Act in 1673, requiring all government officials to profess allegiance to the Church of England and in effect disavow Catholic doctrine. Then in 1678, Parliament precipitated the so-called Exclusion Crisis by explicitly denying the throne to a Roman Catholic. This action was aimed at the king's brother and heir, James, an open convert to Catholicism. Charles refused to allow it to become law.

The dynastic crisis over the succession of a Catholic gave rise to two distinct factions in Parliament: the Tories, who supported a strong, hereditary monarchy and the restored ceremony of the Anglican church, and the Whigs, who advocated parliamentary supremacy and toleration for Protestant dissenters such as Presbyterians. Both labels were originally derogatory: *Tory* meant an Irish Catholic bandit; *Whig* was the Irish Catholic designation for a Presbyterian Scot. The Tories favored James's succession despite his Catholicism, whereas the Whigs opposed a Catholic monarch. The loose moral atmosphere of Charles's court also offended some Whigs, who complained tongue in cheek that Charles was father of his country in much too literal a fashion (he had fathered more than one child by his mistresses but produced no legitimate heir).

Upon Charles's death, James succeeded to the throne as James II (r. 1685–1688). James pursued pro-Catholic and absolutist policies even more aggressively than his brother. When a male heir—who would take precedence over James's two adult Protestant daughters and be reared a Catholic—was born, Tories and Whigs banded together. They invited the Dutch ruler William, prince of Orange and the husband of James's older daughter, Mary, to invade England. James fled to France, and hardly any blood was shed. Parliament offered the throne jointly to William (r. 1689–1702) and Mary (r. 1689–1694) on the condition that they accept a bill of rights guaranteeing Parliament's full partnership in a constitutional government.

In the Bill of Rights (1689), William and Mary agreed not to raise a standing army or to levy taxes without Parliament's consent. They also agreed to call meetings of Parliament at least every three years, to guarantee free elections to parliamentary seats, and to abide by Parliament's decisions and not suspend duly passed laws. The agreement gave England's constitutional government a written, legal basis by formally recognizing Parliament as a self-contained, independent body that shared power with the rulers. Victorious supporters of the coup declared it the **Glorious Revolution**. Constitutionalism had triumphed over absolutism in England.

The propertied classes who controlled Parliament prevented any resurgence of the popular turmoil of the 1640s. The Toleration Act of 1689 granted all Protestants freedom of worship, though non-Anglicans were still excluded from the universities; Catholics got no rights but were more often left alone to worship privately. When the Catholics in Ireland rose to defend James II, William and Mary's troops brutally suppressed them. With the Whigs in power and the Tories in opposition, wealthy landowners now controlled political life throughout the realm. Differences between the factions had become minor; the Tories simply enjoyed less access to the king's patronage.

■ **REVIEW:** *What differences over religion and politics caused the conflict between king and Parliament in England?*

Other Outposts of Constitutionalism

When William and Mary came to the throne in England in 1689, the Dutch and the English put aside the rivalries that had brought them to war against each other in 1652–1654, 1665–1667, and 1672–1674. Under William, the Dutch Republic and England together led the coalition that blocked Louis XIV's efforts to dominate continental Europe. The two states had much in common: oriented toward commerce, especially overseas, they were the successful exceptions to absolutism in Europe. Also among the few outposts of constitutionalism in the seventeenth century were the British North American colonies, which developed representative government while the English were preoccupied with their revolutions at home. Constitutionalism was not the only factor shaping this Atlantic world; as constitutionalism developed in the colonies, so, too, did the enslavement of black Africans as a new labor force.

The Dutch Republic

When the Dutch Republic gained formal independence from Spain in 1648, it had already established a decentralized, constitutional state. Rich merchants called *regents* effectively controlled the internal affairs of each province and through the Estates General (an assembly made up of deputies from each province) named the *stadholder,* the executive officer responsible for defense and for representing the state at all ceremonial occasions. They almost always chose one of the princes of the house of Orange, but the prince of Orange resembled a president more than a king.

The decentralized state encouraged and protected trade, and the Dutch Republic soon became Europe's financial capital. The Bank of Amsterdam offered interest rates less than half those available in England and France. Praised for their industriousness, thrift, and cleanliness—and maligned as greedy, dull "butterboxes"—the Dutch dominated overseas commerce with their shipping (Map 13.3). They imported products from all over the world: spices, tea, and silk from Asia; sugar and tobacco from the Americas; wool from England and Spain; timber and furs from Scandinavia; grain from eastern Europe. A widely reprinted history of Amsterdam that appeared in 1662 described the city as "risen through the hand of God to the peak of prosperity and greatness. . . . The whole world stands amazed at its riches and from east and west, north and south they come to behold it."

The Dutch rapidly became the most prosperous and best-educated people in Europe. Middle-class people supported the visual arts, especially painting, to an unprecedented degree. Artists and engravers produced thousands of works, and Dutch artists were among the first to sell to a mass market. Whereas in other countries, kings, nobles, and churches bought art, Dutch buyers were merchants, artisans, and shopkeepers. Engravings, illustrated histories, and oil paintings, even those of the widely acclaimed Rembrandt van Rijn (1606–1669), were relatively

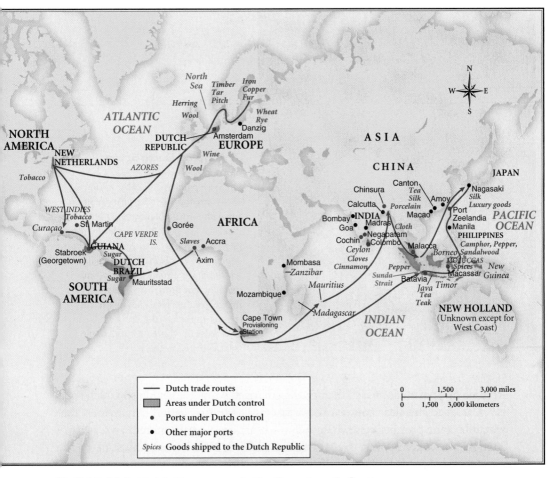

■ MAP 13.3 Dutch Commerce in the Seventeenth Century

Even before gaining formal independence from the Spanish in 1648, the Dutch had begun to com-
pete with the Spanish and Portuguese all over the world. In 1602, a group of merchants established
the Dutch East India Company, which soon offered investors an annual rate of return of 35 percent
on the trade in spices with countries located on the Indian Ocean. Global commerce gave the Dutch
the highest standard of living in Europe and soon attracted the envy of the French and the English.
For more help analyzing this map, see the map activity for this chapter in the ONLINE STUDY
GUIDE at bedfordstmartins.com/huntconcise.

inexpensive. The pictures reflected the Dutch interest in familiar daily details: children at play, winter landscapes, and ships in port.

The family household, not the royal court, determined the moral character of
this intensely commercial society. Dutch society fostered public enterprise in men
and work in the home for women, who were expected to filter out the greed and
materialism of commercial society by maintaining domestic harmony and virtue.

■ A Typical Dutch Scene from Daily Life

Jan Steen painted The Baker Arent Oostward and His Wife *in 1658. Steen ran a brewery and tavern in addition to painting, and he was known for his interest in the details of daily life. Dutch artists popularized this kind of "genre" painting, which showed ordinary people at work and play.* **For more help analyzing this image,** see the visual activity for this chapter in the ONLINE STUDY GUIDE at bedfordstmartins.com/huntconcise. (Rijksmuseum, Amsterdam.)

Relative prosperity decreased the need for married women to work, so Dutch society developed the clear contrast between middle-class male and female roles that would become prevalent elsewhere in Europe and in America more than a century later. As one contemporary Dutch writer explained, "The husband must be on the street to practice his trade; the wife must stay at home to be in the kitchen."

Extraordinarily high levels of urbanization and literacy created a large reading public. Dutch presses printed books censored elsewhere (printers or authors censored in one province simply shifted operations to another), and the University of Leiden attracted students and professors from all over Europe. Dutch tolerance extended to the works of Benedict Spinoza (1633–1677), a Jewish philosopher and biblical scholar who was expelled by his synagogue for alleged atheism but was left alone by the Dutch authorities. Spinoza strove to reconcile religion with science and mathematics, but his work scandalized many Christians and Jews because he seemed to equate God and nature. Like nature, Spinoza's God followed unchangeable laws and could not be influenced by human actions, prayers, or faith.

Dutch learning, painting, and commerce all enjoyed wide renown in the seventeenth century, but this luster proved hard to maintain. The Dutch lived in a world of international rivalries in which strong central authority gave their enemies an advantage. Though inconclusive, the naval wars with England drained the state's revenues. Even more dangerous were the land wars with France, which continued into the eighteenth century. The Dutch survived these challenges but increasingly depended on alliances with other powers, such as England. By the end of the seventeenth century, the regent elite had become more exclusive, more preoccupied with ostentation, less tolerant of deviations from strict Calvinism, and more concerned with imitating French styles than with encouraging their own.

Freedom and Slavery in the New World

The French and English also increasingly overshadowed the Dutch in the New World colonies. While the Dutch concentrated on shipping, including the slave trade, the seventeenth-century French and English established settler colonies that would eventually provide fabulous revenues to the home countries. Many European governments encouraged private companies to vie for their share of the slave trade, and slavery began to take clear institutional form in the New World in this period. While whites found in the colonies greater political and religious freedom than in Europe, they subjected black Africans to the most degrading forms of bondage.

After the Spanish and Portuguese had shown that African slaves could be transported and forced to labor in South and Central America, the English and French endeavored to set up similar labor systems in their new Caribbean island colonies. White planters with large tracts of land bought African slaves to work fields of sugarcane, and as they gradually built up their holdings, the planters displaced most of the original white settlers, who moved to mainland North American colonies. After 1661, when Barbados instituted a slave code that stripped all Africans of rights under English law, slavery became codified as an inherited status that applied only to blacks. The result was a society of extremes: the very wealthy whites, about 7 percent of the population in Barbados; and the enslaved, powerless black majority. The English brought little of their religious or constitutional practices to the Caribbean. Other Caribbean colonies followed a similar pattern of development. Louis XIV promulgated a "black code" in 1685 to regulate the legal status of slaves in the French colonies. Although one of his aims was to prevent non-Catholics from owning slaves in the French colonies, the code had much the same effect as the English codes on the slaves themselves: they had no legal rights.

The highest church and government authorities in Catholic and Protestant countries alike condoned the gradually expanding slave trade; the governments of England, France, Spain, Portugal, the Dutch Republic, and Denmark all encouraged private companies to traffic in black Africans. The Dutch West India Company was the most successful of them. In the early 1600s, about 9,500 Africans were exported from Africa to the New World every year; by 1700, this figure had increased nearly fourfold to 36,000 annually. Historians advance several different factors for the increase in the slave trade: some claim that improvements in muskets made European slavers more formidable; others cite the rising price for slaves, which made their sale more attractive for Africans; still others focus on factors internal to Africa, such as the increasing size of African armies and their use of muskets in fighting and capturing other Africans for sale as slaves. Whatever the reason, the way had been prepared for the development of an Atlantic economy based on slavery.

Virtually left to themselves during the upheavals in England, the fledgling English colonies in North America developed representative government on their own. Almost every colony had a governor and a two-house legislature. The colonial legislatures constantly sought to increase their power and resisted the efforts of Charles II and James II to reaffirm royal control. William and Mary reluctantly allowed emerging colonial elites more control over local affairs. The social and political elite among the settlers hoped to impose an English social hierarchy dominated by rich landowners. Ordinary immigrants to the colonies, however, took advantage of plentiful land to carve out their own farms using white servants and, later, in some colonies, African slaves.

For native Americans, the expanding European presence meant something else altogether. They faced death through unfamiliar disease and warfare and the accelerating loss of their homelands. Unlike white settlers, native Americans believed that land was a divine gift provided for their collective use and not subject to individual ownership. As a result, Europeans' claims that they owned exclusive land rights caused frequent skirmishes. In 1675–1676, for instance, three tribes allied under Metacomet (called King Philip by the English) threatened the survival of New England settlers, who savagely repulsed the attacks and sold their captives as slaves. Whites portrayed native Americans as conspiring villains and sneaky heathens, akin to Africans in their savagery.

▪ **REVIEW:** *How could outposts of constitutionalism coexist with slavery?*

The Search for Order in Elite and Popular Culture

The early success of constitutionalism in England, the Dutch Republic, and the English North American colonies would help to shape a distinctive Atlantic world in the eighteenth century. Just how constitutionalism was linked to the growing commerce with the colonies remains open to dispute, however, because the constitutional governments, like the absolutist ones, avidly pursued profits in the burgeoning slave trade. Freedom did not mean liberty for everyone. One of the great debates of the time—and of much of the modern period that followed—concerned the meaning of freedom: for whom, under what conditions, and with what justifiable limitations could freedom be claimed?

There was no freedom without order to sustain it, and most Europeans feared disorder above all else. Political theories, science, poetry, painting, and architecture all reflected in some measure the attempts to ground authority—to define the relation between freedom and order—in new ways. Authority concerned not just rulers and subjects but also the hierarchy of groups in society. As European states consolidated their powers, elites worked to distinguish themselves from the lower classes. They developed new codes of correct behavior for themselves and tried to teach order and discipline to their social inferiors.

Social Contract Theory: Hobbes and Locke

The turmoil of the times prompted a major rethinking of the foundations of all authority. Two figures stood out prominently amid the competing voices: Thomas Hobbes and John Locke. Their writings fundamentally shaped the modern subject of political science. Hobbes justified absolute authority; Locke provided the rationale for constitutionalism. Yet both argued that all authority came not from divine right but from a **social contract** between citizens.

Thomas Hobbes (1588–1679) was a royalist who sat out the English civil war of the 1640s in France, where he tutored the future king Charles II. Returning to England in 1651, he published his masterpiece, *Leviathan* (1651), in which he argued for unlimited authority in a ruler. Absolute authority could be vested in either a king or a parliament; it had to be absolute, he insisted, in order to overcome the defects of human nature. Believing that people are essentially self-centered and driven by the "right to self-preservation," Hobbes made his case by referring to science, not religion. To Hobbes, human life in a state of nature—that is, any situation without firm authority—was "solitary, poor, nasty, brutish, and short." He believed that the desire for power and natural greed would inevitably lead to unfettered competition. Only the assurance of social order could make people secure enough to act according to law; consequently, giving up personal liberty, he maintained, was the price of collective security. Rulers derived their power, he concluded, from a contract in which absolute authority protects people's rights.

Hobbes's notion of rule by an absolute authority left no room for political dissent or nonconformity, and it infuriated both royalists and supporters of Parliament. He enraged royalists by arguing that authority came not from divine right but from the social contract between citizens. Parliamentary supporters resisted Hobbes's claim that rulers must possess absolute authority to prevent the greater evil of anarchy; they believed that a constitution should guarantee shared power between king and parliament and protect individual rights under the law. Like Machiavelli before him, Hobbes became associated with a cynical, pessimistic view of human nature, and future political theorists often began their arguments by refuting Hobbes.

Rejecting both Hobbes and the more traditional royalist defenses of absolute authority, John Locke (1632–1704) used the notion of a social contract to provide a foundation for constitutionalism. Locke experienced political life firsthand as physician, secretary, and intellectual companion to the earl of Shaftesbury, a leading English Whig. In 1683, Locke fled with Shaftesbury to the Dutch Republic when Charles II clamped down on those conspiring to prevent his Catholic brother from succeeding him. There Locke continued work on his *Two Treatises of Government*, which, when published in 1690, served to justify the Glorious Revolution of 1688. Locke's position was thoroughly anti-absolutist. He denied the divine right of kings and ridiculed the common royalist idea that political power in the state mirrored the father's authority in the family. Like Hobbes, he posited a state of nature that applied to all people. Unlike Hobbes, however, he thought people were reasonable and the state of nature peaceful.

Locke insisted that government's only purpose was to protect life, liberty, and property, a notion that linked economic and political freedom. Ultimate authority rested in the will of a majority of men who owned property, and government should be limited to its basic purpose of protection. A ruler who failed to uphold his part of the social contract between the ruler and the populace could be justifiably resisted, an idea that would become crucial for the leaders of the American Revolution a century later. For England's landowners, however, Locke helped validate a revolution that consolidated their interests and ensured their privileges in the social hierarchy.

Locke defended his optimistic view of human nature in the immensely influential *Essay Concerning Human Understanding* (1690). He denied the existence of any innate ideas and asserted instead that each human is born with a mind that is a *tabula rasa* (blank slate). Everything humans know, he claimed, comes from sensory experience, not from anything inherent in human nature. Locke's views promoted the belief that "all men are created equal," a belief that challenged absolutist forms of rule and ultimately raised questions about women's roles as well. Not surprisingly, Locke devoted considerable energy to rethinking educational practices; he believed that education crucially shaped the human personality by channeling all sensory experience. Although he himself owned shares in the Royal African Company and justified slavery, Locke's writings were later used by abolitionists in their campaign against slavery.

Newton and the Consolidation of the Scientific Revolution

New breakthroughs in science lent support to Locke's optimistic view of human potential and at the same time reaffirmed the underlying order of the natural world. Building on the work of Copernicus, Kepler, and Galileo (see Chapter 12), the English scientist Isaac Newton (1642–1727) finally synthesized astronomy and physics with his law of universal gravitation, further enhancing the prestige of the new science. A Cambridge University student at the time of Charles II's restoration, Newton was a pious Anglican who aimed to reconcile faith and science. By proving that the physical universe followed rational principles, Newton argued, scientists could prove the existence of God and so liberate humans from doubt and the fear of chaos. Newton applied mathematical principles to formulate three physical laws: (1) in the absence of external force, an object in motion continues in a straight line; (2) the rate of change in the motion of an object is a result of the forces acting on it; and (3) the action and reaction between two objects are equal and opposite. The basis of Newtonian physics thus required understanding mass, inertia, force, velocity, and acceleration—all key concepts in modern science.

Extending these principles to the entire universe in his masterwork, *Principia Mathematica* (1687), Newton united celestial and terrestrial mechanics—astronomy and physics—with his **law of universal gravitation**. This law held that every body in the universe exerts over every other body an attractive force directly proportional to the product of their masses and inversely proportional to the square of the distance between them. The law of gravitation explained Kepler's elliptical planetary orbits just as it accounted for the motion of ordinary objects on earth. Once set in motion, the universe operated like clockwork, with no need for God's continuing intervention. Gravity, though a mysterious force, could be expressed mathematically. In Newton's words, "From the same principles [of motion] I now demonstrate the frame of the System of the World." The English poet Alexander Pope later captured the intellectual world's appreciation of Newton's accomplishment:

> *Nature and Nature's laws lay hid in night*
> *God said, Let Newton be! and all was light.*

Newton's science was not just mathematical and deductive; he experimented with light and helped establish the science of optics. Even while making these fundamental contributions to scientific method, Newton carried out alchemical experiments in his rooms at Cambridge University and spent long hours trying to calculate the date of the beginning of the world and of the second coming of Jesus. Not all scientists accepted Newton's theories immediately, especially on the continent of Europe, but within a couple of generations his work was preeminent, partly because of experimental verification. His "frame of the System of the World" remained the basis for all physics until the advent of relativity theory and quantum mechanics in the early twentieth century.

Although not all Newton's peers immediately accepted the validity of his work, absolutist rulers quickly saw the potential of the new science for enhancing their prestige and glory. Frederick William, the Great Elector of Brandenburg-Prussia, for example, set up agricultural experiments in front of his Berlin palace, and various German princes supported the work of Gottfried Wilhelm Leibniz (1646–1716), one of the inventors of calculus. A lawyer, diplomat, and scholar who wrote about metaphysics, cosmology, and history, Leibniz helped establish scientific societies in the German states. Government involvement in science was greatest in France, where it became an arm of mercantilist policy; in 1666, Colbert founded the Royal Academy of Sciences, which supplied fifteen scientists with government stipends.

Constitutional states supported science less directly but nonetheless provided an intellectual environment that encouraged its spread. The English Royal Society, the counterpart to the Royal Academy of Sciences in France, grew out of informal meetings of scientists at London and Oxford rather than direct government involvement. It received a royal charter in 1662 but maintained complete independence. The society's secretary described its business to be "in the first place, to scrutinize the whole of Nature and to investigate its activity and powers by means of observations and experiments; and then in course of time to hammer out a more solid philosophy and more ample amenities of civilization." Whether the state was directly involved or not, thinkers of the day now tied science explicitly to social progress.

Because of their exclusion from most universities, women only rarely participated in the new scientific discoveries. In 1667, nonetheless, the English Royal Society invited Margaret Cavendish—a writer of poems, essays, letters, and philosophical treatises—to attend a meeting to watch the exhibition of experiments. She attacked the use of telescopes and microscopes because she detected in the new experimentalism a mechanistic view of the world that exalted masculine prowess and challenged the Christian belief in freedom of the will. She nonetheless urged the formal education of women, complaining that "we are kept like birds in cages to hop up and down in our houses." "Many of our Sex may have as much wit, and be capable of Learning as well as men," she insisted, "but since they want Instructions, it is not possible they should attain to it."

Freedom and Order in the Arts

Even though Newtonian science depicted an orderly universe, most artists and intellectuals had experienced enough of the upheavals of the seventeenth century to fear the prospect of chaos and disintegration. The French mathematician Blaise Pascal vividly captured their worries in his *Pensées* ("Thoughts") of 1660: "I look on all sides, and I see only darkness everywhere. Nature presents to me nothing which is not a matter of doubt and concern. . . . It is incomprehensible that God should exist, and incomprehensible that He should not exist." Poets, painters, and architects all tried to make sense of the individual's place within what Pascal called "the eternal silence of these infinite spaces."

The English Puritan poet John Milton (1608–1674) responded to the turmoil of the times by giving priority to individual liberty. In 1643, in the midst of the civil war between king and Parliament, he published writings in favor of divorce. When Parliament enacted a censorship law aimed at such literature, Milton countered in

1644 with one of the first defenses of freedom of the press, *Areopagitica* ("Tribunal of Opinion"). Forced into retirement after the restoration of the monarchy, Milton published in 1667 his epic poem *Paradise Lost*. He used Adam and Eve's Fall to meditate on human freedom and the tragedies of rebellion. Although Milton wanted to "justify the ways of God to man," his Satan, the proud angel who challenges God, is so compelling as to be heroic. In the end, Adam and Eve learn to accept moral responsibility. Individuals learn the limits to their freedom, yet personal liberty remains essential to their definition as human.

The dominant artistic styles of the time—the baroque and the classical—both submerged the individual in a grander design. The baroque style proved to be especially suitable for public displays of faith and power that overawed individual beholders. The combination of religious and political purposes in baroque art is best exemplified in the architecture and sculpture of Gian Lorenzo Bernini (1598–1680), the papacy's official artist. His architectural masterpiece was the gigantic square facing St. Peter's Basilica in Rome (1656–1671). His use of freestanding colonnades and a huge open space is meant to impress the individual observer with the power of the popes and the Catholic religion. Bernini also sculpted tombs and statues for the popes and for private patrons too. In 1665, Louis XIV hired Bernini to plan the rebuilding of the Louvre palace in Paris but then rejected his ideas as incompatible with French tastes.

Although France was a Catholic country, French painters, sculptors, and architects, like their patron Louis XIV, preferred the standards of classicism to

■ **Gian Lorenzo Bernini, *Ecstasy of St. Teresa of Ávila* (c. 1650)**
In this baroque sculpture, Bernini captures the drama and sensationalism of a mystical religious faith. He based his figures on a vision of an angel reported by St. Teresa: "In his hands I saw a great golden spear, and at the iron tip there appeared to be a point of fire. This he plunged into my heart several times so that it penetrated my entrails. When he pulled it out I felt that he took them with it, and left me utterly consumed by the great love of God."
(Scala/Art Resource, NY.)

■ **French Classicism**

This painting by Nicolas Poussin, Discovery of Achilles on Skyros *(1649–1650), shows the French interest in classical themes and ideals. In the Greek story, Thetis hid her son Achilles on the island of Skyros so he would not have to fight in the Trojan War. When a chest of treasures is offered to the women, Achilles reveals himself (he is the figure on the far right) because he cannot resist the sword. In telling the story, Poussin emphasizes harmony and almost a sedateness of composition, avoiding the exuberance and emotionalism of the baroque style.*
(Photograph ©2006 Museum of Fine Arts, Boston.)

those of the baroque. French artists developed classicism to be a national style, distinct from the baroque style that was closely associated with France's enemies, the Austrian and Spanish Habsburgs. As its name suggests, **classicism** reflected the ideals of the art of antiquity; geometric shapes, order, and harmony of lines took precedence over the sensuous, exuberant, and emotional forms of the baroque. Rather than being overshadowed by the sheer power of emotional display, in classicism the individual could be found at the intersection of converging, symmetrical, straight lines. These influences were apparent in the work of the leading French painters of the period, Nicolas Poussin (1594–1665) and Claude Lorrain (1600–1682), both of whom worked in Rome and tried to re-create classical Roman values in their mythological scenes and Roman landscapes.

Art might also serve the interests of science. One of the most skilled illustrators of insects and flowers was Maria Sibylla Merian (1646–1717), a German-born

■ European Fascination with Products of the New World

In this painting of a banana plant, Maria Sibylla Merian offers a scientific study of one of the many exotic plants and animals found by Europeans who traveled to the colonies overseas. Merian was fifty-one when she traveled to the Dutch South American colony of Surinam.

(Courtesy of Hunt Institute for Botanical Documentation, Carnegie Mellon University, Pittsburgh, PA.)

painter-scholar whose engravings were widely celebrated for their brilliant realism and microscopic clarity. Merian eventually separated from her husband and joined a sect called the Labadists (after its French founder, Jean de Labadie), whose members did not believe in formal marriage ties and established a colony in the northern Dutch province of Friesland. After moving there with her daughters, Merian went with missionaries from the sect to the Dutch colony of Surinam in South America and painted watercolors of the exotic flowers, birds, and insects she found in the jungle around the cocoa and sugarcane plantations. In the seventeenth century, many women became known for their still lifes and especially their paintings of flowers. Paintings by the Dutch artist Rachel Ruysch, for example, fetched higher prices than works by Rembrandt.

Women and Manners

Poetry and painting imaginatively explored the place of the individual within a larger whole, but real-life individuals had to learn to navigate their own social worlds. Manners—the learning of individual self-discipline—were essential skills of social navigation, and women usually took the lead in teaching them. Under the tutelage of their mothers and wives, nobles learned to hide all that was crass and to maintain a fine sense of social distinction. In some ways, aristocratic men were expected to act more like women. Just as women had long been expected to please men, now aristocratic men had to please their monarch or patron by displaying proper manners and conversing with elegance and wit. Men as well as women had to master the art of pleasing—which included foreign languages (especially French), dance, a taste for fine music, and attention to dress.

As part of the evolution of new aristocratic ideals, nobles learned to disdain all that was lowly. The upper classes began to reject popular festivals and fairs in favor of private theaters, where seats were relatively expensive and behavior was formal. Clowns and buffoons now seemed vulgar; the last king of England to keep a court fool was Charles I. The greatest French playwright of the seventeenth century, Molière (the pen name of Jean-Baptiste Poquelin, 1622–1673), wrote sparkling comedies of manners that revealed much about the new aristocratic behavior. Molière's play *The Middle-Class Gentleman*, first performed at the royal court in 1670, revolves around the yearning of a rich, middle-class Frenchman, Monsieur Jourdain, to learn to act like a *gentilhomme* (meaning both "gentleman" and "nobleman" in French). By making fun of Jourdain's outlandish aspirations, the play seemed to reassure the nobles at court: only true nobles by blood can hope to act like nobles. But the play also showed how the middle classes were learning to emulate the nobility; if one could learn to *act* nobly through self-discipline, could not anyone with some education and money pass himself off as noble?

As Molière's play demonstrated, new attention to manners trickled down from the court to the middle class. A French treatise on manners from 1672 explained:

> *If everyone is eating from the same dish, you should take care not to put your hand into it before those of higher rank have done so. . . . Formerly one was permitted . . . to dip one's bread into the sauce, provided only that one had not already bitten it. Nowadays that would be a kind of rusticity. Formerly one was allowed to take from one's mouth what one could not eat and drop it on the floor, provided it was done skillfully. Now that would be very disgusting.*

The key words *rusticity* and *disgusting* reveal the association of unacceptable social behavior with the peasantry, dirt, and repulsion.

Courtly manners often permeated the upper reaches of society by means of the *salon*, an informal gathering held regularly in private homes and presided over by a socially eminent woman. In 1661, one French author claimed to have identified 251 Parisian women as hostesses of salons. Although the French government occasionally worried that these gatherings might be seditious, the three main topics of conversation were love, literature, and philosophy. Hostesses often worked hard to encourage the careers of budding authors. Before publishing a manuscript, many authors would read their compositions to a salon gathering. Corneille, Racine, and even Bishop Bossuet sought female approval for their writings.

Women who wrote on their own faced many obstacles. Marie-Madeleine de La Vergne, known as Madame de Lafayette, wrote several short novels that were published anonymously because it was considered inappropriate for aristocratic women to appear in print. After the publication of *The Princess of Clèves* in 1678, she denied having written it. Hannah Wooley, the English author of many books on domestic conduct, published under the name of her first husband. Women were known for writing wonderful letters (Marie de Sévigné was a prime example), many of which circulated in handwritten form; hardly any appeared in print during their authors' lifetimes. In the 1650s, despite these limitations, French women began to turn out best sellers in a new type of literature, the novel. Their success prompted the philosopher Pierre Bayle to remark in 1697 that "our best French novels for a long time have been written by women."

The new importance of women in the world of manners and letters did not sit well with everyone. Although the French writer François Poulain de la Barre (1647–1723), in a series of works published in the 1670s, used the new science to assert the equality of women's minds, most men resisted the idea. Clergy, lawyers, scholars, and playwrights attacked women's growing public influence. Women, they complained, were corrupting forces and needed restraint. Women were accused of raising "the banner of prostitution in the salons, in the promenades, and in the streets." Molière wrote plays denouncing women's pretension to judge literary merit. English playwrights derided learned women by creating characters with names such as Lady Knowall, Lady Meanwell, and Mrs. Lovewit. A real-life target of the English playwrights was Aphra Behn (1640–1689), one of the first professional woman authors, who supported herself by journalism and wrote plays and poetry. Her short novel *Oroonoko* (1688) told the story of an African prince mistakenly sold into slavery. The story was so successful that it was adapted by playwrights and performed repeatedly in England and France for the next hundred years. Behn responded to her critics by arguing that there was "no reason why women should not write as well as men."

Reforming Popular Culture

The illiterate peasants who made up most of Europe's population had little or no knowledge of the law of gravitation, upper-class manners, or novels, no matter who authored them. Their culture had three main elements: the knowledge needed to work at farming or in a trade; popular forms of entertainment such as village fairs and dances; and their religion, which shaped every aspect of life and death. In the seventeenth century the division between elite and popular culture widened as elites insisted on their difference from the lower orders and pushed forward the ongoing effort to instill religious and social discipline in their social inferiors.

Building upon campaigns against popular "paganism" that began during the sixteenth-century Protestant and Catholic reform movements, Protestant and Catholic churches alike pushed hard to change popular religious practices. Puritans in England tried to root out maypole dances, Sunday village fairs, gambling, taverns, and bawdy ballads because they interfered with sober observance of the Sabbath. In Lutheran Norway, pastors denounced a widespread belief in the miracle-working powers of St. Olaf. The word *superstition* previously meant "false religion" (Protestantism was a superstition for Catholics, Catholicism for Protestants). In the seventeenth century, it took on its modern meaning of irrational fears, beliefs, and practices, which anyone educated or refined would avoid. *Superstition* became synonymous with popular or ignorant beliefs.

The Catholic campaign against superstitious practices found a ready ally in Louis XIV. While he reformed the nobles at court through etiquette and manners, Catholic bishops in the French provinces trained parish priests to reform their flocks by using catechisms in local dialects and insisting that parishioners attend Mass. The church faced a formidable challenge. One bishop in France complained in 1671, "Can you believe that there are in this diocese entire villages where no one has even heard of Jesus Christ?" In some places, believers sacrificed animals to the Virgin, prayed to the new moon, and worshiped at the sources of streams as in pre-Christian times.

Like its Protestant counterpart, the Catholic campaign against ignorance and superstition helped extend state power. Clergy, officials, and local police worked together to limit carnival celebrations (festivities before the beginning of Lent that often had a riotous character), to regulate pilgrimages to shrines, and to replace "indecent" images of saints with more restrained and decorous ones. In Catholicism, the cult of the Virgin Mary and devotions closely connected with Jesus, such as the Holy Sacrament and the Sacred Heart, took precedence over the celebration of more popular saints who seemed to have pagan origins or were credited with unverified miracles. Reformers everywhere tried to limit the number of feast days on the grounds that they encouraged lewd behavior.

The campaign for more disciplined religious practices helped generate a new attitude toward the poor. Poverty previously had been closely linked with charity and virtue in Christianity: it was a Christian duty to give alms to the poor, and Jesus and many of the saints had purposely chosen lives of poverty. In the sixteenth and seventeenth centuries, the upper classes, the church, and the state increasingly regarded the poor as dangerous, deceitful, and lacking in character.

IMPORTANT DATES			
1642–1646	Civil war between King Charles I and Parliament in England	1678	Marie-Madeleine de La Vergne (Madame de Lafayette) anonymously publishes *The Princess of Clèves*
1648	Peace of Westphalia ends Thirty Years' War; the Fronde revolt challenges royal authority in France; Ukrainian Cossack warriors rebel against the king of Poland-Lithuania	1683	Austrian Habsburgs break the Turkish siege of Vienna
		1685	Louis XIV revokes toleration for French Protestants granted by the Edict of Nantes
1649	Execution of Charles I of England; new Russian legal code enacted	1687	Isaac Newton publishes *Principia Mathematica*
1651	Thomas Hobbes publishes *Leviathan*	1688	Parliament deposes James II and invites his daughter, Mary, and her husband, William of Orange, to take the English throne
1660	Monarchy restored in England		
1661	Slave code set up in Barbados		
1667	Louis XIV begins the first of many wars that continue throughout his reign	1690	John Locke publishes *Two Treatises of Government* and *Essay Concerning Human Understanding*
1670	Molière publishes *The Middle-Class Gentleman*		

"Criminal laziness is the source of all their vices," wrote a Jesuit expert on the poor. The courts had previously expelled beggars from cities; now local leaders, both Catholic and Protestant, tried to reform their character. In the sixteenth century, local and state officials began to levy taxes for more organized poor relief; after the mid-seventeenth century officials began to transform hospitals into houses of confinement for beggars. In Catholic France, upper-class women's religious associations, known as confraternities, set up asylums that confined prostitutes (by arrest if necessary) and rehabilitated them. Confraternities also founded hospices where orphans learned order and respect. Such groups advocated harsh discipline as the cure for poverty.

Although hard times had increased the numbers of poor people and the rates of violent crime as well, the most important changes were attitudinal. The elites wanted to separate the very poor from society either to change them or to keep them from contaminating others. Hospitals became holding pens for society's unwanted members, where the poor joined the disabled, the incurably diseased, and the insane. The founding of hospitals demonstrates the connection between these

■ MAPPING THE WEST Europe at the End of the Seventeenth Century

A map can be deceiving. Although Poland-Lithuania looks like a large country on this map, it had been fatally weakened by internal conflicts. In the next century it would disappear entirely. The Ottoman Empire still controlled an extensive territory, but outside Anatolia its rule depended on intermediaries. The Austrian Habsburgs had pushed the Turks out of Hungary and back into the Balkans. At the other end of the scale, the very small Dutch Republic had become very rich through international commerce. Size did not always prove to be an advantage.

attitudes and state building. In 1676, Louis XIV ordered every French city to establish a hospital, and his government took charge of their finances. Other rulers soon followed the same path.

■ REVIEW: *In what ways did elite and popular culture become more separate during the second half of the seventeenth century?*

Conclusion

The search for order in the wake of religious warfare and political upheaval took place on various levels, from the reform of the disorderly poor to the establishment of more regular bureaucratic routines in government. The biggest factor shaping the search for order was the growth of state power. Whether absolutist or constitutionalist in form, seventeenth-century states all aimed to penetrate more deeply into the lives of their subjects. They wanted more men for their armed forces, higher taxes to support their projects, and more control over foreign trade, religious dissent, and society's unwanted.

Some tearing had begun to appear, however, in the seamless fabric of state power. In England, the Dutch Republic, and the English North American colonies, property owners successfully demanded constitutional guarantees of their right to participate in government. In the eighteenth century, moreover, new levels of economic growth and the appearance of new social groups would exert pressures on the European state system. The success of seventeenth-century rulers created the political and economic conditions in which their critics would flourish.

■ MAKING CONNECTIONS

1. *What are the most important differences between absolutism and constitutionalism as political systems?*

2. *Why was the search for order a major theme in science, politics, and the arts during the second half of the seventeenth century?*

■ FOR FURTHER EXPLORATION

For further reading and online research ideas, see the Suggested References on page SR-7 at the back of the book.

For practice quizzes, a customized study plan, and other study tools, see the ONLINE STUDY GUIDE at **bedfordstmartins.com/huntconcise**.

For additional primary-source material from this period, see Chapter 13 in *Sources of THE MAKING OF THE WEST: A CONCISE HISTORY*, Second Edition.

The Atlantic System and Its Consequences

1690–1740

J OHANN SEBASTIAN BACH (1685–1750), composer of mighty organ fugues and church cantatas, was not above amusing his Leipzig audiences, many of them university students. In 1732 he produced a cantata about a young woman in love with coffee. Her old-fashioned father rages that he won't find her a husband unless she gives up the fad. She agrees, secretly vowing to admit no suitor who will not promise in the marriage contract to let her brew coffee whenever she wants. Bach offers this conclusion:

> *The cat won't give up its mouse,*
> *Girls stay faithful coffee-sisters*
> *Mother loves her coffee habit,*
> *Grandma sips it gladly too—*
> *Why then shout at the daughters?*

Bach's era might well be called the age of coffee. European travelers at the end of the sixteenth century had noticed Middle Eastern people drinking a "black drink," *kavah.* Few Europeans sampled it at first, and the Arab monopoly on its production kept prices high. This changed around 1700 when the Dutch East India

■ **London Coffeehouse**
This gouache (a variant on watercolor painting) from about 1725 depicts a scene from a London coffeehouse located in the courtyard of the Royal Exchange (merchants bank). Middle-class men (wearing wigs) read newspapers, drink coffee, smoke pipes, and discuss the news of the day. The coffeehouse draws them out of their homes into a new public space.
(British Museum/Bridgeman Art Library.)

Company introduced coffee plants to Java and other Indonesian islands. Coffee production then spread to the French Caribbean, where African slaves provided the plantation labor. In Europe, imported coffee spurred the development of a new kind of meeting place: London's first coffeehouse opened in 1652, and the idea spread quickly to other European cities. Coffeehouses became gathering places for men to drink, read newspapers, and talk politics. As a London newspaper commented in 1737, "There's scarce an Alley in City and Suburbs but has a Coffeehouse in it, which may be called the School of Public Spirit, where every Man over Daily and Weekly Journals, a Mug, or a Dram . . . devotes himself to that glorious one, his Country."

European consumption of coffee, tea, chocolate, and other novelties increased dramatically as European nations forged worldwide economic links. At the center of this new world economy was an **Atlantic system** that bound together western Europe, Africa, and the Americas. Europeans bought slaves in western Africa, transported and sold them in their colonies in North and South America and the Caribbean, bought the commodities such as coffee and sugar that were produced by the new colonial plantations, and then sold the goods in European ports for refining and reshipment. This Atlantic system first took clear shape in the early eighteenth century; it was the hub of European expansion all over the world.

Coffee drinking was one example among many of the new social and cultural patterns that took root between 1690 and 1740. Improvements in agricultural production at home reinforced the effects of trade overseas; Europeans now had more disposable income for "extras," and they spent their money not only in the new coffeehouses and cafés that sprang up all over Europe but also on newspapers, musical concerts, paintings, and novels. A new middle-class public began to make its presence felt in every domain of culture and social life.

Although the rise of the Atlantic system gave Europe new prominence in the global context, European rulers still focused most of their political, diplomatic, and military energies on their rivalries within Europe. A coalition of countries succeeded in containing French aggression, and a more balanced diplomatic system emerged. In eastern Europe, Prussia and Austria had to contend with the rising power of Russia under Peter the Great. In western Europe, both Spain and the Dutch Republic declined in influence but continued to vie with Britain and France for colonial spoils in the Atlantic. The more evenly matched competition among the great powers encouraged the development of diplomatic skills and drew attention to public health as a way of encouraging population growth.

In the aftermath of Louis XIV's revocation of the Edict of Nantes in 1685, a new intellectual movement known as the Enlightenment began to germinate. French Protestant refugees began to publish works critical of absolutism in politics and religion. Increased prosperity, the growth of a middle-class public, and the decline in warfare after Louis XIV's death in 1715 all fostered the development of this new critical spirit. Fed by the popularization of science and the growing interest in travel literature, the Enlightenment encouraged greater skepticism about religious and

The remaining 80 percent were African slaves, as most indigenous people died fighting Europeans or the diseases brought by them.

Enslaved women and men suffered terribly. Most had been sold to European traders by Africans from the west coast who acquired them through warfare or kidnapping. The vast majority were between fourteen and thirty-five years old. Before they were crammed onto the ships for the three-month trip, their heads were shaved, they were stripped naked, and some were branded with red-hot irons. Men and women were separated. Men were shackled with leg irons. Sailors and officers raped the women whenever they wished and beat those who refused their advances. In the cramped and appalling conditions aboard ship, as many as one-fourth of the slaves died in transit.

Once they landed, slaves were forced into degrading and oppressive conditions. As soon as masters bought slaves, they gave them new names, often only first names, and in some colonies branded them as personal property. Slaves had no social identities of their own; they were expected to learn their master's language and to do any job assigned. Slaves worked fifteen- to seventeen-hour days and were fed only enough to keep them on their feet. Brazilian slaves consumed more calories than the poorest Brazilians do today, but that hardly made them well fed. The death rate among slaves was high, especially in Brazil, where quick shifts in the weather, lack of clothing, and squalid living conditions made them susceptible to a variety of deadly illnesses.

Not surprisingly, despite the threat of torture or death on recapture, slaves sometimes ran away. In Brazil, runaways hid in *quilombos* (hideouts) in the forests or backcountry. When it was discovered and destroyed in 1695, the quilombo of Palmares had thirty thousand fugitives who had formed their own social organization complete with elected kings and councils of elders. Outright revolt was uncommon, especially before the nineteenth century, but other forms of resistance included stealing food, breaking tools, and feigning illness or stupidity. Slaveholders' fears about conspiracy and revolt lurked beneath the surface of every slave-based society. In 1710, the royal governor of Virginia reminded the colonial legislature of the need for unceasing vigilance: "We are not to Depend on Either Their Stupidity, or that Babel of Languages among 'em; freedom Wears a Cap which Can Without a Tongue, Call Together all Those who Long to Shake off the fetters of Slavery." Masters defended whipping and other forms of physical punishment as essential to maintaining discipline. Laws called for the castration of a slave who struck a white person.

Plantation owners often left their colonial possessions in the care of agents and collected the revenue to live as wealthy landowners back home, where they built opulent mansions and gained influence in local and national politics. William Beckford, for example, had been sent from Jamaica to school in England as a young boy. When he inherited sugar plantations and shipping companies from his father and older brother, he moved the headquarters of the family business to London in the 1730s to be close to the government and financial markets. His holdings formed

state authority. Eventually the movement would question almost every aspect of social and political life in Europe. The Enlightenment began in western Europe in those countries—Britain, France, and the Dutch Republic—most affected by the new Atlantic system. It, too, was a product of the age of coffee.

The Atlantic System and the World Economy

Although their ships had been circling the globe since the early 1500s, Europeans did not draw most of the world into their economic orbit until the 1700s. Western European trading nations sent ships loaded with goods to buy slaves from local rulers on the western coast of Africa; then transported the slaves to the colonies in North and South America and the Caribbean and sold them to the owners of plantations producing coffee, sugar, cotton, and tobacco; and bought the raw commodities produced in the colonies and shipped them back to Europe, where they were refined or processed and then sold to other parts of Europe and the world. The Atlantic system and the growth of international trade helped create a new consumer society.

Slavery and the Atlantic System

Spain and Portugal had dominated Atlantic trade in the sixteenth and seventeenth centuries, but in the eighteenth century European trade in the Atlantic rapidly expanded and became more systematically interconnected (Map 14.1, inset). By 1630, Portugal had already sent 60,000 African slaves to Brazil to work on the new **plantations** (large tracts of lands farmed by slave labor), which were producing some 15,000 tons of sugar a year. Realizing that plantations producing staples for Europeans could bring fabulous wealth, the European powers grew less interested in the dwindling trade in precious metals and more eager to colonize. Large-scale planters of sugar, tobacco, and coffee displaced small farmers who relied on one or two servants. Planters and their plantations won out because slave labor was cheap and therefore able to produce mass quantities of commodities at low prices.

State-chartered private companies from Portugal, France, Britain, the Dutch Republic, Prussia, and even Denmark exploited the 3,500-mile coastline of West Africa for slaves. Before 1675, most blacks taken from Africa had been sent to Brazil, but by 1700 half of the African slaves landed in the Caribbean (Figure 14.1). Thereafter, the plantation economy began to expand on the North American mainland. The numbers stagger the imagination. Before 1650, slave traders transported about 7,000 Africans each year across the Atlantic; this rate doubled between 1650 and 1675, nearly doubled again in the next twenty-five years, and kept going until the 1780s. In all, more than 11 million Africans, not counting those who died at sea or in Africa, were transported to the Americas before the slave trade began to wind down after 1850. Many traders gained spectacular wealth, but companies did not always make profits. The English Royal African

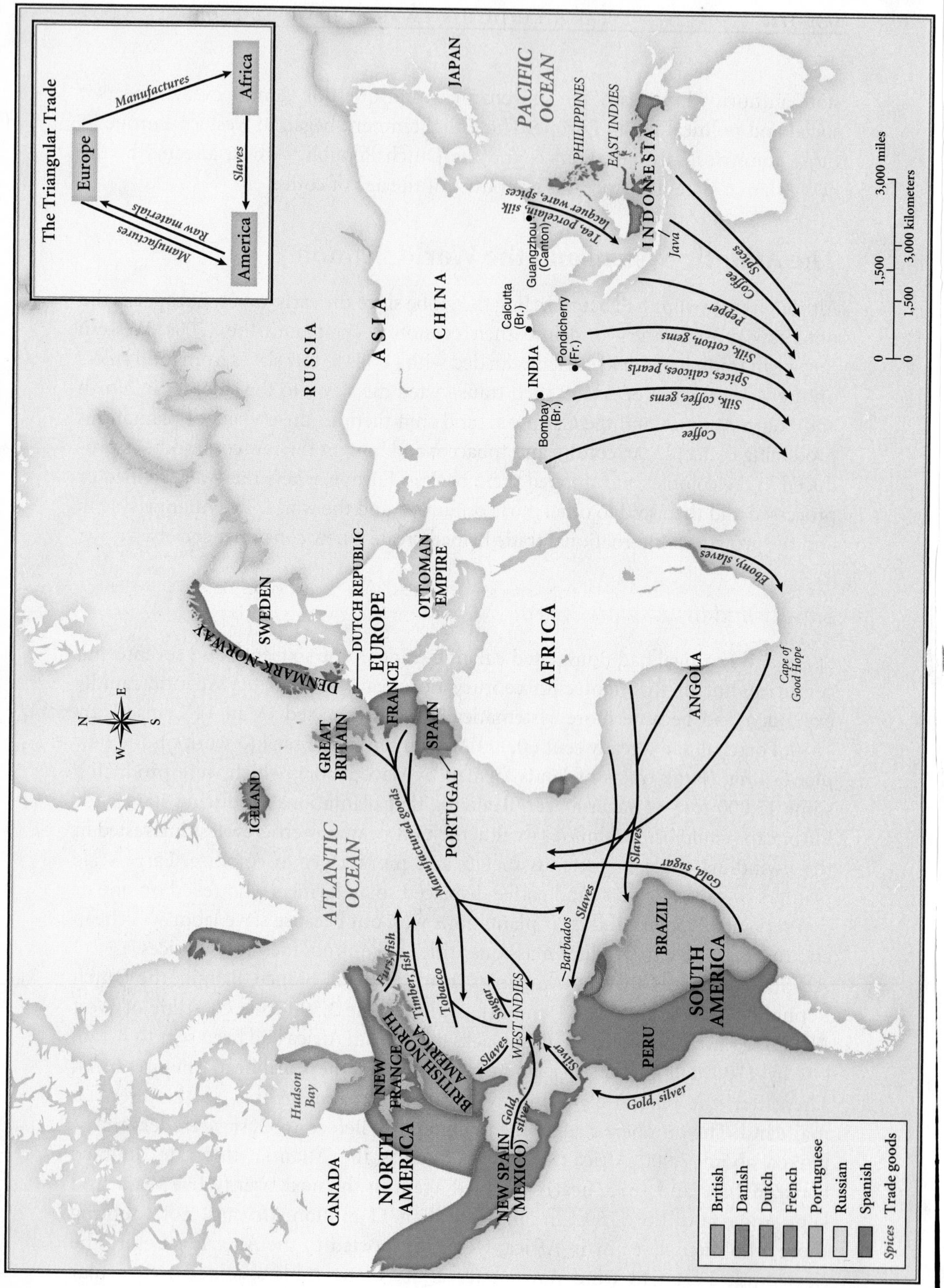

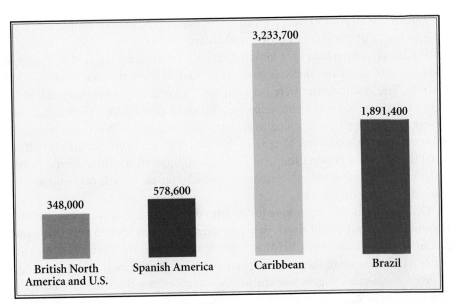

■ **FIGURE 14.1 African Slaves Imported into American Territories, 1701–1810**

During the eighteenth century, planters in the newly established Caribbean colonies imported millions of African slaves to work the new plantations. The vast majority of African slaves transported to the Americas ended up either in the Caribbean or in Brazil.

Company, for example, delivered 100,000 slaves to the Caribbean and imported 30,000 tons of sugar to Britain, yet lost money after the few profitable years following its founding in 1672.

The balance of white and black populations in the New World colonies was determined by the staples produced. New England merchants and farmers bought few slaves because they did not own plantations. Blacks—both slave and free—made up only 3 percent of the population in eighteenth-century New England, compared with 60 percent in South Carolina. On the whole, the British North American colonies contained a higher proportion of African Americans from 1730 to 1765 than at any other time in American history. The imbalance of whites and blacks was even more extreme in the Caribbean; in the early 1700s, the British sugar islands had a population of about 150,000 people, only 30,000 of them Europeans.

■ **MAP 14.1 European Trade Patterns, c. 1740**

By 1740, the European powers had colonized much of North and South America and incorporated their American colonies into a worldwide system of commerce centered on the slave trade and plantation production of staple crops. Europeans still sought spices and luxury goods in China and the East Indies, but outside of Java, few Europeans had settled permanently in these areas. **For more help analyzing this map,** *see the map activity for this chapter in the* ONLINE STUDY GUIDE *at* bedfordstmartins.com/huntconcise.

■ Caribbean Sugar Mill

This seventeenth-century engraving of a sugar mill or grinder makes the work seem much less diffi-cult than it was in practice. Slaves cut the sugarcane and then hauled it from the fields to the mill, where it was crushed. Many slaves lost fingers or hands in the process. The slaves then collected the juice (bottom center) and carried it to the boilers, shown at the bottom left and right. The sap was poured into molds and dried. Then the bricks of raw sugar were exported to Europe for refining.
(The Granger Collection, NY.)

the single most powerful economic interest in Jamaica, but he preferred to live in England, where he could collect art for his many luxurious homes, hold political office (he served as lord mayor of London and in Parliament), and even lend money to the government.

The slave trade permanently altered consumption patterns for ordinary people. Sugar had been prescribed as medicine before the end of the sixteenth century, but the development of plantations in Brazil and the Caribbean made it a standard food item. By 1700, the British sent home 50 million pounds of sugar a year, a figure that doubled by 1730. During the French Revolution of the 1790s, sugar shortages would become a cause for rioting in Paris. Equally pervasive was the spread of tobacco; by the 1720s, Britain imported two hundred shiploads of tobacco from Virginia and Maryland every year, and men of every country and class smoked pipes or took snuff.

The traffic in slaves disturbed many Europeans. As a government memoran-dum to the Spanish king explained in 1610: "Modern theologians in published books commonly report on, and condemn as unjust, the acts of enslavement which take place in provinces of this Royal Empire." Between 1667 and 1671, the French Dominican monk Father Du Tertre published three volumes in which he denounced the mistreatment of slaves in the French colonies.

In the 1700s, however, slaveholders began to justify their actions by demeaning the mental and spiritual qualities of the enslaved Africans. White Europeans and colonists sometimes described black slaves as animal-like, akin to apes. A leading New England Puritan asserted about the slaves: "Indeed their *Stupidity* is a *Discouragement*. It may seem, unto as little purpose, to *Teach*, as to *wash an Aethiopian* [Ethiopian]." One of the great paradoxes of this time was that talk of liberty and self-evident rights, especially prevalent in Britain and its North American colonies, coexisted with the belief that some people were meant to be slaves. Although Christians believed in principle in a kind of spiritual equality between blacks and whites, the churches often defended or at least did not oppose the inequities of slavery.

World Trade and Settlement

The Atlantic system helped extend European trade relations across the globe. The textiles that Atlantic shippers exchanged for slaves on the west coast of Africa, for example, were manufactured in India and exported by the British and the French East India Companies. As much as one-quarter of the British exports to Africa in the eighteenth century were actually re-exports from India. To expand its trade in the rest of the world, Europeans seized territories and tried to establish permanent settlements. The eighteenth-century extension of European power prepared the way for western global domination in the nineteenth and twentieth centuries.

In contrast to the sparsely inhabited trading outposts in Asia and Africa, the colonies in the Americas bulged with settlers. The British North American colonies, for example, contained about 1.5 million nonnative (that is, white settler and black slave) residents by 1750. While the Spanish competed with the Portuguese for control of South America, the French competed with the British for control of North America. Spanish and British settlers came to blows over the boundary between the British colonies and Florida, which was held by Spain.

Local economies shaped colonial social relations; men in French trapper communities in Canada, for example, had little in common with the men and women of the plantation societies in Barbados or Brazil. Racial attitudes also differed from place to place. The Spanish and Portuguese tolerated intermarriage with the native populations in both America and Asia. Sexual contact, both inside and outside marriage, fostered greater racial variety in the Spanish and Portuguese colonies than in the French or the English territories (though mixed-race people could be found everywhere). By 1800, **mestizos**, children of Spanish men and Indian women, accounted for more than a quarter of the population in the Spanish colonies, and many of them aspired to join the local elite. Greater racial diversity seems not to have improved the treatment of slaves, however, which was probably harshest in Portuguese Brazil.

Where intermarriage between colonizers and natives was common, conversion to Christianity proved most successful. Although the Indians maintained many of their native religious beliefs, the majority of Indians in the Spanish colonies had come to consider themselves devout Catholics by 1700. Indian carpenters and artisans in the villages produced innumerable altars, retables (painted panels), and sculpted images to adorn their local churches, and individual families put up domestic shrines. Yet the clergy remained overwhelmingly Spanish: the church hierarchy concluded that the Indians' humility and innocence made them unsuitable for the priesthood.

In the early years of American colonization, many more men than women emigrated from Europe. At the end of the seventeenth century, the sex imbalance began to decline but remained substantial; two and one-half times as many men as women were among the immigrants leaving Liverpool, England, between 1697 and 1707, for example. Women who emigrated as indentured servants ran great risks: if they did not die of disease during the voyage, they might end up giving birth to illegitimate children (the fate of at least one in five servant women) or being virtually sold into marriage.

The uncertainties of life in the American colonies provided new opportunities for European women and men willing to live outside the law, however. In the 1500s and 1600s, the English and Dutch governments had routinely authorized pirates to prey on the shipping of their rivals, the Spanish and Portuguese. Then, in the late 1600s, English, French, and Dutch bands made up of deserters and crews from wrecked vessels began to form their own associations of pirates, especially in the Caribbean. Called **buccaneers** from their custom of curing strips of beef, called *boucan* by the native Caribs of the islands, the pirates governed themselves and preyed on everyone's shipping without regard to national origin. After 1700, the colonial governments tried to stamp out piracy. As one British judge argued in 1705, "A pirate is in perpetual war with every individual and every state. . . . They are worse than ravenous beasts."

White settlements in Africa and Asia remained small and almost insignificant, except for their long-term potential. Europeans had little contact with East Africa and almost none with Africa's vast interior. A few Portuguese trading posts in Angola and Dutch farms on the Cape of Good Hope provided the only toeholds for future expansion. In China, the emperors had welcomed Catholic missionaries at court in the seventeenth century, but the priests' credibility diminished as they squabbled among themselves and associated with European merchants, whom the Chinese considered pirates. "The barbarians [Europeans] are like wild beasts," one Chinese official concluded. In 1720, only one thousand Europeans resided in Guangzhou (Canton), the sole place where foreigners could legally trade for spices, tea, and silk (see Map 14.1).

■ **India Cottons and Trade with the East**
This brightly colored cotton cloth was painted and embroidered in Madras in southern India in the late 1600s. The male figure with a mustache may be a European, but the female figures are clearly Asian. Europeans—especially the British—discovered that they could make big profits on the export of Indian cotton cloth to Europe. They also traded Indian cottons in Africa for slaves and sold large quantities in the colonies. (V&A Images/Victoria and Albert Museum.)

Europeans exercised more influence in Java in the East Indies and in India. Dutch coffee production in Java and nearby islands increased phenomenally in the early 1700s, and many Dutch settled there to oversee production and trade. In India, Dutch, English, French, Portuguese, and Danish companies competed for spices, cotton, and silk; by the 1740s the English and French had become the leading rivals in India, just as they were in North America. Both countries extended their power as India's Muslim rulers lost control to local Hindu princes, rebellious Sikhs, invading Persians, and their own provincial governors. A few thousand Europeans lived in India, though many thousands more soldiers were stationed there to protect them. The staple of trade with India in the early 1700s was calico—lightweight, brightly colored cotton cloth that caught on as a fashion in Europe.

Europeans who visited India were especially struck by what they viewed as exotic religious practices. In a book published in 1696 of his travels to western India, an Anglican minister described beggars of alms, "some of whom show their devotion by a shameless appearance, and walking naked." Such writings increased European interest in the outside world, but they also fed a European sense of superiority that helped excuse violent forms of colonial domination.

The Birth of Consumer Society

Worldwide colonization produced new supplies of goods, from coffee to calico, and population growth in Europe fueled demand for them. Beginning first in Britain, then in France and the Italian states, and finally in eastern Europe, population surged, growing by about 20 percent between 1700 and 1750. The gap between a fast-growing northwest and a more stagnant south and central Europe now diminished as regions that had lost population during the seventeenth-century downturn recovered. Cities, in particular, grew. Between 1600 and 1750, London's population more than tripled, and Paris's more than doubled.

Although contemporaries could not have realized it then, this was the start of the modern "population explosion." It appears that a decline in the death rate, rather than a rise in the birthrate, explains the turnaround. Three main factors contributed to this decline in the death rate: better weather and hence more bountiful harvests, improved agricultural techniques, and the plague's disappearance after 1720.

By the early eighteenth century, the effects of economic expansion and population growth brought about a **consumer revolution**. The British East India Company began to import into Britain huge quantities of calicoes. British imports of tobacco doubled between 1672 and 1700; at Nantes, the center of the French sugar trade, imports quadrupled between 1698 and 1733. Tea, chocolate, and coffee became virtual necessities. In the 1670s, only a trickle of tea reached London, but by 1720 the East India Company sent 9 million pounds to England—a figure that rose to 37 million pounds by 1750. By 1700, England had two thousand coffeehouses; by 1740, every English country town had at least two. Paris got its first cafés at the end of the seventeenth century; Berlin opened its first coffeehouse in 1714; Bach's Leipzig boasted eight by 1725.

The birth of consumer society did not go unnoticed by eyewitnesses. In the English economic literature of the 1690s, writers began to express a new view of humans as consuming animals with boundless appetites. Such opinions gained a wide audience with the appearance of Bernard Mandeville's poem *Fable of the Bees* (1705), which argued that private vices might have public benefits. Mandeville insisted that pride, self-interest, and the desire for material goods (all Christian vices) in fact promoted economic prosperity: "every part was full of Vice, Yet the whole mass a Paradise." Many authors attacked the new doctrine of consumerism, and the French government banned the poem's publication. But Mandeville had captured the essence of the emerging market for consumption.

■ **REVIEW:** *How is consumerism related to slavery?*

New Social and Cultural Patterns

The impact of the Atlantic system and world trade was most apparent in the cities, where people had more money for consumer goods. But rural changes also had significant long-term influence, as a revolution in agricultural techniques made it possible to feed more and more people with a smaller agricultural workforce. As population increased, more people moved to the cities, where they found themselves caught up in innovative urban customs such as attending musical concerts and reading novels. Along with a general increase in literacy, these activities helped create a public that responded to new writers and artists. Social and cultural changes were not uniform across Europe, however; as usual, people's experiences varied depending on whether they lived in wealth or poverty, in urban or rural areas, or in eastern or western Europe.

Agricultural Revolution

Although Britain, France, and the Dutch Republic shared the enthusiasm for consumer goods, Britain's domestic market grew most quickly. In Britain, as agricultural output increased 43 percent over the course of the 1700s, the population increased by 70 percent. The British imported grain to feed the growing population, but they also benefited from the development of techniques that together constituted an **agricultural revolution**. No new machinery propelled this revolution—just more aggressive attitudes toward investment and management. The Dutch and the Flemish had pioneered many of these techniques in the 1600s, but the British took them further.

Four major changes occurred in British agriculture that eventually spread to other countries. First, farmers increased the amount of land under cultivation by draining wetlands and by growing crops on previously uncultivated common lands (acreage maintained by the community for grazing). Second, farmers who could afford to do so consolidated smaller, scattered plots into larger, more efficient units. Third, livestock raising became more closely linked to crop growing, and the yields of each increased. (See "Taking Measure," page 579.) For centuries, most farmers had rotated their fields in and out of production to replenish the soil. Now farmers planted carefully chosen fodder crops such as clover and turnips that added nutrients to the soil, thereby eliminating the need to leave a field fallow (unplanted) every two or three years. With more fodder available, farmers could raise more livestock, which in turn produced more manure to fertilize grain fields. Fourth, selective breeding of animals combined with the increase in fodder to improve the quality and size of herds. New crops had only a slight impact; potatoes, for example, were introduced to Europe from South America in the 1500s, but because people feared they might cause leprosy, tuberculosis, or fevers, they were not grown in quantity until the late 1700s. By the 1730s and 1740s,

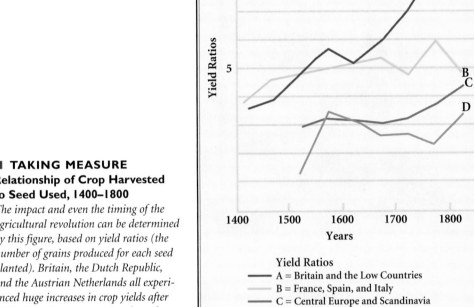

■ TAKING MEASURE
Relationship of Crop Harvested
to Seed Used, 1400–1800
The impact and even the timing of the
agricultural revolution can be determined
by this figure, based on yield ratios (the
number of grains produced for each seed
planted). Britain, the Dutch Republic,
and the Austrian Netherlands all experi-
enced huge increases in crop yields after
1700. Other European regions lagged
behind right into the 1800s.

agricultural output had increased dramatically, and prices for food had fallen because of these interconnected innovations.

Changes in agricultural practices did not benefit all landowners equally. The biggest British landowners consolidated their holdings in the "enclosure movement." They put pressure on small farmers and villagers to sell their land or give up their common lands. The big landlords then fenced off ("enclosed") their property. Because enclosure eliminated community grazing rights, it frequently sparked a struggle between the big landlords and villagers, and in Britain it normally required an act of Parliament. Such acts became increasingly common in the second half of the eighteenth century, and by the century's end six million acres of common lands had been enclosed and developed. "Improvers" produced more food more efficiently and thus supported a growing population.

Contrary to the fears of contemporaries, small farmers and cottagers (those with little or no property) were not forced off the land all at once. But most villagers could not afford the litigation involved in resisting enclosure, and small landholders

■ Treatment of Serfs in Russia
Visitors from western Europe often remarked on the cruel treatment of serfs in Russia. This drawing by one such visitor shows the punishment that could be inflicted by landowners. Serfs could be whipped for almost any reason, even for making a soup too salty or neglecting to bow when the lord's family passed by. Their condition actually deteriorated in the 1700s, as landowners began to sell serfs much like slaves. New decrees made it illegal for serfs to contract loans, enter into leases, or work for anyone other than their lord. Some landlords kept harems of serf girls. Although the Russian landlords' treatment of serfs was more brutal than the treatment they experienced in the German states and Poland, upper classes in every country regarded the serfs as dirty, deceitful, brutish, and superstitious.
(New York Public Library/Art Resource, NY.)

consequently had to sell out to landlords or farmers with larger plots. Landlords with large holdings leased their estates to tenant farmers at constantly increasing rents, and the tenant farmers in turn employed the cottagers as salaried agricultural workers. In this way the English peasantry largely disappeared, replaced by a more hierarchical society of big landlords, enterprising tenant farmers, and poor agricultural laborers.

The new agricultural techniques spread slowly from Britain and the Low Countries (the Dutch Republic and the Austrian Netherlands) to the rest of western Europe. Outside a few pockets in northern France and the western German states, however, subsistence agriculture (producing just enough to get by rather than surpluses for the market) continued to dominate farming in western Europe and Scandinavia. In southwestern Germany, for example, 80 percent of the peasants produced no surplus because their plots were too small. Unlike the populations of the highly urbanized Low Countries (where half the people lived in towns and cities), most Europeans, western and eastern, eked out their existence in the countryside.

In eastern Europe, the condition of peasants worsened in the areas where landlords tried hardest to improve their yields. To produce more for the Baltic grain market, aristocratic landholders in Prussia, Poland, and parts of Russia drained wetlands, cultivated moors, and built dikes. They also forced peasants off lands the peasants worked for themselves, increased compulsory labor services (the critical element in serfdom), and began to manage their estates directly. Some eastern landowners grew fabulously wealthy. The Potocki family in the Polish Ukraine, for example, owned three million acres of land and had 130,000 serfs. In parts of Poland and Russia, the serfs hardly differed from slaves in status, and their "masters" ran their huge estates much like American plantations.

Social Life in the Cities

Because of emigration from the countryside, cities grew in population and consequently exercised more influence on culture and social life. Between 1650 and 1750, cities with at least 10,000 inhabitants increased in population by 44 percent. From the eighteenth century onward, urban growth would be continuous. Along with the general growth of cities, an important south-to-north shift occurred in the pattern of urbanization. Around 1500, half of the people in cities of at least 10,000 residents could be found in the Italian states, Spain, or Portugal; by 1700, the urbanization of northwestern and southern Europe was roughly equal. Eastern Europe, despite the huge cities of Istanbul and Moscow, was still less urban than western Europe. London was by far the most populous European city, with 675,000 inhabitants in 1750; Berlin had 90,000 people, Warsaw only 23,000.

Many landowners kept a residence in town, so the separation between rural and city life was not as extreme as might be imagined, at least not for the very rich. At the top of the ladder in the big cities were the landed nobles. Some of them filled their lives only with conspicuous consumption of fine food, extravagant clothing, coaches, books, and opera; others held key political, administrative, or judicial offices. However they spent their time, these rich families employed thousands of artisans, shopkeepers, and domestic servants. Many English peers (highest-ranking nobles) had thirty or forty servants at each of their homes.

The middle classes of officials, merchants, professionals, and landowners occupied the next rung down on the social ladder. London's population, for example, included about twenty thousand middle-class families (constituting, at most, one-sixth of the city's population). In this period, the middle classes began to develop distinctive ways of life that set them apart from both the rich noble landowners and the lower classes. Unlike the rich nobles, the middle classes lived primarily in the cities and towns, even if they owned small country estates. They ate more moderately than nobles but much better than peasants or laborers. For breakfast, the British middle classes ate toast and rolls and, after 1700, drank tea. Dinner, served midday, consisted of roasted or boiled beef or mutton, poultry or pork, and vegetables. Supper was a light meal of bread and cheese with cake or pie. Beer was the main drink in London, and many families brewed their own. Even children drank beer because of the lack of fresh water.

In contrast to the gigantic and sprawling country seats of the richest English peers, middle-class houses in town had about seven rooms, including four or five bedrooms and one or two living rooms, still many more than the poor agricultural worker. New household items reflected society's increasing wealth and its exposure to colonial imports: by 1700, the middle classes of London typically had mirrors in every room, a coffeepot and coffee mill, numerous pictures and ornaments, a china collection, and several clocks. Life for the middle classes on the European continent was quite similar, though wine replaced beer in France.

Below the middle classes came the artisans and shopkeepers (most of whom were organized in professional guilds), then the journeymen, apprentices, servants, and laborers. At the bottom of the social scale were the unemployed poor, who survived by intermittent work and charity. Women married to artisans and shopkeepers often kept the accounts, supervised employees, and ran the household as well. Every home from the middle classes to the upper classes employed servants; artisans and shopkeepers frequently hired them, too. Women from poorer families usually worked as domestic servants until they married. Four out of five domestic servants in the city were female. In large cities such as London, the servant population grew faster than the population of the city as a whole.

Social status in the cities was readily visible. Wide, spacious streets graced rich districts; the houses had gardens, and the air was relatively fresh. In poor districts, the streets were narrow, dirty, dark, humid, and smelly, and the houses were damp and crowded. The poorest people were homeless, sleeping under bridges or in abandoned homes. A Neapolitan prince described his homeless neighbors as "lying like filthy animals, with no distinction of age or sex." In some districts, rich and poor lived in the same buildings; the poor clambered up to shabby, cramped apartments on the top floors.

Like shelter, clothing was a reliable social indicator. The poorest workingwomen in Paris wore woolen skirts and blouses of dark colors over petticoats, bodice, and corset. They also donned caps of various sorts, cotton stockings, and shoes (probably their only pair). Workingmen dressed even more drably. Many occupations could be recognized by their dress: no one could confuse lawyers in their dark robes with masons or butchers in their special aprons, for example. People higher on the social ladder were more likely to sport a variety of fabrics, colors, and unusual designs in their clothing and to own many different outfits. Social status was not an abstract idea; it permeated every detail of daily life.

The Growing Public for Culture

The ability to read and write also reflected social differences. People in the upper classes were more literate than those in the lower classes; city people were more literate than peasants. Protestant countries appear to have been more successful at promoting education and literacy than Catholic countries, perhaps because of the

Protestant emphasis on Bible reading. Widespread popular literacy was first achieved in the Protestant areas of Switzerland and in Presbyterian Scotland, and rates were also very high in the New England colonies and the Scandinavian countries. In France, literacy doubled in the eighteenth century thanks to the spread of parish schools, but still only one in two men and one in four women could read and write. Despite the efforts of some Protestant German states to encourage primary education, primary schooling remained woefully inadequate almost everywhere in Europe: few schools existed, teachers received low wages, and no country had yet established a national system of control or supervision.

Despite the deficiencies of primary education, a new literate public arose, especially among the middle classes of the cities. More books and periodicals were published than ever before. Britain and the Dutch Republic led the way in this powerful outpouring of printed words. The trend began in the 1690s and gradually accelerated. In 1695, the British government allowed the licensing system, through which it controlled publications, to lapse, and new newspapers and magazines appeared almost immediately. The first London daily newspaper came out in 1702, and in 1709 Joseph Addison and Richard Steele published the first literary magazine, *The Spectator*. They devoted their magazine to the cultural improvement of the increasingly influential middle class. By the 1720s, twenty-four provincial newspapers were published in England. In the London coffeehouses, an edition of a single newspaper might reach ten thousand male readers. Women did their reading at home. Newspapers on the continent lagged behind and often consisted mainly of advertising with little critical commentary. France, for example, had no daily paper until 1777.

The new literate public did not just read newspapers; its members now pursued an interest in painting, attended concerts, and besieged booksellers in search of popular novels. Because increased trade and prosperity put money into the hands of the growing middle classes, a new urban audience began to compete with the churches, rulers, and courtiers as chief patrons for new work. As the public for the arts expanded, printed commentary on them emerged, setting the stage for the appearance of political and social criticism. New artistic tastes thus had effects far beyond the realm of the arts.

Developments in painting reflected the tastes of the new public. The **rococo** style challenged the hold of the baroque and classical schools, especially in France. Like the baroque, the rococo emphasized irregularity and asymmetry, movement and curvature, but it did so on a much smaller, subtler scale. Many rococo paintings depicted scenes of intimate sensuality rather than the monumental, emotional grandeur favored by classical and baroque painters. Personal portraits and pastoral paintings took the place of heroic landscapes and large ceremonial canvases. Rococo paintings adorned homes as well as palaces and served as a form of interior decoration rather than as a statement of piety. Its decorative quality made rococo art an ideal complement to newly discovered materials such as stucco and porcelain, especially the porcelain vases now imported from China.

■ **Rococo Painting**

In this painting, the Venetian artist Rosalba Carriera (1675–1757) reveals Europeans' growing interest in the outside world and their misunderstanding of the actual experience of colonized peoples. Africa (the title of the work) is represented by a young black woman wearing a bejewelled turban and calmly holding a handful of writhing snakes; the scorpion that dangles from her necklace competes with an enormous pearl earring for the fascinated viewer's attention. Known for her use of pastels, Carriera journeyed in 1720 to Paris, where she became an associate of Antoine Watteau and helped inaugurate the rococo style in painting. **For more help analyzing this image,** see the visual activity for this chapter in the ONLINE STUDY GUIDE at bedfordstmartins.com/huntconcise.

(Staatliche Kunstsammlungen Dresden, Gemaldegalerie Alte Meister.)

Rococo, like *baroque*, was an invented word (from the French word *rocaille*, meaning "shellwork") and originally a derogatory label, meaning "frivolous decoration." But the great French rococo painters, such as Antoine Watteau (1684–1721) and François Boucher (1703–1770), were much more than mere decorators. Although both emphasized the erotic in their depictions, Watteau captured the melancholy side of a passing aristocratic style of life, and Boucher painted middle-class people at home during their daily activities. Both painters thereby contributed to the emergence of new sensibilities in art that increasingly attracted a middle-class public.

Music as well as art grew in popularity. The first public music concerts were performed in England in the 1670s, becoming much more regular and frequent in the 1690s. City concert halls typically seated about two hundred, but the relatively high price of tickets limited attendance to the better-off. Music clubs provided entertainment in smaller towns and villages. In continental Europe, Frankfurt organized the first regular public concerts in 1712; Hamburg and Paris began holding them within a few years. Opera continued to spread in the eighteenth century; Venice had sixteen public opera houses by 1700, and in 1732 Covent Garden opera house opened in London.

The growth of a public that appreciated and supported music had much the same effect as the extension of the reading public: like authors, composers could now begin to liberate themselves from court patronage and work for a paying audience. This development took time to solidify, however, and court or church patrons still commissioned much eighteenth-century music. Bach, a German Lutheran, wrote his *St. Matthew Passion* for Good Friday services in 1729 while he was organist and choirmaster for the leading church in Leipzig. He composed secular works (like the "Coffee Cantata") for the public and a variety of private patrons.

The composer George Frederick Handel (1685–1759) was among the first to grasp the new directions in music. He began his career playing second violin in the Hamburg opera orchestra and then moved to Britain in 1710, where he eventually turned to composing oratorios, a form he introduced in Britain. The oratorio combined the drama of opera with the majesty of religious and ceremonial music and featured the chorus over the soloists. Handel's most famous oratorio, *Messiah* (1741), reflected his personal, deeply felt piety but also his willingness to combine musical materials into a dramatic form that captured the enthusiasm of the new public. In 1740, a poem published in the *Gentleman's Magazine* exulted: "His art so modulates the sounds in all, / Our passions, as he pleases, rise and fall." Music had become an integral part of the new middle-class public's culture.

But nothing captured the imagination of the new public more than the novel, the literary genre whose very name underscored the eighteenth-century taste for novelty. Over three hundred French novels appeared between 1700 and 1730. During this unprecedented explosion, the novel took on its modern form and became more concerned with individual psychology and social description than with the picaresque adventures popular earlier (such as Cervantes's *Don Quixote*). The novel's popularity was closely tied to the expansion of the reading public, and novels were available in serial form in periodicals or from the many booksellers who popped up to serve the new market.

Women figured prominently in novels as characters, and women writers abounded. The English novel *Love in Excess* (1719) quickly reached a sixth printing, and its author, Eliza Haywood (1693?–1756), earned her living turning out a stream of novels with titles such as *Persecuted Virtue, Constancy Rewarded,* and *The History of Miss Betsy Thoughtless*—all showing a concern for the proper place of women as models of virtue in a changing world. Haywood had first worked as an actress when her husband deserted her and her two children, but she soon turned to writing plays and novels. In the 1740s, she began publishing a magazine, *The Female Spectator,* which argued in favor of higher education for women.

Haywood's male counterpart was Daniel Defoe (1660?–1731), a merchant's son who had a diverse and colorful career as a manufacturer, political spy, novelist, and social commentator. Defoe's novel about a shipwrecked sailor, *Robinson Crusoe* (1719), portrayed the new values of the time: to survive, Crusoe had to meet every challenge with fearless entrepreneurial ingenuity. He had to be ready for the unexpected and be able to improvise in every situation. He was, in short, the model for the new man in an expanding economy. Crusoe's patronizing attitude toward the black man Friday now draws much critical attention, but his discovery of Friday shows how the fate of blacks and whites had become intertwined in the new colonial environment.

Religious Revivals

Despite the novel's growing popularity, religious books and pamphlets still sold in huge numbers, and most Europeans remained devout, even as their religions were changing. In this period, a Protestant revival known as **Pietism** rocked the complacency of the established churches in the German Lutheran states, the Dutch Republic, and Scandinavia. Pietists believed in a mystical religion of the heart; they wanted a more deeply emotional, even ecstatic religion. They urged intense Bible study, which in turn promoted popular education and contributed to the increase in literacy. Many Pietists attended catechism instruction every day and also went to morning and evening prayer meetings in addition to regular Sunday services.

Catholicism also had its versions of religious revival. A Frenchwoman, Jeanne Marie Guyon (1648–1717), attracted many noblewomen and a few leading clergymen to her own Catholic brand of Pietism, known as Quietism. Claiming miraculous visions and astounding prophecies, she urged a mystical union with God through prayer and simple devotion. Despite papal condemnation and intense controversy within Catholic circles in France, Guyon had followers all over Europe.

Even more influential were the Jansenists, who gained many new adherents to their austere form of Catholicism despite Louis XIV's harassment and repeated condemnation by the papacy. Under the pressure of religious and political persecution, Jansenism took a revivalist turn in the 1720s. At the funeral of a Jansenist priest in Paris in 1727, the crowd who flocked to the grave claimed to witness a series of miraculous healings. Within a few years, a cult formed around the priest's tomb, and clandestine Jansenist presses reported new miracles to the reading public. When the French government tried to suppress the cult, one enraged wit placed a sign at the tomb that read "By order of the king, God is forbidden to work miracles here." Some believers fell into frenzied convulsions, claiming to be inspired by the Holy Spirit through the intercession of the dead priest. After midcentury, Jansenism became even more politically active as its adherents joined in opposition to crown policies on religion.

■ **REVIEW:** *What were the social and cultural consequences of the agricultural revolution?*

Consolidation of the European State System

The spread of Pietism and Jansenism reflected the emergence of a middle-class public that now participated in every new development, including religion. The middle classes could pursue these interests because the European state system gradually stabilized. Warfare settled three main issues between 1690 and 1740: a coalition of powers held Louis XIV's France in check on the continent; Great Britain emerged from the wars against Louis as the preeminent maritime power; and Russia defeated Sweden in the contest for supremacy in the Baltic. After Louis XIV's death in 1715, Europe enjoyed the fruits of a more balanced diplomatic system, in which warfare became less frequent and less widespread. States could then spend their resources establishing and expanding control over their own populations, both at home and in their colonies.

The Limits of French Absolutism

Lying on his deathbed in 1715, the seventy-six-year-old Louis XIV watched helplessly as his accomplishments continued to unravel. Not only had his plans for territorial expansion been thwarted, but his incessant wars had exhausted the treasury, despite new taxes. In 1689, Louis's rival, William III, prince of Orange and king of England and Scotland (r. 1689–1702), had set out to forge a European alliance that eventually included Britain, the Dutch Republic, Sweden, Austria, and Spain. The allies fought Louis to a stalemate in the War of the League of Augsburg, sometimes called the Nine Years' War (1689–1697), and when hostilities resumed four years later, they finally put an end to Louis's expansionist ambitions.

The War of the Spanish Succession (1701–1713) broke out when the mentally and physically feeble Charles II (r. 1665–1700) of Spain died without a direct heir. The Spanish succession could not help but be a burning issue. Even though Spanish power had declined steadily since Spain's golden age in the sixteenth century, Spain still had extensive territories in Italy and the Netherlands and colonies overseas. Before Charles died, he named Louis XIV's second grandson, Philip, duke of Anjou, as his heir, but the Austrian emperor Leopold I refused to accept Charles's deathbed will. In the ensuing war, the French lost several major battles and had to accept disadvantageous terms in the Peace of Utrecht of 1713–1714 (Map 14.2). Although Philip was recognized as king of Spain, he had to renounce any future claim to the French crown, thus barring unification of the two kingdoms. Spain surrendered its territories in Italy and the Netherlands to the Austrians and Gibraltar to the British; France ceded possessions in North America (Newfoundland, the Hudson Bay area, and most of Nova Scotia) to Britain. France no longer threatened to dominate European power politics.

At home, Louis's policy of absolutism had fomented bitter hostility. Nobles fiercely resented his promotions of commoners to high office. The duke of Saint-Simon complained that "falseness, servility, admiring glances, combined with a dependent and cringing attitude, above all, an appearance of being nothing without him, were the only ways of pleasing him." On his deathbed, Louis XIV gave his blessing and some sound advice to his five-year-old great-grandson and successor, Louis XV (r. 1715–1774): "My child, you are about to become a great King. Do not imitate my love of building nor my liking for war."

Map Legend

Territories gained after the Peace of Utrecht, 1714

- French Bourbon lands
- Spanish Bourbon lands
- Austrian Habsburg lands
- Prussian lands
- Great Britain
- To Great Britain
- To the Austrian Empire
- The Jacobite rising of 1715
- Main areas of fighting during the War of the Spanish Succession, 1701–1713
- Boundary of the Holy Roman Empire

Inset map: English and French Claims after the Peace of Utrecht, 1714

■ **MAP 14.2 Europe, c. 1715**

Although Louis XIV succeeded in putting his grandson Philip on the Spanish throne, France emerged considerably weakened from the War of the Spanish Succession. France ceded large territories in Canada to Britain, which also gained key Mediterranean outposts from Spain as well as a monopoly on providing slaves to the Spanish colonies. Spanish losses were catastrophic: Philip had to renounce any future claim to the French crown and give up considerable territories in the Netherlands and Italy to the Austrians.

After being named regent, the duke of Orléans (1674–1723), nephew of the dead king, revived some of the parlements' powers and tried to give leading nobles a greater say in political affairs. Financial problems plagued the Regency as they would beset all succeeding French regimes in the eighteenth century. In 1719, the regent appointed the Scottish adventurer and financier John Law to the top financial position of controller-general. Law founded a trading company for North America and a state bank that issued paper money and stock (without them, trade depended on the available supply of gold and silver). The bank was supposed to offer lower interest rates to the state, thus cutting the cost of financing the government's debts. The value of the stock rose rapidly in a frenzy of speculation, only to crash a few months later. With it vanished any hope of establishing a state bank or issuing paper money for nearly a century.

France finally achieved a measure of financial stability under the leadership of Cardinal Hercule de Fleury (1653–1743), the most powerful member of the government after the death of the regent. Fleury aimed to avoid adventure abroad and keep social peace at home; he balanced the budget and carried out a large project for road and canal construction. Colonial trade boomed. Peace and the acceptance of limits on territorial expansion inaugurated a century of French prosperity.

British Rise and Dutch Decline

The British and the Dutch had formed a coalition against Louis XIV under their joint ruler William III, who was simultaneously stadtholder of the Dutch Republic and, with his English wife, Mary (d. 1694), ruler of England, Wales, and Scotland. After William's death in 1702, the British and Dutch went their separate ways. Over the next decades, England incorporated Scotland and subjugated Ireland, becoming "Great Britain." At the same time Dutch imperial power declined, even though Dutch merchants still controlled a substantial portion of world trade. English relations with Scotland and Ireland were complicated by the problem of succession: William and Mary had no children. To ensure a Protestant succession, Parliament ruled that Mary's sister, Anne, would succeed William and Mary and that the Protestant House of Hanover in Germany would succeed Anne if she had no surviving heirs. Catholics were excluded. When Queen Anne (r. 1702–1714) died leaving no children, the elector of Hanover, a Protestant great-grandson of James I, consequently became King George I (r. 1714–1727). The House of Hanover—renamed the House of Windsor during World War I in response to anti-German sentiment—still occupies the British throne.

Support from the Scots and Irish for this solution did not come easily because many in Scotland and Ireland supported the claims to the throne of the deposed Catholic king, James II, and, after his death in 1701, his son James Edward. Out of fear of this "Jacobitism" (from the Latin *Jacobus* for "James"), Scottish Protestant leaders agreed to the Act of Union of 1707, which abolished the Scottish Parliament and affirmed the Scots recognition of the Protestant Hanoverian succession. The

Scots agreed to obey the Parliament of Great Britain, which would include Scottish members in the House of Commons and the House of Lords. A Jacobite rebellion in Scotland in 1715, aiming to restore the Stuart line, was suppressed. The threat of Jacobitism nonetheless continued into the 1740s (see Map 14.2).

The Irish—90 percent of whom were Catholic—proved even more difficult to subdue. When James II had gone to Ireland in 1689 to raise a Catholic rebellion against the new monarchs of England, William III responded by taking command of the joint English and Dutch forces and defeating James's Irish supporters. James fled to France, and the Catholics in Ireland faced yet more confiscation and legal restrictions. By 1700, Irish Catholics, who in 1640 had owned 60 percent of the land in Ireland, owned just 14 percent. The Protestant-controlled Irish Parliament passed a series of laws limiting the rights of the Catholic majority: Catholics could not bear arms, send their children abroad for education, establish Catholic schools at home, or marry Protestants. Catholics could not sit in Parliament, nor could they vote for its members unless they took an oath renouncing Catholic doctrine. These and a host of other laws reduced Catholic Ireland to the status of a colony; one English official commented in 1745, "The poor people of Ireland are used worse than negroes." Most of the Irish were peasants who lived in primitive housing and subsisted on a meager diet that included no meat.

The Parliament of Great Britain was soon dominated by the Whigs. In Britain's constitutional system, the monarch ruled with Parliament. The crown chose the ministers, directed policy, and supervised administration, while Parliament raised revenue, passed laws, and represented the interests of the people to the crown. The powers of Parliament were reaffirmed by the Triennial Act in 1694, which provided that Parliaments meet at least once every three years (this was extended to seven years in 1716, after the Whigs had established their ascendancy). Only 200,000 propertied men could vote, out of a population of more than 5 million people, and not surprisingly, most members of Parliament came from the landed gentry. In fact, a few hundred families controlled all the important political offices.

George I and George II (r. 1727–1760) relied on one man, Sir Robert Walpole (1676–1745), to help them manage their relations with Parliament. From his position as First Lord of the Treasury, Walpole made himself into first or "prime" minister, leading the House of Commons from 1721 to 1742. Although appointed initially by the king, Walpole established an enduring pattern of parliamentary government in which a prime minister from the leading party guided legislation through the House of Commons. Walpole also built a vast patronage machine that dispensed government jobs to win support for the crown's policies. Walpole's successors relied more and more on the patronage system and eventually alienated not only the Tories but also the middle classes in London and even the North American colonists.

The partisan division between the Whigs, who supported the Hanoverian succession and the rights of dissenting Protestants, and the Tories, who had backed the Stuart line and the Anglican church, did not hamper Great Britain's pursuit of

■ **Sir Robert Walpole at a Cabinet Meeting**
Sir Robert Walpole and George II developed government by means of a cabinet, which consisted of Walpole as first lord of the treasury, the two secretaries of state, the lord chancellor, the chancellor of the exchequer, the lord privy seal, and the lord president of the council. Walpole's cabinet was the predecessor of modern cabinets in both Great Britain and the United States. Its similarities to modern forms should not be overstated, however. The entire staff of the two secretaries of state, who had charge of all foreign and domestic affairs other than taxation, numbered twenty-four in 1726.
(The Fotomas Index, U.K.)

economic, military, and colonial power. In this period, Great Britain became a great power on the world stage by virtue of its navy and its ability to finance major military involvement in the wars against Louis XIV. The founding in 1694 of the Bank of England—which, unlike the French bank, endured—enabled the government to raise money at low interest for foreign wars. By the 1740s, the government could borrow more than four times what it could in the 1690s.

By contrast, the Dutch Republic, one of the richest and most influential states of the seventeenth century, saw its power eclipsed in the eighteenth. When William of Orange (William III of England) died in 1702, he left no heirs, and for forty-five years the Dutch lived without a stadtholder. The merchant ruling class of some two thousand families dominated the Dutch Republic more than ever, but they presided over a country that counted for less in international power politics. In some areas, Dutch decline was only relative: the Dutch population was not growing as fast as populations elsewhere, for example, and the Dutch share of the Baltic trade decreased from 50 percent in 1720 to less than 30 percent by the 1770s. After 1720, the Baltic countries—Prussia, Russia, Denmark, and Sweden—began to ban imports of manufactured goods to protect their own industries, and Dutch trade in particular suffered. The output of Leiden textiles dropped to one-third of its 1700 level by 1740. Shipbuilding, paper manufacturing, tobacco processing, salt refining, and pottery production all dwindled as well. The biggest exception to the downward trend was trade with the New World, which increased with escalating demands for sugar and tobacco. The Dutch shifted their interest away from great-power rivalries toward those areas of international trade and finance where they could establish an enduring presence.

Russia's Emergence as a European Power

The commerce and shipbuilding of the Dutch and British so impressed Russian tsar Peter I (r. 1689–1725) that he traveled incognito to their shipyards in 1697 to learn their methods firsthand. Known to history as Peter the Great, he dragged Russia kicking and screaming all the way to great-power status. Although he came to the throne while still a minor (on the eve of his tenth birthday), grew up under the threat of a palace coup, and enjoyed little formal education, his accomplishments soon matched his seven-foot-tall stature. Peter transformed public life in Russia and established an absolutist state on the western model. His **Westernization** efforts ignited an enduring controversy: did Peter set Russia on a course of inevitable Westernization required to compete with the West, or did he forever and fatally disrupt Russia's natural evolution into a distinctive Slavic society?

Peter reorganized government and finance on western models and, like other absolute rulers, strengthened his army. With ruthless recruiting methods, which included branding a cross on every recruit's left hand to prevent desertion, he forged an army of 200,000 men and equipped it with modern weapons. He created schools for artillery, engineering, and military medicine and built the first navy in Russian history. Not surprisingly, taxes tripled.

The tsar allowed nothing to stand in his way. He did not hesitate to use torture and executed thousands. He allowed a special guards regiment unprecedented power to expedite cases against those suspected of rebellion, espionage, pretensions to the throne, or just "unseemly utterances against him." Opposition to his policies reached into his own family: because his only son, Alexei, had allied himself with Peter's critics, he threw him into prison, where the young man mysteriously died.

To control the often restive nobility, Peter insisted that all noblemen engage in state service. A Table of Ranks (1722) classified them into military, administrative, and court categories, a codification of social and legal relationships in Russia that would last for nearly two centuries. All social and material advantages now depended on serving the crown. Because the nobles lacked a secure independent status, Peter could command them to a degree that was unimaginable in western Europe. State service was not only compulsory but also permanent. Moreover, the male children of those in service had to be registered by the age of ten and begin serving at fifteen. To increase his authority over the Russian Orthodox church, Peter allowed the office of patriarch (supreme head) to remain vacant, and in 1721 he replaced it with the

■ **Peter the Great Modernizes Russia**

In this popular print, a barber forces a protesting noble to conform to Western fashions (the barber is sometimes erroneously identified as Peter himself). Peter ordered all nobles, merchants, and middle-class professionals to cut off their beards or pay a huge tax to keep them. An early biographer of Peter, the French writer Jean Rousset de Missy (1730), claimed that those who lost their beards saved them to put in their coffins, fearing that they would not enter heaven without them.
(Collection, Visual Connection.)

Holy Synod, a bureaucracy of laymen under his supervision. To many Russians, Peter was the Antichrist incarnate.

With the goal of Westernizing Russian culture, Peter set up the first greenhouses, laboratories, and technical schools and founded the Russian Academy of Sciences. He ordered translations of Western classics and hired a German theater company to perform the French plays of Molière. He replaced the traditional Russian calendar with the Western one,* introduced Arabic numerals, and brought out the first public newspaper. He ordered his officials and the nobles to shave their beards and dress in Western fashion, and he even issued precise regulations about the suitable style of jacket, boots, and cap (generally French or German). He published a book on manners for young noblemen and experimented with dentistry on his courtiers.

Peter built a new capital city, named St. Petersburg after him. It symbolized Russia opening to the West. Construction began in 1703 in a Baltic province that had been recently conquered from Sweden. By the end of 1709, forty thousand recruits a year found themselves assigned to the work. Peter ordered skilled workers to move to the new city and commanded all landowners possessing more than forty serf households to build houses there. In the 1720s, a German minister described the city "as a wonder of the world, considering its magnificent palaces, . . . and the

---

*Peter introduced the Julian calendar, then still used in Protestant but not Catholic countries. Later in the eighteenth century, Protestant Europe abandoned the Julian for the Gregorian calendar. Not until 1918 was the Julian calendar abolished in Russia, at which point it had fallen thirteen days behind Europe's Gregorian calendar.

short time that was employed in the building of it." By 1710, the permanent population of St. Petersburg reached eight thousand. At Peter's death in 1725, it had forty thousand residents.

As a new city far from the Russian heartland around Moscow, St. Petersburg represented a decisive break with Russia's past. Peter widened that gap by every means possible. At his new capital, he tried to improve the traditionally denigrated, secluded status of women by ordering them to dress in European styles and appear publicly at his dinners for diplomatic representatives. Imitating French manners, he decreed that women attend his new social salons of officials, officers, and merchants for conversation and dancing. A foreigner headed every one of Peter's new technical and vocational schools, and for its first eight years the new Academy of Sciences included no Russians. Every ministry was assigned a foreign adviser. Upper-class Russians learned French or German, which they often spoke even at home. Such changes affected only the very top of Russian society, however; the mass of the population had no contact with the new ideas and ended up paying for the innovations either in ruinous new taxation or by building St. Petersburg, a project that cost the lives of thousands of workers. Serfs remained tied to the land, completely dominated by their noble lords.

Despite all his achievements, Peter could not ensure his succession. In the thirty-seven years after his death in 1725, Russia endured six different rulers, including a boy of twelve, an infant, and an imbecile. Recurrent palace coups weakened the monarchy and enabled the nobility to loosen Peter's rigid code of state service. In the process, the status of the serfs only worsened. They ceased to be counted as legal subjects; the criminal code of 1754 listed them as property. They not only were bought and sold like cattle but also had become legally indistinguishable from them. Westernization had not yet touched their lives.

The Balance of Power in the East

Peter the Great's success in building up state power changed the balance of power in eastern Europe. Overcoming initial military setbacks, Russia eventually defeated Sweden and took its place as the leading power in the Baltic region. Russia could then turn its attention to eastern Europe, where it competed with Austria and Prussia. Formerly mighty Poland-Lithuania became the playground for great-power rivalries.

Sweden had dominated the Baltic region since the Thirty Years' War and did not easily give up its preeminence. When Peter the Great joined an anti-Swedish coalition in 1700 with Denmark, Saxony, and Poland, Sweden's Charles XII (r. 1697–1718) stood up to the test. Still in his teens at the beginning of the Great Northern War, Charles first defeated Denmark, then destroyed the new Russian army, and quickly marched into Poland and Saxony. After defeating the Poles and occupying Saxony, Charles invaded Russia. Here Peter's rebuilt army finally defeated him at the battle of Poltava (1709).

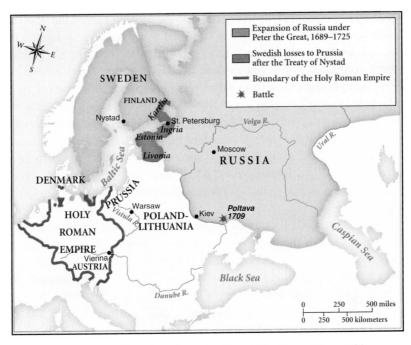

■ MAP 14.3 Russia and Sweden after the Great Northern War, 1721

After the Great Northern War, Russia supplanted Sweden as the major power in the north. Although Russia had a much larger population from which to draw its armies, Sweden made the most of its advantages and gave way only after a great military struggle.

The Russian victory resounded everywhere. The Russian ambassador to Vienna reported, "It is commonly said that the tsar will be formidable to all Europe, that he will be a kind of northern Turk." Prussia and other German states joined the anti-Swedish alliance, and when Charles XII died in battle in 1718, the Great Northern War finally came to an end. By the terms of the Treaty of Nystad (1721), Sweden ceded its eastern Baltic provinces—Livonia, Estonia, Ingria, and southern Karelia—to Russia. Sweden also lost territories on the north German coast to Prussia and the other allied German states (Map 14.3). An aristocratic reaction against Charles XII's incessant demands for war supplies swept away Sweden's absolutist regime, essentially removing Sweden from great-power competition.

Prussia had to make the most of every military opportunity, as it did in the Great Northern War, because it was much smaller in size and population than Russia, Austria, or France. King Frederick William I (r. 1713–1740) doubled the size of the Prussian army; though much smaller than the armies of his rivals, it was the best-trained and most up-to-date force in Europe. By 1740, Prussia had Europe's highest proportion of men at arms (1 of every 28 people, versus 1 in 157 in France and 1 in 64 in Russia) and the highest proportion of nobles in the military (1 in 7 noblemen, as compared with 1 in 33 in France and 1 in 50 in Russia).

The army so dominated life in Prussia that the country earned the label "a large army with a small state attached." So obsessed was Frederick William with his soldiers that the five-foot-five-inch-tall king formed a regiment of "giants," the Grenadiers, composed exclusively of men over six feet tall. Royal agents scoured Europe trying to find such men and sometimes kidnapped them right off the street. Frederick William, the "Sergeant King," was one of the first rulers to wear a military uniform as his everyday dress. He subordinated the entire domestic administration to the army's needs. He also installed a system for recruiting soldiers by local district quotas. He financed the army growth by subjecting all the provinces to an excise tax on food, drink, and manufactured goods and by increasing rents on crown lands. Prussia was now poised to become one of the major players on the continent of Europe.

During the War of the Polish Succession (1733–1735), Prussia stood on the sidelines, content to watch the bigger powers fight each other. The war showed how the balance of power had changed since the heyday of Louis XIV: France had to maneuver within a complex great-power system that now included Russia, and Poland-Lithuania no longer controlled its own destiny. When the king of Poland-Lithuania died in 1733, France, Spain, and Sardinia went to war against Austria and Russia, each side supporting rival claimants to the Polish throne. After Russia drove the French candidate out of Poland-Lithuania, France agreed to accept the Austrian candidate; in exchange, Austria gave the province of Lorraine to the French candidate, the father-in-law of Louis XV, with the promise that the province would pass to France on his death. France and Britain went back to pursuing their colonial rivalries. Prussia and Russia concentrated on shoring up their influence within Poland-Lithuania.

Austria did not want to become mired in a long struggle in Poland-Lithuania because its armies still faced the Turks on its southeastern border. Even though the Austrians had forced the Turks to recognize their rule over all of Hungary and Transylvania in 1699 and occupied Belgrade in 1717, the Turks did not stop fighting. In the 1730s, the Turks retook Belgrade, and Russia now claimed a role in the struggle against the Turks. Moreover, Hungary, though "liberated" from Turkish rule, proved less than enthusiastic about submitting to Austria. In 1703, the wealthiest Hungarian noble landlord, Ferenc Rákóczi (1676–1735), raised an army of seventy thousand men who fought for "God, Fatherland, and Liberty" until 1711. They forced the Austrians to recognize local Hungarian institutions, grant

Habsburg dominions, 1657
Habsburg Hungary, 1657
Expansion to 1699
Expansion to 1718
Regained by Ottoman Empire
Battle

POLAND-LITHUANIA

HUNGARY
AUSTRIA
Vienna
1683
Transylvania

Belgrade
1717

Adriatic Sea

OTTOMAN EMPIRE

0   250   500 miles
0   250   500 kilometers

Austrian Conquest of Hungary, 1657–1730

amnesty, and restore confiscated estates in exchange for confirming hereditary Austrian rule.

The Power of Diplomacy and the Importance of Numbers

No single power emerged from the wars of the first half of the eighteenth century clearly superior to the others, and the idea of maintaining a balance of power guided both military and diplomatic maneuvering. The Peace of Utrecht had explicitly declared that such a balance was crucial to maintaining peace in Europe, and in 1720 a British pamphleteer wrote, "There is not, I believe, any doctrine in the law of nations, of more certain truth . . . than this of the balance of power." It was the law of gravity of European politics. This system of equilibrium often rested on military force, such as the leagues formed against Louis XIV or the coalition against Sweden. All states counted on diplomacy, however, to resolve issues even after fighting had begun.

To meet the new demands placed on it, the diplomatic service, like the military and financial bureaucracies before it, had to develop regular procedures. The French set a pattern of diplomatic service that the other European states soon imitated. By 1685, France had embassies in all the important capitals. Nobles of ancient families served as ambassadors to Rome, Madrid, Vienna, and London, whereas royal officials were chosen for Switzerland, the Dutch Republic, and Venice. Most held their appointments for at least three or four years, and all went off with elaborate written instructions that included explicit statements of policy as well as full accounts of the political conditions of the country to which they were posted. The ambassador selected and paid for his own staff. This practice could make the journey to a new post very cumbersome, because the staff might be as large as eighty people, and they brought along all their own furniture, pictures, silverware, and tapestries. It took one French ambassador ten weeks to get from Paris to Stockholm.

By the early 1700s, French writings on diplomatic methods were read everywhere. François de Callières's manual *On the Manner of Negotiating with Sovereigns* (1716) insisted that sound diplomacy was based on the creation of confidence, rather than deception: "The secret of negotiation is to harmonize the real interests of the parties concerned." Callières believed that the diplomatic service had to be professional— that young attachés should be chosen for their skills, not their family connections. These sensible views did not prevent the development of a dual system of diplomacy, in which rulers issued secret instructions that often negated the official ones sent by their own foreign offices. Secret diplomacy had some advantages because it allowed rulers to break with past alliances, but it also led to confusion and, sometimes, scandal, for the rulers often employed unreliable adventurers as their confidential agents. Still, the diplomatic system in the early eighteenth century proved successful enough to ensure a continuation of the principles of the Peace of Westphalia (1648); in the midst of every crisis and war, the great powers would convene and hammer out a written agreement detailing the requirements for peace.

Adroit diplomacy could smooth the road toward peace, but success in war still depended on sheer numbers—of men and muskets. Because each state's strength depended largely on the size of its army, the growth and health of the population increasingly entered into government calculations. The publication in 1690 of the Englishman William Petty's *Political Arithmetick* quickened the interest of government officials everywhere. Petty offered statistical estimates of human capital—that is, of population and wages—to determine Britain's national wealth. In 1727, Frederick William I of Prussia founded two university chairs to encourage population studies, and textbooks and handbooks advocated state intervention to improve the population's health and welfare.

Public Hygiene and Health Care

Physicians used the new population statistics to explain the environmental causes of disease, another new preoccupation in this period. Petty devised a quantitative scale that distinguished healthy from unhealthy places largely on the basis of air quality, an early precursor of modern environmental studies. Cities were the unhealthiest places because excrement (animal and human) and garbage accumulated where people lived densely packed together. Paris seemed to a visitor "so detestable that it is impossible to remain there" because of the smell; even the façade of the Louvre palace in Paris was soiled by the contents of night commodes that servants routinely dumped out of windows every morning. Only the wealthy could escape walking in mucky streets, by hiring men to carry them in sedan chairs or to drive them in coaches.

After investigating specific cities, medical geographers urged government campaigns to improve public sanitation. Everywhere, environmentalists gathered and analyzed data on climate, disease, and population, searching for correlations to help direct policy. As a result of these efforts, local governments undertook such measures as draining low-lying areas, burying refuse, and cleaning wells, all of which eventually helped lower the death rates from epidemic diseases.

Hospitals and medical care underwent lasting transformations. Founded originally as charities concerned foremost with the moral worthiness of the poor, hospitals gradually evolved into medical institutions that defined patients by their diseases. The process of diagnosis changed as physicians began to use specialized Latin terms for illnesses. The gap between medical experts and their patients increased, as physicians now also relied on postmortem dissections in the hospital to gain better knowledge, a practice most patients' families resented. Press reports of body snatching and grave robbing by surgeons and their apprentices outraged the public well into the 1800s.

Despite the change in hospitals, individual health care remained something of a free-for-all in which physicians competed with bloodletters, itinerant venereal disease doctors, bonesetters, druggists, midwives, and "cunning women," who specialized in home remedies. The medical profession, with nationwide organizations and licensing, had not yet emerged, and no clear line separated trained physicians from quacks. Physicians often followed popular prescriptions for illnesses because they had nothing better to offer. Patients were as likely to die of diseases caught in the hospital as to be cured there. Antiseptics were nearly unknown.

The various "medical opinions" about childbirth highlight the confusion people faced. Midwives delivered most babies, though they sometimes encountered criticism even from within their own ranks. One consulting midwife complained that ordinary midwives in Bristol, England, made women in labor drink a mixture of their husband's urine and leek juice. By the 1730s, female midwives faced competition from male midwives, who were known for using instruments such as forceps to pull the baby out of the birth canal. Women rarely sought a physician's help in giving birth, however; they preferred the advice and assistance of trusted local midwives. In any case, trained physicians were few in number and almost nonexistent outside cities.

Hardly any infectious diseases could be cured, though inoculation against smallpox spread from the Middle East to Europe in the early eighteenth century, thanks largely to the efforts of Lady Mary Wortley Montagu, who learned about the technique while living in Constantinople. After 1750, physicians developed successful procedures for wide-scale vaccination, although even then many people resisted the idea of inoculating themselves with a disease. Other diseases spread quickly in the unsanitary conditions of urban life. Ordinary people washed or changed clothes rarely, lived in overcrowded housing with poor ventilation, and got their water from contaminated sources, such as refuse-filled rivers.

Until the mid-1700s, most people considered bathing dangerous. Public bathhouses had disappeared from cities in the sixteenth and seventeenth centuries because they seemed a source of disorderly behavior and epidemic illness. In the eighteenth century, even private bathing came into disfavor because people feared the effects of contact with water. Fewer than one in ten newly built private mansions in Paris had baths. Bathing was hazardous, physicians insisted, because it opened the body to disease. One manners manual of 1736 admonished, "It is correct to clean the face every morning by using a white cloth to cleanse it. It is less good to wash with water, because it renders the face susceptible to cold in winter and sun in summer." The upper classes associated cleanliness not with baths but with frequently changed linens, powdered hair, and perfume, which was thought to strengthen the body and refresh the brain by counteracting corrupt and foul air.

■ **REVIEW:** *What were the consequences of the stabilization of the balance of power in Europe at the start of the eighteenth century?*

The Birth of the Enlightenment

Economic expansion, the emergence of a new consumer society, and the stabilization of the European state system all generated optimism about the future. The intellectual corollary was the **Enlightenment**, a term used later in the eighteenth century to describe the loosely knit group of writers and scholars who believed that human beings could apply a critical, reasoning spirit to every problem they encountered in this world. The new secular, scientific, and critical attitude first emerged in the 1690s, scrutinizing everything from the absolutism of Louis XIV to the traditional role of women in society. After 1740, criticism took a more systematic turn as writers provided new theories for the organization of society and politics, but even by the 1720s and 1730s, established authorities realized they faced a new set of challenges.

Popularization of Science and Challenges to Religion

The writers of the Enlightenment glorified the geniuses of the new science and championed scientific method as the solution for all social problems. One of the most influential popularizations was the French writer Bernard de Fontenelle's *Conversations on the Plurality of Worlds* (1686). Presented as a dialogue between an aristocratic woman and a man of the world, the book made the Copernican,

■ A Budding Scientist
In this engraving, Astrologia, *by the Dutch artist Jacob Gole (c. 1660–1723), an upper-class woman looks through a telescope to do her own astronomical investigations. Women were not allowed to attend university classes in any European country, yet the Italian Laura Bassi (1711–1778) still managed to become professor of physics at the University of Bologna. Because many astronomical observatories were set up in private homes rather than public buildings or universities, wives and daughters of scientists could make observations and even publish their own findings.*
(Bibliothèque nationale de France.)

sun-centered view of the universe available to the literate public. By 1700, mathematics and science had become fashionable pastimes in high society, and the public flocked to lectures explaining scientific discoveries. Journals complained that scientific learning had become the passport to female affection: "There were two young ladies in Paris whose heads had been so turned by this branch of learning that one of them declined to listen to a proposal of marriage unless the candidate for her hand undertook to learn how to make telescopes." Such writings poked fun at women with intellectual interests, but they also demonstrated that women now participated in discussions of science.

Interest in science spread in literate circles because it offered a model for all forms of knowledge. As the prestige of science increased, some developed a skeptical attitude toward attempts to enforce religious conformity. A French Huguenot refugee from Louis XIV's persecutions, Pierre Bayle (1647–1706), launched an internationally influential campaign against religious intolerance from his safe haven in the Dutch Republic. His *News from the Republic of Letters* (first published in 1684) bitterly criticized the policies of Louis XIV and was quickly banned in Paris and condemned in Rome. After attacking Louis XIV's anti-Protestant policies, Bayle took a more general stand in favor of religious toleration. No state in Europe officially offered complete tolerance, though the Dutch Republic came closest with its tacit acceptance of Catholics, dissident Protestant groups, and open Jewish communities. In 1697, Bayle published the *Historical and Critical Dictionary*, which cited all the errors and delusions that he could find in past and present writers of all religions. Even religion must meet the test of reasonableness: "Any particular dogma, whatever it may be, whether it is advanced on the authority of the Scriptures, or whatever else may be its origins, is to be regarded as false if it clashes with the clear and definite conclusions of the natural understanding [reason]." Although Bayle claimed to be a believer himself, his insistence on rational investigation seemed to challenge the authority of faith. As one critic complained, "It is notorious that the works of M. Bayle have unsettled a large number of readers, and cast doubt on some of the most widely accepted principles of morality and religion." Bayle asserted, for example, that atheists might possess moral codes as effective as those of the devout. Bayle's *Dictionary* became a model of critical thought in the West.

Other scholars challenged the authority of the Bible by subjecting it to historical criticism. Discoveries in geology in the early eighteenth century showed that marine fossils dated immensely farther back than the biblical flood. Investigations of miracles, comets, and oracles, like the growing literature against belief in witchcraft, urged the use of reason to combat superstition and prejudice. Comets, for example, should not be considered evil omens just because such a belief had been passed on from earlier generations. Defenders of church and state published books warning of the dangers of the new skepticism. The spokesman for Louis XIV's absolutism, Bishop Bossuet, warned that "reason is the guide of their choice, but reason only brings them face to face with vague conjectures and baffling perplexities." Human beings, the traditionalists held, were simply incapable of subjecting everything to reason, especially in the realm of religion.

State authorities found religious skepticism particularly unsettling because it threatened to undermine state power, too. The extensive literature of criticism was not limited to France, but much of it was published in French, and the French government took the lead in suppressing the more outspoken works. Forbidden books were then often published in the Dutch Republic, Britain, or Switzerland and smuggled back across the border to a public whose appetite was only whetted by censorship.

The most influential writer of the early Enlightenment was a Frenchman born into the upper middle class, François-Marie Arouet, known by his pen name, Voltaire (1694–1778). In his early years, Voltaire suffered arrest, imprisonment, and exile, but he eventually achieved wealth and acclaim. His tangles with church and state began in the early 1730s, when he published his *Letters Concerning the English Nation* (the English version appeared in 1733), in which he devoted several chapters to Newton and Locke and used the virtues of the British as a way to attack Catholic bigotry and government rigidity in France. Impressed by British toleration of religious dissent (at least among Protestants), Voltaire spent two years in exile in Britain when the French state responded to his book with yet another order for his arrest.

Voltaire also popularized Newton's scientific discoveries in his *Elements of the Philosophy of Newton* (1738). The French state and many European theologians considered Newtonianism threatening because it glorified the human mind and seemed to reduce God to an abstract, external, rationalistic force. So sensational was the success of Voltaire's book on Newton that a hostile Jesuit reported, "The great Newton, was, it is said, buried in the abyss, in the shop of the first publisher who dared to print him. . . . M. de Voltaire finally appeared, and at once Newton is understood or is in the process of being understood; all Paris resounds with Newton, all Paris stammers Newton, all Paris studies and learns Newton." The success was international, too. Before long, Voltaire was elected a fellow of the Royal Society in London and in Edinburgh, as well as to twenty other scientific academies. Voltaire's fame continued to grow, reaching truly astounding proportions in the 1750s and 1760s (see Chapter 15).

Travel Literature and the Challenge to Custom and Tradition

Just as scientific method could be used to question religious and even state authority, a more general skepticism also emerged from the expanding knowledge about the world outside of Europe. During the seventeenth and eighteenth centuries, accounts of travel to exotic places dramatically increased as travel writers used the contrast between their home societies and other cultures to criticize the customs of European society.

In their travels to the new colonies, visitors sought something resembling "the state of nature"—that is, ways of life that preceded sophisticated social and political organization—although they often misinterpreted different forms of society and politics as having no organization at all. Travelers to the Americas found "noble savages" (native peoples) who appeared to live in conditions of great freedom and equality; they were "naturally good" and "happy" without taxes, lawsuits, or much organized government. In China, in contrast, travelers found a people who enjoyed prosperity and an ancient civilization. Christian missionaries made little headway in China, and visitors had to admit that China's religious systems had flourished for four or five thousand years with no input from Europe or from Christianity. The basic lesson of travel literature in the 1700s, then, was that customs varied: justice, freedom, property, good government, religion, and morality all were relative to the place. One critic complained that travel encouraged free thinking and the destruction of religion: "Some complete their demoralization by extensive travel, and lose whatever shreds of religion remained to them. Every day they see a new religion, new customs, new rites."

Travel literature turned explicitly political in Montesquieu's *Persian Letters* (1721). Charles-Louis de Secondat, baron of Montesquieu (1689–1755), the son of an eminent judicial family, was a high-ranking judge in a French court. He published *Persian Letters* anonymously in the Dutch Republic, and the book went into ten printings in just one year—a best seller for the times. Montesquieu tells the story of two Persians, Rica and Usbek, who leave their country "for love of knowledge" and travel to Europe. They visit France in the last years of Louis XIV's reign, writing of the king: "He has a minister who is only eighteen years old, and a mistress of eighty. . . . Although he avoids the bustle of towns, and is rarely seen in company, his one concern, from morning till night, is to get himself talked about." Other passages ridicule the pope. Beneath the satire, however, was a serious investigation into the foundation of good government and morality. Montesquieu chose Persians for his travelers because they came from what was widely considered the most despotic of all governments, in which rulers had life-and-death powers over their subjects. In the book, the Persians constantly compare France to Persia, suggesting that the French monarchy itself might verge on despotism.

The paradox of a judge publishing an anonymous work attacking the regime that employed him demonstrates the complications of the intellectual scene in this period. Montesquieu's anonymity did not last long, and soon Parisian society lionized him. In the late 1720s, he sold his judgeship and traveled extensively in Europe, including an eighteen-month stay in Britain. In 1748, he published a widely influential work on comparative government, *The Spirit of Laws*. The Vatican soon listed both *Persian Letters* and *The Spirit of Laws* in its index of forbidden books.

Raising the Woman Question

Many of the letters exchanged in *Persian Letters* focused on women, marriage, and the family because Montesquieu considered the position of women a sure indicator of the nature of government and morality. Although he was not a feminist, his depiction of Roxana, the favorite wife in Usbek's harem, struck a chord with many women. Roxana revolts against the authority of Usbek's eunuchs and writes a final letter to her husband announcing her impending suicide: "I may have lived in servitude, but I have always been free, I have amended your laws according to the laws of nature, and my mind has always remained independent." Women writers used the same language of tyranny and freedom to argue for concrete changes in their status. Feminist ideas were not entirely new, but they were presented systematically for the first time and represented a fundamental challenge to the ways of traditional societies.

The most systematic of these women writers was the English author Mary Astell (1666–1731), the daughter of a businessman and herself a supporter of the Tory party and the Anglican religious establishment. In 1694, she published *A Serious Proposal to the Ladies*, in which she advocated founding a private women's college to remedy women's lack of education. Addressing women, she asked, "How can you be content to be in the World like Tulips in a Garden, to make a fine *shew* [show] and be good for nothing?" Astell argued for intellectual training based on Descartes's principles, in which reason, debate, and careful consideration of the issues took priority over custom or tradition. Her book was an immediate success: five printings appeared by 1701. In later works such as *Reflections upon Marriage* (1706), Astell criticized the relationship between the sexes within marriage: "If Absolute Sovereignty be not necessary in a State, how comes it to be so in a family? . . . *If all Men are born free*, how is it that all Women are born slaves?" Her critics accused her of promoting subversive ideas and of contradicting the Scriptures.

Astell's work inspired other women to write in a similar vein. The anonymous *Essay in Defence of the Female Sex* (1696) attacked "The Usurpation of Men; and the Tyranny of Custom," which prevented women from getting an education. In 1709, Elizabeth Elstob published a detailed account of the prominent role women played in promoting Christianity in English history. She criticized men who "would declare openly they hated any Woman who knew more than themselves."

Most male writers unequivocally stuck to the traditional view of women, which held that women were less capable of reasoning than men and therefore did not need systematic education. Such opinions often rested on biological suppositions. The long-dominant Aristotelian view of reproduction held that only the male seed carried spirit and individuality. At the beginning of the eighteenth century, however, scientists began to undermine this belief. More physicians and surgeons began to champion the doctrine of ovism—that the female egg was essential in making new

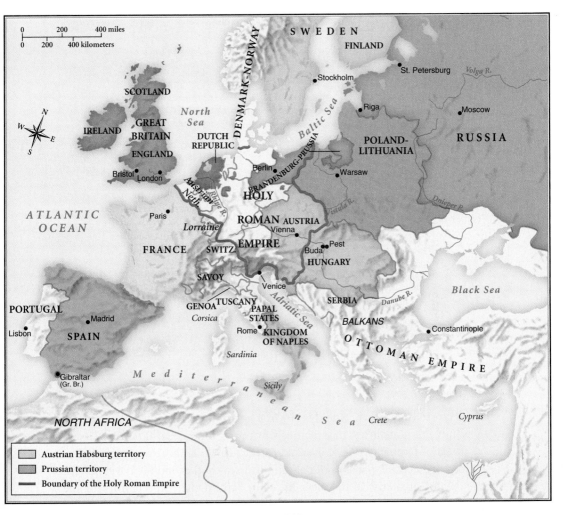

■ **MAPPING THE WEST** Europe in 1740

By 1740 Europe had achieved a kind of diplomatic equilibrium in which no one power predominated. But the relative balance should not deflect attention from important underlying changes: Spain, the Dutch Republic, Poland-Lithuania, and Sweden had all declined in power and influence while Great Britain, Russia, Prussia, and Austria had solidified their positions, each in a different way. France's ambitions had been thwarted, but the combination of a big army and rich overseas possessions made France a major player for a long time to come.

humans. During the decades that followed, male Enlightenment writers would continue to debate women's nature and appropriate social roles.

■ **REVIEW:** *What were the main issues in the early decades of the Enlightenment?*

IMPORTANT DATES			
1690s	Beginning of rapid development of plantations in the Caribbean	1715	Death of Louis XIV
1694	Bank of England established; Mary Astell's *A Serious Proposal to the Ladies* argues for the founding of a private women's college	1719	Daniel Defoe publishes *Robinson Crusoe*
		1720	Last outbreak of bubonic plague in western Europe
1697	Pierre Bayle publishes *Historical and Critical Dictionary*, detailing errors of religious writers	1721	Treaty of Nystad; Montesquieu publishes *Persian Letters* anonymously in the Dutch Republic
1699	Turks forced to recognize Habsburg rule over Hungary and Transylvania	1733	War of the Polish Succession; Voltaire's *Letters Concerning the English Nation* attacks French intolerance and narrowmindedness
1703	Peter the Great of Russia begins construction of St. Petersburg, founds first Russian newspaper	1741	George Frederick Handel composes the *Messiah*
1713–1714	Peace of Utrecht		
1714	Elector of Hanover becomes King George I of England		

Conclusion

Europeans crossed a major threshold in the first half of the eighteenth century. They moved silently but nonetheless momentously from an economy governed by scarcity and the threat of famine to one of ever increasing growth and the prospect of continuing improvement. Expansion of colonies overseas and economic development at home created greater wealth, longer life spans, and higher expectations for the future. In these better times for many, a spirit of optimism prevailed. People could now spend money on newspapers, novels, and travel literature as well as on coffee, tea, and cotton cloth. The growing literate public avidly followed the latest trends in religious debates, art, and music. Everyone did not share equally in the benefits: slaves toiled in abjection in the Americas; serfs in eastern Europe found themselves ever more closely bound to their noble lords; and rural folk almost everywhere tasted few fruits of consumer society.

Politics, too, changed as population and production increased and cities grew. Experts urged government intervention to improve public health, and states found it in their interest to settle many international disputes by diplomacy, which itself became more regular and routine. The consolidation of the European state system allowed a tide of criticism and new thinking about society to swell in Great Britain and France and begin to spill throughout Europe. Ultimately, the combination of the Atlantic system and the Enlightenment would give rise to a series of Atlantic revolutions.

■ **MAKING CONNECTIONS**

1. *How did the rise of slavery and the plantation system change European politics and society?*

2. *Why did the Enlightenment begin just at the moment that the Atlantic system took shape?*

■ **FOR FURTHER EXPLORATION**

For further reading and online research ideas, see the Suggested References on page SR-7 at the back of the book.

For practice quizzes, a customized study plan, and other study tools, see the ONLINE STUDY GUIDE at bedfordstmartins.com/huntconcise.

For primary-source material from this period, see Chapter 14 in *Sources of THE MAKING OF THE WEST: A CONCISE HISTORY*, Second Edition.

Suggested References

CHAPTER 1
Foundations of Western Civilization, to 500 B.C.E.

Archaeological excavation is our best resource for understanding the long period of history from the Stone Age to the rise of the Greek city-state.

Ancient Near Eastern sites: http://www.etana.org/abzu
Ancient Olympic Games: http://www.perseus.tufts.edu/Olympics
*Barnes, Jonathan. *Early Greek Philosophy*. 1987.
Brosius, Maria. *Women in Ancient Persia (559–331 B.C.)*. 1996.
Bryce, Trevor. *The Kingdom of the Hittites*. 1998.
*Dalley, Stephanie, trans. *Myths from Mesopotamia: Creation, the Flood, Gilgamesh, and Others*. 1991.
Ehrenberg, Margaret. *Women in Prehistory*. 1989.
Fisher, Nick, and Hans van Wees, eds. *Archaic Greece: New Approaches and Evidence*. 1998.
Hunt, Norman Bancroft. *Historical Atlas of Ancient Mesopotamia*. 2004.
Nigosian, S. A. *The Zoroastrian Faith: Tradition and Modern Research*. 1993.
Osborne, Robin. *Greece in the Making, 1200–479 B.C.* 1996.
Redford, Donald B., ed. *The Oxford Encyclopedia of Ancient Egypt*. 2000.
Van de Mieroop, Marc. *A History of the Ancient Near East c. 3000–323 B.C.* 2003.
Virtual Museum of Nautical Archaeology (including the Uluburun shipwreck):
    http://ina.tamu.edu/vm.htm

CHAPTER 2
The Greek Golden Age, c. 500–400 B.C.E.

A major challenge in studying the Greek Golden Age is to understand how the period's nearly constant wars affected every part of life.

Davidson, James. *Courtesans and Fishcakes: The Consuming Passions of Classical Athens*. 1998.
Easterling, P. E., and J. V. Muir, eds. *Greek Religion and Society*. 1985.
Ferguson, John. *Morals and Values in Ancient Greece*. 1989.
Fisher, N. R. E. *Slavery in Classical Greece*. 1995.
Greek daily life: http://www.museum.upenn.edu/Greek_World/index2.html
Green, Peter. *The Greco-Persian Wars*. 1996.

---

*Primary sources are indicated with an asterisk.

Hanson, Victor Davis. *The Other Greeks: The Family Farm and the Agrarian Roots of Western Civilization.* 1995.

Lazenby, J. F. *The Spartan Army.* 1985.

*Lefkowitz, Mary R., and Maureen B. Fant, eds. *Women's Life in Greece and Rome: A Source Book in Translation.* 1982.

Martin, Thomas R. *Ancient Greece: From Prehistoric to Hellenistic Times.* 2000.

Parthenon: http://www.perseus.tufts.edu/cgi-bin/vor?lookup=parthenon&collection=

Patterson, Cynthia B. *The Family in Greek History.* 1998.

Pollitt, J. J. *Art and Experience in Classical Greece.* 1972.

Samons II, Loren J. *What's Wrong with Democracy? From Athenian Practice to American Worship.* 2004.

*Strassler, Robert B., ed. *The Landmark Thucydides: A Comprehensive Guide to the Peloponnesian War.* 1996.

CHAPTER 3
From the Classical to the Hellenistic World, c. 400–30 B.C.E.

Research on the transition from the Classical to the Hellenistic Mediterranean world focuses on the imaginative ways in which rulers, thinkers, and artists combined the old and the new, the familiar and the foreign, in the multicultural environment that emerged from the conquests of Alexander the Great.

Ancient Alexandria in Egypt: http://ce.eng.usf.edu/pharos/alexandria

Barnes, Jonathan. *Aristotle.* 1982.

Chauveau, Michel. *Egypt in the Age of Cleopatra.* Trans. David Lorton. 2000.

Collins, John J. *Between Athens and Jerusalem: Jewish Identity in the Hellenistic Diaspora.* 2d ed. 2000.

Gosling, J. C. B. *Plato.* 1973.

Hamilton, J. R. *Alexander the Great.* 1973.

Pomeroy, Sarah B. *Women in Hellenistic Egypt: From Alexander to Cleopatra.* Rev. ed. 1990.

Rogers, Guy MacLean. *Alexander: The Ambiguity of Greatness.* 2004.

*Roisman, Joseph. *Alexander the Great: Ancient and Modern Perspectives.* 1995.

Sharples, R. W. *Stoics, Epicureans, and Sceptics: An Introduction to Hellenistic Philosophy.* 1996.

Shipley, Graham. *The Greek World after Alexander, 323–30 B.C.* 2000.

*Snyder, Jane M. *The Woman and the Lyre: Women Writers in Classical Greece and Rome.* 1989.

Witt, R. E. *Isis in the Greco-Roman World.* 1971.

*Xenophon. *The Persian Expedition.* Trans. Rex Warner. 1950.

CHAPTER 4
The Rise of Rome, c. 753–44 B.C.E.

Our knowledge of the political and economic changes in the Roman republic is being revised by archaeological research linked to close study of the ancient literary sources.

Beard, Mary, et al. *Religions of Rome.* 2 vols. 1998.

Bonfante, Larissa, ed. *Etruscan Life and Afterlife: A Handbook of Etruscan Studies.* 1986.

Bradley, Keith. *Slavery and Society at Rome.* 1994.

*Caesar. *The Civil War.* Trans. John Carter. 1997.

*Cicero. *Philippic Orations.* Trans. Walter C. Ker. 1969.

Daily life (and more): http://www.vroma.org/~bmcmanus/romanpages.html

Earl, Donald. *The Moral and Political Tradition of Rome.* 1967.

Forsyth, Gary. *A Critical History of Early Rome: From Prehistory to the First Punic War.* 2005.

Gardner, Jane. *Women in Roman Law and Society.* 1986.

Goldsworthy, Adrian. *The Punic Wars.* 2000.

Ladder of offices (*cursus honorum*): http://www.vroma.org/~bmcmanus/romangvt.html

Lancel, Serge. *Carthage: A History.* Trans. Antonia Nevill. 1995.
Rosenstein, Nathan. *Rome at War: Farms, Families, and Death in the Middle Republic.* 2004.
Strong, Donald. *Roman Art.* 2d ed. 1988.
Williams, Craig A. *Roman Homosexuality: Ideologies of Masculinity in Classical Antiquity.* 1999.

CHAPTER 5

The Roman Empire, c. 44 B.C.E.–284 C.E.

Modern scholarly work on the principate reveals how the emperors tried to create political legitimacy and social stability through a combination of military, religious, and artistic policy.

Doran, Robert. *Birth of a World View: Early Christianity in Its Jewish and Pagan Contexts.* 1999.
Futrell, Alison. *Blood in the Arena: The Spectacle of Roman Power.* 1997.
Galinsky, Karl. *Augustan Culture.* 1996.
Garnsey, Peter, and Richard Saller. *The Roman Empire: Economy, Society, and Culture.* 1987.
George, Michele, ed. *The Roman Family in the Empire: Rome, Italy, and Beyond.* 2005.
Jackson, Ralph. *Doctors and Diseases in the Roman Empire.* 1988.
*Kraemer, Ross Shephard. *Her Share of the Blessings: Women's Religion among Pagans, Jews, and Christians in the Greco-Roman World.* 1992.
MacMullen, Ramsay. *Christianizing the Roman Empire (A.D. 100–400).* 1984.
Potter, D. S., and D. J. Mattingly, eds. *Life, Death, and Entertainment in the Roman Empire.* 1999.
Roman emperors: http://www.roman-emperors.org
*Suetonius. *The Twelve Caesars.* Trans. Robert Graves. 2003.
Torjesen, Karen Jo. *When Women Were Priests: Women's Leadership in the Early Church and the Scandal of Their Subordination in the Rise of Christianity.* 1993.
Treggiari, Susan. *Roman Marriage: Iusti Coniuges from the Time of Cicero to the Time of Ulpian.* 1991.
Webster, Graham. *The Roman Imperial Army of the First and Second Centuries A.D.* 3d ed. 1985.
Wiedemann, Thomas. *Emperors and Gladiators.* 1995.

CHAPTER 6

The Transformation of the Roman Empire, c. 284–c. 600 C.E.

Recent research has deepened our appreciation of the complexity of the religious transformation of the Roman Empire and the emotional depths that the process stirred up for polytheists and Christians.

Brown, Peter. *The Body and Society: Men, Women, and Sexual Renunciation in Early Christianity.* 1988.
Burns, Thomas. *Barbarians within the Gates of Rome: A Study of Roman Military Policy and the Barbarians, ca. 375–425 A.D.* 1994.
Cavallo, Guglielmo, ed. *The Byzantines.* 1997.
Corcoran, Simon. *The Empire of the Tetrarchs: Imperial Pronouncements and Government, A.D. 284–324.* Rev. ed. 2000.
*Drew, Katherine Fischer. *The Laws of the Salian Franks.* 1991.
*Early Christian literature: http://www.voskrese.info/spl/index.html
Elsner, Jaś. *Imperial Rome and Christian Triumph: The Art of the Roman Empire, A.D. 100–450.* 1998.
Heather, Peter. *The Fall of the Roman Empire.* 2005.
MacMullen, Ramsay. *Christianity and Paganism in the Fourth to Eighth Centuries.* 1997.
Potter, David. *The Roman Empire at Bay A.D. 180–395.* 2004.
Rapp, Claudia. *Holy Bishops in Late Antiquity: The Nature of Christian Leadership in an Age of Transition.* 2005.
Rousseau, Philip. *Pachomius: The Making of a Community in Fourth-Century Egypt.* 1985.
Southern, Pat, and Karen R. Dixon. *The Late Roman Army.* 1996.
Ward-Perkins, Bryan. *The Fall of Rome: And the End of Civilization.* 2005.
Women in Byzantine history bibliography: http://www.wooster.edu/Art/wb.html

CHAPTER 7
The Heirs of the Roman Empire, 600–750

Haldon and Whittow are excellent guides to early Byzantine history; Wood and Geary emphasize different aspects of the Merovingian world. Sells's lyrical translations and commentaries illuminate the Qur'an, and the book includes an audio CD of Qur'an recitations.

Ahmed, Leila. *Women and Gender in Islam: Historical Roots of a Modern Debate.* 1992.
*Bede. *A History of the English Church and People.* Trans. Leo Sherley-Price. 1991.
The Byzantine Studies Page: http://www.fordham.edu/halsall/byzantium
Charles-Edwards, T. M. *Early Christian Ireland.* 2001.
*Fouracre, Paul, and Richard A. Gerberding, eds. *Late Merovingian France: History and Hagiography, 640–720.* 1996.
Geary, Patrick. *Before France and Germany: The Creation and Transformation of the Merovingian World.* 1988.
*Gregory of Tours. *The History of the Franks.* Trans. Lewis Thorpe. 1976.
Haldon, J. F. *Byzantium in the Seventh Century: The Transformation of a Culture.* 1990.
Islamic Sourcebook: http://www.fordham.edu/halsall/islam/islamsbook.html
Kennedy, Hugh. *The Prophet and the Age of the Caliphates: The Islamic Near East from the Sixth to the Eleventh Century.* 2d ed. 2004.
*Murray, Alexander C., ed. and trans. *From Roman to Merovingian Gaul: A Reader.* 2000.
Ousterhout, Robert, and Leslie Brubaker. *The Sacred Image East and West.* 1995.
*Sells, Michael, trans. *Approaching the Qur'an: The Early Revelations.* 1999.
Whittow, Mark. *The Making of Byzantium, 600–1025.* 1996.
Wood, Ian. *The Merovingian Kingdoms, 450–751.* 1994.

CHAPTER 8
Unity and Diversity in Three Societies, 750–1050

Compare Barbero's picture of Charlemagne with Nelson's view of Charles the Bald. Many primary sources for the Carolingian period are translated by Paul Dutton. Political disintegration used to be seen as a bad thing, but recent historians, such as Berkey, Duby, Head, Landes, and Glick, value the diversity and local developments that it permitted.

Barbero, Alessandro. *Charlemagne: Father of a Continent.* Trans. Allan Cameron. 2004.
Berkey, Jonathan P. *The Formation of Islam: Religion and Society in the Near East, 600–1800.* 2003.
Byzantine art: http://witcombe.sbc.edu/ARTHmedieval.html#Byzantine
Duby, Georges. *The Early Growth of the European Economy: Warriors and Peasants from the Seventh to the Twelfth Century.* Trans. H. B. Clark. 1974.
*Dutton, Paul Edward. *Carolingian Civilization: A Reader.* 2d ed. 2004.
Franklin, Simon, and Jonathan Shepard. *The Emergence of Rus, 750–1200.* 1996.
Garland, Lynda. *Byzantine Empresses: Women and Power in Byzantium, A.D. 527–1204.* 1999.
Glick, Thomas. *Islamic and Christian Spain in the Early Middle Ages: Comparative Perspectives on Social and Cultural Formation.* 1979.
Head, Thomas, and Richard Landes, eds. *The Peace of God: Social Violence and Religious Response in France around the Year 1000.* 1992.
Lawson, M. K. *Cnut: The Danes in England in the Early Eleventh Century.* 1993.
McCormick, Michael. *Origins of the European Economy: Communications and Commerce, A.D. 300–900.* 2001.
Medieval and Renaissance manuscripts: http://www.columbia.edu/cu/libraries/indiv/rare/images
Nelson, Janet. *Charles the Bald.* 1987.
*Psellus, Michael. *Fourteen Byzantine Rulers: The Chronographia.* Trans. E. R. A. Sewter. 1966.
Reuter, Timothy. *Germany in the Early Middle Ages, c. 800–1056.* 1991.
Treadgold, Warren. *The Byzantine Revival, 780–842.* 1988.

CHAPTER 9

Renewal and Reform, 1050–1200

Clanchy is excellent on both Abelard and Heloise. The Hildegard of Bingen Web site offers numerous links to her work and works about her. Curiosity about the Crusades has never waned, but Holt shows that there is new interest in their impact.

Clanchy, Michael. *Abelard: A Medieval Life.* 1997.
*The Crusades: http://www.fordham.edu/halsall/sbook1k.html
Daniell, Christopher. *From Norman Conquest to Magna Carta: England, 1066–1215.* 2003.
Epstein, Steven. *Wage Labor and Guilds in Medieval Europe.* 1991.
Glick, Leonard B. *Abraham's Heirs: Jews and Christians in Medieval Europe.* 1999.
Hildegard of Bingen: http://www.healingchants.com/hvb_links.html
Hildegard von Bingen: Ordo virtutum, Deutsche Harmonia Mundi CD, 77394 (music from Hildegard's
    Scivias and the expanded play at its end).
Holt, P. M. *The Crusader States and Their Neighbours, 1098–1291.* 2004.
Hudson, John. *The Formation of the English Common Law: Law and Society in England from the Norman
    Conquest to Magna Carta.* 1996.
Letters of Abelard and Heloise. Trans. Betty Radice. 1974. Includes *History of My Calamities.*
Little, Lester K. *Religious Poverty and the Profit Economy in Medieval Europe.* 1978.
*Lopez, Robert S., and Irving W. Raymond, eds. *Medieval Trade in the Mediterranean World.* 1955.
*Miller, Maureen C., ed. and trans. *Power and the Holy in the Age of the Investiture Conflict: A Brief
    History with Documents.* 2005.
Moore, R. I. *The First European Revolution, c. 970–1215.* 2000.
*Otto of Freising. *The Deeds of Frederick Barbarossa.* Trans. C. C. Mierow. 1953.
Riley-Smith, Jonathan. *The Crusades. A Short History.* 1987.

CHAPTER 10

An Age of Confidence, 1200–1340

Bartlett and Christiansen take up the physical expansion of Europe, while Dante and Thomas Aquinas demonstrate its intellectual range. Bynum deftly ties together religious, theological, and gender issues. The politics of the period always had religious implications, and religious movements always had political ramifications, as Jordan, R. I. Moore, and John C. Moore show in different ways.

Bartlett, Robert. *The Making of Europe: Conquest, Colonization, and Cultural Change,
    950–1350.* 1993.
Boyle, John A. *The Mongol World Empire, 1206–1370.* 1977.
Bynum, Caroline Walker. *Holy Feast and Holy Fast: The Religious Significance of Food to Medieval
    Women.* 1987.
Christiansen, Eric. *The Northern Crusades.* 2d ed. 1997.
*Dante. *The Divine Comedy.* Many editions; recommended are translations by Mark Musa, John Ciardi,
    and Robert Pinsky.
*Fourth Lateran Council: http://www.fordham.edu/halsall/basis/lateran4.html
Jones, Philip J. *The Italian City-State: From Commune to Signoria.* 1997.
Jordan,William Chester. *The French Monarchy and the Jews: From Philip Augustus to the
    Last Capetians.* 1989.
Moore, John C. *Pope Innocent III (1160/61–1216): To Root Up and to Plant.* 2003.
Moore, R. I. *The Formation of a Persecuting Society: Power and Deviance in Western Europe,
    950–1250.* 1987.
O'Callaghan, Joseph F. *The Cortes of Castile-León, 1188–1350.* 1989.
*Polo, Marco. *The Travels.* Trans. Ronald Latham. 1958.
Rubin, Miri. *Corpus Christi: The Eucharist in Late Medieval Culture.* 1991.

*Thomas Aquinas: http://www.fordham.edu/halsall/source/aquinas1.html (Questions 1 and 2 from the
    Summa Theologiae)
*William of Puylaurens. The Chronicle of William of Puylaurens: The Albigensian Crusade and Its
    Aftermath, trans. W. A. Sibly and M. D. Sibly. 2003.

CHAPTER 11
Crisis and Renaissance, 1340–1500

The old view associated the Renaissance primarily with Florence, but now the Renaissance is seen as a European movement (Kirkpatrick; *The Renaissance in Europe*) and even part of Ottoman culture (Jardine and Brotton). Similarly, the traditional view of "Europe discovering the world" has been replaced by a more nuanced and complex discussion that includes non-European views and uses Asian, African, and Mesoamerican sources.

Aberth, John. *From the Brink of the Apocalypse: Confronting Famine, War, Plague, and Death in the Later
    Middle Ages*. 2001.
Bisaha, Nancy. *Creating East and West: Renaissance Humanists and the Ottoman Turks*. 2004.
The Black Death. Ed. and trans. Rosemary Horrox. 1994.
Crabb, Ann. *The Strozzi of Florence: Widowhood and Family Solidarity in the Renaissance*. 2000.
Epstein, Steven A. *Speaking of Slavery: Color, Ethnicity, and Human Bondage in Italy*. 2001.
*Froissart, Jean. *Chronicles*. Trans. Geoffrey Brereton. 1968.
Jardine, Lisa, and Jerry Brotton. *Global Interests: Renaissance Art between East and West*. 2000.
Jordan, William Chester. *The Great Famine: Northern Europe in the Early Fourteenth Century*. 1996.
Kirkpatrick, Robin. *The European Renaissance, 1400–1600*. 2002.
Nirenberg, David. *Communities of Violence: Persecution of Minorities in the Middle Ages*. 1996.
Plague and public health in Renaissance Europe: http://jefferson.village.virginia.edu/osheim/intro.html
Renaissance art links: http://witcombe.sbc.edu/ARTHLinks2.html
The Renaissance in Europe: An Anthology. Eds. Peter Elmer, Nicholas Webb, and Roberta Wood. 2000.
Russell-Wood, A. J. R. *A World on the Move: The Portuguese in Africa, Asia, and America,
    1415–1808*. 1992.
Thomas, Hugh. *Rivers of Gold: The Rise of the Spanish Empire, from Columbus to Magellan*. 2003.

CHAPTER 12
Struggles over Beliefs, 1500–1648

Painstaking archival research has enabled historians to reconstruct the demographic, economic, and social history of this period. Recently, attention has focused more specifically on women, the family, and the early history of slavery.

Ashton, Trevor H., ed. *Crisis in Europe*. 1965.
Bonney, Richard. *The Thirty Years' War*. 2002.
Bouwsma, William J. *John Calvin: A Sixteenth-Century Portrait*. 1988.
Carney, Jo Eldridge, ed. *Renaissance and Reformation, 1500–1620: A Biographical Dictionary*. 2001.
Essential Works of Erasmus. Ed. W. T. H. Jackson. 1965.
The Galileo Project: http://galileo.rice.edu
*Hillerbrand, Hans J., ed. *The Protestant Reformation*. 1969.
Holt, Mack P. *The French Wars of Religion, 1562–1629*. 1995.
Hsia, R. Po-chia. *The World of the Catholic Renewal*. 1997.
Jacob, James. *The Scientific Revolution*. 1998.
Kamen, Henry. *Philip of Spain*. 1997.
Martin Luther's life and thought: http://www.luther.de/en
Mattingly, Garrett. *The Defeat of the Spanish Armada*. 2d ed. 1988.

CHAPTER 13
State Building and the Search for Order, 1648–1690

Recent studies have insisted that absolutism could never be entirely absolute because the king depended on collaboration to enforce his policies. Some of the best sources for Louis XIV's reign are the letters written by important noblewomen.

Barkey, Karen. *The Ottoman Route to State Centralization.* 1994.
*Beik, William. *Louis XIV and Absolutism: A Brief Study with Documents.* 2000.
Collins, James B. *The State in Early Modern France.* 1995.
Davis, Natalie Zemon. *Women on the Margins: Three Seventeenth-Century Lives.* 1995.
*Forster, Elborg, trans. *A Woman's Life in the Court of the Sun King: Elisabeth Charlotte, Duchesse d'Orléans.* 1984.
Gaunt, Peter, ed. *The English Civil War: The Essential Readings.* 2000.
Hill, Christopher. *The World Turned Upside Down: Radical Ideas during the English Revolution.* 1972.
Israel, Jonathan. *Dutch Primacy in World Trade, 1585–1740.* 1989.
Kivelson, Valerie A. *Autocracy in the Provinces: The Muscovite Gentry and Political Culture in the Seventeenth Century.* 1996.
*Pincus, Steven Carl Anthony. *England's Glorious Revolution and the Origins of Liberalism: A Documentary History of Later Stuart England.* 1998.

CHAPTER 14
The Atlantic System and Its Consequences, 1690–1740

Historians have become increasingly interested in the workings of the Atlantic system in recent years. The definitive study of the early Enlightenment is the book by Hazard, but many others have contributed biographies of individual figures, or, more recently, studies of women writers.

Age of Enlightenment: http://www.fordham.edu/halsall/mod/modsbook10.html
Blackburn, Robin. *The Making of New World Slavery: From the Baroque to the Modern, 1492–1800.* 1997.
Brewer, John. *The Sinews of Power: War, Money, and the English State, 1688–1783.* 1990.
Brockliss, Laurence, and Colin Jones. *The Medical World of Early Modern France.* 1997.
Bushkovitch, Paul. *Peter the Great.* 2001.
Handel's Messiah: The New Interactive Edition (CD-ROM). 1997.
Harms, Robert. *The Diligent: A Voyage Through the Worlds of the Slave Trade.* 2003.
Hazard, Paul. *The European Mind: The Critical Years, 1680–1715.* 1990.
*Hill, Bridget. *The First English Feminist: Reflections upon Marriage and Other Writings by Mary Astell.* 1986.
Hunt, Margaret R. *The Middling Sort: Commerce, Gender, and the Family in England, 1680–1780.* 1996.

Additional Acknowledgments

Chapter 1, page 18: Figure 1.2: Egyptian Hieroglyphs. Print of chart from *Detail of Book of the Dead–18th Dynasty. Tomb of Thutmosis III, Valley of the Kings.* Reproduced by permission of Bridgeman-Giraudon/Art Resource, NY.

Chapter 2, page 84: Taking Measure: Military Forces of Athens and Sparta at the Beginning of the Peloponnesian War. From *Ancient Greece: Using Evidence* by Pamela Bradley. Published 1990 by Edward Arnold Publishers.

Chapter 4, page 151: Taking Measure: Census Records of Adult Male Roman Citizens during the First and Second Punic Wars. From *An Economic Survey of Ancient Rome,* Vol. 1, by Frank Tenney. Originally published in 1959 by Pageant Books/Hamish Hamilton (Ltd). Reprinted by permission of The Johns Hopkins University Press.

Chapter 5, page 207: Taking Measure: The Value of Roman Imperial Coinage, 27 B.C.E–300 C.E. Print of Roman Imperial Silver Coinage chart. From *The Archeology of the Roman Empire* by Kevin Greene. Originally published by Salamander Books Limited (B. T. Batsford Ltd., 1986).

Chapter 8, page 321: Taking Measure: Viking Coin Hoards, c. 865–895. From *An Atlas of Anglo-Saxon England* by David Hill.

Chapter 9, page 376: Figure 9.2: Floor Plan of a Cistercian Monastery. Adaptation of three figures (8a, 8b, and 8c) from p. 75 in *Monasteries of Western Europe: The Architecture of the Orders* by Wolfgang Braunfels. Princeton University Press, 1972, p. 75. Reprinted courtesy of DuMont Literatur und Kunst Verlag.

Chapter 10, page 393: Taking Measure: Sentences Imposed by an Inquisitor, 1308–1323. From J. Given, "A Medieval Inquisitor at Work," in *Portraits of Medieval and Renaissance Living* by Samuel K. Cohn Jr. and Steven A. Epstein. Copyright © 1996. Reprinted with permission from the University of Michigan Press. **Page 417:** Figure 10.1: Elements of a Gothic Cathedral. From *Gothic Art: Glorious Visions* by Michael Camille. Abrams, 1996.

Chapter 11, page 429: Taking Measure: Population Losses and the Plague, 1340–1450. From *Fontana Economic History of Europe: The Middle Ages* edited by Carlo M. Cipolla. Originally published by HarperCollins/Fontana Books, 1974, p. 36.

Chapter 12, page 504: Taking Measure: The Rise and Fall of Silver Imports to Spain, 1550–1660. From *American Revolution and the Price Revolution in Spain, 1501–1650,* edited by Earl J. Hamilton. Courtesy of Harvard University Press.

Chapter 13, page 534: Taking Measure: The Seventeenth-Century Army. *Armées et societiés en Europe de 1494 à 1789* by André Corvisier. Universitaires de France, 1976, 126. Reprinted with permission of the publisher.

Chapter 14, page 571: Figure 14.1: African Slaves Imported into American Territories, 1701–1810. From *The Atlantic Slave Trade: A Census* by Philip D. Curtin. © 1969. Reprinted by permission of The University of Wisconsin Press. **Page 579:** Taking Measure: Relationship of Crop Harvested to Seed Used, 1400–1800. From *World Trade since 1431: Geography, Technology, and Capitalism* by Peter J. Hugill. © 1993. Reprinted with the permission of The Johns Hopkins University Press.

Glossary of Key Terms

This glossary of key terms contains definitions of words and ideas that are central to your understanding of the material covered in this textbook. Each term in the glossary is in **boldface** in the text when it is first defined. We have also included the page number on which the full discussion of the term appears so that you can easily locate the complete explanation to strengthen your historical vocabulary.

For words not defined here, two additional resources may be useful: the index, which will direct you to many more topics discussed in the text, and a good dictionary.

Abbasids (296): The caliphal dynasty that came to power in 750. The Abbasids built their capital at Baghdad, where they exercised considerable power over the entire Islamic world until the late ninth century.

absolutism (524): A system of government in which the ruler claimed sole and uncontestable power.

agora (61): The central market square of a Greek city-state; a popular place to gather for conversation.

agricultural revolution (578): Increasingly aggressive attitudes toward investment in and management of land that increased production of food in the 1700s; this revolution developed first in England and then spread to the continent.

Anabaptists (479): Sixteenth-century religious dissenters who believed that humans have free will and that people must knowingly select the Christian faith through rebaptism as adults. They advocated radical separation from society; though originally pacifist, some chose violent paths to religious renewal.

Anglo-Saxon England (286): England *after* the invasions of the Angles and Saxons (which began in the 440s) and *before* the Norman conquest in 1066.

apocalypticism (32): A religious belief about the end of the world; literally, "uncovering the future."

apostate (223): Literally, "renegade from the faith"; the emperor Julian (r. 361–363), who rejected Christianity and tried to restore traditional religion as the state religion, was given the nickname "the Apostate."

apostolic succession (201): The principle by which Christian bishops traced their authority back to Jesus' apostles.

Arianism (227): The Christian doctrine named after Arius, who argued that Jesus was "begotten" by God and did not have an identical nature with his Father.

asceticism (231): The practice of self-denial of pleasure (from the Greek *askesis,* "training"), as in the lives of monks; a doctrine for Christians emphasized by Augustine.

Atlantic system (568): The triangular pattern of trade established in the 1700s that bound together western Europe, Africa, and the Americas. Europeans sold slaves from western Africa and bought commodities such as coffee and sugar that were produced by the new colonial plantations in North and South America and the Caribbean.

auctoritas (175): Literally, "moral authority"; the authority derived from respect on which the Roman princeps' power rested.

Augustus (174): The title meaning "divinely favored" that Rome's Senate granted Octavian and that became shorthand for "Roman imperial ruler."

auto da fé (447): Literally, "demonstration of faith"; the ritual of public confession that was one of the punishments given to heretics by the Inquisition in the fifteenth century.

ban (326): The rights to collect taxes, hear court cases, levy fines, and muster men for defense. It was largely understood as a complex of royal rights, but around 1000, local rulers as well as kings began exercising the ban as well.

baroque (510): An artistic style of the seventeenth century that featured curves, exaggerated lighting, intense emotions, release from restraint, and even a kind of artistic sensationalism; like mannerism, it departed from the Renaissance emphasis on harmonious design, unity, and clarity.

buccaneers (575): Pirates of the Caribbean who governed themselves and preyed on international shipping.

bureaucracy (529): A network of state officials carrying out orders according to a regular and routine line of authority.

Byzantine Empire (218): Historians' name for the eastern Roman Empire from about 500 to 1453, derived from Byzantium, the original name of Constantinople.

castellan (326): A person who controlled a castle. After around 1000, these castles were the seats of local power in France.

chivalry (369): The proper, ideal comportment of a knight, who was constrained by a code of refinement, fair play, and piety.

Christ (196): Greek for "anointed one" (the corresponding English word is *Messiah*); in apocalyptic religious thinking, the agent of God sent to conquer the forces of evil.

city-state (9): A state consisting of an urban center exercising political and economic control over the countryside around it.

civilization (5): A way of life that includes political states based on cities with dense populations, large buildings constructed for communal activities, diverse economies, a sense of local identity, and some knowledge of writing.

classicism (558): A style of painting and architecture that reflected the ideals of the art of antiquity; in classicism, geometric shapes, order, and harmony of lines took precedence over the sensuous, exuberant, and emotional forms of the baroque.

Colosseum (187): Rome's giant amphitheater for gladiatorial shows and other spectacles.

commercial revolution (340): The economic transformation of Europe, especially western Europe, from rural to urban and from gift-based to cash-based.

commune (345): Sworn associations of citizens who formed a legal corporate body. Communes were the normal institution of self-government in many medieval towns.

constitutionalism (524): A system of government in which rulers had to share power with parliaments made up of elected representatives.

consumer revolution (577): The rapid increase in consumption of new staples produced in the Atlantic system as well as of other items of daily life, such as mirrors, that were previously unavailable or beyond the reach of ordinary people.

conversos (447): Jews in the Iberian peninsula who converted to Christianity in the fifteenth century.

cuneiform (11): The earliest form of writing, invented in Mesopotamia and formed with wedge-shaped characters.

curials (220): The social elite in the Roman Empire's towns who were responsible for collecting taxes for the imperial government and paying for any shortfalls themselves.

debasement of coinage (206): Putting less silver in a coin without changing its face value; practiced during the third-century crisis in Rome, which contributed to inflation.

Delian League (57): The naval alliance headed by Athens after the Persian Wars, and the basis of Athenian empire.

dominate (215): Roman rule from Diocletian (r. 284–305) onward; a blatantly authoritarian style of rule; derived from *dominus* ("master"; "lord") and contrasted with principate (172).

dualism (96): The concept that spiritual being and physical being are separate.

Edict of Milan (221): Constantine and Licinius's proclamation of religious toleration that also expressed their favoring of Christianity.

empire (5): A political unit in which one or more formerly independent territories or peoples are ruled by a single sovereign power.

Enlightenment (600): The eighteenth-century intellectual movement whose proponents believed that human beings could apply a critical, reasoning spirit to every problem. Based on a popularization of scientific discoveries, the movement often challenged religious and secular authorities.

Epicureanism (116): The philosophy initiated by Epicurus of Athens to help people achieve pleasure (meaning an "absence of disturbance") in their lives.

epigrams (113): Short poems covering a variety of themes, especially love, and a favorite genre of Hellenistic women poets.

fealty (325): The promise of faithfulness that a vassal made to his lord.

First Triumvirate (164): The coalition formed in 60 B.C.E. by Gnaeus Pompey, Licinius Crassus, and Julius Caesar (the word *triumvirate* means "a group of three").

flagellants (446): A group of Christians who whipped themselves publicly as a form of penance during the fourteenth century.

friars (379): "Brothers" of the mendicant orders, such as the Franciscans and Dominicans.

Fronde (525): A series of revolts in France, 1648–1653, that challenged the authority of young Louis XIV and his minister Mazarin.

gift economy (281): System of give-and-take that determined most seventh- and eighth-century economic transactions; kings and other powerful people amassed large treasuries and foodstuffs that they distributed at will to mark their power, boost their prestige, and demonstrate their generosity.

Glorious Revolution (547): The events when the English Parliament deposed King James II in 1688 and replaced him with William, prince of Orange, and James's daughter Mary.

Golden Horde (397): The name for the Mongol Empire in Russia.

Gothic (416): A style of architecture characterized by pointed arches, ribbed vaults, and large stained-glass windows.

Great Persecution (221): The violent program initiated by Diocletian in 303 to make Christians convert to traditional religion or risk confiscation of their property and even death.

Great Schism (348, 442): The term *Great Schism* refers to two different periods in the history of the Christian church. The first, in 1054, refers to the separation of the Latin Catholic church and the Greek Orthodox church; the second, to the period from 1378 to 1417, when the church had two separate popes, one in Rome and one in Avignon, France.

Gregorian reform (349): The movement for church reform—including clerical celibacy and an end to lay investiture—associated with Pope Gregory VII.

guilds (344): Religious, economic, and trade associations. They regulated, protected, and policed their membership, setting up standards for professional practices.

heliocentrism (514): The view articulated by Polish clergyman Nicolaus Copernicus that the earth and planets revolve around the sun; Galileo Galilei was condemned by the Catholic church for supporting this view.

Hellenistic (92): An adjective meaning "Greek-like" that is today used as a chronological term for the period 323–30 B.C.E.

hierarchy (4): Social system that ranks certain people as more important and more dominant than others; the earliest evidence of social differentiation comes from the Paleolithic period.

hubris (81): The Greek term for excessive arrogance, especially when an overconfident human being goes against the will of the gods.

Huguenots (489): The name given to Calvinists in France after 1560; its linguistic origin remains uncertain.

humanism (450): A literary and intellectual movement that arose in the early fifteenth century to valorize the writings of Greco-Roman antiquity; it was so named because its practitioners studied and supported the liberal arts, or humanities.

humanitas (154): Cicero's ideal of "humaneness," meaning generous and honest treatment of others based on natural law.

iconoclasm (267): Literally, "icon breaking"; the destruction of icons, or images of holy people (e.g., Christ, Mary, the saints). Byzantine emperors banned icons from 726 to 787; a modified ban was revived in 815 and lasted until 843.

indulgences (474): In Roman Catholic doctrine, a remission of sin earned by performing certain religious tasks to avoid purgatory after death; indulgences were in use by the thirteenth century. The Catholic clergy's practice of selling indulgences came under fire during the Reformation.

Inquisition (392): The court of inquiry permanently set up by the church in 1233; its purpose was to ferret out and punish heretics.

Investiture Conflict (350): The conflict between Pope Gregory VII and Henry IV over the right of laymen to appoint bishops and install them in their office.

Koine (120): The "common" or "shared" form of the Greek language that became the international language in the Hellenistic period.

ladder of offices (145): The series of Roman elective government offices from quaestor to consul.

law of universal gravitation (555): Newton's law uniting celestial and terrestrial mechanics held that every body in the universe exerts over every other body an attractive force directly proportional to the product of their masses and inversely proportional to the square of the distance between them.

madrasa (309): A school located within or attached to a mosque.

mannerism (510): A late-sixteenth-century style of painting in which a distorted perspective created bizarre and theatrical effects that contrasted with the precise, harmonious lines of Renaissance painting.

manor (317): A great estate consisting (normally) of arable fields, vineyards, meadows, and woodland, ordinarily owned by a lord (which could as easily be a monastery or a church as a layperson) and cultivated by serfs.

martyr (200): Greek for "witness," designating someone who dies for his or her religious belief.

materialism (116): The philosophical doctrine that only things made of matter truly exist and thus deny the existence of the soul or any nonmaterial phenomena.

mercantilism (529): The doctrine that governments must intervene to increase national wealth by whatever means possible.

Merovingian dynasty (285): The dynasty that ruled as kings of the Franks from about 486 to 751.

mestizos (574): People born to Spanish fathers and native American mothers.

metaphysics (96): Ideas about the ultimate nature of reality beyond the reach of human senses.

metic (72): A foreigner granted a permanent residency permit in a Greek city-state in return for obligations to pay taxes and do military service.

monotheism (22): The belief in only one god, as in Judaism, Christianity, and Islam.

mos maiorum (131): Literally, "the way of the ancestors"; the set of Roman traditional values.

motet (415): A two- or three-part polyphonic song that interweaves vernacular and sacred texts.

mystery cult (66): A set of prayers, hymns, ritual purification, sacrifice, and other forms of worship undertaken to gain divine protection; each cult was connected to a particular divinity and centered on initiation into secret knowledge about the divine and human worlds.

Neoplatonism (204): The spiritual philosophy developed by Plotinus (c. 205–270) that was based on Plato's ideas, and was very influential for Christian intellectuals.

ostracism (59): Athenian democracy's annual procedure to block tyranny by sending a citizen into exile for ten years by a vote of six thousand citizens in the assembly.

parlements (525): High courts in France (the term comes from the French *parler,* "to speak"). Each region had its parlement; the parlements could not propose laws, but they could review laws presented by the king and refuse to register them (the king could also insist on their registration).

patria potestas (134): Literally, "father's power"; the legal right of a father in ancient Rome to own the property of his children and slaves and to control their lives.

patriarchy (10): Social system in which men exert control over political, social, and economic life.

patron-client system (132): The interlocking network of mutual obligations between Roman patrons (social superiors) and clients (social inferiors).

Pax Romana (172): The period of "Roman peace" under the principate in the first and second centuries C.E.

Peace of God (328): A movement begun by bishops in the south of France first to limit the violence done to property and later (with the Truce of God) to limit fighting between warriors.

Pietism (586): A Protestant revivalist movement that emphasized deeply emotional individual religious experience.

plantations (529): Large tracts of land producing staple crops such as sugar, coffee, and tobacco; farmed by slave labor; and owned by a colonial settler who emigrated from western Europe.

plebiscites (144): Laws passed by the Plebeian Assembly in the Roman republic.

polis (38): The Greek term for an independent city-state based on citizenship.

politiques (490): Political advisers during the French Wars of Religion who argued that compromise in matters of religion—limited toleration for the Calvinists—would strengthen the monarchy.

polyphony (415): Music that consists of two or more melodies performed simultaneously.

polytheism (10): The worship of multiple gods.

praetorian guard (175): The group of soldiers stationed in Rome under the emperor's control; first formed by Augustus.

predestination (480): John Calvin's doctrine that God preordained salvation or damnation for each person before creation; those chosen for salvation were considered the "elect."

primogeniture (328): The right to inheritance of the firstborn.

principate (172): The political system invented by Augustus as a disguised monarchy with the *princeps* ("first man") as emperor.

proletarians (144): In the Roman republic, the mass of people so poor that males were not eligible to serve in the army.

Protestants (473): Members of the Christian branch that formed when Martin Luther and his followers broke from the Catholic church in 1517; the name was first used in 1529 in an imperial diet by German princes who protested Emperor Charles V's edict to repress religious dissent.

Puritans (495): Strict Calvinists who opposed all vestiges of Catholic ritual in the Church of England.

radical democracy (59): The ancient Athenian system of democracy, established in the 460s and 450s B.C.E., that extended direct political power and participation in the court system to the mass of adult male citizens.

raison d'état (503): French for "reason of state." The political doctrine, first proposed by Cardinal Richelieu of France, that held that the state's interests should prevail over those of religion; Richelieu, for example, allied with the Lutheran king of Sweden even though he himself was a leading official of the Catholic church.

rationalism (46): The philosophic idea that people must justify their claims by logic and reason.

reconquista (348): The Christian reconquest of Spain.

redistributive economy (10): A system in which state officials control the production and distribution of goods.

rococo (583): A style of painting that emphasized irregularity and asymmetry, as well as movement and curvature, but on a smaller, more intimate scale than the baroque.

Romanesque (374): The term for the art and architecture in western Europe of the period before around 1150, characterized by monumentality and solidity enlivened by sculpture and painting.

Romanization (190): The spread of Roman law and culture in the provinces of the Roman Empire.

Roman republic (140): A system of government based on shared political decision making and the election of male officials by assemblies organized by social hierarchy; the republic lasted from 509 to 287 B.C.E.

ruler cults (121): Cult that involved worship of a Hellenistic ruler as a savior god.

Sassanid Empire (261): The empire of the Sassanid dynasty of Persia, which lasted from 224 until its conquest by Islamic armies from 637 to 651.

scholasticism (411): The body of theological and philosophical thought of the scholastics, the scholars of the medieval universities.

scientific method (516): A combination of experimental observation and mathematical deduction to determine the laws of nature; it became the secular standard of truth and as such challenged the hold of both the churches and popular beliefs.

Seljuk Turks (353): A Sunni Muslim Turkic group whose migration westward, into areas that had been controlled by Byzantium and various local Muslim rulers, set off the First Crusade.

serfs (325): Semi-free peasants. Serfs could not legally leave the land they tilled; they owed labor services and either produce or money to their lord. Yet they were not slaves: they had the right to marry, to keep part of their produce, and to remain on the land.

simony (347): Derived from the name of Simon Magus, a magician in the New Testament who offers St. Peter money to have the power to confer the Holy Spirit (Acts 8:9–24), the term came to mean the giving of gifts or money for church offices.

social contract (553): The doctrine found in the writings of Hobbes and Locke that all political authority derives not from divine right but from an implicit contract between citizens and their rulers.

Socratic method (77): Socrates' method of conversation, in which he asked probing questions to make his listeners examine their most cherished assumptions before drawing conclusions.

Sophists (65): Competitive intellectuals and teachers who offered a new form of education and new philosophical and religious ideas beginning about 450 B.C.E.

Stoicism (116): The most influential Hellenistic philosophy, which taught the goal of living a virtuous life in harmony with nature.

struggle of the orders (143): Turmoil between elite Roman families (patricians) and the rest of Rome's population (plebeians) that centered on social and economic issues and resulted in greater sharing of political power between 509 and 287 B.C.E.

subjectivism (74): The belief, especially associated with the Sophist Protagoras, that there is no absolute reality behind and independent of appearances.

successor kings (106): Alexander's commanders (Antigonus, Seleucus, and Ptolemy) who took over portions of his empire to create personal monarchies after his death.

summa (412): A scholastic treatise. These characteristically took up a topic and explored it exhaustively, resulting in a "summary" of all opinions and their resolution.

symposium (plural: symposia) (71): A drinking party for Greek men with entertainment ranging from philosophical conversation to hired female companions.

tertiaries (410): Laypeople who affiliated themselves with the friars and adopted many of their pious practices while living in the world.

tetrarchy (216): Literally, "rule by four"; devised by Diocletian to put into practice his principle of subdivision of power in ruling the Roman Empire.

tithe (326): A tax, taken by the church, equivalent to one-tenth of the parishioner's annual income.

tsar (439): The Russian imperial title first taken by Muscovite prince Ivan III (r. 1462–1505); also spelled *czar,* from *Caesar.*

Umayyad caliphate (274): The successors of Muhammad who traced their ancestry to Umayyah, a member of Muhammad's tribe. The dynasty lasted from 661 to 750.

ummah (269): The community of believers in Islam.

vassals (324): Free warriors who pledged homage and fealty to a lord, thereby creating a bond that implied mutual obligations, among them to fight for one another.

wergild (244): Under Frankish law, money or goods a murderer had to pay as compensation for his crime; most went to the victim's kin, but the king received about one-third.

Westernization (592): The effort, especially in Peter the Great's Russia, to make society and social customs resemble counterparts in western Europe, especially France, Britain, and the Dutch Republic.

Index

Aachen (A kuhn), 311, 312, 314
Abandonment of children. *See* Infanticide
Abbasid Caliphate (AB a sid) (750–c. 950),
    303–307, 306(*m*), 336–337
  Carolingians and, 296, 309, 317
Abd al-Rahman (caliph; r. 912–961), 306
Abelard, Peter (AH beh lard) (1079–1142), 370,
    372–373, 411–412
Abolitionist movement (antislavery
    movement), 554
Abortion, 265
Abraham (Hebrew patriarch), 31, 250
Absolutism
  in France, 524–533, 537, 540, 546, 568, 587,
    588(*m*), 600–601
  in Germany, 533–535
  in Russia, 533, 537–539
Absolutism (absolute authority), 513, 524–540, 565
  in central and eastern Europe (1648–1699),
    532–540, 535(*m*)
    Austrian Habsburgs and Ottoman Turks,
      533, 535–537
    Brandenburg-Prussia, 532–534
    Poland-Lithuania, 533, 539–540
    Russia, 533, 537–539
    Sweden, 534–535
  Hobbes on, 553–554

  Louis XIV and, 524–533, 568, 587, 589,
    600–601
  in Russia, 592–594
Académie française (French Academy), 526
Academy (Athens), 95–97, 96(*i*), 224
  closing of (530), 255
Accius (c. 170–80 B.C.E.), 138
Achilles, 37
Achilles Tatius, 192
Acropolis (Athens), 58(*i*), 62(*m*), 63(*i*)
Actium, battle of (AK tee uhm) (31 B.C.E.), 173,
    183
Act of Supremacy (1529), 495
Act of Union (United Kingdom; 1707), 589–590
Adam and Eve, 230, 231
Addison, Joseph (1672–1719), 583
Administration (administrative structure). *See
    also* Bureaucracy; Law(s)
  of Alexander the Great, 103, 105
  in ancient Egypt, 20–21
  in Byzantine Empire, 248–249, 250
  under Carolingian emperors, 311–313
  in France
    under Louis IX, 399–401, 400(*m*), 409
    under Philip Augustus (r. 1180–1223),
      398–400

(continued)

in Hellenistic Kingdoms, 108
in Ottoman Empire, 437
papal (curia), 352, 441, 443
in Persian Empire, 28–29
in Roman Empire, 189–190, 216–217
Adrianople, battle of (378), 238
Adultery, 180, 252, 265
Advancement of Learning, The (Bacon), 516
Aediles (EE dilz), 145
Aegean Sea, 33, 33*(m)*, 39*(m)*, 57
Aeneas, 176*(f)*, 183
Aeneid (Virgil), 183, 189
Aeschines (ES kin eez) (c. 397–322 B.C.E.), 105
Aeschylus (ES kil us) (525–456 B.C.E.), 80
Affair of the Placards (1534), 480
Afghanistan, 92, 121
Africa (Africans), 5, 15, 468*(i)*
    Catholic church in, 485–486
    exploration and colonies in, 426, 463, 465,
        465*(m)*, 466, 471, 485–486, 492, 493*(m)*
    missionaries in, 485–486
    slaves and. *See* Slaves and slavery
Afterlife
    in Ancient Greece, 68
    Egyptian belief in, 6, 20, 23, 23*(i)*
Afyeh, 17
Agape, 199*(i)*
Agasse, Guillaume, 393
Agbar (Osrhoëne; r. 179–216), 229*(i)*
Agincourt, battle of (1415), 431, 432*(m)*
Agnosticism, 74
Agora (ag OH ra), 61, 62*(m)*
Agrarian reform, in Rome, 158–159
Agriculture. *See also* Farming; Peasants; Serfs;
        Plantations
    in Byzantine Empire, 265, 299
    in Carolingian period, 317–318
    in early Middle Ages, 280
    Egyptian, 16
    in eighteenth century, 578–581, 579*(f)*
    increased production and, 340–343, 377
    invention of (Neolithic Revolution), 3–4, 6–8
    in post-Carolingian age, 325
    seventeenth-century economic crisis and,
        504–506, 507*(i)*, 508
    three-field system, 318, 325
Agrippa, Marcus (ah GRIP ah), 174*(i)*, 178
Ahura Mazda (ah HOOR uh MAZ duh), 29–30
Aix-la-Chapelle, Treaty of (AYKS la shah PELL)
        (1668), 530
Akhenaten (**Amenhotep IV**) (Egyptian pharaoh;
        fourteenth century B.C.E.), 22
Akkadia (uh KAY dee uh) (Akkadian Empire), 5,
        12–14

Alaric (AHL uhr ihk), 230, 231, 239
Albania (Albanians), 8*n*
Alberti, Leon Battista (1404–1472), 455
Albertus Magnus (c. 1200–1280), 412
Albigensian Crusade (1209–1229), 391–393, 404
Albigensians (al bee JENS ee uhns), 381
Alcibiades (al si BI ah deez) (c. 450–404 B.C.E.), 85
Alcuin (AL kwin) (c. 732–804), 314–315
Alexander III (pope; r. 1159–1181), 367
Alexander III (**the Great**) (Macedonia;
        r. 336–323 B.C.E.), 52, 94, 97, 102–106,
        103*(m)*, 117, 130, 215*(i)*
Alexander IV (pope; r. 1254–1261), 385
Alexander V, (Antipope), 443
Alexander VI (pope; r. 1492–1503), 447, 466
Alexandria (al ek ZAN dree ah) (Egypt), 103–104,
        109, 112, 118, 120, 122–123, 192, 245, 255
Alexei (Russia; r. 1645–1676), 538
Alexiad (Anna Comnena), 359–360
Alexius (claimant to Byzantine throne), 389
Alexius I (Byzantine emperor; r. 1081–1118),
        353*(m)*, 354, 359
Alfonso IX (Castile-León; r. 1188–1230), 408
Alfonso X (Castile-León; r. 1252–1284), 408
Alfred (**the Great**) (Wessex; r. 871–899), 321,
        330*(m)*, 330–331, 331*(i)*
Algebra, 307
Ali (caliph; c. 600–661), 274
Ali al-Hasan (**Alhazen**) (d. 1038), 307–308
Allah, 269
Almohades, 388*(m)*, 390–391
Almoravids, 390
Alphabets. *See also* Writing
    Canaanite, 24, 25, 37
    Cyrillic, 302
    Roman, 142
Alsace (AHL says), 501
Altar of Augustan Peace, 174*(i)*, 184*(i)*
Ambrose (AM broz) (bishop of Milan;
        c. 339–397), 230, 253
American Revolution (War of Independence)
        (1775–1783), 554
Americas, the (New World; Western Hemisphere),
        511. *See also* North America; South
        America; Spain, American colonies of
    Christianity in, 467–470
    English colonies in, 548, 551–552
    European exploration and conquests in
        (sixteenth century), 426, 463, 465*(m)*,
        466–471
    French colonies in. *See also* North America
        Louis XIV and, 530, 551
    slavery in, 606
    Spanish colonies in, 477, 485–486, 551

Amsterdam, 508

Amun-Re, cult of, 22

Anabaptists, 473, 479–480, 480(f), 491

Anatolia (an ah TOL ee ah), 4, 51, 86(m), 88(m), 102, 106, 107(m), 109, 121, 299, 537, 564(m)

   Hittite kingdom in, 15, 22, 24–26

   King's Peace (386 B.C.E.) and, 98

Anatomy, 120, 514–516

Anaxagoras of Clazomenae (an ak SAG or as), 75

Anaximander of Miletus (an ak si MAND er) (c. 610–540 B.C.E.), 46

Andalusia (an da LOOTH yuh) (al-Andalus), 305–307, 306(m), 311, 319(m), 322, 335(m), 348, 367

Angela of Foligno, 411

Angevin kings of England, 362n

Anglican church (Church of England), 495–496, 496(i), 541–543, 590

   in seventeenth century, 544–547

Anglo-Saxon language (Old English), 362

Anglo-Saxons, 240–241, 286(m), 286–288, 321(f), 331

   churchmen, 289, 293, 310, 314

   Norman conquest of England and (1066), 360–362

Angola, 575

Animals. *See also* Hunting

   Aristotle and, 98

   domestication of, 8

   in Egypt, 19

   Livestock raising, in Great Britain, 578

   sacrifice of, 66–67

Anjou, 398(m), 398–399

Anna Comnena (1083–c. 1148), 359–360

Annals (Ennius), 154

Annals (Tacitus), 193

Anne (Great Britain; r. 1702–1714), 589

Anne, grand princess of Kiev, 303

Anne of Austria (r. 1056–1075), 500, 525

Anno (archbishop of Cologne) (r. 1056–1075), 357

Anselm, St. (archbishop of Canterbury; 1033–1109), 362, 377

Anticlericalism, 444–446, 474, 476–478

Antigone (an TIG on ee) (Sophocles), 81

Antigonids, 106

Antigonus (an TIG on uhs) (c. 382–301 B.C.E.), 106, 121

Antioch (AN ti ok) (Syria), 192, 297, 298(m), 355

Antiochus I (an TI ok uhs) (Seleucid king; c. 324–261 B.C.E.), 108

Antiochus IV (Seleucid king; r. 175–164 B.C.E.), 124–125, 196

Anti-Semitism, 540

in eleventh and twelfth centuries, 356–358

in fourteenth and fifteenth centuries, 444(i), 446–448, 471

Antoninus Pius (an to NI nuhs PI uhs) (Roman emperor; r. 138–161), 187

Antony (Christian ascetic) (c. 251–356), 232, 233

Antony, Mark (83–30 B.C.E.), 173

Antwerp, 494, 494(m), 508, 512(i)

Aphrodite (af ro DI tee), 66, 113, 114

Apocalypticism (uh pahk uh LIHP tih sihzuhm), 32, 196, 197

Apollinaris, Sidonius (ap o LOH nahr uhs) (c. 430–479), 239

Apollo, 66, 224(i), 526

   Oracle at Delphi and, 118

Apollonis (Pergamum; r. c. 165 B.C.E.), 111

Apostles, Jesus', 197, 201–202

Apostolic succession (ahp uh STAHL ihk), 201

Apprenticeships, 344, 453

Apuleius (ahp yuh LEE uhs) (c. 125–170), 180, 193, 203

Aqueducts, Roman, 148, 149(i), 177

Aquinas, St. Thomas (ah KWIE nehs) (c. 1225–1274), 411(i), 412–414

Aquitaine (A kwi tayn), 276(m), 398, 398(m), 430, 433(m)

Arabia, in Muhammad's lifetime, 269(m)

Arabic language and literature, 273, 274, 275, 307, 367, 371

Arabic numerals, 308, 333, 593

Arabs. *See also* Islam

   Byzantine Empire and, 259, 260, 262–263, 267, 273, 290, 292

   Roman Empire and, 259

Aragon, 368(i), 388(m), 390–391, 391(m), 396, 459

Aramaeans (ah rah MAY anz), 26

Aramaic language (a rah MAY ic), 26

Arawaks, 467

Arcadius, 218

Archaic Age (Greece; c. 750–500 B.C.E.). *See* Greece, Ancient

Archilochus of Paros (ahr KI lo kuhs) (early seventh century B.C.E.), 46

Archimedes of Syracuse (ar kih MEE deez) (287–212 B.C.E.), 118

Architecture. *See also* Building(s); Housing; Palaces; Pyramids, in ancient Egypt; Temples

   ancient, 4, 8, 22, 27, 34, 35

   Athenian, 52, 61–65, 62(m), 63(i), 64(f)

      column styles, 63, 64(f)

   Gothic, 414(i), 415–421, 417(i)

   Renaissance (fifteenth century), 455–456

   Roman, 129(i), 192(i)

Areopagitica (Milton), 557
Areopagus Council (ay ree O pah guhs), 59
Ares, 45*(i)*, 66
Aretê (ar e TAY) (excellence), 36–37, 108
Argos, 98
Arianism, 228, 242, 288–290
Aristarchus (ar is TAHRK uhs)
     (Socrates' friend), 93
Aristarchus of Samos (third century B.C.E.),
     118–119
Aristides (ar is TI deez) (c. 525–465 B.C.E.),
     56, 60–61
Aristocracy (nobility). *See also* Hierarchy;
     Upper classes
     Austrian Habsburgs and, 535–537
     in Brandenburg-Prussia, 533
     Carolingian, 310, 313, 315, 316–317, 317
     in France, 332, 399
         Louis XIV and, 524–528
     in Germany, 333
     as government, 513
     manners and (seventeenth century), 559–562
     Merovingian, 278, 280–285, 310
     in Poland, 539–540
     post-Carolingian, 323–328
     Roman, 145
     in Russia, 539, 592–594, 593*(i)*
     in Sweden, 534
     in twelfth century, 360, 362, 367–369
Aristophanes (ar i STOF ah neez)
     (c. 455–385 B.C.E.), 77, 82, 83*(i)*
Aristotelian philosophy, in the Middle Ages,
     412–414
Aristotle (AR is taw tuhl) (384–322 B.C.E.), 93,
     97–98, 105, 255
     on the city-state, 40, 41
     in Middle Ages, 307, 360, 371, 412–414
     on slaves, 41
     teachings of, 514–516, 604
Arius (uh RIH uhs) (c. 260–336), 228
Arles (France), 276*(m)*, 278
     amphitheater at, 277*(i)*
Armed forces. *See also* War; Warriors; Weapons
     and military technology
     Abbasid, 305
     in ancient Greece, 40–41, 43
     in Byzantine Empire, 265, 297
     eighteenth-century, 598
     English, 534*(f)*, 541, 543
     French, 530–532, 605*(m)*
     in Hellenistic kingdoms, 108
     Macedonian, 101
     in Peloponnesian War (431–404 B.C.E.), 84*(f)*
     Prussian, 595–596

Roman Empire, 219, 220
     under Augustus, 175
     Christianity and, 225
     economic factors, 205–206
     in Golden Age (96–180 C.E.), 189
Roman Republic, 142, 156
     first client armies, 160–161, 162, 165
Russian, 534*(f)*, 538, 592, 595*(m)*
Sassanid, 261–262
     seventeenth-century, 533–537, 534*(f)*, 565
     Thirty Years' War and, 501, 503, 520, 541
Arnolfo di Cambio (d. 1302), 404*(i)*
Arsinoe II (ahr SI no ee) (c. 316–270 B.C.E.),
     110, 111*(i)*
Art and artists. *See also* Painting(s); Sculpture
     in ancient Greece, 37, 45
     Carolingian renaissance, 309, 314*(i)*, 314–315
     Dutch, 548–550, 550*(i)*
     Egyptian, 21
     Flemish school of, 454–456, 456*(i)*
     in Golden Age Athens, 52, 65
     Hellenistic, 112–115
     under Louis XIV, 526–527
     Paleolithic and Neolithic, 6, 6*(i)*, 8
     in Renaissance (fifteenth century),
         452–457, 471
     Roman, 155–156
     in seventeenth century, 556–559
Artemia, 285
Artemis (AR tuh mihs), 66
Artemisia (ar tuh MIHZH ee uh), 55–56
Arthur, King, legend of, 369, 414
Artisans, 344, 382
Art of Love (Ovid), 183
Art of Measurable Song (Franco of
     Cologne), 415
Asceticism, Christian, 232–234
     Augustine's view of, 231
Asclepius (uh SKLEE pee uhs), 121, 122, 137
Ashoka (ah SOK ah) (Afghanistan;
     r. c. 268–232 B.C.E.), 121
Ashurbanipal (a shur BA nuh pal) (Neo-Assyria;
     r. 680–626 B.C.E.), 27
Asia
     Alexander the Great's conquests in, 103, 103*(m)*
     trade and, 439, 463, 466, 574
Asia Minor, Romans and (first century B.C.E.),
     137, 151, 152, 161, 162, 201*(m)*
Aspasia (ah SPAY zhuh), 72
Assemblies, Roman, 144, 161
Assembly of the Land (Russia; 1649), 538
Assyria (uh SIHR ee uh) (Assyrians), 13–14
     Neo-Assyrian Empire (c. 900–650 B.C.E.),
         26*(m)*, 26–27

Astarte, 142

Astell, Mary (1666–1731), 604

Astrolabes (AHS truh laybs), 308

Astrology, 204(i)
  in Hellenistic period, 121
  in Mesopotamia, 15

Astronomy, 15, 514–515, 554–555, 600(i), 601
  Babylonian, 46
  Chaldean (Neo-Babylonian), 27–28
  in Hellenistic period, 118–119, 119(i), 121

Asturlabi, al-, 308

Aten, cult of, 22

Athaulf (Visigoth king; r. 410–415), 244

Atheists, 601

Athena, 62–65, 66, 67, 137

Athens. *See also* Greece, ancient
  alliances in, 56–58
  democracy in, 44, 52, 54, 57, 59–61, 73–75, 85,
    86–87, 93, 97, 98
  disunity of Greece after Peloponnesian War
    and, 93–95
  economy of, 44, 58
  Golden Age and Classical period
    (c. 500–323 B.C.E.)
    decline of Classical Greece
      (c. 400–350 B.C.E.), 93–99
    democracy, 73–75, 85, 86–87, 97, 98
    education and intellectual innovation, 52,
      73–78
    end of the Golden Age (431–404 B.C.E.),
      83–87
    establishment of the Athenian Empire
      (479–c. 460 B.C.E.), 56–59
    historical writing, 78
    medicine, 78
    Peloponnesian War (431–404 B.C.E.),
      84–86, 93
    Persian wars (499–479 B.C.E.), 52, 53(m),
      54–56
    radical democracy and Pericles' leadership
      (461–445 B.C.E.), 59–61
    religion, 66–68
    Socrates, 75–78
    sophists, 74–75
    Thirty Tyrants period (404–403 B.C.E.),
      86–87, 93, 95
    tragic drama and comedy, 79–83, 80(i), 83(i)
    urban architecture and art, 61–65, 62(m),
      63(i), 64(f)
    women, 43, 65, 68–72, 77, 82–83, 93
  Philip II of Macedonia and, 99–101
  Sparta and, 51

Atlantic system, 507–508, 568–577, 570(m),
  578, 606

slave trade and, 552, 568–575
world trade and settlement and, 552, 574–577

Atomic theory of matter, 75, 116, 154

Attalid kingdom, 107, 107(m), 159

Attalus I (Pergamum; r. 241–197 B.C.E.), 115(i)

Attalus III (Attalid king; d. 133 B.C.E.), 152

Attila (AT i lah) (Hun leader; r. c. 440–453), 238

Augustine (missionary; archbishop of
  Canterbury) (r. 601–604), 286

Augustine, St. (bishop of Hippo; 354–430), 225,
  230–232, 255, 286, 287, 290, 311, 330

Augustinian order, 476

Augustinus (Jansen) (609 B.C.E.), 528

Augustus (Octavian) (aw GUHS tuhs) (Roman
  emperor; 63 B.C.E.–14 C.E.), 110, 129 (i),
  168(m), 172–177, 184(i), 188(m), 196, 203,
  209(m), 223
  arts and literature under, 182–184
  life in Rome under, 177–182
  principate and, 172–177, 184–185
  public expenditures under, 175

Aurelian (aw REE lee an) (Roman emperor;
  r. 270–275), 208, 209(m)

Austrasia (aw STRAY zhuh), 276(m), 285,
  310, 311

Austrian Empire (to 1867), 395, 535(m),
  535–537, 536(i), 558, 564(m).
  See also individual emperors
  conquest of Hungary (1657–1730), 596(m),
    596–597
  Habsburgs and, 477, 493(m), 501, 502(m),
    519(m), 605(m)
  Ottoman Empire and (eighteenth century), 596

Auto da fé, 447

Avars, 261, 261(m), 262, 263, 311

Avicenna (Ibn Sina) (980–1037), 308

Avignon papacy (ah vee NYON) ("Babylonian
  Captivity"; 1309–1378), 405–406, 440–443,
  442(m), 450

Aztecs, 469–470

Babylon (Babylonia), 24, 27, 28, 105, 109. *See also*
  Neo-Babylonian Empire
  Hammurabi's code, 13–15

"Babylonian Captivity." *See* Avignon papacy

Bach, Johann Sebastian (1685–1750), 567,
  577, 585

Bacon, Sir Francis (1561–1626), 516

Bactria, 103, 107

Badr, battle of (624), 269(m), 271

Baghdad, 353, 396
  as Abbasid capital, 296, 304, 306(m),
    307, 336

Bahamas, 467

Balance of power
    doctrine of, 597
    in eastern Europe (eighteenth century),
      594–597
Baldwin of Flanders (Latin emperor of
    Constantinople; r. 1204–1205), 390
Balkans, the, 7*n*, 298*(m)*, 487*(m)*, 564*(m)*
    c. 850–950, 302*(m)*
    Byzantine Empire and, 260, 262, 263, 359
    Ottomans and, 436*(m)*, 436–437, 537
Ball, John, 435
Balthild (BALT hild) (Frankish queen;
    d. c. 680), 284*(i)*
Baltic region, 534, 587, 591, 594, 595*(m)*
    Hanseatic League in, 406–407
    Northern Crusades in, 386, 387, 388*(m)*
Banks and bankers, 439–440, 457, 458
    Amsterdam, 548
    England, 591
    France, 589
    seventeenth-century, 505, 548
    sixteenth-century, 489
Baptists, 543
Barbados, 551, 574
Barcelona, 500
Baroque style (ba ROWK), 510–511, 511*(i)*,
    512*(i)*, 537, 557*(i)*, 557–558, 558*(i)*,
    583–584
Basil I (Byzantine emperor; r. 867–886), 299
Basil II (Byzantine emperor; r. 976–1025),
    302, 303
Basil (the Great) of Caesarea (c. 330–379), 234
Basset, Ralph, 364*(i)*
Bassi, Laura (1711–1778), 600*(i)*
Bathing, 599
Baths, public, in Rome, 178, 207
Bavaria, 501
Bayeux (by YOO) "tapestry," 361*(i)*
Bayle, Pierre (1647–1706), 561, 601
Becket, Thomas (1118–1170), 365, 382
Beckford, William (1760–1844), 572
Bede (673–735), 288, 314
Bedouins (BEHD oo ihnz), 268, 271, 282,
    292, 468
Beguines (be GEENS), 379, 410
Behn, Aphra (1640–1689), 561
Belarus, 438
Belgium, 277, 316. *See also* Austrian Netherlands
Benedict XIII (pope; r. 1394–1417), 443
Benedict Biscop (c. 630–690), 287, 288, 314
Benedictine rule, 234, 310, 315–316, 373, 376,
    376*(i)*, 379
Benedict of Aniane (an YAHN) (c. 750–821), 315
Benedict of Nursia (c. 480–553), 234

Benefices, 428, 440–441, 445
Benevento, Duchy of, 289, 289*(m)*, 290–291
Benignus, St., 280
Berbers, 305, 390
Berlin, 577, 581
Bern, 407, 407*(m)*
Bernard, St. (c. 1090–1153), 362, 371*(i)*, 375,
    377, 382, 387
Bernini, Gian Lorenzo (1598–1680), 557, 557*(i)*
Bes, 23
Bible. *See also* New Testament; Old Testament; Torah
    English-language, 481, 496
    the Enlightenment and, 601
    Latin Vulgate, 314, 481
    vernacular translations of, 481, 483
Bill of Rights (England; 1689), 547
Bishops, 328, 332, 333, 345–346
    in Byzantine Empire, 266
    early Christian church and, 201–202,
      226–227
    in early Middle Ages, 282–283, 285, 286,
      288, 290
    German, 333
    monasteries and, 235
    Nestorian, 228
    reforms of 1050–1150 and, 346–352, 357
Black Death. *See* Plague
"Blood libel," 358
Boccaccio, Giovanni (bo KAH cho, jo VAH nee)
    (1313–1375), 428, 448–449, 450
Bodin, Jean (1530–1596), 512–513, 517
Boethius, 242
Bohemia (boh HEE mee uh) (Bohemians),
    333–334, 437, 469*(m)*
    religious dissent and popular revolt in
      (fifteenth century), 443, 445–446
    in seventeenth century, 535–536
    religious conflicts, 498–499
    Thirty Years' War and, 498–499, 501,
      502, 502*(m)*
Boleslaw the Brave (Poland; r. 992–1025),
    334, 336
Boleyn, Anne (boh LIHN) (1507–1536), 495
Bologna (Italy), law education at, 370–372, 402
Bonaparte, Napoleon. *See* Napoleon Bonaparte
Boniface (bishop) (BAHN i fuhs) (680–754), 310
Boniface VIII (pope; r. 1294–1303), 401, 404*(i)*,
    404–405, 407, 422
Boniface IX (pope; r. 1389–1404), 436
Book of Common Prayer, 542, 544, 545
Book of Psalms, 265
Book of the City of Ladies, The (Christine de
    Pisan), 449
Book of the Dead (Egypt), 23

Books and publishing industry.
  See also Literature
  in Augustan Rome, 183
  in Byzantine Empire, 253–254
  in eighteenth century, 583, 585
  in fifteenth century, 451–452
Bora, Katharina von (1499–1550), 484
Bosnia-Herzegovina, 7*n*
Bossuet, Bishop Jacques-Benigne (baws WAY)
  (1627–1704), 528, 561, 601–602
Boston (Massachusetts), 508
Boucher, François (boo SHAY, frahn SWAH)
  (1703–1770), 584
Bourbon dynasty (France), 489–490, 588*(m)*
Bourgeoisie. *See* Middle class(es)
Bouvines, battle of (boo VEEN) (1214), 398*(m)*,
  399, 401
Brahe, Tycho (bra) (1546–1601), 514–515
Brandenburg-Prussia, 501, 502*(m)*, 529, 532–534,
  535*(m)*, 539, 555, 564*(m)*
Brasidas (BRA sid as) (d. 422), 86*(m)*
Brazil, 466, 468, 470, 486
  slavery and slave trade in, 569, 570*(m)*, 571*(f)*,
  572–575
Britain (British Isles). *See also* England;
  Great Britain
  Anglo-Saxon invasion of, 240
  early Middle Ages, 286–288
  Viking invasions (eighth to tenth centuries),
  319*(m)*, 320–321, 330
British East India Company, 574, 577
Brittany, 362, 363*(m)*, 398, 398*(m)*, 400*(m)*
Bronze Age, 5, 12
Brothers of St. Francis, 379–380, 383
Bruges (broozh), 439
Brunelleschi, Filippo (1377–1446), 456
Bruno of Cologne (c. 1030–1101), 339–340, 355,
  375, 379, 381, 383
Brussels, 456*(i)*
Brutus, Lucius Junius (sixth century B.C.E.), 143, 167
Brutus, Marcus Junius (85–42 B.C.E.), 167
Bubonic plague. *See* Plague
Buccaneers, 575
Building(s) (construction). *See also* Architecture;
  Housing
  in twelfth century, 374, 375*(i)*, 376*(i)*, 378*(i)*
Bulgaria (Bulgarians; Bulgars), 8*n*, 261, 261*(m)*,
  262, 296–297, 298*(m)*, 301–303, 302*(m)*,
  322, 436
Bureaucracy. *See also* Administration
  under Louis XIV, 529–530, 532
  in Russia, 537–538
  Thirty Years' War and, 503
Burgundofara, 283–284

Burgundy (Burgundians), 276*(m)*, 285, 431–433,
  433*(m)*, 435, 437, 456, 459
Burgundy, duke of, 425*(i)*, 431–433, 433*(m)*
Burial practices
  Egyptian, 20, 23*(i)*, 23–24
  Mesopotamian, 10
  Paleolithic (hunter-gatherer societies), 6
  Roman, 137, 181, 182*(i)*
Business and commerce, 13–14. *See also* Trade
  revolution in (eleventh and twelfth centuries)
  business arrangements, 343–344
  centers of commerce, 340–346
  self-government of towns, 345–346
  trade routes, 341*(m)*
Byblos (BIHB luhs), 24
Byzantine Empire (Byzantium), 214, 218, 243*(m)*,
  245–255, 272*(m)*. *See also specific emperors*
  c. 600, 254*(m)*, 261*(m)*, 292–293
  c. 700, 263(m)
  c. 750, 336–337
  Christianity and Christians in, 245–246, 248
    classical literature and, 245, 251, 265
    icons and iconoclasm, 266*(i)*, 266–267,
    290–291, 293, 299, 315
    ninth and tenth centuries, 301–303
  classical literature and education in, 252–255,
    260, 265, 266
  Islam (Muslims) and, 268, 275, 296–297
  Leo IX and, 347–348
  Magyars and, 319*(m)*, 322
  Ottomans and, 436*(m)*, 436–437
  pope and, 290–291, 310–311, 312*(m)*
  renewed strength and influence of (750–1050),
    296–303
    expansion of (860–1025), 297–303, 298*(m)*
    Macedonian renaissance (c. 870–c. 1025),
    297, 299–300, 301*(i)*, 307, 314*(i)*, 315
    new states under the influence of Byzantium,
    301–303
  Roman identity in, 246, 247
  Sassanid Persia and, 250, 261*(m)*,
    261–262, 262*(i)*, 269*(m)*, 272*(m)*, 273,
    274*(i)*, 296–297
  society in, 245–249, 248
  urban decline in, 263–265
  wars against invaders (c. 570–750), 261–263, 359

Cabot, John (c. 1450–1499?), 464*(m)*, 470
Cabral, Pedro Alvares (kuh BRAL) (1467–1520),
  466, 470
Caesar, Julius (SEE zahr, JOOL yuhs)
  (100–44 B.C.E.), 153*(m)*, 172, 173, 176*(f)*
  coin portrait of, 165*(i)*
  downfall of republic and, 159, 163–167, 168*(m)*

Calendar, 593*n*
  Egyptian, 22
  Islamic, 271
  Muslim, 308*(i)*
  Roman, 167
  Russian, 593
Caligula (ca LIG yoo lah) (Roman emperor;
    r. 37–41 C.E.), 185–186
Caliphs, 268, 272*(m)*, 273–275, 293, 322. *See also
    specific caliphs*
  Abbasids and, 296, 303–307
Calvin, John (1509–1564), 479–481, 480*(f)*
Calvinism (Calvinists), 519*(m)*. *See also* Puritans
  in Brandenburg-Prussia, 533
  in England, 481, 486, 542
  in France (Huguenots), 480–481, 489–491,
    490*(m)*, 528–529
  in Netherlands (Dutch Republic), 481, 493–494,
    494*(m)*, 551
  Peace of Augsburg (1555) and, 491
  Scottish, 481, 497
  Thirty Years' War and, 498–499, 501–502
Cambyses (kam BI seez) (Persia; r. 529–522 B.C.E.),
    55*(m)*
Canaanite alphabet, 24, 25, 37
Canada, 470, 509
  French, 530, 574, 588*(m)*
Cannae (KAN eye), battle of (216 B.C.E.), 150
Canon law, 347, 348, 352, 371, 403–404, 443, 483
Canon of Medicine (Avicenna), 308
Canterbury, 286, 288
Canterbury Tales (Chaucer), 449
Cape of Good Hope, 465, 570*(m)*, 575
Capetian kings (cap EE shuhn), 332, 392, 398–401
Capitals, Greek, 64*(f)*
Caracalla (ca rah KAH lah) (Roman emperor;
    r. 211–217), 207–208
Carchemish (KAR kuh mihsh), battle of
    (605 B.C.E.), 27
Cardinals, 441–443
Caribbean colonies
  French. *See* Americas, the, French colonies in
  slavery and slave trade in, 568, 569–575,
    570*(m)*, 571*(f)*, 573*(i)*
Caribbean region, 464*(m)*, 467, 469,
    508–509, 551
Caribs, 467, 509, 575
Caroline minuscule, 315
Carolingian Empire (Carolingians) (kar oh LIN
    jee un), 285, 295, 296, 309–315, 312*(m)*,
    332, 343
  economy, 317–318
  invasions by Vikings, Muslims, and Magyars,
    309, 318–323, 319*(m)*

Carolingian renaissance (c. 790–c. 900), 309,
    314*(i)*, 314–315
Carriera, Rosalba (1675–1757), 584*(i)*
Carthage, 55, 88, 142, 148–152, 166, 241*(i)*
Carthusian order (kar THOO zhuhn), 339, 339*(i)*,
    355, 375, 383
Cartier, Jacques (1491–1557), 470
Casimir III (Poland; r. 1333–1370), 437–438
Cassiodorus (cas i o DOH ruhs) (c. 490–585),
    242, 245
Cassius Dio (c. 164–230), 174
Castellans (CAS tel ens), 326–327, 332, 345,
    357, 392
Castiglione, Baldassare (1478–1529), 504
Castile (kas TEEL), 368*(i)*, 388*(m)*, 390–391,
    391*(m)*, 442, 456*(i)*
Castile-León (kas TEEL lay ON), 391*(m)*,
    394*(m)*, 408
Castles, 323, 326–327, 328, 332, 363, 366, 387. *See
    also* Castellans
Castor and Pollux, Temple of (Rome), 129*(i)*
Catacombs, 199*(i)*
Catalonia (Catalans), 500
Cateau-Cambrésis (kah TO kahm bray SEE),
    peace treaty of (1559), 488
Catena, Vincenzo, 473*(i)*
Cathars, 381, 383, 392
Catherine of Alexandria (saint; fourth
    century C.E. ?), 233*(i)*
Catherine of Aragon (d. 1536), 495
Catherine de Medicis (duh MEHD ih chee)
    (1519–1589), 489–490
Catherine of Siena (see YEN ah) (1347–1380), 443
Catholic church. *See* Roman Catholic church
Catholic League (France), 490
Cato, Marcus Porcius (KAY toh) (234–149 B.C.E.),
    135, 150, 154, 166
Catullus (kuh TUL uhs) (c. 84–54 B.C.E.), 154
Cavaliers, 542–543
Cavendish, Margaret, 556
Celibacy, clerical, 202, 232, 283, 290, 347, 351–352,
    372, 382
Celts (kelts), in Britain, 240
Censors, 145
Censuses, 151*(f)*, 459
Centuriate Assembly, 144
Cervantes, Miguel de (suhr VAHN teez)
    (1547–1616), 497, 585
Ceuta (SYOO tuh), 465
Chaeronea (ki ron AY ah), battle of (338 B.C.E.), 101
Chalcedon, Council of (451), 229, 252
Chaldeans (kal DEE ans), 27–28
Chandragupta (India; r. 323–299 B.C.E.), 107
Chariots, 24, 26, 120, 181, 246

Charities (charitable organizations), 505–506,
    562–564, 598
Chariton (second century C.E.), 192
Charlemagne (SHAR luh mayn) (Frankish king;
    r. 768–814), 295, 296, 304, 311–315,
    311–317, 312(m), 365
    successors of (814–911), 315–317, 332
Charles I (England; r. 1625–1649), 541–545
Charles I (the Bald) (Frankish king and
    Carolingian emperor; r. 843–877), 295,
    296, 312(m), 316
Charles II (England; r. 1660–1685), 545–546, 552,
    553–554
Charles II (Spain; r. 1665–1700), 587
Charles IV (Holy Roman emperor; r. 1347–1378),
    444–445, 446
Charles V (France; r. 1364–1380), 442–443,
    487–489
Charles V (Holy Roman emperor and Spain as
    Charles I; r. 1520–1558), 477–478, 480(f),
    487–489, 491–492, 492, 492(i), 495
Charles VII (France; r. 1422–1461), 431, 433, 435
Charles IX (France; r. 1560–1574), 489, 490, 492
Charles XII (Sweden; r. 1697–1718), 594, 595
Charles of Anjou (Naples and Sicily;
    r. 1266–1285), 396
Charles Martel (mayor of palace in Merovingian
    kingdom; 715–741), 310
Charles the Simple (or Straightforward)
    (Carolingian king; r. 893–923), 321
Chartres (SHAHR truh) cathedral, 416, 420
Chartreuse, La (shar TROOZ), 339, 339(i)
Chaucer, Geoffrey (CHAW suhr) (c. 1342–1400),
    448–449, 450
Cheops (KEE ahps) (Egypt; 2590–2567 B.C.E.),
    19–20
Chiefdoms, Germanic, 237
Childbearing
    in Florence (fifteenth century), 460(i), 460–462
    in Golden Age Athens, 68, 71
    in Roman Empire, 194
Childbirth, 68, 506, 599
    in Roman Empire, 194
Child care, in the Renaissance (fifteenth century),
    460–462
Children. *See also* Education; Family; Infanticide;
    Schools
    in Golden Age Athens, 69, 71, 72
    in Hellenistic kingdoms, 110–111
    in Rome, 180, 183, 194–195
    in Sparta, 43–44
China, 4, 245, 304, 427, 451
    Christian missionaries in, 486
    Europeans in, 571(m), 575

Mongol conquest of, 385, 397(m),
    397–398, 463
trade and, 385(i), 397(m), 397–398, 470,
    570(m), 583
travel literature in 1700s and, 603
Chingiz Khan (c. 1162–1227), 385, 396, 397(m)
Chivalry, 369, 401, 430, 435, 449, 497
Chocolate, 568, 577
Chosroes II (koss ROH) (Sassanid king;
    r. 591–628), 262
Chrétien de Troyes (KRAY tyahn duh TRWAH)
    (c. 1150–1190), 369
Christ. *See* Jesus
Christian IV (Denmark; r. 1596–1648), 499
Christian church ("the church"). *See also* Bishops;
    Christianity, Roman Empire and; Roman
    Catholic church
    Carolingian renaissance and, 309, 314(i),
        314–315
    humanism and, 451
    orthodoxy and heresies, 228–229
    reform of (1050–1150), 346–358
        beginnings of, 346–348
        early crusades and crusader states, 352–356
        Gregorian reform and Investiture Conflict
            (1073–1085), 349(m), 349–351,
            366–367, 382
        Jews and, 356–358
        sacraments and, 351, 443–445
Christianity (Christians). *See also* Christian
    church; Monasticism; Protestantism
    in Americas, 467–470, 574–575
    in British Isles, 286–288
    in Byzantine Empire, 245–246, 248
        classical literature and, 252–255, 265
        icons and iconoclasm, 266(i), 266–267,
            290–291, 293, 299, 315
        Kievan Russia, 302–303
        ninth and tenth centuries, 301–303
    classical literature and, 282, 309, 311
    conversion to
        in American colonies, 574–575
        Czechs and Poles, 333
        Magyars, 335
        Russians, 302–303
        Scandinavia, 322
        in the sixteenth century, 484–486
        Vikings, 320–322, 330
    early, 195–205, 214, 225
    Jews and, 195–205
    Hellenistic period and, 92–93
    influences on, 30, 32, 122, 125
    in Ireland, 286–288

(continued)

Islam and, 268, 269, 272, 273–275, 388(m),
  390–391, 391(m), 394
Jews and (twelfth century), 356–358, 380(m), 383
in late third century C.E., 201(m)
poverty and, 562–563
Roman Empire and, 171, 195–205, 222–235
  appeal of religious and social values, 225
  Constantine's conversion, 214, 221
  development as new religion, 199–202
  Jesus and spread of his teachings, 196–198
  Jews and, 224–225
  the military and, 225
  persecution of Christians, 200, 208–210, 221
  polytheism and, 202–204, 221, 222(i),
    222–224, 226(m)
  spread of (300–600), 222–227, 226(m)
  as state religion, 224, 225
science and, 514
in twelfth and thirteenth centuries, 373–383,
  380(m)
women and, 295(i), 604
  early Christianity, 198, 202, 225–226
  monasteries, 234, 280, 283–285, 284(i), 286,
    288, 333
  virginity and sexual renunciation, 232
Christian missionaries
  Arianism and, 228
  in China, 575
  in England, 286–288, 293, 310
  Jesuit, 484–486, 485(i)
  in Scandinavia, 322
  thirteenth-century, 392
Christina (Sweden; r. 1632–1654), 534
Christine de Pisan (pee ZAHN) (1364–c. 1430),
  449(i), 449–450
Chrysippus (kris IP uhs) (c. 280–206 B.C.E.), 116
Church, the. See Christian church
Churches (buildings)
  Byzantine, 245, 263
  Gothic, 386, 414(i), 416–421, 417(i)
  Italian, 329
  Ottonian dynasty and (Germany), 333
  in post-Carolingian age, 325–326
  Romanesque, 374, 375(i), 376, 378(i), 414(i)
Church of England (Anglican church), 495–496,
  496(i), 508, 541–543
  in seventeenth century, 544–547
Church of the Holy Wisdom (Hagia Sophia), 250,
  251(i), 437
Cicero (SIHS uh roh) (106–43 B.C.E.), 135, 136,
  139, 147, 154–155, 182, 253, 278, 450
Circumcision, 198
Cistercians (sih STUR shuhnz), 362, 375–379,
  376(i), 378(i), 383

Cîteaux (see TOH), 375
Cities. See also Towns; Urbanization
  in Byzantine Empire, 260, 263–265, 273,
    281, 292
  in eighteenth century, 577, 578, 581–583,
    598–599, 606
  in Hellenistic kingdoms, 108–109, 118
  in Italy, 323, 329–330, 341, 341(m), 343, 395,
    408. See also Florence; Milan;
    Rome; Venice
  communes and, 345–346, 350, 366–367,
    406, 457
  Mesopotamian, 8–13, 14–15
  of Roman Empire, 292–293
  trade and, 339–340, 342(i), 382
Citizenship
  in ancient Greece, 39–41, 44, 60–61, 70, 72
  Roman, 133(i), 139–140, 148, 159, 166, 189
    under Caracalla, 207–208
    slaves and, 180
    Social War (91–87 B.C.E.), 160
  Stoicism and, 117
City of God (Augustine), 230, 231, 311
City-states
  Canaanite, 24
  conflict within, 51, 52
  Greek (polis), 38–47. See also Athens; Sparta
    Alexander the Great and, 104–105
    citizenship in, 39–44
    disunity after Peloponnesian War, 98–99
    Hellenistic period (323–30 B.C.E.), 92,
      107(m), 108
    Philip II of Macedonia and, 99–101
  Mesopotamian, 8–13, 9
Civilizations, early (to 1000 B.C.E.), 3–25
Civil rights. See Religious tolerance/intolerance
Civil war(s)
  in England
    1139–1153, 362
    1460–1485 (War of the Roses), 435
    1642–1646, 541–545, 542(m), 556
    thirteenth century, 409
  in Germany (1075–1122), 346, 350, 366
  Islamic (seventh and eight centuries), 274,
    304–305
  in Roman Empire
    305–324, 218, 219, 221
    first century C.E., 186
    second and third centuries C.E., 172, 173,
      205–206, 208–210, 209(m), 214
  in Roman Republic (49–45 B.C.E.), 159,
    161–163
Clairvaux (monastery of), 375
Clans, Germanic, 237

Clare, St., 379
Class differences. *See* Hierarchy
Classical literature and learning, 483
  in Byzantine Empire, 252–255, 265, 359–360
  Carolingian renaissance and, 309, 311, 314(*i*),
    314–315
  in England and Ireland, 287–288
  Islam and, 307–309, 371
  Macedonian renaissance (c. 870–c. 1025) and,
    297, 299–300, 301(*i*), 314(*i*)
  in Renaissance (fifteenth century), 425–426,
    448–451, 471
  in sixth century, 282
Classicism, 583
  French, 557–558, 558(*i*)
Claudius (KLAW dee uhs) (Roman emperor;
    r. 41–54 C.E.), 186
Cleisthenes (KLYIS then eez) (c. 508 B.C.E.), 44, 59, 60
Clement VII (pope; r. 1523–1534), 442–443, 495
Cleon (KLEE ahn) (d. 422 B.C.E.), 82
Cleopatra VII (klee o PAT rah) (69–30 B.C.E.), 92,
    110, 124(*m*), 166, 173, 203
Clergy (priests and priestesses). *See also* Bishops;
    Christian missionaries; Papacy
  in American colonies, 574–575
  anti-Semitic persecutions and, 446–448
  celibacy of, 283, 290, 347, 351–352, 372, 382
  Roman, 139, 174(*i*)
  Roman Catholic
    in Bohemia, 445–446
    Fourth Lateran Council and (1215), 389(*i*),
      403–404
    taxation of, 404(*i*), 404–405
Climate (climate change)
  ancient Egypt, 21
  fourteenth century, 426–427
  Neolithic Revolution and, 7
  seventeenth century, 505
Clothar II (Austrasia; r. 613–623), 285
Clothing
  in Byzantine Empire, 247
  in eighteenth century, 582
Clotilda (Frankish queen; d. 545), 242
Clovis (KLOH vis) (Frankish king; r. 485–511),
    242, 244, 288
Cluny, 322
  Benedictine monastery of, 339(*i*), 346–347,
    370, 373
Cnidos, 114
Cnut (k NOOT) (**Canute**) (England, Denmark,
    and Norway; r. 1017–1035), 322, 331
Codex (Byzantine legal code), 251, 254–255
Coffee, 567(*i*), 567–569, 576, 577, 606
Coffeehouses, 567(*i*), 567–568, 577, 583

Coins (coinage)
  Arabic, 274, 274(*i*)
  Carolingian economy and, 317
  debasement of, 206, 207(*f*)
  invention of, 10
  Roman, 165(*i*), 175, 206, 207(*f*), 219
  Viking coin hoards (c. 865–895), 321(*f*)
Colbert, Jean-Baptiste (kohl BEHR)
    (1619–1683), 529–530, 556
Coligny, Gaspard de, 489
Collection in 74 Titles (canon law textbook), 348
Colleges and universities, 422
  sixteenth-century, 483, 484
  thirteenth-century, 370–372, 387, 401,
    409–413
Colloquies (Erasmus), 475
Collot, Jacques (koh LOH, zhahk), 500(*i*)
Cologne (kuh LOHN), 357, 430, 452
Coloni (tenant farmers), 219, 236–237
Colonies (colonialism; colonized peoples). *See also*
    Americas, The; North America, English
    (British) colonies in; North America,
    French colonies in; Spain, American
    colonies of
  in Africa, 465, 465(*m*)
  Alexander the Great and, 103
  competition for (seventeenth century),
    507–509, 568
  consumer society and (eighteenth
    century), 577
  Greek, 38–39
  mercantilism and, 508, 530
  Roman, 148, 159–160, 166, 173
Colosseum (Rome), 187
Columbanus, St. (d. 615), 282–283
Columbus, Christopher (1451–1506), 464(*m*),
    466–467
Comedies
  Athenian, 81–82, 83(*i*)
  Hellenistic, 113–114
  Roman, 153–154, 155(*i*)
Commenda, 343
Commerce. *See* Business and commerce;
    Mercantilism; Trade
Common law, English, 364(*i*)
Communes
  Italian, 345–346, 350, 366–367, 382,
    406, 457
  Swiss, 407, 407(*m*)
Comnena, Anna (1083–c. 1148), 359–360
Comnenian dynasty (Byzantine;
    1081–1185), 359
Compagnia (kohm PAHN yuh), 343, 382
Companions, in Athens, 71–72

Conciliarists, 443, 458
Concordance of Discordant Canons (Decretum)
    (Gratian), 352
Concordat of Worms (1122), 350
Confessions (Augustine), 231
Confraternities, 563
Confucianism, 486
Congregationalism, 542
Constantine (Byzantine emperor; r. 306–337),
    215*(i)*, 215–218, 219, 220, 222, 224*(i)*
    Arianism and, 228
    conversion to Christianity, 214, 221
Constantine VII Porphyrogenitos (Byzantine
    emperor; r. 913–959), 297–298, 299–300,
    300*(i)*, 301*(i)*
Constantine Palaeologus (Byzantine emperor;
    r. 1449–1453), 437
Constantinople, 218, 221, 238, 245, 290, 292, 299,
    353*(m)*, 599
    conquest of (1204), 386–390, 388*(m)*, 422
    cultural renaissance in, 296–297, 300*(i)*,
        301*(i)*, 307
    in eleventh and twelfth centuries, 359–360
    under Justinian, 249–252
    Latin empire of (1204–1261), 390, 394*(m)*
    Ottoman conquest of (1453), 425, 425*(i)*,
        436*(m)*, 436–437, 451
    walls of, 264*(i)*, 275
Constantius II (Roman emperor;
    r. 337–361), 228
Constitutionalism, 514, 524, 565
    in Dutch Republic, 548–552
    in England (Great Britain), 540–547,
        552–554, 590
    civil war of 1642–1646, 540–545, 542*(m)*
    Cromwell and, 543–545, 545*(i)*
    Glorious Revolution of 1688, 545–547
    in Poland-Lithuania, 539–540
Constitutions of Melfi (Frederick II), 395
Consuls, 144, 145, 160, 161, 163, 175
Consumerism (consumer society; consumer
    capitalism), 600, 606
    in eighteenth century, 577, 578
Contado, 343, 346
Contraception, 194
Contracts, 344
Conversations on the Plurality of Worlds (de
    Fontenelle), 600–601
Conversos (Jewish converts to Christianity),
    447–448
Copernicus, Nicolaus (koh PUR nih kuhs)
    (1473–1543), 514–515, 554, 600
Córdoba, 391, 391*(m)*
    emirate (caliphate) of, 306–307

Corinth, 56, 83–84, 98, 152, 166
Corneille, Pierre (cor NAY) (1606–1684), 527,
    532, 561
Corsica, 148, 150
Cortés, Hernán (1485–1547), 469–470
Cortes (KOR tez), Spanish, 408
Cossacks, 538–540
Council of 500 (Athens), 59–61, 73
Council of Chalcedon (451), 229, 252
Council of Clermont (1095), 354
Council of Constance (1414–1418),
    443–444, 446
Council of Fifteen, 409
Council of Lyon (1245), 395
Council of Nicaea (325), 228
Council of Pisa (1409), 443
Council of Reims (1049), 348
Council of Soissons (1121), 373
Council of Trent (1545–1563), 484
Counter-Reformation, 484–486, 498, 507, 510
Counts, 323–328, 332, 398–399
Court culture
    under Louis XIV, 523–528
    twelfth-century, 367–369
Courtly love, 368–369
Court of Star Chamber (England), 542
Court system. *See* Judicial system
Covenant with God, Hebrew, 31–32
Cranmer, Thomas (1489–1556), 495
Crassus, Marcus Licinius (c. 115–53 B.C.E.), 163,
    164, 165
Crécy, battle of (1346), 432*(m)*
Crete, 33–36, 33*(m)*, 35*(i)*, 297, 298*(m)*
Crimea, 427, 427*(m)*
Critias, 95
Croatia (Croats), 7*n*, 301, 302*(m)*, 535, 537
Croesus, 45*(i)*
Cromwell, Oliver (1599–1658), 543–545, 545*(i)*
Cromwell, Thomas (1485–1540), 495
Crusader states, 352–356, 355*(m)*, 380*(m)*,
    388*(m)*, 465
Crusades, 352–356, 354*(i)*, 355*(m)*, 370, 380*(m)*,
    382, 383, 386, 400, 422
    1150–1300, 386–391, 388*(m)*, 389*(i)*
    Albigensian (1209–1229), 391–393
    First (1096–1099), 353*(m)*, 353–355, 357, 359
    Fourth (1202–1204), 387–390, 388*(m)*, 393
    Northern, 387, 388*(m)*
    against Ottomans, 436, 436*(m)*
    Second (1147–1149), 356, 362, 387, 399
    Third (1189–1192), 356, 387, 388*(m)*
Ctesibius of Alexandria (te SIB ee uhs)
    (b. c. 310 B.C.E.), 119
Ctesiphon (TES e fon), 272*(m)*, 273, 304

Cult(s)
in Hellenistic period, 121–123
imperial (emperor worship), 186–187, 190,
199, 201
mystery
Athenian, 66–68
Hellenistic, 121, 122
of relics, 233, 279(i), 279–280, 284(i), 287, 290,
325, 329, 336, 348, 374, 377, 389, 410,
414(i), 416, 477(i), 562, 586
in Roman Empire, 137, 139, 202–204
ruler, 121
Culture(s) (cultural factors). See also Art and
artists; Education; Intellectuals;
Language(s); Literature; Philosophy
borrowing in, 4
court
under Louis XIV, 523–528
twelfth-century, 367–369
in eighteenth century, 578–586
agricultural revolution, 578–581
cities, 578, 581–583
public, 582–586
religious revivals, 586
Hellenistic, 112–125
the arts, 112–115
languages, 120, 121, 123
philosophy, 115–118
religion, 121–125
the sciences, 118–120
popular. See Popular culture
Roman society and, 130–139
education for public life, 136
family, 134–136
in the Golden Age (96–180 c.e.),
189–195
Greek influence on literature and art, 130,
153–156
patron-client system, 132–134
religion, 137–139, 142
Romanization of provinces, 190–195,
191(m), 192, 192(i)
Cuneiform writing (kyu NEE e form), 11–13,
12(i), 13(f)
Curia (papal government), 352, 441, 443
Curials (curiales), 190, 193, 220, 225, 227, 264,
265, 293
Currency. See also Coins
in Roman Empire, 206, 219
Cynicism (philosophy), 117–118
Cyril (Byzantine missionary), 302
Cyrillic alphabet, 302
Cyrus (SY ruhs) (Persia; r. 559–530 b.c.e.), 28,
29(m), 32, 104

Czechs (chehks), 333–334, 445–446, 536
religious conflicts and
fifteenth century, 477
seventeenth century, 498–499

Dacia (DA shee uh), 187
Da Gama, Vasco (dah GAM uh, VAHSH koh)
(1460?–1524), 464(m), 465
Dalmatia (Croatia), 215
Damascus, 245, 259(i), 262, 272(m), 274–275, 296,
304, 357, 396
Damian, Peter (1007?–1072), 348
Damis, 105
Danegeld, 321
Danelaw, 321, 321(m)
Danes. See Vikings
Dante Alighieri (DAHN tay ah lee GYE ree)
(1265–1321), 413–414, 420, 448
Darius I (da RY us) (Persia; r. 522–486 b.c.e.),
28–29, 29(m), 51, 52, 53(m), 54, 262
Darius III (Persia; r. 336–330 b.c.e.), 102,
104(i), 114
Dark Age, in ancient Greece (c. 1000–750 b.c.e.),
25, 33, 36–38
David (Michelangelo), 454, 455(i)
Decameron (Boccaccio), 449
Decius (DEE shus) (Roman emperor;
r. 249–251), 208
Declaration of Indulgence (1673), 546
Decline and Fall of the Roman Empire, The
(Gibbon), 240
Decretum (Concordance of Discordant Canons)
(Gratian), 352
Decurions (curiales), 190, 193
Defender of the Peace, The (Marsilius), 441
Defenestration (Prague; 1618), 498
Defoe, Daniel (1660?–1731), 585
Deir el Bahri (Egypt), 22
Deities. See Gods and goddesses
Delian League, 57, 57(m), 59–61, 62, 83
Delos, 57, 110
Demeter, 66–68, 203
Demetrius (c. 336–283 b.c.e.), 121
Democracy. See also Legislative bodies
Athenian, 44, 54, 73–75, 79, 85, 86–87,
97–98, 98
radical democracy and Pericles' leadership
(461–445 b.c.e.), 59–61, 82, 83, 84, 85
resistance movement in, 87
natural law and, 513–514
Democritus of Abdera (dee MOK rit uhs), 75
Demosthenes (384–322 b.c.e.), 100, 101
Denmark, 303, 322, 508, 591, 594
Denmark-Norway, absolutism in, 534

Descartes, René (day CART, re NAY)
   (1596–1650), 516–517, 604
Des Prez, Josquin (day PRAY, zhos KIHN)
   (1440–1521), 456
Dhuoda (doo OH duh), 295, 296, 316–317
Dia, Contessa de (fl. c. 1160), 368
Dias, Bartholomeu, 464(*m*), 465
Diaspora, Jewish, 32, 198
Didymus (DID im uhs) (c. 80–10 B.C.E.), 113
Diet of Regensburg (1541), 491
Diet of Worms, 477
Digest (Byzantine legal code), 251
Diggers, 543
Diocletian (di o KLEE shuhn) (Roman emperor;
   r. 284–305), 172, 210, 214–218, 217(*m*),
   219, 220–221
Diogenes (dy AW jen eez) (d. 323 B.C.E.), 117
Dionysius of Halicarnassus, 137
Dionysus (dy o NY sus), theater of (Athens), 66,
   67(*i*), 79, 80(*i*), 100(*i*), 122
Diplomatic service
   eighteenth-century, 587, 597–598, 606
   Renaissance (fifteenth-century), 458–459
Discrimination. *See* Race
Diseases and epidemics, 599. *See also* Medicine;
   Plague
   in Athens (430–426 B.C.E.), 85
   in Augustan Rome, 178
   in Byzantine Empire (540s), 250
   early Middle Ages, 280
   in eighteenth century, 598–599
   seventeenth-century economic crisis and,
      505–506, 509
Divine Comedy (Dante Alighieri), 413–414, 420, 448
Divine right of kings, 28–29, 503, 523, 524, 528,
   553–554
Division of labor by gender, 8, 14, 237
Divorce, 484, 556
   in Babylon, 14
   in Byzantine Empire, 265
Domesday Book (DOOMZ day), 361–362
Domestication of animals, 3–4, 8
Domestic servants, 440, 581, 582
   in Florence (fifteenth century), 459, 462
   slaves as, 459, 462, 467–468, 468(*i*)
Dominate, Roman, 215–216
Dominic, St. (1170–1221), 380–381, 392
Dominicans (Dominican order), 380–381, 383,
   392, 409, 411(*i*), 411–412, 441, 443
Domitian (do MI shuhn) (Roman emperor
   r. 81–96), 187, 205, 236(*m*)
Donatello (don uh TEL oh) (1386–1466), 453
Donation of Constantine, 313
Donation of Pippin (756), 310–311

Donatism, 228–229
Donatus, 229
Don Quixote (don kee HO tay) (Cervantes),
   497, 585
Dowry 43, 69, 272, 281, 282, 458, 461, 462
Drama. *See also* Comedies; Theater
   in Golden Age Athens, 52, 79–80, 81–84
Dualists (dualism), 381, 391. *See also* Albigensians
   Plato's concept of, 96–97
Duchies, in Germany, 333, 366
Dufay, Guillaume (doo FAY, gee YOHM)
   (1400–1474), 455–456
Duns Scotus, John (c. 1266–1308), 413
Dürer, Albrecht (1471–1528), 468(*i*)
Dutch East India Company, 549(*m*), 567–568
Dutch Republic (United Provinces), 494
   Atlantic system and, 569
   constitutionalism in, 524, 548–551, 565
   economy (seventeenth century), 505–508,
      509, 521
   in eighteenth century, 578, 579(*f*), 580, 587,
      589, 591–592, 605(*m*)
   English war against (1652–1654), 544, 546,
      550–551
   Louis XIV and, 530–532, 531(*m*)
   in seventeenth century, 548–551, 549(*m*), 575
   Thirty Years' War and, 499–500, 501
Dutch West India Company, 551
Du Tertre, Father, 574

Easter, date of, 286–287
Eastern Europe, 260
   balance of power in (eighteenth century),
      594–597
   in fifteenth century, 437–439, 438(*m*)
   peasants in, 580–581, 606
   population growth and, 577, 581
   rise of Russia, 568
   state building in (1648–1699), 532–540,
      535(*m*). *See also* Absolutism, in central and
      eastern Europe
East India Company
   British, 574, 577
   Dutch, 549(*m*), 567–568
East Indies, 571(*m*), 576
Eberbech, 378(*i*)
Ebla, 12–13
Economy (economic conditions). *See also*
      Business and commerce; Inflation;
      Taxes; Trade
   Byzantine Empire, 250
   Carolingian, 317–318
   early Middle Ages, 280–282, 324
   in fourteenth and fifteenth centuries, 440–441

gift, 281–282, 343, 374
Greek, after Peloponnesian War, 94–95
Minoan, 34, 36
in Neolithic Revolution, 8
profit-based, 340–343, 347, 375
seventeenth-century crisis, 504–509, 524
Edessa, 229(i), 355, 355(m)
Edgar (England; r. 959–975), 331
Edict of Milan (313), 221
Edict of Nantes (1598), 490–491, 528–529, 533, 568
Edict of Restitution (1629), 499
Edict on Maximum Prices (301), 219
Education. *See also* Colleges and universities; Schools
in ancient Athens, 52, 73–78
in Byzantine Empire, 252–253, 260, 265, 266
Carolingian renaissance and, 309, 314–315, 315(i)
in eighteenth century, 582–583, 585–586
of women, 136, 485, 556, 585, 600(i), 604
Edward (the Confessor) (England; r. 1042–1066), 360
Edward I (England; r. 1272–1307), 404, 409
Edward III (England; r. 1327–1377), 430, 439
Edward IV (England; r. 1461–1483), 435
Edward VI (England; r. 1547–1553), 495
Egalitarianism, 6, 40, 44, 60–61, 75
Egypt (Egyptian civilization), 4
ancient, 15–25, 17(m)
Alexander the Great and, 103
Hebrews in, 31
Hellenistic period (323–30 B.C.E.), 106
Hyksos invasion and rule (c. 1670–1567 B.C.E.), 21–22
Middle Kingdom (c. 2050–1786 B.C.E.), 21
New Kingdom (c. 1567–1085 B.C.E.), 15–16, 22–25
Old Kingdom (c. 3100–2181 B.C.E.), 16–21
Ptolemaic kingdom, 107–111, 111(i), 113, 121–122, 123, 123(i), 135, 166, 173
pyramids, 16, 19–20, 20(i)
religion in, 16–24
Roman Empire and, 166, 173, 188(m)
Einhard (EYN hahrt) (c. 770–840), 311, 313
Elba, 12
Eleanor of Aquitaine (A kwi tayn) (c. 1122–1204), 362, 363(m), 367, 369
Elections, Roman, 144–145, 166
Elements of the Philosophy of Newton (Voltaire), 602
Elephants, war, 150, 152(i)
Eleusis, 68
El Greco (c. 1541–1614), 510, 511(i)

Elisabeth of Hungary (1207–1231), 410
Elisabeth de Valois (1545–1568), 492
Elizabeth I (England; r. 1558–1603), 495–497, 496(i), 510, 541
Elstob, Elizabeth, 604
Emperor worship (imperial cult), Roman, 186, 187, 190, 199, 201
Empire, 5
Empiricism, 116
Enclosure movement (Great Britain), 579
Encomium Moriae (Erasmus), 475n
England. *See also* Britain; Great Britain; *individual monarchs, political leaders, and specific events and topics*
civil war(s) in
1139–1153, 362
1642–1646, 541–545, 542(m), 556
thirteenth century, 409
constitutionalism in, 524, 540–547, 552–554, 565, 590
French wars with (seventeenth century), 530, 532
Hundred Years' War (1337–1453) and, 430–435, 432(m), 433(i)
Magna Carta and, 401–402, 402(i), 407–408
medieval poetry in, 448–449
in Middle Ages
Anglo-Saxon, 286(m), 286–288, 293, 321(f), 331
ninth to eleventh centuries, 323, 326, 329–332, 330(m)
Norman conquest (1066), 360(m), 360–362, 361(i)
twelfth and thirteenth centuries, 401–402
Vikings, 319(m), 320–321, 321(f), 330–331
monarchy in. *See* Monarchy, in England
Parliament, 408–409, 435
religion and church in, 365, 540. *See also* Church of England
Catholicism, 287, 494–497, 541–542, 544–547, 589, 602
English-language Bibles, 481
Lollardy, 444–445
new sects, 543–544
Protestant Reformation, 482(m), 492, 494–497, 529
Puritans, 495–496, 509, 541–545, 556, 562
seventeenth century, 541–547
taxing the clergy, 404–405
Test Act (1673), 546
seventeenth-century economy, 504–509, 521
women in. *See* Women, in England
English language, 362
Enheduanna, 12

Enlightenment, the, 568–569, 600–606
  popularization of science and, 600–602
  religion and, 601–602
  travel literature and, 602–603, 606
  women and, 604–605
Enlil, 10, 13
Ennius (EN ee us) (d. 169 B.C.E.), 153, 154
Entertainment. *See also* Popular culture
  in Byzantine Empire, 246
  in Rome, 181, 187
Environment, 8
Ephesus (EF us sus), 263
Ephialtes (ef ee ALT eez), 59
Epic of Creation (Mesopotamia), 3, 10–11, 37
Epic of Gilgamesh (Mesopotamia), 10–11, 27
Epic poetry, 367, 448
Epicureanism, 116
Epicurus (e pi KEW rus) (341–270 B.C.E.), 116, 154
Epidemics. *See* Diseases and epidemics
Equites (EK wih teez) (equestrians), 160, 180
Equity, in Roman law, 193–194
Erasmus, Desiderius (e RAS moos, deh sih DAY
    ree oos) (c. 1466–1536), 475, 476, 481
Eratosthenes of Cyrene (er a TAWS then eez)
    (c. 275–194 B.C.E.), 119
Ermengard (wife of Louis the Pious), 316
Essay Concerning Human Understanding
    (Locke), 554
Essay in Defence of the Female Sex
    (Anonymous), 604
Estates General (France), 407, 408n
Estonia, 387, 388(m), 499, 534, 595
Ethics
  Aristotle's views on, 98
  Hellenistic, 116
  Jewish, 30–32
  Plato's views on, 95–97
  Socrates and, 75–76
Ethnic groups. *See also* Race
  in Rome, 140
Etiquette. *See also* Manners
  court, 367–369, 504, 526, 562
Etruscans, 47(m), 141(m), 141–142, 143(i)
Eucharist (holy communion), 358, 377,
    403, 411
  Czech dissenters and, 445–446
  Luther and Zwingli's views of, 479
  transubstantiation and, 403, 414, 479, 484
Euclid (yew KLID) (fourth century B.C.E.), 118
Eulalius, count, 284
Eunuchs, 297
Euphrates River, 4, 8
Euripides (yoo RIP i deez) (c. 485–406 B.C.E.), 68,
    80, 81

Europe
  c. 400 B.C.E., 88(m)
  c. 600, 254(m), 261(m)
  c. 750, 291(m)
  c. 1050, 335(m)
  c. 1340, 420(m)
  c. 1500, 469(m)
  c. 1715, 588(m)
  in 1740, 605(m)
  at the end of seventeenth century, 564(m)
  religious divisions of (c. 1648), 519(m)
  trade patterns (c. 1740), 571(m)
  thirteenth-century, 394(m)
  twelfth-century, 363(m)
  as the West, 4
  witchcraft trials in, 517(i), 517–520
Eusebius (yoo SEE bee us) (c. 260–340), 221
Evans, Sir Arthur (1851–1941), 34
Evelyn, John, 546(i)
Everard, Count, 328
Exarchate (EKS ar kate) of Ravenna, 262,
    289(m), 291
Exclusion Crisis (1678), 546
Exodus (Ezechiel), 114
Exodus, book of, 31
Exposure (abandonment), 72, 111, 134, 194–195
Eyres, 364
Ezechiel (ih ZEE kee uhl), 114

Fabius Pictor, 152
Fable of the Bees (Mandeville), 577
Faithfulness (*fides*), Roman view of, 131–132, 139
Family (family life)
  in ancient Greece, 41, 82
  in Byzantine Empire, 265
  in Carolingian period, 295(i), 295–296,
      317–318
  eighteenth century, 604
  in Florence (fifteenth century), 460(i), 460–463
  in Islam, 269
  patrilineal, 328
  in post-Carolingian age, 327–328, 329
  Roman, 134–136
  seventeenth-century economic crisis and,
      506–507, 507(i)
Farming (farmers). *See also* Agriculture; Peasants
  in Byzantine Empire, 265
  in Hellenistic kingdoms, 110
  Roman, 156–158, 160
  tenant, in Roman Empire, 219, 237
Fathers. *See* Patriarchy
Fatimah (FAT im uh) (Muhammad's daughter),
    274, 305
Fatimids (FAT uh midz), 305, 306(m), 307, 335(m)

Fealty, 316, 325, 327, 331, 395, 403
Feiken, Hille, 473, 473(i), 480
Female Spectator, The, 585
Ferdinand I (Holy Roman emperor;
    r. 1558–1564), 492
Ferdinand II (Aragon; r. 1479–1516), 447, 467, 495
Ferdinand II (Bohemia, Holy Roman emperor;
    r. 1619–1637), 498, 499
Ferrer, Vincent (1350–1419), 443
Fertile Crescent, 6–7, 8
Festivals, Athenian, 66–68, 79–83
Feudalism, 324, 324n
Ficino, Marsilio (fee CHEE no, mahr SEE lyo)
    (1433–1499), 451
Fideles, 309, 324
Fiefs, 324, 327, 348, 355, 361
    French monarchy and, 399, 430
Finland, 387, 534
Fire, used for cooking, 6
Fire department, first, 178
First Crusade (1096–1098), 353(m), 353–355,
    357, 359
First Punic War (264–241 B.C.E.), 149–150, 151(f)
First Triumvirate (tree UHM ver et), 164, 165
Flagellants, 446
Flamininus (flam ih NY nus), 151
Flanders, 341(m), 342, 345, 346, 362, 398–399,
    431, 465
    plague in, 427, 427(m), 429(f), 430
Fleury, Cardinal Hercule de (1653–1743), 589
Floods
    in Egypt, 16–18, 19, 21, 203, 233
    in Mesopotamia, 8
Florence, 439–440
    Renaissance (fifteenth century), 450–451, 453,
        454(i), 455(i), 456–462
Fontenelle, Bernard de (1657–1757), 600
Food (food supply). *See also* Agriculture
    in eighteenth century, 581–582
    in hunter-gatherer societies, 5–6
    in Minoan Civilization, 34
    in post-Carolingian age, 325
    in post-war Athens, 94
    in Rome, 157, 159, 178–179, 191(m), 208
    seventeenth-century economic crisis and,
        505–507, 507(i)
Forum of Augustus, 175, 176(f)
Fourth Crusade (1202–1204), 387–390,
    388(m), 393
Fourth Lateran Council (1215), 389(i), 403–404,
    409, 422
France, 277, 316. *See also* Gaul(s); *individual
    monarchs, political leaders, and specific
    events and topics*

Atlantic system and, 569
Catholic church in
    Inquisition, 386, 392–393, 393(f)
    under Louis IX, 400–401
    under Louis XIV, 528–529, 602
    seventeenth century, 562–564
    taxing the clergy, 404(i), 404–405
    wars of religion (sixteenth century), 489–491
colonialism and imperialism, 574. *See also
    specific colonies*
    New World colonies of. *See* Americas, the,
        French colonies in; North America, French
        colonies in
in eighteenth century, 605(m), 606. *See also*
    French Revolution
    culture, 582, 583–585
    diplomatic service, 597
    War of the Polish Succession
        (1733–1735), 596
    Hundred Years' War (1337–1453) and, 429(f),
        430–435, 432(m), 433(i)
Jews in, 357–358, 398, 400–401, 403, 448
literacy in, 583
monarchy in. *See* Monarchy, in France
under Napoleon Bonaparte, 532
peasant rebellion in, 434–435
population growth in, 577
Protestants (Huguenots) in, 480–481, 489–491,
    490(m), 492, 528–529
Renaissance in, 456, 456(i)
in seventeenth century, 506–509
    economy of, 507, 509
in sixteenth century, 487(m), 487–492, 490(m)
    church reform and, 481
    religious wars, 489–491
in thirteenth and fourteenth centuries,
    398–401, 399(m), 400(m)
Thirty Years' War and, 497, 499–503, 502(m),
    506, 521, 525
women in, seventeenth century, 560–561, 563
Franciscans. *See* Friars
Francis I (France; r. 1515–1547), 487–489, 503
Francis II (France; r. 1559–1560), 489, 496
Francis of Assisi, St. (c. 1182–1226), 370,
    379–381, 411
Francis Xavier, St., 486
Franco of Cologne, 415
Franco-Turkish alliance (sixteenth century), 488
Frankfurt-am-Main, 452
Frankfurt Book Fair, 452
Franks (Frankish kingdoms), 242, 276–280,
    284(i), 286, 288, 289, 291(m), 292, 295,
    296, 309, 311, 312(m), 313, 319(m),
    320–322, 324, 332

Frederick (the Wise) (Prince of Saxony; r. 1486–1525), 477
Frederick I (Prussia; r. 1688–1713), 534–535
Frederick I Barbarossa (Germany and Holy Roman emperor; r. 1152–1190), 356, 363(m), 366–367, 393
Frederick II (Sicily and Germany, Holy Roman emperor; r. 1212–1250), 391, 393–396, 394(m), 405
Frederick V of the Palatinate (Bohemia; r. 1616–1623), 498
Frederick William (Great Elector of Brandenburg-Prussia; r. 1640–1688), 555
Frederick William I (Prussia; r. 1713–1740), 595–596, 598
Frederick William of Hohenzollern (Great Elector of Brandenburg-Prussia; r. 1640–1688), 533
Free Spirits, 444
Free will, Stoic view of, 116–117
French Revolution (1789–1799), 573
French Wars of Religion (1562–1598), 489–491
Friars (Franciscans and Dominicans), 379–381, 383, 392, 409–410, 411(i)
Froissart, Jean (frwah SAHR) (1333?–c. 1405), 433(i), 434, 449, 450
Fronde (1648–1653), 525, 525(m)
Fugger, Jakob (the Rich) (FOO ger) (1459–1525), 489
Fugger bank, 489
Fulbert, 372
Fulk Nera, count of Anjou (987–1040), 326–327
Funerals. See Burial practices
Fur trade, 530, 548

Galen (130?–200?), 515
Galileo Galilei (1564–1642), 255, 515, 554
Gallo-Romans, 278–279
Garden of Eden, 230, 231
Gaul(s), 114, 115(i)
  Franks and Frankish kingdoms in, 276
  Germanic peoples and kingdoms in, 242, 288, 289, 293
  Rome and, 147, 152, 164, 165, 166, 186, 189
Gender differences (gender roles). See also Men; Women
  division of labor by, 8, 14, 237
  in Dutch society, 549–550
  in postwar Athens, 94
  in Renaissance (fifteenth century), 461–463
  Roman children and, 195
  Roman values and, 134, 234–235
Geneva, Calvinism in, 479–481, 480(f), 486
Geometry, 118

George I (Great Britain; r. 1714–1727), 589, 590
George II (Great Britain; r. 1727–1760), 590, 591(i)
Gerbert (Sylvester II), 333
Germanic peoples and kingdoms, 277–278, 311, 318
  Roman Empire and, 187, 205, 208
Germany (German states), 322, 323, 326. See also individual monarchs, political leaders, and specific events and topics
  Carolingians and, 310, 312(m), 316, 332
  civil war in (1075–1122), 346, 350, 366
  Hohenstaufen dynasty and, 366
  Jews in, 357–358, 446–447
  militaristic absolutism in, 533–535
  monarchy in
    eleventh and twelfth centuries, 366–367
    tenth and eleventh centuries, 331–335, 332(m), 334(i), 335(m), 337
    thirteenth century, 394–396
  in seventeenth century, 506, 508, 533–534
  Thirty Years' War in, 499, 501, 502(m), 518
  women in, 461–462
Gerson, Jean (ger SOHN) (1363–1429), 443
Geta, 207
Ghent, 341(m), 345, 427(m), 430
Gibbon, Edward (1737–1794), 240
Gibraltar, 587
Gift economy, 281–282, 343, 374
Gilbert (bishop of Poitiers; d. 1154), 371(i), 419(i)
Gilbert of Liège, 370
Gilgamesh, Epic of, 10–11
Giotto (JOT oh) (1266–1337), 419(i), 421, 453
Gla, palace at, 36
Gladiators, 146, 181, 182(i)
Glanvill (treatise), 364
Glorious Revolution (1688), 545–547, 554
Gods and goddesses. See also Polytheism; Religion
  Athenian, 63, 63(i), 64–65, 66–68, 79, 81
  Babylonian, 27–28
  Chaldean (Neo-Babylonian), 27
  Christian God, 196, 205, 228
    disputes about the nature of, 228
    divine right doctrine and, 503
    Newton's view of, 554–555
    scholastics and, 412–414
    Spinoza's view of, 550
  Egyptian, 18–19, 23
  Greek, 42(i), 46–47, 52, 79
  Hebrew (Yahweh), 31–32, 124
  Hittite, 24
  in Homer and Hesiod, 37
  in Islam, 269–272

Mesopotamian, 3, 13
Persian, 30
polytheism and, 202–204
Roman, 131, 132, 137–139, 138(i), 208, 209, 221
    Julian's restoration of (361–363), 223
    Roman imperialism and, 147
Sumerian, 10–11
Gold, 465(m), 465–469, 470, 492, 504–505, 504(f)
Golden Ass, The (Apuleius), 193, 203
Golden Horde, 397
Gole, Jacob (c. 1660–1723), 600(i)
Gonzaga Palace, 455
Gonzaga tapestries, 453
Gordion, 102
Gospels, Christian, 197
    Lindisfarne Gospels, 287(i)
Gothic architecture, sculpture, and painting, 409,
    414(i), 415–421, 417(i), 448
Government (the state). *See also* Absolutism;
    Administration; Legislative bodies;
    Monarchy
    Augustine's *City of God* and, 230, 231
    Machiavelli on, 457
    religious conflict and (1500–1618), 486–497
    Roman Empire, 172
    Roman Republic
        early republic (509–287 B.C.E.), 143–146
        religion and, 139
        Senate, 140, 145–146, 150, 152, 159–160, 161,
            162, 164, 167, 172, 175, 180, 185
        social elite and, 158–160
    Thirty Years' War and growth, 503–505
Gracchus, Gaius Sempronius (GRAK us)
    (d. 121 B.C.E.), 135, 158–160
Gracchus, Tiberius (d. 133 B.C.E.), 135, 158–160
Granada, 391, 391(m), 447, 447(m)
Gratian (GRAY shun) (Roman emperor;
    r. 375–383 in the west), 223
Gravitation, law of (Newton), 554–555
Great Britain (United Kingdom)
    Act of Union (1707), 589–590
    Catholic church in. *See* Roman Catholic
        church, in England
    colonialism and imperialism, 574, 576, 576(i),
        596. *See also* North America, English
        (British) colonies in; *and specific colonies*
    in eighteenth century, 587–592, 605(m), 606
        agriculture in, 578–580, 579(f)
        enclosure movement, 579
    Parliament, 408–409
        Charles II and, 545–546
        in the eighteenth century, 589–590
        Exclusion Crisis (1678), 546
        Glorious Revolution (1688), 547

    in the seventeenth century, 541–547, 556
    in the sixteenth century, 495, 497
    Peace of Utrecht and, 588(m)
Great Depression (1930s)
Great Northern War (1700–1718), 495(m),
    594–495
Great Persecution (303), 221
Great Pyramid at Giza (Egypt), 19, 20, 20(i)
Great Schism (1054), 348, 352
Great Schism (1378–1417), 426, 442(m),
    442–443, 458
Greece, ancient (Greek civilization). *See also*
    Athens; Sparta
    c. 1500 B.C.E., 33(m)
    c. 400 B.C.E., 88(m)
    Aegean Sea and, 33(m), 34
    Archaic Age (c. 750–500 B.C.E.), 38–47, 39(m)
    citizenship in, 39–41
    Dark Age (c. 1000–750 B.C.E.), 36–38
    Etruscans and, 141–142
    Golden Age and Classical period
        (c. 500–323 B.C.E.), 51–89. *See also* Athens,
        Golden Age and Classical period
    decline of Classical Greece
        (c. 400–350 B.C.E.), 83–87, 93–99
    Persian wars (499–479 B.C.E.), 54–56
    in Hellenistic period (323–30 B.C.E.), 107–110
    Persian wars (499–479 B.C.E.), 51, 53(m)
    philosophy, 45–47
        Socrates, 75–78
        sophists, 74–75
    polis (city-states), 108. *See also* Athens; Sparta
        Alexander the Great and, 104–105
        citizenship (political rights), 38–44, 39(m)
        disunity after Peloponnesian War, 98–99
        Hellenistic period (323–30 B.C.E.), 92, 108
        Philip II of Macedonia and, 99–101
    religion, 42(i), 42–43, 121–125
        Golden Age Athens, 66–68
        Minoan and Mycenaean period, 37
    Roman literature and art and, 152–156
    Rome and, 151–152
    slavery and, 41–42
    women in
        Athens, 65, 68–72, 82–83
        comedies, 82–83
        companions, 71–72
        legal and political status, 40, 43
        Olympics and, 38
        after Peloponnesian War, 93–94
        religious functions of, 42(i), 42–43
        social and economic roles, 40, 42–44,
            68–72
        Spartan, 44

Greece, modern, under Byzantine rule, 260, 301, 302(m)
Greek culture, 152–156
   in Byzantine Empire, 265
   in eastern provinces of Roman Empire, 192
Greek language, 92, 108, 120, 121, 123, 288, 450–451
   in Byzantine Empire, 247
   in eastern provinces of Roman Empire, 191(m), 192
   Mycenaean, 35
   in Rome, 136
Greek Orthodox Church, 355, 380(m), 440, 519(m)
   Great Schism (1054) and, 348, 352
Greeks
   in ancient Italy, 141
   Archaic Age settlements, 38–39, 41
   in Hellenistic kingdoms, 92–93, 103, 108–110, 109(i), 115, 120
Greenland, Viking settlement of, 319(m), 320
Gregorian calendar, 593n
Gregorian reform, 349
Gregory (bishop of Tours; r. 573–c. 594), 278–281, 283, 285
Gregory I (the Great) (pope; r. 590–604), 286, 290, 310, 330
Gregory VII (Hildebrand) (pope; r. 1073–1085), 346, 348, 349–350, 351
Gregory XI (pope; r. 1371–1378), 441
Gregory XII (pope; r. 1406–1415), 443
Grotius, Hugo (GROH shee uhs) (1583–1645), 512–514
Guangzhou (Canton, China), 574
Guarino of Verona, 450
Guilds, 334–335, 344–345, 357, 372, 382, 386, 387, 402(i), 406, 416, 430, 530
Guinea, 465
Gustavus Adolphus (guhs TAY vuhs ah DOHL foos) (Sweden; r. 1611–1632), 499, 503, 534
Gutenberg, Johannes (c. 1400–1470), 451
Gutians, 13
Guyon, Jeanne Marie (1648–1717), 586
Gymnasia, 73
Gymnasia, Protestant, 483
Gynaeceum, 318

Habsburgs (Habsburg dynasty), 395, 407, 437, 588(m), 596(m). See also Holy Roman Empire
   Louis XIV and, 530–532
   in seventeenth century, 533–537, 535(m)
   in sixteenth century, 477, 487(m), 487–489, 488(i), 492–493, 493(m)
   Thirty Years' War and, 498, 501–502, 502(m)

Hadrian (HAY dree uhn) (Roman emperor; r. 117–138), 187, 188(m), 203, 205, 224
Hadrian I (pope; r. 772–795), 313
Hagia Sophia. See Church of the Holy Wisdom
Hajj, 271
Hamlet (Shakespeare), 510
Hammurabi (hah moo RAH bee) (Babylon; r. c. 1792–1750 B.C.E.), 14–15, 31
Handel, George Frederick (1685–1759), 585
Hannibal (247–182 B.C.E.), 150, 152(i), 159
Hanover, House of, 589
Hanseatic League, 406–407
Hanukkah, 124
Harold (earl of Wessex; mid-eleventh century), 360, 360(m)
Harun al-Rashid (Abbasid caliph; r. 786–809), 304–305
Harvey, William (1578–1657), 516
Hastings, battle of (1066), 360, 360(m)
Hatshepsut (Egypt; fifteenth century B.C.E.), 22
Hattusili III (Hittite king; c. 1286–c. 1265 B.C.E.), 25
Haywood, Eliza (1693?–1756), 585
Health care, in eighteenth century, 598–599, 606
Hebrew Bible (Old Testament), 123, 197, 198, 225. See also Torah
   Luther's translation of, 481
   monotheism and, 30–32
   translated into Greek (the Septuagint), 123
Hebrew language, 281, 367
Hebrews (Israelites), 25. See also Jews; Judaism
   exile of, 32
   monotheism and, 30–32
Heliocentrism, 118, 514–515, 600–601
Hellenic League, 54–56
Hellenistic period (323–30 B.C.E.), 91–126, 107(m), 124(m)
   culture in, 112–125
      the arts, 112–115
      languages, 120, 121, 123
      philosophy, 115–118
      religion, 121–126
      the sciences, 118–120
   kingdoms, structure of, 106–110, 107(m)
   society in, 110–112
Hellespont, 54
Heloise (EHL uh weez) (c. 1100–c. 1163/1164), 372–373
Helots (HE lots), 43, 44, 98
Henry (the Navigator) (prince; 1394–1460), 465
Henry I (England; r. 1100–1135), 362
Henry I (Germany; r. 919–936), 332
Henry II (England; r. 1154–1189), 357, 362–365, 363(m), 382, 398–399, 401, 408

Henry II (France; r. 1547–1559), 489
Henry II (Germany and Holy Roman emperor;
  r. 1002–1024), 333
Henry III (England; r. 1216–1272), 396, 408–409
Henry III (France; r. 1574–1589), 490, 492
Henry III (Germany and Holy Roman emperor;
  r. 1039–1056), 347, 349
Henry IV (Germany and Holy Roman emperor;
  r. 1056–1106), 346, 349–350, 357
Henry IV (Henry of Navarre) (France;
  r. 1589–1610), 489–491, 529
Henry V (England; r. 1413–1422), 431
Henry V (Germany; r. 1106–1125), 366
Henry VI (England; r. 1422–1461), 435
Henry VII (Henry Tudor) (England;
  r. 1485–1509), 435
Henry VIII (England; r. 1509–1547), 475, 480(f),
  494–495
Henry the Younger, 362
Hephaestus (heh FEHS tuhs), 66
Hera, 38, 66, 137
Heracles (Hercules), 68
Heraclius (her uh KLIH uhs) (Byzantine
  emperor; r. 610–641), 259, 262, 265
Herculaneum (hur kyuh LAY nee uhm), 179(i), 187
Heresies (heretics), Christian, 202, 359, 371(i),
  379, 380(i), 381, 383, 426.
    See also Inquisition, Catholic
  anti-heretic campaigns (1150–1300), 391–393
  Arianism, 228
  in Bohemia, 443, 445–446
  in Byzantine Empire, 248
  Catholic church and, 481, 528
  Donatism, 228–229
  early church and, 227–229
  fourteenth and fifteenth centuries, 441,
    443–445
  Free Spirits, 444
  Hussitism, 443–446
  Justinian and, 253
  Monophysite, 229
  Nestorianism, 228
  thirteenth-century, 386, 391–395
    Albigensian Crusade, 391–393, 404
    Fourth Lateran Council (1215), 389(i),
      403–404, 422
    penitent heretics, 393
Hero (Alexandrian scientist), 119
Hero cults, Athenian, 66, 67
Herod Antipas, 197
Herodotus (c. 485–425 B.C.E.), 28, 78
Herod the Great (Judea; r. 37–4 B.C.E.), 196
Herophilus of Chalcedon (b. c. 300 B.C.E.), 120
Hesiod (HEE see ud), 36–37

Hierapolis (hy uh RAP uh lihs), 111
Hierarchy (social status; class differences), 4.
    See also specific social classes
  in Byzantine Empire, 248, 249
  in Egypt, 20–21
  in Florence (fifteenth century), 459–463
  in hunter-gatherer societies, 4, 6
  in Neolithic Revolution, 8
  in Roman Empire, 180, 193–194
  in Roman Republic, 143, 144, 157
  in Sumerian society, 9–10
Hieroglyphs, Egyptian, 17, 18, 18(f), 91(i)
Hijra, 270, 271, 273
Hildegard of Bingen (1098–1179), 373
Hindus, 576
Hipparchia (hip AHR kee ah), 117–118
Hippias (Athenian tyrant; 527–510 B.C.E.), 54
Hippocrates (hip OK rah teez) (c. 460–377
  B.C.E.), 78, 122
Hispaniola, 467
Historia calamitatum (Abelard), 372
Historical and Critical Dictionary (Bayle), 601
Histories (Gregory), 279
Histories (Herodotus), 78
History of the Peloponnesian War (Thucydides), 78
Hittite kingdom (Anatolia), 15–16, 22–25
Hiung-nu people, 238
Hobbes, Thomas (1588–1679), 553–554
Hohenstaufen dynasty, 366
Hohenzollern dynasty, 501, 533
Holy Land. See Levant
Holy Roman Empire. See also individual emperors
  c. 1273, 395
  c. 1340, 405, 420(m), 427(m), 443, 445, 446
  in fifteenth century, 458, 459, 469(m)
  in seventeenth century, 531(m), 531–532, 533,
    535(m), 535–536
  in sixteenth century, 476–479, 482(m), 490(m),
    492, 493(m)
  Thirty Years' War and, 498–502, 502(m), 518, 536
Holy Synod (Russia), 593
Homage, 327, 334(i)
Homer (fl. 850 B.C.E.), 36–37, 79
  Iliad, 37, 102, 183, 255
  Odyssey, 37, 152–153, 183, 255
Homo sapiens, 5
Homosexuality (homosexuals)
  in ancient Greece, 43–44, 73–74
  in Byzantine Empire, 252
  in Florence (fifteenth century), 462
Honor, Roman view of, 131–132, 145, 161, 162
Honorius (ho NAW ri uhs) (Roman emperor;
  r. 395–423 in the west), 213(i), 214, 218,
  239, 247

Hoplites (HOP lytz), 40–41, 41(i), 51(i), 55(i), 84(f)
  Persian Wars and (499–479 B.C.E.), 54–55, 56
Horace (65–8 B.C.E.), 112, 183
Horatius (ho RAY shus), legend of, 143
Horses, in warfare (ninth to eleventh
    centuries), 327
Hospitals
  in eighteenth century, 598–599
  in seventeenth century, 563–564
Housing (dwellings)
  in Athens, 61
  in Augustan Rome, 177–178
  in eighteenth century, 581–582
Hubris, 81
Hugh Capet (France; r. 987–996), 332
Hugh of St. Victor, 351
Huguenots (HYOO geh nots) (French
    Protestants), 480, 489–491, 490(m),
    528–529, 533, 601
Humanism, 426
  Christian, 474–475, 498, 520
  Renaissance, 448–452, 471
Humanitas, Cicero's doctrine of, 154–155
Humbert of Silva Candida, 348
Humors, medical theory of, 78
Hundred Years' War (1337–1453), 426, 429(f),
    430–435, 432(m), 433(i), 439, 449
Hungary, 301, 303, 335(m), 335–336, 436, 437,
    438(m), 469(m), 487(m), 488, 488(i),
    519(m)
  Austrian conquest of (1657–1730), 596(m),
    596–597
  Mongol invasion of, 385, 396, 397(m)
  Ottoman Turks and, 535, 535(m), 537, 564(m)
Huns, 235–238, 236(m)
Hunter-gatherers, 3, 5–6
Hunting, in Neo-Assyrian kingdom, 26–27
Hus, Jan (hoos, yon) (d. 1415), 443–446,
    477, 499
Hussites (Hussitism), 443–446
Hyksos, 21–22

Iaroslav the Wise (Russian prince;
    r. 1019–1054), 303
Ibn Sina (Avicenna) (980–1037), 308
Iceland, Viking settlement of, 319(m), 320
Icons and iconoclasm, 266(i), 266–267, 274,
    290–291, 293, 299, 315, 539
Idylls (Theocritus), 113
Ignatius (ig NAY shus) (bishop of Antioch;
    c. 35–107 C.E.), 200
Ignatius of Loyola (1491–1556), 484
Île-de-France (eel duh FRAHNS), 332, 358, 365,
    392, 398, 398(m)

Iliad (IL ee ad) (Homer), 37, 102, 183, 255
Illegitimate children, in Florence (fifteenth
    century), 462
Illidius, St., 280
Illiteracy, in eighteenth century, 582–583
Illyrians, 101
Immigrants. *See* Migrations
Immortality, in ancient Egypt, 15
Imperial cult, 202
  Roman, 186–187, 190
Imperialism. *See also* Colonies
  Roman (fifth to second centuries B.C.E.)
    expansion in Italy, 146–148
    social consequences of wars, 156–158
    wars with Carthage, 148–152
Inanna (Ishtar), 10, 12, 27
Incas (IHN kuhs), 469–470
India, 245, 464(m), 465–466, 492, 493(m)
  Alexander the Great in, 104
  Europeans in, 574, 576(i), 576–577
  religious practices of, 576–577
Indian Ocean, 463, 464(m), 465, 549(m)
Indians, American. *See* Native
    Americans
Indo-European languages, 24
Indulgences, sale of, 474–475, 476
Indus Valley, 28
Infanticide, 272, 460
  by exposure (abandonment), 72, 111, 134,
    194–195, 462
Inflation
  in Roman Empire, 205–206, 219–220
  in seventeenth century, 503, 504–505
Ingria, 595
Inheritance, 328, 329, 332–333, 337, 355, 461
  in ancient Greece, 43, 69
  Islamic women and, 272, 281
  in Merovingian period, 281–284
  in non-Roman societies, 237
  in northern Europe (fifteenth century),
    461–462
Innocent III (pope; r. 1198–1216), 387, 389(i),
    390, 392, 393, 402–403, 404(i)
Inquisition, Catholic, 386, 392–393, 393(f), 404, 515
  in Germany, 444
  in Spain, 447–448
Institutes (ins tih TOO tays) (Byzantine law
    textbook), 251
Institutes of the Christian Religion, The
    (Calvin), 480
Institutions (Cassiodorus), 245
Instruction of Ptahhotep, 21
Insulae (IN sool eye) (Roman apartment
    buildings), 177

Interim (Germany) (1548), 491
Intermarriage, in American colonies, 574–575
Investiture Conflict (c. 1070–1122), 349(m),
 349–351, 366, 367
Ionia (ee OH nee uh), 37, 46, 46(m), 47, 51, 52, 54
Ionian Revolt (499–490 B.C.E.), 52–54, 53(m)
Iran, 7, 8n, 28. See also Persia
 Islam and, 307
 Mongol invasion of, 396, 397(m)
Iraq, 7, 261, 304, 306(m)
Ireland
 Catholic church and Catholics in, 547, 590
 Christianity in, 286–288
 in seventeenth century, 544, 545(i), 547
 Vikings in, 319(m), 320
Irish missionaries, in England, 286
Iron metallurgy, 38
Irrigation, 8–9
 in Mesopotamia, 8
Isabella I (Castile; r. 1474–1504), 447–448, 467, 495
Isabella of Bavaria (consort of Charles VI of
 France), 449(i)
Ishtar (Inanna), 10, 27
Isis (EYE sis), 19, 121, 122–123, 123(i), 193, 223
 cult of, 203
Islam (is LAHM or is LAM) (Muslims), 30, 32,
 260, 261, 268–275, 272(m), 291(m),
 380(m), 303–309
 c. 1000, 306(m)
 Abbasid Caliphate (750–c. 950), 303–307,
  306(m), 336–337
 Christianity and, 268, 269, 272, 273–275,
  306–307, 422
  crusades against, 352–357, 353 (m),
   383, 488
 classical literature and learning and,
  307–309, 371
 Muhammad's successors (632–750), 273–275,
  293
 Ottoman Empire and, 436(m), 436–439,
  438(m), 442(m)
 Qur'an, 269, 270(i), 273, 275, 287, 292
 regional diversity in, 305–307
 renaissance of (c. 790–c. 1050), 307–309, 314
 rise and development of (c. 610–632), 268–273,
  292–293, 298(m)
 Roman Empire and, 259, 274(i), 275, 281
 Shi'ite, 274, 304, 305
 in Spain, 268, 273, 289, 291(m), 305–307,
  306(m), 371, 426, 466
  Christian reconquest (reconquista), 348, 386,
   388(m), 390–391, 391(m), 447–448
  Moriscos, 492–493
 Sunni, 274, 305, 353, 356

Israel, 7, 8n, 16. See also Jerusalem
 ancient, 32
Istanbul, 218, 581. See also Constantinople
Italian language, 414
Italy, 316. See also Etruscans; Roman Empire;
  Roman Republic; Rome
 ancient, 140–141, 141(m)
 Byzantine Empire and, 260, 359
 under Diocletian, 216–217
 fifth century B.C.E., 147(m)
 Justinian and, 249, 250
 Lombards in. See Lombardy
 in Middle Ages, 311, 312(m), 313
  business agreements, 343–344
  communes, 406
  early medieval kingdoms, 289(m), 289–293
  at end of thirteenth century, 395(m)
  Frederick I Barbarossa, 363(m), 366–367
  Investiture Conflict and, 349–351
  papal-imperial conflicts, 393–396, 394(m),
   395(m)
  peasants, 326, 343
  post-Carolingian age, 319(m), 322, 323, 326,
   329–330
  urban self-government, 345–346
 Renaissance in, 425–426
 Social War (91–87 B.C.E.), 161
Ivan III (ee VAHN) (Muscovite tsar; r.
 1462–1505), 439
Ivan IV (the Terrible) (Russia; r. 1533–1584), 499

Jacobitism, 588(m), 589–590
Jacquerie (1358), 434–435
Jagiellonian dynasty, 438
Jamaica, 572–573
James Edward (pretender to British throne), 589
James I (England; r. 1603–1625), 496–497, 503,
 541, 589
James II (England; r. 1685–1688), 546–547, 552,
 589–590
Janissaries (JAHN ih sehr ees), 437, 488(i)
Jan of Leiden (yahn uv LY den) (1626–1679), 479
Jansen, Cornelius (1585–1638), 528
Jansenists (Jansenism), 528, 586
Japan, Christian missionaries in, 485(i), 486
Java, 568, 571(m), 576
Jerome (theologian; c. 345–420), 151, 230, 234,
 255
Jerome, St., 287
Jerome of Prague (d. 1416), 445
Jerusalem, 123, 188, 197
 crusades and, 353(m), 354, 355, 355(m), 356,
  380(m), 388, 388(m)

(continued)

Muslims and, 271
    as Roman colony, 188, 196–197, 224
    temple in, 31, 32, 124, 163, 196, 198
Jesuits (JEHZH oo ihts) (Society of Jesus),
        484–486, 485(i), 498
    in North America, 530
Jesus (Christ) (c. 4 B.C.E.–30 C.E.), 196–198, 224, 562
    depictions of, 224(i), 253, 512
    disputes about nature of, 228–229
    Islam and, 260
    twelfth- and thirteenth-century views of, 377,
        379, 411, 421
Jewish law, 196–198, 225
Jews. See also Anti-Semitism; Judaism
    Byzantine Empire and, 259, 299
    in Dutch Republic, 494, 550, 601
    in early Middle Ages, 281
    in eleventh and twelfth centuries, 342, 355–358,
        357(i), 380(m), 383
    emergence of Christianity and, 195–205
    in fourteenth and fifteenth centuries, 446–448
    Fourth Lateran Council and (1215), 403
    in France, 357–358, 398, 400–401, 448
    in Germany, 357–358, 446–447
    in Hellenistic kingdoms, 109, 123–125
    Islam and, 268, 269, 270–272, 275, 306, 307
    persecution of, 444(i), 446–448
    Roman Empire and, 163, 195–205, 224–225
    in Russia and Soviet Union, 302
    in Spain, 426, 447–448
    in thirteenth century, 422
Jihad (jih HAD), 271, 273
Joan of Arc (1412?–1431), 431–433, 432(m), 434(i)
Jogaila (yo GAY lo) (Jagiellon) (Lithuanian
        prince; fourteenth century), 438
John (England; r. 1199–1216), 399, 401–402,
        402(i), 422
John II (Portugal; r. 1481–1495), 465
John XXII (pope; r. 1316–1334), 441
John XXIII (antipope; r. 1410–1415), 443
John of Damascus, St., 267
John the Baptist, 197
Jolliet, Louis (zhoh LYAY) (1645–1700), 530
Jordan, 7, 16
Joseph (biblical figure), 31
Journalism. See Newspapers
Judaea, 195, 196
Judah, 32
Judah the Maccabee, 124
Judaism, 225. See also Jews
    early Christianity and, 195, 196, 199, 200
    Hebrew Bible and, 30
    in Hellenistic period, 123–125
    monotheism and, 25, 30–32, 292

Judicial system (court system)
    Athenian, 59–61
    in England, 363–365, 364(i)
    in France, 398–401
    Roman, 145, 146, 160
Judith (consort of Louis I; early ninth century),
        316
Julia (Julius Caesar's daughter), 164,
        165, 185
Julian (Roman emperor; r. 361–363),
        223, 249
Julian calendar, 593n
Julio-Claudians, 185, 193
Julius II (pope; r. 1503–1513), 495, 510
Julius Nepos, 241
Junkers (YUN kers), 533
Juno, 137
Jupiter, 137, 139, 189, 203, 216
Justice
    in ancient Greece, 37, 44, 96, 97
        Socrates' views of, 75–78
    divine, 196
    Roman, 144
Justin (c. 100–165), 200
Justinian (juh STIHN ee un) (Byzantine emperor;
        r. 527–565), 233(i), 243(m), 245, 246(i),
        249–252, 254(m), 260, 300, 312, 437
Justinian II (Byzantine emperor; r. 685–711),
        289–290
Juvenal (JOO vuh nuhl) (c. 65–130), 177,
        178, 193

Kadesh (KAY desh), battle of (c. 1274 B.C.E.), 25
Karelia, 595
Karlowitz, Treaty of (1699), 537
Kent, 286, 286(m)
Kepler, Johannes (1571–1630), 515, 554–555
Khadija, 269, 270
Khwarizmi, al- (KWAR ihz mee)
        (c. 780–850), 308
Kiev, 396, 539
Kievan Russia, 302–303, 335(m)
King James Bible, 496
King Lear (Shakespeare), 510
King Philip's War (1675–1676), 552
King's Peace (386 B.C.E.), 98
Knights, 325, 327, 329, 335, 355, 359, 361(i), 364,
        368(i), 369, 399, 401, 430–431, 435,
        440, 444(i)
Knights, The (Aristophanes), 82
Knights Templar, 355, 356(i)
Knossos (NAHS uhs), 34, 35
Koine (koy NAY) (Greek language), 120
Kore (KOR ay) (Persephone), 68

Kosovo (KOSS oh voh), battle of (1389),
  436, 436(m)
Krak-des-Chevaliers, 356(i)
Krum, Khagan (Bulgaria; r. c. 803–814),
  301–302

Labadie, Jean de, 559
Labadists, 559
Labor force. See Workers
Ladder of offices, 145
Lafayette, Madame de (Marie-Madeleine de La
  Vergne), 526, 561
Lancelot, 369
Lancelot (Chrétien de Troyes), 367
Landownership (landowners; landlords). See also
  Tenant farmers
  Byzantine, 297, 299
  Carolingian economy and, 317–318
  in England (Great Britain), 331, 579–580
  Huns and, 238
  Merovingian economy and, 288, 310, 317–318
  in post-Carolingian age, 324–327, 337
  Roman, 140, 148, 156–158
Language(s). See also specific languages
  in Byzantine Empire, 247
  in Hellenistic period, 108, 122
  of Roman world, 191(m)
  vernacular, 330, 331(i), 367–369, 511, 515
    Renaissance (fifteenth-century), 448–450
Languedoc (lang DAWK), 381, 392,
  393(f), 400
Lares (LAHR eez), 137, 138(i)
La Salle, Sieur de (1643–1687), 530
Las Casas, Bartolomé de (lahs KAH sahs, bahr
  toh loh MAY day) (1474–1566), 486
Las Navas de Tolosa, battle of (1212), 388(m),
  391, 391(m)
Latifundia (la tih FUN dee ah), 158
Latin America. See Spain, American colonies of
Latin language, 141, 148, 153, 154, 191(m), 255,
  278–279, 281, 282, 288, 323, 367, 370–371,
  450–451, 475, 511, 515. See also Classical
  literature and learning
  in Byzantine Empire, 247–248, 262
  in England, 330
Latin literature
  Byzantine Empire and, 252
  comedies, 153, 155(i)
  in late first and early second centuries C.E., 193
Latin Vulgate, 314, 481
Latium (LAY shum), 140, 141
Latvia, 499, 534
Laud, William (lawd) (archbishop of Canterbury;
  1573–1645), 542

Law(s) (law codes). See also Judicial system
  canon (church law), 347, 348, 352, 371,
    403–404, 443, 483
  Constitutions of Melfi (Frederick II), 395
  in England
    King Alfred, 330
    Magna Carta, 401–402, 402(i), 408, 422
  Hammurabi's, 14–15, 31
  Hebrew (Pentateuchal), 31
  Jewish, 196–198, 225
  Lombard, 289
  Roman, 144–146, 159, 193–194, 216, 243,
    244, 371
    Germanic kings and, 238, 244
  schools of, 371
Law, John (1671–1729), 589
Law of universal gravitation, 555
Lechfeld, battle of (955), 319(m), 322, 332(m)
Lefèvre d'Étaples, Jacques (leh FEHV day TAPL)
  (c. 1455–1536), 481
Legislative bodies (representative institutions).
  See also Democracy; specific legislative
  bodies
  in ancient Greece, 59–61
  in colonial North America, 509, 552
  in Eastern Europe (seventeenth century),
    533–534, 537, 539–540
  Roman, 144–145
  in thirteenth and fourteenth centuries,
    407–409
Legnano (leh NYAH no), battle of (1176),
  363(m), 367
Leibniz, Gottfried Wilhelm (LYB nihts)
  (1646–1716), 555–556
Leo III (pope; r. 795–816), 313
Leo III the Isaurian (r. 717–741), 267, 290
Leo IX (pope; r. 1049–1054), 347–348
Leo X (pope; r. 1513–1521), 494
León (lay OHN), 388(m), 390, 391(m), 408. See
  also Castile-León
Leonardo da Vinci (1452–1519), 452–453
Leontion (le ON tee on), 116
Leopold I (Holy Roman emperor; r. 1658–1705),
  533, 535–537, 587
Leopold of Austria, 355
Leovigild (Visigothic king; r. 569–586), 288
Lepanto, battle of (1571), 492–493,
  493(m), 497
Lepidus (LEP ih dus), 173
Lesbia, 154
Letters Concerning the English Nation (Voltaire),
  602
Leucippus of Miletus (loo KIP us) (c. 500–400
  B.C.E.), 75

Levant (luh VAHNT) (modern Syria, Lebanon, and
     Israel), 16, 16(m), 16n, 17, 17(m), 107, 142
  crusader states in, 353, 355(m), 356, 356(i),
     380(m), 388(m)
  Hittite expansion in, 24
  Romans in, 153(m), 163
Levellers, 543–544
Leviathan (luh VY uh thun) (Hobbes), 553
Lewes, battle of (1264), 409
Liberal arts, 370–371, 450
Libraries, 112, 166
Lindisfarne Gospels, 287(i)
Linear A and B (Mycenaean script), 35
Lippi, Filippo (LEE pee, fee LIHP po)
     (1457–1504), 453
Lisbon, 388(m), 391, 391(m), 465
Literacy/illiteracy, in eighteenth century, 582–583,
     585–586, 606
Literature. See also Books and publishing
     industry; Drama; Novels; Poetry;
     individual authors
  in ancient Egypt, 21
  Byzantine, 245, 252–255, 260
  Chaldean (Neo-Babylonian; wisdom
     literature), 27
  Christian, 252–255
  classical. See Classical literature and learning
  courtly (twelfth century), 367–369
  eighteenth-century, 578, 583, 585–586,
     602–603, 606
  fifteenth-century (Renaissance), 448–450
  Greek, 153, 192
  Hellenistic, 113–114
  Latin
     Byzantine Empire and, 252
     comedies, 153, 155(i)
     in late first and early second
        centuries C.E., 193
  Mesopotamian, 12–13
  novels, 192, 193
     eighteenth-century, 578, 583, 585–586, 606
     seventeenth-century, 561
  Renaissance (fifteenth-century), 448–450
  Roman, 152–155, 183, 245. See also Classical
     literature and learning
  seventeenth-century, 561
  thirteenth-century, 413–415
  travel (eighteenth century), 602–603, 606
Lithuania, 387, 388(m), 437, 438, 438(m)
Liutprand (LYOOT prahnd) (bishop of
     Cremona), 297–298, 322
Livestock, 8, 578
Livius Andronicus, 153
Livonia (Livs), 387, 388(m), 393, 595

Livy (LIHV ee) (59 B.C.E.–17 C.E.), 140, 142, 143,
     144, 151, 183, 450
Local government
  in post-Carolingian age, 323–337
  of towns, 345–346
Locke, John (1632–1704), 513, 553–554, 602
Lodi, Treaty of (1454), 459
Logic, 46, 47, 370–373, 516. See also Reason
  Abelard and, 372–373
  Aristotle on, 97–98, 411–414
  in Hellenistic philosophy, 116
Lollardy, 444–445
Lombard League, 367
Lombardy (Lombards; Lombard kingdom),
     254(m), 261, 261(m), 262, 289(m),
     289–291, 291(m), 332, 458
  Charlemagne and, 311
  papacy and, 290–293, 310–311
London, 509, 542, 597
  in eighteenth century, 577, 581–582, 583, 584
  Great Fire of (1666), 545, 546(i)
Looms, 345. See also Weaving
Lope de Vega (1562–1635), 509
Lorrain, Claude (loh RAYN) (1600–1682), 558
Lorraine, 531(m), 532, 596
Lorris, Guillaume de, 414
Lothar I (Carolingian emperor; r. 840–855),
     312(m), 316
Louis I (the Pious) (Carolingian emperor;
     r. 814–840), 295, 315–316
Louis VI (the Fat) (France; r. 1108–1137),
     365–366, 382, 398, 416
Louis VII (France; r. 1137–1180), 362
Louis IX (St. Louis) (France; r. 1226–1270),
     399–401, 400(m), 405, 414(i), 416
Louis XIII (France; r. 1610–1643), 499–500, 503,
     525
Louis XIV (France; r. 1643–1715), 500, 523(i),
     527(i), 548, 596
  absolutism and, 524–533, 537, 540, 546, 568,
     587, 588(m), 589, 600–601
  bureaucracy, 529–530
  colonies and territorial holdings, 530–532,
     531(m)
  court culture, 523–528
  the Fronde (1648–1653), 525, 525(m)
  mercantilism, 529–530
  religious orthodoxy, 528–529, 546, 586, 601
  reform of popular culture and, 562–564
  wars of, 597
Louis XV (France; r. 1715–1774), 587, 596
Louisiana Territory, 530
Louis of Bavaria (emperor), 441
Louis the Child (Germany; r. 900–911), 332

Louis the German (Carolingian emperor;
    r. 843–876), 312(*m*), 316
Louvre palace, 527–528, 557
Lower classes. *See* Peasants; Poor, the; Serfs; Workers
Lübeck, 406
Lucerne (loo SERN), 407, 407(*m*)
Lucian (LOO shun) (c. 117–180), 192–193
Lucretia (loo KREE shah), 142–143
Lucretius (loo KREE shus) (c. 94–55 B.C.E.), 154
Lupercalia festival, 137–138
Luther, Martin (1483–1546), 473, 474, 476–480,
    477(*i*), 480(*f*), 481, 483, 495, 511
Lutherans (Lutheran church), 519(*m*)
    ninety-five theses and, 476
    in Norway, 562
    spread of, 476–479, 480(*f*), 483, 486, 491
    Thirty Years' War and, 498–499, 501–502
Lützen, battle of (1632), 499, 502(*m*)
Luxembourg, 276(*m*), 277, 316. *See also* Austrian
    Netherlands
Lyceum (ly SEE um) (Peripatetic School; Athens), 97
Lydus, John, 248, 249
Lyon (France), 381, 395
Lyric poetry, Greek, 45–46
Lysias (c. 445–380 B.C.E.), 66, 86–87
Lysimachus (ly SIM uh kus) (Egypt; c. 355–281
    B.C.E.), 110
Lysippus (ly SIP us) (c. 400–300 B.C.E.), 114
Lysistrata (lih SIH strah tuh) (Aristophanes), 82–83

Ma'at (supernatural force), 19
Macbeth (Shakespeare), 510
Macedonia (mass ih DOH nee uh), 7*n*, 93, 151, 152
    rise of (359–323 B.C.E.), 99–106
    under Alexander the Great (r. 336–323
        B.C.E.), 102–106, 103(*m*)
    under Philip II (r. 359–336 B.C.E.), 99–101,
        101(*m*)
Macedonian renaissance (c. 870–c. 1025), 297,
    299–300, 301(*i*), 307, 314(*i*)
Macedonians (mass ih DOH nee uhns)
    in Hellenistic kingdoms, 92
    in territory conquered by Alexander the Great,
        103
Machiavelli, Niccolò (mah kyah VEL lee, nee koh
    LOH) (1469–1527), 457, 512, 553
Macrina, 234
Macrinus (muh KRY nus) (Roman emperor; r.
    217–218), 208
Madeira, 467
Madrasa, 309
Madrid, 509, 597
Magellan, Ferdinand (muh JEL un)
    (1480?–1521), 464(*m*), 465

Magic
    in Ancient Greece, 67(*i*)
    in Egypt, 23
    in Mesopotamia, 15
    in sixteenth and seventeenth centuries, 516–517
Magna Carta, 401–402, 402(*i*), 408, 422
Magyars (MAG yars), 309, 318, 319(*m*), 322–323,
    332, 335, 537
Maieul (may OOL) (abbot of Cluny), 322
Maintenon, marquise de (man tuh NOHN, mahr
    KEEZ duh) (**Françoise d'Aubigné**)
    (1635–1719), 528
Mainz, 357
Majority rule, in Athenian radical democracy, 59
Malta, 148
Mamluks, 305
Mandeville, Bernard, 577
Manius Curius (MAN ee us KYOO ree us)
    (d. 270 B.C.E.), 158
Mannerism, 510, 511(*i*)
Manners. *See also* Etiquette
    in seventeenth century, 559–562
Manors, 317–318, 325–326, 328, 434
Manses, 343
    Carolingian, 317–318
Mantegna, Andrea (man TAY nyah, an DRAY ah)
    (1431–1506), 453, 455
Mantinea, battle of (man tin EE ah) (362 B.C.E.), 99
Manzikert, battle of (1071), 353(*m*), 354, 359
Mapmaking, 15
Marathon, battle of (490 B.C.E.), 52, 53(*m*), 54
Marcel, Étienne (mar SEL, ay TYEHN), 434
Marcian, 229
Marcus Aurelius (Roman emperor; r. 161–180),
    187, 188, 203, 205
Marduk (mythical king), 3, 4, 27–28
Marguerite de Valois (mahr guh REET duh vahl
    WAH) (1553–1615), 489
Marius, Gaius (MAIR ee uhs) (c. 157–86 B.C.E.),
    159–161, 160, 162
Mark Antony, 110, 173
Markets
    in eleventh and twelfth centuries, 340–343,
        341(*m*)
    in ninth and tenth centuries, 329
Marquette, Jacques (1637–1675), 530
Marriage. *See also* Adultery; Divorce; Dowry
    in ancient Greece, 43, 69
    Christianity and, 231–232, 351–352, 483–484
    clerical, 290, 351–352
    early Middle Ages, 282–283
    in eighteenth century, 604
    in Florence (fifteenth century), 460–462

(continued)

interracial, in American colonies, 574–575
Protestant Reformation and, 483(i), 483–484
in Ptolemaic Egypt, 110–111, 111(i)
Roman, 134, 136, 180, 194
in seventeenth century, 506–507
in twelfth century, 354(i)
Mars, Roman Temple to, 175, 176(f)
Marseilles (France), 276(m), 278, 428
Marsilius of Padua (mar SIL ee us)
    (c. 1290–1343), 441
Martin of Tours, St. (c. 316–397), 234, 279–280,
    283
Martin V (pope; r. 1417–1431), 443
Martyrdom, 200
    monasticism as, 232
    virginity and sexual renunciation as, 232
Mary, Virgin (mother of Jesus), 228, 266(i),
    295(i), 377, 414, 416, 418(i), 421, 494, 562
Mary I (Mary Tudor) (England; r. 1553–1558),
    492, 495–496
Mary II (England; r. 1689–1694), 547–548, 552,
    589
Maryland, 508, 573
Mary of Oignies (1177–1213), 379
Mary Stuart (Mary, Queen of Scots) (1542–1587),
    497
Masaccio (muh SAH chee oh) (1401–1428), 453,
    454(i)
Masinissa (mah sin IS ah) (Numidian king;
    r. second century B.C.E.), 152
Mass, sacrament of, 351, 375, 415, 416, 445, 475,
    480, 511, 562. See also Eucharist
    Fourth Lateran Council and (1215), 403
Massachusetts Bay Company, 508
Mass culture. See Popular culture
Materialism, 116
Mathematics, 516, 555, 601
    in Ancient Greece, 46
    in Hellenistic period, 118–119
    Islam and, 308–309
    in Mesopotamia, 12–15
    Pythagoras and, 46
Matthew, St., 314(i)
Matthias Corvinus (muh THY us kohr VY nus)
    (Hungary; r. 1456–1490), 437
Maurice (Duke of Saxony), 491
Mauryan dynasty, 107
Maxentius, 221
Maximianus (bishop of Ravenna), 246(i)
Maximilian I (Holy Roman emperor;
    r. 1493–1519), 458, 489
Mayflower, 508
Mazarin, Cardinal (maz uh RAN) (1602–1661),
    500, 525–526, 529

Mecca, 268, 270–271, 307
Medea (Euripides), 68, 81
Medes (meedz), 27
Medici, Cosimo de' (MEH dih chee)
    (1388–1464), 451, 453, 457
Medici, Lorenzo de' (the Magnificent)
    (1449–1492), 456–457
Medici family, 440, 456–457, 458, 461
Medicine
    in ancient Egypt, 23
    in eighteenth century, 598–599
    in Hellenistic period, 120, 122
    Hippocrates and, 78
    Mesopotamian, 15
    Roman, 194
    in sixteenth and seventeenth centuries, 514–516
Medina (mih DEE nuh), 268, 270–271
Meditations (Marcus Aurelius), 203
Mediterranean polyculture, 34
Mediterranean Sea and region, 7n
    c. 500 B.C.E., 4, 47(m)
    c. 400 B.C.E., 88(m)
    c. 750, 291(m)
    c. 1050, 335(m)
    c. 1350, plague and, 427(m), 428
    in fifteenth century, 463–465
    Greek settlements during Archaic Age, 38–39
    Rome and, 152, 188(m), 190
Megarons, 35
Mehmed II (the Conqueror) (Ottoman sultan;
    r. 1451–1481), 425, 436–437
Memphis (Egypt), 19
Men (men's roles and status). See also Patriarchy
    in ancient Egypt, 21
    in ancient Greece, 36, 38, 76
        Athenian, 59–61
        education and physical fitness, 73–74
        paternalism, 42, 43, 44
        sexual activity, 43–44, 74–75, 81–82
    Bedouin concept of manliness, 268
    eighteenth-century view of women, 604–605
    faithfulness in, 131–132
    as gladiators, 181
    Hebrew, 31
    in hunter-gatherer societies, 5–6
    as Islamic warriors, 271, 273
    Macedonian, 99, 100(i)
    manners and (seventeenth century), 560
    Neo-Assyrian, 26–27
    Paleolithic and Neolithic, 5–8
    Roman, 131, 132, 134, 140, 144, 145
        education of, 183
Menander (meh NAN der) (c. 342–289 B.C.E.),
    113, 114

Menes (MEE neez) (Egypt;
   c. 3100–c. 3040 B.C.E.), 16
Mennonites, 480
Mentuhotep II, 21
Mercantilism, 508
   English, 544
   French, 529–530, 556
Mercenaries
   in Ancient Greece, 92
   Carthaginian, 149
Merchants. *See also* Trade
   Hanseatic League, 406–407
Merian, Maria Sibylla (1646–1717), 558–559,
   559(*i*)
Mérida, battle of (1230), 391, 391(*m*)
Merovingian kingdoms (mer oh VIN jee un)
   (Merovingian society) (c. 485–751),
   242, 244, 276(*m*), 276–286, 293.
   See also Franks
   powerful people in, 281–285, 317–318
Mesopotamia (Mesopotamian civilization), 187,
   188(*m*). *See also* Akkadia; Assyria;
   Babylon; Sumer
   Bronze Age, 5
   cities in, 8–13, 14–15
   cuneiform writing, 11–13, 13(*f*)
   emergence of civilization in, 4
   empire building in, 12
   Epic of Creation, 3
   Hammurabi's laws, 14–15, 31
   religion and mythology in, 3, 4, 10–11
   Sassanid Empire and, 261
   Sumerian (southern Mesopotamian) society,
   8–13
Messiah, 196, 197, 198
Messiah (Handel), 585
Mestizos, 486, 574–575
Metacomet (King Philip), 552
Metals and metallurgy
   agriculture and, 8
   in ancient Egypt, 16
   in ancient Greece, 38, 39
   Assyrian, 26
   Hittite, 24
   in Mesopotamia (Bronze Age), 12
   in Middle Ages, 344
Metamorphoses (Ovid), 183
Metaphysics, 96
Methodius (Byzantine missionary), 302
Metics (noncitizens), 42, 72–73
Metz (Germany), 357
Meulen, Adam Frans van der, 523(*i*)
Meun, Jean de, 414
Mexico, 486, 504

Michelangelo Buonarroti (mik el AN jeh loh,
   bwo nah ROT tee) (1475–1564), 454,
   455(*i*), 510
Middle Ages
   commercial revolution and, 344–345, 369, 377,
   379, 382
   early medieval kingdoms, 275–293, 276(*m*)
   use of term, 260*n*
Middle class(es) (bourgeoisie)
   in Byzantine Empire, 265
   in eighteenth century, 567(*i*), 568, 581–584,
   586, 590
   in fourteenth and fifteenth centuries, 430–431,
   448, 454
   in seventeenth century, 491, 505, 524–525, 543,
   548–550, 560
Middle-Class Gentleman, The (Molière), 560
Middle East. *See also* Near East
   Byzantine Empire and, 260, 273, 296
   meaning of term, 7*n*
Middle Kingdom (Egypt; c. 2061–1665 B.C.E.),
   17(*m*), 21–22
Midrash, 225
Midwives, 195(*i*), 599
Mieszko I (MYESH ko) (prince of Poland;
   r. 963–992), 334
Migrations
   to American colonies, 575
   in Ancient Greece, 72
   Germanic, in fourth century, 235–243, 236(*m*)
Milan, 327, 329, 345–346, 349, 451, 456
   Visconti dynasty and, 450, 453, 458–459
Military. *See* Armed forces; War; Weapons and
   military technology
Milo (athlete), 38
Milton, John (1608–1674), 556–557
Milvian Bridge, battle of the (312), 221
Minerva, 137, 203
Ming dynasty (China), 463
Mining. *See* Metals and metallurgy
Minoan civilization (Minoans; Cretans), 33–36,
   34(*m*), 35(*i*)
Minoan Wall Painting (Thera), 35(*i*)
Minos (MY nus) (Crete), 34, 36
Minotaur, 34, 36
Missi dominici (MEE see doh MIN ih kee),
   312–313, 316, 336
Missionaries, Christian, 422
   Arianism and, 228
   in Balkans, 302
   in China, 397–398, 575, 603
   in England, 286
   in Frisia, 310

(continued)

Jesuit, 484–486, 485(i)
    Portugal and, 485(i), 486
    in Scandinavia, 322
    thirteenth-century, 392
Missy, Jean Rousset de, 593(i)
Mithras (MITH rus) (Mithraism), 204(i)
Mithridates VI (mith rih DAY teez) (Pontus;
    120–63 B.C.E.), 161–162
Moero of Byzantium, 113
Mohács (MO hahch), battle of (1526), 487(m),
    488, 488(i)
Molière (mohl YAYR) (1622–1673), 560–561, 593
Monarchy (kings; queens; emperors). *See also
    specific monarchies and empires*
    absolute. *See* Absolutism
    in ancient Near East, 7(m)
    Byzantine, 245–249, 296–300. *See also specific
        emperors*
    in Central and Eastern Europe (tenth and
        eleventh centuries), 332–336, 335(m)
    Danish, 322
    divine right of, 28–29, 503, 513, 523, 524, 528,
        553–554
    in Eastern Europe, fourteenth and fifteenth
        century, 437–439, 438(m)
    in Egypt, 18–20
    in England (Great Britain), 323, 327, 329–331,
        345, 457
        abolition of (1649), 544–545
        eleventh and twelfth centuries, 360–365,
            363(m)
        fourteenth and fifteenth centuries, 437, 439,
            447, 457
        Hundred Years' War and, 430–435, 433(m)
        King Alfred's law code, 330
        restoration of (1660), 545–546
        sixteenth and seventeenth centuries,
            494–497
        in twelfth and thirteenth centuries, 394(m),
            401–402, 402(i), 404–405, 407–409, 422
    in France, 331–332, 457. *See also* Louis XIV,
        absolutism and
        absolute, 540, 546
        Capetian kings, 332, 392, 394(m), 398–401,
            422
        courtiers in the sixteenth century, 503–504
        eighteenth century, 603
        eleventh and twelfth century, 361, 365–366
        fourteenth and fifteenth century, 437, 440,
            442, 447, 457, 459
        Hundred Years' War and, 430–435, 433(m)
        limits of absolutism (eighteenth century), 587
        post-Carolingian, 326, 326(m), 331–332
        sixteenth and seventeenth century, 490–491

    thirteenth century, 398–401, 400(m), 404–405
    twelfth century, 361, 365–366
    in Germany
        eleventh and twelfth century, 366–367
        post-Carolingian, 332–333, 334(i)
        tenth and eleventh centuries, 323, 332–335
        thirteenth century, 394–396
    Hellenistic period, 92–93, 106–112, 107(m),
        110–112, 111(i)
    Hittite, 24
    Lombard Italy and, 299–293
    Macedonian, 99–101
    Merovingian, 276(m), 281–282, 285, 288, 310
    in Neo-Assyrian Empire, 26–27
    papal
        fourteenth and fifteenth centuries, 440–443
        thirteenth and fourteenth centuries, 402–406
    Persian, 28–29, 30(i)
    in post-Carolingian age, 323–327, 331–337, 343
    revival of (eleventh and twelfth centuries)
        Byzantium, 358–367
        courtly culture, 367–369
        England, 360–365
        France, 365–366
        Germany, 366–367
    Roman (c. 753–509 B.C.E.), 139–142
    Roman principate, 172, 173, 175, 176,
        184–188, 190
        Caesar, 166
    in Russia, 594
    in Spain, 405, 407–408, 447–448, 458
    Sumerian, 10
Monasticism (mo NAS tih sizum) (monasteries
        and convents), 232–235, 233(i), 245,
        281–283, 284(i), 285, 324, 328, 339–340,
        342. *See also specific monastic orders*
    in Byzantine Empire, 265, 266–267
    coenobitic, 233–234
    communities of, 232
    crusaders and, 355, 356(i)
    in eleventh and twelfth centuries, 370,
        373–383
    in England, 286–288, 331
    in Frankish kingdoms, 277(i)
    Irish (Columbanian), 282–283, 286, 310
    in Italy, 289, 411(i)
    Luther and, 476, 477(i)
    reforms and, 315–316, 340, 346–347, 445
    women in, 234, 280–281, 283–285, 284(i), 286,
        288, 410
Monegund (nun), 280
Mongols (Tatars or Tartars), 385–386, 396–398,
        397(m), 420(m), 422, 438(m), 438–439,
        463, 466, 469(m)

Monophysites (muh NAHF uh syts), 229, 233(i), 246, 252, 273
Monotheism, 228, 270, 292
  in ancient Egypt, 22
  Byzantine Empire and, 260
  Hebrew, 25, 30–32
  Zoroastrianism and, 30
Montagu, Lady Mary Wortley (MAHN tah Hyoo) (1689–1762), 599
Montaigne, Michel de (mahn TAYN, mih shel de) (1533–1592), 512–513, 516, 518
Montesquieu, baron de (mahn tess KYOO) (Charles-Louis de Secondat) (1689–1755), 603–604
Monteverdi, Claudio (mahn tuh VAYR dee) (1567–1643), 512
Morality (moral values), 230, 231. See also Virtue(s)
  dualism in, 30
  law codes and, 244
  Plato and, 96–97
  relativism in, 75
  Roman, 130–132, 134, 136, 137, 139, 142, 145–146, 203, 205
    loss of, 158, 161, 162, 163
    males and, 234
  Socrates and, 76–78, 95
  sophists and, 75
Moravia, 535
More, Thomas (1478–1535), 475–476, 495
Moriscos, 492–493
Mosaics
  Alexander the Great at battle of Issus, 104(i)
  Christ as Sun God, 224(i)
  family from Edessa, 229(i)
  Hagia Sophia, 251(i)
  Justinian and his court in Ravenna, 246(i), 250
  mosque at Damascus, 259(i)
  Plato's Academy, 96(i)
  Roman, 171(i)
  Theodora and her court in Ravenna, 247(i)
  upper-class country life (fourth century), 241(i)
Moscow, 581, 594
Moses, 31, 233(i)
Mos maiorum ("the way of the ancestors"), 131, 146
Motets (mo TETS), 415
Mozarabs, 306
Muhammad (muh HAHM id) (prophet; c. 570–632), 268, 269–274, 272(m), 292
  Fatima and, 274, 305
  hadith literature and, 275
  successors of (632–750), 273–275, 293

Muhammad ibn Musa (d. 850), 308
Mühlberg, battle of (1547), 491
Mummification, 19, 23, 121
Munich, 462
Münster (MOON stuhr), Anabaptists in, 473, 473(i), 479–480, 480(f)
Müntzer, Thomas (1468?–1525), 478, 480(f)
Mursili II (Hittite king; r. 1321–1295 B.C.E.), 24
Muscovy (MUS kuh vee), 426, 438(m), 438–439, 469(m), 505, 508
Music, 46
  eighteenth-century, 567, 578, 584–585, 606
  Gregorian chant (plainchant), 373–374, 383
  polyphonic, 415, 452, 455
  Renaissance (fifteenth century), 452, 455–457
  seventeenth-century, 511–512, 527
  thirteenth-century, 386, 415
  written notation, 368(i), 374
Muslim calendar, 308(i)
Mussolini, Benito (moo suh LEE nee) (1883–1945), 174(i)
Mycenaean civilization (my seh NEE an), 33–36
Mystery cults, 66–68, 121, 122
Mythology, 3, 4
  Greek, 11, 34, 36, 37, 105
  Mesopotamian, 10–12

Nabonidus (nah bo NEE dus) (Babylon; r. c. 555–539 B.C.E.), 28
Naevius (NEE vee us) (d. 201 B.C.E.), 153
Nantes (nahnts), 577
Naples, 141, 322
Napoleon Bonaparte (Napoleon I) (BO nuh part) (1769–1821), 532
Naram-Sin (Akkadia; r. c. 2250 B.C.E.), 12–13
Naseby, battle of (1645), 542(m), 543
Native Americans (Indians), 467–470, 530, 552, 572, 603
  conversion to Christianity, 485–486, 574–575
Natural law, Grotius's conception of, 513–514
Natural rights, 514
Navigation. See Ships and navigation
Navigation Act (1651), 544
Navy (naval warfare)
  battle of Lepanto (1571), 492–493, 493(m), 497
  Byzantine, 265
  Delian League and Athens, 56–57, 58(i), 59, 61, 84, 85, 86(m), 98
  Great Britain and, 591
  Persian wars and, 55, 56
  Roman, 173
    First Punic War (264–241 B.C.E.), 149, 150
  Spanish Armada, 497, 505

Near East, 37. *See also* Middle East
　ancient, 7(*m*), 7*n*, 8*n*
　　empires in (to 500 B.C.E.), 25–32
　　science and religion in, 28
　Dark Age (1200–1000 B.C.E.), 25, 38
　Greek art and literature and, 45
　Greek migration to, 92–93
　Hellenistic kingdoms in, 92
　influence of, 45
　knowledge from, 46
　Neolithic Revolution in (c. 10,000–4000 B.C.E.),
　　6–8
Nebuchadnezzar II (neh boo kud NEZ ur) (Neo-
　Babylonian king; r. 605–562 B.C.E.), 27, 32
Nefer-ka-Re (Egypt; r. c. 2300 B.C.E.), 20
Nefertiti (nef ur TEE tee) (Egyptian queen;
　r. fourteenth century B.C.E.), 22
Neo-Assyrian Empire, 25–27, 26(*m*)
Neo-Babylonian Empire, 27–28
Neolithic period (Neolithic Revolution; New
　Stone Age), 3–4, 5–8, 33
Neoplatonism (nee oh PLAY tuh nizum),
　204–205, 255, 307, 359–360
Nepos, Julius, 241
Nero (Roman emperor; r. 54–68), 185, 186, 200
Nerva (Roman emperor; r. 96–98), 187
Nestorianism (Nestorian Christians), 228
Nestorius (bishop of Constantinople; d. 451), 228
Netherlands, 310, 316. *See also* Austrian
　Netherlands; Dutch Republic; Spanish
　Netherlands
　Calvinists in, 493–494
　under Spanish rule, 492–494, 493(*m*), 494(*m*),
　　496–497, 513
　War of Spanish Succession and, 587, 588(*m*)
Neustria (NEW stree ah), 276(*m*), 285, 310
New England, 481, 552, 571, 583
Newfoundland, 470, 587
New Kingdom (Egypt; c. 1569–1081 B.C.E.),
　15–16, 17(*m*), 22, 24, 25
New Model Army, 543
New Plymouth Colony, 508
News from the Republic of Letters (Bayle), 601
Newspapers, eighteenth-century, 583, 606
New Testament, 197, 198, 227, 475, 481
Newton, Isaac (1642–1727), 524, 554–556, 602
New World. *See* Americas, the
Nicaea (ny SEE uh), Council of (325), 228
Nice, 488
Nicephorus I (ny SEF uh rus) (Byzantine
　emperor; r. 802–811), 301, 302
Nicetius (Merovingian bishop), 282, 285
Nicholas V (pope; r. 1447–1455), 465
Nicolaitism, 347

Nicomedia, 218
Nicopolis, battle of (1396), 436, 436(*m*)
Nijmegen, Treaty of (NY may ghen) (1678–1679),
　531, 531(*m*)
Nika Riot (532), 249
Nile River, 16, 17, 17(*m*), 19, 21, 203, 233
Nîmes, aqueduct at, 149(*i*)
Nineveh (NIN uh vuh), 27
Nine Years' War (War of the League of Augsburg)
　(1689–1697), 587
Nippur (nih POOR), 15
Nobility. *See* Aristocracy
Nominalism, 413
Normandy (Normans), 321–322, 348, 359,
　398(*m*), 398–399, 399*n*
　conquest of England (1066), 360(*m*), 360–362,
　　361(*i*)
　Hundred Years' War (1337–1453) and, 431,
　　432(*m*)
North Africa, 8*n*
　Arabs and, 263
　Byzantine Empire and, 260
　city-states in, 55
　Donatism in, 228–229
　Islam and, 268, 305–307, 306(*m*), 390, 391(*m*),
　　488, 493
　Ottoman Empire and, 436(*m*)
　Vandals in, 240
North America. *See also* Native Americans
　colonies in, 570(*m*), 574, 576, 590, 596
　constitutionalism in, 524, 548, 552, 565
　English (British) colonies in, 508–509, 548, 568
　　Caribbean, 551
　　representative government, 509, 552, 565
　　settlement patterns, 574–575
　　slavery and slave trade, 548, 551–552,
　　　568–569, 570(*m*), 571, 571(*m*), 571(*f*), 573
　exploration and settlements (fifteenth and
　　sixteenth centuries), 470
　French colonies in, 509, 568, 587, 588(*m*), 596
　　Canada, 530, 574
Northern Crusades, 387, 388(*m*), 406, 422
Northwest passage, 470
Norway, 303, 322, 562
Nossis of Locri, 113
Nova Scotia, 587
Novels, 192, 193
　eighteenth-century, 578, 583, 585–586, 606
　seventeenth-century, 561
Novgorod (NAHV guh rahd), 428, 438(*m*), 439
Nubia (NOO bee uh), 16–17, 17(*m*), 22
Nur al-Din, 356
Nuremberg, 446, 452, 453
Nystad, Treaty of (1721), 595, 595(*m*)

Oblation, 234, 283

Occitan, 366–367

Ockham, William of (c. 1285–1349), 413, 441

Ockham's razor, 413

Octavian. *See* Augustus

Odoacer (oh doh AH ser) (c. 434?–493), 241, 242

Odyssey (Homer), 37, 153, 183, 255

Ogodei (OH guh day) (Great Khan; 1186–1241), 396

Old Believers (Russia), 538

Old English (Anglo-Saxon language), religious works in, 330, 331(*i*)

Old Kingdom (Egypt; c. 2687–2190 B.C.E.), 16–21

Old Testament (Hebrew Bible), 30–32, 123, 198, 225, 481. *See also* Torah

Oleg (Russian chief; r. c. 900), 302

Oligarchy (AW lih gahr kee), 40, 44, 130

Olympic Games, in ancient Greece, 38

Olympus, Mount, 66

On Agriculture (Cato), 154

On Architecture (Alberti), 455

On the Caesars (Victor), 217(*m*)

On the Church (Wycliffe), 444

On the Construction of the Human Body (Vesalius), 515

On the Manner of Negotiating with Sovereigns (Callières), 597

On the Nature of Things (Lucretius), 154

On the Revolution of the Celestial Spheres (Copernicus), 514

Opera, 511–512, 521, 527, 584–585

Optimates (op tee MAHT ays), 160, 161, 167

Oracles, 102, 118

Orange, princes of, 493

Oratory. *See* Rhetoric

Order. *See* Social order

Order of Christ, 465

Order of Sword Brothers, 387

Oresteia (aw res TY uh) (Aeschylus) (458 B.C.E.), 80–81

Orestes (aw RES teez), 81, 241

Orfeo (Monteverdi), 512

Origen (OH rih jen) (c. 185–255), 203

Original sin, doctrine of, 230

Origins, The (Cato), 154

Orléans, duke of (or lay AHN) (1674–1723), 589

Orléans, siege of, 431, 432(*m*)

Oroonoko (Behn), 561

Orthodoxy

   Christian, 202, 227, 228, 229, 230. *See also* Heresies

   Justinian and, 251–252

Orvieto, cathedral at, 418

Osiris (oh SY ris), 24, 123(*i*), 203

Osman I (Ottoman emperor; r. 1280–1324), 436

Ospedale degli Innocenti (Florence), 462

Osrhoëne, 229(*i*)

Ostracism (AHS trah siz um), 59–60

Ostrogoths, 242, 249, 254(*m*), 289

Oswy (Northumbria; r. c. 665), 287

Otto I (Germany and Holy Roman emperor; r. 936–973), 322–323, 332(*m*), 332–333

Otto II (Germany and Holy Roman emperor; r. 973–983), 333

Otto III (Germany and Holy Roman emperor; r. 983–1002), 332(*m*), 333, 334(*i*)

Ottoman Empire (Ottoman Turks), 420(*m*), 426, 436, 463, 466, 564(*m*). *See also* Turkey

   at Constantinople, 425, 425(*i*), 458

   expansion in fourteenth and fifteenth centuries, 436(*m*), 437–438, 438(*m*), 457, 459, 467–468, 469(*m*), 471

   Hungary and (1657–1730), 596, 596(*m*)

   Jews in, 448

   Peace of Westphalia and, 519(*m*)

   in seventeenth century, 533, 535(*m*), 535–537, 536(*i*), 540

   in sixteenth century, 486–488, 487(*m*), 488(*i*), 492–493

Ottonian dynasty (Germany), 332(*m*), 332–333, 334(*i*), 335(*m*)

Ovid (AHV id) (43 B.C.E.–17 C.E.), 183

Ovism, doctrine of, 604–605

Oxford University, 413, 444

Pachomius, 233

Paganism, 202

Painted Stoa (Athens), 61, 116

Painting(s)

   catacomb, 199(*i*)

   Dutch, 548–550, 550(*i*), 559

   in eighteenth century, 583–584, 606

   Hellenistic, 114

   portraiture and, 583

   red-figure, 42(*i*), 55(*i*)

   Renaissance (fifteenth century), 452–455, 454(*i*), 456(*i*)

   in sixteenth and seventeenth centuries, 510–511, 558(*i*), 558–559, 559(*i*)

   vase, 42(*i*), 51(*i*), 69(*i*), 71(*i*), 94(*i*)

   wall, 141, 157(*i*), 204(*i*)

Palaces

   Cretan (Minoan), 34

   Mycenaean, 35

   Persian, 30(*i*)

   Sumerian, 10

Paleolithic period (Old Stone Age), 5–8
Palestine, 198, 225. *See also* Jerusalem; Levant
    30 C.E., 197 *(m)*
    ancient, 22, 31, 32, 109, 123, 124
Panathenaia, 67
Papacy (popes). *See also individual popes*
    at Avignon (1309–1378; "Babylonian
        Captivity"), 405–406, 440–443, 442*(m)*, 450
    Battle of Lepanto (1571) and, 492
    Byzantium and, 290–292
    Carolingians and, 310–311, 313
    church reform and
        1050–1150, 346–358, 365, 379–382
        Fourth Lateran Council, 403–404, 422
    curia (papal government), 352, 441, 443
    Eastern Europe and, 334–336
    English monarchs and, 495–496
    in fourteenth and fifteenth centuries, 436,
        440–443, 456, 458–459, 471
        Great Schism (1378–1417), 426, 442*(m)*,
          442–443, 458
    Germany and, 366–367, 387, 393–396
    Italy and, 311, 393–396, 394*(m)*, 395*(m)*
    Lombard kings and, 290–293, 310–311
    Luther and, 476–477
    Ottonian Empire and, 333
    patronage of, 510, 557
    Protestantism and, 490–491
Papal States, 441, 469*(m)*
Paper (papermaking), 309, 451
Paracelsus (pah rah SEL sus) (**Theophrastus
    Bombastus von Hohenheim**)
    (1493–1541), 515–517
Paradise Lost (Milton), 557
Parallel Lives (Plutarch), 193
Parenti, Marco, 461
Parenti, Parente, 461
Paris, 285, 366, 407, 415, 584, 598, 602
    in fourteenth and fifteenth centuries, 440, 456
    French parlement in, 399, 400, 401
    Jacquerie in, 434
    population growth in, 577
    University of, 370, 371, 402
Parlements (France), 399, 408*n*, 525, 528, 529, 589
Parliament(s), 407–409, 435
    constitutionalism and, 524
    English (British), 408–409, 408*n*
        Charles II and, 545–546
        in the eighteenth century, 589–590
        Exclusion Crisis (1678), 546
        in the seventeenth century, 541–547, 556
        in the sixteenth century, 495, 497
    Hungarian, 537
    Irish, 590

Parthenon (Athens), 62–65, 224
Parthians (Parthian Empire), 107, 165, 184*(i)*, 205
Partnerships, 343–344
Pascal, Blaise (1623–1662), 528, 556
Pasti, Matteo de, 425, 437
Pastoral Care (Gregory the Great), 331*(i)*
Pastoralists, 8
Pastoral Rule (Gregory the Great), 290
Paternalism, in ancient Greece, 42–43, 44
Patria potestas (PAH tree ah poh TES tuz)
    ("power of a father"), 134
Patriarchy (patriarchal society)
    Babylonian, 14
    in Byzantine Empire, 248
    European, 430
    in Florence (fifteenth century), 461–462
    Germanic, 237
    Islamic, 272
    Sumerian, 10
Patricians, 143, 144, 145, 148, 460–462
Patrick, St. (c. 389–461), 286
Patrilineal families, 328, 329, 332–333, 337, 461
Patristic authors, 230
Patron-client system, Roman, 132, 133, 176
    armed forces and, 161, 162
Paul III (pope; r. 1534–1549), 484
Paul of Tarsus (c. 10–65 C.E.), 196, 198
Pavia, 289
    battle of, 487, 487*(m)*
Pax Romana (PAHKS roh MAHN ah)
    (Roman peace), 172–195
    creating, 173–184
    maintaining, 184–195
Peace movement, in post-Carolingian age, 328–329
Peace of Augsburg (1555), 491, 498, 501
Peace of God, 328–329
Peace of Rijswijk (RICE vike) (1697), 531*(m)*, 532
Peace of Utrecht (1713–1714), 587, 588*(m)*, 597
Peace of Westphalia (1648), 501–503,
    502*(m)*, 519*(m)*, 597
Peasants. *See also* Serfs
    in Byzantine Empire, 299
    in Carolingian estates, 317–318
    in early Middle Ages, 278–281
    in Eastern Europe, 580–581, 606
    in eighteenth century, 580–581, 606
    in eleventh and twelfth centuries,
        340–342, 356*(i)*
    in England, 360–361
    in fourteenth and fifteenth centuries, 440
    in Germany, 333, 533
    in Hellenistic kingdoms, 112
    Hundred Years' War (1337–1453)
        and, 431, 435

in Ireland, 590
in Italy, 329
in Merovingian period, 278–279, 280–281
plague and, 426–429
in Poland, 540
popular culture and, 561–562
in post-Carolingian age, 322–328
in Roman Empire, 220
in Russia and Soviet Union, 538, 539(i)
in seventeenth century, 538, 539(i), 540
    economic crisis and, 497, 503,
    505–507, 507(i)
in sixteenth-century Holy Roman Empire, 478
in Switzerland, 407
Thirty Years' War and, 500, 501
Peasants' War (1525), 478, 478(m), 480(f)
Peloponnese (pel oh poh NEES), 34, 38, 43(m)
Peloponnesian League, 56, 57(m), 61, 84
Peloponnesian War (431–404 B.C.E.), 78, 83,
    84–86, 84(f), 86(m), 88(m),
    92, 93, 94–95
    Golden Age and, 52, 93
Penance, sacrament of, 474
Penates (spirits of the household), 137
Penitent heretics, 393
Pensées (Pascal), 556
Pentateuch (Torah), 31, 32
Pergamum (PUR gah mum), 107, 114, 159
Pericles (PEHR ih kleez) (c. 495–429 B.C.E.),
    59–61, 62, 72, 74, 82, 83–85
Peripatetic School (Athens), 97
Persephone (Kore), 68, 203
Persepolis, 28, 30(i)
Persia (Persian Empire), 28–30, 29(m), 47(m), 51,
    53(m), 463. See also Iran
    Alexander the Great and, 92, 102
    European attitudes toward, 603
    Greece and, 51–56
        Delian League, 57
        invasion of Greece (480–479 B.C.E.),
        54–56, 63(i)
        King's Peace (386 B.C.E.), 98
        Peloponnesian War (431–404 B.C.E.), 85
        wars (499–479 B.C.E.), 51–56, 53(m),
        55(i), 86(m), 101
    in Hellenistic period (323–30 B.C.E.), 107
    in India, 576
    Islam and, 268, 272(m), 273–275, 292
    Philip II of Macedonia and, 101
    Sassanid, 205, 261, 296–297
Persian Letters (Montesquieu), 603–604
Perspective, 454–455, 471, 510, 511(i)
Peter (Portuguese regent; r. 1440–1448), 465
Peter, St. (apostle), 227, 287, 290

Peter I (the Great) (Russia; r. 1689–1725), 568,
    592–595, 593(i), 595(m)
Petition of Right (1628), 541
Petra, 109(i)
Petrarch, Francesco (1304–1374), 440,
    448, 450
Petronius (d. 66 C.E.), 182
Petronius Probus, 213(i)
Petty, William, 598
Pharmacology, 514, 516. See also Medicine
Pharos (Alexandria), 120
Pharsalus (far SAY lus), battle of (48 B.C.E.), 166
Philip I (France; r. 1052–1108), 365
Philip II (Augustus) (France; r. 1180–1223), 356,
    358, 366, 398–401, 400(m), 422
Philip II (Macedonia; r. 359–336 B.C.E.),
    99–101, 101(m)
Philip II (Spain; r. 1556–1598), 490, 492–494,
    493(m), 495–497, 511(i)
Philip III (Spain; r. 1598–1621), 493–494
Philip IV (Spain; r. 1621–1665), 504
Philip IV (the Fair) (r. 1285–1314), 404(i),
    404–405, 407
Philip V (Macedonia; 238–179 B.C.E.), 150, 151
Philip V (Spain; r. 1700–1746), 587, 588(m)
Philip VI (France; r. 1328–1350), 430
Philoponus, John (fil uh PAHN us)
    (c. 490–570), 255
Philosophy
    Greek, 45–47, 93
        Aristotle, 97–98
        Plato, 95–97, 116
        Socrates, 75–78
        sophists, 74–75
    Hellenistic, 115–118
    rationalist, 46–47
    Roman, 154–155
Philoxenus of Eretria, 114
Phoebe (early church deacon), 198
Phoenicians, 47(m)
Phrygia (Asia Minor), 137
Physical fitness, in ancient Greece, 73
Physics
    in Ancient Greece, 46
    in Hellenistic philosophy, 116
    Newtonian, 554–556
Piacenza (Italy), 406
Pietism, 586
Pilgrimage (pilgrims), 370, 377, 382,
    410, 416, 475, 508, 562
    to Holy Land, 352–353, 354(i), 355
    to Mecca, 268, 271
    to Rome, 278, 476
Pippin (son of Louis the Pius), 316

Pippin III (the Short) (Carolingian king;
       r. 751–768), 291–292, 310
Pirates, 575
  in Mediterranean, 163, 322, 463
  Muslim, 322, 463
  in North Africa, 488
  Viking, 320
Pisano, Nicola (c. 1220–1278?), 421
Pius II (pope; r. 1458–1464), 457
Pizarro, Francisco (c. 1475–1541), 469–470
Placita, 329
Plague, 426–430, 427*(m)*, 429*(f)*, 444*(i)*,
       445–447, 449
  of 1628–1632, 505–506, 508
  in 1665 (London), 545
  disappearance of, 577
  in Germany, 501
Plainchant (Gregorian chant), 373–374, 383
Plantagenets, 362*n*
Plantations (plantation economy), 467–468, 509,
       548, 559, 568–574, 570*(m)*, 571*(f)*, 573*(i)*
Plataea (plah TEE uh), battle of (479 B.C.E.), 53*(m)*
Plato (PLAY toh) (c. 429–348 B.C.E.), 76–77, 93,
       95–97, 116, 117, 204, 224, 253, 359–360
  Academy established by, 95, 96*(i)*
  Renaissance and (fifteenth century), 451
Platonic Academy (Florence), 451
Plautus (d. 184 B.C.E.), 153
Plebeian (pleh BEE in) Assembly, 144, 159
Plebeians, 143, 144, 145, 148, 175
Plebiscites (PLEB ih syts), 144, 162
Pliny (PLIN ee) (61–113 C.E.), 194
Pliska, battle of (811), 301, 302*(m)*
Plotinus (plah TY nuhs) (c. 205–270), 204
Plutarch (PLOO tahrk) (c. 50–120), 159, 193
Podestà, 367, 406
Poetry. *See also* Literature; *individual poets*
  Akkadian, 12
  Bedouin, 268, 273
  Chaldean, 27
  Greek, 36–37, 45–46, 81
  Hellenistic, 113–114
  Islamic, 275
  lyric, 45–46
  in Renaissance, 448–450, 449*(i)*
  Roman, 154, 183, 282
  in twelfth and thirteenth centuries,
       367–369, 386, 409, 413–415
Poitiers (pwah tee AY), battle of (1356), 433*(m)*
Poitou, 362, 398*(m)*, 398–399, 400
Poland, 303, 437–438, 438*(m)*, 594
  Jews in, 447, 539–540
  Mongol attacks on, 385, 396
  parliaments in, 407

  peasants in, 580–581
  Reformation in, 481, 482*(m)*, 486
  Roman Catholicism in, 333–334, 438, 443
  in sixteenth century, 508
Poland-Lithuania, 438, 438*(m)*, 469*(m)*
  in eighteenth century, 594, 595*(m)*,
       596, 605*(m)*
  Protestantism in, 499
  in seventeenth century, 524, 533, 564*(m)*
  siege of Vienna and, 537, 540
Polanians, 334
Police force, first, 178
Polis (Greek city-state), 38–43, 39*(m)*, 108.
       See also Athens; Sparta
  Alexander the Great and, 104–105
  citizenship (political rights), 39–43
  disunity after Peloponnesian War, 98–99
  Hellenistic period (323–30 B.C.E.), 92, 108
  Philip II of Macedonia and, 99–101
Politics (political parties). *See also* Democracy;
       specific political parties
  Roman, 159–160
  in seventeenth century, 512–514
Politiques, 490–491, 502–503, 512
Polo, Maffeo, 385
Polo, Marco (1254–1324), 385, 386,
       398, 463, 466
Polo, Niccolò, 385
Polo family, 397
Poltava, battle of (1709), 594, 595*(m)*
Polyphony, 415, 452, 455
Polytheism, 230. *See also* Gods and goddesses
  in Byzantine Empire, 251, 252, 253
  in Golden Age Greece, 66
  Hellenistic, 121
  Islam and, 270
  Mesopotamian, 10
  in Roman Empire, 202–204, 221, 222*(i)*,
       222–224, 226*(m)*
Pompeii, 187
  religious shrine from, 138*(i)*
Pompey, Gnaeus (POMP ee, NEE us)
       (106–48 B.C.E.), 153*(m)*, 159, 163–167, 173
Pontius Pilate (governor of Judea;
       r. 26–36 C.E.), 197
Poor, the (poverty)
  in ancient Greece, 41
  in Augustan Rome, 177, 179, 180, 181, 186
  in Byzantine Empire, 248–249
  Christianity and, 225
  in eighteenth century, 581–582
  monastic orders and, 375–376, 379–381,
       409–411, 411*(i)*
  Protestant reformers and, 562–563

in Ptolemaic Egypt, 112
punishments of, 216
Roman, 156–159, 163, 182
in seventeenth century, 562–565
 economic crisis and, 505–506, 507(i)
Poor Laws, England (1597), 505
Pope, Alexander (1688–1744), 555
Popolo, in Italian communes, 406
Popular culture (mass culture).
 See also Entertainment
in seventeenth century, 561–564
Populares (poh puh LAHR es), 160
Population (population growth or decline).
 See also Migrations
in Archaic Age, 40
census and, 459
in Dark Age, 33, 40
in eighteenth century, 577, 578, 581
in Minoan civilization, 34
Neolithic Revolution and, 7, 9, 34
plague and (1340–1450), 426–429, 429(f)
Roman Empire, 130, 140, 164, 194, 208
 under Augustus, 177
Rome and Italy (300 B.C.E.), 148, 156–157
in sixteenth and seventeenth centuries,
 474, 504–507
in twelfth century, 340–343
Poquelin, Jean-Baptiste. *See* Molière
Porphyry (POR fih ree) (c. 234–305), 223
Portugal, 456(i)
colonies of, 492, 493(m), 508, 549(m), 574–576.
 See also Brazil
in Africa, 575
exploration and settlements (fifteenth and
 sixteenth centuries), 426, 463–466,
 464(m), 465(m), 468, 468(i), 470,
 485(i), 486
Muslims in, 388(m), 390–391, 391(m)
slave trade and, 551, 569, 570(m), 574–575
Thirty Years' War and, 500
Poulain de la Barre, François (1647–1723), 561
Poussin, Nicolas (1594–1665), 558, 558(i)
Praetorian guard, 175
Praetors (PREE tohrz), 144, 145
Prague
 1648 sack of, 501
 defenestration in (1618), 498
 Hus in, 443, 445
Praise of Folly, The (Erasmus), 475
Praxagoras of Cos (fourth century B.C.E.), 120
Praxiteles (prak SIT uh leez)
 (fourth century B.C.E.), 114
Predestination, doctrine of, 480–481
Pregnancy, 232

Presbyterianism (Presbyterians),
 496, 542–544, 547, 583
Press, the. *See* Newspapers
Priests and priestesses. *See also* Clergy
in Athens, 43, 63
influence of, 10
ordaining of, 202, 227
Roman, 139
Primogeniture, 328, 355
Prince, The (Machiavelli), 457
Princeps. See Principate
Princess of Clèves, The (Lafayette), 526, 561
Principate (PRIN sih payt), Roman, 172, 173, 175,
 176, 177, 184–188, 190, 215
Principia Mathematica (Newton), 555
Printing
 Dutch Republic and, 550, 583, 603
 in fifteenth century, 448, 451–452
 Reformation and, 477(i), 481
Proletariat (proletarians). *See also* Workers
 Roman, 144, 161
Property (property rights). *See also* Inheritance;
 Landownership
in ancient Greece, 43–44, 68–69
in Germanic society, 237
Hammurabi's code, 14
in Rome, 134, 136
Proscription, 162, 166
Prostitution, 440, 563
in Byzantine Empire, 248, 252
in Florence (fifteenth century), 462
in Golden Age Athens, 71(i), 72–73
in Rome, 136, 157, 180
Protagoras, 74–75
Protestantism (Protestants). *See also* Calvinism;
 Lutherans; Presbyterianism; Protestant
 Reformation; Puritans
education and, 582–583, 586
in England (Great Britain),
 492, 494–497, 529, 589, 590
 Toleration Act (1689), 547
French (Huguenots), 480, 489–491, 490(m),
 509, 528–529, 568
in Germany, 476–479, 480(f), 481,
 487, 499
in Holy Roman Empire (sixteenth century),
 476–479, 482(m), 490(m), 518, 519(m)
music and, 511
in Poland-Lithuania, 539–540
popular religious practices of seventeenth
 century and, 562–563
in sixteenth century, 473–497, 482(m)
Thirty Years' War and, 498, 499,
 501–502

Protestant Reformation, 473–486, 482(m), 498
    Anabaptists and, 473, 479–480, 480(f), 491
    Calvin and, 479–481, 480(f)
    in England, 492, 494–497
    Luther and, 476–480, 477(i), 480(f)
    marriage and, 483(i), 483–484, 507
    social changes and, 481, 483–484
    vernacular translations of Bible and,
        481, 483
    violence of, 512–513, 520–521
    Zwingli and, 479–480, 480(f)
Provincial Letters (Pascal), 528
Prussia, 387, 388(m), 568, 569, 591, 595(m),
        595–596
    in eighteenth century, 605(m)
    landholders in, 580
Ptahhotep, 21
Ptolemaic Egypt (tawl eh MAY ik), 107–111,
        111(i), 112, 113, 121–122, 123, 123(i),
        135, 166, 173
Ptolemy (TAW luh mee) (astronomer; fl. second
        century), 308(i), 514–515
Ptolemy I (Egypt; c. 367–282 B.C.E.), 106, 122, 123
Ptolemy II (Egypt; r. 282–246 B.C.E.), 111, 113, 123
Ptolemy III (Egypt; d. 221 B.C.E.), 122
Ptolemy V (Egypt; r. 203–180 B.C.E.), 91(i)
Ptolemy XIII (Egypt; 63–47 B.C.E.), 166
Public baths, in Rome, 178, 207
Public health, in eighteenth century, 598–599
Public opinion, in Rome, 144
Public sanitation, in the eighteenth century,
        598–599, 606
Public works
    under Louis XIV, 527–528
    in Roman Republic and Empire, 133, 146, 159,
        166, 190, 219, 220
Publishing industry. See Books and
        publishing industry
Publius Claudius Pulcher, 139
Pulcheria (puhl KER ee uh) (Byzantine emperor;
        r. 414–453), 229
Punic (PEW nik) Wars, 148–152
Puritans, 495–496, 508, 509, 541–545, 556, 562
Pyramids, in ancient Egypt, 15, 19–20, 20(i)
Pyrrho (PIHR ro) (c. 360–270 B.C.E.), 117
Pythagoras (py THAG or as) (sixth century
        B.C.E.), 46, 117

Quadrivium, 371
Quaestor (KWES tohr), 145
Quakers, 543–544
Quebec, French settlement of, 530
Quest of the Holy Grail, 414
Quietism, 586

Qur'an, 32, 269, 270(i), 273, 275, 287, 292, 307,
        308–309
Quraysh tribe, 268, 269, 270, 271

Race (racial discrimination; racism). See also
        Anti-Semitism
    in American colonies, 574–575
    Roman Catholic church and (sixteenth
        century), 485(i), 486
Racine, Jean-Baptiste (1639–1699), 527, 561
Radical democracy, 59–61
Rahman III, Abd al- (caliph; r. 912–961), 306
Raimon de Miraval (fl. 1191–1229), 368(i)
Rákóczi, Ferenc (RAH kot see, FER ents)
        (1676–1735), 596
Ramadan, 271
Ramesses II (RAM uh seez) (Egypt; thirteenth
        century B.C.E.), 25
Ranters, 543
Rape, 462–463
Rape of the Sabine Women, 129
Rationalism (rationality), 46–47.
        See also Logic; Reason
Ravenna, 218, 242, 312
    Exarchate of, 262, 289(m), 291
    Justinian and his Court in, 246(i)
    Theodora and her court in, 247(i)
Raymond VI (count of Toulouse), 392
Raymond VII (count of Toulouse), 392
Razin, Stenka (d. 1671), 538, 539(i)
Reason. See also Logic; Rationalism
    Descartes and, 516–517, 604
    the Enlightenment and, 601–602
    scholastics and, 411–413
Reccared (REK a red) (Visigothic king;
        r. 586–601), 288
Recession
    in fourteenth and fifteenth centuries, 440–441
    in sixteenth and seventeenth centuries,
        504–507
Reconquista (ray con KEE stuh) (Christian
        reconquest of Spain), 348, 386, 388(m),
        390–391, 391(m), 408, 447–448
Redistributive economies, 10, 14, 34–36, 37
Reflections upon Marriage (Astell), 604
Reform (reform movements). See also specific
        reforms and reform movements
    Catholic Church (1050–1300), 346–358, 370
        beginnings of, 346–348
        early crusades and crusader states, 352–356
        Fourth Lateran Council and, 403–404
        Gregorian reform and Investiture Conflict
            (1073–1085), 349(m), 349–351,
            366–367, 382

in fourteenth and fifteenth centuries, 445
Protestant (sixteenth century), 473–486, 477(i), 480(f), 482(m)
Regensburg, Diet of (1541), 491
Regulus, Marcus Atilius (REG yoo lus) (Roman general; d. c. 250 B.C.E.), 156
Reims, 370
    Cathedral of, 431–432
    Council of (1049), 348
Relativism, 75
Relics, cult of, 233, 279(i), 279–280, 284(i), 287, 290, 325, 329, 336, 348, 374, 377, 389, 410, 414(i), 416, 477(i), 562, 586
Religion(s), 25. See also Cult(s); Gods and goddesses; Reform; specific religions
    Assyrian, 27
    in early Middle Ages, 280–283
    Egyptian, 18–24
    the Enlightenment and, 601–602
    Greek, 121
        Golden Age Athens, 66–68
        Minoan and Mycenaean period, 37
        sophists and, 74–75
    Hebrew, 30–32
    in Hellenistic period, 121–125
    Hittite, 24
    major (c. 1200), 380(m)
    Mesopotamian, 3–4, 5
    in North Africa, 263
    Paleolithic, 6
    Persian, 28, 30
    Roman, 131, 137
        Etruscans and, 142
        government and, 139
    in Roman Empire. See also Christianity, Roman Empire and reforms of
        fourth century C.E., 220–221
    seventeenth-century conflicts over, 473–474, 565
    Sumerian, 10–11
    in thirteenth and fourteenth centuries, 409–413
    women's role in, 42–43
Religious revivals (revivalism), eighteenth-century, 586
Religious tolerance/intolerance (religious freedom), 512–514, 601–602
    Archduke Ferdinand's curtailment of, 498
    Constantine and, 221
    in Dutch Republic, 494, 540, 550
    Edict of Nantes (1598) and, 490–491, 528–529, 533
    in England, 540, 545–547
    in sixteenth century, 474, 489–491, 494
    Theodoric and, 242

Rembrandt van Rijn (REM brant van RINE) (1606–1669), 511, 548, 559
Remegius, St., 348
Renaissance
    Carolingian (c. 790–c. 900), 309, 314(i), 314–315
    fifteenth-century, 448–471, 469(m)
        art and music, 452–457
        classical literature and learning of, 425–426, 453, 455(i), 471
        humanism, 448–452, 471
        in Italy, 425, 457–459
    Islamic (c. 790–c. 1050), 307–309, 314
    Macedonian (c. 870–c. 1025), 297, 299–300, 301(i), 307, 314(i)
Reproduction, 604–605. See also Childbearing; Sex and sexuality
    in Ancient Greece, 43
    in Roman Empire, 194–195
Republic, The (Plato), 97
Revenues. See Taxes
Revivalist movements. See Religious revivals
Rhetoric (public speaking)
    in Byzantine Empire, 253
    Roman, 136, 182, 183
Rhineland, 381, 444
    Jews in, 357
Rhode Island, 508
Rich, the. See also Upper classes
    in Ancient Greece, 36, 57–58, 61, 70, 72
    in Byzantine society, 248–249
    in Hellenistic Kingdoms, 108
    Persian, 28
    Roman, 134, 144, 148, 157–158, 177, 179, 180, 182, 183, 195
Richard I (the Lion-Hearted) (England; r. 1189–1199), 401
Richard II (England; r. 1377–1399), 356, 435, 443
Richard III (England; r. 1483–1485), 435
Richelieu, Cardinal (1585–1642), 499–500, 503
Roads, Roman, 148, 148(m)
Robert (Naples; r. 1309–1343), 450
Robinson Crusoe (Defoe), 585
Rococo style, 583–584, 584(i)
Rollo (Viking leader; c. 860–931), 321
Roman Catholic church (Catholicism), 202. See also Bishops; Heresies, Christian; Monasticism; Papacy; Sacraments
    astronomy and, 514–515
    Augustine and, 230
    clergy
        in Bohemia, 445–446

(continued)

Fourth Lateran Council and (1215), 389(i),
        403–404
    taxation of, 404(i), 404–405
Counter-Reformation and, 484–486, 510
crusades and, 352–356, 354(i), 355(m), 380(m),
        383, 386
in Dutch Republic, 494
in Eastern Europe, 303
in eighteenth century, 586
in England (Great Britain), 287, 494–497,
        541–542, 544–547, 602
the Enlightenment and, 603
in France
    Inquisition, 392–393, 393(f)
    under Louis IX, 400–401
    under Louis XIV, 528–529, 557, 562–564
    seventeenth century, 562–563
    taxing the clergy, 404(i), 404–405
    wars of religion (sixteenth century), 489–491
Great Schisms and
    1054, 348, 352
    1378–1417, 426, 442(m), 442–443, 458
in Holy Roman Empire (sixteenth century),
        476–479, 482(m), 490(m), 493(m),
        518, 519(m)
Inquisition and, 386, 392–393, 393(f), 404, 444,
        447–448
in Ireland, 547, 590
in Italy, 289–290
    conversion of Lombards, 289–290
Jansenism and, 528, 586
in Lithuania, 438
marriage and, 351–352, 483–484
missionaries, 484–486, 485(i)
in Poland, 333–334, 438, 443
in Poland-Lithuania, 540
Protestant Reformation and, 475–486,
        482(m), 498
    violence of, 512–513, 520–521
in sixteenth and seventeenth centuries
    Africa and the New World, 485–486
    Counter-Reformation, 484–486, 498, 507
    popular religious practices, 562–563
    religious wars, 487–497
in Spain, 288–289
    reconquista, 447–448
Thirty Years' War and, 498–503
Romance of the Rose, The, 414–415
Romances, 369, 448
Roman Empire, 130, 139, 171–211. See also specific
        emperors
    Arabs and, 259, 289, 292
    under Augustus, 177–182
    Byzantine Empire and, 260, 281, 289–293

Carolingian kingdoms and, 317–318, 323
Christianity and, 171, 181, 195–205,
        222–235
    appeal of religious and social values, 225
    Constantine's conversion, 214, 221
    development as a new religion, 199–202
    Jesus and the spread of his teachings,
        196–198
    Jews and, 225
    the military and, 225
    persecution of Christians, 200, 208–210, 221
    polytheism and, 202–204, 221, 222(i),
        222–224, 226(m)
    spread of Christianity (300–600), 222–227,
        226(m)
    state religion, Christianity as, 224, 225
    women and, 225–226
expansion of
    c. 500–44 B.C.E., 153(m)
    30 B.C.E.–117 C.E., 188(m)
Germanic peoples and, 187, 205, 208
Golden Age of (96–180), 189–195
    armed forces, 189
    financial factors, 189–190
    law, 193–194
    literature, 193
    natural features and languages, 191(m)
    reproduction and marriage, 194–195
    Romanization of provinces, 190–195
Justinian's plan to reunite eastern and western
        empires, 249–252
Merovingian kingdoms and, 276–280, 281, 285,
        286, 288
natural features and languages of, 191(m)
Pax Romana (Roman peace)
    creating, 172–184
    maintaining, 184–195, 205
peoples and kingdoms of (c. 526), 235–245,
        243(m)
principate, 172, 176, 184–188, 193
reorganization of (fourth century C.E.)
    administrative structure, 214–221,
        217(m), 218(m)
    the dominate, 215–216
    financial reform and social consequences,
        219–220
    laws, 216
    religious reform, 220–221
slaves, 147, 156, 158, 180–181, 208
    citizenship, 140
    education and, 136
    ex-slaves, 133(i), 133–134
third-century crisis (c. 284 C.E.), 205–210,
        209(m), 214

defense of frontiers, 205
natural disasters, 208–210
Severan emperors, 206–210
"Year of the Four emperors" (69 C.E.), 186
Romanesque churches, 374, 375(i), 376,
378(i), 414(i)
Roman Forum, 129(i), 133
Romania (Romanians), 6(i), 8n, 537
Romanization, 190–195, 191(m), 192(i)
Roman law, 144–146, 193–194, 216, 244, 292, 371
traditions of, 276, 281, 285, 289, 398
Umayyad caliphate and, 274(i)
Roman literature, 152–155, 183, 245. See also
Classical literature and learning
Roman peace. See Pax Romana
Roman republic, 140, 158–168
c. 44 B.C.E., 168(m)
c. 30 B.C.E., 124(m)
Augustus's "restoration" of (27 B.C.E.–14 C.E.),
172, 174–177, 185
early (509–287 B.C.E.), 142–146
fifth century B.C.E., 147(m)
imperialism and (fifth to second centuries
B.C.E.), 146–158
expansion in Italy, 147–148
social consequences of wars, 147, 156–158
wars with Carthage, 148–152
late republic (c. 133–44 B.C.E.), 158–168
downfall of, 163–167
Gaius Marius and the first client armies,
160–161
Gracchi brothers and factional politics,
158–160
Sulla and civil war, 161–163
social and moral values in, 130–132
Roman society and culture, 130–139
education for public life, 136
family, 134–136
in Golden Age (96–180 C.E.), 189–195
hierarchy in, 132
influences on, 92–93, 152–156
patron-client system, 132
religion, 137–139, 142
Romanization of provinces, 190–195, 191(m),
192(i)
Romanus IV (Byzantine emperor; r. 1068–1071),
353–354
Rome, 597
under Augustus, 177–182
bishops of, 227
classicism and, 558
under Diocletian, 218
Etruscan influence on, 142
family dynasties and, 184–185

fifth century B.C.E., 147(m)
foundation legend, 129–130
geographical advantages of, 140
as kingdom (c. 753–509 B.C.E.), 130, 139–142
living conditions in, 164
papacy in, 313, 440–443
pilgrimage to, 278, 476
Pope Sixtus's renewal of, 455
sack of (410), 239
sack of (1527), 487
Sassanid Empire and, 262(i)
St. Peter's Basilica, 557
Sulla and, 162
Vandal plunder of (455), 240
Romulus, 129, 130, 176(f)
Romulus Augustulus (Roman emperor;
r. 475–476), 241
Rosetta stone, 91(i)
Rothari (Lombardy; r. 636–652), 2889
Roundheads, 542
Rouvroy, Louis de (duc de St.-Simon), 526
Roxane (Bactrian princess; fourth century B.C.E.),
104, 105
Royal Academy of Sciences (France), 556
Royal African Company (England), 554, 569–570
Royalists (England), 553–554
seventeenth century, 542, 542(m), 544
Royal Society (England), 556, 602
Rubens, Peter Paul (1577–1640), 510–511, 512(i)
Rudolph (Holy Roman emperor;
r. 1273–1291), 395
Ruler cults, 121, 122
Rump Parliament (England; 1648–1653), 544–545
Rural areas. See also Agriculture; Peasants
in Byzantine Empire, 263–265
Hellenistic poetry and, 113
Russia, 322. See also individual tsars and political
leaders
absolutism in, 533, 537–539, 592–594
Baltic trade and, 591
Byzantine Empire and, 260, 299
in eighteenth century, 605(m)
balance of power in eastern Europe, 594–597
emergence as European power, 587, 592–595,
595(m)
Great Northern War (1700–1718), 594–595,
595(m)
westernization, 592–594, 593(i)
expansion to Siberia of, 499
Jews in, 302
Kievan, 302–303, 335(m)
Mongols and, 385, 396–397, 397(m), 438–439
Muslims in, 302

(continued)

in ninth and tenth centuries, 301–303
Peter the Great and, 568
rise of, 296
serfs in, 538, 539(i), 580(i), 581
Russian Academy of Sciences, 593, 594
Russian Orthodox church, 439, 538, 592–593
Russo-Polish war (1654–1667), 539
Ruysch, Rachel, 559

Sacraments, 443–445, 474. *See also specific
    sacraments*
eleventh-century church reforms and, 351
Fourth Lateran Council and (1215), 403
Sacrifice
in ancient Greece, 10, 66–67
infant, 149
Roman, 139, 171, 223, 224
Sacrosanctity, 145
St. Bartholomew's Day massacre (1572), 490
St. Catherine, Monastery of (Mount Sinai), 233(i)
St. Denis, church of, 365, 416
St.-Germain-des-Prés, monastery of, 317–318
St. Peter Baptizing (Masaccio), 453, 454(i)
St. Peter's Basilica (Rome), 476, 557
St. Petersburg, 593–594
St.-Savin-sur-Gartempe, 378(i), 414(i)
St.-Simon, duc de (Louis de Rouvroy) (sahn see
    MOHN) (1675–1755), 526, 587
Saints, 279(i), 279–280, 329. *See also* Relics, cult
    of; *individual saints*
Saisset, Bernard (bishop of Pamiers), 404(i), 405
Saladin (sultan of Egypt and Syria;
    1138–1193), 356
Salamis, island of, 53(m), 55
Salem (Massachusetts), witchcraft trials in, 520
Salons, 560–561
in Russia, 594
Samarra, minaret of the Great Mosque at, 304(i)
Sanitation (hygiene), in Augustan Rome, 177–178
Sappho (SAH foh) (fl. c. 600 B.C.E.), 46
Saracens, 305, 395
Sarapis (sar AH pis), 122, 123(i)
Sardinia, 148, 150, 596
Sardis, 51, 52, 109
Sargon (Akkadia; fl. c. 2350 B.C.E.), 12–13
Sassanids (Sassanid Empire) (Persia), 205, 208,
    209(m), 245, 250, 261(m), 261–262, 262(i),
    269(m), 273, 274(i), 296–297, 304
Saturn, 222(i)
Saturnalia (sat ur NAYL ee uh) festival, 138
Satyricon (Petronius), 182
Satyrs, 79, 100(i)
Saxons. *See also* Anglo-Saxons
Charlemagne and, 311

Saxony, 326, 332, 332(m), 387, 477, 491, 594
Scandinavia, 302, 303, 548, 583, 586.
    See also Vikings
agriculture in, 579(f), 580
Anglo-Saxons and, 321(f), 331
Christianity in, 319
Reformation in, 482(m), 486
Schmalkaldic League, 491
Scholars (scholarship)
Byzantine, 309, 360
Carolingian renaissance and, 309, 314(i),
    314–315
Islamic, 308–309, 371
Renaissance, 450–452
in twelfth century, 369–373, 382
Scholastica, 234
Scholastics (Scholasticism), 411–416, 418
Schools. *See also* Education
Carolingian, 314–315
Islamic, 309, 315
Protestant reformers and, 481, 483
twelfth-century, 369–373, 382
Schott, Johann, 477(i)
Science(s). *See also specific sciences*
Alexander the Great and, 105
Aristotle and, 97–98
the Enlightenment and, 600–602
in Hellenistic period, 118–120
Islam and, 308
rationalism and, 46
in sixteenth and seventeenth centuries, 474,
    509, 514–521, 554–556
in thirteenth and fourteenth centuries, 412
Scientific method, 514, 516–517, 521
Scientific revolution, 514–521, 524
Scipio Africanus (SKIP ee oh ahf ree KAHN us)
    (fl. c. 200 B.C.E.), 150
Scipio Nasica (SKIP ee oh nah SEE kah), 159
Scivias (Hildegard), 373
Scotland, 320, 583
British incorporation of, 589–590
Calvinists in, 497
Christianity in, 286, 442
seventeenth-century religious conflicts and,
    542, 544
Scribes, 11–12, 13(f), 253
Script. *See* Writing
Scriptoria, 451
Sculpted Tomb, 133(i), 182(i)
Sculpture, 21, 25, 76(i), 83(i), 111
Gothic, 418(i), 419–421, 448
Greek, 45, 45(i), 64–65, 64(f)
Hellenistic, 114, 115(i)
in Neo-Assyrian Empire, 26–27

Persian, 28, 30(i)
relief, 58(i), 115, 174(i), 182(i), 222(i), 361
Renaissance (fifteenth century), 454, 455(i)
Roman, 123(i), 135(i), 155–156, 184, 184(i),
   215(i)
Romanesque, 374, 374(i), 375(i)
Sassanid Empire and, 262(i)
seventeenth-century, 557, 557(i)
Sea Peoples (c. 1200–1000 B.C.E.), 25, 36
Second Crusade (1147–1149), 356, 362, 387, 399
Second Punic War (218–201 B.C.E.), 150, 151(f)
Second Triumvirate, 173
Secularization, 509, 521
Seekers, 543
Sejm (Polish parliament), 540
Seleucid (seh LOO sid) kingdoms, 106–107,
   107(m), 121, 123, 124, 163, 196
Seleucus (se LEWK uhs) (c. 358–281 B.C.E.), 106
Self-government of towns, 345–346, 351
Seljuk Turks, 353–355, 355(m), 359
Senate (senators), Roman, 140, 145–147, 150, 152,
   156, 158, 161, 162, 164, 167, 180
  Augustus and, 172, 173, 177
  Gaius Marius and, 160
  Julius Caesar and, 165
  taxes and, 219
Seneca (SEN ek ah) (4 B.C.E.–65 C.E.), 203
Sennacherib (sen AHK uh rib) (Neo-Assyrian
   king; r. 704–681 B.C.E.), 27
Septimius Severus (Roman emperor; r. 193–211),
   181, 206, 207, 208, 218
Serbs (Serbia), 301–303, 322, 436–437, 438(m), 537
  rise of, 296
Serfs (serfdom), 325, 435, 508, 594, 606
  abolition of, 478, 540
  Jews as, 357
  in Russia, 538, 539(i), 580(i), 581
Sergius I (pope; r. 687 or 689–701), 290
Serious Proposal to the Ladies, A (Astell), 604
Servetus, Michael (1511–1553), 481
Sévigné, Marie de (say vee NYAY) (1626–1696),
   523, 524, 526, 561
Seville, 391, 391(m), 508, 509
Sex and sexuality. See also Adultery; Celibacy;
   Homosexuality
  in ancient Greece, 43–44, 71–74, 81, 100(i)
  Augustine's view of, 231–232
  Christian view of, 231–232
  Cynics and, 117
  Justinian and, 252
  Plato's view of, 97
  in Renaissance (fifteenth century), 462–463
  in Roman poetry, 154
  in seventeenth century, 506–507

Seymour, Jane (England; r. 1536–1537), 495
Sforza, Bianca Maria (SFOR tsa), 458
Sforza, Francesco (1401–1466), 458–459
Sforza, Ludovico, 458
Shaftesbury, Earl of, 554
Shakespeare, William (1564–1616), 193, 510–511
Shamash, 14
Shapur I (Sassanid king; r. c. 240–270 C.E.), 208,
   209(m)
Shi'ite Muslims, 274, 304, 305
Ships and navigation
  in fifteenth century, 466
  Greek, 58(i)
  Vikings and, 320, 320(i)
Shrines, Roman, 137, 138(i)
Shtetls, 540
Siberia, 499
Sic et Non (Abelard), 372, 411
Sicily, 39, 86(m), 88(m), 150, 428
  city-states in, 55
  Islam and, 306, 322, 371
  in thirteenth century, 386, 394(m), 394–396,
   395(m)
  in twelfth century, 363(m)
Sidonius Apollinaris (c. 430–479), 239
Siege tactics and weapons, 26. See also Weapons
   and military technology
  Alexander the Great and, 102
  in Hellenistic period, 120
Sigismund (Holy Roman emperor; r. 1410–1437),
   443, 446
Signoria, 406
Sikhs, 576
Silesia, 535
Silk trade and industry, 189, 299, 427, 548,
   575, 576
Silver
  Carolingian economy and, 317
  imports to Spain, 504–505, 504(f)
  Italian economy and, 439
  Kutnà Hora mine, 445
  in Roman coins, 206, 207(f)
Simon de Montfort (c. 1208–1265), 409
Simon IV de Montfort l'Amaury
   (1165?–1218), 392
Simons, Menno (1469–1561), 480
Simony, 346, 347, 348, 476
Sinai, Mount, 31, 233(i)
Sisters of St. Francis, 379
Sistine Chapel, 510
Six Books of the Republic, The (Bodin), 513
Sixtus IV (pope; r. 1471–1484), 455
Sixtus V (pope; r. 1585–1590), 497
Skeptics (Skepticism), 117, 513, 516, 568, 601, 603

Slaves and slavery, 31, 231, 488. *See also* Slave trade
  abolition of, 554
  African, 465, 465(m), 467–468, 468(i), 576(i)
  in ancient Egypt, 20
  in ancient Greece, 41, 41(i), 42, 43, 51(i), 72–73,
      85, 95, 98
  in Brazil, 569, 570(m), 571(f), 572–575
  in Florence (fifteenth century), 459, 462, 463
  in fourteenth and fifteenth centuries, 437, 440
  in Hellenistic kingdoms, 110, 116
  Islamic society and, 307
  Mamluks and, 305
  in Merovingian period (c. 485–751), 277–278,
      279, 281, 283, 317–318
  in New World, 538, 548, 551–552, 588(m), 606
  in Roman Republic and Empire, 147, 148, 156,
      158, 180–181, 186, 193, 208
    citizenship, 140
    education and, 136
    ex-slaves, 133(i), 133–134, 138
    rebellion of, 163
  in Sparta, 43
  in Sumerian society, 9–10
Slave trade, 465(m), 467–468
  1701–1810, 571(f)
  Atlantic system and, 552, 568–575
  in eighteenth century, 568–575, 571(m), 571(f)
    conditions on slave ships, 572
  in seventeenth century, 548, 551–552
Slavs (Slavic peoples and states), 261, 262, 263,
      322, 332, 445, 468
  Byzantine Empire and, 297, 301–303
Slovenia, 7n
Smallpox, 599
Sobieski, Jan (sob YES kee, yahn) (Poland-
      Lithuania; r. 1674–1696), 536(i), 540
Social classes. *See also* Hierarchy; Middle class(es);
      Upper classes
  curiales, 190, 220, 225, 264, 265, 293
  in eighteenth century, 581–583
  in Florence (fifteenth century), 457, 459–463
  racial discrimination and, 486
Social contract theory, 553–554
Social elites. *See* Upper classes
Social order
  Augustine's view of, 231
  Justinian and, 249
  in seventeenth century, 552–565
    the arts, 556–559
    reforming popular culture, 561–564
    social contract theory, 553–554
    women and manners, 559–561
Social War (91–87 B.C.E.), 161
Society of Jesus. *See* Jesuits

Socrates (SAW krah teez) (469–399 B.C.E.), 65,
      75–78, 76(i), 93, 95
Socratic method, 77
Sogdiana (sog dee AH nah), 104
Solar system, Hellenistic models of, 118–119
Soldiers. *See* Armed forces
Solomon (Israel; r. c. 961–922 B.C.E.), 31, 32
Solon (SOHL on) (c. 638–559 B.C.E.), 44
Sophia (daugher of Tsar Alexei), 538
Sophists, 65, 74–75
Sophocles (SOF o kleez) (c. 496–406 B.C.E.), 80, 81
Soranus (sor AH nus), 194
South America
  African slaves in, 569
  colonies in, 570(m), 574
    Dutch, 559, 559(i)
    Spanish, 504, 508, 551, 568
  exploration of (sixteenth century), 465(m)
Spain, 39, 509, 596
  American colonies of, 477, 485–486, 492,
      493(m), 508, 511, 568
    settlement patterns, 574–575
    silver imports, 504–505, 504(f)
    slavery and, 551
  baroque style and, 558
  Catholic church in, 288–289
    reconquista, 447–448
  Charlemagne and, 311, 312(m)
  in eighteenth century, 605(m)
  exploration and settlements (fifteenth and
      sixteenth centuries), 426, 463, 464(m),
      466–470
  Jews in, 358, 403, 426
  Louis XIV and, 525, 530–532
  monarchy in
    fifteenth century, 447–448
    thirteenth century, 405, 407–408
  Muslims (Moors) in, 289, 291(m), 305–307,
      306(m), 371, 422, 426
    Christian reconquest (*reconquista*), 348, 386,
      388(m), 390–391, 391(m), 408, 447–448
    Moriscos, 492–493
  Netherlands and, 492–494, 493(m), 494(m),
      496–497, 513, 548, 549(m)
  Roman Empire and, 148, 150, 166, 220
  in sixteenth century, 477, 487, 487(m), 490,
      492–497, 493(m)
  slave trade and, 467–468, 468(i), 569, 570(m),
      571(f), 574
  Thirty Years' War and, 499–501, 503
  unification of (late fifteenth century),
      447, 447(m)
  Visigothic, 239(i), 240, 288–290, 293
  War of Spanish succession and, 587, 588(m)

Spanish Armada, 497, 505
Spanish Fury (1576), 494
Spanish Netherlands, 510–511, 530–531, 531(m)
Sparta, 51
    c. 750–500 B.C.E., 43(m)
    c. 400 B.C.E., 88(m)
    alliances in, 56–58
    citizenship (political rights) in, 44
    disunity of Greece and (390s to 370s B.C.E.),
        93, 98–99
    homosexuality and, 43–44
    Peloponnesian League and, 56, 57(m), 61
    Peloponnesian War (431–404 B.C.E.) and,
        84–86, 84(f), 86(m), 93
    Persian invasion and (480–479 B.C.E.), 55,
        56–58
    Thirty Tyrants period in Athens and, 86–87,
        93, 95
Spartacus (SPAHRT ah kus) (d. 71 B.C.E.), 163
Spectator, The (magazine), 583
Speyer (Germany), 357
Spice trade, 189, 245, 341(m), 342, 398, 427, 465,
    466, 548, 549(m), 571(m), 575–576
Spinoza, Benedict (1633–1677), 550
Spirit of the Laws (Montesquieu), 603
Spoleto, Duchy of, 289, 289(m), 290–291, 335(m)
Sports, Olympic Games, 38
State. See Government
Statues. See Sculpture
Ste.-Chapelle, 414(i)
Steele, Sir Richard (1672–1729), 583
Steen, Jan (1626?–1679), 550(i)
Stephen I (Magyar king; r. 997–1038), 335–336
Stephen II (pope; r. 752–757), 292
Stigmata, 379
Stoas, 61
Stoicism (STO ih sizum), 116–117, 154, 202,
    203, 223
Stone Age, 3–4
Story of Sinuhe, The (Egypt), 21
Strasbourg, 484
    cathedral in, 418(i)
    Louis XIV's seizure of (1681), 532
    printing in, 452, 477(i)
Strozzi, Alessandra (STROT zee), 461
Strozzi, Caterina, 461
Strozzi, Filippo, 461
Strozzi family, 453, 461
Struggle of the orders, 143
Stuart dynasty (Great Britain), 589–590
Students
    clerical status of (thirteenth and fourteenth
        centuries), 411–413
    in twelfth century, 369–373

Styria, 535
Subjectivism, 74–75
Successor kings, 106
Sudan, 22
Suetonius (swee TOH nee us) (c. 70–130), 173,
    186, 217(m), 314
Sufi, al-, 308(i)
Sugar production and trade, 467–468, 509, 548,
    551, 559, 568–572, 570(m), 573, 573(i),
    577, 592
Suger (abbot of St. Denis; 1081–1152), 365–366,
    382, 416
Suleiman I (the Magnificent) (Ottoman sultan;
    r. 1520–1566), 488
Sulla, Lucius Cornelius (SUHL uh) (c. 138–78
    B.C.E.), 161–163
Sumer (Sumerians), 8–13
Summa, 412
Summa Theologiae (Thomas Aquinas), 412–413
Sunni Muslims, 274, 305, 353, 356
Superstition, seventeenth-century campaign
    against, 562
Surinam, 559, 559(i)
Swabia, 367
Sweden, 322
    absolutist consolidation in, 533–535
    in eighteenth century, 597, 605(m)
    decline, 587, 591, 593, 594, 595, 595(m)
    French wars with, 432, 530
    mercantilism and, 508
    Poland-Lithuania and, 539–540
    Thirty Years' War and, 499, 501–503,
        502(m), 534
Swiss Confederation, 407, 407(m), 501
Switzerland, 277, 279(i), 316, 597
    education in, 583
    religious reform and, 479–480, 482(m)
Sylvester II (pope; r. 999–1003), 333
Symeon the Stylite (SIM me un) (390–459), 232
Symmachus, Aurelius (SIM uh kus) (c. 340–402),
    223, 230
Symposia, in Athens, 71, 71(i), 73
Synagogues, 225
Synod of Sutri (1046), 347
Synod of Whitby (664), 287
Syracuse, 55
Syria, 12, 16, 22, 163, 208
    Arabs and, 263, 292
    in Hellenistic period (323–30 B.C.E.), 106
    Islam and, 272(m), 273–275, 274(i), 305, 308
    trade and, 281

Table of Ranks (1722), 592
Taborites, 446

Tacitus (TAS ih tuhs) (c. 56–120 C.E.), 177, 187, 193, 200, 450
Taifa, 307, 348, 390
Talmud, 225
Tarquin the Proud (Rome; r. late sixth century B.C.E.), 143
Tartars. *See* Mongols
Taxes (revenues)
  Abbasid, 305
  in Byzantine Empire, 249–250, 290, 297, 359
  Delian League and, 62
  in early Middle Ages, 283, 285, 289, 325–326
  in Egypt, 21
  in England, 321, 331, 361, 401
    Hundred Years' War (1337–1453) and, 435
    seventeenth century, 541–542, 545, 547
  in France, 366, 399, 503
    Louis XIV, 525, 529, 531–532
  in Germany, 367, 395, 533
  Hebrew, 32
  in Hellenistic kingdoms, 103, 108–109
  in Islam, 271, 273, 274(i), 275, 293
  in Italy, 406, 459
  on Jews, 357–358
  in Mesopotamia, 10
  Mongol system of, 397
  in Ottoman Empire, 437
  papal, 441
  on peasants, 343
  in Persian Empire, 28
  protests against, 445
  in Prussia, 596
  Roman Catholic clergy and, 404(i), 404–405, 478
  in Roman Empire, 148, 175, 189–190, 208, 219, 220
  in Roman Republic, 161
  in Russia and Soviet Union, 538, 592
  in seventeenth century, 538, 541–542, 545, 547, 565
  in Spain, 407
  Thirty Years' War and, 505, 520, 524
Tea trade, 548, 568, 575, 577, 606
Technology (technological advances)
  metallurgical, 4
  trade and, 6
Tell, William, legend of, 407
Temples. *See also* Architecture
  Egypt, 22
  Etruscan, 142
  Greek, 62–65, 63(i), 64–65
  Israelite, 31, 32
  Mesopotamia, 9, 10, 11(i)
  Roman, 137, 158

Tenant farmers
  in England, 580
  in Roman Empire, 219, 237, 244
Ten Commandments, 31, 32, 233(i)
Tenochtitlán, 470
Terence (c. 190–159 B.C.E.), 153
Tertiaries, 410
Tertullian (tur TUHL ee an) (c. 160–240), 181, 200
Test Act (1673), 546
Tetradia, 284
Tetrarchy, 216, 218
Teutonic Knights, 387, 406, 438, 469(m)
Textiles (textile industry), 398, 505, 548, 606
  in ancient Greece, 94
  in Byzantine Empire, 264
  Dutch Republic and, 591
  in fourteenth century, 429–430, 458
  in France, 530
  in India, 574, 576(i), 576–577
  in Middle Ages, 344, 345
Thales (thay LEEZ) (c. 625–545 B.C.E.), 46
Thamugadi, arch at, 192(i)
Theater. *See also* Comedies; Drama; Tragedy
  in Golden Age Athens, 65, 79–83, 80(i)
  Hellenistic, 113–114
  under Louis XIV, 527
  in sixteenth and seventeenth centuries, 509–510, 521, 538
Thebes, 22, 93, 98, 101, 102
Themes (military districts), 297, 359
Themistocles of Athens (theh MIS toh kleez) (c. 528–462 B.C.E.), 55
Theocracy, Sumerian, 10
Theocritus (thee OK rit us) (c. 300–260 B.C.E.), 113
Theodora (thee uh DOH ruh) (Byzantine empress; d. 548), 247(i), 249
Theodore (archbishop; r. 669–690), 287
Theodoric the Great (Ostrogothic king; r. 493–526), 242, 246(i)
Theodorus the Atheist, 117–118
Theodosius (Roman emperor; r. 379–395 in the east), 224, 238
Theodosius II (Roman emperor; r. 408–450), 264(i)
Theophrastus (c. 370–285 B.C.E.), 116, 118
Theopompus of Chios, 101
Theotokopoulos, Domenikos. *See* El Greco
Thera (Santorini), 35(i)
Thermopylae (ther MAH pill ee), battle of (480 B.C.E.), 55
Theseus of Athens (THEE see us), 36
Thessalonika, 436, 436(m), 448

Theuderic, 279(i)

Third Council of Toledo (587), 288

Third Crusade (1189–1192), 356, 387, 388(m)

Third Punic War (149–146 B.C.E.), 150

Thirty-Nine Articles of Religion (Church of England; 1563), 496

Thirty Tyrants' period (Athens), 86–87, 95

Thirty Years' War (1618–1648), 473–474, 498–505, 500(i), 516, 525, 533, 534, 535(m), 536, 541

  Germany and, 499, 501, 502(m), 518

  origins and course of, 498–503

  peace negotiations and treaty, 501–503, 502(m)

  recession after, 504–508, 520–521, 524

  Sweden and, 594

Thrace, 28, 29(m)

Three-field system, 318, 325

Thucydides (thoo SID ih deez) (c. 455–399 B.C.E.), 57, 85

  on Peloponnesian War, 78, 84(f)

Thuringia (Germany), 429, 478

Tiamat, 3

Tiberius (Roman emperor; r. 14–37 C.E.), 185, 190

Tiglathpileser III (Assyria; r. 745–727 B.C.E.), 32

Tigris River, 4, 8

Timbuktu (Africa), 307

Tithe, 326

Titian (1477–1576), 492(i)

Titus (TY tus) (Roman emperor; r. 79–81 C.E.), 187

Tobacco, 509, 548, 569, 573, 577, 592

Toledo, 288

Toleration Act (1689), 547

Tombs and graves, 143(i), 229(i). *See also* Burial practices

  ancient Egyptian, 22, 23

  Etruscan, 141

  Mycenaean, 34, 36

  Roman, 182(i)

  Sumerian, 10

Topkapi Saray Palace, 425, 437

Torah (Pentateuch), 31, 32, 50. *See also* Hebrew Bible

Tordesillas (tor day SEE yahs), Treaty of (1494), 464(m), 466

Tories, 547, 590

Torture, 513, 515, 520, 592

Tours, 278–280, 283

Towns

  medieval, walled, 340, 342(i)

  self-government of, 345–346

Trade. *See also* Business and commerce; Mercantilism

  in ancient Egypt, 16

  ancient trade routes, 22, 24

  with Asia, 439, 463, 466

  Assyrian, 26

  Atlantic system and, 507–508, 552, 568–577, 570(m), 578

  Byzantine Empire, 264, 299, 302

  Carolingian, 317

  with China, 245, 304, 385, 385(i), 397(m), 397–398, 470

  Dutch, 507–508, 530, 544, 548–551, 549(m), 575, 589, 591–592

  in early Middle Ages, 281

  Etruscan, 141–142

  Greek, 37, 39

    Athens, 44, 61

    Minoan and Mycenaean period, 33–35

  Hanseatic league and, 406–407

  Hittite, 24

  India, 576(i), 576–577

  Iraqi, 304

  iron metallurgy and, 37–38

  Islamic, 307, 317

  medieval routes in eleventh and twelfth centuries, 340–342, 341(m), 382

  Mediterranean (fifteenth century), 463–465

  Neolithic, 4, 5, 6, 7–8

  in North American colonies, 530

  silk, 189, 427

  sixteenth and seventeenth centuries, 493(m), 494, 544, 548, 549(m), 551

  slave. *See* Slave trade

  spice, 189, 245, 341(m), 342, 398, 427, 465, 466, 548, 549(m), 571(m), 575–576

  Sumerian, 9–10

  in textiles, 398

  thirteenth century, 422

  Vikings and, 321

Tragedy, Greek, 79–81

Trajan (Roman emperor; r. 98–117 C.E.), 187, 188(m), 190, 192(i), 193

Transportation, in the eleventh century, 342

Transubstantiation, doctrine of, 403, 414, 479, 484

Transylvania, 488(i), 535(m), 539, 596

Travel, in Merovingian period (c. 485–751), 277–278

Travel literature, eighteenth-century, 602–603, 606

Travels of Marco Polo, The (Polo), 466

Triangular Trade, 570(m)

Tribunes, Roman, 144, 145, 159, 175

Triennial Act (1694), 590

Trier, 278

Triremes (TRY reemz), 57, 58(i), 84(f)

Trivium, 370–371

Trojan War, 37, 80
Troubadours, 368(i), 368–369, 448
Truce of God, 329
Truth (Protagoras), 74–75
Tsar, defined, 439
Tullia (TUHL ee ah) (c. 79–45 B.C.E.), 135
Tunis, battle of (1535), 487(m), 488
Tunisia, 142, 305
Turkey, 7, 8n. See also Ottoman Empire
    Byzantine Empire and, 260
Turks
    Ottoman. See Ottoman Empire
    Seljuk, crusades and, 353–355, 355(m), 359
Tuscany, 459–460
Tustari brothers, 307
Tutankhamun (r. 1361–1352 B.C.E.), 22
Twelve Tables, 144
Two Treatises of Government (Locke), 554
Tyche (TY kee) (Chance), 121
Tyndale, William (1495–1536), 481
Tyranny, 40
    in ancient Greece, 44
Tyre, 24, 109
    capture of (332 B.C.E.), 102

Ubayd Allah, 305
Ugarit (OO gah reet), 24
Ukraine, 302, 438, 538, 539
Ulster, 544
Umayyad dynasty (oo MAY ahd) (Umayyad
    period), 272(m), 273–275, 274(i), 287,
    291(m)
    overthrow of, 296, 304, 306
Ummah (OO ma), 269, 308
Unam Sanctam (1302), 405
Underclass, in the fourteenth and fifteenth
    centuries, 440
United Kingdom. See Great Britain
United Provinces. See Dutch Republic
Universities. See Colleges and universities
University of Bologna, 370–372, 600(i)
University of Leiden, 550
University of Paris, 370, 371, 412, 413,
    441, 443
University of Wittenberg, 476
Upper classes. See also Aristocracy; Hierarchy
    in ancient Greece, 36, 56, 57–58, 59, 80, 86
    in Byzantine Empire, 260, 264
    Christian missionaries and, 486
    in Florence (fifteenth century), 450, 460–462
    in France, 489–490
    in Hellenistic kingdoms, 92, 108–109,
        110–112, 114
    in Italian cities, 323, 450, 460–462

Macedonian renaissance (c. 870–c. 1025)
    and, 299
    manners and (seventeenth century), 553,
        559–563
    mosaic of country life (fourth century), 241(i)
    in Muslim society, 308–309
    Persian Wars and, 56, 57
    in Roman Republic and Empire, 140, 142, 143,
        157–158, 180, 189–190, 192–193, 220, 223,
        244–245
    Visigoths and, 239
Ur (oor), 3, 9, 10, 31
    Ziggurat of, 11(i)
Urban II (pope; r. 1088–1099), 354–355, 359
Urban V (pope; r. 1360s), 436, 444
Urban VI (pope; r. 1378–1389), 441–443
Urban areas. See Cities
Urbanization, 273–274
Ur-Nammu (Ur; r. 2112–2095 B.C.E.), 11(i)
Ursula, St., Company of (Ursulines), 485
Uruk, 9, 10
Usury, 344, 357, 411(i)
Uthman (caliph; r. 644–656), 273–274
Utopia (More), 475–476
Utopias, 97
Utraquists (OO truh kwists), 445–446

Vaccination, 599
Václav (duke of Bohemia; r. 920–929), 333–334
Valencia, 388(m), 390, 391(m)
Valens (Roman emperor; r. 364–378), 238
Valerian (Roman emperor; r. 253–260), 208,
    209(m)
Valois (vahl WAH), 487(m), 487–490
Vandals, 240, 241(i), 244, 249, 254(m)
Van de Venne, Adriaen Pietersz, 507(i)
Vassals (vassalage), 324–329, 353(m), 355, 398
    Carolingians and, 316
    in England, 361, 362, 401
    in France, 332, 359, 365–366, 369, 399
    in Germany, 333, 366, 395
    oath of fealty and, 316, 325, 327, 395, 403
    in Ottoman Empire, 437
    in Sicily, 348, 395
    in Spain, 390
Vatican, 224(i), 458. See also Papacy
Venice (Venetians), 291, 298(m), 299, 355, 440,
    508, 584, 597
    Battle of Lepanto (1571) and, 492
    in fourteenth and fifteenth centuries, 451,
        457–458, 462, 469(m)
    Fourth Crusade (1202–1204) and, 388(m),
        388–390
    in seventeenth century, 564(m)

trade and, 385, 385(i), 397, 425
Turks and, 457, 463
"Venus" figurines, 6(i)
Verdun, Treaty of (843), 312(m), 316, 333
Vernacular languages and literature, 330, 331(i),
    367–369, 515
  music and, 511
  Renaissance (fifteenth-century), 448–450
  translations of Bible into, 481, 483
Versailles, palace at, 523(i), 527(i), 527–528
Vesalius, Andreas (vih SAY lee us) (1514–1564), 515
Vesconte, Pietro, 385(i)
Vespasian (ves PAY shun) (Roman emperor;
    r. 69–79 C.E.), 178, 186, 187
Vespucci, Amerigo, 464(m), 467
Vesta, shrine of, 137
Vestal Virgins, 137
Vesuvius, Mount (veh SOO vee us), 179(i), 187
Veto, in Rome, 145
Vibia Perpetua, 171, 171(i), 172
Victor, Sextus Aurelius, 217(m)
Vienna, 437, 597
  Jews in, 403
  siege of (1683), 536(i), 537, 540
Vikings (Danes), 317, 387
  coin hoards (c. 865–895), 321(f)
  in England, 319(m), 320–321, 321(f), 330–331
  invasions of ninth and tenth centuries, 302,
    309, 318–323, 319(m), 330–331
Villages
  early medieval, 278–279
  post-Carolingian, 325–326
Villani, Matteo, 430
Villeneuve St.-Georges, 317–318
Villiers, George, 541
Violence
  efforts to contain, in post-Carolingian age,
    328–329
  Roman, 159, 162, 165, 166, 209, 249
    as entertainment, 181
Virgil (70–19 B.C.E.), 183, 189, 193, 282, 314, 414
Virginia, 508, 573
Virginity, Christianity and, 232, 234
Virgin Mary (mother of Jesus), 228, 266(i),
    295(i), 377, 414, 416, 418(i), 421, 494, 562
Virtue(s). See also Morality
  Plato on, 96
  Roman view of, 132
  Socrates on, 77, 95
  Stoic view of, 116–117
Visconti dynasty (vees KON tee), 450, 458–459
Visigoths (VIS ih gawths), 238–240, 254(m),
    261(m), 293, 311
  in Spain, 288–289

Visual perspective, 454–455, 471, 510, 511(i)
Vitry, Jacques de, 379
Vladimir (grand prince of Kiev and all Russia;
    r. c. 980–1015), 303
Voltaire (vohl TAYR) (François-Marie Arouet)
    (1694–1778), 602
Vulgate (bible translation), 314, 481

Waldensians, 381
Waldo, 381
Wales, 286, 544, 589
Walid, al- (Umayyad caliph), 259(i)
Wallenstein, Albrecht von (1583–1634), 499
Walpole, Sir Robert (1676–1745), 590, 591(i)
War (warfare). See also Armed forces; Weapons
    and military technology; specific wars
  Alexander the Great and, 103(m), 105
  in ancient Near East, 7(m)
  cultural interaction and, 13
  in fourteenth and fifteenth centuries, 440
  influence of, 4
  Louis XIV and, 533–532, 591
  Mongols' military tactics, 396
  Neo-Assyrian kingdom, 26, 27
  New Kingdom (Egypt), 22, 24
  in ninth to eleventh centuries, 327–329
  between Persians and Greeks, 28, 51–56
  Roman, 140, 144, 146, 147, 150, 156–158,
    159, 161
  in twelfth-century poetry, 369
War of Independence (American). See American
    Revolution
War of the League of Augsburg (Nine Years' War)
    (1689–1697), 587
War of the Polish Succession (1733–1735), 596
War of the Roses (1460–1485), 435
War of the Spanish Succession (1701–1713),
    587, 588(m)
Warriors (warrior class)
  crusaders as, 388, 392
  Islam and, 271, 273
  knights as, 367, 434
  in Merovingian period, 280, 282
  Mongolian, 385
  in post-Carolingian age, 323, 327–329
Warsaw, 581
Water power, 344–345
Water supply, 148, 149(i)
Watteau, Antoine (1684–1721), 584, 584(i)
Wealthy, the. See Rich, the; Upper classes
Weapons and military technology. See also War
  Alexander the Great and, 102
  in Ancient Greece, 56

                                (continued)

artillery, 488(i), 488–489
battering rams, 26
gender roles and, 12
in Golden Age Greece, 58
in Hellenistic kingdoms, 108, 120
Hittite, 24
in Mesopotamia (Bronze Age), 12
Neo-Assyrian kingdom, 26
in ninth to eleventh centuries, 327
under Philip II, 101
Weaving, 94, 345. See also Textiles
Welfare (social welfare programs), 483–484
Wergild (VER gilt), 244
Wessex, 321, 330, 330(m)
West, The, idea of, 4
Western Europe, 260, 275
  c. 600, 254(m), 261(m)
  c. 750, 291(m)
  Byzantine Empire and, 262, 295–296,
    310, 312(m)
  Charlemagne's conquests in, 311–312, 312(m)
  early medieval kingdoms, 275–293
    British isles, 286–288
    economic activity in a peasant society,
      280–282
    Frankish kingdoms, 275–280, 317, 319(m),
      320–322
    Italy, 289–291
    Merovingian society, 281–285
    Spain, 288–289
  Frankish kingdoms, 276–280, 317, 319(m),
    320–322, 332
  local rule in post-Carolingian society, 323–337
    public power and private relationships,
      323–328
  profit economy and, 340–343, 347, 375
  Russia and, 303
  Viking, Muslim, and Magyar invasions of ninth
    and tenth centuries, 318–323, 319(m)
Westernization of Russia, 592–594, 593(i)
West Indies, 509
Weyden, Rogier van der (c. 1400–1464),
  454, 456(i)
Whigs, 547, 554, 590
Whitby, Synod of (664), 287
White Mountain, Battle of (1620), 498–499,
  502(m)
Why God Became Man (St. Anselm), 377
William (prince of Orange; d. 1584), 494
William I (the Conqueror) (England;
  1027–1087), 360(m), 360–362, 361(i)
William III (prince of Orange, king of England
  and Scotland; r. 1689–1702), 547–548, 552,
  587, 589–591

William IX (duke of Aquitaine; 1071–1126),
  367–368
Winchester Cathedral (England), 362
Windsor, House of, 599
Wisdom literature, Egyptian, 21, 22, 27, 32
Witches and witchcraft, 517(i), 517–520
Wladyslaw II (Poland; r. 1386–1434), 438
Women. See also Divorce; Family; Gender
    differences; Marriage; Prostitution; Sex
    and sexuality
  Alexander the Great and, 102
  in American colonies, 575
  in ancient Egypt, 21
  in ancient Greece, 38, 98
    Athens, 43, 60–61, 65, 67, 68–72, 73, 82–83
    comedies, 82–83
    companions, 71–72
    fetching water, 94(i)
    legal and political status of, 40, 42, 43
    after Peloponnesian War, 93–94
    religious functions of, 42(i), 42–43
    roles of, 42, 42(i)
    social and economic roles of, 44, 68–72
    Sparta, 44
  in Byzantine Empire, 249, 265, 267
  Christianity and, 295(i), 604
    early Christianity, 202, 225–226
    monasteries, 234, 280–281, 283–285, 284(i),
      286, 288, 333
    virginity and sexual renunciation, 232
  in city-states, 40
  division of labor by gender, 8, 14, 237
  as domestic servants, 440, 459, 462, 467, 468(i)
  education of, 485, 556, 600(i), 604
    eighteenth century, 585, 604
    in Rome, 136
  in eighteenth century, novels and, 585
  in England (Great Britain), 461–462, 543–544,
    556, 582, 585
  the Enlightenment and, 600, 600(i), 604–605
  in Florence (fifteenth century), 459–463
  in France, seventeenth century, 560–561, 563
  guilds and, 334–335, 430
  Hebrew, 31
  in Hellenistic kingdoms
    medical view of, 120
    philosophy and, 116–117, 118
    poetry and, 113
    social and economic status, 110–111
  Indo-European, 24
  inheritance and, 272, 281, 329
  Islam and, 269, 272
  in Mesopotamia, 12, 14
  in Middle Ages

Carolingian period, 295(i), 318
commercial revolution and, 344–345
courtly literature, 368–369
crusades and, 355
early Middle Ages, 280–285, 284(i)
fourteenth and fifteenth centuries, 430,
437, 440
monastic orders, 373, 375–376, 379, 382
post-Carolingian age, 324, 328, 333
religion, 410–411
Neo-Assyrian kingdom, 27
in northern Europe (fifteenth century),
461–462
novels and, 561, 585
in Paleolithic and Neolithic periods, 5–6, 6(i), 7
in patriarchal society. See Patriarchy
Plato's view of, 97
Protestant Reformation and, 483(i), 483–484
in Roman Republic and Empire
childbearing, 194–195
education, 136
family and household, 134–136
gladiators, 181
independence of, 134–135
moral values, 131–132, 135
property, 135(i), 136
reproduction, 194–195
as slaves, 180
Vestal Virgins, 137
in Russia and Soviet Union, 594
in science, 308
in seventeenth century, 549–550, 556
artists, 558–559, 559(i)
authors, 561
manners, 559–561
novels, 561
salons, 560–561
witches (witchcraft) and, 517(i), 517–520
Wonders of the World, The (Callimachus), 113
Woolen industry, 362, 430. See also Textiles
Wooley, Hannah, 561
Workers (working class)
in ancient Egypt, 23
in Roman Empire, 219–220

Works and Days (Hesiod), 37
Worms, 357
Concordat of (1122), 350
Diet of, 477
Writing (script), 5. See also Alphabets
Arabic, 270(i), 275
cuneiform, 11–13, 13(f)
demotic, 18
Greek, 36, 37
hieroglyphs, 17, 18, 18(f), 91(i)
Kufic, 270(i)
Linear A and B, 35
Roman, 183
Wycliffe, John (c. 1330–1384), 444–445

Xenophanes (zen OFF uh neez) (c. 580–480
B.C.E.), 47
Xenophon (c. 430–355 B.C.E.), 72–73, 99
Xerxes I (ZUHRK seez) (r. 486–465 B.C.E.),
53(m), 54–55, 262

Yahweh, 31–32, 124
Yangzhou (China), 397, 427
Year of the Four emperors (69 C.E.), 186
Ypres (EE pruh), 341(m), 345, 427(m), 430
Yuan dynasty (China), 463
Yugoslavia, 8n, 537

Zachary (pope; r. 741–752), 291–292, 310
Zama, battle of (202 B.C.E.), 150
Zara, 388(m), 389
Zarathustra (Zoroaster) (sixth century B.C.E.), 30
Zell, Katharina, 484
Zengi (Seljuk chieftain; fl. 1145), 355
Zeno (philosopher) (335–263 B.C.E.),
116–117, 203
Zeno (Roman emperor; r. 474–491), 241, 242
Zenobia (zih NO bee uh) (Palmyra; r. 269–272), 208
Zeus, 37, 38, 66, 105, 123(i), 137
Ziggurat of Ur in Sumer (ZIG uh rat), 10, 11(i)
Zoroastrianism (zohr oh AHS tree uh nizum), 30
Zurich, 407, 479
Zwingli, Huldrych (TSVING lee, HOOLD rik)
(1484–1531), 479–480, 480(f)

Elevation

Feet	Meters
Over 13,120	Over 4,001
6,561–13,120	2,001–4,000
1,641–6,560	501–2,000
661–1640	201–500
0–660	0–200
Below sea level	Below sea level

⍟ National capital

• Major city

0   150   300 miles

0   150   300 kilometers

NORWAY

SWEDEN

Bergen

Oslo ⍟

Stockholm ⍟

Göteborg

SCOTLAND

Glasgow   Edinburgh

NORTHERN
IRELAND

Belfast

North Sea

Aarhus

Baltic Sea

Dublin ⍟

IRELAND

UNITED

DENMARK

Copenhagen ⍟

RUSSIA

Kaliningrad

Liverpool

KINGDOM

Berlin ⍟

Gdańsk

Cork

Birmingham

Elbe R.

WALES   ENGLAND

NETHERLANDS

POLAND

Thames R.

Amsterdam ⍟

GERMANY

Oder R.

London

English Channel

Antwerp

Rotterdam

Rhine R.

Frankfurt

Prague ⍟

Cracow

Paris ⍟

Brussels

BELGIUM

CZECH REP.

Brno

SLOVAKIA

A T L A N T I C
O C E A N

Luxembourg ⍟

LUXEMBOURG

LIECHTENSTEIN

Munich

Vienna ⍟

Bratislava

Miskolc

Seine R.

Zurich

Vaduz

AUSTRIA

Budapest ⍟

*Bay of
Biscay*

FRANCE

Loire R.

Bern ⍟

SWITZERLAND

Innsbruck

Graz

HUNGARY

Lyon

Rhône R.

A   L   P   S

Milan

SLOVENIA

Ljubljana ⍟

Zagreb

ANDORRA

Po R.

CROATIA

Belgrade ⍟

Oporto

PYRENEES

Andorra
la Vella

San
Marino

BOSNIA AND

Lisbon ⍟

PORTUGAL

Ebro R.

Marseille

MONACO

A
P
E
N
N
I
N
E
S

SAN
MARINO

HERZEGOVINA

Sarajevo

Split

Madrid ⍟

Corsica

Adriatic Sea

SERBIA AND
MONTENEGRO

SPAIN

Barcelona

Tirana ⍟

Seville

BALEARIC IS.

Sardinia

Rome ⍟

ITALY

*Tyrrhenian
Sea*

Naples

ALBANIA

Gibraltar
(Br.)

Algiers

Tunis

*Ionian
Sea*

Rabat ⍟

Palermo

Sicily

MOROCCO

TUNISIA

Valletta ⍟

M e d i t e r r a n e a n

MALTA

Tripoli

ALGERIA

LIBYA

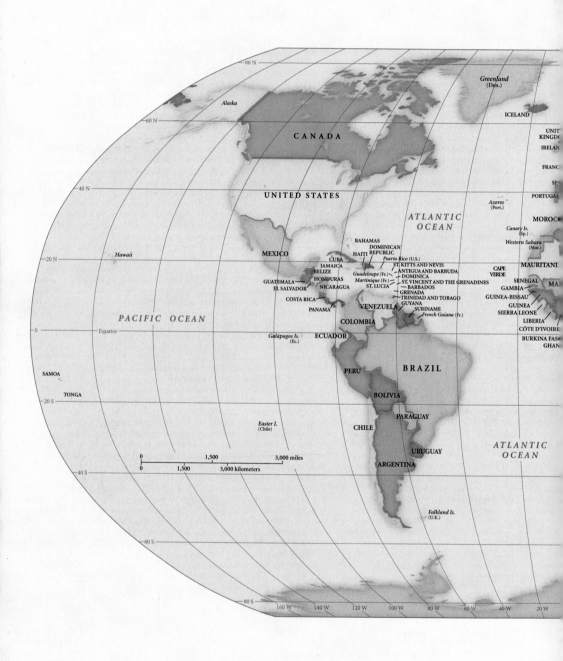

80 N

Greenland
(Den.)

Alaska

ICELAND

60 N

CANADA

UNIT
KINGD

IRELAN

FRANC

40 N

SP

PORTUGAL

ATLANTIC
OCEAN

Azores
(Port.)

MOROC

UNITED STATES

Canary Is.
(Sp.)

Western Sahara
(Mor.)

BAHAMAS

20 N

Hawaii

MEXICO

DOMINICAN
REPUBLIC

HAITI

CAPE
VERDE

MAURITANI

CUBA

Puerto Rico (U.S.)

ST. KITTS AND NEVIS

SENEGAL

MA

JAMAICA

BELIZE

Guadeloupe (Fr.)

ANTIGUA AND BARBUDA

DOMINICA

GUATEMALA

HONDURAS

Martinique (Fr.)

ST. VINCENT AND THE GRENADINES

GAMBIA

GUINEA-BISSAU

EL SALVADOR

NICARAGUA

ST. LUCIA

BARBADOS

GRENADA

GUINEA

COSTA RICA

TRINIDAD AND TOBAGO

SIERRA LEONE

LIBERIA

PANAMA

VENEZUELA

GUYANA

SURINAME

CÔTE D'IVOIRE

PACIFIC OCEAN

COLOMBIA

French Guiana (Fr.)

BURKINA FAS

GHAN

0

Equator

Galápagos Is.
(Ec.)

ECUADOR

SAMOA

PERU

BRAZIL

TONGA

20 S

BOLIVIA

Easter I.
(Chile)

PARAGUAY

CHILE

URUGUAY

ATLANTIC
OCEAN

| 0 | 1,500 | 3,000 miles |

| 0 | 1,500 | 3,000 kilometers |

ARGENTINA

40 S

Falkland Is.
(U.K.)

60 S

80 S

160 W   140 W   120 W   100 W   80 W   60 W   40 W   20 W

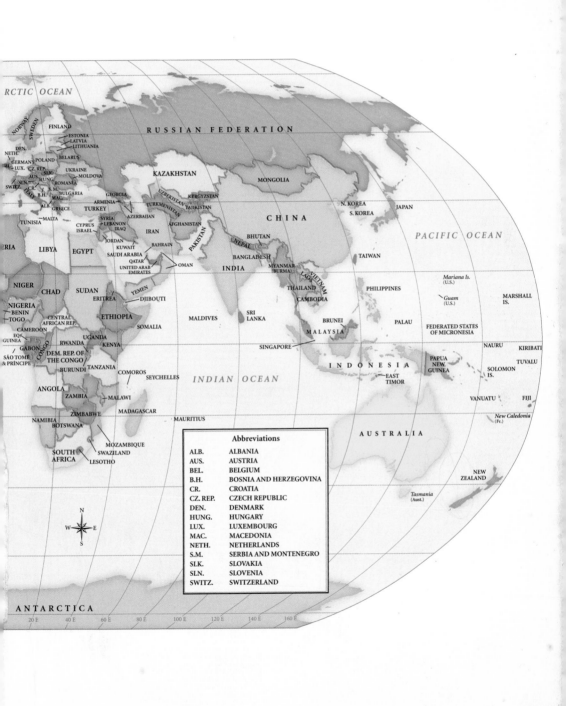

RCTIC OCEAN

NORWAY
SWEDEN
FINLAND
DEN.
NETH.
GERMANY POLAND
LUX.
CZ. REP.
AUS.
SLK.
SLN.
HUNG.
SWITZ.
CR.
ITALY
B.H.
S.M.
MAC.
ALB.
GREECE
TUNISIA
MALTA

RUSSIAN FEDERATION

ESTONIA
LATVIA
LITHUANIA
BELARUS
UKRAINE
MOLDOVA
ROMANIA
BULGARIA
GEORGIA
ARMENIA
TURKEY
AZERBAIJAN
SYRIA
CYPRUS LEBANON
ISRAEL
JORDAN
KUWAIT
IRAQ
IRAN

KAZAKHSTAN

UZBEKISTAN
TURKMENISTAN
KYRGYZSTAN
TAJIKISTAN
AFGHANISTAN

MONGOLIA

CHINA

N. KOREA
S. KOREA

JAPAN

PACIFIC OCEAN

ERIA
LIBYA
EGYPT

SAUDI ARABIA
BAHRAIN
QATAR
UNITED ARAB
EMIRATES
OMAN

PAKISTAN

NEPAL
BHUTAN

INDIA
BANGLADESH
MYANMAR
(BURMA)
LAOS
VIETNAM

TAIWAN

NIGER
CHAD
SUDAN
YEMEN
ERITREA
DJIBOUTI

THAILAND
CAMBODIA

Mariana Is.
(U.S.)

Guam
(U.S.)

MARSHALL
IS.

NIGERIA
BENIN
TOGO
CAMEROON
CENTRAL
AFRICAN REP.
ETHIOPIA
SOMALIA

MALDIVES

SRI
LANKA

BRUNEI

PHILIPPINES

PALAU

FEDERATED STATES
OF MICRONESIA

EQ.
GUINEA
GABON
CONGO
SÃO TOME
& PRÍNCIPE
DEM. REP. OF
THE CONGO
RWANDA
UGANDA
KENYA
BURUNDI
TANZANIA

SINGAPORE

MALAYSIA

INDONESIA

NAURU

KIRIBATI

PAPUA
NEW
GUINEA

EAST
TIMOR

SOLOMON
IS.

TUVALU

COMOROS
SEYCHELLES

INDIAN OCEAN

ANGOLA
ZAMBIA
MALAWI
ZIMBABWE
MADAGASCAR
NAMIBIA
BOTSWANA
MAURITIUS

VANUATU

FIJI

New Caledonia
(Fr.)

AUSTRALIA

MOZAMBIQUE
SWAZILAND
SOUTH
AFRICA
LESOTHO

NEW
ZEALAND

Tasmania
(Aust.)

N
W   E
S

Abbreviations

ALB.	ALBANIA
AUS.	AUSTRIA
BEL.	BELGIUM
B.H.	BOSNIA AND HERZEGOVINA
CR.	CROATIA
CZ. REP.	CZECH REPUBLIC
DEN.	DENMARK
HUNG.	HUNGARY
LUX.	LUXEMBOURG
MAC.	MACEDONIA
NETH.	NETHERLANDS
S.M.	SERBIA AND MONTENEGRO
SLK.	SLOVAKIA
SLN.	SLOVENIA
SWITZ.	SWITZERLAND

ANTARCTICA

20 E   40 E   60 E   80 E   100 E   120 E   140 E   160 E

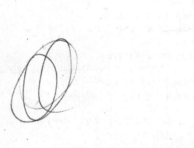